Rights and Right-Holding

Rights and Right-Holding

A Philosophical Investigation

MATTHEW H. KRAMER
University of Cambridge

OXFORD
UNIVERSITY PRESS

OXFORD
UNIVERSITY PRESS

Great Clarendon Street, Oxford, OX2 6DP,
United Kingdom

Oxford University Press is a department of the University of Oxford.
It furthers the University's objective of excellence in research, scholarship,
and education by publishing worldwide. Oxford is a registered trade mark of
Oxford University Press in the UK and in certain other countries

Published in the United States of America by Oxford University Press
198 Madison Avenue, New York, NY 10016, United States of America

British Library Cataloguing in Publication Data

Data available

Library of Congress Control Number: 2024937037

ISBN 978–0–19–889122–2

DOI: 10.1093/oso/9780198891222.001.0001

The manufacturer's authorised representative in the EU for product safety is
Oxford University Press España S.A. of El Parque Empresarial San Fernando
de Henares, Avenida de Castilla, 2 – 28830 Madrid (www.oup.es/en or
product.safety@oup.com). OUP España S.A. also acts as importer into Spain
of products made by the manufacturer.

Preface

As is discussed in my opening chapter, this book largely though not entirely supersedes my previous publications on rights and right-holding. Albeit some sound lines of reasoning scattered through those previous writings are not incorporated into this volume, most of the sound lines of reasoning from those earlier publications have been re-elaborated herein (usually with considerable amplifications or modifications), and any unsound arguments have been replaced or discarded and in some instances have been explicitly repudiated. Moreover, numerous strands of this book are unparalleled by anything in my past ruminations on rights and right-holding. Chapter 1, in its final main section, will comment further on this matter.

I should here note two points of terminology that are applicable throughout this volume. First, I use the terms "duty" and "obligation" interchangeably. Second, I use the noun "interest" to denote a stake—whether individual or collective—in the occurrence of some event(s) or the existence of some state(s) of affairs. I do not use that noun to denote an attitude of curiosity or inquisitiveness. Many additional points of terminology will emerge in the chapters that follow.

I am most grateful to Kezia Johnson, Reyman Joseph, and Brian Stone for their roles in bringing this book through the editorial and production processes at the Oxford University Press, and I am likewise grateful to two anonymous readers for their valuable comments. I owe thanks as well to several other people who have read portions of this book during my writing of it: Joseph Chan, Rowan Cruft, Luis Duarte d'Almeida, Visa Kurki, Agnes Lindberg, Mark McBride, Anna Peters, Gopal Sreenivasan, and Siegfried van Duffel. I am also greatly obliged to the students from the course on Topics in Legal and Political Philosophy which I have taught at Cambridge for many years.

Matthew H. Kramer
Cambridge, England
September 2023

Contents

1. Introduction 1
  1.1 The Scope of the Book 1
  1.2 A Note on Formalization 3
  1.3 A Note on Methodology and on the Standards for Success 5
    1.3.1 A Misunderstanding of Appeals to Ordinary Understandings 7
    1.3.2 *Tu Quoque* 9
    1.3.3 Conjectures from an Armchair 9
    1.3.4 More from Wenar's Armchair 10
    1.3.5 Standards for Success 11
  1.4 Past Publications 13

2. The Hohfeldian Analysis of Legal and Moral Relationships 16
  2.1 Some Remarks on General Terminology 17
  2.2 Correlativity 21
  2.3 The Diagonals: Duality and Contradictoriness 22
  2.4 Claim-Rights and Duties 24
    2.4.1 Contents and Conduct 26
    2.4.2 Deontic Conflicts 28
    2.4.3 Contradictions 34
    2.4.4 Unenforcedness and Unenforceability 39
  2.5 Liberties and No-Rights 43
    2.5.1 Unpaired Liberties and Paired Liberties 45
    2.5.2 The Contents of Liberties 49
    2.5.3 Exercises Protected by Claim-Rights 51
    2.5.4 Claim-Rights without Liberties 55
    2.5.5 Quantification over Parties 58
      2.5.5.1 Some Clarification of Disjunctive Universal Quantification 59
      2.5.5.2 Liberties and Distributive Universal Quantification 64
    2.5.6 Limits on Duality 66
    2.5.7 No-Rights 70
      2.5.7.1 Hohfeld's Misstep 71
      2.5.7.2 The Reality of No-Rights 72
  2.6 Powers and Liabilities 77
    2.6.1 More on Evaluative Neutrality 81
    2.6.2 Quasi-Powers and Quasi-Liabilities 83
      2.6.2.1 Insentient Forces and Entities 83
      2.6.2.2 The Applicability of General Norms 86
    2.6.3 Quantification Afresh 87

2.6.3.1 Quantification over Sets of Conditions for Changes in Legal Relationships 88
2.6.3.2 Quantification over Sets of Changes 89
2.6.3.3 Quantification over Potential Bearers of Liabilities 91
2.7 Immunities and Disabilities 92
2.7.1 The Importance of Immunities: Bills of Rights 93
2.7.1.1 A Qualification: Wrongdoing in Law-Administration 93
2.7.1.2 Disabilities Imposed on Lawmakers 94
2.7.2 The Importance of Immunities: Securing Other Entitlements 97

3. In Defense of the Correlativity Axiom 99
3.1 A Glimpse of the Interest Theory of Right-Holding 100
3.2 The Axiomaticity of the Correlativity Axiom 102
3.2.1 Compliance with Legal Requirements 102
3.2.1.1 Claim-Rights Held Only by a System of Governance 103
3.2.1.2 Collectivities as Holders of Claim-Rights 104
3.2.1.3 A Counterexample? 109
3.2.2 Conformity to Moral Requirements 111
3.3 Justificatory Priorities 113
3.4 Misrepresentations of the Correlativity Axiom 119
3.5 Eleemosynary Duties 120
3.6 More Mistakes by MacCormick 123
3.7 Generality versus Concreteness 125
3.8 Claim-Rights versus Interests 128
3.9 Stages of Emergence 131
3.10 No Wrongs without Claim-Rights 135
3.10.1 A Preliminary Clarification 136
3.10.2 A Third-Party-Beneficiary Contract 138
3.10.3 A Cheated Prizewinner 142
3.10.4 Overhearing a Falsehood 146
3.10.4.1 Another Misrepresentation of a Legal Judgment 147
3.10.4.2 Ostensible Concessions and Untenable Assertions 148
3.10.4.3 The Correlativity Axiom Disowned? 153
3.10.5 The *Palsgraf* Problem 154
3.10.6 Examples from the Bard 158
3.10.6.1 Much Ado about Nothing 159
3.10.6.2 Julius Caesar 161
3.10.6.3 The Killing of a Child by a Drunken Driver 162
3.10.7 Cornell's General Theoretical Reflections 164
3.10.7.1 Discreditable Origins? 164
3.10.7.2 Motivation versus Obligation 166
3.10.7.3 An Explosive Example 167
3.10.7.4 The Derivativeness of the Claim-Rights of Third Parties 170
3.10.7.4.1 A First Rejoinder 170
3.10.7.4.2 A Second Rejoinder 172

3.10.7.4.3 A Third Rejoinder 173
3.10.7.5 The Interest/Will Controversy 174
3.10.8 Conclusion 177

4. In Praise of the Interest Theory of Right-Holding 178
4.1 The Interest Theory of Right-Holding 179
4.1.1 Evaluative Tenets in the Interest Theory for the Holding of Legal Claim-Rights 181
4.1.1.1 Objectivity versus Subjectivity 182
4.1.1.2 Legal Claim-Rights versus Moral Claim-Rights 183
4.1.2 The Overexpansiveness of the Interest Theory? 187
4.1.2.1 Bentham's Test 188
4.1.2.2 An Illustration of Bentham's Test 189
4.1.2.3 A Second Illustration: Back to the Third-Party-Beneficiary Contract 190
4.1.3 The Underinclusiveness of the Interest Theory? 193
4.1.3.1 A Third Illustration of Bentham's Test: Another Vignette from Sreenivasan 194
4.1.3.2 Bentham's Test and the Personal/Vicarious Distinction 196
4.1.4 The Inordinate Flexibility of the Interest Theory? 203
4.1.4.1 The Misplacing of a Quantifier 203
4.1.4.2 The Matter of Categorization 205
4.2 The Interest Theory in Connection with the Holding of Moral Claim-Rights 208
4.2.1 An Additional Clause? 208
4.2.2 An Additional Evaluative Premise 211
4.2.3 A Misconceived Criterion 213
4.3 The Interest Theory of Right-Holding versus the Razian Interest Theory of Rights 214
4.3.1 On Balance versus Typically 217
4.3.2 Raz's Commitment to the Justificatory Priority of Victims' Interests 218
4.3.2.1 Punitive Torture and Monstrous Wrongdoers 219
4.3.2.2 Purposes of Perpetrators versus Interests of Victims 220
4.3.2.3 The Inappositeness of Raz's Justificatory Focus 222
4.4 The Capacious Version of the Interest Theory of Right-Holding 225
4.4.1 Wenar's First Worry about the Capacious Version of the Interest Theory 228
4.4.2 A Second Set of Complaints by Wenar 230
4.4.3 Conflating Non-Justificatory Questions with Justificatory Questions 232
4.4.4 The Discretion of a Parent Redux 234
4.4.5 Some Further Putative Counter-examples 238
4.4.6 Arrangements for Marriages 240
4.4.7 The Message to Be Gathered 241

4.4.7.1 Rousseau and Marx 242
4.4.7.2 Jesus of Nazareth 242
4.4.8 Some Problematic Legal Liberties 243
4.4.8.1 Paternalistic Legal Prohibitions 243
4.4.8.1.1 Inconclusiveness at Best 244
4.4.8.1.2 An Invalid Conclusion 246
4.4.8.2 Legal Liberties in a Dire Condition 247
4.4.9 Claim-Rights and Other Entitlements 250
4.5 Objections to the Will Theory of Right-Holding 255
4.5.1 A First Set of Objections 257
4.5.1.1 A Claim-Right Not to Be Murdered or Rendered Comatose 257
4.5.1.2 No Claim-Rights of Victims under the Criminal Law 258
4.5.1.3 Minimum-Wage Laws 259
4.5.1.4 The Class of Potential Holders of Claim-Rights 260
4.5.1.5 Fundamental Rights 265
4.5.2 The Near-Eliminativism of the Will Theory 268
4.5.2.1 Two Default Rules 270
4.5.2.2 Two Situations Governed by the First Default Rule 271
4.5.2.2.1 A Limited Time for a Lawsuit 271
4.5.2.2.2 Unlimited Time for a Lawsuit 272
4.5.2.3 Two Situations Governed by Versions of the Second Default Rule 273
4.5.2.3.1 The Second Default Rule at the Post-Violation Stage 273
4.5.2.3.2 A Variant of the Second Default Rule at the Pre-Violation Stage 275
4.5.2.3.3 Steiner and the Conflation of Powers and Immunities 277
4.5.2.3.4 No Begging of the Question 278
4.5.2.3.5 Some Possible Rejoinders 279
4.5.3 A Further Critique of the Will Theory 284
4.6 A Short Summary 290

5. Potential Holders of Claim-Rights 292
5.1 The Need for This Chapter 294
5.2 An Expansive Conception of Interests 298
5.2.1 Bowen's Worries about My Account of Interests 298
5.2.1.1 Bowen's First Substantive Query: The Univocality of a Theory 299
5.2.1.2 A Second Substantive Objection by Bowen: No Justification 301
5.2.2 Dworkin on Foetuses and Interests 302
5.2.2.1 An Excessively Controversial Position 303

5.2.2.2 Dworkin's First Argument: Begging the Question and Missing the Point 305
5.2.2.3 Dworkin's Second Argument: Missing the Target 306
5.2.2.4 Dworkin's Third Argument: Begging the Question and Missing the Target Afresh 307
5.2.2.5 Dworkin's Final Argument: Familiar Errors 308
5.3 Distinct Issues 309
5.4 A Discourse on Value 313
5.4.1 Instrumental Value 313
5.4.2 Constitutive Value 314
5.4.3 Intrinsic Value 315
5.4.4 Ultimate Value 317
5.4.4.1 Foreign Wording 317
5.4.4.2 No Specific Attitudes 318
5.4.4.3 Some of the Main Exclusions 318
5.4.4.4 Another Significant Exclusion 322
5.4.4.5 The Level of Application 323
5.4.4.6 Human Collectivities and Ultimate Value 327
5.5 Warranted Self-Respect and the Class of Potential Holders of Claim-Rights 329
5.5.1 A Community without Institutions 330
5.5.2 Non-Paradigmatic Members in the Community of Potential Holders of Claim-Rights 333
5.5.2.1 Inanimate and Insentient Entities 334
5.5.2.2 Non-Human Animals 338
5.5.2.3 Non-Human Animals and Ultimate Value 339
5.5.2.3.1 The Inclusion of Many Animals 339
5.5.2.3.2 The Exclusion of Certain Animals 344
5.5.2.3.3 Holding Claim-Rights and Bearing Duties 348
5.5.2.4 Infants and People with Mental Incapacities 350
5.5.2.5 Permanently Comatose People and Anencephalic Infants 353
5.5.2.6 Foetuses 356
5.5.2.7 Dead People 359
5.5.2.7.1 The Overall Trajectory of a Life 359
5.5.2.7.2 Do Dead People Belong to the Community of Potential Holders of Claim-Rights? 363
5.5.2.7.3 How Long? 365
5.5.2.7.4 Bowen's First Objection 366
5.5.2.7.5 A Second Line of Attack by Bowen 368
5.5.2.7.6 A Third Line of Attack by Bowen 370
5.5.2.7.7 A Query Borrowed from Kurki 372
5.5.2.7.8 Purposes Mistook and Fall'n on the Inventor's Head 373

5.5.2.8 Future Generations 374
5.5.2.8.1 Are Future Generations Assimilable Now to the People They Will Be? 375
5.5.2.8.2 When Are the Claim-Rights of Future Generations Held? 380
5.5.2.8.3 Universal Quantification in the Holding of Claim-Rights 382
5.5.2.8.4 The Non-Identity Conundrum? 384
5.6 A Laconic Conclusion 387

References 389
Index 399

1
Introduction

This book endeavors to explicate the nature of rights and to specify the general conditions under which anyone holds a right. That simple statement of the book's aims, however, conceals a multitude of complexities. As will rapidly become apparent, the term "rights" is problematically ambiguous both in everyday discourse and in juristic discourse. Indeed, the disambiguation of that term is one of the chief concerns in the first half of the book, and it was one of the foremost concerns of the American jurist Wesley Hohfeld whose analysis of legal relationships will figure saliently throughout my discussions. Without the precision and clarity that can be gained through Hohfeld's analyses, ruminations on rights almost inevitably land in confusion. Still, even before we have proceeded through the labors of disambiguation that will result in such precision and clarity, my opening statement of this book's objectives can signal what will not be attempted herein as well as what will be attempted.

1.1 The Scope of the Book

Not all matters pertaining to rights and to the holding of rights are tackled within this volume. One way of framing the distinction between the issues included and the issues excluded is that this book grapples with formal matters rather than with substantive matters in its efforts to pin down the general nature of rights and the essential conditions for the holding of rights. That "formal"/"substantive" terminology is by no means entirely inapposite, for the topics to be addressed in my subsequent chapters are within the purviews of deontic logic and modal logic or are otherwise focused on properties of rights and right-holding that transcend specific contents and contexts. Nevertheless, although such terminology is helpful in quite a few respects, it can be very misleading if it is not construed with due caution. It might convey the impression, for example, that all the issues to be pondered in this book are austerely analytical and that they are thus in sharp contrast with the ethical questions which I would contemplate if I were treating of the substantive problems that are debated in the philosophy of rights. Any impression along those lines would be simplistic at best. For one thing, this book will probe the nature and holding of moral rights as well as the nature and holding of legal rights, and all aspects of moral rights are moral matters even when they are also conceptual matters. Moreover, although many aspects of legal rights are indeed analytical

Rights and Right-Holding. Matthew H. Kramer, Oxford University Press. © Matthew H. Kramer 2024.
DOI: 10.1093/oso/9780198891222.003.0001

rather than ethical, certain other important aspects of such rights are ethical. While some of the germane ethical considerations are thinner and less controversial than those that would be at stake in disputation over substantive questions about rights and right-holding, we shall find—especially in the second half of this volume—that some other ethical considerations pertaining to the nature and holding of legal rights are partly convergent with the considerations that would be adduced in substantive disputation. Hence, illuminating though the division between formal matters and substantive matters is as a *point d'appui* for delimiting the scope of this book, the task of delimitation is better performed with a somewhat different orientation.

In lieu of the distinction between the substantive and the formal, we should differentiate between justificatory questions and non-justificatory questions in the philosophy of rights. When we raise questions of the former kind, we are asking (for example) what sorts of legal rights people should have or what sorts of moral rights people do have or how legal rights should be distributed or how moral rights are distributed. We are asking how moral rights should be given effect through legal relationships and mechanisms. When addressing these and kindred questions, philosophers enquire into the moral foundations of rights. Their theses about those foundations form their accounts of distributive and commutative justice. Now, although I have wrestled with such problems at length in some of my previous books (Kramer 2011; 2014; 2017a; 2021), they are not the matters with which the present volume is principally concerned. Admittedly, as has already been stated, such enquiries into the foundations of justice do converge in some respects with the ethical considerations that will be invoked at certain junctures in this book. Nonetheless, even within those areas of convergence, this book will not be directly coming to grips with justificatory questions of the sorts that have just been broached. Instead, it will focus on prior matters such as the problem of ascertaining what sorts of beings can hold rights at all. More broadly, the book will seek to answer an array of questions which are prior to the justificatory inquiries in that one's answers to the former questions will be presupposed by one's responses to those latter inquiries. In addition to venturing to specify the types of beings who are capable of holding rights at all, I will be setting out to explain what rights are and what the holding of them consists in and how rights are logically related to other legal or moral positions. Although a complete theory of rights would combine answers to those questions with answers to the justificatory inquiries from which this volume largely prescinds, the matters covered herein are sufficiently knotty and far-reaching to be worthy of this separate book-length investigation—which can salutarily be read in conjunction with the tomes where I ponder sundry justificatory issues.

Of course, not all philosophers would entirely endorse the justificatory/non-justificatory distinction as I have dilated upon it here. Some philosophers, most prominently Joseph Raz and his followers, submit that any satisfactory explication of the phenomenon of right-holding is justificatory in character. We shall examine Raz's account of the holding of rights in Chapters 3 and 4 of this book, where its inadequacies will become plain. For the moment, we should simply note that one shortcoming of the account is the way in which it runs together the two sets of questions which I have distinguished in the preceding paragraph. Those two sets of questions are not hermetically sealed off from each other—and indeed several of my arguments against Raz will be moral arguments—but the questions are not linked as extensively and straightforwardly as the Razian exposition of right-holding has contended.

Another crucial element in the demarcation of the ambit of this book is that its aspirations and methods are philosophical rather than social-scientific or historical. Its theses about the nature of rights and of right-holding are not confined to systems of law that do exist or have existed, and its methods are analytical (and, especially in the final chapter, ethical) rather than empirical. It does not profess to recount the legal rights that are currently possessed by people in any particular jurisdiction, nor does it profess to recount how the distribution and contents of the legal rights held by people in any jurisdiction have developed over time. My analyses are of course applicable to such empirical configurations and developments—and indeed will be invaluable for anyone who wants to understand such phenomena with precision—but my analyses are likewise applicable to the rights and the instances of right-holding that obtain in any possible society, whether actually existent or not. Because my explications of the nature of rights and the nature of right-holding transcend the divide between the actual and the merely possible, they are not focused on only the "actual" side of that divide. Most of my illustrative examples throughout the book are thought-experiments rather than situations from the actual world, since the former are at least as serviceable as the latter for my philosophical purposes. Variegated though the distributions and contents of rights are in any comparisons among a throng of possible worlds, the fundamental character of rights and the fundamental character of right-holding are invariant across all those worlds. With an orientation toward those fundaments rather than toward the details of multitudinous contingencies, this book is an exercise in philosophical elucidation rather than an exercise in empirical chronicling.

1.2 A Note on Formalization

While my methods in this volume are those of analytic philosophy with some sustained reflections on logical quantification, I only very sparingly employ the notation of formal logic. Such notation is vital in some philosophical contexts, of course, and there have been a number of efforts over the past several decades to formalize the Hohfeldian schema of legal relationships that will be expounded in the first half of this book.[1] Although some of the more recent contributions to the formalization of that schema have improved over the error-riddled attempts that emerged during the 1960s and 1970s, there are good reasons for my declining to unfold a formal apparatus within this book.

In the first place, even the best of the quite recent efforts to formalize Hohfeld's framework have been unsatisfactory in some major respects—and they have been so because the veracity of any formal apparatus is dependent on the solidity of the philosophical convictions that are explicitly or implicitly incorporated into it. For example, if the axioms of a logical calculus exclude the possibility of deontic conflicts (situations instantiated whenever someone is under a moral obligation or legal obligation to φ and is simultaneously under a moral obligation or legal obligation not to φ), then the calculus is *pro tanto* systematically distortive rather than an aid to understanding. My concern in this volume is to present a philosophically sound account of the nature of rights and the nature of right-holding. Such an account will eschew the bevy of misapprehensions that varyingly imbue even the strongest of the attempts that have been made heretofore to formalize the Hohfeldian matrix. The avoidance of those misapprehensions is central to every chapter of this book, as is the construction of an illuminatingly accurate theory that is free of them. A theory thus purified is indispensable as the basis for any satisfactory representation of Hohfeld's schema in logical notation. It is the most important stage of such a representation.

Second, whereas an accurate exposition of the nature of rights is essential as a basis for the success of any formalization of Hohfeldian relationships, there is no comparable dependence in the other direction. Although quite a number of the points advanced throughout this book involve subtle logical distinctions and logical quantification, the points can be made and the distinctions can be drawn with only a very modest use of formal notation. To be sure, the systematic parlaying of such notation into a full-scale formalization could be valuable as a supplement to my theorizing in certain contexts—contexts in which the Hohfeldian categories are brought to bear on the intricacies of legal or moral relationships in the world, for example. I am scarcely here denying that the provision of a supplement of that kind would be salutary. Rather, my contention is merely that the provision of such a supplement is unnecessary for the accomplishment of the purposes of this book. Those purposes can all be achieved in prose, which (with some regimentation) is sufficiently nuanced and resourceful as a medium for the elaboration of a philosophical theory of rights and right-holding.

Third, given that the aims of this volume can be realized in prose, they should be so pursued—because any extensive recourse to formal notation would put off some readers whom I am hoping to reach. On the one hand, this book is a work of

[1] See, for example, Anderson 1962; Fitch 1967; Hurd and Moore 2018; Kanger and Kanger 1966; Makinson 1986; Mullock 1972; Oliveira Lima et al. 2021; Saunders 1990. See also Heinze 2003.

legal and moral philosophy, and philosophers in those areas of the discipline are my prime audience. Most such philosophers would not be daunted by a formal apparatus (provided, of course, that the elements of the apparatus are explained lucidly). On the other hand, this book is also addressed to legal theorists and even to jurists. Hohfeld himself, whose writings during his short lifetime were all published as articles in law journals, took legal theorists and jurists to be his prime audience. *Rights and Right-Holding* is more heavily philosophical and is clearly oriented predominantly toward philosophers. Notwithstanding, also included among its addressees are readers of the kinds whom Hohfeld sought to enlighten. After all, as Luis Duarte d'Almeida has recently underscored with reference to a decision by the Supreme Court of Ireland (Duarte d'Almeida 2016, 554, 564), jurists continue to commit errors like those which Hohfeld exposed and condemned. Hence, there are strong reasons for continuing to strive to persuade the readers whom Hohfeld most wanted to influence. Those readers, however, are unlikely to be enticed by a book that teems with formal notation.

Fourth, even if there were strong reasons for making more extensive use of such notation than I have made in this volume, most of my arguments would have to be articulated in prose. Especially in the portions of the book where I engage in ethical reflections, but also in most of the analytical portions, a lot of the requisite distinctions and apposite conclusions cannot be captured straightforwardly or illuminatingly in logical notation. Although the distinctions and conclusions are of course consistent with all genuine logical constraints, those constraints in themselves are far from sufficient to determine the answers to many philosophical and ethical questions. Trying to encapsulate all the aforementioned distinctions and conclusions in the notation of formal logic is thus not only unnecessary but also futile.

1.3 A Note on Methodology and on the Standards for Success

As can be inferred from what has been said already, the methodology of this book is uncompromising. *Rights and Right-Holding* will distill individually necessary and jointly sufficient conditions for the existence of any instance of right-holding as such, and it will likewise distill such conditions for any claim-right or liberty or power or immunity as such. Its ambitions are therefore essentialist, in that it sets forth to specify the essence of every instance of right-holding and the essence of every entitlement that is correctly classifiable as a "right" (in the capacious sense of that term, rather than only in the narrower sense which I will commend in due course). Accordingly, the methodology of this volume is bolder than the approaches followed in quite a few other works of contemporary philosophy. Among the main alternatives to essentialism as modes of conceptual analysis are central-instance approaches, Wittgensteinian family-resemblance enquiries, and cluster-concept investigations. There is no need for me here to expound each of those alternatives, but what should be noted is that each of them designedly stops short of specifying a set of individually necessary and jointly sufficient conditions for the existence of every instance of any phenomenon that is under investigation.

My embrace of an essentialist methodology in this book is not doctrinaire. Each phenomenon (or each concept that corresponds to a phenomenon) should be probed with methodological open-mindedness. There are no grounds for thinking that a single mode of conceptual analysis is decisively pertinent across the board. For example, I believe that a family-resemblances approach is apposite for coming to grips with the phenomenon of games on which Ludwig Wittgenstein himself concentrated, and in my 2014 book on torture I have specified some necessary conditions but no single set of necessary and sufficient conditions for the status of any course of conduct as an instance of torture.[2] Not every phenomenon lends itself to an essentialist analysis; the way in which a concept picks out some phenomenon does not have to consist in the distillation of a set of individually necessary and jointly sufficient conditions. Still, some phenomena do indeed lend themselves to essentialist analyses, as I have maintained in my philosophical investigation of the rule of law (Kramer 2007, 184–5) and as the present book maintains in its philosophical investigation of rights and right-holding. Though the essentialist ambitions outlined in my preceding paragraph are not realizable in every area of philosophical enquiry, they are realizable in the areas plumbed by the subsequent chapters of this volume.

And so we arrive at the matter of fixing upon the standards of success for the theorizing which this book undertakes. How should we gauge the soundness of a theory of rights and right-holding, or the superiority of such a theory to the competing accounts of those phenomena? Some philosophers, most stridently Leif Wenar, have presumed that the key factor in this regard is the degree of congruence between a theory's conclusions and the judgments that are asserted or presupposed in ordinary discourse. Wenar insists that, if some implications of a theory of rights and right-holding do not coincide with the assertions or assumptions routinely made by competent ordinary users of the language of "rights," the theory that carries those implications is *pro tanto* defective. He declares that "[t]he 'data' of ordinary understanding are ... significantly less contentious than the 'data' of what rights there really are, and focusing on ordinary understanding allows debates over the nature of rights to refer to a common set of facts to be explained" (Wenar 2008, 252). He contends that "both sides [of the debates between the proponents of the Interest Theory and the proponents of the Will Theory of right-holding] take extensional fit with ordinary usage as a primary standard of success—that is, both aim to present theories that capture all and only rights-assertions that make

[2] See Kramer 2014, 114. For the essay that has convinced me of the correctness of Wittgenstein's meditations on the concept of games, see Geras 2009.

sense to competent users of the language. This standard of success is accepted here" (Wenar 2013, 202–3). He similarly proclaims that "[t]heorists of rights have, in the main, taken an ordinary understanding of rights to set the phenomena to be explained. For example, a rights theorist will reject any theory that ascribes rights to tomato plants, or to ant colonies, because such a theory is incompatible with an ordinary understanding of rights" (2008, 252). This standard for theoretical success trumpeted by Wenar, which takes ordinary usage to be a definitive lodestar, is vulnerable to a number of criticisms. Before we examine a far better alternative set of standards, we should mull over the weaknesses of Wenar's position.

1.3.1 A Misunderstanding of Appeals to Ordinary Understandings

Wenar in his 2013 article does not offer any citations to back up his allegation that Interest Theorists and Will Theorists are determined to arrive at conclusions that match those of ordinary speakers, nor does he there address the passages in which they disavow any such methodological stricture. By contrast, his 2008 essay does endeavor to deal with those points. Although I have obviously not yet expounded in this book my Interest Theory of right-holding to which Wenar is retorting, my encounter with him here on this matter of methodology can fruitfully precede my exposition of that theory in Chapter 4.

Despite his statements quoted above, Wenar eventually acknowledges that I do not in fact regard ordinary linguistic usage as some sort of template with which any tenable theory of rights must fit unswervingly. As I have emphasized since my earliest publications on rights and right-holding, ordinary discourse is marked by too much imprecision and too many inconsistencies to be serviceable as such a template. Moreover, even if everyday usage were more rigorous and discriminating than it is, it would scarcely be an unchallengeable point of reference. As I have already remarked in this chapter, and as I will argue at length in Chapters 4 and 5—broadly in line with what I have contended in Kramer 2001, 29–57—some aspects of my Interest Theory of right-holding are straightforwardly oriented toward ethics rather than toward patterns of linguistic usage. For example, contrary to what Wenar asserts in my final quotation from him above, ethical considerations rather than linguistic considerations determine the answer to the question whether tomato plants and ant colonies are potential holders of rights. Hence, not only are some departures from ordinary usage and some regimentation of ordinary usage inevitable in any satisfactory theory of right-holding, but so too are touchstones for theorizing that go beyond a focus on the patterns of ordinary discourse.

Wenar complains that I "attempt to cast enough aspersions on ordinary 'rights-talk' that there will appear to be no option but to shift from an ordinary to a technical explanandum" (Wenar 2008, 264), and he submits that there is a tension if not a downright inconsistency between those aspersions and my appeals to ordinary understandings in some of my animadversions on the Will Theory of right-holding. He condemns me along with other philosophers (2008, 264):

> They ... insist that ordinary rights-talk is vague and inconsistent in order to attempt to shift attention toward their favoured technical recharacterizations of the term "rights." Yet when attention is so shifted, they once again attempt to embrace an ordinary understanding of rights as the guarantor of their theory's superiority. This position holds the ordinary understanding of rights to be so irremediably vague and inconsistent as to be useless as the object of theoretical explanation, but not so corrupt as to be useless in mediating between artificially constructed definitions of "rights."

Wenar has misunderstood the point of the invocations of ordinary understandings which he reports. There is no tension whatsoever between (1) insisting that some regimentation of ordinary linguistic usage is unavoidable in any coherent philosophical theory of right-holding and (2) commending one's theory of right-holding for capturing far more of ordinary usage than does the main rival theory. Moreover, and relatedly, nobody has ever denied that ordinary understandings are an important anchor for one's theorizing about rights and right-holding. As I stated two-and-a-half decades ago in my first main essay on the topic (Kramer 1998, 22–3; Kramer and Steiner 2007, 296–7), one's theorizing about rights would be unintelligible if its key terms did not have a solid rooting in ordinary discourse. My next chapter will show that Hohfeld's disambiguation of the notion of rights into four entitlements is apt in this respect as in many other respects, for the terms with which Hohfeldians label those disambiguated entitlements—"claim-rights," "liberties," "powers," and "immunities"—are all salutarily rooted in ordinary discourse.[3] Without any inconsistency, one can commend this aspect of Hohfeld's analytical framework while also insisting that ordinary discourse is too loose and multifarious to be reproduced fully by that framework or by any coherent philosophical account of rights.

Also worth noting here is that the philosophers who call for some regimentation of ordinary usage are doing so only in relation to philosophical and juristic discourse. Nobody has been suggesting that everyday discussions of these matters should be similarly regimented. Any suggestion along those lines would be risibly futile.

[3] Hohfeld himself usually employed the term "privilege" to denote the entitlement which most Hohfeldians (including me) generally designate as a "liberty." Most Hohfeldians prefer the latter designation precisely because it corresponds better to ordinary usage. By contrast, as I will explain in Chapter 2, the term "privilege" is often misleading. Despite the emphasis placed by Wenar on conformity to ordinary usage, he himself generally follows Hohfeld in employing the term "privilege."

1.3.2 *Tu Quoque*

As Wenar remarks, and as will become apparent in my next chapter, the cardinal way in which I seek to enhance the language of "rights" for philosophical theorizing is to confine it to Hohfeldian claim-rights (accompanied by Hohfeldian immunities against the termination or suspension of the claim-rights). He states: "Interest theorists ... stipulate that their theories are not meant to account for rights as commonly understood, but only for 'rights' defined as Hohfeldian claim-rights" (Wenar 2008, 262). Wenar takes exception to this mode of regimentation: "Kramer wishes to work within a sphere of discourse in which the referent of 'rights' is claim-rights.... Kramer faces the difficulty that ordinary discourse does not line up with his technical definition" (2008, 263). Apart from the fact that Wenar ignores my arguments where I explain why the language of "rights" should be restricted to Hohfeldian claim-rights—arguments which I have advanced previously and which I will amplify later in this book—the main peculiarity of his criticism of such a restriction is that it leaves him vulnerable to an obvious "*tu quoque*" retort. His 2013 article begins with the following sentence: "This is a new analysis of rights, particularly of the paradigm: the claim-right" (Wenar 2013, 202). The rest of the article is very much in keeping with that opening sentence, as Wenar focuses his analysis on claim-rights throughout. Having upbraided Hohfeld and me for contending that the term "rights" is applicable in its strictest sense to claim-rights (Wenar 2008, 263–4), Wenar himself now declares that that term is applicable in its paradigmatic sense to claim-rights. At one juncture he accuses his opponents of resembling a person who suffers from a mental illness that leads her to embrace and repudiate something simultaneously (2008, 264–5), but he could more accurately have leveled that misdirected gibe against himself.

1.3.3 Conjectures from an Armchair

Wenar's sundry assertions about patterns in the ordinary usage of the language of "rights" are patently empirical contentions. Many of those assertions are sufficiently clear-cut to be in no need of empirical substantiation, but some of them are less straightforward. Consider, for example, the following statement: "Few thoughtful laymen would insist that it is a conceptual impossibility ... for the comatose to have rights against bodily mutilation" (Wenar 2008, 255). Though the adjective "thoughtful" might be taken to indicate that this statement is not really an empirical supposition and that it is instead a partial explication of the ethical property of thoughtfulness, Wenar cannot rely on such an interpretation. The sentence which leads into the quoted statement makes clear that he purports to be recounting an element of the "ordinary understanding of rights" (2008, 255). Hence, he is indeed propounding an empirical hypothesis here. He marshals no evidence whatsoever in support of that empirical conjecture, yet evidence is sorely needed—for the correctness of his hypothesis is by no means obvious when judged *in abstracto*. On a matter as elusive as the question whether participants in everyday discourse accept that comatose people can hold legal rights, Wenar's surmises are inadequate.

Worth noting here also, in accordance with what I have already suggested, is that those surmises are in any event largely irrelevant. Whether comatose people belong to the class of potential holders of legal rights is something determined by ethical factors rather than by patterns of ordinary discourse. Although the conclusions generated by those ethical factors may very well be aligned with the conclusions that would be endorsed in ordinary discourse, any such congruity is beside the point. Regardless of whether any such congruity obtains, the ethical factors are dispositive. We shall return to those factors in much greater detail in Chapter 5 of this book.

1.3.4 More from Wenar's Armchair

Wenar proclaims that philosophers of rights have not established that quotidian understandings of rights are in need of regimentation, and he declares from his armchair that those understandings are frequently if not always precise and unconfused. He writes as follows (2008, 265):

> [T]echnical rights theorists have not in fact established that ordinary discourse is frequently vague and contradictory, instead of being a discourse that systematically assigns different meanings to the same word in different contexts. Such systematic variation in meaning is familiar in common speech. For example there is nothing vague or contradictory in the statement that "in a free market one is free to lend money interest-free." "Free" in this statement takes three different but determinate meanings, the meaning of each occurrence being determined by the context. Similarly in ordinary discourse one often hears the word "right" used to refer variously to privilege-rights, claim-rights, power-rights, and immunity-rights, with the intended referent made clear by the context. Interpretations of ordinary speech that find vagueness or inconsistency instead of precise and determinate variation in usage are often just poor interpretations of ordinary speech.

Short of conducting a full-scale empirical study, the only way to support complaints about paralogisms and inconsistencies in ordinary discourse is to adduce examples of such missteps. Contrary to the impression conveyed here by Wenar, Hohfeld adduced a plethora of such examples involving both jurists and legal theorists. In my 1998 essay "Rights without Trimmings," I have marshaled a number of more recent instances involving legal philosophers. Such examples hardly amount to a systematic survey, but they do reveal that confusion and equivocation in the discourse of "rights" are not outlandishly uncommon even among highly sophisticated people.

By contrast, Wenar does not supply any evidence whatsoever to support his empirical pronouncements about the precision and clear-sightedness of ordinary usage. He simply states that he often hears precise and unconfused invocations of the language of "rights." No examples are provided. Of course, I do not doubt that he could have come up with some examples if he had sallied forth from his armchair to do so; nobody has ever suggested that everyday discourse is *always* muddled. My point is that he has not taken even a single step toward substantiating his broad empirical contentions. His *ipse dixits* do not constitute such a step.

1.3.5 Standards for Success

In short, the patterns of ordinary usage that characterize the language of "rights" are not a determinative set of touchstones for gauging the correctness of a theory of rights and right-holding. On the one hand, as has already been said, the patterns of ordinary usage are important; a theory of rights and right-holding that abounds in sweeping departures from those patterns would be incomprehensible as such a theory (Schauer 2022, 108, 110–11). On the other hand, everyday discourse is not the template which Wenar supposes it to be. What, then, are the standards for success that serve as the appropriate alternative to Wenar's misguided methodology?

Here we need to distinguish between legal rights and moral rights. As has already been stated, every aspect of moral rights is a moral matter. Although this book will be prescinding from the justificatory questions that are outlined in §1.1 above, the non-justificatory questions that will be tackled herein are all fundamentally moral insofar as they pertain to moral rights and the holding of moral rights. Thus, the standards for the correctness of answers to those questions in relation to such rights are moral principles. Indeed, the basic moral principles that determine the correctness or incorrectness of one's theorizing about such matters are the same as the basic moral principles that determine the correctness or incorrectness of one's responses to the justificatory questions that will not be addressed in this volume. Unsurprisingly, then, some of my subsequent chapters will advert to those principles and draw upon them. To be sure, there will not arise any need within this book for me to probe the relevant moral considerations in nearly the same depth that would be required if I were grappling with the justificatory questions about rights and right-holding. Still, the standards by reference to which we can appositely gauge the soundness or unsoundness of a theory of moral rights are ethical as well as conceptual.

With regard to legal rights, the situation is more involuted. Most of the non-justificatory questions pertaining to such rights are not ethical matters, and can be addressed without recourse to moral principles. The values that are the polestars for coming to grips with those questions are theoretical-explanatory rather than ethical. When we turn to the *holding* of legal rights, the foci for my enquiries are more complicated. Throughout, whenever my Interest Theory of right-holding is brought to bear on specific circumstances—whether actual or hypothesized—it has to proceed from evaluative assumptions concerning what is typically beneficial or detrimental on balance. Nevertheless, although the evaluative assumptions are indispensable, they are thin in a sense closely akin to that invoked by John Rawls in his elaboration of a thin theory of the good (Rawls 1999, §60). As Rawls wrote, "the theory of the good used in arguing for the principles of justice is restricted to the bare essentials. This account of the good I call the thin theory."[4] In other words, the evaluative assumptions that undergird the Interest Theory of right-holding are virtually platitudinous. They do not include the much more contestable evaluative commitments that are carried by thicker accounts of what is beneficial or detrimental.

My exposition of the holding of legal rights will have to delve more deeply into matters of ethics when I mull over questions about the sorts of beings who can hold legal rights at all. Nobody doubts that sane human adults belong to the class of potential holders of such rights, but disagreements among philosophers of rights emerge as soon as any other types of beings are considered: babies, infants, insane or demented people, comatose people, dead people, foetuses, future generations of people, non-human animals, and so forth. Any adequate arguments for the inclusion of such beings in the class of potential holders of rights are grounded straightforwardly on ethical considerations, and any arguments against the inclusion of such beings would likewise have to resort to ethical considerations. As will be seen, the relevant ethical considerations involve distinctions among kinds of value, and they draw on some of the same basic moral principles that ultimately determine the answers to any justificatory questions about rights. Although I will not have to explore the implications of those principles as searchingly as I would if I were pursuing the justificatory questions directly, the problem of delimiting the class of potential holders of rights will take this book quite far into the domain of ethics—even in connection with the holding of legal rights, and *a fortiori* in connection with the holding of moral rights.

In sum, the standards for the correctness of philosophical accounts of rights and right-holding are far more complex than Wenar's methodological precepts imply. Even if we leave aside the fact that his musings are speculations delivered from an armchair, and even if we leave aside the fact that the patterns of ordinary discourse are often marked by inexactitude and muddles, the standard for success championed by Wenar would be of no avail in a few key parts of this book's theorizing. Evaluative questions and ethical questions are to be answered not

[4] Rawls 1999, 348. For a broader defense of Rawls's thin theory of the good, see Kramer 2017a, 325–33.

through one's striving to arrive at conclusions that correspond to the deliverances of ordinary usage, but instead through one's striving to arrive at conclusions that correspond to the implications of evaluative or ethical principles. Of course, those implications might themselves tally with the deliverances of ordinary usage; patently, there is no inherent inconsistency between the former and the latter. Nonetheless, any such convergence between them is incidental. Whenever the conclusions enshrined in ordinary understandings are at variance with those that follow from correct evaluative or ethical principles, one's recourse to ordinary understandings as a source of guidance for one's answers to evaluative or ethical questions would be perverse.

Before moving on, I should emphasize anew that I am not dismissing altogether the import that attaches to everyday uses of the language of "rights." On the contrary, I will occasionally refer to some of those uses in this book. For example, as has already been adumbrated in this chapter, and as will become evident in Chapter 4, some powerful objections against the Will Theory of right-holding are centered on the fact that it clashes so markedly with everyday understandings of rights and right-holding. All the same, as will also become evident, those objections—powerful though they be—are less telling than some other lines of criticism that are not similarly dependent on appeals to ordinary discourse. Vital though the strands of such discourse are as points of departure for one's theorizing about rights and right-holding, the guidance provided by them falls far short of what Wenar envisages.

1.4 Past Publications

Over the past quarter of a century, since the appearance of "Rights without Trimmings" in 1998,[5] I have published quite a number of essays on rights and right-holding. This introductory chapter will conclude by very briefly delineating the relationship between the present monograph and those earlier publications. First, whenever the arguments and conclusions in this volume are at odds with those in any of my previous writings, the positions herein supersede the previous stances and reasoning. Indeed, the supersession of some of my original ideas has been occurring for quite some time, as most of my essays on rights and right-holding since 1998 have refined or rescinded or amplified certain aspects of the theses propounded in "Rights without Trimmings." Those changes have been both methodological and substantive. Though the chapters in this book go well beyond

[5] See Kramer 1998. Even earlier (in Kramer 1997, 15–23), I published an overview of the Hohfeldian analysis of rights. For some of my main writings on rights and right-holding after 1998, see Kramer 2000; 2001; 2004, 249–94; 2008, 415–21; 2010; 2012, 127–9; 2013; 2017a, 134–44, 148–50; 2017b; 2019; 2022, 363–401; Kramer and Steiner 2007.

any of my other publications in undertaking such changes, the chapters are the culmination of a process that began many years ago. Sometimes the differences between this book's positions and my positions in "Rights without Trimmings" involve outright retractions of the stances which I adopted in 1998, but much more often I have sought to bolster those initial stances by salutarily modifying them. Even more frequently, this volume enlarges the scope of my reflections on rights and right-holding by investigating a host of issues and complexities which I have not addressed heretofore.

Second, as is suggested by the last two sentences of the preceding paragraph, the transformations in my thinking about rights and right-holding are accompanied by numerous continuities. My 1998 essay defended the Hohfeldian analysis of rights and the Interest Theory of right-holding, which are the two general doctrines that are likewise defended in the present book. Albeit my elaboration of the Hohfeldian schema and the Interest Theory has become much more refined and wide-ranging than my original elaboration of them, the intellectual allegiances of this monograph are largely the same as those of "Rights without Trimmings." On many matters of detail as well, this book is in harmony with my earlier reasoning and conclusions.

Third, at some junctures in this volume I will expressly note how my views on certain topics have shifted or how they have been amplified since "Rights without Trimmings." Much more frequently, however, the positions that emerge from the shifts and amplifications will simply be presented as constituents of an overall philosophical account of rights and right-holding—without my drawing attention to the ways in which those positions diverge from, or go far beyond, stances which I have taken in the past. After all, the topic of this book is rights and right-holding, rather than the intellectual history of Matthew Kramer. In this volume, I will advert to my past ideas only when my doing so is conducive to shedding light on the nature of rights and right-holding.

Fourth, although this book supersedes my earlier publications insofar as it alters or augments their analyses, those earlier publications are not entirely superseded—partly because there are many continuities between them and the present monograph, but even more because some portions of my previous essays have addressed a number of matters that are not covered herein. Most notably, "Rights without Trimmings" doggedly rebuts a myriad of misconceived criticisms that had been directed against the Hohfeldian analysis of rights during the second half of the twentieth century. When I wrote "Rights without Trimmings" in late 1995, the torrent of objections to Hohfeld's logical framework—objections that were mostly fatuous—had not abated. I therefore felt obliged to counter all the caviling, at length. Fortunately, the situation has greatly improved during the two-and-a-half decades since the publication of "Rights without Trimmings." Benighted carping against the insights of Hohfeld has largely (though not quite entirely) ceased, and the incorporation of those insights into theorizing on a variety of topics has become more widespread than ever among philosophers and legal scholars and political scientists. Thus, although this book will occasionally joust with critics of Hohfeld, it will devote less attention and energy to that endeavor than I devoted to it in "Rights without Trimmings." *Rights and Right-Holding* will not recapitulate my rejoinders to the fog of misconceptions that had to be dispelled in the mid-1990s. Its intermittent tussling with critics of Hohfeld will be mainly confined to more recent writers, and my engagements with those writers will be greatly overshadowed by my exploration of facets of Hohfeld's framework that have hitherto been neglected both by opponents and by proponents of that framework. However, the fact that I will forbear in this volume from rehashing the aforementioned rejoinders is not a sign of my dissatisfaction with them. On the contrary, my disinclination to revisit those 1998 ripostes is due chiefly to my being content with most of them. Far from being superseded, then, those ripostes stand as having accomplished the purposes for which I undertook them a quarter of a century ago. Anyone inclined to contemplate the merits of the sundry objections to Hohfeld that were raised during the second half of the twentieth century is well advised to consult "Rights without Trimmings."

It is fitting that this chapter has concluded with some remarks in defense of the Hohfeldian analysis, since the first half of this book will commendatorily expound that analysis in depth. My exposition will not be uncritical, but the criticisms will be supportive rather than hostile. Thereafter, the book will crucially supplement the Hohfeldian table of legal relationships by coupling it with the Interest Theory of right-holding. To those tasks we now turn.

2
The Hohfeldian Analysis of Legal and Moral Relationships

Wesley Hohfeld, an American legal theorist who died in 1918 at the age of thirty-nine,[1] devised a table of legal relationships that has been enormously influential since its first appearance. Hohfeld believed that the eight positions delineated in his table were fundamental and that the table as a whole was comprehensive. As will be seen in this chapter and in some subsequent chapters, the attribution of fundamentality to the Hohfeldian categories is defensible so long as it is construed with due caution. Also partly defensible is the notion that the Hohfeldian analytical framework as a whole is comprehensive; that framework does indeed encompass all legal and moral relationships, when we take account of the fact that the Hohfeldian categories can be combined in often intricate ways. However, as will become apparent, there are many aspects of the structures and operations of legal systems that cannot be subsumed under those categories. A full understanding of such systems, and of the positions occupied within them, has to recognize the limits of the Hohfeldian analysis as well as its remarkable breadth.

A key insight of Hohfeld was that every position within his schema of legal entitlements and correlates is thoroughly relational, in that each such position constitutes—and is constituted by—any other position(s) to which it is related. Before we start to examine each type of legal position in depth, we should scrutinize the Hohfeldian matrix as a whole in order to fathom the relationships that are central to it. Notwithstanding that Hohfeld himself presented his network of legal positions in a slightly different format, Table 2.1 can suitably convey to readers the relationships just mentioned.

Table 2.1 Hohfeldian Table of Legal Positions

Entitlements	claim-right (or claim)	liberty	power	immunity
Correlates	duty	no-right	liability	disability
	First-order positions		*Higher-order positions*	

[1] For some interesting discussions of Hohfeld's life and career, see Hull 1997, 97–115 and Schlegel 2022. By contrast, quite remarkably, there is almost nothing about Hohfeld in Duxbury 1995.

Rights and Right-Holding. Matthew H. Kramer, Oxford University Press. © Matthew H. Kramer 2024.
DOI: 10.1093/oso/9780198891222.003.0002

Although this schema is labeled as the "Hohfeldian Table of Legal Positions" (in accordance with Hohfeld's own understanding of it), and although I shall be differentiating between legal positions and moral positions at quite a few junctures in this book, my present discussion cuts across any division between the legal and the moral. My remarks here are applicable to moral positions as much as to legal positions.

2.1 Some Remarks on General Terminology

To each of the four positions in the upper half of Hohfeld's framework, the umbrella term "entitlement" applies. Hohfeld himself revealed that, in everyday discourse and in juristic discourse, the noun "right" is very frequently employed to denote each of the positions in the upper half of the framework. As I have mentioned in my opening chapter, one of his principal concerns was to disambiguate that noun by distinguishing carefully among the four types of entitlements to which it is commonly attached. Given how he strove to elucidate the term "right" and to warn against the confusion bred by the use of that term as a catch-all label, any such use of it within this book should be sparing. I have in fact employed the noun "right" expansively in the title of the book and in my opening chapter—which, of course, has foregone my presentation of the Hohfeldian table of relationships here—and I shall at times also employ it expansively in this chapter and in the second half of the volume, where I discuss a capacious version of the Interest Theory of right-holding. For the most part, however, this book abides by Hohfeld's strictures about the need for regimentation of the noun "right" in philosophical and juristic discourse. As has already been noted in my opening chapter, that noun is usually confined herein to Hohfeldian claim-rights coupled with Hohfeldian immunities. However, precisely because the term "right" or "rights" is usually not employed capaciously in this book to cover each of the four positions in the top row of the Hohfeldian table, some other overarching label is required. For that purpose, the term "entitlement" or "entitlements" can serve admirably.

Like the noun "right," the noun "entitlement" is frequently used in everyday discourse and in juristic or philosophical discourse to cover each of the four positions in the upper half of the Hohfeldian matrix. As will become evident when we go through each of those positions in depth—and, indeed, as might already be evident from one's pre-theoretical acquaintance with those positions and with the language applied to them—formulations along the lines of "I am entitled to" are as idiomatic as "I have a right to" in statements that ascribe to oneself any of those top four positions. Nevertheless, the term "entitlement" or "entitlements" used in this book as an umbrella label for those positions is a bit of technical parlance. We should not presume that the appropriateness of it as such a label is due to something which all of the top four positions have in common. In particular, we should not suppose that instances of those positions are always or typically advantageous for the parties who possess them. Hohfeld himself floated just such a supposition when he wrote that the word "right" in its capacious sense is "used generically and indiscriminately to denote any sort of legal advantage, whether claim, privilege, power, or immunity."[2] As will become evident subsequently in this chapter and in Chapter 4, a supposition about the typically advantageous character of entitlements would be correct in application to the left-hand half of Hohfeld's schema but not in application to the right-hand half. In keeping with what Hohfeld himself observed at a different juncture (1923, 60 n. 90), we shall find that numerous instances of the entitlements on the right-hand half of the Hohfeldian matrix are not even typically beneficial for the parties who hold them. All that can be said at an abstract level about the right-hand entitlements, then, is that the numerous instances just mentioned are coexistent with many other instances that are typically beneficial for the parties who hold them. This point will be explained and amplified later in this chapter.

Despite what has just been said, there is a clear sense in which Hohfeld was correct to suggest that each legal position commonly designated as a "right" is typically advantageous for anyone who holds it. As we shall discover in Chapter 4 when I explore a capacious version of the Interest Theory of right-holding, any particular legal or moral position that would indeed be idiomatically designated as a "right" is of a kind that is normally beneficial for someone who occupies it. Much the same is true of any particular legal or moral position that would idiomatically be designated as an "entitlement." Nonetheless, precisely that aspect of common usage is what has led me in the preceding paragraph to emphasize that the term "entitlement" as it is used in this book is broader than the term in its everyday applications. As an overarching label, that term covers not only every claim-right or liberty and not only every power or immunity that is typically beneficial for the holder thereof, but also every power or immunity that is typically detrimental or neutral for its holder. That overarching designation encompasses all instances of the four positions in the upper half of the Hohfeldian table, rather than only the subset of instances that would be characterized as "rights" or "entitlements" in ordinary discourse. Hence, as has been stated, that designation is a bit of technical parlance; it has a strong rooting in everyday usage, but it is considerably more expansive.

As for the noun "correlates," it too is a bit of technical parlance—though with a more tenuous rooting in ordinary discourse. It comprehends all instances of each of the four positions in the lower half of Hohfeld's matrix. However, just as the

[2] Hohfeld 1923, 71. For a similar suggestion, see Morris 1993, 830: "It would not be inaccurate to analyze [Hohfeldian] legal entitlements merely by saying that every entitlement is a legal advantage of some kind." See also Kennedy and Michelman 1980, 752, where we are told that Hohfeld supplied "a lexicon for distinguishing among several discrete types of legal advantages (entitlements, as we now commonly say)."

entitlements on the right-hand side of that matrix differ from those on the left-hand side in that many instances of them are not typically beneficial for the parties who hold them (even though many other instances of them are typically beneficial for the parties who hold them), so too the correlates on the right-hand side differ from those on the left-hand side in that many instances of them are not typically disadvantageous for the parties who bear them (even though many other instances of them are typically disadvantageous for the parties who bear them). Until we probe each of the Hohfeldian positions in depth, the preceding sentence might strike some readers as rather opaque. What warrants attention at this juncture is simply that the appropriateness of the umbrella label "correlates"—like the appropriateness of the umbrella label "entitlements"—is not due to any straightforward linkages between the positions covered by that label and the interests of the parties who occupy those positions. Numerous Hohfeldian entitlements are not typically beneficial for their holders, and numerous Hohfeldian correlates are not typically disadvantageous for their bearers.

Instead of being focused on any evaluative considerations like the ones just mentioned, my choice of "correlates" as a term that encompasses all instances of the four positions in the lower half of Hohfeld's schema is focused on a logical consideration. That is, each of those four positions is logically correlated with the position directly above it in the table. That logical relationship of correlativity within each of the four columns of Hohfeld's schema will be expounded in §2.2 and invoked repeatedly thereafter.

Before we move on, we should note one further pair of phrases in the Hohfeldian framework above: "first-order positions" and "higher-order positions." Those phrases together indicate another important division between the left-hand half of the Hohfeldian table and the right-hand half. The four positions on the left-hand side are classified as "first-order" because the contents of many instances of those positions do not refer to any other legal or moral positions. For example, if John owes David a duty not to punch him in the face, the content of that duty is John's not punching David in the face. That content, which adverts simply to the non-occurrence of a certain mode of physical conduct, does not itself make reference to any other legal or moral positions. Similarly, if David is at liberty vis-à-vis John to walk along Grange Road every morning, the content of David's liberty is his walking along Grange Road every morning. That content, which adverts simply to the occurrence of a pattern of physical conduct, does not itself make reference to any other legal or moral positions.

By contrast, the content of every instance of each position on the right-hand half of the Hohfeldian schema does refer to some other legal or moral position(s). Although this point will not become fully clear until the nature of each position on the right-hand side of the schema has been thoroughly elucidated, a couple of terse examples can clarify it adequately for now. Just as the preceding paragraph has relied on one's pre-theoretical grasp of the nature of duties and liberties, this paragraph can rely on one's pre-theoretical grasp of the nature of powers and disabilities. If Mary has a legal power to waive a legal duty owed to her by Sally, the content of her power is the extinguishing of Sally's duty. That content makes reference to some other legal position—namely, Sally's duty. Likewise, if Jennifer is legally disabled from terminating Alison's legal liberty to walk along Grange Road each morning, the content of Jennifer's disability is her terminating Alison's liberty to walk along Grange Road. That content, too, makes reference to some other legal position: namely, Alison's liberty.

My exposition of the "first-order"/"higher-order" terminology in the two foregoing paragraphs has perhaps conveyed the impression that the division between the left-hand half and the right-hand half of the Hohfeldian table is tidier than it is. Although the contents of many instances of the positions on the left-hand half of the table do not refer to any other legal or moral positions, the contents of quite a few other instances of the positions on the left-hand half of the table do so refer. For example, if a legal-governmental official is under a legal duty to exercise a certain legal power under specified conditions, the content of the official's duty makes reference to some other legal position—namely, the official's power. Hence, while all instances of the positions on the right-hand half of the Hohfeldian matrix have contents that refer to other legal or moral positions, some instances of the positions on the left-hand half of the matrix have contents that likewise so refer. In that respect, the first-order/higher-order distinction is not quite as straightforward as it might initially appear.

Of course, somebody might demur at my first-order/higher-order taxonomy and might maintain that the higher-order category should instead encompass every instance of a Hohfeldian position that has a content which makes reference to some other Hohfeldian position(s). Under that alternative taxonomy, all first-order legal positions would be on the left-hand side of the Hohfeldian table, but not all instances of the positions on the left-hand side of the table would be classified as first-order. Conversely, all instances of the positions on the right-hand side of the schema would be classified as higher-order, but not all instances of higher-order positions would be on the right-hand side; certain positions on the left-hand half of the schema, such as the duty of a legal-governmental official to exercise some legal power under specified circumstances, would be classified as higher-order.

Now, within the purposes of this book, the alternative taxonomy just outlined could be readily countenanced. As far as the purposes of this book are concerned, the divergence between that alternative taxonomy and the taxonomy presented in my chart of the Hohfeldian relationships is purely classificatory or terminological. It is not a divergence of philosophical substance. My point in demarcating the first-order/higher-order distinction is merely to draw attention to the fact that many instances of the legal or moral positions on the left-hand half of the Hohfeldian framework differ from all instances of the legal or moral positions on the right-hand half of the framework—in that many instances of the left-hand positions have contents that do not refer to any other legal or moral positions. That difference, which is philosophically important, is recognized both by the first-order/higher-order taxonomy broached in the preceding paragraph and by my preferred first-order/higher-order taxonomy in the Hohfeldian table above. Hence, the only point of contrast between those two approaches is a matter of classification in regard to the instances of the left-hand Hohfeldian positions that have contents which do refer to other legal or moral positions. That classificatory matter is not something of philosophical importance.

2.2 Correlativity

As has already been observed, the four positions in the lower half of the Hohfeldian matrix are designated as "correlates" because each of them is logically correlated with the position directly above it in the matrix. "Correlativity" and cognate terms such as "correlates" and "correlations" are elements of the vocabulary that Hohfeld employed. In the terminology of standard logic, the relationship between the two positions in each of the four columns of the Hohfeldian table is that of biconditional entailment. Each column delineates a type of legal or moral relationship where each end of any such relationship is fully constituted by, and fully constitutive of, the other end. Neither end of such a relationship can ever exist unless the other end exists. Each side of the relationship obtains if and only if the other side obtains; the existence of each side is a necessary and sufficient condition for the existence of the other side. Thus, for example, if and only if John owes Mary a legal duty to pay her $10 on a certain day, Mary holds a legal claim-right vis-à-vis John to be paid $10 by him on the specified day. His legal duty to pay her exists if and only if her legal claim-right to be paid by him exists. If either the claim-right or the duty has ceased to obtain, then *ipso facto* the other has likewise ceased to obtain.

Of course, the relationship of biconditional entailment within each column of the Hohfeldian table is scarcely unique to the deontic and normative positions that are comprehended by that table. For instance, the fact that John is six inches shorter than Harry entails the fact that Harry is six inches taller than John, and vice versa. Neither of those facts can ever obtain unless the other obtains. Similarly the fact that a certain slope inclines upward at a specified angle is constituted by, and constitutive of, the fact that the slope inclines downward at that specified angle. Neither of those facts can ever obtain unless the other obtains.

Let us briefly ponder a further example of Hohfeldian correlativity. If Alicia has a legal power to bring about some specified change X in the legal positions of Vincent, then Vincent is legally liable to undergo X through Alicia's exercise of her power. Vincent's liability to undergo the change at the hands of Alicia is constituted by, and constitutive of, her power to bring it about. Neither of those legal positions can exist unless the other exists. Each is a necessary and sufficient condition for the other.

Although the relationship of correlativity as biconditional entailment within each column of the Hohfeldian schema can initially seem obvious and incontestable, it has been more frequently assailed than any other aspect of the Hohfeldian analysis. Queries have been raised especially often about the correlativity of claim-rights and duties. Some of the objections are the badly confused criticisms which I have rebutted in my 1998 essay "Rights without Trimmings." Having mentioned those criticisms near the end of the opening chapter of this book, I shall not revisit them in the present volume—because, as I have stated in Chapter 1, my refutations of them a quarter of a century ago are satisfactory. However, some other objections do merit attention in this volume. I shall therefore devote Chapter 3 to them, in connection with claim-right/duty relationships. As will be seen, some of the worries will prompt me to meditate upon subtleties in logical quantification. Quantification is pivotal in several ways for the Hohfeldian analysis, and it is essential for any thorough defense of the proposition that claim-rights and duties are correlative in the manner indicated by that analysis. We shall enter into those complexities subsequently, but for the moment this chapter is simply endeavoring to outline the basic logical features of the framework which Hohfeld propounded. For that latter purpose, the following general statement can suffice at present as a summary of Hohfeldian correlativity. The existence of either of the two positions in any column of the Hohfeldian table, with a certain content and obtaining between parties P and Q, entails the existence of the other position in that column with the same content and obtaining between parties Q and P.

2.3 The Diagonals: Duality and Contradictoriness

Whereas correlativity between the two positions in each column of the Hohfeldian framework is a logical feature that obtains in every column, the diagonal relationships between the two columns on the left-hand half of the framework are different from the diagonal relationships between the two columns on the right-hand half. In other words, the relationships between claim-rights and no-rights and between duties and liberties are different from the relationships between powers and disabilities and between liabilities and immunities. Whereas the relationship between duties and liberties and the relationship between claim-rights and no-rights each consist in logical duality, the relationship between powers and disabilities and the relationship between liabilities and immunities each consist in logical contradictoriness.[3]

The distinction between logical duals and logical contradictories can best be explicated with an example. Let us ponder the proposition that Sally owes Joe a

[3] My discussion of logical duality in Kramer 2019 is confusedly criticized in Halpin 2020. For a bracing corrective to Halpin's confusion, see McBride 2021.

legal duty to pay him $10 on a certain day, and the proposition that Sally is legally at liberty vis-à-vis Joe not to pay him $10 on the specified day. Each of those propositions is true if and only if the other is false. Each proposition is the negation of the other, and the content of the deontic predicate (that is, the content of the duty or liberty) in each proposition is the negation of the content of the deontic predicate in the other proposition. These twofold instances of negation, the negation at the level of the proposition and the negation at the level of the predicated content—which are often classified as external negation and internal negation—are characteristic of logical duals.

This point about the negation of the predicated content is crucial because "Sally owes Joe a legal duty to pay him $10 on a certain day" is logically consistent with "Sally is legally at liberty vis-à-vis Joe to pay him $10 on the specified day." Indeed, the latter proposition will usually be true when the former proposition is true. Only when the content of the deontic predicate in each proposition is the negation of the content of the deontic predicate in the other proposition, will each proposition itself be the negation of the other proposition. Whereas "Sally owes Joe a legal duty to pay him $10 by a certain date" is logically consistent with "Sally is legally at liberty vis-à-vis Joe to pay him $10 by the specified date," it is the negation of "Sally is legally at liberty vis-à-vis Joe *not* to pay him $10 by the specified date."[4]

Different from logical duals are logical contradictories, for in the latter the only negation is at the level of the proposition. Again, let us proceed with an example. "Peter is legally liable to undergo some change C in his legal positions brought about through the performance of some action A by Brenda" is the negation of "Peter is legally immune from undergoing the specified change C in his legal positions that could otherwise have been brought about through Brenda's performance of A." Each of those propositions is true if and only if the other is false. Yet, whereas there is clearly negation at the level of the proposition, there is no negation at the level of the content of the predicate. The content of the liability in the first of those propositions—a content that consists, of course, in Peter's undergoing of C through Brenda's performance of A—is the same as the content of the immunity in the second of the propositions. Hence, those two propositions are contradictories rather than duals.

In §2.1 we have encountered one major difference between the left-hand half and the right-hand half of the Hohfeldian schema, in the form of the distinction between first-order legal or moral positions and higher-order legal or moral positions. Here we have encountered another significant difference between the two halves of the schema, in the form of the distinction between diagonal relationships of logical duality and diagonal relationships of logical contradictoriness. We shall

[4] Among the theorists who have missed this point is Pavlos Eleftheriadis, who writes as follows: "The existence of a [claim-right] and duty over some act . . . means the absence of a no-right and liberty over the same act" (2008, 109–10).

encounter some further differences as we go along. Notwithstanding that the relationship of correlativity or biconditional entailment between the two positions in each column is the same across the whole array of four columns, some of the other logical relationships operative in the Hohfeldian framework are divergent between its two sectors.

Although a number of other logical aspects of the Hohfeldian analysis will emerge in this chapter and my next chapter, the relationship of correlativity within each column and the diagonal relationships between the positions in adjacent columns on each half of the Hohfeldian table are especially salient. With those relationships delineated, we can start to go through the eight positions in Hohfeld's framework. One thing that should be emphasized at this juncture is that the relationship of biconditional entailment within each column is not paralleled by any relationships of biconditional entailment across the columns. Similarly, the relationships of logical duality or logical contradictoriness between the diagonal positions on each half of the framework are not paralleled by any further relationships of duality or contradictoriness within that framework. These points should be kept in mind throughout my discussions because—as we shall see—many philosophers have erroneously presumed that certain types or instances of Hohfeldian positions across the columns are biconditionally entailing, or have presumed that certain duties (conflicting duties) are logically inconsistent. Detecting the illusiveness of those putative logical relationships is as important as recognizing clear-sightedly the genuine logical relationships that have been explicated heretofore in this chapter.

2.4 Claim-Rights and Duties

Whereas Hohfeld usually applied the term "right" or "claim" to the first of his four entitlements, I in this book usually designate that entitlement as a "claim-right" (with the term "right" itself largely reserved for any claim-right that is combined with sundry immunities against the elimination or suspension of the claim-right). A claim-right is a position of deontic protectedness; when someone holds a claim-right, some aspect of his or her situation is deontically protected against interference or uncooperativeness. Both the notion of interference and the notion of uncooperativeness are to be understood very broadly here. Interference occurs whenever there befalls some event that worsens the situation of somebody in any way, and uncooperativeness occurs whenever there does not befall some event that would have improved the situation of somebody in any way. Although countless types of interference or uncooperativeness can be legally and morally permissible, any types that fall within the protective ambit of a claim-right are legally or morally impermissible.[5]

As will be highlighted in Chapter 3's defense of the proposition that claim-rights and duties are always correlative, the holder of a claim-right can be a collectivity as well as an individual. Likewise, the party vis-à-vis whom a claim-right is held can be a collectivity. In Chapter 5 of this book, where I seek to delimit the class of potential holders of claim-rights, we shall find that many non-human animals are similarly in that class. Also to be noted here is that the party who holds a certain claim-right can be the same as the party who bears the correlative duty. In other words, the holder of a claim-right and the bearer of the correlative duty can be the same party in two different statuses. Duties owed to oneself are not typical in the realm of law, but—both in the realm of morality and in the realm of law—they are far from outlandishly uncommon. We shall return to this point about self-directed duties in considerably greater depth in Chapters 3 and 4.

The protection afforded by a claim-right is deontic, as it consists in making certain types of interference or uncooperativeness impermissible legally or morally. Deontic protection is here contrasted with physical protection, but of course claim-rights that are enforced through governmental mechanisms or other means of coercion do also involve physical protection. Though the claim-rights themselves are not physically protective, the processes of enforcement that back them up do provide some physical security. In some cases, the physical security ensues from anticipatory measures that preclude outright the proscribed interference or uncooperativeness. More often, however, the physical security that ensues from the functioning of mechanisms of legal enforcement is due to the deterrent effects of those mechanisms. Because regularity in the operations of the institutions of enforcement supplies potential malefactors with good grounds for knowing that they are likely to be subjected to legal sanctions if they perpetrate the wrongs which they might otherwise be inclined to perpetrate, the incidence of wrongdoing will typically be reduced substantially by such regularity. As a consequence, the physical security of people who may have been the victims of the wrongdoing (if it had occurred) will *pro tanto* have been enhanced. Still, that increase in physical protection is attributable not to any legal claim-rights themselves but instead to the processes whereby they are regularly given effect. Claim-rights themselves—whether legal or moral—furnish their holders with deontic protection rather than with physical protection.

Correlative to any claim-right held by some party X vis-à-vis some party Y is a duty with the same content owed to X by Y. A legal or moral duty is a requirement that makes some type(s) of interference or uncooperativeness impermissible. In

[5] Hohfeldian categories are applicable not only to legal and moral positions but also to the positions that are operative in activities such as games and linguistic communication. Within this book, however, I concentrate almost entirely on the legal and moral realms.

other words, some type(s) of non-interference or cooperativeness will have been rendered mandatory—whether legally or morally—by the existence of any duty. A bearer of a duty is legally or morally accountable for the fulfillment of that duty.

2.4.1 Contents and Conduct

Most frequently the fulfillment of a duty consists in the duty-bearer's performing some action or refraining from the performance of some action, but—contrary to what some philosophers have presumed[6]—not every duty has such a content. A duty-bearer's conduct is almost always involved, but sometimes only in bringing about the existence of a duty rather than in bringing about what the duty requires. Suppose for example that Phineas, who has been consulted by Hephzibah because he is endowed with meteorological expertise, has stoutly and repeatedly assured her that the weather throughout the following day will be agreeably sunny and that she can therefore safely array some expensive works of art on her lawn during the morning of that day for an exhibition in the afternoon. Phineas in these circumstances has placed himself under a moral duty that will be breached if the weather on the afternoon of the following day turns out to be miserably rainy rather than sunny. We can assume furthermore that the doctrines of contract law and tort law in the relevant jurisdiction are such that there is now incumbent on him a legal duty with the same content as that of the moral duty under which he has placed himself. (If Hephzibah has paid Phineas for his meteorological advice, he has imposed on himself a contractual duty under the law of the jurisdiction. If she has not made any payment, then his legal duty—which will have been breached only if he has acted negligently in his proffering of the advice—is imposed on him under the law of tort rather than under the law of contract.) Although the conduct of Phineas is patently involved in bringing into existence the duties which he owes to Hephzibah, the content of each of those duties does not make any reference to his conduct. Rather, the content pertains only to the climatic conditions on the following afternoon. Hence, the satisfaction of the duty consists in the materializing of those conditions rather than in any instances of Phineas's conduct.

When some philosophers too sweepingly presume that what is made mandatory by any duty is always some conduct on the part of the duty-bearer, they really are concerned to deny that conduct on the part of the holder of the correlative claim-right is what is made mandatory by a duty. On that point, those philosophers are almost always correct. Even when someone owes a duty to herself, any conduct

[6] See, for example, Finnis 1972, 380; Gilbert 2018, 48; Saunders 1990, 478; Sumner 1987, 25; Williams 1956, 1145. In Kramer 1998, 13, I myself committed such a misstep. I first corrected that misstep in Kramer 2005, 352 n 8. See also Kramer 2009a, 75–6. I have subsequently extended my correction by showing that, in unusual circumstances, someone can be under a moral or legal duty that makes mandatory the occurrence of a logically impossible event. See Kramer 2016, 178–9.

made mandatory by the existence of the duty is not her own conduct in her status as the holder of the correlative claim-right; rather, it is her own conduct in her status as the bearer of the duty. Furthermore, even in most versions of the following special situation, it is not the case that the conduct of someone as the holder of a claim-right is made mandatory by the correlative duty. Suppose that Ruth is a singer who often experiences severe anxiety about plying her trade in public, and suppose that her career will be set back if she withdraws from a major recital that has been arranged for her. She enters into a contract with Boaz, who specializes in hypnosis and other techniques of mind-control through which he overcomes people's inhibitions. According to the terms of the contract, Boaz is required to ensure that Ruth sings at the recital which has been scheduled for her. Should we conclude that the contractual duty incumbent on Boaz makes mandatory some conduct on the part of Ruth as the holder of the correlative claim-right? Regardless of the specific wording of the contract, the answer to this question will almost always be negative.

Let us here prescind from any circumstances in which Ruth's singing at the recital is precluded by some adventitious event such as a fire that burns down the venue in which the recital would have occurred. In virtually every jurisdiction, the contract will be interpreted as not requiring of Boaz the non-occurrence of such an event. If the fire has ignited through no fault of his, it will not have contravened his contractual duty—because the duty does not cover any circumstances of that kind. What is required under the contract, rather, is simply that Boaz ensures that Ruth is not prevented by her anxiety or other inhibitions from going ahead with her performance. In any case, even in a peculiar jurisdiction where the contract would be interpreted as requiring of Boaz the non-occurrence of any adventitious calamities, the duty incumbent on him can go unbreached without any singing by Ruth. If his techniques of mind-control do indeed remove all her inhibitions, and if she nonetheless decides for some other reason to refrain from performing, his duty under the contract will have been fulfilled. That duty does not make mandatory any conduct on the part of Ruth.

If instead the duty incumbent on Boaz is accurately interpretable as requiring him to envelop the mind of Ruth in such a blanketing form of control that she is rendered unable to reach any decision to refrain from singing, then what the duty makes mandatory is not any conduct by her but instead some movements of her body that are brought about by Boaz. Those movements occur independently of her volitions, and are thus akin to reflexes that respond to certain stimuli such as a doctor's tapping of a mallet against a knee. Hence, notwithstanding that the duty imposed on Boaz does make mandatory the occurrence of certain movements of Ruth's body—when the contract is interpreted in this latter way—it still does not make mandatory any instances of conduct on her part. Taking place under Boaz's comprehensive control of her mind, her singing is an array of bodily movements that occur willy-nilly. Those movements are thus not instances of her conduct.

They are directly attributable to actions performed by Boaz rather than to actions performed by Ruth.[7]

Still, there could be a fanciful contract between Ruth and Boaz which states explicitly—or which will be interpreted as if it states explicitly—that what is strictly required of Boaz is Ruth's singing at the recital of her own volition without the blanket control of her mind that has been envisaged in the preceding paragraph. Let us suppose that the contract expressly provides that the requirement incumbent on Boaz will remain fully binding even if an adventitious catastrophe occurs and even if Ruth uninhibitedly decides against singing. Such a contract would be quite bizarre, and there might well be jurisdiction-specific obstacles that disallow its legal bindingness in any particular country; but there would not be any logical barriers to its existence and legal bindingness. Thus, although philosophers are almost entirely correct when they submit that volitional actions on the part of the holder of a claim-right CR are not ever made mandatory by a duty that is correlative to CR, they fall slightly short of being entirely correct. In some highly unusual but logically possible circumstances, just such actions on the part of the holder of a claim-right are indeed made mandatory by a correlative duty.

2.4.2 Deontic Conflicts

Somebody can be under a legal or moral duty to φ and can simultaneously be under a legal or moral duty not to φ. In such circumstances, the two duties incumbent on him or her are in conflict. Their contents are contradictories, and therefore the two duties cannot ever be jointly fulfilled. At any given time, one and only one of them will be fulfilled.

Another type of deontic conflict occurs when somebody is under a duty to do X and is simultaneously under a duty to do Y, where doing X excludes doing Y and vice versa. In such a situation, the contents of the duties are contraries rather than contradictories. Ergo, although the two duties cannot ever be jointly satisfied, they can be jointly unsatisfied. At any given time, at least one of them will be unsatisfied.

Let us ponder briefly an example of a deontic conflict of the second kind just outlined. Suppose that Jeremy has formed a contract with Susan whereby he undertakes to be present at a conference hall in New York for an in-person lecture on a certain day during a certain stretch of time. Suppose further that he subsequently forms—or has previously formed—a contract with Melanie whereby he undertakes to be present at a conference hall in Los Angeles for an in-person lecture on the specified day during the specified stretch of time. Each of his contractual

[7] Of clear relevance to this paragraph are my reflections on mind-control in Kramer 2003, 23–4, 255–60. As is evident, the comprehensive mind-control which I envisage in the latter half of the paragraph is a matter of science fiction rather than something that is technologically feasible at present.

partners has spent money for costly arrangements in reliance on the undertaking received, and neither of them has had any grounds for knowing of the agreement between Jeremy and the other contractual partner. (It does not matter, for my purposes, whether Jeremy has been devious or has instead been remissly forgetful when he enters into the second contract.) Now, in these circumstances, the judges or other officials responsible for giving effect to legal requirements could undoubtedly handle the conflict between Jeremy's contractual duties by holding that only one of those duties actually exists. They might, for example, declare that his first contract takes priority over the second. Nonetheless, although a conflict-resolving approach of the sort just mentioned or of some other sort would manifestly be feasible, it most likely would be grossly unfair to one or the other of Jeremy's two contractual partners. In the absence of special mitigating factors, Jeremy should not so leniently be absolved of the burden of dealing with the quandary in which he has placed himself. His moral agency is not compromised by his being required to live up to the obligations which he has incurred. Inevitably, of course, he will breach at least one of those two obligations. His presence at either of the specified locations during the specified span of time will entail his absence from the other specified location during that span of time. Accordingly, regardless of how he acts, he will incur at least one additional legal obligation to remedy a breach of duty (most likely through the payment of compensation). In the circumstances depicted, however, such an outcome is entirely fair to all parties concerned.

Doubtless, although a ruling that holds Jeremy to be under both of his conflicting legal obligations is admirably fair in the circumstances envisioned, there can be other situations where the existence of conflicting legal duties would be unfair to anyone who might bear those duties. After all, somebody under such duties is bound to commit a legal wrong irrespective of how she acts. There can be sundry credible situations in which the unavoidability of committing a legal wrong would be unjust for anyone who faces such a prospect. Accordingly, judges or other legal-governmental officials can frequently be warranted in taking steps to avert conflicts between legal duties (Fuller 1969, 66–9; Williams 1956, 1140–1). Through appropriate interpretive methods or other techniques, the adjudicators or administrators in a system of law can smooth away a deontic conflict by holding in effect that one of the clashing duties does not exist, and they can clearly sometimes be justified in adopting such an approach.

However, three things should be said in response to the preceding paragraph. First, although there can undoubtedly be situations in which maneuvers by adjudicators or administrators to avert conflicts between legal duties are morally justified, there are other circumstances in which such maneuvers would not be morally justified. My scenario of Jeremy and Susan and Melanie in the penultimate paragraph above depicts one set of circumstances in which any maneuvers of that sort would not be warranted. Second, whether or not the adjudicators in the relevant jurisdiction would hold that Jeremy owes both of two conflicting *legal* obligations, Jeremy patently does face a conflict between two *moral* obligations that are incumbent on him. Deontic conflicts in the realm of morality are even more common than deontic conflicts in the realm of law. I have ruminated upon conflicts between moral duties at length in some of my past writings (Kramer 2004, 280–5; 2014, 2–19; 2016). Third, and most important in the present context, is that deontic conflicts are logically possible regardless of their fairness or unfairness. Although it is logically impossible for two conflicting duties to be fulfilled simultaneously, there is nothing logically amiss about the coexistence of those duties. Indeed, the very fact that deontic conflicts are straightforwardly possible as a matter of logic is why adjudicators or administrators employ certain techniques to avert such conflicts between legal duties in various circumstances. Whereas duties and liberties are logical duals, duties with contradictory or contrary contents are not inconsistent with each other at all.

Quite baffling, then, is that standard deontic logic—the system of logic that supposedly encapsulates the fundamental features of obligations and permissions—has long deemed the occurrence of deontic conflicts to be logically impossible. That aspect of standard deontic logic has been uncritically endorsed by numerous philosophers over the years.[8] For example, L.W. Sumner errs when he proclaims that "an act is permitted if it is required" and that a "liberty to do something … is entailed by a duty to do it" (Sumner 1987, 23, 33). Andrei Marmor similarly goes astray when he declares: "A duty to do wrong is surely an oxymoron" (Marmor 1997, 5). Joel Feinberg likewise blundered when he wrote of "the permission trivially entailed by duty" (Feinberg 1973, 69). Hillel Steiner joins this chorus of mistakes as he proclaims that "a duty to do an action implies a liberty to do it," and as he insists that "obligatory actions form a subset of permissible actions" (Steiner 1994, 86; 1998, 268 n. 55). These and many other comparably misguided pronouncements reveal the correctness of my observation in Chapter 1 that the veracity of any logical framework as a representation of the domain which it purports to formalize is dependent on the solidity of the philosophical assumptions that are incorporated into the framework. Regardless of how often philosophers have asserted that the occurrence of deontic conflicts is logically impossible, their assertions remain false. Quite risible is the notion that adjudicators or administrators would be envisaging a logically impossible state of affairs if they were to hold that Jeremy in the scenario above is indeed under two legal duties that cannot be jointly fulfilled.

[8] For a small sample of the philosophical writings that endorse this aspect of standard deontic logic, see Alchourrón and Bulygin 1971; Anderson 1962, 39, 45; Conee 1982; Dworkin 2006, 110–11; Feinberg 1980, 235, 237; Fitch 1967; Hare 1972; Hare 1981, 25–43; Hill 1996, 177; Hughes and Cresswell 1996, 43; Hurd and Moore 2018; McConnell 2010, §4; Mullock 1971, 159–60, 161–2; Raz 1990, 89–90; Simester 2008, 292 n. 10; Vallentyne 1987, 119–20; Vallentyne 1989. See also Bobbitt 2008, 363–5; Curzer 2006, 45; Gross 2004, 1498; Himma 2007, 240–1; Paskins 1976, 143; Posner and Vermeule 2006, 676–7. I have assailed such views in many of my previous writings. See, for example, Kramer 1998, 17–20; 1999, 52–3; 2001, 73–4; 2004, 280–3; 2005, 336–40; 2007, 125–7; 2009a, 117–26; 2009b, 203–6; 2014, 2–19; 2016; 2018, 198–9; 2021, 4–5, 307–11.

Readers might reasonably wonder why numerous philosophers have embraced the canard about the impossibility of deontic conflicts. Having addressed that query elsewhere at length (Kramer 2014, 2–19; 2016), I will here adduce only a few tersely stated considerations. First, the confusion has sometimes stemmed from a failure to differentiate between "obligated not to φ" and "not obligated to φ." Whereas there is no logical inconsistency whatsoever in a situation where Raphael vis-à-vis Michael is morally obligated to φ and at the same time is morally obligated not to φ, there can never as a matter of logic be a situation where Raphael vis-à-vis Michael is morally obligated to φ and at the same time is not morally obligated to φ. That elementary distinction should be unmistakably apparent to anyone with even a modicum of logical training, but some estimable philosophers have failed to heed it. For instance, in an essay published in 1989, Richard Hare wrote as follows: "If I say 'I ought, but there is someone else in exactly the same circumstances, doing it to someone who is just like the person I should be doing it to, but he ought not to do it,' then logical eyebrows will be raised; it is *logically inconsistent* to say, of two exactly similar people in exactly similar situations, that the first ought to do something and the second ought not" (Hare 1989, 179, emphasis in original). Seeking to expose a logical inconsistency, Hare located the negation in the wrong place. Whereas "I ought to φ" logically contradicts "It is not the case that I ought to φ," it is logically consistent with "I ought not to φ." In other words, "not ought" rather than "ought not" is the contradictory of "ought." Given that the structure of a deontic conflict comprises "I ought to φ" and "I ought not to φ," and given that no role is played in any deontic conflict by "It is not the case that I ought to φ," there are no logical inconsistencies in such a conflict. As a logical matter, the occurrence of deontic conflicts is entirely unproblematic.

Second, although a disinclination to recognize the possibility of conflicts between moral duties has been prominent on each side of the division between consequentialists and deontologists, it has been far more widespread among consequentialists. On the deontological side, a disinclination of that type is confined chiefly to Kantians. By contrast, most consequentialists of sundry stripes have been intent on gainsaying the reality of moral conflicts. Though some versions of consequentialism can take account of the occurrence of moral conflicts, the general consequentialist prioritization of the good over the right is largely antithetical to any clear recognition of such conflicts. Every thoroughly consequentialist doctrine takes some overarching desideratum or set of desiderata as an objective that is a touchstone for the rightness or wrongness of any mode of conduct (in accordance with the tendency of the conduct to promote or impede the realization of the objective). Under such a doctrine, one's sole fundamental moral obligation is to contribute maximally to the realization of the commended objective. Hence, when contemplating a clash between moral duties where one duty is more stringent than the other, the supporters of such a doctrine are disposed by it to perceive the less stringent duty as merely ostensible and thus as not genuinely a moral duty at all. They typically believe that, although the factors which constitute the less stringent obligation do *tend* toward the existence of a moral obligation, those factors fall short of actually giving rise to such an obligation on the occasion under consideration. Actions in accordance with those factors, at the expense of alternatives that are more strongly promotive of some consequentialist objective, would produce the net effect of detracting from the realization of that objective. Accordingly, consequentialists are disposed to maintain that such actions are morally non-obligatory as well as morally impermissible. In the eyes of consequentialist theorists, the lone source of moral obligatoriness is the conduciveness of any mode of conduct to the maximal attainment of the desideratum or set of desiderata which the theorists favor. If the net effect of some mode of conduct MC would be to detract from the attainment of the specified desideratum or set of desiderata—because some alternative mode of conduct would be more conducive to that attainment—then MC does not partake of the aforementioned source of moral obligatoriness. By the reckoning of consequentialists, then, MC is neither morally obligatory nor morally permissible. By their reckoning, a person faced with the possibility of performing MC in these circumstances is not under any moral duty to perform it and is thus not confronted with any moral conflict that involves such a duty. In short, because of the emphasis of consequentialism on the balancing of considerations that respectively tend toward the existence of moral duties, consequentialists are not well equipped to recognize the reality of moral conflicts. Hence, as I have submitted elsewhere (2014, 11–14), and as Bas van Fraassen observed half a century ago (1973, 12), the inclinations of the founders of standard deontic logic to deny the possibility of deontic conflicts were very likely due in part to the consequentialist predilections of most of those founders.

Third, the clear ambition of the devisers of standard deontic logic was to have it parallel modal logic very closely. Quite unexceptionable is the proposition that the necessity of the occurrence of some event entails the possibility of its occurrence, and likewise unexceptionable is the proposition that the necessity of the non-occurrence of some event entails the possibility of its non-occurrence. However, when the property of necessity is replaced with the property of obligatoriness, and when the property of possibility is replaced with the property of permissibility, there are no entailments homologous to those just stated. Consequently, the project of assimilating deontic logic to modal logic has been partly responsible for the blindness of so many deontic logicians to the possibility of deontic conflicts.

Fourth, because moral theories and principles are supposed to provide answers to questions about the correct courses of conduct in multitudinous sets of circumstances, one complaint sometimes voiced about the specter of moral conflicts is that we would have no grounds for deciding what to do when confronted with clashing obligations (Dworkin 2011, 90; McConnell 2010, §§4 and 7). In other words, moral conflicts are thought to leave people bereft of action-guidance. Any anxiety along those lines is largely baseless. In most moral conflicts, the clashing duties are of unequal stringency; hence, the uniquely correct response to such a conflict is to fulfill the more stringent duty. Of course, the adjective "correct" here does not denote permissibility. Within a moral conflict, no morally permissible course of conduct is available. Nonetheless, although the uniquely correct mode of conduct in such circumstances is itself morally impermissible—and although the adoption of that course of conduct will therefore give rise to remedial duties—it is indeed uniquely correct in that the non-adoption of it would be an even graver wrong. Accordingly, there is no lack of action-guidance in any such moral conflict. Morality determinately prescribes the mode of conduct that is to be undertaken as the less gravely wrong way of dealing with the quandary which such a moral conflict presents. Furthermore, even when we ponder a moral conflict where the clashing duties are evenly balanced in their stringency or are incommensurably counterpoised, we should still conclude that the fulfillment of either duty will amount to a breach of the other and will thus impose remedial obligations on anyone who has committed the breach (Nussbaum 2000, 1009). Hence, although neither the fulfillment of the duty-to-φ nor the fulfillment of the duty-not-to-φ in a conflict of this latter kind is a morally better course of conduct than the other, we are not wholly devoid of guidance in a situation of this sort. Anyone aware of the nature of a moral conflict that confronts her has grounds for knowing that, regardless of whether she complies with her duty to φ or with her duty not to φ, she will have incurred a further moral obligation to remedy the wrong that she has thereby done.

Fifth, most of the founders of standard deontic logic believed that norms are non-propositional. Those founders were therefore inclined to cash out the logical relationships between norms by reference to the fulfillment-conditions thereof. However, as I have maintained elsewhere (2018, 198–9, 203, 214 n. 16), such an approach disastrously conflates the fulfillment-conditions and the existence-conditions of norms. That is, it conflates the conditions under which duty-imposing norms are satisfied and the conditions under which duty-imposing norms are operative. In any situation of deontic conflict, where someone is simultaneously under an obligation to φ and under an obligation not to φ, the bearer of those conflicting obligations cannot fulfill both of them. The joint fulfillment of conflicting duties is a logical impossibility. All the same, the conflicting duties can perfectly coherently coexist. A bearer of such duties will inevitably breach one or the other of them, but the very reason for the inevitability of a breach in one direction or the other is that the duties are simultaneously binding. Hence, a system of logic that gauges the logical relationships between norms (or between the duties imposed by norms) with reference to their fulfillment-conditions is fundamentally distortive.[9]

[9] That distortive method antedates the advent of standard deontic logic. It is also characteristic of Jeremy Bentham's "logic of the will," which is ably expounded in Hart 1982, 111–17.

Sixth, and finally, with regard to the realm of morality there have arisen concerns about unfairness or excessive onerousness that parallel the concerns about unfairness or excessive onerousness in the legal realm. Michael Moore has raised such a concern when he explains why he hopes to show that moral conflicts are very uncommon. On the one hand, Moore does briefly acknowledge the potential for conflicts between deontological duties, and he allows that "[i]t may not be, as Kant famously proclaimed, that a conflict of such obligations is literally 'inconceivable'" (2007, 37). On the other hand, he declares that "it would be unfortunate for us in the extreme if morality often confronted us with choices where we will be 'damned if we do and damned if we don't.' The distinctions we shall examine hold out the possibility of so limiting our stringent obligations as to minimize or even eliminate such situations of moral conflict" (2007, 37–8).

Moore's ambition to establish the infrequency of moral conflicts is focused not on the problem of action-guidance but instead on the onerousness or unfairness of a world in which someone often finds that every mode of conduct open to her is morally wrong. Such a worry is pertinent, of course, but Moore draws an inapt conclusion from it. Instead of indulging in the puerility of wishful thinking by trying to expound the general structure of morality in a manner that whisks most moral conflicts out of sight, we should quite frequently seek to act in ways—and to arrange our institutions in ways—that will reduce the incidence of such conflicts (Marcus 1980). Acting in conformity to a practically oriented conclusion of that sort is the best means of allaying the anxiety felt by Moore and others about the prospect of unavoidable wrongness. To act in such a fashion, one needs to be alert to the possibility and actuality of moral conflicts in a diversity of settings.

In other words, the consternation engendered by the specter of unavoidable wrongness should incline us away from the wishful thinking which Moore recommends. Far from trying to delineate the contours of morality in a manner that will obscure the emergence of moral conflicts, we should be seeking to grasp those contours with keen sensitivity to the likelihood of such conflicts. Only thus can we informedly fix upon the practical steps that are best suited to avert predicaments of unavoidable wrongness (insofar as they can and should be averted).

2.4.3 Contradictions

Unlike deontic conflicts, which can and do occur both in the realm of morality and in the realm of law, contradictions between moral positions or between legal positions cannot ever genuinely occur. Positions that contradict each other cannot coexist. This point applies to the right-hand half of the Hohfeldian table as much as to the left-hand half, but it is best broached here—because the contrast between the possibility of deontic conflicts and the impossibility of contradictions is illuminating, and because purported discoveries of contradictions among the norms of any particular legal system (or warnings against such contradictions) are usually focused on situations involving claim-right/duty relationships.

Of course, frequently the putative discoveries of contradictions stem from outright confusion as theorists fail to differentiate between contradictions and deontic conflicts. For instance, as I have remarked elsewhere (2007, 125–30), Lon Fuller persistently ran together contradictions and conflicts as he professed to be discussing the former while providing examples of the latter. Similarly, both Hans Kelsen and Eugenio Bulygin were sometimes guilty of such conflations. For example, near the outset of Bulygin's ruminations on Kelsen's thesis that there cannot ever be genuine contradictions between any of the norms of a legal system that are in effect at a given time, we encounter the following passage (Bulygin 2013, 225, quoting Kelsen 1967, 328):

> This thesis states that no two legal norms that belong to the same system can ever contradict each other. In other words, no two contradictory norms can be simultaneously valid. "It is not possible," Kelsen writes, "to describe a normative order by asserting the validity of the norms '*a* ought to be' and at the same time '*a* ought not to be.' "

Although Kelsen was correct in espousing his thesis about the impossibility of contradictions among the laws that are simultaneously valid in any system of governance, and although Bulygin went astray in trying to impugn that thesis, the quotation here from Kelsen muddies the water by encapsulating a deontic conflict rather than a contradiction.[10] Had Kelsen's thesis about consistency been aimed against the possibility of deontic conflicts within a legal system, it would have been badly misguided—for, as has just been argued, such conflicts are abidingly possible and are sometimes actual. Fortunately for Kelsen, however, his thesis was in fact aimed against the possibility of contradictions within a legal system. So directed, the thesis was indeed sound. There cannot ever be a situation where one norm in a legal system L makes it the case that Ezekiel owes Obadiah a duty to φ, while another norm in L simultaneously makes it the case that Ezekiel vis-à-vis Obadiah is at liberty not to φ. Those two deontic upshots cannot coexist within a single legal system.

At least as common as the conflation of conflicts and contradictions is another misstep that has led some philosophers to believe that contradictions are possible among the laws that are in effect in any particular jurisdiction. Often, such philosophers have failed to distinguish adequately between the legal norms in a jurisdiction and the formulations of those norms. Ironically, Kelsen was

10 I am here construing the normative auxiliary verb "ought" as a deontic auxiliary verb of obligation. If that auxiliary is instead construed as non-deontic, then the situation recounted by Kelsen involves neither a contradiction nor a conflict.

guilty of just such a failure—and furthermore of running together conflicts and contradictions yet again—even while he affirmed the impossibility of contradictions among the laws of any system of governance. He committed the norms/formulations muddle both in the passage quoted above and in the following passage: "Contradictions are also banned within the sphere of [law and morality]. Just as it is logically impossible to assert both 'A is' and 'A is not', so it is logically impossible to assert both 'A ought to be' and 'A ought not to be' " (Kelsen 1945, 374–5). Even if we leave aside the conflation of conflicts and contradictions in this statement, Kelsen erred in proclaiming that it is impossible to assert two contradictory propositions. Anybody can assert two such propositions, even though the state of affairs jointly denoted by them can never possibly obtain. I can easily assert that some specified mathematical theorem is provable, even if that putative theorem subsequently turns out to be false and therefore unprovable. In such an event, the proposition which I asserted was necessarily false, but there were no logical barriers or other impediments to my asserting it. Similarly, the lawmakers (whether legislative or adjudicative or administrative) in some system of governance can bring into existence various legal materials—statutes, regulations, ordinances, rulings, and so forth—which formulate norms that would be in contradiction if those norms were simultaneously in effect. The simultaneous existence of those contradictory formulations is entirely possible, just as my assertion about the provability of the mathematical theorem is entirely possible. What is impossible, of course, is the coexistence of the two norms that are denoted by the contradictory formulations. Those two norms cannot ever both be in effect at the same time, notwithstanding that the formulations of them are simultaneously "on the books" as some of the legal materials which the lawmakers of a jurisdiction have brought into existence. A promulgated norm-formulation which ordinarily denotes an operative norm can become a referentially empty formulation in the presence of a contradictory norm-formulation promulgated by the same system of legal governance. The contradictory norm-formulations can be "on the books" simultaneously, but at any given time one or the other of them is referentially empty whenever they are simultaneously on the books.

My latest quotation from Kelsen is especially puzzling because he himself proceeded straightaway to make the very point which I have just made about the importance of distinguishing between legal norms and the formulations of those norms (Kelsen 1945, 375):

> It is one of the main tasks of the jurist to give a consistent presentation of the material with which he deals. Since the material is presented in linguistic expressions, it is *a priori* possible that it may contain contradictions. The specific function of juristic interpretation is to eliminate these contradictions by showing that they are merely sham contradictions.

Kelsen here rightly highlighted the distinction between norms and norm-formulations, and the concomitant distinction between genuine contradictions and ostensible contradictions. Because the materials of a legal system are presented in written or spoken formulations, they can contain contradictions and inconsistencies. Nonetheless, the contradictions in the materials never correspond to contradictions between the norms that are simultaneously valid within the system. In a given jurisdiction, there might be one statute which purports to place anyone like Ezekiel under a duty-to-φ owed to anyone like Obadiah, and there might be another statute which purports to endow anyone like Ezekiel with a liberty-not-to-φ that is held vis-à-vis anyone like Obadiah. However, the legal norms respectively denoted by those two statutes cannot ever be in effect simultaneously. One or the other of those norms is in effect at any particular time, and the remaining one of them is not in effect at that time. The point here is not simply that the two norms are insusceptible to being implemented jointly—in that the effectuation of the first statute would result in the imposition of sanctions on Ezekiel for his not φ-ing, whereas the effectuation of the second statute would result in the withholding of any sanctions against Ezekiel for his not φ-ing. Although the norms denoted by the two statutes obviously cannot be implemented jointly, my point here is more deeply that the deontic upshot of each norm excludes the deontic upshot of the other. Not only can the two norms never be *given* effect jointly when Ezekiel does not φ, but additionally they can never be *in* effect jointly. It can never be the case that, within a single jurisdiction, Ezekiel owes Obadiah a legal duty to φ and simultaneously does not owe Obadiah any legal duty to φ. Consequently, the norm-formulations "on the books" in the relevant jurisdiction are not in congruity with the norms that are actually in effect there.

As I have remarked in a somewhat different context (2003, 66), the term "laws" is ambiguous in everyday discourse and in philosophical discourse. In some contexts it refers to norm-formulations such as the texts of statutes, and in other contexts it refers to the norms that are encapsulated by those formulations. That ambiguity does not inevitably engender confusion, since the distinct senses of "laws" can be kept suitably separate. Nonetheless, confusion can readily arise—as theorists who come upon some contradictions among laws in the first sense are tempted to infer that they have discovered some contradictions among laws in the second sense. Any such inference is to be resisted, for the incoherence that is possible at the level of norm-formulations is not ever paralleled at the level of deontic relationships that are actually in effect.

As Kelsen suggested in my latest quotation from him, a jurist or theorist who does encounter some contradictions at the level of the norm-formulations in a particular jurisdiction is faced with the task of explaining how the legal relationships in the jurisdiction are free of contradictions. One tack, which Kelsen seemed to have in mind, is to reconstrue the norm-formulations themselves with the aim of showing that the contradictions therein are only apparent and are not genuine even at the level of the formulations. Thus, for example, a jurist or theorist might interpret one of the two seemingly contradictory formulations in a way that reconciles it with the other such formulation. In many jurisdictions, these reconciliatory interpretations are commonly undertaken by adjudicative or administrative officials who are confronted with what appear to be contradictory provisions in the statutes or regulations or other materials which they are called upon to construe (Twining and Miers 2010, 146). In a closely related vein, the officials might conclude that one of two contradictory norm-formulations has superseded or precluded the operativeness of the other formulation. They might maintain, for instance, that a later enactment supersedes any portions of an earlier enactment with which it is in contradiction—even if the supersession is not explicitly signaled in the later enactment. Or the officials might conclude that, in the absence of any such explicit signal, the earlier enactment takes precedence over any portions of the later enactment which contradict it. Techniques of these kinds can often quite plausibly be wielded to resolve apparent contradictions at the level of the norm-formulations in a jurisdiction.

Still, there are of course no guarantees that those techniques or other cognate approaches will be plied by the officials in any particular set of circumstances where the legal materials in a jurisdiction contain some contradictory formulations. In a situation where a contradiction between formulations has not been explicitly addressed through any such techniques, legal scholars and philosophers will have to try to ascertain which of the formulations denotes a norm that is currently in effect and which of them denotes a norm that is not currently in effect. The most obvious tack for such an enquiry resides in examining the patterns of implementation pertaining to the contradictory formulations. Let us consider again a situation in which one enactment E_1 purports to place anybody like Ezekiel under a duty-to-φ owed to anyone like Obadiah, while another enactment E_2 in the same jurisdiction purports to endow anybody like Ezekiel with a liberty-not-to-φ that is held vis-à-vis anyone like Obadiah. Suppose that, whenever Ezekiel or anyone else like him in the jurisdiction has not φ-ed, the legal-governmental officials there take no steps whatsoever to give effect to the legal duty that has supposedly been imposed on Ezekiel and on everybody else like him by E_1. Observing such a pattern of wholesale non-enforcement, legal theorists can quite safely conclude that the norm denoted by E_1 is not currently in effect in the relevant jurisdiction—and that the norm denoted by E_2 is instead in effect there. Such a conclusion is importantly different from the conclusion that would be warranted if there were no E_2 "on the books." Without the presence of any E_2, legal theorists who observe the wholesale absence of enforcement pertaining to the duty imposed under the norm denoted by E_1 are warranted only in concluding that the norm denoted by E_1 is regularly unenforced. They would lack any basis for concluding that that norm is not currently in effect as a valid law of the jurisdiction.

As has already been suggested, the reason for this difference between the conclusion warranted in the absence of E_2 and the conclusion warranted in the presence of E_2 is that the deontic upshot of E_2 cannot coexist with the deontic upshot of E_1. The norms denoted by those enactments cannot ever simultaneously be in effect within a single jurisdiction, because Ezekiel cannot ever simultaneously owe Obadiah a legal duty to φ and not owe Obadiah any legal duty to φ within a single jurisdiction. Consequently, when E_2 is "on the books," and when the pattern of law-administration is along the lines envisaged in the preceding paragraph, the appropriate conclusion is that the norm denoted by E_2 is currently in effect and that the norm denoted by E_1 is not currently in effect within the jurisdiction where those two enactments are both "on the books." Accordingly, any duties that would have been imposed under the norm denoted by E_1 are currently non-existent. By contrast, when E_1 is "on the books" whereas E_2 is not, and when the pattern of law-application is along the lines envisaged in the preceding paragraph, the apposite conclusion is that the duties imposed under the norm denoted by E_1 are existent but are regularly unenforced. Although those duties are *in* effect, they are not *given* effect. Perhaps they are unenforceable, or perhaps they are simply unenforced; in either case, the bindingness of the duties as a deontic matter is not currently backed up by the wielding of sanctions or other measures through which a system of governance can seek to secure compliance with legal requirements.

2.4.4 Unenforcedness and Unenforceability

In my discussion of the impossibility of contradictions among the legal norms or legal positions that are in effect at any given time within a system of governance, we have just glimpsed the matter of legal duties that are regularly unenforced. Although the topic of legal powers to enforce legal duties will figure saliently in Chapter 4 of this book, and although the power/liability axis in Hohfeld's table of legal relationships will be examined later in this chapter, we can fruitfully consider now the matter of unenforcedness and unenforceability. That matter is an ingredient in any full explication of the claim-right/duty axis in the Hohfeldian table.

Whether merely unenforced or also unenforceable, a legal duty that does not receive any backing from the mechanisms of a system of governance through sanctions or preventative measures is nonetheless in existence as a legal duty. The deontic upshot of the law that imposes the duty does obtain, even though that deontic upshot is not accompanied by any measures of material implementation in response to contraventions of it. For example, suppose that a municipality enacts an ordinance that prohibits jaywalking on the streets of the city. Suppose further that acts of jaywalking never or almost never trigger any responses from the administrative officials (such as constables) who are responsible for enforcing the city's laws. In such circumstances, the duty imposed on each person under the terms of the ordinance is regularly unenforced. All the same, that duty incumbent on each person is existent as a genuine legal duty. Until the ordinance is repealed either expressly or implicitly, its deontic upshot resides in legally obligating everyone within the municipality to refrain from acts of jaywalking. That upshot is not undone by the sheer fact that the obligation in question is regularly unenforced. Indeed, as I will explain shortly, a duty that is regularly unenforced can nevertheless be of considerable practical importance.

Before we explore that point about practical importance, however, we should ponder the difference between mere unenforcedness and unenforceability. In the scenario of the anti-jaywalking ordinance, the duty incumbent on each person to refrain from acts of jaywalking is very likely enforceable even though it is persistently unenforced. That is, very likely the constables of the municipality and other local officials are legally empowered to give effect to the ordinance by apprehending and fining people who jaywalk on the streets of the city. Though the constables and other officials do not exercise their powers of enforcement in response to breaches of the anti-jaywalking ordinance, they could do so if they were differently inclined. Hence, the ordinance is not legally unenforceable. By contrast, some other readily envisioned laws are unenforceable as well as persistently unenforced.

For instance, suppose that a law in some jurisdiction J places every school in J under a legal duty to have inner doors that are all made entirely of wood, and suppose that there is no law in J which provides that each school there is legally at liberty not to have inner doors that are all made entirely of wood. Let us suppose further that some of the schools in J have inner doors that are made of glass rather than of wood. In response to this situation, no measures of enforcement whatsoever are undertaken. Though the absence of any such measures could have stemmed simply from the disinclination of the officials in J to exercise powers of law-enforcement with which they are vested, it in fact stems instead from their not being endowed with any such powers that would cover the situation of the schools. Neither any general authorization nor any specific authorization empowers the officials in J's system of governance to proceed against schools in connection with violations of construction-safety laws. Moreover, when a student suffers an injury to her hand through the shattering of a portion of a glass door in her school, and when she pursues legal proceedings against the school to recover damages for her injury, the courts in J correctly hold that—in the absence of any negligence on the part of the school—there is no basis, under the law of J, for an injunction or an award of damages against the school. Under the law of J, the sheer fact that the construction-safety enactment has been breached is not such a basis. Neither through public-law administrative measures nor through private-law adjudicative proceedings, then, are there any legal powers to enforce the duty which requires that all the inner doors of each school in J be made entirely of wood. That legal duty is unenforceable rather than merely unenforced. Nonetheless, it is a perfectly genuine legal duty. Its deontic upshot, or the deontic upshot of the law that imposes it, is not dissolved or precluded by its unenforceability. Every school in J is legally obligated to have inner doors that are all made entirely of wood. A school in J will be committing a legal wrong if it does not have such doors.

No functional system of law could operate entirely or predominantly through duties that are unenforceable. As H.L.A. Hart maintained in *The Concept of Law* (1994, 193–200), the need for sanctions as means of giving effect to legal duties is something that follows from certain elementary characteristics of human nature. Still, any functional system of governance can operative effectively while a small proportion of the duties imposed by it are not only unenforced but also unenforceable. In J, the effectiveness of the overall operations of its system of governance is compatible with the fact that the law pertaining to the composition of the inner doors of schools is not enforceable by any of the coercive mechanisms of that system.

Still, although the overall system of governance in J can function effectively despite the unenforceability of its legal requirement pertaining to the doors of schools, some readers might wonder about that requirement itself. Why should it be classified as a genuine legal duty, given that it cannot be enforced at all by J's legal-governmental officials? Two replies to this question are appropriate. First, even if every unenforceable legal duty were devoid of all significance on a quotidian practical level, the deontic upshot of each such duty would abide. As has been stated in the penultimate paragraph above, the placing of a party (such as each school in J) under a legal duty to φ will have made it legally wrong for that party not to φ. For such a party, φ-ing is legally mandatory. Precisely because that deontic upshot ensues from the imposition of a legal duty-to-φ even when the duty in question is unenforceable, the law which imposes the duty will have been repealed or suspended—implicitly if not explicitly—by another law that is in contradiction with it. If no deontic upshot were produced by the imposition of an unenforceable legal duty-to-φ on any party P, then the law imposing such a duty could coexist with a law that makes it legally permissible for P not to φ. However, given that the upshot of legal obligatoriness is indeed produced by a legal duty-to-φ even when the duty is unenforceable, the two laws just mentioned cannot coexist as valid legal norms. Only one of them can be in effect at a given time, since it can never be the case that some mode of conduct or some state of affairs is both legally impermissible and legally permissible for any party simultaneously within a single system of law.

Second, as a result of generating the deontic upshot that has been summarized here, a law that imposes unenforceable duties can be of considerable significance on an everyday level in its guiding and influencing of the behavior of the parties to whom its duties are applicable. At that level, the difference between the existence of a law that imposes unenforceable duties-to-φ and the absence of any law that imposes duties-to-φ can be far from inconsequential. When a law that imposes unenforceable duties-to-φ has been brought into existence, the prevailing system of governance has deemed φ-ing to be legally mandatory and has thereby set a standard of conduct for the parties to whom the law is addressed. For any such party, not φ-ing is legally impermissible. That deontic upshot will not inevitably yield significant consequences at the level of everyday guidance and influence, but the occurrence of such consequences is always possible and is far from outlandish. In some contexts, the occurrence of such consequences can be highly likely. For instance, although the schools in J will not incur any sanctions if they fail to comply with the law which requires them to have inner doors that are all made entirely of wood, the administrators who run the schools in J may well be inclined to bring their institutions into compliance with that law (or to keep their institutions in compliance with it). Especially if the system of governance that presides in J is a liberal democracy, the status of some mode of conduct as legally mandatory can be a powerful stimulus for the adoption of that mode of conduct. Duty-imposing legal norms and the formulations that denote them can serve to channel and direct the behavior of people even when the duties established by the norms are unenforceable. When those effects of channeling and directing occur, they are of course not due to any prospect of sanctions for contraventions of unenforceable obligations (since there is no such prospect). Instead, they are due both to the prestige of the law in fixing upon authoritative standards and to the closely related role of the law in furnishing people with focal points that can overcome coordination problems. At least in societies with systems of governance that are robustly liberal-democratic, those features of the law are often operative. At least in such societies, then, some unenforceable legal requirements can significantly influence the conduct of people in the matters to which those requirements pertain. For example, if J is a society over which a liberal-democratic system of governance presides, the administrators of schools in J may well be inclined to comply with the construction-safety law pertaining to the inner doors of their buildings. They may well wish to avoid the classifiability of their schools as lawbreakers. Such an effect is not inevitable, of course, but it is far from fanciful.

Are unenforceable legal requirements, with their channeling and directing effects, essentially the same as the aspirations specified in a set of voluntary guidelines issued by a system of governance? If this question is construed as asking about the ways in which (or the extent to which) the behavior of people is influenced by the unenforceable requirements and by the voluntary guidelines respectively, then it is broaching a complex matter of individual and social psychology that cannot be explored here. That empirical matter is better tackled in a work of social science than in a work of philosophy. Alternatively, however, the question above can be construed as asking about the requirements and guidelines themselves—rather than about their effects. So interpreted, the question is broaching a philosophical matter. Is the hortatory tenor of the guidelines assimilable to the deontic tenor of the requirements? As should be manifest from what has been said already, the answer to this question is negative. Whether a duty-imposing law is enforceable or unenforceable, certain modes of conduct or certain states of affairs are made legally mandatory by the obligations which that law establishes. Those obligations legally disallow any contrary modes of conduct or any contrary states of affairs. By contrast, the specifications of guidelines in a voluntary code implicitly or explicitly disclaim the mandatoriness of what they prescribe. Though the exhortative force of the specifications may be strong, it does not render anything legally obligatory. Deviations from the guidelines are not legal wrongs.

Exactly because the guidelines in a voluntary code do not establish any legal requirements, they can coexist with laws which permit modes of conduct or states of affairs that are contrary to what the guidelines prescribe. Whereas the legal norm in J that imposes on each school an unenforceable legal duty pertaining to the composition of inner doors will be negated or suspended as a valid norm by the introduction of another law which permits each school not to have inner doors that are all made entirely of wood, a law of the latter kind would not negate or suspend a voluntary guideline in J that recommends against the use of substances other than wood for the inner doors of schools. Such a guideline would be entirely consistent with the permission-conferring law, since it would not legally disallow anything which the permission-conferring law allows. Indeed, the recommendation in the guideline would not legally disallow anything, period. Devoid of any duty-imposing upshot, the voluntary guideline would not clash with the deontic upshot of any permission-bestowing law. By contrast, the law that imposes the unenforceable duty on each school in J would be inconsistent with a law in J that confers upon each school a legal liberty not to have inner doors that are all composed entirely of wood. Those two laws cannot simultaneously be valid, for the deontic upshot of each is logically inconsistent with the deontic upshot of the other. That logical inconsistency obtains irrespective of the unenforceability of the duties that are incumbent on the schools with regard to their inner doors. What matters for the deontic upshot of a law is whether that law makes some mode of conduct legally mandatory, rather than whether the mandatoriness is materially backed up by measures of enforcement and prevention. Accordingly, even if the conformity-eliciting effects of an unenforceable duty-imposing law are broadly similar to those of a voluntary guideline, the general character of that law is unassimilable to the general character of the guideline.

2.5 Liberties and No-Rights

Much more remains to be said about claim-rights and duties, and much more will be said in this book. For one thing, as has already been stated, Chapter 3 will defend the Correlativity Axiom—the proposition that every claim-right entails a duty with the same content and that every duty entails a claim-right with the same content—in response to various objections and queries that have been leveled against it. My defense of the Correlativity Axiom will bring to bear some of the quantificational apparatus that is crucial for a sound analysis of the positions in Hohfeld's table of deontic and normative relationships. Furthermore, even as we move on for the moment to examine the liberty/no-right column in Hohfeld's table, the roles of claim-rights and duties will continue to figure saliently. Some of the matters to be contemplated in one's probing of the complexities of liberties and no-rights are centered on the interplay between the claim-right/duty axis and the liberty/no-right axis in Hohfeld's schema. While now proceeding to come to grips with the second of those axes, we will not have left the first of them behind.

A Hohfeldian liberty is a permission. When somebody is legally or morally at liberty to φ, the applicable laws or the applicable moral principles permit her to φ. Either in the realm of law or in the realm of morality (or in each realm), she is not under any duty to refrain from φ-ing. A Hohfeldian liberty is an instance of freedom, but the freedom is deontic rather than modal; it consists in someone's being allowed to φ, rather than in her being able to φ. Of course, very often somebody is able to do what she is permitted to do. In many other cases, however, her Hohfeldian liberty to φ is not accompanied by any ability of hers to φ. Conversely, very often someone is capable of doing things which she is not legally or morally at liberty to do. The concept of deontic freedom as Hohfeldian liberties and the concept of modal freedom as abilities are extensionally as well as intensionally non-equivalent. Permissions and abilities frequently coincide but likewise frequently diverge.

As is indicated by my assertion in the preceding paragraph that a Hohfeldian liberty to φ involves the absence of a duty not to φ, and as I have already explained in §2.3 above, duties and liberties are logical duals rather than logical contradictories. "Leah owes Ethan a moral duty not to punch him in the face" is equivalent to "It is not the case that Leah is morally at liberty vis-à-vis Ethan to punch him in the face," because "Leah owes Ethan a moral duty not to punch him in the face" and "Leah is morally at liberty vis-à-vis Ethan to punch him in the face" are logical duals. Each of the propositions in the latter pair is the negation of the other, and the content of the deontic predicate in each of those two propositions is the negation of the content of the deontic predicate in the other proposition. Disastrous confusion can ensue when theorists do not take account of the negation at the level of the predicated content as well as the negation at the level of the proposition. Unlike "Leah owes Ethan a moral duty not to punch him in the face" and "Leah is morally at liberty vis-à-vis Ethan to punch him in the face," "Leah owes Ethan a moral duty not to punch him in the face" and "Leah is morally at liberty vis-à-vis Ethan not to punch him in the face" are perfectly consistent propositions. Though this point about the twofold levels of the negation in the relationship between any logical duals may seem obvious when it is highlighted, quite a few philosophers in the past have overlooked it or have baselessly accused Hohfeld of overlooking it.[11] For

[11] For various references, see Kramer 1998, 13 n 4.

example, when ruminating on the Hohfeldian analysis, Richard Flathman wrote that "the [negation] of *A*'s having a liberty to do *X* is for him to have a duty to do *X*" (Flathman 1976, 39). Much earlier, only a few years after Hohfeld's death, Albert Kocourek misguidedly complained that under the Hohfeldian analysis a person "may have a [Hohfeldian liberty] and a Duty as to the same act.... In other words, Duty and *No*duty are the same thing—a rather unusual result even for an unusual system of terminology" (Kocourek 1922, 239, emphasis in original). Albeit Hohfeld himself did not employ the technical language of "logical duality," he not only avoided Flathman's and Kocourek's blunders but also in fact emphasized the twofold levels of the negation in the relationship between duties and liberties (Hohfeld 1923, 39).

2.5.1 Unpaired Liberties and Paired Liberties

One's Hohfeldian liberty to φ consists in one's being legally or morally permitted to φ. In itself, an ascription of a liberty-to-φ to a person P leaves open the question whether P is also at liberty not to φ. P might of course hold both a liberty to φ and a liberty not to φ, but alternatively she might hold only a liberty to φ and might lack any liberty not to φ (or vice versa). If P does hold only a liberty to φ and does lack any liberty not to φ, she is both duty-bound to φ and at liberty to φ. As a matter of logic—rather than as a matter of jurisdiction-specific constraints that might be in place—a liberty to φ and a duty to φ can be combined just as readily as can a liberty to φ and a liberty not to φ. When a liberty to φ is coupled with a duty to φ, it is an unpaired liberty; contrariwise, when a liberty to φ is coupled with a liberty not to φ, each of them is a paired liberty. Any Hohfeldian liberty can be either paired or unpaired. (As is evident from my reflections on deontic conflicts in §2.4.2 above, P can lack a liberty-to-φ while also lacking a liberty-not-to-φ. In that event, P is under a duty not to φ and is simultaneously under a duty to φ.)

Joab might hold a liberty to φ and a liberty not to φ vis-à-vis Absalom, while holding only a liberty to φ or only a liberty not to φ vis-à-vis Zebulun. For example, suppose that Joab and Zebulun have entered into a contract whereby Joab has undertaken to deliver a certain package to Zebulun's home by 5:00pm on a specified day. Under the terms of the contract, Joab vis-à-vis Zebulun still holds a liberty to deliver the package but no longer holds a liberty not to deliver it. Joab vis-à-vis Zebulun is now legally and morally obligated to deliver the package. Vis-à-vis Zebulun, then, Joab's liberty to deliver the package is unpaired rather than paired. Vis-à-vis Absalom, however, Joab continues to hold both a liberty to deliver the package and a liberty not to deliver it. His legal duty to deliver the package is owed to Zebulun (and to the prevailing system of governance) rather than to Absalom. Thus, vis-à-vis Absalom, Joab's liberty to deliver the package is paired with his liberty not to deliver it.

In sum, whenever we ask whether somebody's liberty to φ is unpaired or paired, we need to specify the party (or parties) vis-à-vis whom the liberty to φ is held. Joab's liberty vis-à-vis Zebulun to deliver the package to Zebulun's home is an unpaired liberty, whereas Joab's liberty vis-à-vis Absalom to deliver the package to Zebulun's home is a paired liberty. Vis-à-vis Zebulun, the liberty of Joab to deliver the package is coupled with a duty to deliver it; vis-à-vis Absalom, the liberty of Joab to deliver the package is coupled with a liberty not to deliver it. Of course, someone might not owe to anybody at all a legal or moral duty to φ. If so, vis-à-vis everyone, she holds a legal or moral liberty not to φ. We can then ask whether that legal or moral liberty-not-to-φ held vis-à-vis everyone is paired with a legal or moral liberty-to-φ that is also held vis-à-vis everyone. Even here, however, we are quantificationally specifying the parties vis-à-vis whom each liberty is held. Ascriptions of liberties (whether paired or unpaired) that involve quantification over the parties in the correlative positions are something to which we shall return shortly in this chapter.

Some philosophers have rather curiously maintained that the noun "liberty" is inapposite for an unpaired permission. As I have mentioned in Chapter 1, Hohfeld himself more often employed the term "privilege" than the term "liberty" for the entitlement in the second column of his table. Strangely, some philosophers have felt that the former term is better for an unpaired permission and that the term "liberty" should be reserved for paired permissions. For example, David Adams has opined as follows (1985, 87–8):

> [T]he widespread propensity on the part of Hohfeld's critics to substitute "liberty" for "privilege" [is] certainly a chief source of confusion. Simply put, the problem here is that it does not seem to follow from the assertion that I am "privileged" to do p that I am "at liberty" to do p: the latter seems to make a stronger claim. To say that I am at liberty to do something suggests ... that I am permitted to do it and permitted not to do it. ...Thus it appears that on any reasonable theory of liberty the expressions "having a liberty" or "being at liberty" will say something stronger than "having a privilege" or "being privileged."

Contrary to what Adams submits, the substitution of "liberty" for "privilege" is salutary and is not in any way a source of confusion. Moreover, the reason for the salutariness of that substitution is unrelated to the paired/unpaired distinction. Most modern commentators on Hohfeld (including me) prefer the word "liberty" because the word "privilege" conveys the impression that an entitlement denoted by it is a prerogative vested distinctively in one person or in each member of some special class of people. That person or each member in that class of people is privileged by dint of being singled out to hold the entitlement in question. Because the noun "privilege" so strongly carries this connotation of someone's having been set apart from all or most other people through the holding of a special prerogative not enjoyed by those others, it is inapt as a label for the entitlement in the second axis of Hohfeld's schema.[12]

Some Hohfeldian liberties (whether paired or unpaired) are privileges in the sense just outlined, of course, but countless other Hohfeldian liberties are not privileges in that sense. Let us quickly ponder a couple of examples. First, Mabel is like everyone else in any ordinary circumstances in that she is legally and morally *at liberty* to refrain from punching Edward in the face. She is of course also like everyone else in any non-pugilistic circumstances in that she is legally and morally *obligated* to refrain from punching Edward in the face. Her liberty to refrain from punching Edward in the face is therefore not paired with a liberty to punch him in the face, but her liberty to refrain from punching him in the face is decidedly not a privilege in the sense limned by my preceding paragraph. It is scarcely a prerogative that sets Mabel apart from her fellow citizens. Second, every motorist in any ordinary circumstances is legally and morally *at liberty* to refrain from proceeding through a red light at any intersection, and every motorist in any ordinary circumstances is also legally and morally *obligated* to refrain from proceeding through a red light at any intersection. Hence, the holding of that unpaired liberty by each motorist does not distinguish him or her from anybody else. One's designation of that liberty as a privilege would thus be highly misleading.

Conversely, some paired liberties are indeed privileges in the sense specified by the penultimate paragraph above. For instance, the law of a given jurisdiction might invest a particular person or company with a liberty to charge a toll for the use of a certain road by motorists. That person or company is also legally at liberty to refrain from charging a toll to motorists. Although everybody else in the jurisdiction is likewise legally at liberty to refrain from charging any toll to motorists for the use of the specified road, nobody else there is legally at liberty to charge a toll. Hence, the liberty of the chosen person or company to charge a fee is a paired liberty and is nonetheless a privilege in the sense summarized above.

In short, Adams's terminological quibbling is baseless. The unpairedness of many Hohfeldian liberties is not a consideration that tells in favor of the highly misleading term "privileges" as a label for those liberties. Still, pointless misgivings about the terminology of "liberties" as applied to unpaired permissions are not unique to Adams. One of the earliest critics of Hohfeld, Kocourek, not only failed to grasp that duties and liberties are logical duals—for which I have criticized him already—but also failed to grasp that unpaired permissions are indeed liberties. Kocourek wrote as follows: "If an owner is under a *duty* to stay off his own land how can it be said, if we are talking of law, that he has a *liberty* to stay off the

[12] In a related sense, the term "privilege" in everyday discourse denotes something that is a source of particular honor or gratification for the person who is endowed with it. For example, a politician upon his retirement might declare that his service as an elected legislator has been a great privilege for him. The unpaired Hohfeldian liberties recounted by my next paragraph are not privileges in this latter sense any more than in the sense sketched above.

land? ... If one is under a duty to perform or omit an act, freedom of action is superseded."[13] To this travesty of an argument by Kocourek, the obvious riposte is that a duty to stay off some land and a liberty to stay off that same land are patently compatible. Somebody vested with the specified liberty is legally permitted to fulfill the specified duty. In the second sentence of this quotation, Kocourek seems again to be fundamentally confused about the logical duality of duties and liberties. One's legal duty to φ does supersede one's legal liberty not to φ, but it scarcely supersedes one's legal liberty to φ. Of course, that latter liberty will itself not exist if the person under a legal duty to φ is simultaneously under a legal duty not to φ. A deontic conflict of that kind is of course possible, but its occurrence is decidedly not preordained by the sheer fact that the person is under a legal duty to φ. *Pace* Kocourek, one's bearing of a duty to φ does not entail one's bearing of a duty to abstain from φ-ing.

A far more sophisticated commentator on Hohfeld, Luis Duarte d'Almeida, does not harbor any of the pointless terminological anxiety displayed by these other writers. However, a comment by Duarte d'Almeida can help to reveal why such anxiety is so misplaced (2016, 557):

> Hohfeldian liberties, in other words, are "single" liberties; a liberty to φ is compatible either with a liberty not to φ or with a duty to φ. The ordinary, non-technical notion of being at liberty to φ, with its implicature of freedom to either φ or not φ, is analysable as a conjunction—a "pair"—of Hohfeldian liberties.

Perhaps Duarte d'Almeida is correct when he suggests that a pre-theoretical understanding of one's possession of a liberty to φ carries a defeasible presupposition that one is both at liberty to φ and at liberty not to φ. However, even if such a suggestion is correct, the defeasibility or cancelability of the presupposition is crucial. Unless that presupposition is indeed defeasible or cancelable, an ordinary conception of the nature of a legal liberty to φ would be committed to the proposition that every set of circumstances within the ambit of any system of governance is either a situation of paired liberties or a situation of deontic conflict. After all, if the pre-theoretical understanding of a legal liberty-to-φ is that no such liberty exists unless it is paired with a legal liberty not to φ, then the pre-theoretical understanding presumes that everyone at any time *either* is legally at liberty to φ and legally at liberty not to φ *or else* is both under a legal duty not to φ and under a legal duty to φ. Now, there are ample reasons for thinking that any ordinary conception of one's possession of a liberty to φ does not preposterously carry such a commitment to a stark dichotomy between paired liberties and deontic conflicts. There are thus

[13] Kocourek 1922, 238, emphases in original. For a couple of much more recent articles that express some broadly similar terminological reservations, see Nascimento 2019; Oliveira Lima et al. 2021, 21–3.

ample reasons for insisting that, if Duarte d'Almeida is correct in suggesting that an ordinary conception of one's possession of a liberty to φ does carry an implicature about the pairing of that liberty with a liberty not to φ, the implicature is readily defeasible or cancelable.

2.5.2 The Contents of Liberties

In §2.4.1 above, I have argued against the notion that the content of every duty perforce makes reference to the conduct of the duty-bearer. Because duties and liberties are logical duals, that point about the contents of duties is applicable *mutatis mutandis* to the contents of liberties. Though the contents of countless liberties do refer to actions or omissions by the liberty-holders, the contents of countless other liberties do not so refer. Let us consider again the scenario from the opening paragraph of §2.4.1. Phineas in that scenario has come to owe a legal or moral duty to Hephzibah, where the content of the duty pertains to the sunniness of the weather on the following afternoon. Notwithstanding that the conduct of Phineas (specifically, his provision of assurances about the weather) has played an indispensable role in giving rise to the duty that is incumbent on him, the content of that duty does not make any reference to his conduct. Now, given that every duty is the dual of a liberty with a content that is the negation of the content of the duty, the dual of the duty owed by Phineas to Hephzibah is a liberty pertaining to the occurrence of inclement weather on the following afternoon. Phineas owes his duty to Hephzibah if and only if, vis-à-vis her, he does not hold a liberty with the content just specified. That content, of course, does not make any reference to his conduct.

Liberties with contents that do not refer to any actions or omissions by the people who hold the liberties, then, are innumerable. Whenever somebody has not come to be under a duty with the same content as that of the duty owed by Phineas to Hephzibah, he or she holds a liberty—vis-à-vis everyone else—with regard to the occurrence of inclement weather on the following afternoon. In other words, liberties of that kind are pervasive. So too are myriads of other liberties with contents that do not refer to any actions or omissions by the holders of those liberties. Insofar as somebody has not undergone the imposition of a duty vis-à-vis someone else with regard to the occurrence of some natural event (or with regard to the occurrence of some humanly caused event in which he is not a participant), he holds a liberty with a content that is the negation of the content of any such duty. Ubiquitous, therefore, are liberty/no-right relationships between people with contents that are not focused at all on any actions or omissions by the holders of the liberties.

Of course, there very seldom arise any contexts in which people need to advert to any of the liberty/no-right relationships that have just been broached. In almost all circumstances, those relationships can safely be taken for granted instead of being invoked or pondered. However, the fact that those relationships can suitably go unmentioned in nearly all contexts is not an indication that they are unimportant. On the contrary, they are of enormous importance—for, without them, people would be under crushingly onerous legal or moral duties at all times. In being at once hugely important and very safely taken for granted and left unspoken on nearly all occasions, the existence of these multitudinous liberty/no-right relationships is somewhat like the continued presence of oxygen in the atmosphere of the planet Earth. In the vast majority of contexts where human beings are pursuing their projects and planning their activities, they do not have to pay any attention explicitly to the fact that oxygen will continue to be present in the atmosphere of Earth. They can safely take that fact for granted, instead of adverting to it directly. Still, the continuation of the presence of oxygen in the atmosphere of Earth is manifestly vital for all those projects and activities. In a roughly parallel fashion, the liberty/no-right relationships adumbrated here are essential for keeping each person's deontic burdens to manageable levels, yet there is hardly ever an occasion for invoking any of those relationships. In nearly all circumstances they can safely remain in the background, tacitly but pervasively.

In the respect just noted, the liberties with contents that do not refer to actions or omissions by the holders of those liberties are not fundamentally different from most liberties with contents that do refer to such actions or omissions. Though some liberties of the latter kind will be invoked in quite a few credible contexts, countless other such liberties can and do remain tacitly in the background. Suppose that Sharon is a resident of the United Kingdom and that she is legally at liberty vis-à-vis everyone else in the United Kingdom to hold her left arm above her head for the next twenty minutes. She is furthermore legally at liberty, vis-à-vis everyone else in the United Kingdom, to rotate that arm either clockwise or counter-clockwise. She is likewise legally at liberty, vis-à-vis everyone else in the United Kingdom, to keep her arm lowered on her desk for the next twenty minutes. There will not arise any occasion for Sharon to invoke any of these liberties or even to reflect fleetingly on the fact that she is endowed with them. In that regard, those liberties are akin to her sundry liberties with contents that do not refer to her own conduct. In virtually every context, they can remain unnoticed in the backdrop of her life.

Moreover, as will become apparent when this chapter arrives at the right-hand half of Hohfeld's schema, countless immunities are also akin to the liberties that have been touched upon here. Multitudes of Hohfeldian immunities remain unglimpsed, even though they are vital components of the moral fabric and legal fabric of people's lives. Indeed, as will be seen, some immunities are partly constitutive of all other Hohfeldian legal and moral positions. Nevertheless, despite the crucial roles of these vast arrays of immunities in the moral and legal dimensions of people's lives—or perhaps precisely because of the ubiquity of those roles—the immunities are almost all taken for granted. Seldom if ever are there any occasions for people to advert to them directly. Thus, although liberties with contents that do not refer to any actions or omissions by the liberty-holders are almost always taken for granted instead of being invoked or directly discerned, they do not thereby differ from numerous other Hohfeldian entitlements. Their existence and importance and pervasiveness are not at all placed in doubt by their remaining unmentioned and unnoticed nearly everywhere.

2.5.3 Exercises Protected by Claim-Rights

Although claim-rights and liberties are obviously quite different from each other as first-order Hohfeldian entitlements, and although their disjoinability will be highlighted in my next subsection, they can and frequently do combine in ways that have been remarked upon—though not always accurately characterized—in the philosophy of rights. A Hohfeldian liberty to φ does not in itself provide any deontic protection for the ability of its holder to exercise the specified liberty by φ-ing. As a permission to φ, where the permission consists in the absence of a duty not to φ, a liberty to φ can exist in a situation where its holder is permissibly thwarted from exercising it. For example, Ithamar can be legally at liberty to win a two-mile race against Hermione, and Hermione can be legally at liberty to win that race against Ithamar. If Ithamar succeeds in exercising his liberty to win the race by outrunning Hermione without contravening any of the rules of the event, he will permissibly have precluded Hermione from exercising her cognate liberty to win the race. Conversely, if Hermione succeeds in exercising her liberty to win the race by outrunning Ithamar without contravening any of the rules, she will permissibly have stymied Ithamar from exercising his homologous liberty. Any number of further examples could be adduced to illustrate this point, of course.

Nonetheless, although a liberty to φ does not in itself provide any deontic protection for the ability of its holder to φ, a liberty to φ will always be accompanied by some claim-rights that do supply such deontic protection. Indeed, the scenario in the preceding paragraph exemplifies the ways in which claim-rights that accompany liberties can serve to furnish deontic protection for the exercising of those liberties. I have talked there about outrunning a rival without contravening any of the rules of the event. Under the rules of virtually any race, each competitor will be endowed with sundry claim-rights vis-à-vis any other competitor(s). Each competitor will hold claim-rights against being shot or stabbed or thrown to the ground or deliberately tripped, and each competitor will have claim-rights against the wielding of various other techniques through which any rival(s) might cheat. Many of those institutional claim-rights coincide in their contents with certain legal claim-rights held by each competitor vis-à-vis any other competitor(s), and all of those institutional claim-rights coincide in their contents with moral claim-rights held by each competitor. Ithamar holds such claim-rights vis-à-vis Hermione, and Hermione holds such claim-rights vis-à-vis Ithamar. What is deontically protected by those claim-rights is not the liberty of Ithamar or of Hermione to win the race, but instead the ability or effort of each of them to win the race. In other words, the exercise of that liberty—rather than the liberty itself—is what receives deontic protection from the claim-rights vested in each competitor against the use of unfair tactics by the other competitor(s). Because of the existence of those claim-rights, the only permissible way for each competitor to win the race lies in outrunning the other competitor(s).

As has been underscored, claim-rights of the sort contemplated at this juncture do not deontically protect the liberties which they accompany. Instead, they deontically protect the exercising of those liberties by the holders thereof. (The liberties themselves are protected chiefly by immunities, as we shall see later.) This distinction is surprisingly often overlooked in the philosophical literature on rights and right-holding. Let us glance at just a few examples. Rowan Cruft, a highly perceptive contributor to that literature, has written as follows (2019, 83–4):

> [B]are Hohfeldian [liberties] are constituted simply by the absence of directed duties, and hence are not violable or infringeable. Insofar as we talk of the violation or infringement of a [liberty] right (such as my right to walk on a beach), we are referring to violation or infringement of the Hohfeld[ian] claims protecting it.

Siegfried van Duffel twice commits a similar misstep in the following passage (2017, 194, emphases in original, footnote omitted):

> When we recognize liberties as rights, we do so because they are protected by a collection of more general duties that are not correlative to the liberty, but that constitute—in Hart's terminology—a protective perimeter that protects us from *certain kinds of* interference. Call these "protected liberties." The normative constraints thesis would then hold that liberties which are not *vested* must be *protected* by such general duties if they are to be recognized as rights.

James Penner, another theorist who has contributed insightfully to the philosophical literature on rights and right-holding, is equally guilty of carelessness on this point. He writes that "having the right to [some garden gnomes] is normally regarded as comprising not only the right to non-interference by others, but that this claim-right both protects and to some extent goes hand in hand with the liberty-right to destroy the gnomes" (Penner 2017, 101). Peter Westen likewise declares that a person's "claim-right vis-à-vis all [other] persons—including the state—to defend himself means that no one may interfere with his liberty-right to defend himself."[14]

[14] Westen 2018, 461 (italics removed). For two quite recent articles that repeatedly fail to mark the distinction between deontically protecting a liberty and deontically protecting the exercise of a liberty, see Halpin 2019 and Spena 2012.

Sometimes a person's liberty to φ is accompanied by a claim-right or a set of claim-rights against all ways of preventing the person from φ-ing, but more frequently a person's liberty to φ is accompanied by claim-rights against various ways of preventing the person's φ-ing rather than against all ways. As has been widely recognized in the philosophical literature on these matters (Kramer 1998, 12 n. 3), the abilities of people to exercise any number of liberties are deontically protected to considerable degrees by the basic claim-rights with which people are endowed under any functional system of governance: claim-rights against being subjected to murder, assault and battery, arson, theft, serious fraud, and so forth. In the scenario of the two-mile race between Ithamar and Hermione, for example, the elementary legal claim-rights of each competitor provide a substantial degree of deontic protection for the ability of each competitor to exercise his or her liberty to win the race. Very likely, some further deontic protection is supplied by the rules of the competition. On the one hand, the deontic protection is not comprehensive. It does not disallow every means of preventing the rival runner from exercising his or her liberty to win the race, since each runner remains legally and morally at liberty to outpace the other competitor. On the other hand, although the deontic protection falls short of being comprehensive, it is very wide-ranging. As has already been suggested, outrunning the other competitor is probably the only way of exercising the aforementioned liberty that is legally and morally permissible for each participant in the race, and it is therefore probably the only way of permissibly thwarting the exercise of the cognate liberty held by the rival participant.

This chapter has already observed that there are no relationships of logical entailment between one's liberty to φ and one's claim-rights against being prevented from φ-ing. Nevertheless, although there are no logical entailments between those entitlements, the accompaniment of legal liberties by legal claim-rights against specific ways of preventing the exercise of those liberties is not a mere contingency. While committing the error which I have criticized in the penultimate paragraph above, Alessandro Spena further stumbles when he attributes to Hohfeldians the following view: "Even though a liberty is normally 'supported' by claim-rights that 'protect' it, this 'protection' should be regarded as a mere empirical accident, a coincidence" (Spena 2012, 162). The claim-rights which Spena has in mind are protective not of liberties themselves but instead of acts of exercising those liberties, and the accompaniment of legal liberties by such legal claim-rights is scarcely coincidental or accidental. It is not a matter of logical necessity, but it is a matter of metaphysical necessity.

After all, as has been recounted in the penultimate paragraph above, the abilities of people to exercise their legal liberties are deontically protected to quite considerable degrees by their elementary legal claim-rights against being subjected to major modes of mistreatment. The fact that people hold those elementary claim-rights is hardly a coincidence or an accident. Rather, as Hart contended in a line of argument to which I have already briefly referred in §2.4.4 above, all or most people within the jurisdiction of any functional system of governance will hold those legal claim-rights (Hart 1994, 193–200; Kramer 2018, 164–72). No such system could endure more than fleetingly if it failed to impose and effectuate the legal duties that are the correlates of those claim-rights, since the effectuation of such duties is essential for the very cohesiveness of any society. As Hart submitted, the indispensability of those duties and their correlative claim-rights for the sustainability of any system of governance is due to some fundamental features of human beings and of the world in which they live. In other words, it is due to the nature of human beings or to the nature of the human condition. Hart himself characterized the indispensability of those elementary duties and their correlative claim-rights as a matter of "natural necessity," but in the parlance of contemporary philosophy it is best characterized as a matter of metaphysical necessity. It is something that follows from the fact that human beings are as they everywhere are. As a matter of metaphysical necessity, then, all or most people within the jurisdiction of any functional system of governance hold legal claim-rights that are conferred upon them by the laws of the system which proscribe major forms of misconduct. Now, given that those claim-rights deontically protect the abilities of people to exercise their legal liberties, and given that the universal or very widespread holding of those claim-rights under any functional system of governance is a matter of metaphysical necessity, the fact that people's abilities to exercise their legal liberties are deontically protected by accompanying legal claim-rights is itself a matter of metaphysical necessity. Legal liberties exist as such only when a functional system of governance is in existence, and as a matter of metaphysical necessity a functional system of governance is in existence only when the legal liberties of people are accompanied by legal claim-rights that serve to protect the abilities of the holders of those liberties to exercise them. Hence, far from being coincidental or accidental, the accompaniment of legal liberties by legal claim-rights in every jurisdiction is intrinsic to the human condition.

Lest the reflections in the foregoing paragraph be misunderstood, a caveat should be attached. Although the nature of human beings is such that every functional system of governance has to proscribe the perpetration of major types of misconduct, the specifics of the legal prohibitions can vary to some degree from one system to another. Even in regard to the most serious types of misconduct, such as homicide, the specifics of the prohibitions can vary to some degree. For example, systems of governance can obviously differ in their specifications of the circumstances (such as situations of self-defense) in which the killing of a person by another is legally permissible, and they can likewise differ over the question whether an absence of culpability is itself sufficient to exclude an instance of homicide from the scope of a prohibition on such misconduct. These variations and numerous other relatively minor variations are manifestly possible among systems of governance that are all robustly durable. Thus, when I maintain that the accompaniment of legal liberties by legal claim-rights is a matter of metaphysical necessity, I am not suggesting that a precisely delimited set of legal claim-rights must obtain uniformly across jurisdictions. Nor am I contending that the details of the throngs of legal claim-rights in any particular jurisdiction are a matter of metaphysical necessity. Those details are always shaped in part by contingencies. Instead my assertions about metaphysical necessity are focused on the fact that, in every jurisdiction, people's legal liberties—which exist only when a functional system of governance is in existence—are accompanied by some legal claim-rights against major modes of misconduct that would prevent the exercising of those liberties. Such assertions are fully consistent with the fact that there are variations across jurisdictions in the assemblages of basic legal claim-rights with which people are endowed.

2.5.4 Claim-Rights without Liberties

As has been remarked, there are no relationships of logical entailment between any Hohfeldian liberty to φ and any Hohfeldian claim-right(s) against being prevented from exercising that liberty. Similarly, there are no relationships of logical entailment in the opposite direction. Indeed, a party X can owe another party Y a legal duty not to φ and can simultaneously hold vis-à-vis Y a broad legal claim-right to Y's abstention from preventing X's φ-ing. Such situations are not common, but there are no logical barriers to their occurrence. Let us ponder here a somewhat modified version of a scenario which I introduced a quarter of a century ago (Kramer 1998, 15–17).

Before we mull over that scenario directly, a few preliminary comments on it are advisable. It involves a pair of lawsuits, but nothing hinges on the sequence in which those lawsuits are pursued. Though I will of course specify a sequence in which one lawsuit follows the other, the ordering of them could have been reversed without detracting at all from the message of my vignette. Likewise inessential to that message is the nature of the remedies granted in the respective lawsuits. I shall proceed here on the assumption that the remedy in each case is an award of damages, but that assumption is dispensable. Even if the remedy in each case were injunctive relief or something else, the point made by my thought-experiment would remain sound. Immaterial as well, for my purposes, is the question whether the damages are to be paid recurrently or instead as a lump sum. Similarly dispensable is any assumption about which of the parties in my thought-experiment arrived first at the lake where they eventually come into conflict. Indeed, I shall not need to take a position on that aspect of the situation at all. Finally, although my specifications of the contents of the two chief claim-right/duty relationships in the scenario are accurate, neither of those specifications is uniquely accurate. The content of each claim-right/duty relationship could be specified in alternative ways, and a court that handles each of the lawsuits might well be inclined to adopt one or more of those alternative formulations. Still, as has been stated, my formulation of the content of each such relationship is accurate and is therefore entirely consistent with any accurate formulation that would be adopted by a court.

Consider, then, a factory that has long been operating on the shore of a large lake. Vital to the factory's processes of manufacturing is the discharge of effluents into the lake. Without the continual discharges, those processes would very quickly grind to a halt. Also availing themselves of the lake, albeit at quite a distance and for a very different set of purposes, are some fishermen who have plied their trade for many years on its waters. Over a lengthy period of time, the emissions of noxious substances into those waters from the factory are cumulatively sufficient to reduce sharply the number and diversity of the fish in the lake. As a consequence of that steep decline, the fishermen are no longer able to earn their livelihoods from their trawling. After expostulations with the owner of the factory have proved to be fruitless, the fishermen pursue a lawsuit against the owner to seek damages for the losses which they have undergone. Their litigation is successful, as the court holds that the factory owner is under a legal duty vis-à-vis the fishermen to abstain from releasing the toxic pollutants into the lake. Hence, the factory owner vis-à-vis the fishermen does not have a legal liberty to discharge those substances into the lake.

Perhaps because the fishermen are dissatisfied with the amount of the damages awarded to them by the court, or perhaps simply because of their anger about the loss of their trade, they subsequently take matters into their own hands by occluding the outlet pipes of the factory at night. Because the emissions of the effluents from the pipes have been obstructed so effectively, the operations of the factory have to cease for several weeks. A new instance of litigation arises, with the factory owner as the plaintiff and with the fishermen as the defendants. Like the lawsuit brought by the fishermen against the factory owner, the lawsuit brought by the factory owner against the fishermen eventuates in an award of damages. Noting that discharges of noxious substances generated by the factory's processes of production are essential for the continuation of those processes, the court holds that the factory owner vis-à-vis the fishermen has a claim-right to their not preventing the discharges. Because the fishermen have contravened the factory owner's claim-right through their actions of obstruction, they are now legally obligated to compensate the owner for the losses which those actions have occasioned.

In sum, the upshot of the situation is (1) that the factory owner vis-à-vis the fishermen is not legally at liberty to emit the toxic contaminants into the lake, and (2) that the factory owner vis-à-vis the fishermen has a legal claim-right against their preventing him from emitting the contaminants into the lake. Vis-à-vis the fishermen, the factory owner lacks a legal liberty to φ but holds a legal claim-right against their prevention of his φ-ing. Whether or not a configuration of legal positions along these lines is desirable, it is plainly possible as a matter of the logic of Hohfeldian entitlements. Of course, in a jurisdiction-specific manner, a particular system of governance could rule out the occurrence of any such configurations of legal positions. However, quite apart from the fact that I am unaware of any system of governance that does rule out such configurations, a jurisdiction-specific restriction of that sort would scarcely be something that follows inexorably from the logic of Hohfeldian legal positions.

As I have remarked in "Rights without Trimmings" (1998, 16), a scenario like that of the factory owner and the fishermen is sometimes very loosely characterized as depicting a party who has "a right to commit a wrong." Such phrasing is best eschewed, notwithstanding its piquancy, for it is both inapposite and sloppily imprecise. It is inapposite because, as I have already explained in §2.4.1 above, the content of a claim-right/duty relationship does not refer primarily to an action or omission on the part of the holder of the claim-right.[15] Such a content can of course refer to the duty-bearer's not preventing some action by the holder of the claim-right, but the primary reference therein is to the bearer's non-prevention rather than to the holder's action; it is the former rather than the latter that is made mandatory by the existence of the specified claim-right/duty relationship. What is more, the "right to commit a wrong" wording is sloppily imprecise and misleading. Because the general term "right" is frequently employed in everyday discourse and philosophical discourse to refer to Hohfeldian liberties or indeed to any of the Hohfeldian entitlements, the "right to commit a wrong" phraseology can all too readily incline readers to infer oxymoronically that the factory owner vis-à-vis the fishermen is legally at liberty to commit a legal wrong. To avoid such tomfoolery and to specify precisely the Hohfeldian legal positions that are occupied by somebody like the factory owner, we should abjure the "right to commit a wrong" formulation and should instead say that the factory owner vis-à-vis the fishermen holds a legal claim-right against their prevention of his recurrent breaches of a legal duty which he owes to them. Vis-à-vis them, he does not hold any legal liberty-to-φ that would accompany his legal claim-right to their not preventing his φ-ing. Hence, my vignette of the fishermen and the factory owner illustrates the point enunciated by Andrew Halpin when he asserts that "[t]here is a significant set of cases where the law prohibits interference by the aggrieved party with a forbidden activity" (2019, 248).

[15] I here leave aside any weird contract of the sort contemplated in the closing paragraph of §2.4.1.

2.5.5 Quantification over Parties

Quantification will be operative at several junctures in my exposition of the Hohfeldian analysis of legal and moral positions, and we have here reached the first of those junctures (though in fact quantification could equally well have been introduced during my discussions of the first column in the Hohfeldian schema). A quantifier is a function that determines how a given property or entity is assigned among the members of some domain. Here the term "domain" simply denotes the set of things over which a quantifier ranges. At this juncture in my exposition, the domain on which I shall chiefly concentrate is the set of beings who are potential parties to legal or moral relationships. Those beings are capable of holding Hohfeldian entitlements or of occupying the positions correlative to such entitlements.

Quite a number of quantifiers have been developed by logicians and other philosophers, but the most prominent are the universal quantifier and the existential quantifier. One of my principal concerns here is to disambiguate the universal quantifier, but we can begin with a glance at the existential quantifier. When a proposition is governed by an existential quantifier, the quantifier indicates that at least one member of the relevant domain possesses the property or satisfies the requirement articulated by the proposition. Let us consider, for example, the existentially quantified proposition "There are squirrels residing regularly in the United Kingdom." We can suppose that the relevant domain comprises all animals. In that event, the proposition asserts that there is at least one animal which possesses both the property of being a squirrel and the property of residing regularly in the United Kingdom. For an example more directly pertinent to a theory of rights and right-holding, we can ponder the existentially quantified proposition "Miranda is legally at liberty, vis-à-vis somebody else, to walk down Grange Road in Cambridge this evening." We can suppose that the relevant domain comprises every potential party to legal relationships, in which case the proposition asserts that there is at least one such party vis-à-vis whom Miranda is legally at liberty to walk down Grange Road this evening.

Even more important for my purposes in this book is the universal quantifier. As I have already suggested, we need to attend here to three distinct ways in which the universal quantifier can be construed. In ordinary English, the differences among those ways approximately correspond to the differences among "all," "each" or "every," and "any." Throughout this book I shall label these three distinct modes of universal quantification as "aggregative," "distributive," and "disjunctive." When a proposition is governed by an *aggregative* universal quantifier, it ascribes some property to all the members of the relevant domain as an overarching collectivity or assemblage. That property might not be accurately ascribable or even meaningfully ascribable to any member of the domain in isolation, but—if the proposition governed by an aggregative universal quantifier is true—the property is accurately ascribable to all the members of the domain taken together. When a proposition is governed instead by a *distributive* universal quantifier, it ascribes some property to every member of the relevant domain taken individually. Here the ascribed property is possessed (or is said to be possessed) by each member of the domain rather than by all the members as an overarching collectivity or aggregate. Of course, the specified property might also be correctly ascribable to all the members of the domain taken together. However, even if it is correctly ascribable in that fashion through aggregative universal quantification, its being so is not a corollary of the sheer fact that it can correctly be ascribed to each member through distributive universal quantification. Finally, another possibility is that a proposition is governed by a *disjunctive* universal quantifier. If such a proposition is predictive or descriptive, the disjunctive universal quantifier is equivalent to the existential quantifier—since the proposition so quantified will be true if at least one member of the domain over which the quantifier ranges is possessed of the property which the proposition ascribes. However, if a proposition governed by a disjunctive universal quantifier is prescriptive, the quantifier is not equivalent to the existential quantifier. For such a proposition, the prescription asserted by it will be satisfied if at least one member of the domain over which the disjunctive universal quantifier ranges is treated in the manner specified by the proposition.

2.5.5.1 Some Clarification of Disjunctive Universal Quantification

Although this book will say considerably more about each of these types of universal quantification, and although my focus in a moment will be on the distributive variety, we should first briefly contemplate a couple of examples of propositions that are governed by disjunctive universal quantifiers. After all, whereas the distinction between aggregative universal quantification and distributive universal quantification will be familiar to most philosophers as largely similar to the medieval distinction between generality *in sensu composito* and generality *in sensu diviso*,[16] the disjunctive universal quantifier is probably less familiar. Moreover, given that the disjunctive universal quantifier is equivalent to the existential quantifier for predictive and empirical propositions, its role as a distinctive quantifier for deontic propositions is in need of clarification. A couple of examples, one involving a predictive proposition and the other involving a deontic proposition, will help to dispel any unclarity.

Let us consider the predictive proposition "On any day next week, the temperature in Cambridge (England) will rise above 30 degrees Celsius." In the domain over which the quantifier ranges are the days of next week. Here the disjunctive universal quantifier is clearly equivalent to the existential quantifier, as the

[16] For a well-known discussion of the distinction between generality *in sensu composito* and generality *in sensu diviso*, albeit with a focus quite different from my own, see Lewis 2002, 64–8. For some reflections on that distinction with a focus closer to my own, see Cohen 1983, 14 *et passim*.

proposition governed by the quantifier is true if and only if there is at least one day next week on which the temperature in Cambridge rises above 30 degrees Celsius. Perhaps because the disjunctive universal quantifier is equivalent to the existential quantifier when attached to a proposition that is predictive or empirical, the distinctiveness of disjunctive universal quantification has often been overlooked. We should therefore turn to an example involving a deontic proposition, where the distinctiveness of such quantification becomes manifest.

Suppose that the system of governance in some country has enacted a law that requires every adult with an annual income above the level of $30,000 to donate at least 10% of his or her after-tax earnings each year to any of the charities on the official register of such organizations. In that country, then, the following proposition is true: "Every adult in this jurisdiction with an annual income above the level of $30,000 is legally obligated to donate at least 10% of his or her after-tax earnings each year to any of the officially registered charities in this jurisdiction." I shall designate this proposition as the "Eleemosynary Obligation Proposition." As is evident, more than one universal quantifier is operative in that proposition. A distributive universal quantifier ranges over a domain comprising human adults in the jurisdiction, and another distributive universal quantifier ranges over a domain comprising the years during which the relevant law is in effect. However, my focus here is on the disjunctive universal quantifier that ranges over a domain comprising the charities that are listed in the official register. Incumbent on every adult in the jurisdiction with an income each year above the specified level is an eleemosynary duty. To whom is that duty owed? Let us leave aside for now the fact that every legal duty is owed at least to the system of governance that has imposed it. (I shall return to that fact in Chapters 3 and 4.) There is no overarching collectivity of the charities to which a duty would be owed, nor is the duty requiring the payment of at least 10% of one's after-tax income owed to each charity individually—as if each charity would be legally wronged whenever somebody chooses to donate the requisite amount to some other charity instead. Rather, the duty is owed to the charities disjunctively. In other words, it is owed not to an overarching collectivity nor to each charity discretely but instead to a disjunction of the charities. Precisely because the duty is so owed, it will be satisfied by any bearer of it who pays at least 10% of her after-tax earnings to any single charity; and the duty will likewise be satisfied by any bearer of it who spreads such a payment across two or more charities. If someone owes that duty, she will have fulfilled it if and only if she makes a payment in either of the two ways just mentioned.

A few quick observations about the Eleemosynary Obligation Proposition are germane here. First, the truth-value of that proposition obviously does not depend on anyone's fulfillment of the legal duty which it articulates. Its truth-value is determined instead by the accuracy or inaccuracy of its encapsulation of what has been imposed under the enactments that have issued from the presiding system of governance. That encapsulation can be fully accurate even if the duty recounted in it is seldom satisfied by anybody.

Second, as can be inferred from the closing two sentences of the penultimate paragraph above, I am construing the disjunctive universal quantification in the Eleemosynary Obligation Proposition as inclusive rather than exclusive. That is, I am taking as given that one's choice of any particular charitable organization as a recipient of one's legally required largesse does not exclude one's also choosing some other such organization(s) to share in that largesse. The disjuncts in the disjunction are not mutually exclusive. As a consequence, the duty specified in the Eleemosynary Obligation Proposition can in principle be satisfied by everyone in the jurisdiction even if no donor has bestowed as much as 10% of her after-tax income upon any single charity. Of course, the disjunctive universal quantification in that proposition could alternatively have been construed as exclusive rather than inclusive. So interpreted, the Eleemosynary Obligation Proposition would be asserting that each adult with earnings above the specified level is legally required to bestow at least 10% of his or her after-tax income upon any one charity. Such an interpretation is perfectly coherent, but I have implicitly dismissed it because the disjunctive universal quantification in the Eleemosynary Obligation Proposition is much more plausibly construable as inclusive. Very likely, the duty articulated in that proposition is intended and understood to require each duty-bearer to choose between conferring the requisite payment on any single charity and spreading the requisite payment among any two or more charities. (There are undoubtedly some deontic propositions with disjunctive universal quantifiers that are aptly construable as exclusive, but I shall not explore any such propositions here.)

Third, and most important for my present purposes, the duty envisaged here reveals the unwisdom of Hohfeld's insistence that every legal duty borne by some party is correlated with a legal claim-right held by some other single party. Countless legal duties are so correlated, of course, but not every legal duty is. In particular, when a legal duty is imposed by a norm that universally quantifies in a disjunctive fashion over the parties to whom the duty is owed, that duty is not correlated with a legal claim-right held by any single party. (At present, I am continuing to prescind from the fact that every legal duty is owed at least to the system of governance that has imposed it. When that fact is taken into account, a version of Hohfeld's insistence can be salvaged. However, my prescinding from that point at present is not even slightly unfair to Hohfeld—because there is no basis for thinking that he agreed with me about the owing of every legal duty to the system of governance that has imposed it. Indeed, given that he denied that claim-rights are ever genuinely held by collectivities, he was committed to disagreeing with me. I shall return to the matter of collectivities as holders of claim-rights in my next few chapters.)

Disjunctive universal quantification is different from the aggregative and distributive varieties of universal quantification in its posing of difficulties for Hohfeld's thesis about one-to-one correlations between claim-rights and duties and between holders of claim-rights and bearers of duties. When a legal duty is imposed by a norm that universally quantifies in an aggregative fashion over the parties to whom the duty is owed, the parties constitute a collectivity which holds the claim-right correlative to that duty. Although Hohfeld himself denied that claim-rights or other entitlements are ever genuinely held by collectivities, my next chapter will argue that he erred in so doing. Once his mistakes on that topic are rectified, his thesis about one-to-one correlations between claim-rights and duties and between holders of claim-rights and bearers of duties is unthreatened by the existence of a norm that contains an aggregative universal quantifier which ranges over a domain comprising the parties to whom any duty imposed by the norm is owed. A duty imposed by such a norm is correlated with a claim-right held by the parties as a collectivity.

Even more clearly, the Hohfeldian thesis about one-to-one correlations is unthreatened by the existence of a norm that contains a distributive universal quantifier which ranges over a domain comprising the parties to whom any duties imposed by the norm are owed. A duty imposed by such a norm is correlated with a claim-right held by each of those parties. Hohfeld himself maintained that every duty imposed by such a norm is owed in tandem with an indefinitely expansive array of cognate duties, each of which is correlated with a claim-right held by one of the parties in the domain over which the quantification has ranged.[17] He designated those homologous duties as "multital." As he affirmed, "instead of there being a single [duty] with a single correlative [claim-right] resting on all the persons against whom the [duty] avails, there are many separate and distinct [duties], actual and potential, each one of which has a correlative [claim-right] resting upon some one person" (Hohfeld 1923, 92). As I have submitted in "Rights without Trimmings" (1998, 9–10 n. 2), Hohfeld's approach to this matter is tenable. It is in keeping with my analysis of distributive universal quantification. However, as I also observe in "Rights without Trimmings," Hohfeld's approach is not uniquely tenable. In numerous contexts where a duty is imposed by a norm that contains a distributive universal quantifier which ranges over a domain comprising the parties to whom the duty is owed, the duty can best be construed as ramifyingly correlated with claim-rights that are held respectively by the members of that domain. In other words, in numerous contexts, the duty is best construed as a single duty that is directed to the parties distributively. Because the universal quantification over those parties is distributive, the duty directed to them through the quantification is correlated with an indefinite multiplicity of claim-rights where

[17] Hohfeld 1923, 72, 91–6. Hohfeld in fact wrote about multital claim-rights rather than about multital duties, but his analysis of the matter applies (*mutatis mutandis*) to the latter as much as to the former. Inversely, of course, my own analysis of distributive universal quantification applies (*mutatis mutandis*) to norms that universally quantify distributively over potential bearers of legal duties as much as to norms that universally quantify distributively over potential holders of legal claim-rights.

each such claim-right is held by a distinct party. Although Hohfeld vigorously resisted this way of understanding such a duty, and although it is inconsistent with his thesis about one-to-one correlations between duties and claim-rights—since it presents a single duty as correlated with multiple claim-rights—such an understanding is appropriate in a host of contexts. Nonetheless, given that Hohfeld's alternative understanding is also tenable (though less illuminating) even in those contexts, his thesis about one-to-one correlations is compatible with the existence of any duty that is imposed by a norm containing a distributive universal quantifier which ranges over a domain that comprises the parties to whom the duty is owed.

Quite different is the existence of a norm containing a *disjunctive* universal quantifier that ranges over a domain which comprises the parties to whom any duty imposed by the norm is owed. Quite different, in other words, is the existence of a norm like the one that is encapsulated in the Eleemosynary Obligation Proposition. Unlike distributive universal quantification, disjunctive universal quantification does not lend itself to any analysis that will square it with Hohfeld's thesis about one-to-one correlations between bearers of duties and holders of claim-rights. In regard to the eleemosynary duty owed by each adult whose income is above the specified level, there is no tenable analysis under which the owing of that duty is correlated uniquely with the holding of a claim-right by any particular charity. Each bearer of the eleemosynary duty owes it to the registered charities disjunctively, rather than to any particular charity or to each particular charity. If a bearer of the eleemosynary duty fails to comply with it, no single charity will have been legally wronged. No charity has a legal claim-right to be paid anything by any adult, for no adult owes a legal duty to pay anything to this or that particular charity. At the same time, no charity has a legal claim-right requiring each adult with an income above the specified level to pay the requisite amount to *some* registered charity or another. Although each such adult does bear a legal duty with that content, the duty is owed to the registered charities disjunctively rather than to any charitable organization(s) individually. There is claim-right/duty correlativity, but the position correlative to the eleemosynary duty of each adult is occupied by the registered charities disjunctively. It is not occupied by any charitable organization(s) individually.

At present, when I deny that the position correlative to the eleemosynary duty is occupied by any charitable organization(s) individually, and when I contend that it is instead occupied by the registered charities disjunctively, I might seem to be advancing a sheer assertion in lieu of marshaling an argument in support of that assertion. However, as will be seen in Chapter 4 when I unfurl my Interest Theory of right-holding, the assertion just mentioned is something that follows straightforwardly from the Interest Theory. Far from being an unsupported dogma, it is a conclusion entailed by the correct account of what constitutes the holding of a claim-right. That conclusion will be reaffirmed in this book when the Interest Theory of right-holding has been fully expounded.

Indeed, the current discussion looks ahead not only to my presentation of the Interest Theory in Chapter 4 but also to my defense of the Hohfeldian Correlativity Axiom in Chapter 3. My efforts to vindicate that axiom will proceed partly by rejecting some of the dubious contentions which Hohfeld attached to it. In keeping with what I have said earlier in this subsection about aggregative universal quantification, I shall impugn Hohfeld's insistence that collectively held entitlements are reducible to individually held entitlements. And in keeping with what I have maintained in the last few paragraphs above, I shall contest Hohfeld's thesis that every legal duty is correlated with a legal claim-right held by a discrete party. (Likewise unsustainable is the converse thesis that every legal claim-right is correlated with a legal duty borne by a discrete party.) As will be observed in Chapter 3, one of the most frequently invoked reasons for doubting the correctness of the Correlativity Axiom is that people are often under eleemosynary duties, whether legally or morally. To respond adequately to any objections along those lines, a defender of the Correlativity Axiom needs to recognize that sometimes a claim-right is not correctly ascribable to any discrete party and is instead correctly ascribable to an array of parties disjunctively. Not at all coincidental, then, is the fact that my ruminations on disjunctive universal quantification in this subsection have been concerned chiefly with duties requiring donations to charities. With such a focus, this subsection has not only helped to elucidate the nature of disjunctive universal quantification but has also prepared much of the ground for some of my arguments in Chapter 3.

2.5.5.2 Liberties and Distributive Universal Quantification

Whereas the preceding subsection has attended mainly to some claim-right/duty relationships and has devoted more scrutiny to disjunctive universal quantification than to distributive universal quantification, this subsection will concentrate on the latter type of quantification and will return my focus to Hohfeldian liberties. In particular, we should here contemplate propositions that universally quantify distributively over a domain comprising the potential occupants of the positions correlative to liberties. Those positions are of course Hohfeldian no-rights, which I have not yet expounded. Nevertheless, because the purpose of the present discussion is to shed light on the nature of liberties rather than on the nature of no-rights—and because, in any event, my exposition of no-rights will emerge quite soon in this chapter—we can aptly proceed to explore this matter now, in advance of my reflections on no-rights.

Every Hohfeldian liberty to φ is of course relational, in that it is held by some party vis-à-vis some other party. Consequently, Pedro can be legally at liberty vis-à-vis Martin to walk down Grange Road this afternoon, even while he is not legally at liberty vis-à-vis Jacqueline to walk down Grange Road this afternoon. Because the Hohfeldian schema does in this way take every liberty-to-φ to be a position held by a discrete party vis-à-vis another discrete party, it enables philosophers and jurists to attain an admirable degree of fine-grained precision in their analyses of people's legal or moral statuses. However, philosophers and jurists and ordinary people frequently are concerned not only with the fine-grained analyses but also with deontic categories at a higher level of generality. Instead of asking solely whether Pedro is at liberty to φ vis-à-vis some other particular party, philosophers and jurists and ordinary people are often inclined to ask whether Pedro is at liberty to φ *tout court*. An inquiry of the latter sort is sometimes said to be about permissibility in a non-relational sense (Duarte d'Almeida 2016, 562), but such a characterization of the matter is inapposite. Permissibility *tout court* is also relational, but the relationality is channeled through distributive universal quantification. In any assertion that Pedro is at liberty to φ *tout court*, there is operative—implicitly or explicitly—a distributive universal quantifier that ranges over a domain comprising all potential bearers of no-rights. Given the truth of such an assertion about Pedro, everyone who can bear a no-right does bear a no-right with regard to Pedro's φ-ing. A person P is at liberty to φ *tout court* if and only if everyone who can bear a no-right does bear a no-right with regard to P's φ-ing.

This analysis of being at liberty to φ *tout court* can illuminatingly be contrasted with an analysis of being obligated to φ *tout court*.[18] In any assertion that Pedro is obligated to φ *tout court*, there is implicitly or explicitly operative a disjunctive universal quantifier that ranges over a domain comprising all potential holders of claim-rights. Such an assertion is true if and only if at least one member of that domain does hold a claim-right to Pedro's φ-ing. In other words, such an assertion is true if and only if someone who can hold a claim-right does hold a claim-right to Pedro's φ-ing. A person P is obligated to φ *tout court* if and only if someone who can hold a claim-right does hold a claim-right to P's φ-ing. (Here, of course, "someone" is to be construed as "at least one party.")

Because of the difference between the distributive universal quantification operative in assertions about one's being at liberty to φ *tout court* and the disjunctive universal quantification operative in assertions about one's being obligated to φ *tout court*, the connection between one's being at liberty to φ *tout court* and one's holding a Hohfeldian liberty to φ is the inverse of the connection between one's being obligated to φ *tout court* and one's bearing a Hohfeldian duty to φ. One's being at liberty to φ *tout court* entails one's holding a Hohfeldian liberty to φ vis-à-vis every particular party, whereas one's holding a Hohfeldian liberty to φ vis-à-vis this or that particular party does not entail one's being at liberty to φ *tout court*. By contrast, one's being obligated to φ *tout court* does not entail one's bearing a Hohfeldian duty to φ vis-à-vis this or that particular party, whereas one's bearing a Hohfeldian duty to φ vis-à-vis this or that particular party entails one's being obligated to φ *tout court*. One's being at liberty to φ *tout court* is sufficient but not

[18] The contrast to which I advert here is aptly recognized in Van Duffel 2012, 112–13, though his way of explicating the contrast is quite different from my own.

necessary for one's holding a Hohfeldian liberty to φ vis-à-vis this or that particular party, whereas one's holding a Hohfeldian liberty to φ vis-à-vis this or that particular party is necessary but not sufficient for one's being at liberty to φ *tout court.* By contrast, one's being obligated to φ *tout court* is necessary but not sufficient for one's bearing a Hohfeldian duty to φ vis-à-vis this or that particular party, whereas one's bearing a Hohfeldian duty to φ vis-à-vis this or that particular party is sufficient but not necessary for one's being obligated to φ *tout court.*

2.5.6 Limits on Duality

Although the limits recounted in this subsection are applicable to both halves of the Hohfeldian table—and to all eight positions therein—they are best broached now with reference to the logical duality of liberties and duties. As has been contended in §2.3, a person P is legally at liberty to φ vis-à-vis some other person Q if and only it is not the case that P owes Q a legal duty to refrain from φ-ing. That relationship of duality between liberties and duties or between claim-rights and no-rights does indeed obtain, but it does so within boundaries. Those boundaries are operative because they are limits to the very existence of Hohfeldian positions. Throughout the wide-ranging expanse inside those boundaries, the absence of a legal duty to φ constitutes the existence of a legal liberty not to φ. Beyond that expanse, however, the absence of a legal duty to φ is not equivalent to the existence of a legal liberty to abstain from φ-ing.[19] (The limits on the existence of Hohfeldian legal positions overlap with the limits on the existence of Hohfeldian moral positions, but they are not the same. Hence, to a greater extent than some other portions of this chapter, my cogitations in the current subsection will have to differentiate between the legal and the moral.)

One set of limits on the incidence of any Hohfeldian legal positions is that no such positions exist when there is no legal system in existence. This point applies to liberties and no-rights as much as to claim-rights and duties. Whenever no legal system is in existence in the world as a whole or in any portion of the world, legal liberties and no-rights do not exist there—just as legal claim-rights and duties do not exist there. In such a state of affairs, the absence there of any legal duty to φ is not constitutive of any legal liberty to abstain from φ-ing, and the absence there of any legal claim-right to someone's φ-ing is not constitutive of any legal no-right with regard to someone's abstention from φ-ing.

A second set of limits is related but broader, and it pertains to Hohfeldian moral positions as much as to Hohfeldian legal positions. No such Hohfeldian

[19] The limitedness of the expanse within which the logic of the Hohfeldian schema obtains is highlighted intermittently in Oliveira Lima et alia 2021. However, I mull over some limits beyond the ones which those scholars contemplate.

positions are ever occupied by any non-human entities that are inanimate or insentient. For example, the fact that the Milky Way Galaxy does not owe the Andromeda Galaxy any legal or moral duty to swirl in some specified direction is scarcely a ground for inferring that the Milky Way Galaxy holds a legal liberty and a moral liberty vis-à-vis the Andromeda Galaxy not to swirl in that specified direction. Because no Hohfeldian positions are ever held or borne by inanimate entities such as galaxies, the absence of any legal or moral duty incumbent on the Milky Way Galaxy is not constitutive of any legal or moral liberty held by that galaxy. Non-human inanimate entities on the planet Earth are likewise, of course, never the holders or bearers of Hohfeldian positions. A rock cannot ever hold a claim-right to be left undisturbed, for example. No duty is owed to the rock by anybody to leave it undisturbed, but the absence of any such duty does not mean that everybody holds a liberty vis-à-vis the rock to disturb it. Rocks are never parties to Hohfeldian relationships, whether those relationships be legal or moral. Similarly, no Hohfeldian positions are ever held or borne by insentient entities such as trees and grass. People do not ever owe any legal or moral duties to such entities, but the absence of any duties owed to them is not constitutive of any legal or moral liberties held vis-à-vis them. Like inanimate non-human entities, insentient non-human organisms are outside all Hohfeldian relationships. They are never parties to liberty/no-right relationships any more than to claim-right/duty relationships. (Three short caveats should be attached to this paragraph. First, I shall say much more in the latter half of this book about the class of potential occupants of Hohfeldian positions. Chapter 5 will present arguments to support my assertions here that inanimate and insentient non-human entities do not belong to that class. Second, as will readily be acknowledged in the latter half of this book, countless legal and moral relationships pertain to inanimate and insentient entities. For instance, people are frequently under legal and moral duties to refrain from defacing works of art or to refrain from cutting down grand trees. Nonetheless, although such Hohfeldian relationships pertain to inanimate or insentient entities, those entities are not parties to the relationships. Third, when the present chapter moves on to the power/liability column in Hohfeld's table, I will discuss some of the ways in which the workings of inanimate entities and forces can alter people's legal and moral relationships. Still, as will be argued there, the abilities of such entities and forces to bring about changes in legal and moral relationships are not Hohfeldian powers. They are instead quasi-powers which affect legal and moral relationships from the outside.)

Another set of limits on the existence of Hohfeldian legal and moral positions is that some matters within the scope of the law of a jurisdiction or within the scope of the correct principles of morality are not determinately settled by the current laws or by the applicable principles. Although the incidence of indeterminacy in the realm of law or in the realm of morality has been overestimated by some philosophers, there is inevitably some indeterminacy in each of those realms.[20] Whenever some question about the existence of a legal or moral duty to φ is not determinately answerable, neither an affirmative answer nor a negative answer to that question is determinately correct. In such circumstances, the proposition "It is not determinately the case that the specified duty to φ exists" does not entail "The specified duty to φ does not exist" and therefore does not entail "A liberty to refrain from φ-ing exists." Conversely, of course, in such circumstances there is no entailment between "It is not determinately the case that the specified duty to φ does not exist" and "The specified duty to φ exists." Accordingly, in such circumstances, there is no entailment between "It is not determinately the case that the specified duty to φ does not exist" and "A liberty to refrain from φ-ing does not exist." In regard to any matters that are indeterminate, the usual diagonal relations of logical duality on the left-hand side of Hohfeld's schema—and the usual diagonal relations of logical contradictoriness on the right-hand side of the schema—do not obtain. Consequently, any Hohfeldian positions that would determinately exist if those matters were determinately resolved are not determinately existent. Nor, of course, are they determinately inexistent! (The factors that can lead to indeterminacy in the realm of law or in the realm of morality are multiple. In the past books of mine which I have just cited in note 20 of this chapter, I explore all the main such factors.)

A final source of limits on the existence of Hohfeldian legal or moral positions is that any ascription of such a position presupposes the past or present or future existence of the party to whom the position is ascribed. As has been stated at the outset of the discussion in this subsection, the relationship of duality between duties and liberties is such that a person P is legally or morally at liberty to φ vis-à-vis some other person Q if and only if it is not the case that P owes Q a legal or moral duty to refrain from φ-ing. However, suppose that the domain covered by the "Q" variable were to include leprechauns or the god Apollo or the mythical lumberjack Paul Bunyan. Each person P would not bear a legal or moral duty to φ vis-à-vis any of those imaginary beings, but would likewise not hold a legal or moral liberty to refrain from φ-ing vis-à-vis any of them. Given the chimericalness of any being such as Paul Bunyan, there is no entailment between "I do not owe Paul Bunyan any legal or moral duty to φ" and "I am legally or morally at liberty vis-à-vis Paul Bunyan to refrain from φ-ing." Just as the chimericalness of Paul Bunyan precludes him from holding a claim-right that would be correlative to someone's duty to φ, so too it precludes him from bearing a no-right that would be correlative to someone's liberty not to φ. Hence, the domain of parties over which the relevant quantifiers

[20] In a few of my previous books, I have written at length about indeterminacy in the legal realm and the moral realm: Kramer 2007, 14–38, 201–30; 2009a, 86–128; 2018, 112–17, 128–30, 133–47. In the ruminations of Alchourrón and Bulygin 1971 and Oliveira Lima et alia 2021, indeterminacy is the principal source of limits on the existence of Hohfeldian positions.

and variables range in ascriptions of Hohfeldian positions does not include any mythical or imaginary parties. Only within a domain marked by such an exclusion, will "P is legally or morally at liberty to φ vis-à-vis Q" be inferable from "It is not the case that P owes Q a legal or moral duty to refrain from φ-ing." As has already been mentioned, Chapter 5 of this book will say far more about the class of potential holders of claim-rights. Though future generations and some dead people are within that class, no mythical or imaginary beings are within it.

These limits on the existence of Hohfeldian positions and relationships are of direct relevance to some contemporary debates about the reality of Hohfeldian liberties and no-rights as positions constituted by the absence of other Hohfeldian positions. Some philosophers, such as Heidi Hurd and Michael Moore, have submitted that liberties and no-rights as sheer absences are purely negative and are thus too phantasmal to be genuine deontic positions in any way.[21] As they declare, Hohfeldian "liberties are no things at all—no more than an absent elephant is a ghostly kind of elephant, or an absence of two elephants is a ghostly herd of ghostly elephants" (Hurd and Moore 2018, 339). I shall engage more sustainedly with Hurd and Moore in my reflections on no-rights shortly, but for the moment we should simply note that their dismissal of the reality of Hohfeldian liberties is thoroughly heedless of the points which I have just been making about the limited domains within which the logical duality of duties and liberties is operative. To contend that Hohfeldian liberties are unreal as sheer absences is to ignore the difference between the following two situations: a situation in which I do not owe Shirley a legal duty to φ, because the prevailing system of governance does not impose any such duty on me vis-à-vis her; and a situation in which I do not owe Shirley a legal duty to φ, because the prevailing system of governance has completely disintegrated and has not been replaced by any new system. In the former situation the absence of a legal duty to φ is constitutive of a legal liberty not to φ, whereas in the latter situation the absence of a legal duty to φ is not constitutive of any such legal liberty. Likewise, Hurd and Moore ride roughshod over the difference between my not owing Miranda Fricker a duty to pay her $100 and my not owing Paul Bunyan a duty to pay him $100. Whereas the absence of the former duty is constitutive of a liberty held by me vis-à-vis Miranda Fricker not to pay her $100, the absence of the latter duty is not constitutive of any liberty held by me vis-à-vis Paul Bunyan. In other words, what Hurd and Moore overlook is that the absence of a duty is constitutive of a liberty only within a deontic relationship. When no relevant deontic relationship is in existence—for any of the reasons distilled in this subsection—the absence of a duty to φ is a sheer absence rather than a deontic position. By contrast, when none of the considerations delineated in this subsection is applicable, the absence of a duty to φ is not a sheer absence

[21] This theme is prominent both in Hurd and Moore 2018 and in Hurd and Moore 2019. See also Halpin 1997, 34, 41; Husik 1924, 267–8. For ripostes, see Green 2021; Kramer 2019.

and is instead constitutive of a liberty to abstain from φ-ing. That absence is not a sheer absence in such circumstances, because it is itself a position within a deontic relationship between parties. Tiresome quips by Hurd and Moore about elephants obfuscate the difference between the existence and the inexistence of any such relationship, and they therefore obfuscate the difference between situations within the boundaries of Hohfeldian logic and situations beyond those boundaries.

2.5.7 No-Rights

No-rights, the correlates of liberties, are more often neglected than are any of the other entries in Hohfeld's table. Doubtless, one reason for the relative dearth of attention accorded to the no-right is that Hohfeld devised a hyphenated neologism to designate it. Each of the other positions in the Hohfeldian schema is designated by a term with a solid grounding in everyday discourse and juristic discourse—though Hohfeld greatly precisified and regimented each of those terms for his analysis, by attaching a univocal or nearly univocal meaning to each of them—whereas the hyphenated term "no-right," in contrast with the unhyphenated phrase "no right," does not have any comparable grounding either in ordinary discourse or in juristic discourse. That neologism is almost never employed by anyone outside the confines of discussions of Hohfeld's categories, and it is often not employed even within those confines. Notwithstanding the abundance of philosophical and juristic lucubrations devoted to Hohfeld's analytical framework since its elaboration in the second decade of the twentieth century, the term "no-right" has found little favor in philosophical or juristic circles. Moreover, on the rather rare occasions when the term is used rather than merely mentioned, it is almost always misused.

The persistent misuse of the term "no-right" is directly connected to the differences between that term and the phrase "no right." Whereas "right" is a word within the phrase "no right," it is only a component of a word (a free morpheme, but not itself a word) within the term "no-right." Consequently, the morphological differences between the phrase and the term are accompanied by logical differences; the phrase and the term cannot correctly be used interchangeably. We can have inferred as much from the closing paragraph in §2.5.6 above—for the phrase "no right" can denote a sheer absence, whereas the term "no-right" always denotes a deontic position.

More specifically, as has already been stated, the term "no-right" designates a legal or moral position that is correlated with a legal or moral liberty. Any two such correlated positions make up a liberty/no-right nexus that obtains between some specified parties with a specified content. That is, if a liberty and a no-right are indeed correlated, the content of each of them is the same as the content of the other (and the parties between whom either of them obtains are transposedly the same as the parties between whom the other one of them obtains). If the content of a liberty is not the same as that of a no-right, then the liberty and the no-right are not correlated with each other, and they therefore do not form a single relationship.

2.5.7.1 Hohfeld's Misstep

The foregoing terse reflections are sufficient to enable us to discern that Hohfeld and many eminent proponents of the Hohfeldian analysis have failed to use the term "no-right" correctly. Having elsewhere drawn attention to some of the stumbles by various expositors of the Hohfeldian analysis (Kramer 2019, 217–19), I shall here concentrate on a misstep by Hohfeld himself. In his only relevant remark about no-rights, Hohfeld wrote as follows (1923, 39):

> [T]he correlative of [a liberty] is a "no-right," there being no single term available to express the latter conception. Thus, the correlative of X's right that Y shall not enter on the land is Y's duty not to enter; but the correlative of X's [liberty to enter the land] is manifestly Y's "no-right" that X shall not enter.

Hohfeld here went astray in more than one respect. In the first place, he erred in asserting that there is "no single term available" to designate the correlate of a liberty. Unlike the phrase "no right," the hyphenated term "no-right" is indeed a single term. Its having been coined as a technical neologism is fully consistent with its status as a single term. Also consistent with that latter status, of course, is the hyphenatedness of "no-right."

Hohfeld committed an even worse mistake in the second sentence of this quotation, where he employed the word "no-right" as if it were the phrase "no right." Had he employed that phrase, the expression "X shall not enter" would correctly have encapsulated the content of the claim-right that is the dual of the relevant no-right. Hohfeld would have been asserting, correctly, that Y does not have any claim-right with that content. However, having used the term "no-right" rather than the phrase "no right," Hohfeld specified the content incorrectly. Just as the content of any liberty is the negation of the content of the duty that is the dual of that liberty, so too the content of any no-right is the negation of the content of the claim-right that is the dual of that no-right. X's liberty to enter the land is the dual of X's duty not to enter the land, and Y's no-right concerning X's entering the land is the dual of Y's claim-right to X's not entering the land. Whereas the content of Y's no-right is the same as the content of X's liberty, the content of Y's no-right is the negation of the content of the claim-right which Y would possess if he didn't bear the no-right which he bears.

As is evident from the penultimate sentence in the preceding paragraph, the term "no-right" does not connect very elegantly to a specification of the content of the position which that term denotes. In this regard, "no-right" differs from "liberty" or "duty" or "claim-right." Each of those last three words is readily joinable to a specification of the content of the position which each word respectively designates. Consider for example X's liberty to enter the land, held vis-à-vis Y. Here the term "liberty" is smoothly linked to a specification of the content of the position which that term designates, through the use of an infinitive verb phrase: "to enter the land." Much the same is true, *mutatis mutandis*, when we contemplate the duty of Mary to pay John $10. As for the claim-right of John to be paid $10 by Mary, the term "claim-right" can be connected in several ways to a specification of the content of the position which the term designates. One such way is illustrated in the opening clause of the preceding sentence, where I have used a passive infinitive verb phrase ("to be paid $10 by Mary"). Another such way is illustrated in the statement that John has a claim-right to Mary's paying him $10. In this latter formulation, a nominalized verb phrase is connected to "claim-right" through the preposition "to." Yet another possibility is exemplified in the statement that John has a claim-right that Mary pay him $10. Here the specification of the content of the claim-right is a subordinate clause that is joined to "claim-right" through the subordinate conjunction "that."

All of the foregoing ways of linking the designations of Hohfeldian legal or moral positions to formulations of the contents of those positions are familiar from quotidian contexts. By contrast, largely because the term "no-right" is itself alien to such contexts, there is no really smooth way of connecting it to a specification of the content of the position which it denotes. Hohfeld's conflation of "no-right" with "no right" stemmed in part from his failure to recognize this very point. In the second sentence of the passage from Hohfeld quoted above, the content of Y's no-right is formulated as a subordinate clause connected to "no-right" through the subordinate conjunction "that"; such a construction would be appropriate for the phrase "no right" but is inapposite for the term "no-right." For the hyphenated term, the link to the content of its designated position has to be formulated slightly more ponderously through words such as "concerning" or "regarding" or through phrases such as "in relation to" or "pertaining to" or "in respect of." Thus, instead of writing that the correlate of X's liberty to enter the land is Y's no-right that X shall not enter, Hohfeld should have written that the correlate is Y's no-right concerning X's entering the land (or Y's no-right in respect of X's entering the land, and so forth). When the link to the content is formulated suitably, the content itself can then be specified straightforwardly and accurately.

2.5.7.2 The Reality of No-Rights

As we have beheld in §2.5.6, Hurd and Moore seek to cast doubt upon the reality of Hohfeldian liberties. Wholly unsurprising, then, is that they also strive to cast doubt upon the reality of no-rights as the correlates of Hohfeldian liberties. Their first line of thought is as follows: "Hohfeld uses the phrase 'no-right,' as if the term labelled some thing. But it is plain from his usage that what he means to designate is the *absence* of some thing, namely, the absence of a claim right" (Hurd and Moore 2018, 307, emphasis in original). Both sentences in this quotation are deeply problematic. Contrary to what the opening clause of the first sentence presupposes, "no-right" is a word rather than a phrase, and it does label something. That is, it labels a position within a deontic relationship. Constituted by the absence of a claim-right, something correctly classifiable as a "no-right" is a position of rightlessness within a deontic relationship that situates it as the correlate of a liberty—and so the second sentence quoted here relies on a false dichotomy. When the absence of a claim-right is constitutive of a no-right, the absence is not a sheer absence. It is occurrent within the boundaries of the logic of Hohfeldian relationships rather than beyond those boundaries.

Hurd and Moore try to bolster their stance in a lengthy footnote. Let us examine only two sentences from that note:

> Kramer distinguishes a "no right" (which does indeed designate an absence of a claim-right by one person that a [liberty-holder] not do the act he is [at liberty] to do, as we say in the text) from a "no-right" which supposedly designates an actual [position], one that Kramer calls a ["position of rightlessness"].... So construed, Kramer's "no-right" would still designate an absence of a status in the "no-right" holder, not a status itself.[22]

Hurd and Moore stumble by using the indefinite article "a" before "no right," for my chief point in distinguishing between the term "no-right" and the phrase "no right" is to indicate that the term denotes a position in a deontic relationship whereas the phrase does not. That point is missed again by Hurd and Moore when they assert that "no-right" designates "an absence of a status ..., not a status itself." Although the status or position designated by "no-right" is constituted by the absence of a claim-right, it is indeed a status or position within a deontic relationship. The insistence of Hurd and Moore to the contrary appears to derive from a concern which they express slightly later, when they declare that a no-right "is not a special, ghostly kind of claim right that someone can possess; rather, it is the absence of there being any such right" (2018, 313). A no-right is of course not a special kind of claim-right. Rather, it is a position in a deontic relationship—a position of rightlessness—constituted by the absence of any claim-right and correlated with the presence of a liberty. Worries about ghostliness or mysteriousness would be apposite if no-rights were being presented here as somehow akin to claim-rights. However, given that claim-rights and no-rights are correctly presented here as logical duals with no formal features or substantive features in common,[23] worries

[22] Hurd and Moore 2018, 307 n. 29. The first two bracketed insertions are alterations of terminology for the sake of clarity. The other two bracketed insertions are my corrections of some egregious typographical errors committed by Hurd and Moore.

[23] Between a claim-right and the no-right that is its dual, there is only one thing in common (apart from the fact that each of them is a deontic position): the person who holds the claim-right is the person who bears the no-right, and the person who bears the duty correlative to the claim-right is the person who holds the liberty correlative to the no-right.

about the ghostliness or mysteriousness of no-rights are themselves mysterious and wearisome.

Because the effort by Hurd and Moore to dismiss the genuineness of no-rights is so closely bound up with their effort to dismiss the genuineness of liberties, we should here glance again at that latter endeavor. On the one hand, they assert that "[i]t is no part of our thesis to deny that [Hohfeldian] liberties can exist." On the other hand, especially since their article is focused predominantly on moral positions, their treatment of liberties amounts to a retraction of this initial disavowal. Quite remarkably, they declare that a Hohfeldian liberty "is naked in the sense that renders it devoid of any moral significance." They then deny the very reality of Hohfeldian liberties, in a passage which I have partly quoted in §2.5.6 above: "[A Hohfeldian liberty is] only the absence of obligation on the part of the option holder, and the absence of rights on the part of everyone else. Unlike double negation in logic, two absences do not make for a presence. Morally speaking, naked liberties are no things at all—no more than an absent elephant is a ghostly kind of elephant, or an absence of two elephants is a ghostly herd of ghostly elephants" (Hurd and Moore 2018, 339). Hurd's and Moore's worries about the ghostliness of liberties are no less peculiar than their worries about the ghostliness of no-rights. Nobody has ever suggested that a Hohfeldian liberty is a kind of duty—a ghostly kind. Rather, a Hohfeldian liberty is a deontic position constituted by the absence of the duty that is the logical dual of the liberty.

Having proclaimed that Hohfeldian liberties are "devoid of any moral significance," Hurd and Moore concede in a footnote that such a proclamation is false (2018, 339 n. 110):

> Granted, [Hohfeldian] liberties can have other kinds of moral significance. For example, one owes no duties of corrective or of retributive justice with respect to some harm caused to another by one's doing of some act if one did no wrong in doing such [an] act, i.e., if one violated no obligation not to do the act causing that harm. That one was nakedly at liberty to act as one did can have this kind of moral significance).

Quite bewildering is the fact that Hurd and Moore treat this immense moral significance of any Hohfeldian liberty as a trifling matter or an afterthought that is to be consigned to a footnote. At any rate, their footnote reveals why their dismissal of the reality of Hohfeldian liberties—their dismissal of the reality of such liberties, "[m]orally speaking"—should itself be discountenanced.

As I have remarked, the insistence by Hurd and Moore on the unreality of Hohfeldian liberties is directly connected to their insistence on the unreality of Hohfeldian no-rights. Given that the relationship between a Hohfeldian liberty and its correlative no-right is a relationship of biconditional entailment, philosophers who reject the reality of no-rights are obliged to reject the reality of liberties. In each case, the rejection stems from a failure to differentiate between the reality of a no-right or a liberty as a deontic position and the unreality of a no-right or a liberty as (respectively) a ghostly claim-right or a ghostly duty. A no-right is not a claim-right of any kind, and a liberty is not a duty of any kind, but each of them is a perfectly genuine deontic position. A no-right is a position that consists in being rightless within the scope of its content, and a liberty is a position that consists in being obligation-free within the scope of its content.

Hence, my seemingly pedantic distinction throughout §2.5.7 between "no-rights" and "no rights" (a distinction between a term that is a label for deontic positions of a certain type and a phrase that is not such a label) is crucial for a vindication of the reality of liberties as well as for a vindication of the reality of no-rights. Moreover, the import of that distinction goes even further—for the Hurd/Moore approach, if correct, would undermine the reality of every Hohfeldian position. Consider a counterfactual world in which Wesley Schmofeld has propounded an analysis of normative positions where the first of the four axes in his table is the claim-right/no-liberty relation. Schmofeld knows that a no-liberty could be labeled as a "duty" or an "obligation," but he prefers the symmetry with "no-right." His analytical table is otherwise the same as Hohfeld's in the actual world. Suppose that the counterparts of Hurd and Moore in this counterfactual world contemplate the first axis in the Schmofeldian analysis. While so doing, they persistently conflate "no liberty" with "no-liberty." Believing correctly that the phrase "no liberty" does not designate any deontic position, they conclude that the same is true of "no-liberty." *Mutatis mutandis*, they say the same things about no-liberties that have been said in the actual world by Hurd and Moore about no-rights and liberties. They assert that, although "no-liberty" might seem to designate some thing, it in fact designates only the absence of some thing: namely, the absence of a liberty. They assure their readers that a no-liberty is not a special ghostly kind of liberty, and they proclaim that no-liberties are devoid of moral significance. The immense moral significance of no-liberties is fleetingly mentioned by them as an afterthought in a footnote, but it surfaces only there and not in their main analyses at all. Having emphatically denied the reality of no-liberties, they proceed to deny the reality of claim-rights as positions that are correlated with no-liberties. They assert that a claim-right is simply the absence of a no-right borne by the holder of the claim-right and that it is simply the absence of a liberty held by the person vis-à-vis whom the claim-right is directed. They inform their readers that two absences do not make up a presence, and they contend that a claim-right is no more a ghostly no-right than an absent elephant is a ghostly elephant. They conclude that claim-rights are akin to no-liberties in not being genuine deontic positions. After all, one's claim-right not to be prevented from φ-ing is consistent with one's not being at liberty to φ.

We could mull over some additional counterfactual worlds in which the counterparts of Hurd and Moore deny the reality of each of the four normative positions on the right-hand side of the Hohfeldian table. And so Hurd and Moore and their counterparts end up with the conclusion that none of the eight positions in the Hohfeldian framework is genuinely a normative position. Hurd and Moore have committed themselves to such an unpalatable conclusion because they have sought to derive metaphysical inferences from some premises about purely logical relations among Hohfeldian positions. Although the logical relations in the two halves of the Hohfeldian framework are not entirely symmetrical—in that the diagonals are duals on the left-hand side and contradictories on the right-hand side—there is sufficient symmetry between them to render the reasoning of Hurd and Moore applicable to each of the four axes in the Hohfeldian table alike. If that reasoning were correct in application to any of the four axes, it would be correct in application to every one of them.

What pretty clearly impels Hurd and Moore to concentrate on the liberty/no-right axis—while not applying their reasoning to any other axis in the Hohfeldian table—is their adherence to certain metaphysical assumptions which are never expounded and defended in their long article on Hohfeld's schema.[24] Having argued elsewhere at length that those metaphysical assumptions are unfounded in any explorations of deontic and normative phenomena (Kramer 2009a, 190–212, 270–1; 2018, 23–31), I shall not here recapitulate my reflections on that point. Rather, the message of this discussion is that Hurd and Moore cannot vindicate their metaphysical preconceptions about deontic positions by appealing to logical relations among those positions. Their attempt to do so has committed them to the proposition that none of the eight Hohfeldian positions is real. That proposition can be avoided by anyone who properly attends to the distinction between "no-rights" and "no rights." Somebody who marks that distinction will recognize that there is nothing ghostly about no-rights, which are deontic positions just as solidly as are claim-rights and duties and liberties.

What should be re-emphasized at the close of these remarks is that, when Hurd and Moore dismiss no-rights as ghostly, they are blinding themselves to the difference between absences of deontic positions occasioned by the limits recounted in §2.5.6 and absences of deontic positions that occur within the realm of deontic relationships. When the absence of a specified Hohfeldian claim-right in some situation is attributable to any of the aforementioned limits, the absence is not constitutive of any Hohfeldian no-right. It is a sheer absence that reflects the constraints on the domains over which the quantifiers and variables range in the logic of Hohfeldian relationships. By contrast, when the absence of a Hohfeldian claim-right is situated within the boundaries of that logic, it is constitutive of a

[24] I will not conjecturally endeavor here to identify the assumptions, but I presume that they are redolent of the naturalistic outlook to which Hurd and Moore adhere (that is, an outlook in which the only entities recognized as real are those which are causally efficacious). Naturalistic dogmas pervade Moore's work in moral philosophy and the philosophy of causation. See, for example, Moore 1982; 1992; 2009.

Hohfeldian no-right. It is a perfectly genuine deontic position, whether moral or legal or institutional. It carries deontic significance—precisely the inverse of the deontic significance that would be carried by the claim-right of which it is the dual. With irksomely unfunny jests about ghosts and elephants, Hurd and Moore obscure the crucial difference between the import of absences within the bounds of Hohfeldian duality and the import of absences outside those bounds.

2.6 Powers and Liabilities

We can now examine the higher-order legal and moral positions on the right-hand half of Hohfeld's table. While these positions are of course normative, they are not deontic, and—as has already been explained—the logical structure of the right-hand side of the table is subtly different from that of the left-hand side. Although the relationship of biconditional entailment between the two positions in each column on the right-hand half is the same as the relationship of biconditional entailment between the two positions in each column on the left-hand half, the diagonal relationships between the columns on the right-hand half are of logical contradictoriness rather than of logical duality. These general points will become further apparent as we move through the specifics of the higher-order positions.

A legal power in the Hohfeldian sense is an ability to effect changes, through one's actions, in one's own legal positions or in the legal positions of other people. Hohfeld himself provided quite a detailed formulation of the nature of a legal power (1923, 50–1):

> A change in a given legal relation may result (1) from some superadded fact or group of facts not under the volitional control of a human being (or human beings); or (2) from some superadded fact or group of facts which are under the volitional control of one or more human beings. As regards the second class of cases, the person (or persons) whose volitional control is paramount may be said to have the (legal) power to effect the particular change of legal relations that is involved in the problem.

Though Hohfeld left his first class of cases unexplored, we shall investigate them in due course. At present, however, we should concentrate on the second class of cases. As is evident from Hohfeld's formulation, legal powers are abilities of people to bring about changes in legal relationships. Not fully explicit in that formulation is whether the abilities in question are exercisable only through actions or also through omissions, but the reference to "some superadded fact or group of facts" strongly suggests that powers are exercisable only through actions. In any event, whatever Hohfeld thought on that point, the philosophically correct understanding of Hohfeldian powers is that they are indeed abilities to effect changes in legal or moral relationships through one's actions. We shall see that changes in such relationships which occur through omissions are to be analyzed differently. Of course, an understanding of legal and moral powers along these lines has to rely on a demarcation between actions and omissions. Having elsewhere supplied at length some expositions of a rigorous criterion for that demarcation (Kramer 2003, 324–42; 2014, 77–97), I do not need to rehash those expositions here. For the purposes of this book, a pre-theoretical grasp of the distinction between actions and omissions is adequate. If a more sophisticated grasp of that distinction is needed in any other contexts in the philosophy of rights and right-holding, my previous expositions of the distinction can be drawn upon.

One notable feature of the Hohfeldian conception of legal and moral powers is its expansiveness. Under that conception, every ability to alter legal or moral relationships through one's actions is a legal or moral power. Whether or not the possession of some specific ability of that kind is typically beneficial for a party who possesses it (or is typically desired by a party who possesses it), the ability counts as a Hohfeldian power. Thus, for example, somebody whose actions contravene a legal requirement has thereby exercised some legal powers to alter her own legal positions and the legal positions of certain other people such as law-enforcement officers; she has made herself liable to undergo arrest or other measures of enforcement, and she has invested certain people with legal powers and legal liberties to resort to such measures. Scenarios of this sort have led many philosophers to adopt narrower conceptions of legal powers within their own theories. Perhaps the most famous example is Hart, who was admiringly acquainted with Hohfeld's work but who propounded his own conception of legal powers that was more circumscribed than the Hohfeldian understanding of them. Hart did not delimit the contours of his conception with any precision in *The Concept of Law*, but he appeared to confine the category of powers to Hohfeldian powers that are normally beneficial for the people who are endowed with them. In other words, being vested with a legal power (in the relevant sense) is normally better for a holder of the power than is not being vested with it.[25] When the class of legal powers is restricted in this fashion, it obviously does not encompass the ability of a criminal or a tortfeasor to alter her legal positions in the detrimental ways mentioned above.

Some other philosophers of law have similarly felt a need to come up with analyses of legal powers that are less wide-ranging than Hohfeld's analysis. For example, Joseph Raz was worried not just about the ability of a lawbreaker to alter her own legal positions through contraventions of the law, but also about the ability of someone to alter her own legal positions by shifting her residence from

[25] See Kramer 2018, 36–7. For a different (though compatible) construal of Hart's conception of legal powers in *The Concept of Law*, see MacCormick 2008, 97–8. Of course, I am not suggesting that Hart assumed that the *justification* for a power-conferring law will always reside in the fact that the powers conferred are typically beneficial for the people who hold them. Any such justificatory assumption would be particularly outlandish in connection with laws that confer public powers.

one location to another. As Raz proclaimed: "By changing my residence from one town to another, or from one country to another, I change my rights and duties, but I do not have a legal power to effect these changes by such action" (1972, 80). Though the scenario of the person who moves from one dwelling to another is not nearly as straightforward as the scenario of the criminal or tortfeasor, the abilities of a person to alter her legal relations through such a relocation might not fall under the concept of legal powers as Hart construed it. Although those normative abilities exercised in moving to a new abode are not typically detrimental for the person who possesses them, they might likewise not typically be beneficial for such a person. Instead, as a general matter, they might be evaluatively neutral.

In a sophisticated recent discussion of these complexities, Visa Kurki (2017) has for some purposes endorsed Hohfeld's understanding of legal powers and has for other purposes favored a narrower conception. Although the specifics of my analyses are different from those in the ruminations by Kurki, I concur with him about the advisability of embracing a bifurcated approach. Throughout the first half of this book and in some portions of the second half, I adhere to a broad Hohfeldian understanding of legal and moral powers. One of the virtues of such an understanding is that it helps to accentuate the distinction between the left-hand side and the right-hand side of Hohfeld's schema. Whereas the categories on the left-hand side are deontic, those on the right-hand side are modal. Given the modal character of Hohfeldian powers and immunities, Hohfeld's broad conception of powers is pertinent in that it tends to highlight the affinities between them and other abilities. Although normative abilities are obviously different from physical and psychological abilities in some salient respects, one of the major similarities between them is that exertions of them can frequently lead to typically detrimental results as well as to typically beneficial results. That feature of normative abilities is kept in view when the category of legal and moral powers is not confined to the powers that are typically beneficial for the people who possess them.

All the same, the more restrictive Hartian conception of legal and moral powers will figure in the second half of this book when I contemplate why some powers and immunities are generally classified as "rights" in the overarching sense. As will become apparent there, a version of the Interest Theory of right-holding that extends to all four Hohfeldian entitlements rather than only to claim-rights is in need of Hart's cabined conception of powers—and a similarly cabined conception of immunities. Although many Hohfeldian powers are typically detrimental for the people who hold them, and although many other Hohfeldian powers are typically beneficial for the people who hold them, only the latter powers are aptly designated as "rights" in the overarching sense. Even in the most capacious sense of that term, a criminal or a tortfeasor does not exercise a right when he renders himself liable to the imposition of punitive or compensatory sanctions. Hence, although there are solid grounds for my retention of the wide-ranging Hohfeldian category of powers in most parts of this book, the more constricted Hartian category will also play an important role.

A legal liability in the Hohfeldian sense is a position of susceptibility to the occurrence of changes in one's legal positions brought about through the exercise of a legal power by oneself or by somebody else. Just as a claim-right/duty relationship can exist between a party as the holder of the claim-right and that same party as the bearer of the duty, so too a power/liability relationship can obtain between a party as the holder of the power and that same party as the bearer of the liability. In keeping with what has just been said about Hohfeldian powers—some of which are typically beneficial for their holders and some of which are typically detrimental for their holders—some Hohfeldian liabilities are typically detrimental for their bearers whereas other Hohfeldian liabilities are typically beneficial for their bearers. Hohfeld himself underscored this point: "We are apt to think of liability as exclusively an onerous relation of one party to another. But, in its broad technical significance, this is not necessarily so." He offered the example of each person's liability to receive certain liberties and certain powers-to-acquire-ownership through the abandonment of a wristwatch or some other valuable item by somebody else (Hohfeld 1923, 60 n. 90, italics omitted):

> But such a liability instead of being onerous or unwelcome, is quite the opposite. As regards another person, M, for example, it is a liability to have created in his favor ... a [liberty] and a power relating to the watch—that is, the [liberty] of taking possession and the power, by doing so, to vest a title in himself.

In this regard, the term "liability" as an element of Hohfeld's parlance is different from that term in everyday discourse and in much of juristic discourse. Both in quotidian settings and in juristic settings, the term "liability" usually signals something that is unwelcome or deleterious. For example, if I remark that the presence of some specified player on a basketball team is a liability for the team, I am thereby indicating that the overall effect of the inclusion of the player as a member of the team is detrimental. Similarly, if a judge rules that one party P is liable to pay damages to another party Q, the term "liability"—as a designation for what is imposed on P—refers to something that is highly unwelcome (from the perspective of P). A Hohfeldian liability is quite different. In Hohfeld's vocabulary, the term "liability" is evaluatively neutral. Some positions of susceptibility to changes in one's legal relationships are typically inimical to the interests of the people who occupy those positions of susceptibility, but other such positions of susceptibility are typically promotive of the interests of the people in those positions. Everything depends on the specifics of the changes that would be brought about through the exertions of the powers that are correlative to the liabilities.

2.6.1 More on Evaluative Neutrality

Let us probe a bit further into the feature of Hohfeldian powers and liabilities that has just been highlighted: their evaluative neutrality. Although many specific types and particular instances of powers and liabilities are of course not evaluatively neutral—in that those specific types and particular instances are either typically beneficial or typically detrimental for the people who hold or bear them—the broad categories of Hohfeldian powers and liabilities are evaluatively neutral. Merely from the fact that someone holds a power or bears a liability, we cannot know whether the person's situation is thereby affected in a way that is typically beneficial or typically adverse. Only when we know the content of the power or of the liability can we safely draw any inference about its typically beneficial or typically adverse character. Why are the categories of Hohfeldian powers and liabilities evaluatively neutral in this fashion?

The key to answering this question lies in attending to the difference between the right-hand side and the left-hand side of the Hohfeldian schema. On the right-hand half of the schema, as has been emphasized, the positions are modal rather than deontic. Legal power/liability relationships pertain to changes in legal positions that are possible through the performance of certain actions, while legal immunity/disability relationships pertain to changes in legal positions that are not possible through the performance of certain actions. To ascertain whether some person P holds a specified legal power vis-à-vis somebody else, we do not need to rely on any evaluative assumptions concerning the typically beneficial or typically detrimental upshot of holding such a power. Instead, we simply need to ascertain whether P can bring about the specified changes in legal positions through his performing of the specified action(s). Because the distinctive functioning of legal powers consists in exercises of abilities, the presence or absence of such a power is detectable independently of any propositions about its agreeableness or disagreeableness for a party who holds it.

As Chapter 4 of this book will explore, legal claim-right/duty relationships are importantly different from legal power/liability relationships in the respect that has been outlined here. Though this matter will be fully investigated hereafter, a preview of it now will help to clarify and accentuate the relevant divergence between the left-hand side and the right-hand side of Hohfeld's schema. Consider, then, the following pair of legal duties imposed by the system of governance in some country. First, every adult in the jurisdiction below the age of sixty-five with an income above a specified level is legally obligated to pay at least $5,000 per annum to each parent who is still alive. Second, every adult in the jurisdiction is legally obligated to inform upon his or her parents to a domestic surveillance agency whenever the parents utter any sentiments of dissatisfaction with the prevailing system of governance. John, a citizen of the country in question, is thus under a legal duty to pay at least $5,000 every year to each of his parents and is also under a legal duty to inform upon either of his parents if either of them evinces any sense of unhappiness about the presiding system of governance. Given that each of these duties incumbent on John is a legal obligation, and given that Chapters 3 and 4 will argue that every legal obligation is owed at least to the system of governance that has imposed it, we can here take for granted that each of John's duties is owed to that system (or to some unit of the system). Does anyone else hold a claim-right correlative to either of John's duties? In particular, do his parents hold claim-rights correlative to those duties? With regard to the first of John's duties, the answer to each of these questions is affirmative. John owes each of his parents a legal duty to pay each of them at least $5,000 per annum. Each parent holds a legal claim-right, vis-à-vis John, to be paid at least $5,000 by him. In regard to the second of John's legal duties, however, the answer to each of the foregoing questions is negative. Neither parent holds a legal claim-right to be informed upon by John to a domestic surveillance agency. John's duty to inform upon the parents is owed to the prevailing system of governance and more specifically to the surveillance agency, but it is not owed to either of the parents or to anyone else.

Chapter 4, with its elaboration of the Interest Theory of right-holding, will present a full explanation of the difference between the upshots of these situations. An explanation is needed, for in each case John owes a legal duty with a content that pertains squarely to his parents. Without yet venturing into the intricacies of the Interest Theory, we can simply note here that the best way of accounting for the difference between the aforementioned upshots is to observe that being paid at least $5,000 per annum is typically beneficial for the recipient whereas being informed upon to a domestic surveillance agency is typically detrimental for the person who has been betrayed. Such an observation is not a moral judgment, but it is an evaluative judgment. Here the judgment has been stated explicitly, but often the evaluative judgments that inform one's ascriptions of legal claim-rights are left implicit. Still, such judgments are always operative when somebody is identifying the holders of any legal claim-rights that are correlated with specified legal duties. In that regard, the matter of identifying the holders of legal claim-rights is in contrast with the matter of identifying the holders of legal powers. No evaluative judgments are needed when we are posing the question whether some party P is able to effect certain changes in specified legal relationships by performing some specified actions. If the answer to such a question is affirmative, then we can correctly maintain that P is endowed with a legal power to bring about such changes through those actions. If instead the answer to such a question is negative, then we can correctly maintain that P lacks the specified legal power. We can reach either of those answers without further asking whether the ability to induce the envisioned changes will typically be beneficial or typically be detrimental for someone who possesses that ability.

Thus, with reference to the broad category of Hohfeldian legal powers, we cannot correctly say that such powers are typically beneficial on balance for the people who hold them—nor, of course, can we correctly say that such powers are typically detrimental on balance for the people who hold them. All that can accurately be said is that many Hohfeldian legal powers are typically beneficial on balance for the people who hold them and that many Hohfeldian legal powers are typically detrimental on balance for the people who hold them. Similarly, all that can accurately be said about the evaluative bearings of Hohfeldian legal liabilities is that many such liabilities are typically beneficial on balance for the people who bear them and that many other such liabilities are typically detrimental on balance for the people who bear them. By contrast, all claim-rights as deontic protections are typically beneficial on balance for the people who hold them, and liberties as permissions are likewise typically beneficial on balance for the people who hold them. When we undertake the transition from the deontic properties of the positions delineated on the left-hand side of Hohfeld's schema to the modal properties of the positions delineated on the right-hand side, we thereby undertake a transition from evaluative definiteness to evaluative open-endedness.

2.6.2 Quasi-Powers and Quasi-Liabilities

In §2.5.6, I have referred *en passant* to quasi-powers and quasi-liabilities. We should probe two main types of quasi-powers, the first of which was recognized but left unexplored by Hohfeld.[26] Together, these two categories of quasi-powers cover the main ways in which sundry alterations of people's legal or moral relationships can be brought about through routes other than exertions of legal or moral powers. A quasi-liability is, of course, a position of susceptibility to the transformative effects of the workings of a quasi-power. Such a position of susceptibility can be occupied by everyone who is a potential occupant of any of the standard Hohfeldian legal positions.

2.6.2.1 Insentient Forces and Entities

First, as has been mentioned in §2.5.6, the alterations in people's legal or moral relationships can be brought about through the workings of insentient forces or through the actions of insentient organisms. For example, if Penelope is struck and injured quite badly by a bolt of lightning while she is standing outdoors, her legal and moral positions will have been changed by that force of nature. For one thing, she now has a moral claim-right and perhaps also a legal claim-right to be assisted by anyone in her proximity who is able to help. In addition, her legal and moral relationship with her insurer or with the public health-care system in her locality will have altered. If Penelope has been killed by the bolt of lightning, her

[26] I have explored the first category of quasi-powers in Kramer 2009a, 78–82; 2022, 366–8. I also advert to it quite briefly in Kramer 1998, 102–3.

legal and moral positions will have been transformed even more sweepingly. Her entitlements as an owner of any assets will have been transferred to her estate for distribution to her heirs, or will have been transferred to public coffers. In most jurisdictions, her death will have deprived her of her legal claim-rights not to be defamed. In these ways, and in a host of other ways, an event involving natural forces or entities can change the legal and moral relationships among people. These alterations are effected not by exercises of powers but instead by exercises of quasi-powers. Although the parties who occupy the quasi-liabilities correlative to those quasi-powers are within the vast matrices of legal and moral relationships that join people (and many non-human animals) to one another, the exertions of the quasi-powers impinge on those matrices—often far-reachingly—from the outside.

Exertions of quasi-powers occur not only through dramatic events such as bolts of lightning and earthquakes and monsoons. They occur also, multitudinously, in more mundane forms. For example, if Helena dies of natural causes through some illness, the microorganisms in her body that kill her will have transformed her legal and moral relationships in much the same ways as a lethal bolt of lightning. Vis-à-vis those microorganisms, she bears quasi-liabilities to undergo the changes in her legal and moral positions which the microorganisms can induce through the termination of her life.

In many cases, the workings of quasi-powers operate independently of the designs pursued by human beings. For example, if Penelope has been reasonably cautious and has not sought to be struck by lightning while she is walking or standing outdoors, her mishap that involves her being felled by a bolt of lightning is not something sought or arranged by anybody. Nor is it due to culpability—negligence or recklessness or malice—on the part of Penelope or on the part of anyone else. In some other cases, by contrast, the existence or efficacy of a quasi-power as such is due to the designs or culpability of somebody. Especially in a case of the latter kind, but also in most cases of the former kind, the placing of some person or class of persons under a quasi-liability is due to an exercise of a Hohfeldian power. Such an exercise of a Hohfeldian power has resulted not in the creation of any Hohfeldian legal or moral positions but instead in the creation of a quasi-liability vis-à-vis some insentient force or entity.

Let us glance at a few examples. Suppose that, even though Penelope has been reasonably cautious and has not sought to be struck by lightning, her going outside has made a decisive difference between a situation in which she is vulnerable to a flash of lightning and a situation in which she is not vulnerable to such an occurrence. In that event, her going outside is the exercise of a Hohfeldian power (held vis-à-vis herself) through which she has placed herself under a quasi-liability to undergo the changes in her legal and moral relationships that will be effected by a bolt of lightning which strikes her. *Ex hypothesi*, she has exercised that Hohfeldian power inadvertently rather than designedly. Nevertheless, a Hohfeldian power can be exerted without any intention on the part of the power-holder to exert it. Even though Penelope has not been remiss and has not sought to place herself in harm's way, her action of going outside has played a key role in rendering the flash of lightning efficacious as a force endowed with a quasi-power. Her action of going outside has been the exercise of a power to impose on herself a quasi-liability correlative to the quasi-power of the bolt of lightning.

Of course, the action of Penelope in going outside will even more clearly be the exercise of a power (held vis-à-vis herself) if she has been foolhardy or if she has intentionally exposed herself to the perils of a fierce electrical storm. Through that action, she has deliberately or recklessly made herself vulnerable to the workings of a quasi-power—which is to say that she has deliberately or recklessly imposed on herself a quasi-liability to undergo the multiple changes in her legal relationships that will be induced by those workings insofar as they materialize. Not every quasi-power gains its efficacy as such from the exercise of a Hohfeldian power that leads into it, but many quasi-powers do indeed become efficacious in such a fashion. (For an example of some quasi-powers that are efficacious independently of any exercise of a Hohfeldian power, we can envisage anew the death of Helena through the workings of fatal microorganisms in her body. If the presence and operations of those microorganisms in her body are not due to her actions or to the actions of anybody else, the efficacy of those deadly operations in changing her legal and moral positions is not attributable to any exertions of Hohfeldian powers.)

Furthermore, in some other situations the very existence of quasi-powers as such is due to the actions of people who have thereby exercised Hohfeldian powers to subject themselves or other people to quasi-liabilities. Consider, for instance, the following observation by Laura Donohue (2022, 19): "Sophisticated algorithms, machine learning, and artificial intelligence are being used with legal effect. Criminal risk assessment algorithms, for example, are being employed to determine whether individuals are granted parole, altering their liberty rights." As is evident, the quasi-powers recounted here by Donohue—that is, the abilities of computerized machines to alter people's legal relationships by arriving at certain determinations—have been brought into existence deliberately by legal-governmental officials who, with the aid of technicians, have put into place the arrangements for the functioning of the machines. Hence, the actions of those officials in settling the arrangements are exercises of legal powers that impose on each person in the relevant jurisdiction some quasi-liabilities to undergo changes in his or her legal relationships through the determinations of the computerized machines. Any changes brought about through those determinations are not directly engendered by exercises of Hohfeldian powers, but the quasi-powers which (when exerted) do directly engender such changes are themselves the products of certain exercises of Hohfeldian powers. Exercises of those powers obviously do involve choices and actions by human beings, even though the quasi-powers established through those exercises of powers are exerted by non-human contraptions.

2.6.2.2 The Applicability of General Norms

Many further alterations in the legal and moral relationships of people take place not through exertions of Hohfeldian powers but instead through the applicability of general laws and moral principles. For example, when a statute of limitations has prescribed the span of time during which lawsuits can be pursued or prosecutions can be brought, the applicability of that statute to the situations of people will very frequently result in modifications of their legal positions. If somebody possesses a legal power (or a set of legal powers) to pursue successfully a lawsuit against a tortfeasor or against the breacher of a contractual duty, and if she declines to pursue any such lawsuit, she will cease to possess that power (or set of powers) when the time prescribed by the statute has elapsed. That change in her legal positions, and in the legal positions of anyone whom she could have sued successfully, is brought about not through any exercise of a Hohfeldian power but instead through the operation of the statute. Though the existence of the statute is of course due to exertions of legal powers by the members of a legislature, the effect of the statute in depriving the potential claimant of her power(s) to pursue a lawsuit successfully does not itself involve any such exertions. It has occurred through the inaction of the potential claimant, and—as has been stated—omissions are not exercises of Hohfeldian powers.

Many other changes in people's legal relationships likewise occur through the applicability of general norms rather than through exertions of legal powers. For example, a statute in some jurisdiction might prescribe that anyone who finds a lost item of property will gain entitlements of ownership over that item if it has not been claimed by its current owner within six months of the posting of advertisements (in specified publications) about its having been found. By discovering some lost chattel and by posting suitable advertisements about the discovery, John will have exercised some legal powers through which he has placed himself under quasi-liabilities to acquire entitlements over the chattel after six months have passed. *Pari passu*, John will have placed the current owner under quasi-liabilities to be deprived of those entitlements. John's acquisition of the entitlements after the elapsing of six months is not itself occasioned by any further exercise of a legal power. Instead, it is due to the operation of a general statute whose applicability is triggered by the sheer passing of time rather than by some further action on the part of John. (Of course, if the item of found property is valuable, John at the end of the six-month period might have to obtain some official document that attests to his newly acquired ownership. His action of obtaining such a document is the exercise of a legal power, but that very power will have been vested in him by the combination of the statute and the sheer passing of time.)

Like the workings of natural forces, then, the operations of general laws can produce changes in people's legal relationships that are not produced directly by exercises of legal powers. Now, Hohfeld himself did not discuss quasi-powers and quasi-liabilities at all, even though he briefly adverted to their existence. Should we conclude, consequently, that there are gaps in the comprehensiveness of the Hohfeldian framework even within the boundaries delineated by §2.5.6 above? Neither an unequivocally negative answer nor an unequivocally affirmative answer to this question is apposite. On the one hand, the comprehensiveness of Hohfeld's framework of legal and moral relationships pertains to the multifarious such relationships that exist among the potential holders of legal and moral entitlements. Although some quasi-powers originate from exercises of legal powers held by human beings, the quasi-powers themselves are not possessed by human beings; *ex hypothesi*, they are possessed by insentient entities and forces or by general laws and moral principles. Those entities and forces and laws and principles do not belong to the class of potential holders of Hohfeldian entitlements. Accordingly, although any quasi-liability as the correlate of a quasi-power is borne by a member of that class, it is not borne vis-à-vis some other member thereof. Hence, unlike a power/liability relationship, a quasi-power/quasi-liability relationship does not obtain between potential holders of Hohfeldian entitlements. Rather, it obtains between a potential holder of Hohfeldian entitlements and some insentient thing(s) or force(s) or some general law(s) or moral principle(s). Hence, any quasi-power/quasi-liability relationship is not among the countless relationships which Hohfeld sought to encompass within his schema.

On the other hand, I readily avow that Hohfeld's failure to discuss quasi-powers and quasi-liabilities is a lacuna in his overall theorizing about jural relationships. Given that exertions of quasi-powers induce changes in the legal or moral relationships that obtain among the occupants of Hohfeldian legal or moral positions, and given that many quasi-powers have arisen through actions that constitute exercises of legal powers, a general theory of legal and moral relationships should take the roles of quasi-powers carefully into account. Still, one's acceptance of that point is perfectly consistent with one's affirmation that Hohfeld's analytical framework is indeed comprehensive as a distillation of the types of legal and moral relationships that can link people to one another and to many non-human animals.

2.6.3 Quantification Afresh

Quantification is crucial for analyses of some major aspects of the positions in all four columns of Hohfeld's table, and its importance specifically for analyses of powers and liabilities has to some degree been recognized within the philosophical literature that has been generated by Hohfeld's work. Kevin Saunders in particular, during a flawed but sophisticated effort to formalize the Hohfeldian analysis, has drawn attention to one aspect of powers and liabilities that is in need of quantification (1990, 483 n. 98). Here I will elaborate on Saunders's insight, and I will also broach some other respects in which quantification is needed for analyses of power/liability relationships. We should here keep in mind the distinctions which

I have drawn in §2.5.5, especially the distinction between disjunctive universal quantification and distributive universal quantification.

2.6.3.1 Quantification over Sets of Conditions for Changes in Legal Relationships

Saunders recognizes that some statements which ascribe legal powers to people do not specify the types of actions through which the powers can be exercised. Implicit if not explicit in any such statement is an existential quantifier. As a first approximation, we can say that the domain under the quantifier comprises the act-types that can be performed by the party to whom the legal power is ascribed. So construed, the statement affirms or presupposes that there is at least one type of action which the party can perform that will bring about a specified change in certain legal positions. Such a construal of the statement is only a first approximation, however, for the existential quantification is really over sets of propositions where each set if true will be minimally sufficient for enabling the exercise of the power in question. Every set of propositions in the domain will include the proposition that an action of some type can be performed by the party who holds the power. Construed in this more precise fashion, the power-ascribing statement affirms or presupposes that there is at least one set of true propositions minimally sufficient for enabling the occurrence of a specified change in legal positions where at least one such set includes the proposition that an action of some type can be performed by the party to whom the legal power is ascribed.

Two main elements of the remarks in the foregoing paragraph should be elucidated here. First, the notion of minimal sufficiency—which will figure conspicuously in Chapter 4 of this book—is to be understood as follows. A set of actually occurrent facts S is minimally sufficient for some effect E if and only if (1) S is sufficient for E and (2) S does not comprise any facts that are unnecessary to make S sufficient for E. In other words, there are no redundant elements in a minimally sufficient set of facts; every element is necessary to make the overall set of facts sufficient for the occurrence of E. Every set of propositions within the domain covered by the existential quantifier in a power-ascribing statement is (if true) minimally sufficient for enabling the exercise of the specified power, and every such set within the domain includes the proposition that an action of some type can be performed by the power-holder. Hence, the fact that an action of some type has been performed by the power-holder is indispensable for her *exercise* of a legal power, and the fact that the power-holder can bring about a change in legal relationships through the performance of such an action is indispensable for her *possession* of a legal power.

Second, some readers may wonder why existentially quantifying over the types of actions that can be performed by the power-holder is not fully suitable. Why is the fully suitable quantification instead over sets of conditions minimally sufficient for enabling the exercise of the specified power, where each such set includes the proposition that the power-holder can perform an action of some type? The reason is that an attempt to exercise a power can be thwarted if defeating conditions materialize, which have the effect of suspending or terminating the existence of the power. Hence, every set of facts minimally sufficient for enabling the exercise of a power will include the fact that no such defeating conditions have materialized.[27] Within the domain covered by the existential quantifier in a power-ascribing statement, every set of minimally sufficient propositions includes a proposition about the absence of defeating conditions.

In short, whenever a power-ascribing statement does not specify the types of actions through which the ascribed power can be exercised, the existential quantifier operative in the statement ranges over a domain comprising every set of propositions which if true will be minimally sufficient for the possession of that power. Every such set includes both (1) the proposition that the holder of the power can perform an action of some type and (2) the proposition that any conditions which would defeat every attempt by the holder to exercise the power are not present. Were the quantification instead only over the types of actions that can be performed by the power-holder, the ascription of the specified legal power would leave open the possibility that the power is possessed by the holder in circumstances where it cannot be exercised by her. Yet the notion of an ability that cannot be exercised is nonsensical. In any circumstances where a legal power cannot be exercised by the person who supposedly holds it, its existence has been either suspended or terminated. Hence, whether an existential quantifier in a power-ascribing statement of the sort envisaged here is implicit or explicit, it covers a domain comprising every set of propositions which if true will be minimally sufficient for enabling the exercise of the specified power by the party to whom the power is ascribed. Such a statement affirms or presupposes that at least one such set of propositions is true.

2.6.3.2 Quantification over Sets of Changes

In the preceding subsection, I have assumed that the element left unspecified in a power-ascribing statement is the action or set of actions through which the ascribed power can be exercised. As is evident, however, that element is not the only thing that might be left unspecified in such a statement. Especially when the legal power ascribed is a broad power to enact statutes or ordinances or other legislation, the changes that can be brought about through the exercise of the power will have to be left largely or wholly unspecified. Implicit or perhaps explicit in a law which establishes such a wide-ranging legal power is a universal quantifier that ranges disjunctively over a domain comprising the multitudinous possible sets of jointly consistent changes that can be effected through exertions of the

[27] Though the analyses in Holton 2002 and 2010 are propounded in response to other philosophical controversies, they shed light on the point articulated here.

power. The disjunctive universal quantification is exclusive rather than inclusive. On any given occasion, only one of the possible sets of jointly consistent changes will be actualized through the exertion of some particular legislative power(s) in a jurisdiction.

Manifold possible changes in legal relationships, though of course not *all* such changes, can be brought about simultaneously. A myriad of distinct sets of jointly consistent possible changes will be the elements of the domain over which the disjunctive universal quantifier ranges. Each such set comprises a unique array of jointly consistent possible changes, albeit of course many of the sets are proper subsets of others. Some sets each comprise only one pair of changes in the positions of a single legal relationship, whereas countless others each comprise multiple changes in multiple legal relationships.

Disjunctive universal quantification over possible sets of jointly consistent changes in legal relationships is likewise operative, implicitly if not explicitly, in laws that endow individuals and organizations with powers to enter into contracts. Although the general character of the changes brought about through exercises of those powers might well be outlined in the relevant laws and doctrines of a jurisdiction, the specifics of the changes are spelled out instead by the contractual parties whenever they exercise those powers. Operative in the relevant laws and doctrines of a jurisdiction, then, are disjunctive universal quantifiers over domains comprising the myriad distinct sets of jointly consistent changes in legal relationships that can be sought by parties who enter into contracts. Again, some of the sets each comprise only one pair of changes in the positions of a single legal relationship, whereas countless other sets each comprise multiple changes in multiple legal relationships between the contractual parties. The nature of the institution of contract law makes inevitable, in the norms which establish and regulate that institution, the (usually implicit) presence of disjunctive universal quantifiers that range over the aforementioned sets.

Of course, the domains to which I have referred in the preceding two paragraphs do not typically comprehend all the sets of jointly consistent changes in legal relationships that could be actualized if the powers of legislators to enact laws and the powers of individuals and organizations to enter into contracts were unrestricted. In most if not all jurisdictions, the powers of legislators to enact laws are limited by constitutional provisions or by other basic constraints. Sometimes the limits take the form of legal duties, but much more often they are imposed through the exclusion of certain types of alterations from the range of alterations that can be brought about by exercises of the powers of legislators. As will be emphasized in §2.7.1 below, many of the guarantees in so-called bills of rights are implemented predominantly through legal immunities and disabilities rather than predominantly through legal duties and claim-rights. Similarly, in most if not all jurisdictions, limitations on the powers of individuals and organizations to enter into contracts are much more often in the form of legal disabilities than in the form of legal duties. Hence, when a disjunctive universal quantifier is operative in a statement that ascribes law-making powers to legislators or contract-forming powers to individuals and organizations, the domain covered by the quantifier is reflective of the limits that have just been broached here.

2.6.3.3 Quantification over Potential Bearers of Liabilities

In my initial reflections on quantification in §2.5.5 above, I have concentrated chiefly on quantification over potential occupants of Hohfeldian positions (especially potential bearers of Hohfeldian no-rights). A comparable focus is pertinent here, for statements that ascribe legal or moral powers to people frequently leave unspecified the parties vis-à-vis whom the powers are held. Often the lack of any such specification indicates that a quantifier is operative. For example, if I ascribe to myself a legal power to vest myself with proprietary entitlements over a book by purchasing the book from a shop, my statement will probably leave unspecified the bearers of the legal liabilities that are correlative to the ascribed power. What is obvious is that the owner of the shop and I bear some of those liabilities, as my exercise of my power alters the owner's legal positions and my own legal positions. Somewhat less obvious, however, is that liabilities correlative to my power are also borne by everyone else in the jurisdiction. My gaining of proprietary entitlements over the book through my action of purchasing it will have altered the legal positions of everyone else in the jurisdiction, since everyone there now owes to me certain legal duties that have thitherto been owed to the bookseller. (Though I concentrate here on the modifications to people's legal duties, other legal positions of theirs will also have shifted. For example, whereas each person previously bore a legal power vis-à-vis the bookseller to acquire ownership of the book by purchasing it from her, each person now bears that power vis-à-vis me to acquire ownership of the book by purchasing it from me.) Thus, unless my power-ascribing statement is explicitly focused solely on the bookseller and myself as the bearers of liabilities correlative to my power, the statement is best construed as containing a distributive universal quantifier that covers a domain comprising everyone in the relevant jurisdiction. The universal quantification is distributive because the legal positions of everyone within the jurisdiction are liable to change in parallel ways through my exercise of the ascribed power.

While the preceding two subsections have focused on quantification in the contents of Hohfeldian power/liability relationships, the current subsection focuses on quantification in the directionality of the relationships. Still, because a full specification of the content of a legal or moral power will advert to the parties whose legal or moral positions would be altered through the exercise of the power, such a specification will have fixed the directionality of the power. Whereas a legal or moral duty can be owed to a party to whom no reference is made in a full specification of the content of the duty, any full specification of the content of a legal or moral power will advert to the parties vis-à-vis whom the power is held.

(The references to those parties will be at least *de dicto* if not *de re*.) Thus, although the distributive universal quantification discussed in the preceding paragraph does of course pertain to the directionality of power/liability relationships, it thereby also pertains to the contents of those relationships. For many a Hohfeldian power, a full specification of its content will incorporate a distributive universal quantifier that ranges over liability-bearers.

2.7 Immunities and Disabilities

We now arrive at the final column in Hohfeld's table, the immunity/disability axis. If some person P holds an immunity vis-à-vis some other person Q in relation to a certain modification of P's legal or moral positions through the performance of some action(s) by Q, then P is insusceptible to undergoing that modification through Q's performance of the specified action(s). As is evident, then, an immunity is the negation of a liability. P is immune from the bringing about of some modification in his legal or moral positions through Q's performance of some specified action(s) if and only if P is not liable to undergo that modification through the performance of the action(s) by Q. An immunity and the liability of which it is the negation are contradictories rather than duals; although each is the negation of the other, the content of each is the same as the content of the other.

Immunities of course vary along several different dimensions. An immunity can be held vis-à-vis only one party or vis-à-vis multiple parties. It can pertain to only a narrowly specified type of modification, or it can pertain to an array of modifications. Legal positions protected by it can be more numerous or less numerous in their extent. Unsurprisingly, given how important quantification is in analyses of power/liability relationships, quantification will often likewise be involved in analyses of immunity/disability relationships along any of the dimensions just broached.

A disability is a position of powerlessness within the scope of its correlative immunity. In the example sketched in the penultimate paragraph above, Q bears a disability vis-à-vis P with regard to Q's modifying of certain legal positions of P through Q's performance of any specified action(s). If Q attempts to modify those legal positions by performing the specified action(s), the attempt will be unavailing. Hence, just as an immunity is the negation of a liability with the same content, so too a disability is the negation of a power with the same content. The content of a disability is not only the same as the content of the power of which the disability is the negation; in addition, that content is of course the same as the content of the immunity of which the disability is the correlate. In that respect, the immunity/disability axis is like each of the other three columns in Hohfeld's schema. In each column, the two correlative positions are endowed with the same content—and the party who occupies either position is the party vis-à-vis whom the other position is held or borne.

2.7.1 The Importance of Immunities: Bills of Rights

Most commentators on Hohfeld's analysis of legal positions tend to say rather little about immunities and disabilities, but immunity/disability relationships are in fact of immense importance. For one thing, many of the entitlements conferred by so-called bills of rights are immunities. For example, the bestowal of immunities on citizens is the prime effect of the First Amendment to the American Constitution with its guarantees of freedom of expression and other liberties. Although the wording of the First Amendment with reference to freedom of expression ("Congress shall make no law . . . abridging the freedom of speech, or of the press") could have been construed as principally duty-imposing, it has in fact been construed as preponderantly immunity-conferring. That is, instead of having been interpreted as imposing legal duties on the US Congress to refrain from enacting laws that abridge people's communicative liberties in certain ways, the First Amendment has been interpreted as bestowing legal immunities on Americans which shield them against Congressional legislation that would abridge such liberties in the disallowed ways.[28] Whereas the American courts do not levy sanctions on the Congress for enacting laws that are at odds with the First Amendment, they hold that those laws—or the relevant provisions of those laws—are invalid. In other words, the courts hold that the Congress by enacting such laws has gone beyond the scope of its legislative powers. Those laws are within the ambit of the disabilities imposed on the Congress by the First Amendment, and are therefore of no effect. In general, the free-speech guarantee under the American Constitution is implemented predominantly through immunity/disability relationships rather than predominantly through claim-right/duty relationships.

2.7.1.1 A Qualification: Wrongdoing in Law-Administration

Worth noting here is that what has just been said is applicable to contraventions of a constitutional free-speech guarantee which occur at the level of statutes or regulations or ordinances or other general laws. In situations where contraventions instead occur at the level of law-administration, the proper responses are different. When laws that are unobjectionable in themselves are given effect by officials in legally and morally objectionable ways, criminal-law proceedings or tort-law

[28] For nearly a century, the US Supreme Court has deemed the First Amendment's free-speech guarantee to be applicable not only to the Congress but also to state legislatures (through the Fourteenth Amendment). My reason for omitting any mention of the state legislatures in the brief discussion in the text is simply that I can thereby avoid cumbersome prose.

proceedings against the officials (and against the governmental agencies that employ them) can be legally and morally justifiable. For example, suppose that some constables in a municipality enforce a breach-of-the-peace statute in a discriminatory manner against certain speakers whose messages are not to the liking of the constables. Some instances of discriminatory enforcement of this kind notoriously occurred during the civil-rights campaigns in the southern half of the United States during the 1960s. Such instances of enforcement were morally wrongful partly because they invested hostile audiences with the authority to determine the range of communicative endeavors that would be legally tolerated, and partly because the overall pattern of enforcement was blatantly invidious. Hence, the wielding of criminal or civil sanctions against the individual constables—as well as against the police forces that employed them—could be morally justified both under the principle of freedom of expression and under a principle of equal protection.

In the contexts just mentioned, and in countless other relevantly similar cases, some administrative or adjudicative officials are giving effect to just laws but are doing so in ways that clash with the constraints of content-neutrality and speaker-neutrality established by the principle of freedom of expression. In contexts where such officials are deliberately deviating from the terms of just laws instead of implementing them selectively, the actions at variance with the aforementioned constraints of neutrality will be even graver; consequently, the remedies that are morally vital for rectifying the wrongs done by those actions will be more onerous. Situations of this kind reveal especially clearly the moral requisiteness of holding law-enforcement officials individually responsible for some transgressions of the principle of freedom of expression. Although the officials *qua* officials are always acting on behalf of their system of governance and more specifically on behalf of the governmental body (such as a police force) that employs them, and although the responsibility for their actions performed within their roles as officials is therefore always collective as well as individual, there are some cases in which the wrongs constituted by transgressions of the principle of freedom of expression will not have been fully rectified without the imposition of sanctions on the individuals who have committed those wrongs. Having violated some of their legal and moral duties, the officials as well as their employer should have to bear the burdens of remedying their misdeeds.

2.7.1.2 Disabilities Imposed on Lawmakers

Although constitutional guarantees (such as the First Amendment to the American Constitution) that correspond more or less closely to the moral principle of freedom of expression are contravened not uncommonly at the level of law-application, the contraventions most frequently under scrutiny in high-profile litigation are at the level of general laws. In a liberal democracy, any remedies suitable for rectifying the wrongs perpetrated at that latter level are almost always directed against collectivities rather than against individuals (where a collectivity targeted by a remedy can be an entire system of governance or some organ of decision-making within that system). Moreover, very often the legal remedies pertinent for rectifying any contraventions of the principle of freedom of expression at the level of general laws are not sanctions.

As has been remarked already, the legal entitlements conferred on individuals and groups by constitutional free-speech guarantees such as the First Amendment are mostly immunities. Those immunities shield individuals and groups against being deprived of their communicative liberties by laws that purport to remove or curtail such liberties. Now, as has also been remarked, legal immunities are effectuated by administrative or adjudicative officials not through legal sanctions but instead through annulments of ostensible exercises of legal powers. Suppose for example that the US Congress were to enact a statute which professes to bar everybody in the United States from discussing the matter of abortion in any location outside a private residence. Such a law would of course be challenged successfully in the courts, but the upshot of the challenge would not be the imposition of any penalties on the Congress or on any members of Congress. Rather, the upshot would be the invalidation of the statute, as the courts would declare that the attempt by the Congress to exercise its law-making powers had been of no avail. Instead of giving effect to any legal duty incumbent on the Congress, the courts would be giving effect to a legal disability that limits the Congress's legislative powers. That Hohfeldian disability is correlated with the immunity of each citizen against being deprived of communicative liberties by laws that contravene the First Amendment.

As is manifest from my exposition of the Hohfeldian analytical framework in this chapter, claim-rights and immunities are not equivalent. Similarly, of course, the duties that correlate with claim-rights and the disabilities that correlate with immunities are not equivalent. Hence, as has been stated in the preceding paragraph, the legal remedy that is most often suitable in response to any contravention of the principle of freedom of expression that occurs at the level of a general law—namely, the invalidation of that law either as a whole or in part—is not a legal sanction levied for a breach of a legal duty. Indeed, such a conclusion follows not only from the Hohfeldian analysis but also from Hart's famous critique of John Austin's jurisprudential theory. In one strand of that critique, Hart cogently argued that the nullity ensuing from an unsuccessful attempt to exercise a legal power is not tantamount to a sanction imposed for a violation of a legal obligation (Hart 1994, 33–5; Kramer 2018, 39–41). Yet, given that disabilities are not equivalent to duties, and given that the nullity which ensues from the implementation of a legal disability is not equivalent to a sanction which ensues from the enforcement of a legal duty, the role of nullity as a remedy for contraventions of the principle of freedom of expression that occur at the level of general laws might seem problematic. After all, those contraventions are breaches of moral duties. How can the effectuation of a legal *disability* be a suitable remedy for a breach of a moral *duty*? Should not instead the suitable remedy be the enforcement of a legal duty?

Three replies to such a worry are apposite here. First, although Hart and Hohfeld were correct to highlight the logical differences between legal duties and legal disabilities, and although Hart was also correct to highlight the functional differences between them, there is a functional overlap between duties and disabilities in contexts where adjudicators are called upon to say whether the efforts of legislators to exercise law-making powers have been successful.[29] In any such context, the invalidation of a statute or an ordinance or some other law—though not equivalent to the levying of a sanction such as a fine—is quite a rebuke to the legislative body whose enactment has been annulled. Such a remedy undoes what the legislature has presumed to accomplish, and it in effect requires the members of that body to expend further time and effort if they wish to come up with some alternative to the enactment that has been nullified. A court that invalidates a law might forbear from using any reproachful language in its presentation of its judgment on the matter, but that judgment does function as a reproach implicitly if not explicitly.

Second, although a general law that clashes with a constitutional guarantee such as the First Amendment should normally be invalidated by the courts without the imposition of legal sanctions, there can be exceptional circumstances in which the imposition of sanctions on a legislative body would be morally suitable and indeed morally requisite. Suppose for example that a local government enacts a succession of nearly identical ordinances, each of which is glaringly in contravention of the principle of freedom of expression (and glaringly in contravention of a constitutional guarantee which corresponds to that principle). After constitutional challenges to several of the successive editions of the ordinance have resulted in the invalidation of all of them, a court will be morally warranted in issuing an injunction that forbids the local government to continue to enact versions of the ordinance that are nearly identical to those which have already been annulled. Such an injunction will place the local government under a legal duty to desist from its cynical pattern of behavior. Under the terms of the injunction, any subsequent enactments must differ from the invalidated versions of the ordinance in ways that duly take account of the unconstitutionality of those previous versions. An enactment by the local government that defies the terms of the injunction will trigger the levying of a sanction such as a fine. In the circumstances envisaged here, where the local government has displayed flagrantly bad faith by declining to heed its constitutional limitations and its moral obligations, the placing of it under a legal duty through the issuance of an injunction can be morally justified. Likewise, of

29 My references to legislators and legislative bodies are to be understood expansively here and elsewhere. Such references encompass any organs of governance that establish general laws, including not only any straightforwardly legislative institutions such as the US Congress and the UK Parliament but also—among others—any administrative agencies that promulgate regulations and any local authorities that enact ordinances or by-laws.

course, the plying of sanctions against the local authorities in the event of their non-compliance with that legal duty can be morally justified.

Third, in the absence of circumstances in which a legislative body has exhibited arrantly bad faith or gross remissness, the effectuation of a legal disability through the nullification of an enactment is the fitting remedy when a transgression of a constitutional guarantee is at the level of a general law. As has been argued, although such a remedy is not a sanction, its function in the context of its occurrence is partly that of a sanction. Moreover, in the absence of egregiously bad faith or gross remissness on the part of a legislative body, the employment of such a remedy avoids both excessive confrontationality and excessive deference. Measures suitable for rectifying any transgressions of constitutional guarantees have to be responsive to the requirements of other major moral precepts such as the principle of democratic legitimacy. Although that latter principle obviously cannot be expounded in depth here, its requirement of respect for the operations of a democratically elected legislative body is binding as a constraint on any remedial response to a violation of a constitutional guarantee. In the absence of strikingly bad faith or blatant remissness in those operations, the respect due is not shown if a legislative body is subjected to legal sanctions when its enactments collide with a constitutional safeguard. In the event of a clash between an enactment and such a safeguard, the invalidation of the enactment upholds the civil liberties protected through the constitutional provision while also serving the ideal of democratic legitimacy by keeping a legislative body within the ambit of its authority.

2.7.2 The Importance of Immunities: Securing Other Entitlements

Apart from the role of legal immunities and disabilities in the effectuation of guarantees of civil liberties—such as the guarantees enshrined in the First Amendment to the American Constitution—legal immunities are crucial for securing the existence and continuity of other legal positions. For example, if Melanie has a legal claim-right against being punched in the face by Luke, and if she does not hold any legal immunities against being divested of that claim-right by Luke through countless elementary means (such as his looking at her or waving at her or smiling at her or uttering some mundane phrase), then her claim-right is almost entirely hollow. Indeed, if she does not hold any legal immunity against being divested of that claim-right through Luke's clenching of his fist or through his movement of his arm toward her face, we shall have to conclude that she does not really hold such a claim-right at all. Given that in those circumstances Melanie can be deprived of her legal claim-right by precisely the sorts of movements of Luke's body that would be involved in his contravening the claim-right, her legal protection against being punched in the face by Luke would be indistinguishable from her not having any legal protection against such misconduct by him. Consequently, the very existence of her claim-right is dependent on its being accompanied by sundry immunities against the extinguishing of that claim-right.

This role of immunities in securing the existence and continuity of other entitlements is pervasive and vital, yet it is almost always taken for granted rather than made explicit. Still, like the presence of oxygen in the atmosphere of Earth—which, as I have observed in §2.5.2 above, is necessary for the continued existence of human beings but is mostly taken for granted in everyday life—the aforementioned role of immunities is no less important for going so often unnoticed. Immunities are central not only to freedom of expression but also to the sway of legal and moral positions more generally.

This role of immunities in securing the existence and continuity of other entitlements is what accounts for my contention (in my opening chapter and near the outset of this chapter) that the noun "right" in its strict sense is properly limited to any claim-right combined with immunities against the discontinuation of that claim-right. Although Hohfeld took "right" in its strict sense to be interchangeable with "claim" or "claim-right," his doing so was very likely attributable to what I have described in the last paragraph above. That is, he was very likely taking for granted that any claim-right will be accompanied by sundry immunities which serve to secure it against being extinguished by routine modes of behavior and especially against being extinguished by the very modes of behavior that would constitute violations of the claim-right. He was of course safe in making such an assumption, but it should not be left implicit. What should be recognized explicitly is that any Hohfeldian claim-right properly designated as a "right" is accompanied by multiple immunities that secure its very existence and its continuity. To be sure, the immunities that accompany any particular claim-right might not be comprehensive in the protection which they bestow. Though some claim-rights are inextirpable—at least during the lifetime of anyone who holds them—other claim-rights can be terminated through a number of routes. Nonetheless, every claim-right appropriately classifiable as a "right" is accompanied by an array of immunities that keep it existent in countless circumstances of a person's life. Unless a claim-right is normatively protected in that manner, it itself does not furnish any meaningful deontic protection and is therefore only an ostensible claim-right.

3
In Defense of the Correlativity Axiom

As my second chapter has recounted, the two positions in each column of Hohfeld's analytical framework are biconditionally entailing. An instance of either position in any column cannot ever exist without an instance of the other position in that column. This relationship of correlativity within each of the four axes of Hohfeld's table is readily apparent when each of the eight deontic or modal positions in that table is expounded, but—as has been signaled in Chapter 2—the relationship of correlativity within the first axis of the Hohfeldian schema has repeatedly been oppugned. Many philosophers take for granted that not all duties are correlated with claim-rights, and some philosophers have marshaled arguments to try to support such an assumption in their reflections on Hohfeld's work. Even when the facile lines of reasoning which I rebutted in "Rights without Trimmings" are left aside, there are some more substantial lines of reasoning that have to be countered in the course of a vindication of the Hohfeldian analysis. Thus, the present chapter will complete my exposition and defense of that analysis by endeavoring to uphold the Correlativity Axiom: the thesis that every claim-right is correlated with at least one duty which partakes of the same content, and that every duty is correlated with at least one claim-right which partakes of the same content. In other words, this chapter will maintain that there are never any legal or moral duties uncorrelated with legal or moral claim-rights (and that there are never any legal or moral claim-rights uncorrelated with legal or moral duties).

Of course, as is evident from my formulation of the Correlativity Axiom and even more from my ruminations on disjunctive universal quantification in §2.5.5.1 of Chapter 2, the thesis defended in this chapter is not the same as Hohfeld's own understanding of the correlativity of claim-rights and duties. Indeed, as has been foreshadowed in §2.5.5.1, my espousal of the Correlativity Axiom in this chapter will depart in multiple respects from the insistence by Hohfeld on one-to-one correlations between claim-rights and duties and between holders of claim-rights and bearers of duties. For one thing, in opposition to Hohfeld, this chapter will argue that claim-rights can be held not only by individuals but also by collectivities. My stance on that matter, which will be further elaborated in Chapter 5, is crucial for a defense of the Correlativity Axiom—since the claim-rights correlated with certain duties are aptly ascribable only to collectivities and not to any individuals. An additional respect in which this chapter dissents from Hohfeld's pronouncements is its acceptance that a single claim-right can be correlated with more than one duty and that a single duty can be correlated with more than one

Rights and Right-Holding. Matthew H. Kramer, Oxford University Press. © Matthew H. Kramer 2024.
DOI: 10.1093/oso/9780198891222.003.0003

claim-right. Hohfeld's insistence on one-to-one correlations between claim-rights and duties is not tenable, and it is not necessary for the sustainability of his key insight into the relationality of duties and the relationality of claim-rights. Also untenable is his insistence on one-to-one correlations between holders of claim-rights and bearers of duties. As we have beheld in §2.5.5.1, and as will be contended afresh in this chapter, those one-to-one correlations between parties break down when a duty is owed to parties disjunctively rather than aggregatively or distributively or singly. Because one of the foremost challenges that must be repelled by a supporter of the Correlativity Axiom is focused on disjunctive universal quantification, any endeavor of salvaging the Correlativity Axiom has to dissociate that Hohfeldian tenet from some of the dubious dogmas which Hohfeld himself attached to it. Instead of taking the Correlativity Axiom to be a thesis about one-to-one correlations between claim-rights and duties and between holders of claim-rights and bearers of duties, this chapter construes it simply as the thesis that every claim-right is correlated with at least one duty which possesses the same content and that every duty is correlated with at least one claim-right which possesses the same content. In so doing, the chapter will be reaffirming Hohfeld's core insistence on the relationality or directionality of every claim-right and every duty.

Before this chapter moves on to grapple with the objections that have been posed against the Correlativity Axiom, it needs to lay some preliminary groundwork. Although the Interest Theory of right-holding is the main topic of Chapter 4, the present chapter has to introduce my principal formulation of that theory—because some of the argumentation in this chapter will be relying upon it. To be sure, the present chapter does not have to explore all the involutions of the Interest Theory that will be fully probed in Chapter 4. Only an outline of my chief version of the theory will be broached here, and for now that outline will indeed merely be broached rather than scrutinized and defended. The tasks of amplifying and elucidating and upholding the Interest Theory will be deferred to my fourth chapter. In addition to providing a sketch of the Interest Theory, this chapter will preface its vindication of the Correlativity Axiom by elaborating on the status of that axiom itself. Although the Correlativity Axiom is indeed axiomatic within the logic of Hohfeldian legal and moral positions, it is not a dogma propounded without any justification. My clarification of that point will really begin my defense of the Correlativity Axiom, for the clarification will on its own suffice to establish that every duty is correlated with at least one claim-right which possesses the same content.

3.1 A Glimpse of the Interest Theory of Right-Holding

As has been stated, several of the arguments in this chapter will ground their conclusions partly on the Interest Theory's criterion for identifying the holders of the claim-rights that are correlative to specified duties. Hence, without yet plumbing any of the complexities and subtleties that will be pondered in Chapter 4, I should here supply my principal formulation of the Interest Theory in order to make explicit a key premise that informs some of my reasoning in the subsequent sections of this chapter. By so doing, I shall be underscoring the interconnectedness of the two halves of this book. While the Interest Theory of right-holding is vital as a supplement to the Hohfeldian analysis of legal and moral positions, it is more than just a supplement. It is integral to my championing of that analysis in response to various difficulties that have been invoked by critics of Hohfeld.

> **Interest Theory of Right-Holding**: Individually necessary and jointly sufficient for the holding of a claim-right by *X* are (1) the fact that the duty correlative to the claim-right deontically and inherently protects some aspect of *X*'s situation that on balance is typically beneficial for a being like *X*, and (2) the fact that *X* is a member of the class of potential holders of claim-rights.

Chapters 4 and 5 will expatiate on many aspects of this formulation, but for the moment the sole phrase that requires some elucidation is "and inherently." What such phrasing indicates is that the content of a specified duty D cannot be realized—and therefore that D cannot be fulfilled—without affecting *X*'s situation in some way that is on balance typically beneficial for beings like *X*. In other words, the reference to the inherency of the deontic protection bestowed by D on some typically beneficial aspect of *X*'s situation is meant to differentiate between protective effects that are fortuitous or incidental and protective effects that are always occurrent through the realization of what D requires. Note that the protection, rather than the derivation of some benefit from the protection, is what is inherent to the satisfaction of the duty. As will be discussed at length in Chapter 4, the protection conferred by D on the situation of the holder of a correlative claim-right is typically beneficial for anyone like that holder but is not invariably so.

These extremely skimpy remarks on the Interest Theory are adequate for now. My aim in this short section of the chapter has simply been to furnish a quick preview of the Interest Theory that will suffice to set the stage for some of the argumentation that follows. When discussing the correlativity of claim-rights and duties, I will recurrently presuppose a certain understanding of the conditions that constitute the holding of a claim-right. My glance at the Interest Theory in this section reveals what that understanding is. Still, although a glance is all that is needed for my purpose in this section, it patently does not amount to a full exposition or a full justification. Indeed, it is only the first small step in such an exposition and such a justification. Hence, just as the current chapter has to be read in conjunction with Chapter 2—of which it is an offshoot—so too it has to be read in conjunction with Chapters 4 and 5, which thoroughly expound and defend the Interest Theory. That is, those subsequent chapters serve to explain and vindicate a theory that pivotally underlies much of the reasoning in this chapter, including the reasoning in my next section.

3.2 The Axiomaticity of the Correlativity Axiom

As has been stated, the Correlativity Axiom is not dogmatically stipulative. It occupies a fundamental place in the logic of Hohfeldian positions, but its correctness in the realm of law rests on jurisprudential considerations, and its correctness in the realm of morality rests on ethical considerations. When Visa Kurki declares that "the question whether all duties entail rights is certainly substantive rather than something that should be settled axiomatically" (2022a, 90), he is to some degree trading on a false dichotomy. On the one hand, he is correct in maintaining that the question which he broaches is something that has to be settled on the basis of jurisprudential considerations and ethical considerations. On the other hand, he conveys a misleading impression when he suggests that the Correlativity Axiom is somehow not axiomatic. Rather, precisely because the germane jurisprudential and ethical considerations establish that every legal or moral duty is correlated with at least one claim-right, a thesis affirming such correlativity can be taken as an axiom in a system of logic that formally encapsulates the fundamental relationships between claim-rights and duties (and also the fundamental relationships between other deontic positions and between normative positions). Let us mull over these matters first in regard to the realm of law and then in regard to the realm of morality.

3.2.1 Compliance with Legal Requirements

At a few junctures in Chapter 2, I have mentioned that every legal duty is owed by its bearer at least to the system of governance that has imposed it. Most legal duties are also owed to other parties, but every such duty is owed at least to the system of governance—or the specific governmental body—whence it emanates. Legal claim-rights which respectively correlate with those duties are correctly ascribable to that system of governance because the satisfaction of legal requirements is typically beneficial for any such system. A legal duty deontically and inherently protects something that is typically beneficial for the system of governance that has brought the duty into existence, in that such a duty makes mandatory the compliance of every addressee with a standard of conduct which that system has prescribed. Although the conformity of the addressees with a prescribed standard can on balance be detrimental to the interests of the system in anomalous cases, the conformity of addressees is typically on balance promotive of those interests—both because the channeling of behavior in accordance with the prescriptions issued by a system of governance is typically conducive to the realization of the objectives which the system pursues, and more broadly because such channeling of behavior serves to manifest and reinforce the authoritative role of the system in setting the limits and general patterns of the interaction among people within its jurisdiction. Hence, by reference to the Interest Theory of right-holding, we can conclude that a system of governance holds a claim-right correlative to each of the legal duties which it imposes on anyone.

3.2.1.1 Claim-Rights Held Only by a System of Governance

As has been suggested, some legal duties in any jurisdiction are such that the sole legal claim-rights which correlate with them are the claim-rights of the prevailing system of governance to compliance by each person with its mandates. Nigel Simmonds somewhat overstates this point when he asserts that under the Interest Theory "a very large number of [legal] rights will fall into the residual category of rights possessed [solely] by the state" (1998, 198), but there are certainly some legal claim-rights that fall into the category which he mentions—as I have recognized and indeed emphasized since my earliest writings on these matters. Let us briefly consider two of the main types of legal duties that are correlated only with legal claim-rights held by the system of governance that has imposed the duties.

First are so-called public duties (Kramer 1998, 58–60). Among the most commonly cited examples of these are the legal duty of everyone with income above a certain threshold to pay an annual income tax, and the legal duty of each person at a certain age to engage in military service or in some comparable public service. Legal duties that require people to pay income taxes are existent in most countries, and legal duties that require people to serve in the military are existent in quite a few countries. In any country where public duties of those kinds or of sundry other kinds exist, they are correlated only with claim-rights held by the system of governance that has established those duties. If any particular individual declines to pay the income tax which he or she owes, the effect on any other individual will be nil; in any sizeable society, the non-compliance of some individual with the income-tax obligation will not in itself increase the tax burdens of anyone else or impair the public services enjoyed by anyone else. Similarly, if an individual does not fulfill the legal duty of military service or public service which she owes under a program of conscription, no other individual will have been adversely affected. Accordingly, neither the duty incumbent on some person to pay income taxes nor the duty incumbent on some person to perform military service inherently protects any typically beneficial aspect of the situation of anybody else. By reference to the Interest Theory of right-holding, then, we should conclude that each of the legal duties just mentioned is not correlated with a legal claim-right held by any individual. Each such duty is instead correlated with a legal claim-right held by the presiding system of governance (and with a legal claim-right held by the members of the public collectively rather than by any member individually).

Alongside public duties in this subsection are legal duties that have been brought into existence for the benefit of imaginary or mythical entities. Suppose for instance that the system of governance in some country has placed every adult in its jurisdiction under a legal obligation to engage in a ritual of prayer and expressions of gratitude to the god Apollo at the start of each month. Were the god Apollo a member of the class of potential holders of claim-rights, the legal duty of each adult would correlate with a legal claim-right held by that deity. However, as has been emphasized in §2.5.6 of Chapter 2, purely imaginary or mythical beings do not belong to that class. Consequently, the legal duty requiring prayers and expressions of gratitude from each adult is correlated only with a legal claim-right to compliance that is held by the system of governance which has imposed the duty. There is no one else in the class of potential holders of claim-rights whose situation is inherently protected by that duty in some aspect which is typically beneficial.

3.2.1.2 Collectivities as Holders of Claim-Rights

At a few junctures in Chapter 2, I have mentioned that Hohfeld discountenanced the notion of collectively held claim-rights that are not reducible to individually held claim-rights. Having argued against his stance on that matter at some length in "Rights without Trimmings" (Kramer 1998, 49–60), I have to return to it here—for the whole of my current discussion manifestly presupposes that a collectivity such as a system of governance can hold claim-rights. Let us begin by glancing at Hohfeld's main comments on the topic.

Hohfeld stated his views on the reducibility of collectively held entitlements most extensively in one of his less renowned essays, dealing with the responsibility of stockholders for corporate debts. He began the relevant portion of his analysis quite unexceptionably by asserting that "it has not always been perceived with perfect clearness that transacting business under the forms, methods, and procedure pertaining to so-called corporations is simply another mode by which *individuals* or *natural persons* can enjoy their property and engage in business" (1923, 197, emphases in original). Much more dubiously, however, he wrote of the "necessity of emphasizing ... the realities of corporate forms, methods, and procedure and of looking beneath the fictional language tending to obscure those realities" (1923, 197 n. 9). In an equally questionable vein, he proclaimed that "[w]hen all is said and done, a corporation is just an association of natural persons conducting business under legal forms, methods, and procedure that are *sui generis*. The only conduct of which the state can take notice by its laws *must* spring from natural persons—it cannot be derived from any abstraction called the 'corporate entity'" (1923, 198, emphasis in original, footnote deleted). He then delivered himself of some starkly reductionist pronouncements, of which only two representative portions will be quoted here. Consider first the statement that "[w]hen, therefore, in accordance with the customary terminology, we speak of the corporation, as such, as contracting in the corporate name, as acquiring, holding, and transferring property, and as suing and being sued, and when we speak of stockholders as mere claimants against the corporation, holding stock, which is a species of personal property—and so on indefinitely—we are merely employing a short and convenient mode of describing the complex and peculiar process by which the benefits and burdens of the corporate members are worked out" (1923, 199–200). Equally heavy-handed is the following contention (1923, 199–200 n. 14):

> In reality when we say that the so-called legal or juristic person [such as a corporation] has rights or that it has contracted, we mean nothing more than what must ultimately be explained by describing the capacities, powers, rights, privileges (or liberties), disabilities, duties and liabilities, etc, of the natural persons concerned or of some of such persons. . . .
>
> Doesn't this roundabout process of explanation necessitated by calling the association a juristic person suggest the same objection that has been made concerning a certain other legal fiction? Is it not like looking at things through smoked glass and then holding a candle on the other side in order to see them? If this be so, it appears even more objectionable to speak of a corporation as an abstract entity or personality distinct from the sum of the stockholders. Is it not better, then, as a matter of words and definitions, to say with emphasis that, as applied to associations of natural persons considered as units, the terms, *right, duty, contract, etc*, should never be used except in a figurative sense—that is, as a sort of legal shorthand?

These lengthy extracts from the arguments by Hohfeld reveal his belief that statements about jural relationships involving any collective person can be reduced to statements about certain jural relationships involving some or all of the individuals who make up that collective person. According to Hohfeld, a statement of the former sort is at best an instance of figural shorthand; any relationship to which it seemingly refers is fictive. According to him, only the statements about relationships between individuals directly refer to anything that is real.

To be sure, we should not lose sight of the sophistication of his perspective on this matter. Hohfeld did not contend that a thesis about a corporation's claim-right with a certain content is perforce reducible to a thesis about a claim-right with that content held by some individual—or even to theses about multiple claim-rights which are each possessed of that content and which are held respectively by various individuals. He more subtly maintained instead that any thesis about a claim-right of a corporation is perforce reducible to a thesis about some set of entitlements held by some individuals (or perhaps occasionally to a thesis about only one entitlement held by one individual). He allowed, in other words, that reducibility does not perforce amount to straightforward homologousness. His aim was to insist upon the unreality of corporate entitlements while recognizing that the task of translating propositions about such entitlements into propositions about individual entitlements is an enterprise that differs from case to case.

Even when misguidedly dismissing the reality of collective entitlements, then, Hohfeld was not lacking in astuteness. All the same, he went badly astray by adopting a reductionist stance on the matter of claim-rights vested in collectivities, since he thereby conflated explicability with reducibility and fictitiousness. To come to grips with the weaknesses of his stance, we should start by attending clear-sightedly to the fact that the holding of a claim-right is a relational property. It consists in being deontically and inherently protected through the existence of a duty that is incumbent on some other party (or on oneself). Hohfeld believed that that relational property of being deontically protected is never non-reducibly ascribable to any collectivity—because he believed that no collectivity ever non-reducibly exists as such. Both his misconceived denial of irreducible ascriptions of claim-rights and his misconceived denial of irreducible collectivities stemmed from his failure to grasp that, in ascriptions of the claim-rights that are held by collectivities and in affirmations of the existence of those collectivities, the universal quantification that implicitly or explicitly operates is aggregative.

On the one hand, the domain over which the universal quantification ranges in any such ascription or affirmation is indeed composed of individuals who make up the relevant collectivity. Any explication of the nature of that collectivity has to make reference to those individuals. On the other hand, because the universal quantification over those individuals is aggregative, any ascription or affirmation containing the quantification makes reference to them not as individuals but instead as an overarching collectivity. Their status as an overarching collectivity is irreducible, even though all the actions and decisions of the collectivity take place through actions and decisions by the individuals who belong to it.

We should have in mind here two broad types of collectivities, both of which are covered by my ruminations in this subsection. First are collectivities which are durable and continuous in their existence and which have relatively elaborate formal rules and procedures in place for their reaching of collective decisions and their performing of collective actions. Such collective entities are frequently designated as "group agents" in the philosophical literature on the topic.[1] Any system of governance is a group agent in this sense, as is each of the institutions that are the components of such a system. Second are collectivities which are relatively ephemeral or episodic and which have few if any formal rules and procedures in place for their reaching of collective decisions and their performing of collective actions. A collectivity of this second kind consists of people acting concertedly, with some common aim(s) in view and with efforts to coordinate their actions through which they can realize the shared aim(s). Unlike a group agent, however, a collectivity of this second kind—which is sometimes designated in the philosophical literature as a "coalition" (Dowding 2011) or a "team" (Simpson 2017)—is transitory or

[1] See, for example, Pettit 2009; Pettit and List 2011; Tuomela 2013. Other closely similar labels are often applied to such collectivities in the philosophical literature.

sporadic and is relatively informal in its organization and functioning. An example of a coalition in this sense would be a group of friends who get together informally to play a game of baseball for an afternoon.

What is notable here is that a collectivity of either of these two types is irreducible in that it possesses certain properties that are correctly ascribable solely to the collectivity and not to any of the members of it individually. Although this point about irreducibility is especially evident in application to group agents, it is applicable also to coalitions. Suppose for example that seven friends act concertedly to push a stalled van up a hill. By shoving mightily with a shared aim and with efforts to coordinate their actions, they manage to get the van to the top of the hill. Any six of the friends would not have been able to accomplish such a feat; only when the seven of them combine their strengths, are they able to succeed in their endeavor. Hence, the ability to push the vehicle to the top of the hill is a property correctly ascribable to the seven friends as a coalition but not to any of them individually and not to any proper subset of them. Of course, that ability is fully explicable by reference to the separate abilities of the seven friends (including the ability of each of them to act concertedly with other people). Nonetheless, the ability to push the van to the top of the hill is possessed only by the friends as a coalition. In any statement which accurately ascribes that ability to the friends, the universal quantification that ranges over them is aggregative rather than distributive or disjunctive.

Now, as has been affirmed, the holding of a legal claim-right is the property of being deontically and inherently protected—in some aspect of one's situation that is typically beneficial—through the existence of a legal duty borne by some other party or by oneself. A defender of Hohfeld's reductionism has to maintain that such a property is unlike the property of being able to push the van to the top of the hill, in that it is never non-reducibly possessed by a collectivity such as a system of governance. Let us consider here afresh the legal claim-right that is correlative to the legal duty of each person to pay a specified amount of tax on his or her income above a certain level. As has been contended, such a claim-right is not held by any individual in the relevant jurisdiction. No typically beneficial aspect of the situation of any individual is deontically and inherently protected through the bearing of the income-tax obligation by any other individual. By contrast, the system of governance which has imposed that duty on each individual does hold a legal claim-right correlative thereto, since some typically beneficial aspects of the situation of such a system—most notably the smoothness or effectiveness of its functioning, and its authoritative role in setting forth standards of conduct for the people within its jurisdiction—are deontically and inherently protected through the existence of the duty. A defender of Hohfeld's reductionism will presumably seek to argue that the benefits typically accruing to a system of governance from the fulfillment of the income-tax obligation by each person who bears such an obligation are reducible to benefits typically accruing to discrete individuals (specifically, benefits typically accruing to the discrete legal-governmental officials who run the system). However, even if we leave aside the fact that any defense of Hohfeld along those lines would be going far afield of what he himself wrote, such a defense will fail.

To discern why any such line of defense for Hohfeld's reductionism will fail, we should take account of a quantifier that has not yet been broached in this book. That is, we should take account of what has sometimes been designated as the "pleonotetic" quantifier (Altham 1991; Geach 1980, 125)—the quantifier that corresponds to "most" in ordinary English. With that quantifier in mind, we should inquire whether a defender of Hohfeld's reductionism would be correct in submitting that the benefits typically accruing to a system of governance from the fulfillment of the income-tax duty by each person who bears that duty are reducible to benefits typically accruing to discrete legal-governmental officials. On the one hand, it may well be that all or most of the officials will each typically benefit derivatively from the benefits that typically accrue directly to their system of governance through the compliance of each individual with the income-tax obligation. On the other hand, whatever be the details of the benefits that will typically flow derivatively to the officials through such compliance, they are not equivalent to the benefits that typically flow directly to the system of governance as a group agent. We need to differentiate here between a direct interest in the effective functioning and authoritativeness of the system and a derivative interest of each official in some benefits that may typically ensue from the effective functioning and authoritativeness. Most or all of the officials might each have a derivative interest of that latter kind, but only as a collectivity do the officials have a direct interest in the effectiveness and vibrancy of their system. That direct interest of the officials *qua* collectivity is not reducible to a welter of derivative interests, both because no congeries of derivative interests can ever add up to a direct interest and because the direct interest can abide even while the derivative interests shift or partly disappear.

To be sure, if no officials or very few officials were benefiting at all from their participation in the running of their system of governance, their collective enterprise of operating that system would be better off discontinued than sustained. In such circumstances, where few if any of the officials would stand to benefit from the effectiveness and continuation of the system, the officials collectively as a group agent would not any longer have a direct interest in the continuation of the system. Contrariwise, when the continuation of a system of governance will produce effects that are typically beneficial for most or all of the officials who are its functionaries, they as a collectivity have a direct interest in the effectiveness and sustainment of the system. That interest can persist even if the derivative interests of the officials are recurrently shifting and for some officials are no longer existent. That direct interest will endure so long as most of the officials stand to gain more than they lose from the continued functioning of the system.

Because the quantifier "most" in the preceding sentence is distributively pleonotetic rather than distributively universal, it signals that the direct interest of a system of governance in its own effectiveness and continuation will have transcended the derivative interests of any particular official who contributes to the running of the system. Distributive pleonotetic quantification, in contrast with distributive universal quantification, does not lend itself to a reductionist analysis. A system of governance as a group agent has a direct interest in its own effectiveness and authoritativeness if most of its officials have derivative interests in the effectiveness and authoritativeness, regardless of which officials are among the majority who do have those derivative interests. Any majority among a disjunction of possible majorities will suffice. Consequently, *pace* any defenders of Hohfeld's reductionism, the benefits typically accruing directly to a system of governance through the compliance of citizens with their income-tax obligations are not reducible to any pattern of benefits enjoyed derivatively by the officials who operate the system. No typically beneficial aspect of the situation of any particular official is *inherently* protected through the existence of those obligations, and therefore no particular official is classifiable under the Interest Theory as a holder of claim-rights correlative to those obligations. Only the system of governance constituted by all the officials as a collectivity is the holder of those claim-rights. This conclusion will be reinforced in Chapter 4, when we explore how the Interest Theory of right-holding is applied.

Before this subsection closes, I should address a point that may have puzzled some readers. This subsection has devoted its attention to deontic protection bestowed on aspects of the situation of a system of governance and on aspects of the situations of the system's officials, but has not devoted any attention to deontic protection bestowed on aspects of the situations of the citizens who are governed by the system. Some readers might be baffled by that pattern of attention and inattention, since the effects of a system of governance on the citizenry over whom it presides are central to any moral assessment of the system. However, my focus currently lies on legal claim-rights rather than on moral claim-rights. As will be explained in Chapter 4, the goodness of complying with correct principles of morality is not an aspect of the situation of any party that will be taken into account when we are ascertaining whether the party holds a legal claim-right correlative to some specified legal duty. Hence, although the effects of a system of governance on citizens are obviously among the chief determinants of the morality of the system's workings, they are deliberately omitted from a discussion that is aimed not at morally appraising such a system but instead at mulling over the conditions that are constitutive of the system's holding of certain legal claim-rights. Chapter 4 will clarify and fully explain that deliberate omission.

3.2.1.3 A Counterexample?

In a recent essay, Kurki has tried to show that my thesis about every legal duty does not follow from the Interest Theory of right-holding (2022a, 89). He retorts that "we could think of an anarchist party winning the majority in a parliamentary election and thereby enacting legislation aimed towards dismantling the state. Would the ensuing duties be correlated by the state's right-to-be-dismantled?" Four rejoinders are appropriate here. First, any duties imposed by the envisioned legislation will have arisen through exercises of legal powers by the prevailing system of governance—where those powers enable the system to introduce authoritative standards of conduct into the society over which it presides. Because compliance with authoritative standards that have been set is typically beneficial on balance for a system of governance that has prescribed those standards, the duties imposed by the anarchist legislation confer inherent protection on an aspect of the situation of the prevailing system of governance that is typically beneficial on balance for such a system. Those duties are therefore correlated with claim-rights to compliance, held by the system.

Second, as is evident even from the small amount that has been said heretofore in this chapter about the Interest Theory of right-holding, the criterion articulated by that theory allows for circumstances in which a typically on-balance beneficial aspect of the situation of some party would in fact not be beneficial on balance for that party. In other words, there can be anomalous cases in which the fulfillment of some legal duties would on balance harm the parties to whom the duties are owed. Hence, if a legal mandate LM is such that the fulfillment of it would be detrimental on balance to the system of governance which has introduced it, LM nonetheless bestows upon that system some legal claim-rights to the conformity of citizens and officials with the requirements of LM—because the conformity of citizens and officials with legal mandates is typically beneficial on balance for a system of governance, even if conformity with LM is an exception to that usual pattern. Accordingly, notwithstanding that obedience to the state-dismantling legislation of the anarchists would perhaps be injurious on balance to the system of governance through which the legislation has been enacted, that system holds claim-rights to such obedience. It does so because compliance with the legislative enactments of such a system is typically conducive on balance to the effectiveness of the system's operations, and because typical conduciveness (rather than invariable conduciveness) is all that is needed under the terms of the Interest Theory of right-holding.

Third, in any event, the fulfillment of the state-dismantling duties that have been imposed by the anarchistic laws might not on balance be detrimental to the system of governance that has enacted the laws. Given the peculiar aims of the anarchists who have democratically gained control of the parliament and the executive branch in the scenario which Kurki propounds, their efforts to dismantle their system of governance through their legislation might be relevantly analogous to the efforts of a terminally ill and pain-racked person to commit suicide. Chapter 4 will submit that, although the interests taken into account by the Interest Theory of right-holding are objectively specified, they include one's interest in attaining the aims which one keenly pursues. A person afflicted irreversibly with a fatal malady and with excruciating pain will on balance have an interest in attaining the death for which he or she keenly yearns. Somewhat analogously, a system of governance that has come under the control of anarchists through democratic procedures can on balance have an interest in the realization of the state-dismantling objectives which the anarchists have pledged to seek. Although dying is not normally in a person's interest on balance, and although the undoing of a system of governance is not normally in the interest of such a system on balance, either of those outcomes could be beneficial on balance in exceptional circumstances.

Fourth, Kurki is not really in a position to invoke the example of the anarchists and their daft legislation. After all, he subscribes to H.L.A. Hart's argument about the minimum content of natural law (Kurki 2022a, 76), and a central theme of that argument—to which I have adverted a few times in Chapter 2—is that no credibly possible society larger than a handful of families can endure for more than the briefest period without a system of governance that will give effect to legal prohibitions on very serious modes of misconduct. From Kurki's own perspective, then, quite chimerical is a situation in which some anarchists take over a system of governance and eliminate without replacement the institutions of law-creation and law-application in a credibly possible (and sizeable) society that continues as a functionally cohesive community. This final point is more than an *ad hominem* retort, of course. Kurki is quite correct in maintaining that the prospect of a sizeable and cohesive society with no legal-governmental institutions is too outlandishly fanciful to be taken seriously in any theory of right-holding.

3.2.2 Conformity to Moral Requirements

We have hitherto pondered the jurisprudential considerations that can be combined with the Interest Theory of right-holding to vindicate the Correlativity Axiom in regard to legal duties and legal claim-rights. Let us now contemplate the ethical considerations that can be combined with the Interest Theory to vindicate the Correlativity Axiom in regard to moral duties and moral claim-rights. Of key importance here is that any operationalization of the Interest Theory has to draw upon some evaluative premises—that is, some premises concerning what is generally beneficial for any potential holders of claim-rights. We here need to ruminate on one such premise that will inform any satisfactory application of the Interest Theory to the holding of moral claim-rights.

As has been mentioned near the end of §3.2.1.2 above, the goodness of acting in conformity to the requirements of the correct principles of morality is not taken into account when we are ascertaining whether a specified *legal* duty inherently protects some aspect of a party's situation that is typically beneficial on balance. By contrast, the goodness of so acting is always taken into account when we pose a similar inquiry about any specified *moral* duty. Chapter 4 will explain why the requisite approach for legal duties on this point is so different from the requisite approach for moral duties. For the moment, we should simply note that the approach for moral duties serves to vindicate the Correlativity Axiom in application to such duties. After all, every moral duty is either an implication of the correct principles of morality or an implication of those principles plus certain empirical propositions. Hence, one's fulfillment of any moral duty amounts to one's acting in conformity with the requirements of the correct principles of morality. As an objective matter, one's acting in compliance with a moral duty is typically beneficial on balance in that it almost always improves the quality of one's life more than would non-compliance with such a duty. To be sure, there can sometimes occur an anomalous situation (most likely involving a moral conflict) in which the fulfillment of a moral duty to φ is not morally the best course of action; however, any such situation is truly exceptional rather than typical. Hence, whenever somebody is under a moral duty to φ, that duty is always owed to himself or herself. Nearly every such duty is also owed to at least one other party, but every such duty borne by any person P is owed to P. A moral duty inherently protects an aspect of its bearer's situation that is typically beneficial on balance for anybody like the bearer—namely, the aspect that consists in his or her conformity with the requirements of the correct principles of morality. Accordingly, everyone who bears any moral duty-to-φ is the holder of a moral claim-right correlative to that duty. Anybody who is morally obligated to φ has a moral claim-right to his or her φ-ing, held vis-à-vis himself or herself. Consequently, the Correlativity Axiom in application to moral duties is true. Every moral duty is correlated with at least one moral claim-right, since every such duty is correlated with a moral claim-right held by the bearer of the duty. And since nobody has ever doubted that the Correlativity Axiom is true with reference to moral claim-rights (in that every moral claim-right is correlated with at least one moral duty which possesses the same content), we can aptly conclude that the Correlativity Axiom is a proper foundation in a schema that distills the logic of first-order moral relationships. In the realm of morality, as in the realm of law—albeit for different reasons—the Correlativity Axiom is indeed solidly axiomatic.

Note again that the premise about the on-balance goodness of acting in conformity to the requirements of the correct principles of morality is applicable even in a context where somebody is confronted with a moral conflict. In such a context, let us recall, the person in question is under a moral duty to φ and is simultaneously under a moral duty not to φ (or is under a moral duty to do X and is simultaneously under a moral duty to do Y, where doing X is inconsistent with doing Y). In such a context, then, acting in conformity to the requirements of the correct principles of morality will always involve acting at variance with the requirements of the correct principles of morality. There is no way to avoid the perpetration of a moral wrong in such a situation. Still, because one's fulfillment of one's moral duty to φ is indeed a way of acting in compliance with a requirement of the correct principles of morality, one holds a moral claim-right correlative to that duty vis-à-vis oneself—even though one simultaneously owes a moral duty-not-to-φ that in turn is correlated with a moral claim-right held by oneself vis-à-vis oneself. One cannot avoid committing a moral wrong in such a predicament, but the wrong is committed against oneself as a holder of moral claim-rights that are respectively correlated with those moral duties. (Almost always, of course, any wrong in such a plight is likewise committed against at least one other party.)

3.3 Justificatory Priorities

This chapter can now proceed to rebut some of the lines of reasoning that have been marshaled against the Correlativity Axiom over the past several decades. As has already been mentioned, this chapter will forbear from engaging afresh with the especially feeble instances of griping about the Correlativity Axiom that have been painstakingly countered in my "Rights without Trimmings." I will instead concentrate here on some new objections, and on a few of the more substantial objections that have been parried in "Rights without Trimmings." Let us begin with one of the latter.

Quite commonly in political and moral philosophy, theorists focus either on the conferral of legal claim-rights or on the imposition of legal duties—rather than on both—when they are arguing in favor of certain legal prohibitions. Though a focus on the conferral of claim-rights can of course be combined with a focus on the imposition of duties, many philosophers in their efforts to justify various legal policies have opted for one focus or the other rather than for both. Some theorists might strive to justify the adoption of a certain law L because they perceive it as essential for the protection of the dignity or autonomy or vital interests of the people on whom legal claim-rights will be bestowed by L. For such theorists, the legal duties that correlate with the legal claim-rights conferred by L are significant and commendable only because they are integral to the existence of those claim-rights. These theorists do not ascribe any independent significance or salutariness to the legal duties that are imposed on people by L. In other words, the justificatory orientation of these theorists is centered on each individual *qua* someone whose dignity or autonomy or vital interests will be protected by L, rather than on each individual *qua* someone whose moral integrity will be upheld by L through the curtailment of his or her legal latitude to inflict harm on others.

Some different philosophers might maintain that the imposition of legal duties on people by L is of paramount significance for the justifiability of L. For these philosophers, the project of championing the adoption of L is properly focused on each individual *qua* someone whose legal leeway to hurt others will have been cabined, rather than on each individual *qua* someone whose dignity or autonomy or vital interests will have been safeguarded through the deontic constraints imposed on others by L. Theorists who adopt this approach to the task of justifying

L can invoke multiple considerations in support of their emphasis on the bearers of legal duties. For example, they might contend that the establishing of those duties serves to uphold the moral integrity or probity of the people on whom the duties are incumbent. Whatever may be the exact considerations that impel a philosopher to favor a duty-centered justification of L, an approach of that kind will advocate the adoption of L by invoking the salutariness of such an enactment for the people whom it will deontically constrain.

Let us briefly contemplate here, as an illustration, a debate over the introduction of a law that would prohibit the use of interrogational torture by any legal-governmental officials in their dealings with criminals and terrorists. A claim-right-centered approach will typically advert to the dignity of the potential victims of torture or to their vital interests in being free from excruciating pain and terror and humiliation. It will advert to the lasting damage, both physical and psychological, that afflicts most victims of torture. By contrast, a duty-centered approach will advert to the degradingness of the practice of torture for the individual officials who perpetrate it and for the system of governance in the service of which those officials are acting when they stoop to such a practice. A rationale for a prohibition on torture along those lines will proclaim that the officials tarnish their own moral integrity and the moral integrity of their system of governance when they resort to desperate and demeaning tactics in their efforts to thwart criminality and terrorism. This duty-centered perspective was nicely encapsulated a couple of decades ago by John McCain in the title of a journal article where he inveighed against the campaign of interrogational torture that had been undertaken by the American government during the Presidency of George W. Bush: "It's About Us" (McCain 2006).

Patently, the two approaches just recounted can be combined. They are not at all mutually exclusive. Still, although they are combinable, they are also disjoinable. Far from denying or contesting their disjoinability, I have sought to highlight it in several of my books as I have championed a predominantly duty-centered perspective on matters ranging from the death penalty to torture to artistic subventions to freedom of expression (Kramer 2011; 2014; 2017a; 2021). What will be oppugned here is neither the genuineness nor the importance of the distinction between claim-right-centered justifications and duty-centered justifications; rather, what will be oppugned is the notion that that genuine and important distinction is somehow problematic for the Correlativity Axiom.

Oddly enough, some philosophers have supposed that the foregoing distinction is indeed at odds with the Correlativity Axiom. Ronald Dworkin, for instance, appeared to presume as much in the following passage (1978, 171):

> [G]oals can be justified by other goals or by rights or duties, and rights or duties can be justified by goals. Rights and duties can also be justified, of course, by other, more fundamental duties or rights. Your duty to respect my privacy, for

> example, may be justified by my right to privacy. I do not mean merely that rights and duties may be correlated, as opposite sides of the same coin. That may be so when, for example, a right and the corresponding duty are justified as serving a more fundamental goal, as when your right to property and my corresponding duty not to trespass are together justified by the more fundamental goal of socially efficient land use. In many cases, however, corresponding rights and duties are not correlative, but one is derivative from the other, and it makes a difference which is derivative from which. There is a difference between the idea that you have a duty not to lie to me because I have a right not to be lied to, and the idea that I have a right that you not lie to me because you have a duty not to tell lies. In the first case I justify a duty by calling attention to a right; if I intend any further justification it is the right that I must justify, and I cannot do so by calling attention to the duty. In the second case it is the other way around.

To be sure, the language in this extract is somewhat ambiguous. Having not mentioned Hohfeld at all, Dworkin *might* have been referring only to justificatory correlativity (and derivativeness) rather than to analytical or existential correlativity (and derivativeness). That is, he *might* have been referring to levels of priority within a justificatory argument only—and not to levels of priority within an analytical exposition or within a legal system. If so, then Dworkin was not contending that the Correlativity Axiom somehow fails to apply to the legal positions commended by duty-centered or claim-right-centered theories. Nonetheless, the quoted remarks are highly misleading at best.

Much less ambiguous are some comments of a broadly similar tenor by Neil MacCormick, who sought to highlight "the possibility that rights are or could be *logically* prior to duties," and who jested that "Austin and Hohfeld might be scandalized" (1982, 161, emphasis added). MacCormick was inclined to affirm the possibility of the logical priority of claim-rights over duties because he wished to support his pronouncement that "it is *because* children have a right to care and nurture that parents have the duty to care for them" (1982, 162, emphasis in original). Such a pronouncement, however, is manifestly justificatory rather than analytical; hence, MacCormick must have believed that the existence of justificational priorities is somehow incompatible with the logical correlativity of claim-rights and duties.

Such a belief about justificational priorities and logical correlativity is even more explicitly and directly voiced by Jeremy Waldron, who declares that "the possibility that rights and duties may stand in generational or justificatory relationships to each other, *rather than relationships of logical equivalence*, provides an opening for the distinction between right-based and duty-based theories" (1988, 69–70, emphasis added). Waldron goes on to insist that "the justificatory role of rights means that they cannot be regarded as strictly correlative to duties, and therefore that statements about rights are not strictly equivalent to statements about duties. The last point is crucial if rights are to be seen as justifications: one statement cannot justify another if the two are equivalent" (1988, 84). Like MacCormick, Waldron supposes that the propounding of claim-right-centered or duty-centered rationales for legal prohibitions is in conflict with the universal sway of claim-right/duty correlativity. According to Waldron, one's ability to adopt a justificatory focus that prioritizes a claim-right over a duty—or a duty over a claim-right—is due to the absence of any mutual entailment between the prioritized element and the subordinated element. As he asserts (1984, 12, emphases in original): "[T]his distinction [between claim-right-centered and duty-centered justifications] is bound to seem mysterious if we simply postulate a *logical* relationship between rights and duties. If P's having a right is *defined* in terms of Q's having a duty, how can some theories be right-based while others are duty-based?"

Andrei Marmor pursues a similarly misguided line of thought when he is discussing Joseph Raz's interest theory of rights, which differs greatly from my Interest Theory of right-holding. Marmor opines as follows (1997, 3): "As opposed to the traditional Hohfeldian analysis which conceived of a right to be *correlative* to a duty, the [Razian] interest theory holds the right to be the *normative ground* for the imposition of duties. In other words, the relation between a right and its corresponding duty (or duties, as we shall see below) is not symmetrical; the relation is a justificatory one. Rights justify the imposition of duties but not vice versa" (1997, 3, emphases in original). There are some weaknesses in this passage from Marmor that will be exposed in my next chapter. At present, the weakness to which we should attend is his assumption that justificatory priorities are somehow inconsistent with the biconditional entailment of claim-rights and duties.

Dworkin and MacCormick and Waldron and Marmor have each gone astray when trying to come to grips with this matter, for a justificational focus on the conferral of legal claim-rights or on the imposition of legal duties is entirely consistent with the Correlativity Axiom. Suppose that the dominant or exclusive consideration which impels some theorist T to support a legal prohibition on the use of interrogational torture by legal-governmental officials is a concern to spare the potential victims from the agony and dread and humiliation which the subjection of anyone to torture inflicts. T does not attach great significance to the ways in which the imposition of legal duties on the potential perpetrators of torture will serve to uphold their moral probity, and she therefore does not highlight those ways in her efforts to justify the legal prohibition. All the same, T can and should recognize that the conferral of the claim-rights on the potential victims is inseparable from the imposition of the duties on the potential perpetrators. Unless the duties are established, the claim-rights are not bestowed; the imposing of a legal duty on P not to subject Q to torture and the vesting of Q with a legal claim-right not to be subjected to torture by P are the mutually constituting sides of a single jural relationship.

If Julia keenly desires a slope in her yard so that she can enjoy the downward perspective from the top, she can and should recognize that the slope stretches upward as well as downward. Perhaps she does not attach much if any importance to the upward perspective from the bottom of the slope (maybe because the terrain there is less agreeable than at the top), in which event her decision to have a slope created in the yard of her house will not have been prompted by any keen desire for the availability of that upward perspective. Nevertheless, although her justification for introducing a slope into the yard is focused solely on the gratifyingness of the top-down perspective, she would be irrational if she were to think that the top-down inclination of the slope is logically or existentially prior to its bottom-up inclination. Strict simultaneity, as opposed to anteriority and posteriority, is what marks the logical and temporal relationship between the downwardness and the upwardness of the slope. That relationship of simultaneity between the upwardness and the downwardness is scarcely undone by a justificatory concentration on one or the other of those two thoroughly simultaneous aspects. The existence of the top-down inclination entails the existence of the bottom-up inclination, and the existence of the bottom-up inclination entails the existence of the top-down inclination.

When a philosopher adopts a claim-right-centered approach to the justification of a legal prohibition on some type of misconduct, she devotes her attention preponderantly if not exclusively to the dignity or interests of the potential victims of the misconduct, and she devotes little if any attention to the moral integrity of the people who might stoop to engage in that misconduct if it is not legally prohibited. Conversely, when a philosopher adopts a duty-centered approach to the justification of a legal prohibition on some type of misconduct, she trains her attention chiefly if not solely on the moral probity of the potential perpetrators of the misconduct, and she trains little if any attention on the dignity or interests of the potential victims thereof. A claim-right-centered justification concentrates on people as beneficiaries of deontic protection, whereas a duty-centered justification concentrates on people as responsible agents whose probity can be preserved through their heeding of vital limits on their doings. However, to focus in one direction or the other for justificatory purposes is hardly to commit oneself to the notion that a claim-right can be conferred without the simultaneous imposition of a duty or that a duty can be imposed without the simultaneous conferral of a claim-right. Just as Julia who relishes the downward inclination of a slope in her yard should recognize that the yard must also contain the slope's upward inclination (by dint of containing its downward inclination), so a person who advocates the imposition of certain legal duties should recognize that he is thereby calling implicitly or explicitly for the creation of certain legal claim-rights—and a person who advocates the creation of certain legal claim-rights should recognize that she is thereby calling implicitly or explicitly for the imposition of certain legal duties.

In short, the Correlativity Axiom is straightforwardly consistent with a justificatory orientation that attaches prime importance either to the bestowal of claim-rights or to the imposition of duties. The Correlativity Axiom affirms a *logical* and *existential* nexus of mutual entailment between claim-rights and duties, in distinction from a nexus of *justificatory* parity. Indeed, one's attentiveness to the Correlativity Axiom helps to improve the wisdom of one's decision-making about the conferral of legal claim-rights and the imposition of legal duties, since it reveals the full deontic implications of those legal positions. Consider, for example, a setting in which some legislators have to decide whether to enact a law that will endow each person with a legal claim-right not to be made miserable by anyone else. If the legislators are insufficiently attuned to the fact that such a claim-right will be correlated with a legal duty incumbent on each person to refrain from making anybody else miserable, they may be prone to overestimate the attractiveness of a law that would confer the claim-right. After all, the benefits accruing to each person *qua* entitlement-holder through the possession of such a claim-right would not be inconsiderable. Yet, if the legislators are enticed by a justificatory argument that highlights the status of each person as the holder of a legal claim-right which would protect him or her against being made miserable, they will almost certainly cease to be so enticed when they take account of the oppressive legal duty that would have to be borne by each person as a result of the bestowal of such a claim-right on everyone else.

Were such a legal claim-right and its correlative legal duty to be brought into existence, then Mary who is deeply beloved by John would be under a legal duty to accede to his overtures even if she feels no love for him at all. (Of course, if the overtures by John render Mary profoundly despondent, then he would be under a legal duty to forbear from them—quite as much as she would be under a legal duty to yield to them, in order to avoid making *him* despondent.) A world in which Mary would have to give herself to the unloved John, and in which countless equally bizarre requirements would arise, is hardly a world that should win the favor of any sensible legislators. Ergo, the vesting of each person with a legal claim-right against being made miserable by others is not something that should win the favor of any sensible legislators. However appealing such a claim-right may seem when the legislators concentrate only on the status of each person *qua* holder of that claim-right, it shows itself to be dreadful when the legislators realize what it logically entails as they reflect upon the status of each person *qua* bearer of a duty that is a correlate of the claim-right held by everybody else. Thus, here and elsewhere, one's attentiveness to the Correlativity Axiom—with its affirmation of the biconditional entailment between claim-rights and duties—can enhance the sophistication of one's claim-right-centered or duty-centered approach to the justification of legal prohibitions.

3.4 Misrepresentations of the Correlativity Axiom

Having stumbled badly by presuming that the correlativity of claim-rights and duties would exclude the possibility of claim-right-centered or duty-centered justifications of legal prohibitions, MacCormick erred further by misrepresenting the nature of correlativity itself. He declared that "[t]o rest an account of claim rights *solely* on the notion that they exist whenever a legal duty is imposed by a law intended to benefit assignable individuals ... is to treat rights as being simply the 'reflex' of logically prior duties. Accordingly, for any statement about rights there could always be substituted a statement about duties which would be at a more fundamental level analytically" (1977, 199, emphasis in original). He continued: "It is however no part of my intention here to advance a theory according to which even 'claim rights' are conceived as being merely the reflex of duties, as though the latter must always be understood as being in every way prior to rights" (1977, 200, footnote omitted). Waldron once again echoes a fallacy propagated by MacCormick, as he submits that Hohfeld analyzed "rights-statements of all sorts in terms of what he appears to regard as the more primitive notion of a duty" (1988, 68). Waldron offers no textual support for this reading of Hohfeld, and indeed there is none. In Hohfeld's writings, correlativity or biconditional entailment is indeed correlativity or biconditional entailment. It is not the priority of one correlative element over the other. Just as a slope's downward direction is not logically or existentially prior to its upward direction, a duty is not logically or existentially prior to the claim-right with which it is correlated. The existence of a claim-right is a necessary and sufficient condition for the existence of its correlative duty, and the existence of a duty is a necessary and sufficient condition for the existence of its correlative claim-right. (Especially curious here is Waldron's phrase "rights-statements of all sorts." If Waldron is suggesting that Hohfeld analyzed ascriptions of powers and immunities by reference to duties, then his assertion is even wider of the mark than I have taken it to be.)

In the background of MacCormick's and Waldron's misrepresentations of correlativity is Hart's well-known insistence that "if to say that an individual has ... a right means no more than that he is the intended beneficiary of a duty, then 'a right' in this sense may be an unnecessary, and perhaps confusing, term in the description of the law; since all that can be said in a terminology of such rights can be and indeed is best said in the indispensable terminology of duty" (Hart 1982, 181–2). What is most objectionable about Hart's comment is its one-sidedness. To be sure, given the correlativity of claim-rights and duties, Hart was correct in saying that every legal relationship accurately describable as the holding of a claim-right by *Q* vis-à-vis *R* can be accurately redescribed as the bearing of a duty by *R* vis-à-vis *Q*. However, a corresponding point applies to every legal relationship accurately describable as the bearing of a duty by *R* vis-à-vis *Q*, which can always be accurately redescribed as the holding of a claim-right by *Q* vis-à-vis *R*. When we probe *Q*'s claim-right vis-à-vis *R* not to be assaulted by *R*, we can indeed recharacterize the legal relationship between those parties as *R*'s duty vis-à-vis *Q* to forbear from assaulting *Q*; but, when we probe *R*'s duty vis-à-vis *Q* to forbear from assaulting *Q*, we again can equally well recharacterize the legal relationship between those parties as *Q*'s claim-right vis-à-vis *R* not to be assaulted by *R*.[2]

3.5 Eleemosynary Duties

In §2.5.5.1 of Chapter 2, where I elucidate the nature of disjunctive universal quantification, my main example is that of a law which imposes a duty of charity on every person in the relevant jurisdiction with an income above a specified level. Under that law, each such person is legally obligated to donate a certain portion of her income to any one or more of the organizations that are included on the list of registered charities. What can be added here is that each such person is in any event under a moral obligation to make a donation of that kind annually. Like the legal duty incumbent on each such person, the moral duty incumbent on her involves disjunctive universal quantification over a domain comprising the organizations that appear on the list of registered charities.

Now, as I have remarked elsewhere,[3] one of the most common objections to the Correlativity Axiom is that it is supposedly incompatible with the existence of any eleemosynary duties of the sort which I have described in the preceding paragraph and in §2.5.5.1. Here the importance of the distinction between my own version of the Correlativity Axiom and Hohfeld's version—a distinction which I have underscored in §2.5.5.1—becomes manifest. As I have argued in Chapter 2, one key reason for rejecting Hohfeld's understanding of the Correlativity Axiom is precisely that his insistence on one-to-one correlations between individual holders of claim-rights and individual bearers of correlative duties is inconsistent with any satisfactory analysis of eleemosynary duties. In other words, his version of the Correlativity Axiom is indeed vulnerable to the objection which I have just mentioned. However, the proper response lies not in abandoning the Correlativity Axiom but instead in embracing a version of it that is shorn of Hohfeld's dogmas about one-to-one correlations between claim-rights and duties and between holders of claim-rights and bearers of duties.

When those dogmas are eschewed, the Correlativity Axiom turns out to be the thesis that every claim-right is correlated with at least one duty which possesses the

[2] I have made this point in Kramer 1998, 26–7 and more tersely in Kramer 1991, 286–7 n. 15.

[3] Kramer 1998, 25 n. 11. For some of the many objections to the Correlativity Axiom that are focused on eleemosynary duties, see Biasetti 2014, 1045; Cruft 2019, 11–12; Edmundson 2012, 80–1; Erk 2017, 154; Feinberg 1970, 244; Jones 1994, 207–8; Kurki 2018, 447 n. 59; Mayo 1965, 226; Nascimento 2018, 153; Thompson 2018, 15; Valentini 2021, 46; Van Duffel 2012, 107; Waldron 1993, 14–16.

same content and that every duty is correlated with at least one claim-right which possesses the same content. Such a thesis, unlike Hohfeld's understanding of correlativity, is not vulnerable to the worry about eleemosynary duties. On the contrary, that thesis is supported rather than belied by the analysis of those duties which I have propounded in §2.5.5.1. As has been maintained there, each person who bears the eleemosynary duty in the relevant jurisdiction owes that duty to the registered charities disjunctively. A claim-right correlative to that duty is therefore held by the registered charities disjunctively. Hence, an eleemosynary duty is like any other duty in that it is indeed correlated with at least one claim-right which possesses the same content.

In fact, as has already been contended in §3.2 above, any eleemosynary duty—whether legal or moral—is correlated with more than one claim-right. Each such duty imposed by a law is correlated not only with a legal claim-right held by the charities disjunctively but also with a legal claim-right held by the prevailing system of governance. As has been argued in §3.2.1, any such system holds a legal claim-right to compliance with each of the legal duties that it has established. If those legal duties include eleemosynary obligations borne by people with incomes above a specified level, then the prevailing system of governance holds a legal claim-right to the fulfillment of each such obligation. Any legal claim-right of that kind is held by the system vis-à-vis each person who bears the legal eleemosynary obligation with which the claim-right is correlated, of course.

As has been argued in §3.2.2, every moral duty is owed by its bearer to himself or herself. In that respect, an eleemosynary moral duty is like any other moral duty. Thus, the bearer of an eleemosynary moral duty owes that duty not only to the registered charities disjunctively but also to himself or herself. Very far from the truth, then, is the notion that such a duty is undirected. Like a legal eleemosynary duty, a moral eleemosynary duty is always multiply directed.

We should note here anew, in keeping with what has been said in §3.2, that the Interest Theory of right-holding undergirds my ascriptions of claim-rights in this subsection. Although a bearer of an eleemosynary duty (whether legal or moral) can fulfill it without affecting the situation of this or that particular charity in any way that is normally beneficial on balance for such an organization, a bearer of an eleemosynary duty who fulfills it will *ipso facto* have affected the situation of the charities disjunctively in a way that is normally beneficial on balance for such organizations. Hence, a claim-right correlative to each such duty is held by the charities disjunctively rather than by this or that particular charity discretely. If the duty in question is a legal duty, then a bearer of the duty who fulfills it has also *ipso facto* affected the situation of the prevailing system of governance in a way that is typically beneficial on balance for such a system. Accordingly, a legal claim-right correlative to that legal duty is also held by the prevailing system of governance. If an eleemosynary duty is a moral obligation, then a bearer of the obligation who fulfills it has *ipso facto* affected his or her own situation in a way that is typically beneficial on balance for a human being. Consequently, a moral claim-right correlative to that moral obligation is held by the bearer of that obligation. (As has already been remarked in this chapter, the evaluative judgments that are stated summarily at this juncture will be expounded fully in Chapter 4 when I discuss the general evaluative assumptions that inform any application of the Interest Theory. As will be explained there, the evaluative assumptions that are associated with the Interest Theory in application to legal claim-rights are not exactly the same as those that are associated with the Interest Theory in application to moral claim-rights.)

In short, contrary to what the opponents of the Correlativity Axiom have frequently proclaimed, duties of charity like the ones envisaged here are not undirected duties. Those opponents have in fact aligned themselves too closely with Hohfeld when they impugn the Correlativity Axiom. First, like him, they appear to presume that a duty is undirected if it is owed to certain parties disjunctively rather than to one particular party. Such a premise is baseless, for any eleemosynary duty of the sort which we have pondered here is correlated with a claim-right held by the registered charities disjunctively. The Interest Theory of right-holding furnishes a criterion whereby we can readily ascertain that each of the eleemosynary duties—far from being undirected—is directed to the charities disjunctively.

Second, the opponents of the Correlativity Axiom have also joined Hohfeld in overlooking the fact that every eleemosynary legal duty is owed to the system of governance that imposes it (as well as to the charities disjunctively). To be sure, Hohfeld's own neglect of that point was at least partly due to his methodological individualism—that is, to his reductionist insistence that every entitlement seemingly ascribable to a collectivity is in fact an array of entitlements held by some individual(s)—which I have sought to confute in §3.2.1.2 above. Opponents of the Correlativity Axiom might or might not endorse Hohfeld's reductionism, but in any event they have been as remiss as Hohfeld himself in neglecting the fact that a legal claim-right to compliance with any eleemosynary legal duty is held by the system of governance responsible for the existence and enforcement of that duty. Those opponents have likewise been remiss in failing to observe that every eleemosynary moral duty is owed by its bearer to himself or herself as well as to the registered charities disjunctively. Indeed, on that point, the critics of the Correlativity Axiom are more neglectful than Hohfeld. He, after all, was not attempting to explicate the nature of moral entitlements; he focused solely on legal entitlements. By contrast, the philosophers who advert to eleemosynary obligations in their contestation of the Correlativity Axiom are focusing primarily on moral entitlements. They are especially at fault, then, for having disregarded the status of every bearer of a moral duty as a holder of a moral claim-right correlative to that duty. Such a status follows from the Interest Theory of right-holding in combination with a premise about the goodness of acting in conformity to the requirements of morality. When we are attuned to that point, we can recognize that every eleemosynary obligation—whether legal or moral—is multiply directed rather than undirected.

3.6 More Mistakes by MacCormick

In his efforts to impugn the Correlativity Axiom, MacCormick referred to a Scottish statute that included the following provision for any situation in which a parent dies without leaving a will: "Where an intestate is survived by children, they shall have right to the whole of the intestate estate" (MacCormick 1982, 200). MacCormick contended that this statutory provision would bestow a legal claim-right on each child of an intestate parent even before any correlative legal duty has come to be borne by an executor of the decedent's estate. At the moment of the intestate's death—so MacCormick believed—each child gains a claim-right to an equal share of the intestate's assets, even though there is not yet at that moment an executor to bear a correlative duty. MacCormick thus presumed that the statute would generate counter-examples to the Correlativity Axiom, since any applications of the statute would give rise to claim-rights that pre-exist any ostensibly correlative duties. As he wrote: "Vesting of the right is temporally prior to the vesting in any other individual of the correlative duty, which can occur only when an executor has in due course been judicially confirmed or appointed" (1982, 200).

MacCormick erred in thinking that the entitlements ensuing from the implementation of the Scottish statute would be at variance with the Correlativity Axiom. Under that statute, each child of an intestate parent acquires certain claim-rights at two separate stages. At the moment of the intestate's death, each child gains a claim-right—held vis-à-vis everyone else—against conduct that would obstruct the prescribed distribution of the estate of the decedent. Subsequently, at the moment when an executor is appointed by a court, each child also acquires a claim-right vis-à-vis the executor to the proper performance of the executorial responsibilities. Other entitlements are doubtless involved as well, but my highlighting of these two claim-rights or sets of claim-rights is sufficient to show that the Correlativity Axiom is scarcely belied by the Scottish law which regulates the disposition of intestates' assets. At each relevant stage (the moment of the intestate's death, and the moment at which an executor is appointed), every child of an intestate parent holds claim-rights that are strictly coeval with the pertinent duties borne by others. Only by mischaracterizing the claim-right that exists from the moment of the death, could MacCormick maintain that a claim-right held vis-à-vis the executor mysteriously antecedes its correlative duty.

MacCormick also emphasized that, under the Scottish law, a child of an intestate was entitled to be preferred over other parties when a court would appoint an executor for the estate. MacCormick declared: "In this case, therefore, it is not only the case that the vesting of a given right is temporally prior to the vesting of the correlative duty, but it is also the case that the vesting of the right in a given individual is a ground for confirming him in that office to which is attached the duty correlative to the like rights of his brothers and sisters; so that in this context right is logically prior to duty as well" (1982, 201). MacCormick's remarks here are dismayingly unclear and confused, but the situation recounted in them is analyzable fully in accordance with the Correlativity Axiom. Apparently, for one of the children of an intestate parent—presumably the eldest child[4]—the claim-right that vests in each of the children at the moment of the death of the intestate person (a claim-right against conduct that would obstruct the prescribed distribution of the estate) is accompanied by a claim-right to be appointed as the executor of the estate in preference to anyone else. That latter claim-right is held vis-à-vis the court that handles the responsibility of appointing an executor. Correlative to such a claim-right is the duty of the court to make the appointment accordingly. Neither that claim-right nor that duty is prior to the other, either logically or temporally; each of them exists only when the other exists, for each of them exists by dint of the other's existence. Both that claim-right held by the eldest child and that duty borne by the court come into existence at the moment of the death of the intestate. Having been duly appointed as the executor, the eldest child thereby comes under legal duties owed to his or her siblings. Each of those siblings is of course the holder of a legal claim-right that correlates with one of the legal duties owed by the eldest child to the siblings. Like the legal claim-right of the eldest child held vis-à-vis the court in regard to his or her being appointed as the executor, the legal claim-right of each sibling held vis-à-vis the eldest child as the executor in regard to the proper distribution of the estate is strictly coeval with the legal duty that is its correlate. Naturally, the legal claim-rights of the siblings held vis-à-vis the eldest child as the executor are posterior to the legal claim-right of the eldest child held vis-à-vis the court. Whereas that claim-right of the eldest child comes into existence at the moment of the death of the intestate, the claim-right of each sibling vis-à-vis the eldest child comes into existence at the moment of the appointment of the eldest child as the executor. MacCormick appeared to think that the temporal priority of the former claim-right over the latter claim-right (or over the duty that is correlative to the latter claim-right) is somehow problematic for the Correlativity Axiom. If he did think as much, however, he bafflingly misunderstood the Correlativity Axiom. Obviously, executorial duties owed by the eldest scion to the siblings upon being appointed as the executor are both temporally and logically posterior to the eldest scion's claim-right vis-à-vis the court to be appointed as the executor, but—equally obviously—none of those executorial duties would ever be perceived by a Hohfeldian theorist as correlated with the claim-right to be appointed. The content of each of the executorial duties is different from the content of the claim-right to be appointed as the executor, and the parties between whom each of those duties

[4] Perhaps MacCormick was suggesting that a claim-right to be appointed as the executor would be ascribable to the children disjunctively rather than only to the eldest of the children. Drawing upon what I have already said in this book about disjunctive universal quantification, I could straightforwardly come to grips with a situation involving a claim-right that is so ascribable. However, for the sake of enhancing the readability of my prose, I will continue to assume that the eldest child is the party whom the intestate's death endows with a claim-right to be appointed as the executor.

obtains are not invertedly the same as the parties between whom the claim-right to be appointed obtains. Given that the Correlativity Axiom is a thesis about any claim-right and duty which possess the same content and which obtain between the same parties invertedly, and given that it is not about any claim-right and duty which possess different contents or which do not obtain between the same parties invertedly, it patently does not carry any implications that are at odds with the legal relationships in the situation which MacCormick envisions. It patently does not imply that the duty of the court to appoint the eldest scion as the executor is correlated with the claim-right of each sibling to the eldest scion's fulfillment of his or her executorial responsibilities. We can therefore conclude that MacCormick, with his highlighting of the non-simultaneity of the duty borne by the court and the claim-right held by each sibling, did not go any way at all toward successfully impugning the Correlativity Axiom.

3.7 Generality versus Concreteness

Some philosophers, including Raz and MacCormick, have assailed the Correlativity Axiom on the ground of its supposed inconsistency with the distinction between general or abstract entitlements and specific or concrete entitlements. A general claim-right comprises an indefinite number of concrete claim-rights that are instantiations or ramifications of it. One's claim-right not to be robbed of one's belongings, for example, encompasses any number of claim-rights not to be robbed of one's belongings in specific ways. Of course, generality or abstraction is a scalar property, as is specificity or concreteness; each such property obtains to varying degrees. Hence, some claim-right CR1 can be general in comparison with some other claim-right CR2 but concrete in comparison with yet another claim-right CR3. For instance, whereas one's claim-right not to be robbed of one's belongings is general in comparison with one's claim-right not to be robbed of one's laptop computer, it is concrete in comparison with one's claim-right not to be deprived maliciously of one's bodily security or belongings.

A salient aspect of the relationship between general legal claim-rights and specific legal claim-rights is that the existence of a general legal claim-right can frequently result in the establishment of new specific legal claim-rights as circumstances evolve. Consider the following excerpt from some reflections by Raz (1984, 199–200):

> The existence of a right often leads to holding another to have a duty because of the existence of certain facts peculiar to the parties or general to the society in which they live. A change of circumstances may lead to the creation of new duties based on the old right. The right to political participation is not new, but only

> in modern states with their enormously complex bureaucracies does this right justify, as I think it does, a duty on the government to make public its plans and proposals before a decision on them is reached ... This dynamic aspect of rights, their ability to create new duties, is fundamental to any understanding of their nature and function in practical thought.

Although Raz's description here of the "dynamic aspect" of legal claim-rights is not entirely felicitous, that aspect itself is something to which any satisfactory account of such claim-rights has to be alert. If we are to believe Raz, however, the Correlativity Axiom obscures that dynamic aspect of general legal claim-rights: "Unfortunately, most if not all formulations of the correlativity thesis disregard the dynamic aspects of rights. They all assume that a right can be exhaustively stated by stating those duties which it has already established" (1984, 200). Raz did not offer any citations or arguments in support of this assertion, and it in fact is unsupportable.

To see that Raz went astray on this matter, we need to keep in view the distinction between abstract legal claim-rights and concrete legal claim-rights. The Correlativity Axiom affirms a relationship of biconditional entailment between any claim-right and any duty which obtain between the same parties invertedly and which possess the same content *and which therefore possess the same degree of specificity or abstraction*. It does not affirm a relationship of biconditional entailment between any claim-right and any duty with differing contents, and indeed it rules out such a relationship—because it maintains that any claim-right has the same content and thus the same degree of specificity as the duty with which the claim-right is correlated. Accordingly, for example, the general legal claim-right of Agatha vis-à-vis Cornelius not to be subjected to malicious invasions of her privacy by him is correlated with the general legal duty owed to Agatha by Cornelius to abstain from malicious invasions of her privacy. It is not correlated with any of the more concrete legal duties that might come to be imposed on Cornelius by dint of his bearing that general legal duty. Agatha's general claim-right is not in a relationship of biconditional entailment with any of those more concrete duties. Her general legal claim-right can serve as a key part of the justificatory basis for the establishing of those more concrete legal duties borne by Cornelius, each of which is then correlated with a concrete legal claim-right held by Agatha. Whenever technological innovations or other changes of circumstances warrant the introduction of new laws for the purpose of upholding each person's general legal claim-right not to be subjected to malicious invasions of his or her privacy, the enactment of those laws will confer some relatively concrete legal claim-rights on Agatha (as well as on everyone else, including Cornelius) and will impose some relatively concrete legal duties on Cornelius (as well as on everyone else, including Agatha). Those concrete legal claim-rights held by Agatha vis-à-vis Cornelius are correlated with those concrete legal duties owed by him to her. In other words, this situation in which a general legal claim-right justificatorily underlies the creation of sundry concrete legal claim-rights is entirely in accordance with the Correlativity Axiom. The general legal claim-right held by Agatha vis-à-vis Cornelius is correlated with the general legal duty owed by him to her, and each of her more specific legal claim-rights held vis-à-vis him on the basis of that general claim-right is correlated with each of his more specific legal duties owed to her on the basis of his general duty.

Raz went amiss, then, when he frowned upon the Correlativity Axiom for "misleadingly suggest[ing] that to every right there corresponds one duty.... Many rights ... may ground many duties not one. A right to personal security does not require others to protect a person from all accidents or injury. The right is, however, the foundation of several duties, such as the duty not to assault, rape or imprison the right-holder" (1984, 199). Indeed, Raz committed two main missteps in this passage. First, and less important in the present context, the Correlativity Axiom does not affirm that every claim-right is correlated with one duty or that every duty is correlated with one claim-right. Rather, it affirms that every claim-right is correlated with *at least one* duty which possesses the same content and that every duty is correlated with *at least one* claim-right which possesses the same content. Second, and more important in this context, a defender of the Correlativity Axiom should readily agree that a general legal claim-right can serve to "ground many [specific legal] duties" and can be a key element of "the foundation of several [specific legal] duties." After all, the grounding relationship between the abstract legal claim-right and the concrete legal duties is not a *correlation* between them. The abstract legal claim-right correlates only with an abstract legal duty, while each concrete legal duty correlates only with a matchingly concrete legal claim-right—a concrete claim-right that has been justificatorily generated with reference to the abstract claim-right. At least as construed by Hohfeldians, correlativity is a logical tie of biconditional entailment rather than a generality/specificity relationship. (That latter relationship is sometimes logical but is frequently instead purely justificatory, and in any event it does not involve *biconditional* entailment.)

One's embrace of the Correlativity Axiom, then, does not at all impede one from taking account of the "dynamic aspect" of general legal claim-rights. Once the role of such claim-rights in justifying the creation of new legal claim-rights is differentiated from the logical relationship of correlativity between a claim-right and a duty with the same content, we can see that neither excludes the other. An abstract legal claim-right is correlated with an abstract legal duty, and it can comprise or justificatorily undergird an array of concrete legal claim-rights. Each of those concrete legal claim-rights will, of course, be correlated with a concrete legal duty. This point has been adequately acknowledged by Waldron, who on the whole is very sympathetic to Raz: "[T]he 'dynamic aspect' could equally be captured by making the [abstract] right correlative to a rather abstract duty and saying that changing circumstances etc might lead to the derivation of different concrete duties from that" (Waldron 1988, 85). When the distinction between general legal claim-rights and specific legal claim-rights is properly explicated, we can retain the rigor of the Hohfeldian analysis and of the Correlativity Axiom while also grasping how a general legal claim-right can figure vitally in the justificatory basis for the creation of further legal claim-rights with more concrete contents.

3.8 Claim-Rights versus Interests

My reflections on the abstract/concrete distinction and on the "dynamic aspect" of legal claim-rights have contended that an abstract legal claim-right can comprise multiple legal claim-rights at greater levels of specificity (and the concrete legal duties that are respectively correlated with those concrete legal claim-rights, of course). I have submitted that, in two main ways, the more specific legal claim-rights can be comprehended by the existence of the general legal claim-right. First, any general claim-right encompasses some concrete claim-rights as its logical corollaries. For example, a general legal claim-right not ever to be defrauded entails a multiplicity of more concrete legal claim-rights such as the legal claim-right not to be defrauded on Tuesdays. Second, and more important, a general legal claim-right can serve to warrant the introduction of specific legal claim-rights that are crucial for the fulfillment of the general claim-right. For instance, the general legal claim-right of each person not to be subjected to interrogational torture by legal-governmental officials can justificatorily underpin a law which confers upon each person a more specific legal claim-right not to be subjected to interrogational water-boarding by such officials. In this situation, the ties between the abstract claim-right and the concrete claim-right are not logical but are instead partly instrumental and partly explicative or interpretive. Ties of those kinds are involved when legal claim-rights (relatively general legal claim-rights) are invoked as justifying reasons for the establishment or recognition of legal claim-rights (relatively specific legal claim-rights).

What has *not* been indicated in any of my references to the justificatory "grounding" of specific legal claim-rights and duties by general legal claim-rights is what Raz sometimes meant when he described a claim-right as a "ground" of duties. At times Raz used such terminology in much the same way in which it has been employed here, but at other times he used it in a way directly opposed to the Correlativity Axiom. He declared, for example, that "the right is the ground of the duty. It is wrong to translate statements of rights into statements of 'the corresponding' duties. A right of one person is not a duty on another. It is the ground of a duty, a ground which, if not counteracted by conflicting considerations, justifies holding that other person to have the duty" (1984, 199). Raz was here articulating his version of the interest theory of rights, which differs sharply from my own Interest Theory of right-holding—as will become evident in my next chapter. I will criticize his interest theory of rights in that chapter, but my concern at present is to avert potential confusion that might lead some philosophers to doubt the correctness of the Correlativity Axiom.

In the sentences which I have just quoted, Raz was obviously not using the term "right" in the way in which I use the term "claim-right." Nor was he using that term overarchingly to cover all four types of entitlements in the upper half of Hohfeld's table. Instead, he was employing the term "right" to refer to certain justificatory considerations which consist in the interests or well-being of a particular party and which militate in favor of the imposition of a legal duty or an institutional duty on some other party. Now, Raz was morally and legally and intellectually at liberty to employ the term "right" as he saw fit for his theoretical purposes. Hence, the sheer fact that his pattern of usage of that term diverged from any Hohfeldian pattern of usage is not what I shall be deploring here. Rather, what should be assailed here briefly are two interconnected vices of the sentences that have just been quoted (and of other similar statements in Raz's meditations on these matters).

First, especially with the assertion that "[i]t is wrong to translate statements of rights into statements of 'the corresponding' duties," Raz conveyed the impression that he was casting doubt upon the Correlativity Axiom. To be sure, his assertion can be construed as simply making a stipulative terminological point. Raz can be construed as indicating that, when the term "rights" is employed as he employed it, it does not refer to legal or moral positions that are correlated with duties in the manner envisaged by Hohfeldians. Such a stipulative terminological point would not be incorrect in itself, since it would be consistent with the Correlativity Axiom about claim-rights and duties. Nonetheless, especially when Raz's pronouncement is interpreted in combination with his other barbs directed squarely against the Hohfeldian analysis, the pronouncement lends itself readily to being understood as a rejection of the Correlativity Axiom. So interpreted, Raz's pronouncement is woefully misguided. The relationship of biconditional entailment encapsulated in the Correlativity Axiom does not pertain to the justificatory considerations which Raz designated as "rights." Accordingly, the fact that those considerations do not biconditionally entail any duties is something that has no bearing on the Correlativity Axiom at all.

Second, Raz's confinement of the term "rights" to the ethically pregnant considerations that justify the imposition of legal or institutional duties upon other parties is promotive of confusion between people's interests and the legal or institutional protections of those interests. In the Hohfeldian analysis and in the Correlativity Axiom which is integral to that analysis, claim-rights are understood as legal or moral or institutional positions of protectedness. Those deontic protections are distinct from the interests which they serve to safeguard deontically. Raz's terminology tends to obscure that distinctness, especially given that interests and entitlements have often been conflated in the philosophical and legal literature on these issues.

Hohfeld himself strove to combat the running together of interests and entitlements. He wrote, for example (1923, 79 n. 34, emphases in original): "[T]here is a very obvious difference—and one vitally important for the solution of problems in the conflict of laws—between a mere *factual interest* and its *legal recognition* (legal claims, privileges, etc.)." James Penner, writing many years after Hohfeld and with specific reference to Raz and MacCormick, has even more forcefully resisted any elision of the distinction between interests and deontic protections of those interests (1997, 306):

> As we have seen, according to Raz rights ground duties. This claim entails, and is taken by both Raz and MacCormick to entail, that the existence of a right is logically prior to the existence of duties which protect it. In other words, rights *qua* interests are independent of duties. This raises a serious problem for the theory, for a more plausible view is that the interest underlying the right serves as the reason for the imposition of a duty. On this latter view, a right is not simply an interest, not even an intermediate consensus version of an interest. The existence of a right does not logically precede the imposition of its correlative duty; it arises with it.

Notwithstanding the efforts of Hohfeld and some later philosophers to counter any conflations of interests and deontic protections, such conflations have been irksomely common. Let us glance at just a few examples. Theodore Benditt has written as follows: "It seems to me to be more perspicuous ... to identify the right with the interest straightaway, for this seems to be the only way ... of preserving the notion that people's rights can sometimes constitute the legal reasons for certain decisions" (1978, 170). Richard Posner has similarly declared that "a right is an important interest presumptively protected against interference by others" (1990, 331). Waldron has repeatedly adopted a comparable stance. He proclaims, for instance, that "[w]e call *rights* those interests which should not simply be thrown into the social calculus along with everything else" (1990, 105, emphasis in original). Nicolas Cornell has gone in a like direction when he opines: "Part of what is attractive about [Raz's] interest theory is precisely that it reduces the idea of a right to the seemingly more basic ideas of interests and the injuries that can be suffered to those interests" (2015, 115). Given these instances and many other instances of the running together of interests and deontic protections in the philosophical literature on rights and right-holding, Raz's terminology—which encourages such confusion—is best eschewed.

What should be underscored, at the conclusion of this section, is that Benditt errs in the quotation above when he submits that the conflating of interests and deontic protections is "the only way ... of preserving the notion that people's rights can sometimes constitute the legal reasons for certain decisions." As has been maintained in §3.7, general legal claim-rights can serve as key parts of the justificatory bases for the introduction of any number of concrete legal claim-rights. The more concrete legal claim-rights can be crucial for the satisfactory fulfillment of the abstract legal claim-rights, especially if technological advances or other changes of circumstances have occurred. Furthermore, moral claim-rights are often straightforwardly invocable as justificatory grounds for the establishment of legal claim-rights that will give jural recognition and effect to those moral entitlements. Of course, Benditt refers to legal reasons for certain decisions. However, in systems of governance where moral principles have been adopted as substantive legal norms or as standards for determining the status of norms as laws[5]—where the adoption of those principles has been effected constitutionally or legislatively or adjudicatively or administratively—the moral claim-rights invocable in favor of the creation of certain legal claim-rights can correctly be classified as legal reasons for the creation of those legal claim-rights. Hence, Benditt's rationale for effacing the distinction between interests and claim-rights is baseless.

3.9 Stages of Emergence

Defenders of Raz's conception of rights might retort that the abandonment of his conception, with its erasure of the difference between interests and deontic protections, will leave us unable to account for some salient features of claim-rights and other entitlements. Both Raz and MacCormick contended, for example, that we can sometimes accurately ascribe to a person a claim-right even if we cannot yet specify the details of the claim-right such as the party or parties vis-à-vis whom it is held (MacCormick 1982, 163; Raz 1984, 211–12). Yet the ascribability of a claim-right in those circumstances may seem to indicate that the claim-right is logically and temporally anterior to any duty that is supposedly correlated with it. Such an ascription may thus seem to vindicate the Razian conception of rights in opposition to the Hohfeldian conception and particularly in opposition to the Correlativity Axiom.

Appearances are deceptive, however, for the state of affairs to which Raz and MacCormick gestured is fully squarable with the Hohfeldian analysis and the Correlativity Axiom. Indeed, the endeavor of showing the consistency between that state of affairs and the Correlativity Axiom can help to avert the running together of interests and deontic protections of interests. Such an endeavor can best proceed by differentiating among three main stages in the emergence and ascribability of legal entitlements (though each of these stages could be subdivided into additional classifications). First are people's interests of various sorts, including their interests in being unrestricted. Second are inchoate legal entitlements. Any

[5] For some of my main explorations of how moral principles can enter into the law of a jurisdiction, see Kramer 2004, 1–140; 2022, 401–7, 422–35; 2024.

ascriptions of such entitlements consist in assertions that certain interests should be given some legal recognition as yet unspecified. Third are established legal entitlements, whether general or concrete, which consist in the forms of legal recognition that are eventually bestowed. For my present purposes, what needs most attention is the second of these stages along with the transition from it to the third stage. When MacCormick referred to situations "in which we are much more certain that children [or others] have a right to something than we are certain about what is the right or the best way of giving effect to it" (MacCormick 1982, 163), he was referring to inchoate legal entitlements rather than to any established legal claim-rights. That is, he was referring to the fact that certain elementary interests of children should be legally recognized and furthered through the bestowal of legal entitlements that have not yet been determined. He made that very point by declaring that children hold certain "rights" even though nobody yet knows what those "rights" will involve. In that vein, to say that every child holds an unspecified "right" to an education is to say merely that every child's interest in receiving an education should be legally recognized and furthered through the bestowal of some legal entitlements. (My discussion in this section might appear to take for granted the correctness of the Interest Theory of right-holding. Three quick points should be noted in response. First, this chapter has indeed at several junctures presupposed the correctness of the Interest Theory; one of my aims in the chapter is to show how my defense of the Hohfeldian analysis is interwoven with my account of right-holding. Second, given that my ripostes in this section are chiefly to Raz and MacCormick, and given that they were proponents of versions of the Interest Theory—albeit versions markedly different from my own, especially in the case of Raz—my ripostes naturally tend to take for granted a general outlook which I have in common with them. Third, my discussion in this section does not in fact beg any questions in favor of the Interest Theory against the Will Theory, because it leaves room for contexts in which the best way of recognizing and furthering someone's interests is to confer a set of legal entitlements upon someone else. Many proponents of the Will Theory have perceived such contexts as indicative of an interest/entitlement gap that tells against the Interest Theory. As my fourth chapter will argue, however, any tenable version of the Interest Theory can straightforwardly allow for such contexts.)

Three related but distinguishable conditions have to be satisfied before an inchoate legal entitlement will have become an established legal entitlement or a set of established legal entitlements. The *kind* of legal recognition, the *content* of such recognition, and the *directionality* or orientation of that recognition all have to be settled. Legal-governmental officials settle the kind and content of the legal recognition that will be conferred, by assigning one or more of the Hohfeldian entitlements to each person whose interests are being furthered. In any given situation, the legal recognition bestowed can range from a single type of entitlement to a complex combination of all four types. A child's unspecified "right" to an education, for example, might eventuate in some of the following components among others: a legal claim-right not to be excluded or greatly hindered from obtaining an education, legal claim-rights to be furnished with adequate pedagogical services and materials, legal liberties to attend school and engage in lessons regularly, legal immunities against being divested of these educational claim-rights and liberties through any non-statutory means, and legal powers to seek the effectuation of these other educational entitlements.

Selecting the types and contents of Hohfeldian positions that will effect a transition from an inchoate entitlement to some established legal entitlements is a matter that obviously resembles the elaboration of a general legal entitlement through its serving as a key part of the justificatory basis for the creation of concrete legal entitlements. Nonetheless, despite the abstractness of the contents of general legal entitlements such as general legal claim-rights not to be excluded or greatly hindered from obtaining an education, they are established entitlements rather than nebulously undelineated. A general legal claim-right is indeed a general legal claim-right and is not a general legal entitlement of some other sort; by contrast, an undelineated "right" is too amorphous to be classified as belonging to any of the columns in the Hohfeldian table. Perhaps the most obvious manifestation of this difference between general legal entitlements and inchoate entitlements is that general legal entitlements can entail certain concrete legal entitlements. For example, a general legal claim-right not ever to be subjected to unprovoked assaults will entail a concrete legal claim-right not to be subjected to unprovoked assaults on Tuesdays. By contrast, inchoate entitlements do not ever logically entail any concrete legal entitlements.

As important as the task of selecting the kinds and contents of legal entitlements that are to be bestowed is the task of specifying the directionality or orientation of each such entitlement—that is, the task of pinning down the party or parties vis-à-vis whom each entitlement is held. Let us here contemplate again a child who has an inchoate "right" to an education. Legal-governmental officials not only have to determine whether each child should have legal claim-rights to be supplied with adequate pedagogical services and materials, for example; they also have to determine who should bear the legal duties to provide any such services and materials. Much the same is true, *mutatis mutandis*, of every established legal entitlement that ensues from the officials' endeavors to flesh out the formless "right." (This need to pin down the directionality of legal entitlements is another major dissimilarity between my current reflections on the stages of the emergence of legal entitlements and my earlier reflections—in §3.7—on general legal entitlements and concrete legal entitlements. Even a highly general legal entitlement, if established, must obtain vis-à-vis some party or parties.[6] Of course, the directedness of an entitlement can involve quantification over the parties vis-à-vis whom the entitlement is held,

[6] Though there is much with which I disagree in James 2003 and O'Neill 1996, 122–53, I converge with them in emphasizing this point.

as we have explored in Chapter 2 and in this chapter. Still, the directionality of any legal entitlement is established if the entitlement itself is established. In this respect, as well as in other respects, an established legal entitlement is specifiable even if its content is general rather than specific. When we accurately ascribe to some person P a general legal entitlement, we are not simply saying that some interest of P should be legally recognized and furthered; we are also able to identify the party or parties vis-à-vis whom the entitlement is held. Likewise, of course, we are able to indicate the content of the entitlement and the column in Hohfeld's table to which the entitlement belongs.)

Whilst the task of selecting the type of an entitlement is analytically separable from the tasks of fixing upon its content and its directionality, and whilst all of those factors are essential for a transition from an inchoate legal entitlement to an established legal entitlement, they are very often settled simultaneously. The appropriate determination of one of those dimensions will almost always significantly affect the appropriate determination of each of the others. In practice, therefore, the settling of each factor is usually linked to the settling of the others. None of the three dimensions has to take precedence over the others; if the type and content and directionality of a legal entitlement are not settled simultaneously, then any of them can be settled in advance of the others.

How, then, does this tripartite analysis of interests and inchoate legal entitlements and established legal entitlements compare with Raz's conflation of rights and interests? Through the triad of categories in my analysis, we can fully take cognizance of the ascribability of inchoate legal entitlements to people without presuming that the ascribability of those entitlements is somehow inconsistent with the Correlativity Axiom. We can thereby give a wide berth to Raz's running together of interests and deontic protections of interests, while taking on board his observations and MacCormick's observations about the phased emergence of legal entitlements. Contrary to what Raz and MacCormick supposed, the Correlativity Axiom is consistent with the sundry features of entitlements which they highlighted and often misdescribed. We have seen as much when examining the "dynamic aspect" of legal claim-rights in §3.7 above, and we have seen as much here.

My arguments against Raz in this section and in the past few sections will be reinforced in Chapter 4, when I adduce some further considerations that tell decisively against his account of rights and right-holding. Here my concern has chiefly been to vindicate the Correlativity Axiom in the face of strictures from Raz that were concomitant to his account of rights and right-holding. That very account will be one of the principal targets of Chapter 4, where I will maintain that Raz committed himself—through his conception of rights and right-holding—to a host of untenable conclusions. Whereas the posture of this chapter has been defensive as I have shown that none of the observations by Raz or MacCormick is worrisome for proponents of the Correlativity Axiom, my next chapter will go on the offensive by exposing the manifold weaknesses in Raz's interest theory. My objections there to his theory will strengthen my responses here to the anti-Hohfeldian pronouncements which he delivered in the course of espousing that theory.

3.10 No Wrongs without Claim-Rights

This chapter will conclude its defense of the Correlativity Axiom by responding at length to a fairly recent article in which Nicolas Cornell has submitted that people can be wronged by the actions of others even though the wronged people have not held any claim-rights to the non-occurrence of those actions. On the one hand, Cornell does not have to impugn the Correlativity Axiom or the Hohfeldian analysis more generally. Indeed, he writes approvingly of that analysis, and only once does he say anything that is inconsistent with the Correlativity Axiom. On the other hand, although Cornell does not have to contest the correlativity of claim-rights and duties, he does at one juncture tentatively contest it, and he much more robustly assails the notion that the wronging of a person P by the conduct of some other person always consists in the contravention of a claim-right held by P. As he declares at the outset of his article, the proposition which he seeks to confute therein is as follows: "X [would wrong] Y by φ-ing if and only if Y has a right that X not φ" (2015, 111). He correctly contends that that proposition—which I will designate as the "No Wrongs Without Claim-Rights Proposition"—is prevalently endorsed by philosophers. I myself have argued sustainedly in favor of that proposition in the final chapter of my book *Where Law and Morality Meet* (2004, 249–94), and numerous other philosophers have likewise embraced it. Cornell believes that all of us have erred in so doing, and he therefore believes that he can generally acknowledge the correlativity of claim-rights and duties while also affirming that Q can be wronged by P's act of φ-ing even in circumstances where no one has owed any duty to Q that would require P to refrain from φ-ing: "One may be wronged, I will argue, without having a right that is violated" (Cornell 2015, 112). Cornell does not deny that, when P acts in a manner that wrongs Q, P's conduct will perforce have contravened a duty; he merely denies that the duty contravened by P must have been owed to Q. He therefore denies that the wronging of Q by P perforce consists in P's contravening of a claim-right held by Q.

Whereas Cornell only once deviates from the Correlativity Axiom while rejecting the No Wrongs Without Claim-Rights Proposition, someone who embraces the latter proposition might react to Cornell's arguments differently. Suppose that such a person is convinced by those arguments about the absence of any duties owed to parties who have been wronged in certain situations. Such a person would then presumably reject the Correlativity Axiom by contending that Q who is wronged through P's act of φ-ing can hold a claim-right to P's refraining from φ-ing even though no one owes any duty to Q that would require P to refrain from φ-ing. Though such a response to

Cornell's arguments is no doubt highly improbable, the conceivability of it warrants my issuance of rejoinders to those arguments in this chapter. Furthermore, given that I champion both the Correlativity Axiom and the No Wrongs Without Claim-Rights Proposition, I am well advised to demonstrate that Cornell's lines of reasoning can best be countered in full consistency with both of those propositions.

The cardinal tack pursued by Cornell lies in his adducing of various scenarios where Q has apparently been wronged by P's action of φ-ing even though Q has ostensibly not held any claim-right to P's refraining from such an action. Cornell does proceed in the second half of his article to furnish some general theoretical ruminations on the conclusions that are to be drawn from his scenarios, but the force of those ruminations is entirely dependent on the persuasiveness of the concrete examples that have led into them. Hence, for Cornell's purposes, those examples are more than intuition pumps. They carry the main weight of his reasoning. I shall therefore probe each of them carefully before coming to grips with his general theoretical contentions. As will be argued, each of his examples either involves a claim-right held by Q vis-à-vis P or else does not involve any wrong to Q inflicted by P. Consequently, each of his scenarios does not go any way toward refuting the No Wrongs Without Claim-Rights Proposition.

To an even greater extent than the rest of this chapter, my engagement with Cornell will draw upon my Interest Theory of right-holding. At quite a number of junctures, Cornell seems to cleave to the account of right-holding propounded by the rival Will Theory. *Pro tanto*, then, my multiple critiques of the Will Theory of right-holding in Chapter 4 are damaging for Cornell as well as for the philosophers who expressly advocate the Will Theory. Indeed, my retorts to Cornell in defense of the Correlativity Axiom and the No Wrongs Without Claim-Rights Proposition partly anticipate a few of the points that will be pressed against the Will Theory of right-holding in my fourth chapter. My retorts to him could plausibly have been located in that chapter, but they equally well belong here. Still, although my rejoinders to Cornell are not located in Chapter 4, their tellingness will be potentiated by my dissection of the Will Theory in that chapter.

3.10.1 A Preliminary Clarification

Before we investigate Cornell's vignettes, I should differentiate them from a class of cases in which P's action of φ-ing does wrong Q even though Q vis-à-vis P has not held any claim-right to P's refraining from φ-ing. These cases are unproblematically consistent with the truth of the No Wrongs Without Claim-Rights Proposition, and they are therefore of no avail to Cornell in his efforts to rebut that proposition. We are thus well advised to take note of these cases in order to differentiate them from the thought-experiments which he adduces. Unlike his examples, any set of circumstances of the sort that will be recounted here is genuinely a situation in which P's action of φ-ing has wronged Q even though Q vis-à-vis P has not held any claim-right to P's abstention from φ-ing. Q in such a set of circumstances has indeed held a claim-right to P's not φ-ing, but the claim-right has been held vis-à-vis another party R rather than vis-à-vis P.

As has been illustrated with my scenario of Phineas and Hephzibah in §2.4.1 of Chapter 2, the content of a legal or moral duty does not always refer to the conduct of the duty-bearer. Though the content of the duty in that illustration involved the meteorological conditions on a certain afternoon, the message of the scenario could have been conveyed just as pertinently with a duty whose content instead referred to the conduct of some third party. Suppose that Percival has stoutly assured Beulah that Herman will not drive his truck past her house tomorrow afternoon when she will be caring for a young child as a babysitter. Herman normally drives his truck past the house of Beulah several times each weekday afternoon as he makes deliveries from a local supermarket, and the roar of his truck as it passes the house is quite cacophonous. Beulah worries that the noise will awaken or frighten the child for whom she will be caring. She consequently makes contact with Herman's manager Percival, who responds affirmatively to her request with his hearty assurances. Percival subsequently forgets about the matter, and he neglects to say anything about it to Herman. As a result, Herman drives past Beulah's house several times on the following afternoon. Herman's driving of his truck past her house has breached a moral duty owed to Beulah, who has held a moral claim-right to his not engaging in that mode of conduct. However, her moral claim-right is held not vis-à-vis Herman but instead vis-à-vis Percival. Hence, although Herman's conduct has contravened a moral duty owed to Beulah, Herman has not contravened any duty owed *by him* to Beulah. Of course, if Percival had remembered to instruct Herman not to drive past Beulah's house, Herman would then have come under a moral duty not to drive past the house. Herman would have owed such a duty both to Percival and to Beulah, and his action of driving past her house on the following afternoon would have breached the duty owed by him to each of them. Nevertheless, given that Percival in fact neglected to inform Herman of the situation, no duty to abstain from driving past Beulah's house has been owed by Herman. His act of driving does contravene a duty owed to Beulah, but the duty is owed solely by Percival. The moral claim-right to Herman's not driving past her house is held by Beulah vis-à-vis Percival but not vis-à-vis Herman. Beulah has been wronged by Percival but not by Herman, even though it is Herman's conduct that has been directly involved in wronging her.

Now, for my present purposes, what is most notable about this situation is that its occurrence is straightforwardly consistent with the Correlativity Axiom and with the No Wrongs Without Claim-Rights Proposition. Beulah has been wronged by Herman's action of driving, but that action has wronged her precisely because it has transgressed a claim-right held by her. The fact that her claim-right has been held vis-à-vis Percival rather than vis-à-vis Herman is no basis whatsoever for concluding that she has been wronged by Herman's act of driving past her house even though she has not held any claim-right to his abstention from driving past her house. On the contrary, she has indeed held a claim-right to his abstention from driving past her house: a claim-right held by her vis-à-vis Percival. Exactly because Herman's act of driving is violative of the claim-right which Beulah holds vis-à-vis Percival, it wrongs her. Thus, the situation envisioned here nicely illustrates—rather than belies—the No Wrongs Without Claim-Rights Proposition.

Perhaps Cornell has not heretofore contemplated any situation of this kind, or perhaps he has recognized that a situation of this kind would not avail him at all in his efforts to refute the No Wrongs Without Claim-Rights Proposition. In either event, he does not mull over any such situation. Instead, he assembles some quite different scenarios to which we shall now turn. Were he correct in his analysis of each of his own scenarios, he would also be correct in rejecting the No Wrongs Without Claim-Rights Proposition. However, as has already been suggested and as will now be argued, he errs in his analysis of each of his scenarios. Whereas my vignette of Percival and Beulah and Herman has portrayed a situation in which Q has been wronged by P's φ-ing even though Q vis-à-vis P has not held a claim-right to P's abstention from φ-ing, the vignettes presented by Cornell do not portray any such upshot (and therefore do not stand any chance of casting doubt upon the No Wrongs Without Claim-Rights Proposition). Instead, in each of his examples, either Q has not been wronged by P's φ-ing or else Q vis-à-vis P has held a claim-right to P's not φ-ing.

3.10.2 A Third-Party-Beneficiary Contract

The first of Cornell's thought-experiments will be familiar to anyone acquainted with the debates between the proponents of the Interest Theory of right-holding and the proponents of the rival Will Theory. We will of course delve into those debates in my next chapter, but—even before entering into them—we can aptly scrutinize now the attempt by Cornell to draw upon a thought-experiment which Hart propounded in the course of those debates. Hart as an advocate of the Will Theory contended that the key to identifying the holder of any legal claim-right resides in ascertaining who holds certain legal powers of control over the legal duty that is correlative to the claim-right. (My fourth chapter will explicate the Will Theory and the Interest Theory more rigorously than is necessary here.) Hart believed that the virtues of his Will Theory and the deficiencies of the Interest Theory become manifest when we ponder a situation involving a third-party-beneficiary contract. He recounted such a situation as follows, in a passage which Cornell quotes:

> X promises Y in return for some favor that he will look after Y's aged mother in his absence. Rights arise out of this transaction, but it is surely Y to whom the promise has been made and not his mother who *has* or *possesses* these rights. Certainly Y's mother is a person concerning whom X has an obligation and a person who will benefit by its performance, but the person *to whom* he has an obligation to look after her is Y. This is something *due to* or *owed to* Y, so it is Y, not his mother, whose right X will disregard and to whom X will have done *wrong* if he fails to keep his promise, though the mother may be physically injured.[7]

Cornell agrees with Hart that Y is the only holder of a claim-right vis-à-vis X under the contract, but he largely disagrees with the view expressed in the final sentence of this quotation. Cornell submits that the mother will have been wronged by X if X neglects to fulfill his responsibilities under the contract, even though the mother does not hold any claim-right to the fulfillment of those responsibilities (2015, 117):

> It seems to me, however, that ... the mother stands to be potentially wronged. She has a stake in the duty that is owed to her son. Suppose that the promise to Y were broken. I think it would be mistaken to say that the mother has no complaint, as though she were akin to any other mere bystander. It would seem perfectly appropriate for her to resent X's failure in such a case. Her son arranged something for her, and as a result of X's malfeasance, she has not received it. Furthermore, one can imagine X apologizing to the mother or the mother forgiving X.

Cornell infers that Hart's view to the contrary about the mother was due to his acceptance of the No Wrongs Without Claim-Rights Proposition.

I naturally concur with Cornell's insistence that the mother—whom I shall designate as "M"—will have been wronged if X does not adequately care for her in accordance with the terms of the contract. However, the reason for the correctness of Cornell's insistence on that point is that M is straightforwardly a holder of a claim-right vis-à-vis X under the terms of the contract. In other words, although Cornell proceeds soundly by distancing himself from Hart on the matter of the wronging of M, he errs by aligning himself with Hart on the matter of the status of M as a holder of a claim-right. According to the Interest Theory as it has been encapsulated in §3.1 above, the contract envisaged by Hart plainly confers upon M a claim-right vis-à-vis X to be assisted adequately. X has been placed under a duty by the contract to care for M, and that duty inherently protects an aspect of M's situation that is normally beneficial for someone like M. Receiving adequate care is normally beneficial for an elderly person, and the duty imposed on X by the contract will not have

[7] Hart 1955, 180, emphases in original. A slightly terser discussion of a third-party-beneficiary contract also appears in Hart 1982, 187.

been fulfilled unless M does receive adequate care. Thus, by the reckoning of the Interest Theory's criterion for the holding of a claim-right correlative to a specified duty, M is straightforwardly a holder of a claim-right correlative to the duty which X bears under the terms of the contract with Y. If X neglects to provide the care which he is contractually obligated to furnish, he will have breached the claim-right held by M (as well as the claim-right held by Y)—and so he will have wronged M, legally or morally. In sum, the situation depicted by Hart is nicely illustrative of the No Wrongs Without Claim-Rights Proposition.

When Cornell concurs with Hart in denying that M has been vested with a claim-right under the terms of the contract, he invokes some considerations associated with the Will Theory of right-holding: "That X did not owe the duty to the mother is evidenced by the fact that she would not control X's performance. She could not demand or excuse performance" (Cornell 2015, 116). By contrast, I have of course drawn upon the Interest Theory in my rejoinder to Cornell. Consequently, the clinching force of my rejoinder will not be fully apparent until Chapter 4, where I shall marshal some lines of reasoning that tell decisively against the Will Theory and in favor of the Interest Theory. Nonetheless, what should already be evident is the unsatisfactoriness of Cornell's first attempt to substantiate his rejection of the No Wrongs Without Claim-Rights Proposition. That attempt rests entirely on his acceptance of the Will Theory's account of what constitutes the holding of a claim-right. As has been mentioned, scenarios of third-party-beneficiary contracts are commonplace in the disputation between Interest Theorists and Will Theorists. Whereas Will Theorists like Hart and Cornell presume that the third-party beneficiary specified by the terms of such a contract is not accurately classifiable as a holder of a claim-right thereunder, Interest Theorists like me maintain that the third-party beneficiary specified by the terms of such a contract is indeed accurately and straightforwardly classifiable as a holder of a claim-right thereunder. Hence, Cornell's presentation of a vignette involving just such a contract is bound to be dialectically unavailing against Interest Theorists. It might be dialectically of some effectiveness against a few of the Hartian Will Theorists, but Interest Theorists will rightly conclude that Cornell has not come up with any grounds for them to harbor doubts about the No Wrongs Without Claim-Rights Proposition. Even before Chapter 4 presents my critiques of the Will Theory of right-holding, then, Interest Theorists can warrantedly maintain that Cornell's opening broadside against the No Wrongs Without Claim-Rights Proposition is futile.

Furthermore, even the Hartian Will Theorists will most likely resist Cornell's opening broadside. More specifically, they are likely to resist his explanation of why M will have been wronged by the non-fulfillment of X's promise to Y—an explanation which I have quoted above. Such philosophers will underscore the distinction between being harmed and being wronged, and will of course readily allow that M in Hart's scenario stands to be directly harmed by X's failure to provide an adequate level of care of the sort required under the terms of the contract. Quite intelligible to the Hartian Will Theorists is the fact that M feels resentment toward X in circumstances where a breach of the contract by X does occur. Precisely because M has been directly harmed by the wrong which X has committed against Y in such circumstances, her perspective is markedly different from that of a mere bystander. In addition to being justified in feeling the indignation of a bystander, she can be justified in feeling aggrieved about the harm which X's wronging of Y has inflicted upon her. Distinguishing firmly between the wronging of M and the harming of M (where the harming of her is appurtenant to the wronging of Y), the Hartian Will Theorists are likely to be unimpressed by the rest of Cornell's explanation of the wrong done by X to M. In the passage which I have quoted above, Cornell observes that M "has a stake in the duty that is owed to her son" and that "[h]er son arranged something for her, and as a result of X's malfeasance [or non-feasance], she has not received it." In the eyes of the Hartian Will Theorists, those considerations militate strongly in favor of concluding that M will have been harmed by the failure of X to comply with the duty which he owes to Y. In the eyes of those theorists, however, Cornell's observations do not militate in favor of concluding that M will have been wronged by X's non-compliance with that duty. Because the duty is owed to Y rather than to M, Y is the party wronged by X's violation of the duty. By contrast, although the violation of the duty undoubtedly harms M—in the ways suggested by Cornell's observations—it does not wrong M, to whom the duty has not been owed. Or so the Hartian Will Theorists are likely to retort when confronted with Cornell's contentions about the wronging of M by X. Moreover, such retorts would not be ad hoc devices for shoring up the No Wrongs Without Claim-Rights Proposition. On the contrary, they would quite closely resemble the animadversions of Will Theorists in response to the Interest Theory of right-holding.

Of course, I disagree with the Will Theorists and agree with Cornell about the wronging of the mother in Hart's scenario. My point in the preceding paragraph has certainly not been to endorse the Will Theorists' ripostes to Cornell. Rather, the point has been to underline the otiosity of Cornell's first concrete example. Neither the Interest Theorists nor the Will Theorists will accept that that example poses any difficulties for the No Wrongs Without Claim-Rights Proposition. A proponent of the Interest Theory of right-holding will maintain that the mother holds a claim-right vis-à-vis X under the terms of the contract, and that X's non-compliance with his duty under the contract will have wronged the mother because it is a violation of her claim-right. A proponent of the Will Theory of right-holding will contend that the mother does not hold a claim-right vis-à-vis X under the terms of the contract, and that X's non-compliance with the duty owed to Y under the contract has therefore not wronged the mother even though it has harmed her. Divergent though the Interest Theorist and the Will Theorist are in their premises and sub-conclusions, they can converge on the conclusion that Cornell with his invocation of the Hartian scenario has not succeeded in his aspiration to disconfirm the No Wrongs Without Claim-Rights Proposition.

What should be emphasized at the close of this discussion of Cornell's first example is that a proponent of the Interest Theory will regard Hart's scenario of a third-party-beneficiary contract as easily analyzable rather than as vexingly knotty. By the reckoning of an Interest Theorist, the fact that the contract bestows a claim-right upon the mother vis-à-vis X is unproblematically discernible rather than imponderable. Cornell muses that an Interest Theorist "might suggest that the mother actually does have some sort of claim—something that is owed to her—though perhaps in some more subtle way. One might argue that our sense that the mother is wronged is based on her entitlement to rely on X or based on a duty of her son to take care of her. Somehow, the thought goes, the mother has a claim of her own that piggybacks on her son's claim" (2015, 117–18). Contrary to what Cornell supposes, an Interest Theorist does not need to resort to any of the desperate tacks which he broaches here. Nor does an Interest Theorist need to show that a claim-right is held by the mother "in some more subtle way." Rather, an Interest Theorist will simply have recourse to the criterion for the holding of a claim-right which I have articulated in §3.1 as the central thesis of the Interest Theory. When that criterion is applied to Hart's scenario, as I have applied it above in my reflections on his scenario, we can conclude without further ado that the mother holds a claim-right vis-à-vis X under the terms of the contract. There is no need for any tortured reasoning about the mother's piggy-backing on the claim-right of her son.

3.10.3 A Cheated Prizewinner

Having supplied his meditations on Hart's vignette, Cornell offers a second vignette (2015, 118–19). He imagines a situation in which a wealthy man—whom I will designate as "Jeffrey"—decides to give away most of his fortune to a worthy recipient. Jeffrey draws up a list of people in his community who, through their professions or their charitable work, have contributed valuably to the good of the community. Although Cornell does not indicate explicitly whether these people are aware of their inclusion on the list for Jeffrey's lottery, and although their knowing of the situation is not an essential component of the scenario, he appears to assume that they are aware of their inclusion on the list. Someone whom Cornell designates as "X" is placed in charge of the mechanized aleatory procedure that will select the name of the winner. That procedure does indeed select a certain person, whom I will designate as "Judith." However, before Judith receives any of her winnings, X absconds with Jeffrey's fortune and deftly escapes to a foreign jurisdiction where he is beyond the reach of law-enforcement officials from the country whence he has fled.

Cornell affirms that Judith has been wronged by X, though he rather oddly frames the matter entirely in terms of her feelings (2015, 118):

> It seems to me that [Judith] will consider [herself] wronged by X. I would. The feeling would not be merely the "Aw, shucks!" attitude that one might have upon discovering that [one's] ticket was one digit away from winning the lottery. [Judith] would feel aggrieved, I think. If [she] ever met X, [she] might have something to say to him.

At any rate, insofar as Cornell is contending that Judith has been morally wronged by X, he is plainly correct. All the same, he goes astray when he proceeds to assert that no claim-right held by Judith has been involved in the wrong committed against her by X. He declares: "Even though it is natural to see [Judith] as wronged, [her] complaint would not have anything to do with any right of [hers]" (2015, 118). Decidedly peculiar is Cornell's attempt to vindicate his assertion about the absence of any relevant claim-right held by Judith: "Although it may feel [to Judith] as though X has stolen money that was 'as good as [hers],' [she] did not actually have a property right. Nor would [her] complaint be based on any reliance ..., because [she] did not rely on receiving the money" (2015, 118–19). Cornell in this latest quotation is quite clearly talking about legal claim-rights. Unless there are any undisclosed special factors pertaining to the lottery arranged by Jeffrey, or unless the law in the relevant jurisdiction is quite different from Anglo-American law, Cornell is correct in submitting that Judith vis-à-vis X holds neither any legal proprietary claim-right nor any legal contractual claim-right to be furnished with her winnings by X. However, the absence of any relevant legal claim-rights held by Judith is paralleled by the absence of any legal wrong committed against her by X. No legal remedy will be available for Judith, though of course a legal remedy will be available for Jeffrey if X can be apprehended and extradited. Unlike Judith, Jeffrey has held relevant legal claim-rights vis-à-vis X and has been legally wronged by X.

Only at the point of the two most recently quoted sentences does Cornell give any intimation that his vignette about Jeffrey and Judith and X is concerned with legal claim-rights and wrongs rather than with moral claim-rights and wrongs. Until that point, his scenario has seemed to be about moral claim-rights and moral wrongs. Whereas Judith has not been legally wronged by X, she has been morally wronged by him. Moreover, whereas Judith vis-à-vis X has not held any legal claim-right to be furnished with her prize, she has held a moral claim-right vis-à-vis X to be so furnished. Initially, after Jeffrey has compiled his list of worthy people and has put into place the arrangement for the mechanized aleatory procedure with X in charge of the implementation of the arrangement, X owes a moral duty to the people on the list disjunctively. (X also of course owes some moral duties to Jeffrey.) The moral duty incumbent on X requires him to oversee the operation of the aleatory procedure fairly, for the purpose of bestowing Jeffrey's fortune upon anyone who is selected by that procedure. When the mechanized device has operated and has selected somebody on the list for Jeffrey's largesse, the moral duty which X owes to the listed people through disjunctive universal quantification is superseded by a moral duty which X now owes to the particular person who has been selected. Such a duty morally requires X to disburse the winnings to that lucky person—Judith—who holds a moral claim-right vis-à-vis X which correlates with X's moral duty. Through his theft of the winnings, X has contravened the moral duty which he owes to Judith and has therefore of course contravened the moral claim-right held by her vis-à-vis him. Exactly because X has contravened the moral duty and its correlative claim-right, X has morally wronged Judith. (Worth noting here, as an aside, is that the moral duty owed by X to Judith has come into existence through the operation of a quasi-power. Although some choices and actions by human beings have led to the existence of the mechanized aleatory procedure with its quasi-power to confer upon the selected person a moral claim-right vis-à-vis X, the selection of Judith produced by the operation of that procedure is not itself directly due to any choices made by human beings.)

In short, whether Cornell's thought-experiment about Jeffrey and Judith and X is construed as focused on legal entitlements and legal wrongs or instead as focused on moral entitlements and moral wrongs, it is smoothly consistent with the No Wrongs Without Claim-Rights Proposition. If legal entitlements and legal wrongs are at issue in the thought-experiment, then the apt conclusions about Judith are that she has not held a legal claim-right vis-à-vis X to be provided with her winnings and that she has not been legally wronged by X. If instead the thought-experiment is focused on moral entitlements and moral wrongs, then the apt conclusions about Judith are that she has held a moral claim-right vis-à-vis X to be provided with her winnings and that she has been morally wronged by him. In either case, far from casting doubt on the No Wrongs Without Claim-Rights Proposition, Cornell's thought-experiment bolsters that proposition.

To finish my discussion of the scenario of Jeffrey and X and Judith, I should remark that Cornell muddies the water in a footnote. He there suggests that his scenario is structurally similar to the 1995 case of *White v Jones*, which was decided by the House of Lords in the United Kingdom. He explains: "Two daughters sued after a solicitor failed to follow their father's instructions in drawing up a modified will. The court found that the solicitor was liable to the daughters even though they were not owed contractual or fiduciary duties" (2015, 118 n. 20). Cornell here conveys the impression that, in the ruling by the House of Lords, the solicitor was held not to have owed any legal duties to the plaintiffs. Cornell thereby conveys the impression that the solicitor was held to have committed a legal wrong against the plaintiffs despite the absence of any legal duties owed to them and thus despite the absence of any legal claim-rights held by the plaintiffs vis-à-vis the solicitor. However, by conveying such an impression—an impression that is essential for his aim of convincing his readers to abandon the No Wrongs Without Claim-Rights Proposition—Cornell has strikingly misrepresented the judgment in *White v Jones*. Although the solicitor sued by the daughters of the testator was held not to have owed any contractual duties to them, he was held to have owed a legal duty of care to each of them under the law of tort. Because he owed such a legal duty of care to each of them, and because each of them therefore held a legal claim-right vis-à-vis him, his failure to revise the will of the testator in a timely fashion was a legal wrong committed against each of the plaintiffs. In other words, far from supporting Cornell's belief that Q can be legally wronged by P's φ-ing even though Q has not held any legal claim-right to P's abstention from φ-ing, the judgment in *White v Jones* is fully supportive of the No Wrongs Without Claim-Rights Proposition. Indeed, that proposition is the one thing on which the Law Lords in the majority and the dissenting Law Lords all agreed.

I should add as a coda that, while John Goldberg and Benjamin Zipursky in a recent essay strongly support the No Wrongs Without Claim-Rights Proposition—albeit not under that label—they err in a manner broadly similar to that of Cornell by purporting to come up with a judgment from the Anglo-American law of negligence which deviates from that proposition (Goldberg and Zipursky 2022, 379–83). They condemn the reasoning by the California Supreme Court in the case of *Rowland v Christian*, as they declare that "the Court in *Rowland* scrapped entirely the idea that the power to obtain damages, in tort, is predicated on the plaintiff having a claim right [vis-à-vis] the defendant, and the defendant owing a relational duty to the plaintiff" (2022, 380). In *Rowland*, so Goldberg and Zipursky assert, "the power to recover damages is detached from claim rights and corresponding duties" (2022, 383). Such contentions by Goldberg and Zipursky are unsustainable, for the California Supreme Court in fact affirmed that a legal duty of care is owed by a proprietor or an occupier to anyone who might enter the proprietor's or occupier's premises. Far from suggesting that no legal duty of care is owed, the Court averred that such a duty is owed to *every*one on the premises; the owing of the duty of care to someone is not dependent on his or her status as a licensee or an invitee rather than a trespasser. Hence, the judgment of the Court is fully consistent with the No Wrongs Without Claim-Rights Proposition, and indeed the judgment takes that proposition for granted. Goldberg and Zipursky go astray on this matter because they incorrectly think that the duty of care articulated by the Court is non-relational. They write that the Court "rejected the idea that tort law contains rules that specify relational duties of conduct and corresponding rights. Instead, [the Court] deemed tort law's primary or substantive duties to be nonrelational—to be owed 'to the world'" (2022, 380). As should be evident from §2.5.5.1 in my second chapter, Goldberg and Zipursky are doubly in error when they suggest that the legal duties of care incumbent on proprietors and occupiers in California are non-relational. In the first place, those duties can be explicated in line with Hohfeld's analysis of the owing of duties "to the world." According to his analysis, applied to this context, every legal duty of care borne by a proprietor or an occupier in California is owed in tandem with an indefinitely expansive array of cognate legal duties of care also borne by that proprietor or occupier. Each of those parallel duties of care is correlated with a legal claim-right held by a party to whom each duty is respectively owed. In short, each such duty is relational rather than non-relational. Furthermore, such a conclusion also follows from my alternative explication of the owing of duties "to the world." As §2.5.5.1 has recounted, any such duty is owed—through distributive universal quantification—to every one of an indefinitely expansive array of parties. In other words, a proposition that ascribes such a legal duty to some party P contains a distributive universal quantifier that picks out everybody else in the relevant jurisdiction as a holder of a legal claim-right correlative to that duty. To each one of those parties the specified duty is separately owed, for a proposition ascribing to each party a correlative claim-right is entailed by the proposition that ascribes to P the duty. Hence, both under Hohfeld's account of the owing of duties "to the world" and under my account thereof, every such duty is relational rather than non-relational. Goldberg and Zipursky stumble when they declare otherwise, and they therefore stumble further when they contend that the California Supreme Court in *Rowland v Christian* abandoned the No Wrongs Without Claim-Rights Proposition.

3.10.4 Overhearing a Falsehood

Cornell next presents a scenario in which a new employee of a retailer overhears a colleague telling a customer that a certain bridge has now been reopened after the repairs on it were completed. Later in the day, the new employee—whom I shall designate as "Nerissa"—needs to get to a hospital in a hurry for the relief of her asthma. She takes a route that involves going over the supposedly reopened bridge, but she discovers that in fact it remains closed. As a result, her arrival at the hospital is delayed, and her distress from her asthma is considerably intensified beyond what it would have been if she had reached the hospital expeditiously by taking a different route. On the following day, Nerissa remonstrates with the colleague whose false statement she had overheard. I shall designate the colleague as "Antonio." He tells Nerissa that, because he dislikes the customer with whom he was interacting, he spoke mendaciously about the reopening of the bridge. According to Cornell, this scenario depicts a situation in which Nerissa has been morally wronged by Antonio even though no moral claim-right of hers has been violated.

The narrative as Cornell unfolds it is underspecified. One thing in need of clarification or precisification is the content of the claim-right/duty relationship which Cornell believes to be non-existent. Presumably, the content does not consist in Antonio's abstention from telling a lie to the customer. Although Nerissa in any ordinary circumstances has indeed not held a moral claim-right to Antonio's abstention from lying to the customer, she has likewise not been morally wronged in such circumstances by the sheer fact that Antonio has gone ahead and told the customer a lie. Rather, if there has been a moral wrong committed against Nerissa by

Antonio, it stems from her having been deceived by what he has said. To ascertain whether her having been so deceived does constitute a moral wrong committed against her by him, we would need to know certain aspects of the situation which Cornell has not recounted. For example, we would need to know whether Antonio had good grounds for being aware of the likelihood of Nerissa's overhearing the statement which he uttered to the customer. Unless he had such grounds, his not having taken any steps subsequently to disabuse Nerissa of her false belief is not itself a moral wrong committed by him against her. Such details are vital for the satisfactoriness of any moral assessment of the situation, but Cornell has not supplied such details.

In any event, what can be affirmed is that Nerissa has held a moral claim-right vis-à-vis Antonio insofar as he has had good grounds for being aware of the likelihood of her overhearing his lie to the customer. If he has had such grounds, she has held a moral claim-right vis-à-vis him to the dispelling of the misconception which the lie has predictably engendered in her. In those circumstances, his not having taken any steps to puncture that misconception does indeed constitute a moral wrong committed by him against her; but that moral wrong consists in his having failed to comply with a moral claim-right held by her vis-à-vis him. Contrariwise, if Antonio has not had any grounds for knowing about the likelihood of Nerissa's overhearing of his lie told to the customer, then Nerissa has not held a moral claim-right vis-à-vis him to be relieved of her misbegotten belief which his lie has induced, and he has not morally wronged her by omitting to dispel that belief. In either case, the wronging of Nerissa through Antonio's not φ-ing is occurrent only when she vis-à-vis him has held a claim-right to his φ-ing. In other words, the vignette of Antonio and Nerissa is an illustration—rather than a refutation—of the No Wrongs Without Claim-Rights Proposition.

3.10.4.1 Another Misrepresentation of a Legal Judgment

Quite strangely, Cornell seeks to shore up his scenario of Antonio and Nerissa by invoking the case of *Randi W v Muroc Joint Unified School District* that was decided by the California Supreme Court in 1997 (Cornell 2015, 120). In that litigation, the former employer of the vice principal of a school was sued by a girl whom the vice principal had sexually molested. The student sued the former employer for having provided her school with some unalloyedly favorable letters of reference even though the former employer knew that the vice principal had been charged in the past with sexual misconduct. She maintained that the prior employer had breached a duty of care owed to her as someone who was vulnerable to being harmed through the hiring of the vice principal on the basis of the favorable references. Agreeing with the plaintiff, the California Supreme Court held that the erstwhile employer of the vice principal had breached a duty of care owed to the plaintiff and to anyone else like her.

In contrast with Cornell's terse summary of the case, my summary here underscores the fact that the *Randi W* lawsuit rested indispensably on the contention by the plaintiff that the prior employer had owed a legal duty of care to her and had breached that duty. The duty of care was correlated with a claim-right held by the plaintiff and by anyone else like her. Had the California Supreme Court not concluded that the former employer did indeed owe a legal duty of care to the plaintiff—a conclusion explained at length in the judgment issued by the Court—it would have held that the former employer did not commit any legal wrong against the plaintiff. Cornell obscures this aspect of the case when he makes no mention of the duty of care and when he simply asserts that the plaintiff "sued alleging that the prior employer had wronged her by lying in the reference that it gave to others. The court found the former employer liable" (2015, 120). Although the plaintiff did of course allege that the prior employer had legally wronged her, she maintained that the wrong consisted in the failure of the prior employer to fulfill the duty of care which it owed to her. By omitting any mention of that duty of care, and by invoking the *Randi W* case in apparent support of his own insistence on the possibility of wrongs that do not involve any violations of claim-rights, Cornell conveys the impression that the case exemplifies that very possibility. In reality, however, the pleadings and the judgment in the case take as given that P's having legally wronged Q through P's φ-ing is dependent on P's having owed a legal duty to Q not to φ. In California and in other American states, as much as in England, the law of negligence is premised on the No Wrongs Without Claim-Rights Proposition.

3.10.4.2 Ostensible Concessions and Untenable Assertions

Focusing afresh on the vignette of Nerissa and Antonio, Cornell delivers a putative concession: "There is, I recognize, an obligation not to spread false information negligently. For example, if one is rehearsing a play that bystanders might mistake for reality, one ought to take precautions to do so in private" (2015, 121). He allows that someone could plausibly advert to such an obligation when contemplating the scenario of Antonio and Nerissa, but he seeks to forestall any such move. His first retort on the matter is curiously conjectural as well as tendentious (Cornell 2015, 121): "[T]his obligation does not seem to be the basis for [Nerissa's] complaint. In asserting [her] grievance, [she] would likely be asking, 'Why did you lie?' It would not simply be, 'Why didn't you make sure that I couldn't hear you?'" Though Nerissa might well pose the former question—whether out of indignation or simply out of curiosity—she would be asking it as a third-party observer rather than as someone who has been wronged by the sheer fact that Antonio told a lie to the customer. Complaints by third parties about wrongs inflicted on others are perfectly intelligible and can be entirely apt, as Cornell recognizes. Of course, in the envisioned circumstances, Nerissa has been misled and harmed and perhaps wronged by Antonio's mendacity. Hence, she is not a completely dispassionate external observer in those circumstances. Nonetheless, even if she had not been misled and harmed, she could aptly have asked Antonio—reproachfully or curiously, as a third-party observer—why he lied. His mendacity in his interaction with the customer has wronged the customer, but in itself it has not wronged Nerissa.

Still, although the question about Antonio's reason for lying does not suffice to single out an aspect of his conduct that has wronged Nerissa, the other question which Cornell broaches ("Why didn't you make sure that I couldn't hear you?") is wooden and silly. Much more pertinent would be the following question from Nerissa to Antonio: "Given that you had good grounds for knowing that I would overhear your lie, why did you not take any steps to clear up the misapprehension which I was likely to form as a result of overhearing you?" Of course, an actual question posed by Nerissa to Antonio would doubtless be slightly pithier. All the same, the question broached by me here does single out an aspect of Antonio's conduct that has wronged Nerissa (if there were indeed good grounds for Antonio to know that she would probably overhear his falsehood).

Bafflingly, Cornell demurs at the notion that the factor of Antonio's negligence toward Nerissa is what constitutes his wronging of her: "One piece of evidence that negligence toward [Nerissa] is not really the issue is that [Antonio] could not answer [Nerissa's] complaint by saying, 'I could never have foreseen that you would overhear me.' Even if that were true—perhaps the room had bizarre acoustics like the whispering galleries in St. Paul's Cathedral and in the U.S. Capitol—it would not really answer the complaint" (2015, 121). Despite Cornell's assertions to the contrary, the posited reply if true would be a full and germane answer to a complaint about the wronging of Nerissa. Of course, if the complaint which Cornell has in mind is the question about the reason for Antonio's telling of a lie to the customer, the posited reply does not adequately answer that question. However, as I have just argued, the question about the reason for his lying does not in itself single out an aspect of Antonio's conduct that has harmed and wronged Nerissa. It is a question that could appositely have been asked by Nerissa as a third-party observer even if she had not been adversely affected by Antonio's mendacity at all (for example, even if she had recognized that his lie was a falsehood, or even if she had had no occasion to use the bridge about which the lie was told, or even if she had not become aware of his utterance until the later juncture when she also learned that it was an untruth). A complaint by Nerissa specifically and aptly about the wronging of her would be along the lines suggested in my preceding paragraph, in which case the reply posited by Cornell would if true be a satisfactory response to her complaint. To be sure, in the course of articulating her complaint, Nerissa might well raise the question about the reason for Antonio's telling of a lie to the customer. After all, an answer from Antonio to that question would assist Nerissa in gauging the gravity of the wrong (if any) committed by him against her. Even so, a reproach focused on his wronging of her would be countered by a true reply of the kind which Cornell posits.

Cornell tries to vindicate his stance by differentiating between the situation of Antonio and the situation of thespians who are rehearsing a play: "Whereas the duty to avoid foreseeably spreading false information exhausts the conduct for which the rehearsing actors can be held accountable, [Antonio] can be held accountable aside from that—for having lied and for the consequences of that lie. In this way, the wrong does not seem to be only about negligence" (2015, 121, footnote omitted). Cornell is here conflating the wrongness of Antonio's conduct overall and the wrongness of his conduct specifically in relation to Nerissa. Antonio can of course properly be held accountable not only for misleading Nerissa through his negligence—if he has indeed been negligent—but also for his having uttered a mendacious statement to the customer in the first place. The wrongness of his conduct overall, therefore, does not arise merely from his having been negligent. In that respect, his situation does differ from the situation of the actors. However, what is at issue is not the wrongness of his conduct overall, but instead his wronging of Nerissa. His wronging of her does arise from his negligence (if he has in fact been negligent), even though it also involves his wronging of the customer through a deliberate untruth. Conversely, if he has not been negligent—either because he has had no grounds for knowing that anyone else would overhear his falsehood, or because he has taken steps that should have been adequate to dispel misconceptions formed by anybody who may have overheard him—then he has not wronged Nerissa, even though he has obviously wronged the customer.

In a footnote, Cornell persists with his effort to establish that the wronging of Nerissa is independent of any negligence on the part of Antonio: "Ordinary negligence involves a failure to guard against foreseeable harms. But in cases like the overheard lie, the wrong is not based on a failure to protect against foreseeable harms—it is based on the consequence, foreseeable or not, of a wrongful action" (2015, 122 n. 26). Cornell's radically revisionary account of the morality of Antonio's conduct is suffused with a myriad of outlandish implications. Let us consider, for example, a variant of the situation on which we have been concentrating here. Suppose that Nerissa recognizes that Antonio is lying to the customer, and that she informs Antonio as much when he subsequently seeks to prevent her from being misled by his untruth. Later in the afternoon, she tells her sister Jessica about the lie. Though Jessica is normally a robust person, she is so surprised by the news of Antonio's dishonesty that she faints and dies of a heart attack. According to Cornell's understanding of the morality of the situation, Antonio has morally wronged Jessica and is morally accountable for her death. Insofar as Cornell's attempt to disconfirm the No Wrongs Without Claim-Rights Proposition is built on scenarios of this sort, the attempt is badly misconceived.

Cornell endeavors to fortify his position on this matter by quoting a gibe from Elizabeth Anscombe in one of her well-known essays, where she denounced the notion that "you can exculpate yourself from the *actual* consequences of the most disgraceful actions, so long as you can make out a case for not having foreseen them" (Anscombe 1958, 12, emphasis in original, quoted in Cornell 2015, 121–2 n. 26). Anscombe's dictum is fully reconcilable with my rejection of Cornell's verdicts. Unlike someone who has committed a relatively minor wrong such as the telling of a lie to a customer, someone who perpetrates a hideous atrocity can indeed aptly be held accountable for unforeseeable bad consequences of that atrocity. Let us contemplate here a real-life example. After Islamist terrorists commandeered four airplanes on September 11, 2001 and flew two of the planes into the World Trade Center in New York and one of the planes into the Pentagon in Washington, reports of those acts of terrorism were quickly broadcast around the world. An elderly cousin of mine in Latvia saw one of the televised reports about the outrages perpetrated in the United States, and she became so upset that she fainted. As she fell, her head smashed upon the corner of a coffee table, and she died almost instantly from the wound. Now, although this fatality in Riga was probably not a foreseeable consequence of the hijackings in the United States, the malefactors who carried out those hijackings are fairly regarded as morally responsible for the death of my cousin. Because of the extreme turpitude of their crimes, their moral responsibility for the consequences of those crimes is commensurately expansive. If they were alive and if they were rebuked by me or by anyone else for the death of my cousin, it would be ludicrous for them to retort that her death in Riga was not a foreseeable effect of their actions. Such a retort would be ludicrous not because it would be inaccurate, but because the unforeseeability of the bad effects of evildoing is immaterial to the question of moral responsibility when the evildoing is extravagantly heinous.

As should be evident, the conduct of Antonio in his interaction with the customer is readily distinguishable from the carnage wrought by the September 11th terrorists. Although Antonio has wronged the customer by deliberately telling an untruth for no adequate reason, he has not committed any atrocities by so doing. His conduct has not been extravagantly iniquitous. Hence, when we confront the question whether Antonio has wronged Nerissa through the misleading of her by his statement to the customer, the factor of foreseeability is decisive. Save in special circumstances that are not applicable to the situation of Antonio and Nerissa as it has been recounted here, Antonio has not owed Nerissa any moral duty to abstain from lying to the customer and has therefore not wronged her by telling the customer a lie. What he does owe to Nerissa is a general moral duty of care. For the question whether he has breached that latter duty, the foreseeability of her overhearing his lie and being misled by it is of central importance.

Cornell might seek to turn the tables on me by alleging that I have conceded, with reference to the September 11th hijackings and the death of my cousin in Latvia, that Q can be morally wronged by P's act of φ-ing even though Q has not held any moral claim-right to P's abstention from φ-ing. My cousin was badly wronged by the September 11th atrocities, yet—Cornell might contend—she did not hold any claim-rights vis-à-vis the terrorists to their abstaining from those outrages. Any riposte of that kind by Cornell would be misjudged, for the very feature of the hijackings that made the perpetrators of them morally responsible for the remote and probably unforeseeable harm suffered by my cousin is something by dint of which she and everyone else had moral claim-rights vis-à-vis the terrorists to the non-occurrence of those crimes. That is, because the acts of commandeering airplanes full of passengers and ramming those airplanes into edifices full of people were extravagantly evil, those acts were crimes against humanity in the sense which I have specified in my work on the ethics of capital punishment (Kramer 2011, 231–49; 2015; 2017c, 340–2; 2022, 508–18). Although the specifics of my account of extravagant evil are far beyond the scope of my present discussion, the key point here is that everyone throughout the world owes everyone else a moral duty not to engage in any extravagantly evil misdeeds. Everyone therefore holds a moral claim-right vis-à-vis everyone else to the non-perpetration of any such misdeeds. In other words, the moral duty of non-perpetration borne by everyone is correlated (through distributive universal quantification) with a moral claim-right held by everyone else, and the moral claim-right to non-perpetration held by everyone is correlated (through distributive universal quantification) with a moral duty owed by everyone else. Hence, each of the September 11th terrorists did owe my cousin in Latvia a moral duty not to participate in the atrocities which those terrorists perpetrated. Her having been morally wronged by their outrages is fully compatible with the No Wrongs Without Claim-Rights Proposition, since she along with everyone else held a moral claim-right to the non-occurrence of those outrages.

Again, the substance of my account of extravagant evil—and of the grounds for classifying extravagantly evil misdeeds as crimes against humanity that wrong everyone—cannot be summarized here even laconically. Suffice it to say that the perpetration of such misdeeds detracts from the conditions under which everyone in any society can be warranted in harboring a strong sense of self-respect. Because the perpetration of such atrocities is a repudiation of those conditions and of humankind and is an attack thereon, the perpetration of the atrocities will have wronged not only the immediate victims but also everyone else. My cousin in Latvia was harmed and wronged more gravely by the September 11th atrocities than were most other people apart from the immediate victims and their families, but everyone else was likewise wronged. Everyone holds a moral claim-right, vis-à-vis any prevailing system of governance and vis-à-vis everyone else, to the realization of the aforementioned conditions under which a strong sense of self-respect can be warranted for everybody in any society. Given that the realization of those conditions is set back by the occurrence of gross iniquities such as the September 11th hijackings, the fact that everyone was wronged through the perpetration of the hijackings is entirely in keeping with the No Wrongs Without Claim-Rights Proposition.

Of course, in the absence of the arguments which I have marshaled elsewhere,[8] the assertions in the preceding paragraph may strike some readers as oracular. However, my purposes in the present context do not require the re-elaboration of those arguments here. My aim has simply been to indicate that, with lines of reasoning which I have developed in quite different contexts, I can concur with Anscombe's remark about the bad consequences of atrocities while maintaining that the lie by Antonio to the customer has wronged Nerissa only if her being misled by the lie was something which he could reasonably have foreseen. Because of the vast difference between the heinousness of the September 11th hijackings and the veniality of Antonio's lie to the customer, the considerations warranting the conclusion that the hijackers wronged my Latvian cousin are not similarly applicable to any unforeseeable effects of Antonio's untruth. Antonio has wronged Nerissa only if the duty of care owed by him to her has been breached.

3.10.4.3 The Correlativity Axiom Disowned?

Continuing to focus on the scenario of Antonio and Nerissa, Cornell at this juncture gives the first and only sign that his attack on the No Wrongs Without Claim-Rights Proposition might extend also into an attack on the Correlativity Axiom. Cornell allows *arguendo* that Antonio has been under a moral obligation to take all reasonable steps to prevent anyone else from being deceived by the falsehood which he has uttered to the customer, but Cornell then floats the idea that such a moral duty is not correlated with any moral claim-right held by Nerissa. He writes: "Supposing that there is an obligation not to spread falsehoods negligently, it is not clear that this is an obligation that is correlative to a right" (2015, 122). When he explains why he doubts that the posited moral duty is correlated with any moral claim-right, his phrasing again becomes peculiarly tendentious: "Although the liar or the actor should perhaps be cognizant of potential bystanders [who are apt to overhear the liar's untruth or the actor's rehearsal of lines], a bystander would not necessarily be able to claim an entitlement to be shielded from the falsehoods, as in, 'You owe it to me to do that behind closed doors'" (2015, 122).

In two respects, this attempt by Cornell to vindicate his position is misconceived. First, he again makes things far too easy for himself by suggesting that the rebuke addressable to Antonio from Nerissa in her status as a holder of a claim-right would be an asinine insistence that any utterance of a falsehood by Antonio to the customer should have been performed behind closed doors. Instead, an apposite rebuke by her would have been along the following lines: "You have owed me a moral duty to keep me from being misled by your utterance of a lie to a customer,

[8] In addition to the works of mine cited in the text of my penultimate paragraph above, see Chapters 6–9 of Kramer 2017a and Chapter 4 of Kramer 2021. In Chapter 5 of the present volume, I shall say more about the moral duty of everyone to contribute to the realization of the conditions under which each member of any society can be warranted in sustaining a hearty sense of self-respect.

in circumstances where you had good grounds for knowing that I was likely to overhear your utterance of that lie." A reprimand along those lines would aptly pinpoint the aspect of Antonio's conduct that has wronged Nerissa. Of course, one way in which Antonio could have fulfilled his duty of care owed to Nerissa was indeed to interact with the customer at a sufficiently far remove from her presence. However, there were also a number of other ways—including, most obviously, his refraining from telling a deliberate untruth to the customer in the first place. When Antonio does tell that untruth to the customer in the proximity of Nerissa, the most evident way in which he can fulfill his duty of care to her is by taking any requisite steps to disabuse her of the misconception which his mendacious statement will likely have fostered in her.

Second, Cornell appears to be relying on the Will Theory of right-holding as he denies that Nerissa has held any relevant claim-right. That is, he appears to be relying on the notion that a necessary condition for Q's holding of a claim-right vis-à-vis P is that Q is empowered—morally or legally—to preserve the correlative duty in existence through the issuance of an admonition to P about the mandatoriness of complying with that duty. This second shortcoming in the remarks by Cornell is even more apparent when he submits that the holding of a relevant claim-right by Nerissa vis-à-vis Antonio would entail that the requisite "precautions [by Antonio] were actions the bystander [Nerissa] could demand in advance" (2015, 122). Insofar as Cornell is adhering to the Will Theory's conception of what the holding of a claim-right involves, he is laying himself open to the objections that will be mustered against the Will Theory in my next chapter.

Furthermore, these two shortcomings in Cornell's argumentation are intertwined in the following sentence from his article: "A commonsense inventory of rights—the things that we might reasonably demand of another person—is unlikely to include a right that others not lie in our proximity, or even more strangely, a right that others take due care in arranging privacy when they decide to promulgate lies" (2015, 122). Here Cornell between the dashes again appears to be invoking the Will Theory's account of the holding of a claim-right, and in the rest of the sentence he again is making things far too easy for himself by formulating ridiculously the content of the relevant claim-right that is held by Nerissa vis-à-vis Antonio. In lieu of either of the contents which Cornell broaches, the pertinent content of that moral claim-right is Antonio's taking due care to prevent Nerissa from being misled by his deceitful interaction with another person. A moral claim-right with that content is readily includable in a "commonsense inventory of rights."

3.10.5 The *Palsgraf* Problem

Cornell next turns his attention to one of the most famous cases in the history of American tort law: *Palsgraf v Long Island Railroad Company* (Cornell 2015,

123–5). A man boarding a train that had started to move was shoved and pulled onto the train by two of the railroad's employees. Jolted by the shoving and pulling, the man dropped a package that turned out to contain fireworks. When the package fell from his hands onto the railway platform, the items within it exploded. Either as a result of the impact of the explosion or as a result of jostling by panicky onlookers, a heavy scale more than ten feet away tumbled over. Helen Palsgraf, who had been waiting on the railway platform for a different train, was injured by the toppling of the scale. She sued the railroad company to recover damages for the injuries that had been caused to her through a chain of events impelled by the negligent actions of the company's employees. When the case reached the highest court in the state of New York, a majority led by Chief Judge Benjamin Cardozo held that Palsgraf's lawsuit should be dismissed. Although the railroad company and its employees had owed a legal duty of care to Palsgraf, and although the actions of the two employees in pulling and shoving the man onto the train may have breached a duty of care owed by the railroad to that man, those actions did not breach the duty of care owed by the railroad and its employees to Palsgraf. Hence, although Palsgraf had been harmed, she had not been legally wronged.

Cornell agrees with Cardozo that no legal duty of care owed by the railroad and its employees to Palsgraf was breached by the actions of the employees in shoving and pulling the unnamed man onto the train. However, he believes that Cardozo erred in inferring therefrom that Palsgraf was not legally wronged by the railroad company. Cornell recognizes that Cardozo was relying squarely on the No Wrongs Without Claim-Rights Proposition. As Cornell states, Cardozo's "inference is premised on precisely the principle [the No Wrongs Without Claim-Rights Proposition] that I mean to challenge.... Cardozo's reasoning—that only a rightholder can be wronged—is deeply mistaken, even if it has become canonical" (2015, 123–4).

Instead of continuing to focus on the facts and judgment in the *Palsgraf* case in an effort to substantiate directly his assertion about the mistakenness of Cardozo's inference, Cornell at this juncture introduces a more recent case from the state of Maine: *Flanders v Cooper* (Cornell 2015, 124–5). In that latter case, the daughter of the plaintiff underwent treatment from a physical therapist—the defendant—for an ailment in her jawbone. The therapist allegedly treated her with highly unorthodox methods, including hypnotic techniques that led her to form false memories of sexual abuse practiced upon her by the plaintiff. What the court needed to determine was whether the defendant had owed the plaintiff a legal duty of care to refrain from treating the plaintiff's daughter with dubious methods that could inflict such damage on the plaintiff. Arriving at the view that no such duty was owed to the plaintiff, the court therefore held that the lawsuit against the physical therapist should be dismissed.

Cornell accepts that the *Flanders* defendant did not owe the plaintiff a legal duty to refrain from employing the ill-advised therapeutic techniques which the defendant used on the plaintiff's daughter. However, Cornell contends that the court erred in holding that—even if the plaintiff's account of the empirical facts was true, as the court assumed—the defendant did not legally wrong the plaintiff. For the judges on the court, that conclusion about the absence of a legal wrong followed straightforwardly from their sub-conclusion that the defendant did not owe the plaintiff any relevant legal duty (a sub-conclusion which Cornell endorses). As I have already remarked in §3.10.4.1 above, the law of negligence in England and the United States is grounded on the No Wrongs Without Claim-Rights Proposition. Cornell, who adverts to the *Flanders* case in support of his striving to challenge that very proposition, naturally dissents from the court's conclusion. He proclaims: "I think that it should seem almost bizarre to claim that the father could not be wronged here. This incident quite possibly ruined his life. Assuming the allegations against the physical therapist to be true, I think we would—and should—say that the therapist wronged the father" (2015, 124). Two rejoinders to Cornell's verdict are appropriate here.

First, important in this context is a distinction that has already been highlighted in §3.10.2 above: the distinction between being wronged and being harmed. In the sentences just quoted, Cornell asserts that—if the plaintiff's account of the empirical facts was true—the therapist wronged the plaintiff. Cornell seeks to back up that assertion by pointing to the serious reputational damage which the plaintiff underwent through the defendant's plying of questionable methods of therapy in the treatment of the plaintiff's daughter. However, the sheer fact that the plaintiff has been seriously harmed by the defendant's actions does not suffice to establish that the plaintiff has been wronged by those actions. Cornell does not invoke any further considerations that would bolster his assertion about the plaintiff's having been wronged. He cannot avail himself of the consideration that would most obviously shore up his assertion. That is, he cannot maintain that the defendant owed the plaintiff a legal duty of care which required the defendant not to treat the plaintiff's daughter with some doubtful therapeutic techniques that posed a risk of harming the plaintiff. After all, Cornell agrees with the court that no such legal duty was owed by the defendant to the plaintiff.

Second, perhaps Cornell is correct in thinking that the plaintiff was legally wronged by the defendant's actions. If he is correct in so thinking, however, then he is incorrect in contending that the defendant did not owe the plaintiff a legal duty to abstain from employing the methods of treatment that led to the infliction of serious harm on the plaintiff. To assess whether the Maine Supreme Court should have ruled that the defendant did owe the plaintiff a legal duty with that content, we would need to know more about the empirical facts of the case than what can be gleaned from the court's judgment. In particular, we would need to know more about the specifics of the techniques which the therapist wielded and about the risks posed to third parties by those techniques. Such matters inexplicably received almost no attention from the court, yet they are crucial for any informed determination concerning whether a duty with the content just mentioned was incumbent on the therapist. Instead of enquiring into those matters, the court leant heavily on considerations of public policy. Those considerations do bear upon the existence of duties of care under the law of negligence both in England and in the United States, but their significance in any given case cannot be adequately gauged in the absence of information about the specifics of the activities that have injured someone and about the risks that were known to be associated with the activities. Given that the Maine Supreme Court supplied precious little information of that kind in its *Flanders* judgment, one should be circumspect in one's appraisal of the court's ruling about the inexistence of a legal duty of care owed by the defendant to the plaintiff. Perhaps that ruling was mistaken. If so, and if the other allegations of the plaintiff were true, then the court was also of course mistaken in concluding that the defendant did not legally wrong the plaintiff. Under such circumstances, a judgment in favor of the plaintiff would have been fully consistent with the No Wrongs Without Claim-Rights Proposition.

Cornell does not exhibit any hesitance in endorsing the Maine Supreme Court's ruling about the absence of a legal duty of care owed to the plaintiff: "While the physical therapist did have a duty not to provide improper treatment, that was something that he owed to the daughter. So I think that we should say—as the court did—that the father did not have a right over what treatment his daughter received" (2015, 125). Cornell then brings together his reflections on *Flanders v Cooper* with his reflections on the *Palsgraf* case as he affirms that both of those cases reveal the falsity of the No Wrongs Without Claim-Rights Proposition (2015, 125):

> I suggest that we should see these two claims—that the father was wronged and that the father was not the rightholder—as compatible. It is true that the duty to provide a responsible treatment was owed to the patient. Similarly, in *Palsgraf*, the duty of care was owed to the passenger, not to Mrs. Palsgraf. But these points about to whom the duty was owed—about who is properly viewed as the rightholder—do not necessarily dictate who stands to be wronged by a transgression.

Particularly objectionable in this passage is Cornell's use of the definite article "the" in each of the twofold instances of the phrase "the rightholder." His use of that phrase—a definite description—implies that there is only one holder of a relevant claim-right in each situation, such that the existence of a relevant claim-right held by the father in *Flanders v Cooper* would exclude the existence of a relevant claim-right held by the daughter and vice versa. There may well have been only one holder of a relevant legal claim-right in the situation that led to the litigation in *Flanders v Cooper*, but that point should not be taken for granted from the outset. As I have just been remarking, any warrantedly confident stance on that point would have to be based upon considerably more information than was provided by the Maine Supreme Court. In any event, even if the court was correct in denying that the physical therapist owed the plaintiff a legal duty not to resort to any methods of treatment that could induce delusions in the plaintiff's daughter, the absence of such a duty does not follow from the sheer fact that the daughter herself was owed a legal duty by the therapist in regard to the safety of his methods of treatment.

In sum, neither the *Palsgraf* case nor the *Flanders* case is supportive of Cornell's attack on the No Wrongs Without Claim-Rights Proposition. Perhaps the Maine Supreme Court erred in the latter case when it held that the defendant had not owed any relevant legal duty to the plaintiff. If so, then the court also erred in concluding that the defendant had not committed any legal wrong against the plaintiff. However, even if the court was in error on each of those points, the key thing here is that the conclusion about no wrong committed against the plaintiff was mistaken only if the sub-conclusion about no relevant legal duty owed to the plaintiff was mistaken. Whereas Cornell wants to postulate the occurrence of a legal wrong even where no relevant legal duty was owed, both the *Palsgraf* court and the *Flanders* court recognized that the inexistence of any relevant legal duty entails the non-occurrence of a legal wrong. Whether or not each court was correct in the specifics of its sub-conclusions and conclusions, each was correct in its embrace of the No Wrongs Without Claim-Rights Proposition.

At the end of his musings on the *Palsgraf* and *Flanders* judgments, Cornell declares: "What cases like *Palsgraf* and *Flanders* suggest is that we can have a stake in what happens to another person without having a right over what happens" (2015, 125). However, this closing declaration once again runs together the property of being harmed and the property of being wronged. If I have a stake in Q's φ-ing, then Q's not φ-ing will worsen my situation or will stymie an improvement in my situation. Hence, if I have a stake in Q's φ-ing, I will be harmed by Q's not φ-ing. In other words, the fact of my having a stake in Q's φ-ing entails the fact that I would be harmed by Q's not φ-ing. By contrast, there is no entailment between the fact of my having a stake in Q's φ-ing and the fact (if it is a fact) that I would be wronged by Q's not φ-ing. Once again, then, a consideration invoked by Cornell as a basis for his rejection of the No Wrongs Without Claim-Rights Proposition is otiose as such a basis. Whether I would be wronged by Q's abstention from φ-ing is dependent on whether I have a claim-right to Q's φ-ing; unless I do hold such a claim-right, I would not be wronged by Q's abstention from φ-ing even if I would be seriously harmed thereby.

3.10.6 Examples from the Bard

Cornell turns to the plays of Shakespeare for the final main set of scenarios which he perceives as militating in favor of his campaign against the No Wrongs Without Claim-Rights Proposition. Quite superfluously observing that Shakespeare was "a great student of life's complexities" (2015, 125), Cornell contends that one of the complexities of life grasped by himself and Shakespeare—and overlooked by nearly all philosophers and jurists—is the occurrence of moral wrongs that are not contraventions of moral claim-rights. He adduces passages from two of the Bard's plays, *Much Ado about Nothing* and *Julius Caesar*, in an effort to substantiate his insistence that such moral wrongs do occur.

3.10.6.1 *Much Ado about Nothing*

To understand the excerpt from *Much Ado about Nothing*, we need to ponder briefly some of the events of the play. Leonato, the governor of Messina, has been visited by Claudio and Don Pedro and other soldiers who sojourn at his residence for some time. Claudio falls in love with Leonato's daughter Hero, who delightedly agrees to marry him. Shortly before the wedding is scheduled to take place, the villainous Don John deceives Claudio into thinking that Hero has been unfaithful to him by amorously consorting with another man on the eve of the nuptials. Hence, when the marital ceremony is about to be administered, Claudio spurns and publicly denounces Hero instead of taking her as his bride. Leonato, after initially berating Hero publicly for her supposed infidelity, has come to the view that Claudio's accusations against her are malicious and baseless. When Leonato subsequently encounters Claudio, in the portion of the text quoted by Cornell, he inveighs against the man who has maligned his daughter:

> Marry, thou dost wrong me, thou dissembler, thou ...
> Know, Claudio, to thy head,
> Thou hast so wronged mine innocent child and me
> That I am forced to lay my reverence by,
> And with gray hairs and bruise of many days
> Do challenge thee to trial of a man.[9]

Cornell informs his readers of the lesson which he draws from Leonato's condemnation of Claudio: "What Shakespeare knew is that our stake in actions done to others often makes us vulnerable to those actions as well. We are wronged not only by what is done to us, but by what is done to our daughters" (2015, 126).

Before I explain how Cornell has badly misrepresented the scene from *Much Ado about Nothing* to which he looks for support, we should note that he has here again conflated the property of being harmed and the property of being wronged. Whereas he declares in the first of his two quoted sentences that somebody has a stake in certain actions or is vulnerable to the occurrence or non-occurrence of those actions, he declares in his second quoted sentence that somebody is wronged

[9] *Much Ado about Nothing*, V.i.53, 62–6. Throughout this book, I have used Shakespeare 1974 for my quotations from the Bard's plays.

by certain actions. As has already been remarked, the fact that Q would be wronged by P's abstention from φ-ing does not follow from the sheer fact that Q would be harmed by P's abstention from φ-ing. Q can have a stake in P's φ-ing even though P would not wrong Q by abstaining from φ-ing.

At least as important in the present context is that Cornell has woefully misrepresented the tenor of Leonato's complaint. In the first place, Mediterranean societies such as Sicily during the late medieval period adhered to highly patriarchal honor codes. Under the conventional ethical creed of such a society, a family grouping was a unit toward whom a suitable level of respect was owed. A wrong committed against a member of a family, especially where the wrong consisted in impeaching the honor of that member, was a wrong committed against the family as a whole and specifically against the father as the head of the family. To a family as a whole, under the conventional ethical creed of the society where Leonato dwells and governs, a duty of respect is owed by everyone else and indeed by each member of the family itself. When Leonato rebukes Claudio in the extract which Cornell quotes, he is adverting partly to a wrong committed against Leonato's family through the traducing of Hero. A duty not to disgrace Hero unfoundedly has been owed by Claudio not only to her but also to the family of which she is a member and particularly to the father who heads that family. A claim-right with that content is accurately ascribable not only to her but also to her family and specifically to her father, under the Sicilian ethical credo. (Of course, the language of "claim-rights" might seldom be used in an honor society such as medieval Sicily. However, even if Hohfeldian labels are not typically employed in the Messina of Leonato and Hero, the Hohfeldian schema can be brought to bear on their situation for the purpose of analyzing it. As has been underscored in Chapter 2, analyses carried out with the categories of the Hohfeldian schema are not aiming to track or match the patterns of discourse in the situations that are subjected to the analyses. Those categories can aptly be drawn upon for identifying the claim-right/duty relationships that obtain between parties, whether or not the parties themselves would be inclined to use the Hohfeldian terminology in that fashion.)

Furthermore, even if we leave aside the status of Leonato as the head of a family in a patriarchal honor society, he himself has been directly wronged by Claudio in the aborted marital ceremony. Claudio publicly humiliates Leonato during that ceremony when he thrusts Hero back to Leonato after she has been formally put forward to Claudio as his bride by her father. Moreover, because Leonato is initially convinced when he is confronted with the accusations that are leveled against Hero by Claudio and Don John and Don Pedro, he joins them in publicly reviling her in the church where her marriage to Claudio has been derailed. Having been both directly humiliated by Claudio and egregiously misled by him, Leonato can rightly profess to have been personally wronged by Claudio through the same misconduct with which Claudio has personally wronged Hero.

Of course, Leonato errs in thinking that Claudio is a dissembler. Having been cozened by Don John, Claudio is a rash and gullible fool rather than a liar. Nonetheless, the extraordinary credulousness and negligence of Claudio have led him to wrong both Hero and Leonato grievously. He has contravened the moral duty of care which he has owed to each of them, and he has thereby wronged each of them. That is, he has contravened a moral claim-right held by each of them vis-à-vis him.

By omitting the sundry elements of *Much Ado about Nothing* which I have adduced here, Cornell tries to present the wrong committed by Claudio against Leonato as wholly derivative of the wrong committed by Claudio against Hero. On the one hand, especially in a patriarchal honor society like that depicted in Shakespeare's play, the wrong to Leonato as the head of a family is partly derivative of the wrong committed against a member of that family. On the other hand, Claudio has also wronged Leonato directly in multiple ways. Like the wronging of Hero, the wronging of Leonato consists in Claudio's failure to comply with elementary moral duties of care. It therefore consists in his failure to comply with the elementary moral claim-rights that are the correlates of those duties. Contrary to what Cornell has hoped to show, the situation portrayed in *Much Ado about Nothing* does not cast any doubt whatsoever upon the No Wrongs Without Claim-Rights Proposition.

3.10.6.2 *Julius Caesar*

In his next attempt to avail himself of the Bard, Cornell turns to the fierce quarrel between Brutus and Cassius in the second and third scenes of Act IV of *Julius Caesar*. At the outset of the main portion of the quarrel, in lines which Cornell quotes, Cassius complains that his exhortations in support of Lucius Pella have been disregarded by Brutus (IV.iii.1–5).

> That you have wronged me doth appear in this:
> You have condemned and noted Lucius Pella
> For taking bribes here of the Sardians;
> Wherein my letters praying on his side
> Because they knew the man, was slighted off.

Cornell again does not supply any of the narrative context for the passage which he quotes, but here the lack of the surrounding context is not as distortive. Even in the passage itself, the tenor of the remonstration which Cassius addresses here to Brutus is plain. Cassius is taking exception not to the sheer fact that Lucius Pella has been condemned, but to the fact that his own expostulations in behalf of Lucius Pella have gone unheeded. He is complaining about an indignity done to himself. Indeed, we cannot tell from this passage (or from anything else in the play) whether Cassius feels that the condemnation of Lucius Pella was also a wrong done to the condemned man. What enrages Cassius about the condemnation is that it reflects poorly upon himself as someone to whom complaisant courtesy has been due from his chief co-conspirator. Though he does not explicitly employ the language of claim-rights and duties, the situation which he recounts can be analyzed straightforwardly with those Hohfeldian categories. Cassius is contending that Brutus has owed him a duty of courtesy and of consequent deference to his letters supporting Lucius Pella, and Cassius is thus contending that he himself has held a correlative claim-right to such treatment at the hands of Brutus. Nothing in his comment on the matter suggests that the wrong done to him has occurred independently of such a claim-right/duty relationship between Brutus and himself. Rather, he is alleging that Brutus's condemnation of Lucius Pella has contravened the duty of courteous obligingness which Brutus has owed to Cassius. (The claim-right/duty relationship implicitly invoked by Cassius is a relationship established under the conventional code of ethics in Rome. Since Cassius undoubtedly believes that that conventional code is correct, he takes himself to be adverting to a duty incumbent on Brutus under the correct principles of morality. Cassius errs in so thinking, but his error on that point does not affect my current discussion at all. We can recognize that the claim-right/duty relationship implicitly invoked by Cassius is a product of the conventional Roman morality only. Even so, the Hohfeldian categories are as germanely illuminating for analyses of the deontic positions occupied by people under conventional moral codes as for analyses of the deontic positions occupied by people under the objectively correct principles of morality.)

3.10.6.3 The Killing of a Child by a Drunken Driver

Having introduced his two extracts from Shakespeare that do not strengthen his arguments at all, Cornell then presents a scenario of his own devising. He asks his readers to imagine a situation in which an inebriated motorist has killed a child through careless driving. What is obvious is that the motorist has violated some moral claim-rights and legal claim-rights of the child. Only slightly less obvious is that the motorist has morally wronged the immediate relatives of the child and has perhaps also legally wronged them. However, Cornell proclaims that the wrongs inflicted on the immediate relatives do not involve any contraventions of claim-rights (2015, 126):

> I think any reasonable person would say that [each parent of the child] is also wronged by the drunk driver—just as Leonato feels wronged in *Much Ado about Nothing*. This is not because the parent has a right that the drunk driver not be negligent toward his or her child. And the parent is not wronged because the drunk driver should have taken due care to be sure that anyone he might kill not have caring family. The parent is wronged even though there is no right of his or hers that has been violated.

Chief among the shortcomings of this passage is that Cornell yet again makes things far too easy for himself by setting up a ridiculous straw man which he then predictably knocks down. He suggests that, if a claim-right is held by a parent of the child, it will be a claim-right to the motorist's taking "due care to be sure that anyone he might kill not have caring family." However, such a formulation of the content of the relevant claim-right held by the parent vis-à-vis the inebriated motorist is outlandish. Instead, the content consists in not being deprived of the companionship of an immediate relative through any lethal failure by the motorist to exercise due care in using the road. With such a content, the duty owed to the parent by the motorist is fulfillable through the same pattern of conduct that will fulfill the duty owed by the motorist to the child. Like the duty incumbent on the motorist vis-à-vis the child not to kill the child through negligent driving,[10] the duty incumbent on the motorist vis-à-vis the parent is activated whenever the motorist is driving in the proximity of the child.

Without its risible formulation of the content of the relevant claim-right, the quoted passage is merely a set of assertions. Cornell assumes that a parent of the child does not hold any relevant claim-right vis-à-vis the motorist, and he gives voice to that assumption repeatedly without adducing any considerations in support of it (apart from his misjudged specification of what the content of the parent's claim-right would be). Cornell's view of the matter is at odds with the assessment that should be reached by anyone who combines the Hohfeldian schema with the Interest Theory of right-holding. Given that my next chapter will argue sustainedly in support of the Interest Theory, and given that Cornell with his example of the drunken accident does not provide any argumentation in favor of his insistence that a parent of the stricken child has not held a relevant claim-right vis-à-vis the intoxicated driver, the example of the accident further weakens Cornell's case for rejecting the No Wrongs Without Claim-Rights Proposition.

Before we move on to Cornell's broader philosophical ruminations, we should note one clarification that anticipates some of my theorizing in Chapter 4. Although the duty owed by the motorist to each parent of the child is always satisfiable through the same pattern of conduct that will satisfy the duty owed by the motorist to the child, the difference in the respective contents of the duties is marked by a difference in what constitutes a breach of each duty. While the behavior of the motorist that constitutes a breach is the same in each case, a breach of the duty owed to each parent involves the additional fact that the person fatally injured by the drunken negligence of the motorist is a child of the parent. Hence, when we inquire what sets of facts would be minimally sufficient to constitute a

[10] The motorist of course owes the child a broader duty not to harm him or her through negligent driving, but that broader duty entails a duty not to kill the child through such driving. Here the entailed duty, the narrower duty, is that on which I am concentrating—since it relates directly to Cornell's scenario.

breach of the duty owed to the child and what sets of facts would be minimally sufficient to constitute a breach of the duty owed to each parent—where minimal sufficiency is to be understood in accordance with my explication of that notion in §2.6.3.1 of Chapter 2—we find that any set of facts of the former kind is less expansive than any set of facts of the latter kind. All the facts in any set of the former kind will be comprised by a set of the latter kind, but also included in every set of the latter kind will be the fact that the person whose death has been caused by the drunken driving of the motorist is a child of the person to whom the latter duty has been owed.

3.10.7 Cornell's General Theoretical Reflections

Having marshaled his scenarios that are supposed to reveal why the No Wrongs Without Claim-Rights Proposition should be repudiated, Cornell proceeds to some more abstract theoretical reflections in which he endeavors to distill certain general ideas from those concrete thought-experiments (2015, 127–34). He begins his reflections by declaring that the significance of claim-rights is due chiefly to their roles in guiding the conduct of the people who bear the duties correlative to the claim-rights. He strangely contends that any claim-rights which might be posited by a defender of the No Wrongs Without Claim-Rights Proposition in response to his scenarios would not be action-guiding in this manner. As he asserts: "If we posit such rights [for example, the claim-rights of the parents of the fatally injured child, which they hold vis-à-vis the drunken motorist], we must give up on the idea that rights are normative—that the presence of rights affects our deliberation about what to do" (2015, 128). He allows that his assertion "may be surprising," but he persists with it as he submits that any potential wrongs akin to those inflicted on parents through the fatal injuring of their children by drunken motorists are "normatively inert [in that] they do not provide us with reasons to think about as we deliberate" (2015, 128). He pursues several tacks in his efforts to clinch his position on this matter.

3.10.7.1 Discreditable Origins?

Cornell first suggests that a claim-right held by a parent of the fatally injured child vis-à-vis the inebriated motorist would be akin to the legal claim-right that has been contravened in a "loss of consortium" case. In a case of the latter type, where a person P has been badly injured by some other party Q, the spouse of P is endowed with a legal claim-right vis-à-vis Q which has required Q not to engage in negligently injurious conduct that would preclude or greatly diminish any further sexual interaction between P and the spouse. That claim-right is violated when Q's negligence results in injuries to P that terminate or severely impair the normal romantic relationship between P and the spouse. Cornell correctly points out that a legal claim-right of this sort originated in English law on the basis of ideas about the proprietary prerogatives of men over their spouses and children. He also notes correctly that the tort of loss of consortium has been eliminated in a number of common-law jurisdictions at least partly because of its discreditable provenance. Much more dubiously, however, he contends that the legal claim-rights contravened by the perpetration of that tort—in the common-law jurisdictions where such conduct continues to be actionable—are inherently tainted by the tort's patriarchal history. He alleges that any such legal claim-right implies that "one has a right over one's spouse," and he frets that a claim-right of that sort is thus "a problematic holdover from a time when wives were seen as [husbands'] property" (2015, 128 n. 37). Cornell thereby leaves his readers to infer that such a legal claim-right lacks any genuine action-guiding force because it is morally so tarnished.

However, such an allegation does not withstand scrutiny. Although the tort of loss of consortium varies in its contours across the jurisdictions in which it continues to exist as a legally recognized type of wrong, most of those jurisdictions do not limit the tort to injuries that terminate or severely impair the ability of spouses to engage in sexual relations. In most of those jurisdictions, the tort extends to injuries that terminate or severely impair the companionship of spouses more generally. In some jurisdictions, moreover, the tort extends beyond spousal relationships as it encompasses also other intimate relationships like that between a parent and a child. In such jurisdictions the legal recognition of the tort confers a legal claim-right upon each person, vis-à-vis everyone else, against being deprived of the companionship and support of a close relative through the negligence or other wrongdoing of anyone else.

More common than the continued recognition of the tort of loss of consortium are wrongful-death statutes such as the Fatal Accidents Act of 1976 in the United Kingdom. Cornell is of course aware of such statutes, but he writes as follows: "Modern wrongful death statutes again create an action for loss of a family member, but should not be read to create a right to one's family member" (2015, 128 n. 37). Yet again, Cornell makes things far too easy for himself by setting up and toppling a straw man. He errs in thinking that the Fatal Accidents Act or any similar statute does not bestow legal claim-rights on individuals, but he is correct in thinking that such a statute does not invest anyone with a claim-right to a family member. Instead of being endowed with that preposterous content, the claim-right bestowed on each member of a family by the Fatal Accidents Act is a claim-right—held vis-à-vis everyone else—not to be deprived of the companionship and support of another member of one's family through the lethal negligence or other lethal wrongdoing of anybody else. In other words, the content of a legal claim-right conferred by the Fatal Accidents Act is largely similar to the content of a legal claim-right conferred by a statute or common-law doctrine that establishes the more capacious version of the tort of loss of consortium which has been mentioned above. In each case, there is nothing morally dubious about the claim-rights bestowed. Only by characterizing the contents of those claim-rights with extraordinary tendentiousness does Cornell suggest otherwise.

3.10.7.2 Motivation versus Obligation

In a couple of footnotes, Cornell distinguishes between the considerations that motivate someone not to φ and the considerations that morally obligate someone not to φ. He is focusing on the latter considerations rather than on the former when he denies that the parents of a child who has been fatally injured by a drunken driver are vested with any relevant claim-rights vis-à-vis the driver. He elaborates as follows: "A person may sometimes be moved to φ by considering the potential wrongs that failing to φ might produce. Telling a serial killer that you have a mother named Doris might shake his intention to kill you, but I do not think that he now has any more reason not to kill you than he had before" (2015, 128 n. 39). Now, although the distinction between motivating considerations and obligation-imposing considerations is perfectly genuine, Cornell misapplies that distinction here.

Let us first note an ambiguity in what Cornell has written. If the consideration that inclines a serial murderer to refrain from slaying a certain person P is that the name of P's mother is "Doris," then the motivating consideration is indeed not among the obligation-imposing reasons for the murderer to refrain from his misdeed. However, apart from the fancifulness of Cornell's example when it is construed in this way, it will have become irrelevant to any analysis of wrongful-death statutes such as the Fatal Accidents Act—since the names of family members are irrelevant under those statutes. Thus, although the second of the quoted sentences is misleadingly written, Cornell's example should be construed as focused not on the name of the mother but instead on her existence. What disposes the serial murderer to abstain from slaying P is the fact that P's mother is still alive (and is perhaps dependent on P in certain respects). Does that fact about the existence of P's mother constitute an obligation-imposing reason for the murderer to desist from his intended act of homicide? Contrary to what Cornell thinks, the answer to this question is affirmative. Although there are already overwhelming obligation-imposing reasons for the murderer to refrain from his envisioned misconduct, the existence of the mother is a further such reason. Even without the existence of the mother, the murderer is of course morally obligated not to proceed with his slaying of P; but the mother's existence constitutes a further reason for his being morally obligated not to proceed, even though the importance of that additional reason is greatly overshadowed by the importance of some of the other reasons for the moral obligation incumbent on the murderer not to proceed. Whether or not the existence of the mother is a consideration that disinclines the murderer to go ahead with his deadly malefaction, it is a consideration that morally obligates him to forgo that malefaction—notwithstanding that some other considerations even more stringently obligate him to forgo such a crime.

Given that Cornell is an admirer of Shakespeare, he ought to have noticed that the Bard frequently highlighted the operativeness of reasons akin to the reason constituted by the existence of P's mother. For example, in *Henry V*, after the eponymous king receives a mocking message from the French Dauphin that will precipitate the invasion of France by the English army, he draws the attention of the French ambassadors to some of the considerations that should have led the Dauphin away from such fleering (I.ii.281–7):

> And tell the pleasant prince this mock of his
> Hath turn'd his [tennis] balls to gun-stones; and his soul
> Shall stand sore charged for the wasteful vengeance
> That shall fly with them: for many a thousand widows
> Shall this his mock mock out of their dear husbands;
> Mock mothers from their sons, mock castles down;
> And some are yet ungotten and unborn
> That shall have cause to curse the Dauphin's scorn.

Henry V does not speak these lines in an attempt to convince the Dauphin, whose imperviousness to persuasion by him has been amply demonstrated through the contumely of the message that has been received. Rather, Henry speaks the lines reproachfully to accentuate some of the factors that have morally obligated the Dauphin to be accommodating in his communications with England. Of course, the recitation of those factors by Henry is self-serving as he comes up with reasons for the Dauphin to have been more obliging. Even so, regardless of whether Henry is correct in the specifics of his pronouncements on the morality of the situation, the point here is that he rightly discerns that the losses which will be inflicted on the mothers and widows of slain soldiers are considerations that morally obligate the Dauphin to endeavor to avoid those losses. They are considerations to which the Dauphin should have been attentive.

3.10.7.3 An Explosive Example

Cornell tries to reinforce his theorizing by adducing yet another example (2015, 128–32). He conjures up a scenario in which someone—whom I shall designate as "Kendricka"—enjoys recreational pyrotechnics. In a secluded area set aside by the local authorities for such avocations, she and her fellow enthusiasts detonate their fireworks and other small explosives. Large signs inform members of the public about the dangerous activities that are conducted there. This hobby pursued by Kendricka is lawful, but she is legally and morally required to issue a loud and sustained warning through a public-address system in advance of each detonation. One day, when she has set up some explosives with a timed detonator that will enable her to get away safely, she neglects to issue the required warning. As she looks back, she espies two children who have wandered from different directions toward her medley of fireworks. Because Kendricka has not sounded any warning, the children are blithely unaware of the peril in their proximity. She has time to rescue either child but not both. One of the children is a girl without any living family members, whereas the other child is the son of two adoring parents who happen not to be with him on this occasion.

Although Cornell's scenario is marked by the artificiality that disfigures much of contemporary moral philosophy, I shall here acquiesce in its contrivedness. Cornell observes that each child has a moral claim-right to be rescued by Kendricka and that each child will consequently be wronged by her in the event of not being rescued. (Cornell does not mention that each of the children has already been morally wronged by Kendricka's negligence, which has endangered each of them.) Cornell submits that, if the parents of the boy have moral claim-rights not to be deprived of the companionship of their son through the negligence or other wrongdoing of anyone else, a choice by Kendricka between leaving the girl unsaved and leaving the boy unsaved will not be evenly balanced. Whereas the former course of conduct in the stipulated circumstances would contravene only the claim-right of the girl, the latter course of conduct in the stipulated circumstances would contravene the claim-rights of the parents as well as the claim-right of the boy. Cornell resists such a conclusion (2015, 129):

> The fact that failing to save the boy would also wrong some related parties does not seem to provide any further reason. It is no reason at all. It would be erroneous—perhaps downright pernicious—to think that the existence of the parents can decide between the otherwise evenly balanced claims of the two children. It is not something that [Kendricka] should think about.

Cornell does not adequately differentiate here between the matter of wrongness and the matter of the gravity of the wrongness. Irrespective of whether Kendricka omits to rescue the boy or omits to rescue the girl, she will have very seriously wronged the child whom she has not saved. That conclusion about her wronging of the unrescued child is not affected at all by the existence of the boy's parents. As has been underlined in §2.4.2 of Chapter 2, neither of the clashing duties in a moral conflict is suspended or canceled by the existence and bindingness of the other one of those duties. Even if one of the duties is more stringent than the other, the less stringent duty continues to be fully binding on the person who is faced with the moral conflict. Hence, the fact that Kendricka bears a moral duty to rescue the girl does not suspend or cancel her moral duty to rescue the boy, nor of course does her bearing of the latter duty suspend or cancel her bearing of the former duty. She will contravene a stringent moral duty and will therefore commit a very serious moral wrong, regardless of how she chooses—given that she cannot succeed in saving both children and will therefore have to select between them, as Cornell has stipulated.

That matter of unavoidable wrongness is to be distinguished from the matter of the gravity of the wrongness. Whereas the existence of the boy's parents has no effect on the fact that Kendricka will be committing a serious moral wrong by failing to rescue either child for the sake of rescuing the other, the existence of the parents does affect the relative gravity of the wrongs. Although Kendricka's declining to rescue the boy would not in itself constitute a graver moral wrong than would her declining to rescue the girl, it will constitute a graver moral wrong overall—because declining to save the boy in order to rescue the girl will have contravened not only the moral claim-right of the boy but also the moral claim-rights of his parents, whereas declining to save the girl in order to rescue the boy will have contravened the moral claim-right of the girl only.

Cornell tends to obscure this crucial distinction between the matter of wrongness and the matter of the gravity of the wrongness, when he adverts to the putative "fact that one should not, on account of the parents, choose the boy over the familyless girl" (2015, 129). Of key importance here is the way in which the normative auxiliary verb "should" is to be construed. If it is to be construed as a straightforwardly deontic auxiliary, such that "one should not" is equivalent to "one morally must not" or "one is morally obligated not to," then the alleged fact to which Cornell refers is indeed a fact. It is indeed the case that Kendricka is morally obligated not to choose the boy over the girl, just as she is morally obligated not to choose the girl over the boy. The existence of the boy's adoring parents is irrelevant to the persistence and bindingness of the moral duty incumbent on Kendricka not to leave the girl unrescued. Kendricka faces a moral conflict—a moral conflict bred by her own negligence—because she is morally obligated to do something that is inconsistent with her doing something else which she is also morally obligated to do.

By contrast, if the auxiliary verb "should" is to be construed as pertaining to the relative gravity of the wrongs between which Kendricka has to choose, such that "one should not" is equivalent to "one has no greater obligation-constitutive reasons to," then the ostensible fact to which Cornell refers is not a fact. Rather, it is a denial of a fact: namely, the fact that the obligation-imposing reasons for Kendricka to save the boy are more stringent than the obligation-imposing reasons for her to save the girl. Though no single moral duty incumbent on Kendricka in the moral conflict that confronts her is more stringent than her moral duty to rescue the girl, she will have incurred greater remedial obligations by leaving the boy unsaved than by leaving the girl unsaved. Cornell's fanciful thought-experiment does not reveal a situation in which the parents who will be morally wronged by Kendricka in the event of her failing to rescue their son are without any moral claim-rights to her undertaking such an act of rescue. Instead, the thought-experiment depicts a situation in which the claim-rights on the clashing sides of a moral conflict are persistently operative and are of unequal stringency.

3.10.7.4 The Derivativeness of the Claim-Rights of Third Parties

While continuing to focus on the scenario of Kendricka and the endangered children, Cornell pursues a further line of thought. He notes that any wrongs which might be done by Kendricka's actions to third parties such as the parents of the boy are derivative of wrongs that might be done to someone (such as the boy) directly affected by her actions. "If there were not something to make the action wrongful antecedently, then there would not be a potential wrong to the third party. A potential wrong to a third party only exists if there are already reasons in place sufficient to dictate one's decision" (2015, 131). As he articulates the same point in a footnote, "the wrong to the family member only comes onto the scene when there is already a direct rights violation, and that direct violation provides all the reasons.... [P]otential wrongs only come onto the scene once there is already decisive reason not to do something" (2015, 131 n. 43).

3.10.7.4.1 A First Rejoinder

Three rejoinders are appropriate here. First, although the claim-rights of the boy's parents are contravened by Kendricka only if she contravenes the claim-right of the boy himself, that feature of the situation is perfectly consistent with the fact that the claim-rights of the parents are additional deontic constraints that require her to save the boy. In the sentences just quoted, Cornell appears to assume that the claim-rights of the parents are superfluous and therefore chimerical because there are already decisive obligation-imposing reasons for Kendricka not to leave the boy unrescued. Such a curious assumption overlooks the abiding possibility and frequent actuality of deontic overdetermination. There can be multiple reasons for someone to φ, each of which is sufficient to render his φ-ing morally obligatory. For example, if Duncan in ordinary circumstances makes a promise to each of several people that he will φ, he now owes each of those people a moral duty to φ. Each of them, vis-à-vis him, holds a moral claim-right to his φ-ing. Yet the fact that each promisee's claim-right is sufficient to render Duncan's φ-ing morally obligatory does not mean that the claim-right of any other promisee is illusory.

Cornell proceeds to modify his line of thought somewhat by concentrating not on the multiplicity of the obligation-constitutive reasons for Kendricka to save the boy, but instead on the derivativeness of the third-party reasons. As he writes: "The fact that an act would wrong someone (or someone additional) does not, I think, count as yet another reason. It is not that the third parties are morally irrelevant, but that, from the deliberative perspective, the wrongs they might suffer are epiphenomenal. If this is correct, then the presence of the third parties is not a reason and does not guide our action" (2015, 131–2). The final sentence of this quotation is an arrant non sequitur. Although in Cornell's scenario the claim-rights of the parents will be contravened by Kendricka only if the claim-right of their son is contravened by her, that aspect of the situation does not negate the existence or the deontic force of their claim-rights. Notwithstanding that Kendricka's declining to rescue the boy would be morally impermissible even if the boy did not have any adoring parents, the fact that his parents do exist is something that intensifies the gravity of the wrong which Kendricka will commit if she declines to save him. What would be a seriously wrongful course of conduct even without the existence of the parents is a still more gravely wrongful course of conduct in a situation where it not only violates a claim-right of the boy but also violates the claim-rights held by his parents.

Cornell resorts to some startling assertions as he tries to counter the notion that the parents of the boy hold claim-rights vis-à-vis Kendricka not to be deprived of the companionship of their son through her negligence: "The potential wrong to the parents is not associated with any ex ante claim on your conduct. The parents could not (properly) demand that you save their child at the expense of the familyless girl. Of course, they would hope for such a choice, but it would be wholly inappropriate to assert that you owe it to them to make such a choice. Nor should you consider yourself to owe it" (2015, 132). Let us here put aside the fact that Cornell again takes for granted the correctness of some version of the Will Theory as an account of what is involved in the holding of a claim-right. As I have already observed, my arguments against Cornell in this chapter will be greatly reinforced by my critiques of the Will Theory in Chapter 4 and by my sustained defense of the Interest Theory. Even when that matter is left aside for now, Cornell's assertions are vulnerable to two main objections. In the first place, Cornell has again made things too easy for himself by misstating the content of each parent's claim-right. Although neither parent has a moral claim-right vis-à-vis Kendricka to her saving the boy *at the expense of the girl*, each parent has a moral claim-right vis-à-vis Kendricka to her *saving the boy*. Of course, in the envisaged circumstances, Kendricka's rescuing of the boy will entail her leaving the girl unrescued. However, that consequence of her action is not something to which either parent has any claim-right and is therefore not to be included in any accurate specification of the content of the claim-right held by each parent. When that element is removed from Cornell's specification of the content, the implausibility of his assertions is palpable. Wholly untenable is the notion that the parents cannot properly demand that Kendricka save their son whom she has endangered and whom she is able to rescue.

Moreover, with the inapposite element in his specification of the content of each parent's claim-right, Cornell has foisted on himself a conclusion that is at variance with what he appositely takes for granted. That is, he appositely takes for granted that each of the two children holds a relevant claim-right vis-à-vis Kendricka. Yet neither of the two children can properly demand to be saved by Kendricka *at the expense of the other child*. Hence, if any relevant claim-right ascribable to each child were correctly specifiable as a claim-right to be rescued by Kendricka *at the expense of the other child*, and if we were to accept Cornell's Will-Theory view that the holding of a claim-right consists at least partly in being empowered and permitted to demand the realization of the content of the claim-right, then we would have to conclude that neither child holds a relevant claim-right vis-à-vis Kendricka. To avoid that outlandish conclusion, which Cornell himself aptly rejects, we need to recognize that the claim-right correctly ascribable to each child is a claim-right to be rescued by Kendricka. Each child can properly demand to be rescued by her, even though neither child can properly demand to be rescued by her *at the expense of the other child*. Given that the relevant claim-right held by each child vis-à-vis Kendricka is correctly specifiable as a claim-right to be rescued by her, so too the relevant claim-right held by each parent of the boy vis-à-vis Kendricka is correctly specifiable as a claim-right to her rescuing of the boy. The content of that claim-right can properly be demanded of Kendricka by each parent, even though neither parent can properly demand of her that the boy be rescued *at the expense of the girl*. A proper demand cannot refer to leaving either child unrescued. Accordingly, under Cornell's own conception of what the holding of a claim-right involves, we can soundly conclude that each parent holds a claim-right vis-à-vis Kendricka to her rescuing of the boy.

3.10.7.4.2 A Second Rejoinder

In the passage which I have quoted at the outset of §3.10.7.4, Cornell declares that a "potential wrong to a third party only exists if there are already reasons in place sufficient to dictate one's decision." Heretofore I have assumed that Cornell is referring to reasons which are sufficient in the circumstances to disallow morally a certain course of conduct such as omitting to rescue the boy or omitting to rescue the girl. When his wording is so interpreted, his vignette of Kendricka and the children does involve such reasons in regard to each of those courses of conduct. Because in the circumstances the rescuing of the boy by Kendricka will entail her failing to rescue the girl, such a course of conduct is morally impermissible. Likewise, because in the circumstances the rescuing of the girl by Kendricka will entail her failing to rescue the boy, such a course of conduct is morally impermissible. Thus, when Cornell's wording is construed as I have hitherto construed it, his vignette of a moral conflict does recount a situation in which there are obligation-imposing reasons for Kendricka not to pursue each rescue-omitting course of conduct that is available to her. In line with what Cornell declares, her wronging of the parents as third parties would be derivative of her acting at odds with the obligation-imposing reasons for her not to leave the boy unsaved.

However, Cornell's wording about "reasons … sufficient to dictate one's decision" is more readily interpreted as referring instead to reasons that are sufficient in the circumstances to make a certain course of conduct morally better than a contrary course of conduct. When his wording is so interpreted, his pronouncement about the derivativeness of wrongs suffered by third parties is inapplicable to his own scenario of Kendricka and the fireworks. After all, Cornell believes that the wrongs that might be suffered by the parents are derivative of the operativeness of the reasons to which he is adverting. Yet, when we prescind from the existence of the parents, we do not find any such reasons. There are reasons that decisively make wrong Kendricka's omitting to rescue the boy, and there are reasons that decisively make wrong Kendricka's omitting to rescue the girl, but—in the absence of any consideration of the existence of the parents—there are no factors that would make one of those courses of conduct a graver wrong than the other. There are no factors that would make one of those courses of conduct a lesser wrong than the other, and there are thus no reasons of the sort envisaged by Cornell under my current interpretation of his wording. Given that there are no such reasons, he (under my current interpretation, the natural interpretation, of his wording) cannot account for the fact that the parents of the boy will be wronged if Kendricka declines to save their son and instead saves the girl.

3.10.7.4.3 A Third Rejoinder

Cornell errs in suggesting that the derivativeness of the claim-rights held by the parents of the boy is somehow inimical to the genuineness of those claim-rights. Furthermore, even if his suggestion were correct, some other third-party scenarios would be unaffected—because the claim-rights of the third parties in those scenarios can be violated without any violations of claim-rights held by the parties who are directly involved. Let us consider the following example. Suppose that Jacqueline is a young woman who approaches Marvin, an employee at a television network, for assistance in landing a job in the entertainment industry. Marvin knows that Jacqueline's parents are dismayed by her determination to pursue a career in the entertainment industry, and he seizes on this opportunity to give effect to his unwarranted dislike of them by assisting Jacqueline in obtaining a job. In these circumstances, Marvin has not contravened any moral claim-rights held by Jacqueline vis-à-vis him. On the contrary, he has aided her in her ambitions which are not themselves morally illegitimate. All the same, by acting spitefully toward Jacqueline's parents as third parties, he has contravened some moral claim-rights held by them. Though Marvin in the absence of any special undertakings has not owed a moral duty to the parents to refrain from assisting the efforts of their daughter to gain a foothold in the entertainment industry, he has owed them an elementary moral duty not to try to cause them distress by acting maliciously toward them. Having breached that elementary duty, Marvin has morally wronged the parents. The occurrence of that wrong, however, has not depended on his having morally wronged Jacqueline—for it has occurred without his having morally wronged her.[11] Hence, even if the derivativeness of claim-rights held by third parties were somehow at odds with the actuality of those claim-rights, some situations marked by harms to third parties would be situations in which those harms are contraventions of claim-rights held by the third parties. In such situations, the contraventions of the claim-rights held by the third parties are not derivative of any contraventions of the claim-rights that are held by the people who are directly affected.

3.10.7.5 The Interest/Will Controversy

Having persistently taken for granted the correctness of some version of the Will Theory as an account of the holding of claim-rights, Cornell near the close of his article turns his attention to the disputes between Will Theorists and Interest Theorists (2015, 134–7). He refers here afresh to Hart's example of a third-party-beneficiary contract, which I have discussed in §3.10.2 above. Cornell reiterates what he perceives as the lesson administered to the proponents of the Interest Theory by Hart's scenario: "[H]aving an interest that is protected by a duty is too weak to ground a right. Such a theory gives out rights too freely. Because parties who are not in a position to claim or waive a duty may nevertheless have an interest in its performance, the interest theory seems overinclusive" (2015, 134–5). As should be evident from what has already been said in this chapter about the Interest Theory of right-holding, and as will be elaborated much more amply in my next chapter, Cornell's objection to the Interest Theory—an objection previously propounded by numerous other philosophers in their own ill-judged critiques of the Interest Theory—is based on a fundamental misunderstanding. It is not the case that the proponents of the Interest Theory maintain that one's holding of a claim-right consists in one's "having an interest that is protected by a duty." Rather, as my formulation of the Interest Theory has indicated in §3.1, the proponents of the theory maintain that one's holding of a claim-right consists in the fact that the duty correlative to the claim-right *inherently* protects some aspect of one's situation that is typically beneficial on balance for anybody like oneself. What is disregarded in Cornell's objection (and in the myriad of similar objections previously advanced by others) is that the protection conferred by the holding of a claim-right is inherent rather than incidental. We shall return to this very matter at length in Chapter 4. For the moment, we should simply note that Cornell's worry about the supposed overexpansiveness of the Interest Theory completely drops

[11] Some readers might object that Marvin has morally wronged Jacqueline by using her as a means to spite her parents. However, he has not used her *solely* as a means; on the contrary, he has treated her in accordance with her wishes. Moreover, we can assume here that his personal acquaintance with her would have led him to assist her in finding a job even if he had not harbored any spiteful motivations. Thus, although those motivations are sufficient to impel him to provide such assistance, he would in any event have provided it.

away when we suitably take on board this point about the inherence of the protection bestowed by the holding of a claim-right.

That point is consistent with what Cornell writes in a footnote where he observes that "harm to interests, narrowly understood, may not be necessary for a wrong. I might violate a duty owed to you, but in a way that does you no harm whatsoever" (2015, 136 n. 50). As will be emphasized in my next chapter, my formulation of the Interest Theory does not assert or imply that the holding of a claim-right is always beneficial on balance for the holder. What is inherently protected by one's holding of a claim-right is some aspect of one's situation that is *typically* beneficial on balance for anybody like oneself. In anomalous circumstances, that aspect of one's situation can on balance be detrimental or neutral rather than beneficial. In such circumstances, a violation of the duty correlative to the claim-right will not on balance cause any harm to the holder of the claim-right.

Although Cornell rejects the Interest Theory as an account of the holding of claim-rights—because of his baseless belief that it is overexpansive—he accepts that, *mutatis mutandis*, it is correct as an account of the undergoing of wrongs. He combines those two appraisals of the Interest Theory, of course, through his renunciation of the No Wrongs Without Claim-Rights Proposition. He summarizes his stance on the matter as follows: "In each of the examples that I have presented, the third party—be it Shakespeare's Leonato, the lottery recipient, the bystander who overhears a lie, or the parent of the child killed by the drunk driver—has a major stake in the action of another. And in each case, the third party is wronged not simply because he or she is harmed but because the other person acts wrongfully. The wrong appears to consist in the unjustifiability of the action in which the third party had some stake" (2015, 136). Two responses to this passage are pertinent. First, although Cornell thinks that the listed examples support his rejection of the No Wrongs Without Claim-Rights Proposition, I have shown at some length that each of those examples is fully consistent with that proposition. When each of them is shorn of misrepresentations and straw men, what becomes apparent is that Cornell has failed to unearth any wrongs that do not amount to contraventions of claim-rights.

Second, having spurned the Interest Theory of right-holding because of its ostensible overexpansiveness, Cornell here propounds a conception of wrongs that is markedly overexpansive. Let us briefly contemplate a scenario that will be probed more deeply in Chapter 4. Suppose that Doris under her contract with her employer has a legal claim-right to be paid £700 each week as her remuneration for her thirty-five hours of toil, and suppose that she spends approximately £150 of her remuneration each week on groceries from a local shop. Without any adequate justification, the employer neglects to pay Doris her remuneration for a couple of weeks. As a result, her spending at the grocery shop dwindles to very little during those weeks. Were we to embrace Cornell's thesis that a wrong to a third party arises from the unjustifiability of some action which has adversely affected that third party, we would have to conclude that the withholding of the weekly wages from Doris by her employer has legally wronged not only her but also the local grocery shop. After all, the grocery shop is harmed by the employer's failure to pay Doris in a timely fashion, and the failure to pay her is legally and morally unjustified. Hence, Cornell has committed himself to the conclusion that the employer legally wrongs the grocery shop when Doris's wages are withheld. In other words, Cornell has committed himself to exactly the sort of overinclusiveness which he incorrectly imputes to the Interest Theory of right-holding. It is rather ironic, then, that at the end of his article he complains about a putative proliferation of claim-rights in the ruminations of legal and political philosophers: "Positing rights runs amok in political discourse. The serious injustices in the world lead to a proliferation of rights talk" (2015, 142). What has run amok is his own positing of wrongs.

Returning for a final time to Hart's scenario of the third-party-beneficiary contract, Cornell contends that we should "say, with the will theory, that the son to whom the contract is made is the rightholder" (2015, 141). Cornell's chief mistake here, like his chief mistake earlier, is his use of the definite article "the" in the phrase "the rightholder." A sensible account of right-holding will concur with the Will Theory in identifying the son as *a* right-holder under the terms of the contract but will not identify him as *the* right-holder—because there is more than one right-holder under those terms. Y's mother holds a claim-right vis-à-vis X under the envisaged contract, just as much as Y himself does.

Cornell asserts: "What is at stake here [in Hart's thought-experiment] is hardly just a matter of labeling. Determining who is a rightholder affects questions about who can waive or demand performance" (2015, 141). On the one hand, Cornell is correct in declaring that the challenge of analyzing the situation broached by Hart is not just a matter of labeling. It is a matter of articulating and sustaining a correct account of what is involved in the holding of a claim-right. On the other hand, Cornell's own explanation of the importance of pinning down whether the mother holds a claim-right is skewed in favor of the Will Theory of right-holding. Like other proponents of the Will Theory, Cornell conflates the holding of a legal claim-right with the holding of some legal powers to waive or enforce a legal duty. We shall see in my next chapter how damaging such a conflation is. As will be observed there, many instances of the holding of claim-rights are not accompanied by the holding of powers of waiver and enforcement, and some instances of the holding of powers of waiver and enforcement are not accompanied by the holding of claim-rights. Cornell remains blind to such states of affairs only by ignoring the sundry criticisms of the Will Theory that have been directed against it during the past few decades—criticisms to which I will be adding greatly in Chapter 4.

3.10.8 Conclusion

Although the article by Cornell contains some further insupportable assertions and arguments, I have already said enough to make clear that his efforts to impugn the No Wrongs Without Claim-Rights Proposition have foundered comprehensively. Neither his general theoretical reflections nor the concrete examples on which he relies inordinately are of any avail for the aforementioned efforts. Had Cornell succeeded in establishing that P can be wronged by Q's φ-ing even though Q's φ-ing has not contravened any claim-rights held by P, he would have provided some grounds for doubting the Correlativity Axiom. He himself at one juncture raises a query about the correlativity of duties and claim-rights. However, given that the No Wrongs Without Claim-Rights Proposition has robustly withstood all his striving against it, my rejoinders to Cornell combine with my other lines of reasoning in this chapter to vindicate the Correlativity Axiom. It is fitting that my ripostes to Cornell have concluded with a subsection on the disputation between Interest Theorists and Will Theorists, because the force of my ripostes will be braced by my exposition and defense of the Interest Theory of right-holding in Chapter 4. The current chapter has served to bolster my presentation of the Hohfeldian analysis in Chapter 2, and Chapters 4 and 5 will serve to bolster my defense of the Correlativity Axiom in this chapter. In turn, the distinctions which I have drawn and the theses for which I have argued in Chapters 2 and 3 will illuminate the points of contention addressed by the next two chapters. Thus, as we proceed now to the Interest/Will controversies, the various layers of this book continue to reinforce one another in their interconnectedness.

4
In Praise of the Interest Theory of Right-Holding

As has been observed at several junctures in Chapter 3, not least at its conclusion, the Interest Theory of right-holding has been crucial for my defense of the Correlativity Axiom which in turn has been crucial for my exposition of the Hohfeldian analysis of legal and moral positions. What is more, the central role of the Interest Theory—its role in providing a criterion for identifying the holders of the claim-rights that are correlative to specified duties—is something that is not fulfilled by the Hohfeldian analysis on its own. An account of the holding of claim-rights is thus essential for the completion of the Hohfeldian analysis. Also essential for that purpose is the elaboration of a more capacious version of the Interest Theory, which will be presented in this chapter. That more capacious rendering of the theory covers the other Hohfeldian entitlements along with claim-rights: all the entitlements, in other words, that are frequently designated as "rights" in juristic parlance and in ordinary discourse. (Likewise necessary for the completion of the Hohfeldian analysis are Chapter 5's meditations on the range of potential holders of claim-rights. Those meditations make clear that a thorough exploration of the non-justificatory dimensions of claim-rights and other entitlements must draw upon moral considerations as well as upon logical considerations. Indeed, some of the germane moral considerations are continuous with those that are central to my reflections in several of my recent books on the justificatory dimensions of claim-rights and other entitlements.)

At the same time, while the Interest Theory vitally supplements the Hohfeldian schema of legal and moral relationships by charting the directionality of those relationships—that is, by specifying the conditions under which various parties occupy the positions in those relationships—the Interest Theory is indispensably informed by the categories in that schema. As will be apparent throughout this chapter, the Interest Theory of right-holding relies again and again on the distinctions that are drawn in the Hohfeldian table. Without those distinctions, the Interest Theory could not even begin to play its key role in supplementing the Hohfeldian table and vindicating the Correlativity Axiom. Hence, the current chapter rests upon the preceding chapters as much as they rest upon it.

Throughout the present chapter, the Interest Theory of right-holding is to be understood partly by way of its opposition to the Will Theory of right-holding. Much

Rights and Right-Holding. Matthew H. Kramer, Oxford University Press. © Matthew H. Kramer 2024.
DOI: 10.1093/oso/9780198891222.003.0004

of my championing of the Interest Theory will be concerned with differentiating it from the Will Theory and with assailing the Will Theory. Still, as has already been signaled, the contrast between the Interest Theory and the Will Theory is not the only major diremption within this chapter. Specifically with regard to the holding of claim-rights, the Interest Theory itself is divided. In a significant respect, the evaluative presuppositions of the Interest Theory in connection with the holding of legal claim-rights are different from its evaluative presuppositions in connection with the holding of moral claim-rights. Furthermore, as has been mentioned above, the Interest Theory for the holding of claim-rights (whether legal or moral) is paralleled by a more expansive version of the theory for the holding of any of the Hohfeldian entitlements. All these distinctions, along with others, will be saliently operative in this chapter.

4.1 The Interest Theory of Right-Holding

Chapter 3 has already presented my formulation of the Interest Theory. Here we have to delve into that formulation much more deeply. Let us begin with it afresh:

> **Interest Theory of Right-Holding**: Individually necessary and jointly sufficient for the holding of a claim-right by *X* are (1) the fact that the duty correlative to the claim-right deontically and inherently protects some aspect of *X*'s situation that on balance is typically beneficial for a being like *X*, and (2) the fact that *X* is a member of the class of potential holders of claim-rights.

Chapter 3 has already briefly explained the phrase "and inherently" in this formulation. That phrase indicates that the protection bestowed on the situation of a holder of a claim-right by the duty correlative to the claim-right is not a matter of happenstance. Rather, whenever that duty exists with its specified content, it confers deontic protection on some aspect of the situation of the right-holder that is typically beneficial on balance for someone like the right-holder. Hence, the conferring of such protection is integral to the existence of the duty with its specified content and is not merely a fortuitous consequence thereof. As will become evident in this chapter, and as has been foreshadowed in my retort to Nicolas Cornell's worry about the putative overinclusiveness of the Interest Theory of right-holding in §3.10.7.5 of Chapter 3, the inherence of the protection bestowed is a pivotal element of the Interest Theory.

The protection conferred by a legal or moral duty-not-to-φ is deontic rather than physical or modal. It consists in the fact that φ-ing is made legally or morally wrong by the existence of the duty, rather than in the fact (if it is a fact) that φ-ing has been prevented. Of course, a legal duty or even a moral duty might be given effect through anticipatory measures of enforcement which do prevent any occurrence that is contrary to the content of the duty. However, the operativeness of such anticipatory measures is entirely contingent and is not inseparable from the existence of the specified duty. (Even when legal duties are well enforced, the enforcement typically consists in the imposition of sanctions *ex post* rather than in the performance of preventative actions *ex ante*.) A legal or moral duty in itself—that is, in abstraction from any processes of enforcement that might accompany it—does not prevent actions or other occurrences that are at odds with what it requires. Instead, it establishes that any such actions or occurrences are legally or morally impermissible.

Also in need of elucidation is the phrase "on balance is typically beneficial." Because nearly every feature of a person's situation is typically beneficial in some respect or another even when that feature is typically detrimental on the whole, the evaluations that are essential for applying the Interest Theory to various situations are about what is beneficial or detrimental on balance. Were those evaluations instead about what is beneficial in some respect or another, they would be almost entirely undiscriminating. As for the qualifying adverb "typically" attached to "beneficial," it too is indispensable for the Interest Theory. As will be emphasized in this chapter, and as has been observed at a few junctures in Chapter 3, the aspects of people's situations inherently protected by the holding of claim-rights can be detrimental on balance in exceptional cases even though they are beneficial on balance in the preponderance of cases. Thus, although one's holding of a claim-right always bestows deontic protection on some aspect of one's situation that is normally beneficial on balance, the aspect that is inherently protected is not always beneficial on balance; it is usually beneficial on balance rather than invariably so.

Even the property of being beneficial on balance is in need of elucidation within this chapter. As has been suggested in Chapter 2, the set of evaluative assumptions informing any application of the Interest Theory will be thin and general rather than thick and concrete. Those assumptions will not tell us whether being skillful in the sport of basketball is better than being skillful in the activity of chess, for example, or whether earning a lofty salary in a stressful and regimented line of work is better than earning a moderate salary in a relaxed and flexible line of work. Concrete evaluative matters of those sorts are not addressed in any satisfactory account of the holding of claim-rights. Rather, the judgments about the typical on-balance advantageousness of sundry aspects of people's situations are pitched at much higher levels of generality. Some brief reflections on the evaluative tenets that underlie such judgments will be serviceable as a point of departure for my detailed investigation of the Interest Theory.

4.1.1 Evaluative Tenets in the Interest Theory for the Holding of Legal Claim-Rights

With regard to the holding of legal claim-rights, the Interest Theory rests on evaluative premises that quite closely parallel the thin theory of the good articulated by John Rawls in *A Theory of Justice* (1999, §§15, 60). In his highly influential account of primary social and natural goods, which I have amplified and defended at length in some of my recent books (Kramer 2017a, 325-33; 2022, 507–8), Rawls maintained that certain basic desiderata are conducive to anyone's pursuit of his or her objectives regardless of what those objectives might be. These desiderata are all-purpose goods in their promotiveness of one's attainment of any other goods, and are "primary" in precisely that sense. Primary social goods are the all-purpose desiderata that can meaningfully be distributed and secured by a system of governance. They amount to an array of entitlements: basic civil liberties and political entitlements and civil rights, opportunities for obtaining positions of power and influence, and entitlements to wealth and income. Any of those sundry entitlements will always or almost always be beneficial on balance for someone who is endowed with them. Always or almost always, even somebody who elects to waive one of those entitlements will have been better positioned as a result of having it.[1]

Primary natural goods are likewise all-purpose desiderata, but they are not meaningfully susceptible to being distributed directly by any system of governance. Among them are health, intelligence, and warranted self-respect. Instead of aiming to control and distribute such desiderata directly, a system of governance should be striving to foster strong levels of them among the citizens over whom the system presides. Like primary social goods, primary natural goods are always or almost always beneficial on balance for people who are endowed with them.

Very general evaluative judgments like those involved in recognizing the serviceability of primary goods for the realization of people's ends are what will be required in any applications of the Interest Theory. In any such evaluative judgment, the relevant comparison is between a party's situation with a certain feature present and a party's situation with that same feature absent. If the presence of that feature will typically improve on balance the situation of the party or will typically on balance avert a worsening of that situation, then the feature is of a kind that is protectable by a legal duty and its correlative legal claim-right. Fine-grained evaluative judgments like those broached in my antepenultimate paragraph above—involving comparisons between different pastimes, for example, or between different detailed ways of life—are beside the point in applications of the Interest Theory. No such detailed judgments are needed, and no such judgments would be pertinent.

[1] I make this point at some length with reference to Francis of Assisi in Kramer 2017a, 330–2.

4.1.1.1 Objectivity versus Subjectivity

My invocation of Rawls's account of primary goods, with my references to the ends pursued by people, may seem to imbue the evaluative underpinnings of the Interest Theory with a subjective tenor. However, both Rawls's account of primary goods and the evaluative underpinnings of the Interest Theory are in fact predominantly objective. Though the primary goods are specified with reference to their serviceability for the pursuit of any ends that people might seek to attain, their all-purpose serviceability is a characteristic of them irrespective of anyone's beliefs about them or anyone's attitudes toward them. Rawls's thin theory of the good is objective in that fashion. Similarly, the evaluative tenets that inform the Interest Theory are predominantly objective in that they ascribe typical on-balance advantageousness or typical on-balance disadvantageousness to various aspects of people's situations irrespective of anyone's beliefs about those aspects or anyone's attitudes toward them. When Interest Theorists ponder whether features of people's situations are typically beneficial on balance or typically detrimental on balance, their assessments are not accommodatingly individualized to match the outlook of each person.

Nonetheless, although the evaluative premises of the Interest Theory of right-holding are preponderantly objective, there is a subjective dimension. That dimension has been adumbrated in §3.2.1.3 of Chapter 3, where I respond to Visa Kurki's scenario of anarchists who democratically gain control of a system of governance. Notwithstanding that multitudinous aspects of people's situations are evaluated by proponents of the Interest Theory in an objectively unaccommodating manner as typically beneficial on balance or typically detrimental on balance, one possible aspect of the situation of anyone lies in attaining what he or she keenly desires. That aspect is typically beneficial on balance, even though it is of course not always beneficial on balance. Hence, for example, somebody who masochistically yearns to be subjected to a specific type of torture can benefit on balance from being subjected to such torture. If a masochistic person Damian enters into a contract that legally obligates his contractual partner Gregory to subject Damian to the specified type of torture—and if the law of the jurisdiction countenances such a contract as a binding agreement instead of invalidating it on grounds of public policy—the aspect of Damian's situation inherently protected by Gregory's contractual duty is the subjection of Damian to the specified type of torture in accordance with his desires. Precisely because his subjection to torture is indeed in accordance with his deeply felt desires, it is an aspect of his situation that is beneficial on balance for Damian even though subjection to torture would be detrimental on balance for just about any non-masochistic person. Consequently, we can correctly ascribe to Damian a legal claim-right to be subjected to the preferred type of torture by Gregory, who is of course under a legal duty correlative to that claim-right. (Proponents of the Interest Theory can also correctly ascribe to Damian such a legal claim-right through a slightly different line of analysis. In the formulation of the Interest Theory, the wording "typically beneficial for a being like *X*" is such that it leaves open the degree of specificity or abstraction with which *X* as the holder of a claim-right is to be categorized. Damian can be categorized quite abstractly as a human being, or he can be categorized more concretely—for example, as a masochist. For the purpose of bringing the Interest Theory to bear on the highly idiosyncratic contract envisaged in this paragraph, we should indeed categorize Damian quite concretely as a masochist. That level of specificity, in contrast with an abstract classification of him as a human being, enables us to make sense of his having entered into such a peculiar contract. When Damian is categorized in this illuminatingly concrete fashion, we can readily conclude that the aspect of his situation inherently protected by Gregory's torture-inflicting duty is typically beneficial on balance for someone like Damian.)

What should be noted here is that this subjective element in the evaluative premises of the Interest Theory of right-holding is itself specified objectively. One of those premises is that the realization of a person's intensely felt desires is typically beneficial on balance for anyone like that person. Such a premise is not dependent on the beliefs of any particular individual about the goodness of realizing his or her keenly held desires, nor is it dependent on the higher-order conative attitudes of any individual toward the realization of his or her intense desires. Accordingly, even when the evaluative underpinnings of the Interest Theory accommodate some of the idiosyncrasies of people, those underpinnings remain objective—for the accommodation is objectively specified.

4.1.1.2 Legal Claim-Rights versus Moral Claim-Rights

At present, my focus lies on the holding of legal claim-rights. One of the main differences between the holding of legal claim-rights and the holding of moral claim-rights pertains to the evaluative premises that are respectively involved in applications of the Interest Theory. As we shall see later, and as has already been remarked in §§3.2.1.2 and 3.2.2 of Chapter 3, the evaluative premises that enable us to identify the holders of moral claim-rights include the basic premise that acting in compliance with the requirements of the correct principles of morality is typically beneficial on balance for a person who so acts. Adherence to those principles, in comparison with non-conformity to them, typically improves the quality of a person's life on balance by enduing that life with uprightness. Admittedly, in a situation of moral conflict, non-compliance with a moral duty-to-φ by some person P can be morally better than compliance with that duty by P—where the non-compliance amounts to P's fulfillment of a more stringent moral duty-not-to-φ. In such a situation, P's non-compliance with the moral duty-to-φ improves the quality of her life more than would her compliance with that duty. However, any such situation of moral conflict is exceptional rather than typical, and in any event the breaching of the duty-to-φ by P in a situation of that kind is undertaken for the purpose of satisfying the correct principles of morality in an even more pressing respect. Thus, the evaluative premises of the Interest Theory in connection with the holding of moral claim-rights will lead us to identify P as the holder of a moral claim-right to her own φ-ing even when her moral duty to φ is in conflict with a more stringent moral duty incumbent on her not to φ.

We shall return in §4.2 below to the Interest Theory in connection with the holding of moral claim-rights. Here my concern is to note afresh and explain the fact that the evaluative underpinnings of the Interest Theory in connection with the holding of legal claim-rights do not include any premise about the typical on-balance advantageousness of conformity to the correct principles of morality. In the sections of Chapter 3 that have been mentioned above, we have glimpsed this stark difference between the two sets of evaluative presuppositions for the Interest Theory. Why do they diverge so sharply on this point? The reason is that, if the evaluative underpinnings of the Interest Theory in connection with the holding of legal claim-rights were to include a premise about the typical on-balance advantageousness of conformity to the correct principles of morality, such a premise would constitute an endorsement of a natural-law doctrine—an anti-positivist doctrine—in debates over the nature of law and of legal systems. That is, the inclusion of such a premise would postulate some important necessary connections between law and morality. It would in effect maintain that certain legal positions occupied by people are not legal claim-rights, because the aspects of the situations of those people inherently protected by the legal positions in question are at variance with what is required under the correct principles of morality. In other words, even though certain ostensible legal claim-rights are indeed recognized as legal claim-rights within the jurisdiction where they exist, their character as genuine legal claim-rights would be undone on the basis of moral considerations. Such is the conclusion to which the proponents of the Interest Theory would be committing themselves if a premise about the typical on-balance advantageousness of adherence to the correct principles of morality were to be among the evaluative underpinnings of the Interest Theory in connection with the holding of legal claim-rights.

Let us briefly contemplate an example. Suppose that Reinhard is an art dealer who has knowingly received several sculptures that were looted from some identifiable Jewish families during the years of Nazi persecution in Germany. Those sculptures have been presented to him as a gift by one of the people involved in plundering them from the Jewish families. Reinhard proudly displays the sculptures on an expanse of land which he keeps open to the public during certain hours on most days. Under the law of the jurisdiction where Reinhard lives, he is legally protected against efforts to deprive him of the sculptures. Some of the legal protections are immunities, and some are claim-rights. Those claim-rights are held vis-à-vis everyone else, including any members or representatives of the families from whom the sculptures were wrongfully taken. Now, the aspect of the situation of Reinhard that is inherently protected by those legal claim-rights is his retention of the stolen sculptures or his not being deprived of the stolen sculptures. By retaining some works of art which he has knowingly acquired as a gift from someone who looted them in circumstances of great evil, Reinhard is behaving immorally. When he declines to acquiesce in the removal of those works of art by the members or representatives of the Jewish families from whom they were pillaged, Reinhard is conducting himself immorally. Hence, although the aspect of his situation that is inherently protected by the relevant legal claim-rights is undoubtedly beneficial for him in other respects, it detracts from the quality of his life decisively through its being in contravention of the correct principles of morality. Of course, Reinhard very likely does not care about that on-balance debasement of the quality of his life, and he probably even relishes it. Nonetheless, my assessment of the quality of his life—for the purpose of applying the Interest Theory of right-holding—is undertaken objectively rather than in an accommodatingly subjective manner. Thus, if the evaluative premises of the Interest Theory in connection with the holding of legal claim-rights were to include a premise about the typical on-balance advantageousness of adherence to the correct principles of morality, an exponent of the Interest Theory would have to conclude that Reinhard vis-à-vis the members of the robbed families does not hold legal claim-rights against their depriving him non-consensually of the sculptures that belonged to them. After all, given that the retention of the sculptures by Reinhard detracts on balance from the quality of his life through the immorality of his obdurateness, any legal duties incumbent on the members of the Jewish families to forbear from non-consensually reappropriating the sculptures do not inherently protect any aspect of the situation of Reinhard that on balance is typically beneficial for someone like him.[2] Furthermore, since the prevailing system of governance is morally obligated to endeavor to facilitate the return of the stolen sculptures to their legitimate owners, the aspect of its situation that is inherently protected by any legal duties incumbent on the members of the families to refrain from depriving Reinhard of the sculptures is detrimental on balance for that system. Given as much, those ostensible legal duties are not correlated with any legal claim-rights held by Reinhard or with any legal claim-rights held by the prevailing system of governance, or so the supporters of the Interest Theory would have to affirm. Since there are no legal claim-rights with which those ostensible legal duties are correlated, and since legal duties are always correlated with legal claim-rights, the ostensible legal duties turn out not to be actual legal duties at all. Such is the startlingly anti-positivist conclusion to which the Interest Theorists would be committed if the evaluative underpinnings of their doctrine in connection with the holding of legal claim-rights were to

[2] As I will indicate shortly, I am assuming that the members of the families would attempt to carry out the reappropriation peacefully—though non-consensually—from the open-air display of the sculptures. However, if Reinhard initiates violence, they will of course be morally permitted to defend themselves.

include a premise about the typical on-balance advantageousness of compliance with the correct principles of morality.

Because the situation depicted in the example of Reinhard and the plundered sculptures is only one of countless potential situations where legal claim-rights protect immoral patterns of behavior on the part of the holders of those claim-rights, the point made by the example is far-reaching in its implications. With regard to a large range of circumstances, the defenders of the Interest Theory would be saddling themselves with the conclusion that—for moral reasons—what appear straightforwardly to be legal claim-rights and legal duties are not genuinely legal claim-rights and legal duties. As is evident, the Interest Theory in connection with the holding of legal claim-rights should not entail an overweeningly anti-positivist doctrine of this sort (a doctrine too strong even for quite a few opponents of legal positivism). Hence, we can infer that the evaluative underpinnings of the Interest Theory in the realm of law do not include any premise about the typical on-balance advantageousness of adherence to the correct principles of morality. We have to prescind from any such premise whenever we are seeking to ascertain whether someone holds a legal claim-right correlative to a specified legal duty. Only thus can we adequately take into account the potential incongruities between what the law of a jurisdiction prescribes and what the correct principles of morality prescribe.

By contrast, as has been remarked in the opening paragraph of this subsection (and as will be explored further in §4.2), a premise about the typical on-balance advantageousness of conformity to the correct principles of morality is always among the evaluative underpinnings of the Interest Theory with regard to the holding of moral claim-rights. Unlike legal claim-rights, moral claim-rights are inherently moral phenomena. In relation to moral claim-rights, the potential incongruities between what the law of a jurisdiction prescribes and what the correct principles of morality prescribe are irrelevant. Reinhard does not hold any moral claim-rights against being deprived of the sculptures non-consensually by the Jewish families who are morally the rightful owners thereof, even though the law of his jurisdiction invests him with legal claim-rights against his being so deprived. He does not hold any such moral claim-rights, because the families are not under any moral duties to forbear from reappropriating the sculptures. (Of course, the families are morally obligated not to remove the sculptures in certain specific ways—for example, by thrashing Reinhard in order to get access to them. However, the families are morally at liberty and indeed legally at liberty vis-à-vis Reinhard to enter the expanse of land on which their works of art are exhibited, and they are morally at liberty vis-à-vis Reinhard to take those works of art away from there without his consent. Correlated with their moral liberties are his moral no-rights with regard to their entering the expanse of land and with regard to their reappropriation of the statues. Those moral no-rights are the logical duals of the moral claim-rights which he does not hold.)

This divergence between the Interest Theory in the realm of law and the Interest Theory in the realm of morality is a product of the foremost difference between those two realms. Whereas the former version of the Interest Theory has to take account of the potential incongruities between legal requirements or permissions and moral requirements or permissions, those potential incongruities are beside the point when we are applying the latter version of the Interest Theory to any particular set of circumstances. Hence, whereas the evaluative groundings of the former version of the theory have to exclude any premise about the typically decisive advantageousness of behaving in compliance with the requirements of the correct principles of morality, the evaluative groundings of the latter version of the theory have to include just such a premise.

4.1.2 The Overexpansiveness of the Interest Theory?

Although some further points about the evaluative premises of the Interest Theory of right-holding will emerge within this chapter, we should now move to the objection that has most commonly been leveled against that theory during the past several decades. We have encountered this objection in §3.10.7.5 of Chapter 3, where I have sought to rebut Nicolas Cornell's contention that the Interest Theory of right-holding is overexpansive in its identifying of parties as holders of claim-rights. Similar contentions have been propounded by a number of other philosophers as well. For example, Gopal Sreenivasan—one of the most sophisticated contemporary theorists of rights and right-holding—has opined that "the ordinary Interest theory does not distinguish third-party interests from other interests in the first place. All interests are on a par. As a result, this version of the Interest theory is infamously liberal in awarding claim-rights to third-party beneficiaries" (2017, 136). Like Cornell, Sreenivasan adverts to H.L.A. Hart's scenario of a third-party-beneficiary contract (2005, 262–3; 2017, 136–7). That scenario has long been perceived by the Will Theorists as a stumbling stone for the Interest Theory, and Sreenivasan is sympathetic to Hart's view that the promisee in the scenario is the sole holder of a legal claim-right vis-à-vis the promisor under the terms of the contract. However, Sreenivasan piquantly goes beyond Hart and Cornell by introducing a further layer of the scenario which he believes to be especially problematic for champions of the Interest Theory. Contemplating a version of the third-party-beneficiary situation in which Xavier promises his brother to pay their sister £100, Sreenivasan writes that "it would certainly be the wrong verdict if Xavier's duty to pay his sister were also owed to *his sister's child*, on whom—let us say—she will spend the £100, so that Xavier's niece had a claim-right against him. But the Interest theory clearly appears to yield that verdict as well" (2017, 137, emphasis in original).

In §3.10.7.5, I have retorted to Cornell's worry about the putative overinclusiveness of the Interest Theory by pointing out that such a worry disregards the inherence of the protection which the holding of a claim-right confers on some aspect of the holder's situation that is typically beneficial on balance for anybody like the holder. When we recognize that the deontic protection is inherent rather than incidental, we can discern that the charge of overinclusiveness lodged by Cornell is misbegotten. A similar retort is apropos here, notwithstanding the ingenuity of Sreenivasan's amplification of Hart's scenario. However, instead of focusing on the words "and inherently" in my formulation of the Interest Theory, we can best approach the matter from the other direction. That is, instead of attending directly to the inherence of the protection conferred by the holding of a legal claim-right that is correlated with some specified legal duty, we often can best attend to that inherence indirectly by probing the conditions under which the specified duty would be contravened.

4.1.2.1 Bentham's Test

In my previous work on this matter, I have applied the label "Bentham's Test" to the criterion which I have elaborated for identifying the holder of any claim-right by attending to the conditions under which the duty correlative to the claim-right would be breached. On the one hand, Kurki is correct when he observes that "[i]t is quite unclear whether [Kramer's] test in its current form should be attributed to Bentham" (2018, 437 n. 30). My refinement of the criterion over the years has removed it quite some distance from anything that Jeremy Bentham ever explicitly wrote. On the other hand, my earliest reflections on this matter were prompted three decades ago by Hart's exegetical meditations on some of Bentham's remarks about the holding of claim-rights by individuals (Hart 1982, 177–81; Kramer 1998, 81–4). Although my early reflections have been superseded by some of my subsequent work and even more by my discussion of Bentham's Test in this chapter, the link to those reflections is sufficient to warrant the retention of the phrase "Bentham's Test" as a handy label.

Bentham's Test provides as follows. To ascertain whether someone holds a legal claim-right correlative to some specified legal duty D, we need to ask what facts would be minimally sufficient to constitute a breach of D. Let "*R*" designate the party who bears D, and let "*Q*" designate some party who is capable of holding legal claim-rights. **If and only if at least one set of facts minimally sufficient to constitute a breach of D includes the fact that the situation of *Q* has been affected by *R* in a way that is normally detrimental for someone like *Q*, *Q* holds a legal claim-right correlative to D.**

As should be evident, Bentham's Test is not an extrinsic supplement to the Interest Theory. Rather, each of them is a notational variation of the other. Thus, Bentham's Test is not a *deus ex machina* that is wheeled out to rescue the Interest Theory from problems (problems of overexpansiveness) which the Interest Theory itself is somehow not able to resolve. On the contrary, when we take due account of the phrase "and inherently" in my formulation of the Interest Theory, we can recognize that Bentham's Test and the Interest Theory generate exactly the same conclusions about the holding of claim-rights by various parties. Nevertheless, although they are extensionally equivalent, they arrive at their conclusions from inverted perspectives. Whereas the Interest Theory concentrates on the inherent deontic protection that is conferred through the existence of a legal duty, Bentham's Test concentrates on the conditions under which a legal duty would be transgressed. Though enquiries into the holding of claim-rights can be conducted with either orientation, the orientation of Bentham's Test is frequently more convenient.

Before we mull over an example that illustrates how Bentham's Test is applied to concrete circumstances, a couple of the elements in my formulation of that test should be elucidated. First is the notion of minimal sufficiency. As has been recounted in §2.6.3.1 of Chapter 2, the property of minimal sufficiency is to be explicated along the following lines. A set of facts S is minimally sufficient for some effect E if and only if (1) S is sufficient for E and (2) S does not comprise any facts that are unnecessary to make S sufficient for E. There are no superfluous elements in a minimally sufficient set of facts; every element is necessary to make the overall set of facts sufficient for the occurrence of E. In the context of Bentham's Test, of course, the effect designated by "E" is a contravention of some specified legal duty.

A second point in need of clarification here is the reference in Bentham's Test to *at least one* minimally sufficient set of facts. That phrasing is needed because there always can arise—and ofttimes will arise—multiple sets of facts where each of those sets is minimally sufficient to constitute a violation of some specified legal duty. We shall see as much shortly, when we return to the scenario of the third-party-beneficiary contract and to Sreenivasan's amplification of that scenario. We shall likewise see as much through some of my further applications of Bentham's Test in this chapter.

4.1.2.2 An Illustration of Bentham's Test

As a first illustration of Bentham's Test, we should re-examine a scenario which I have briefly marshaled against Cornell's conception of wrongs in §3.10.7.5 of Chapter 3. In that vignette, Doris's employer owes Doris a contractual duty to pay her £700 per week for her thirty-five hours of labor. After receiving her remuneration each week, Doris proceeds to spend £150 of it at a local grocery shop. Now, the Interest Theory will straightforwardly classify Doris as a holder of a legal claim-right correlative to her employer's legal duty to pay her £700, and it will straightforwardly deny that the local grocery shop holds a legal claim-right correlative to that legal duty. After all, the employer's legal duty to pay £700 each week to Doris deontically *and inherently* protects an aspect of her situation that is typically advantageous on balance for anyone like her. By contrast, the deontic protection which the employer's legal duty confers on a typically advantageous aspect of the situation of the grocery shop is incidental rather than inherent. Even while that duty of the employer continues to be fulfilled, Doris might forgo her usual spending at the shop—perhaps because she has decided to shift her weekly purchases of food to a different retailer—in which case no typically advantageous aspect of the situation of the local grocery store will any longer be incidentally protected by the existence of the employer's duty.

Let us now behold that Bentham's Test (quite predictably) leads to exactly the same conclusions about Doris and the local grocery shop respectively. At least one set of facts minimally sufficient to constitute a breach of the employer's legal duty to pay Doris her remuneration will include the fact that the employer has not paid her. Indeed, every set of facts minimally sufficient to constitute a breach of that duty will include the fact that Doris has not been paid £700. Because not being paid one's remuneration is typically detrimental on balance for anybody like Doris, Bentham's Test straightforwardly classifies her as the holder of a legal claim-right correlative to the employer's legal duty.

Equally clear-cut under Bentham's Test is that the local grocery shop does not hold any legal claim-right correlated with the legal duty of the employer to provide Doris with her remuneration. Suppose that Doris has toiled in her usual stint of thirty-five hours for a given week, and that her employer neglects to pay her for that week. As a result, Doris goes without her usual purchases at the local grocery shop. Each set of facts minimally sufficient to constitute a breach of the employer's duty will include the fact that Doris has not been paid by the employer. If the fact that Doris has not made her usual purchases at the local grocery shop were to be added, it would be superfluous and would therefore undermine the status of the set of facts as *minimally* sufficient for a breach of the employer's duty. Any such fact about the lack of purchases by her at the local grocery shop would be superfluous because the fact about her not having been paid by her employer—along with sundry background facts such as the existence of the contract of employment and her having worked her usual thirty-five hours during the week for which she has not been paid—will be sufficient to constitute a violation of the employer's duty, without the additional fact about the absence of purchases by her at the shop. Hence, just as Bentham's Test unproblematically classifies Doris as a holder of a legal claim-right correlated with the employer's legal duty to pay her £700, so too it withholds any such classification from the local grocery shop. No set of facts *minimally* sufficient for a violation of that legal duty will include the fact that some aspect of the situation of the grocery shop has been adversely affected.

4.1.2.3 A Second Illustration: Back to the Third-Party-Beneficiary Contract

Let us return now to Sreenivasan's version of the example of the third-party-beneficiary contract. In that version, Xavier has promised his brother to pay their sister £100. According to the Interest Theory, the brother is a holder of a legal claim-right correlative to the legal duty borne by Xavier under the contract, and the sister is likewise a holder of such a claim-right. The existence of Xavier's duty deontically and inherently protects an aspect of the brother's situation that is normally beneficial on balance for anybody like the brother, since the duty makes legally wrong the disrespect or indignity to which the brother as a promisee would be subjected through the non-fulfillment of the promise. Not being subjected to disrespect or indignity is typically advantageous on balance for someone like the brother, and he is therefore a holder of a legal claim-right correlative to Xavier's contractual duty. A similar classification applies to the sister. Xavier's duty inherently protects an aspect of the situation of the sister that is typically beneficial on balance for someone like her, since his duty makes legally wrong any failure by him to pay her £100. Because being paid £100 is normally beneficial on balance for anybody like the sister, the Interest Theory yields the conclusion that she is a holder of a legal claim-right correlative to Xavier's contractual duty.

Unsurprisingly—given that Bentham's Test and the Interest Theory are notational variations of each other—Bentham's Test generates the same conclusions about the brother and the sister. At least one set of conditions minimally sufficient to constitute a breach of Xavier's contractual duty will include the fact that the duty has been incurred through his making of a legally binding promise to someone and the fact that the promise has not been fulfilled. Neither the content of the promise nor the identity of the promisee would be included in such a set of facts, because the inclusion of either of those additional items of information would be superfluous. Nonetheless, anyone applying Bentham's Test to the situation of Xavier and his siblings will be aware that the brother is the promisee and will thus be aware that the non-fulfillment of Xavier's promise has affected the brother as the promisee in a way that is typically detrimental on balance for somebody like the brother. Consequently, Bentham's Test enables us to identify the brother as the holder of a legal claim-right correlative to Xavier's contractual duty.

At least one set of facts minimally sufficient to constitute a breach of the legal duty borne by Xavier will include the fact that the duty requires him to make a payment of £100 to a particular person and the fact that he has failed to pay £100 to that person. Here the content of the legal duty is obviously included, but the nature of that legal duty as contractual is excluded, and the identity of the payee—the identity of the sister, to whom the payment was to be made—is likewise excluded as superfluous. Along with various background facts, the two facts specified here as included will be minimally sufficient to constitute a breach of Xavier's legal duty. Drawing on the evaluative premises of the Interest Theory, moreover, we can easily discern that the breach has affected the payee in a manner that is typically disadvantageous on balance for a person. Because anyone applying Bentham's Test to the situation of Xavier and his siblings will know that the payee is the sister of Xavier (and will also know that Xavier's legal duty is specifically a contractual duty), Bentham's Test enables us to identify the sister as a holder of a legal claim-right correlative to the contractual duty of Xavier.

We have seen here the importance of the final paragraph in §4.1.2.1 above, where I have emphasized that more than one set of facts can be minimally sufficient to constitute a breach of a legal duty. In the two preceding paragraphs of the current subsection, two distinct sets of facts have been adduced; each of those sets has been minimally sufficient to constitute a breach of Xavier's contractual duty, but each set has had to be pondered separately from the other. Had I included both the fact that Xavier has not fulfilled a contractual promise made to some promisee and the fact that Xavier has not paid someone whom his legal duty requires him to pay, the overall set of facts would have included some redundant elements and would therefore not have been *minimally* sufficient to constitute a breach of Xavier's duty under the contract. Only when the situation of the brother as a contractual promisee and the situation of the sister as a payee are considered separately, does the classifiability of each of them as a holder of a legal claim-right correlative to Xavier's legal duty become apparent. Bentham's Test classifies each of them as a holder of such a claim-right because at least one set of facts minimally sufficient to constitute a breach of Xavier's legal duty includes the fact that Xavier has affected the promisee (the brother) in a way that is typically disadvantageous on balance for somebody like the promisee, and because at least one set of facts minimally sufficient to constitute a breach of Xavier's legal duty includes the fact that Xavier has affected the payee (the sister) in a way that is typically disadvantageous on balance for somebody like her.

Let us now contemplate Sreenivasan's clever addition to his version of the Hartian scenario of a third-party-beneficiary contract. Sreenivasan suggests that the defenders of the Interest Theory of right-holding have committed themselves to the proposition that the daughter of the sister—on whom the sister will bestow the £100 after she receives the payment from Xavier—is a holder of a claim-right correlative to Xavier's duty under the contract. As is manifest, however, the position of the daughter is on a par with the position of the local grocery shop in my scenario of Doris and her employer in §4.1.2.2 above. Like the local grocery shop in that scenario, the daughter here does not qualify as a holder of a relevant legal claim-right. No relevant legal claim-right is ascribed to her by the Interest Theory, for the deontic protection which Xavier's legal duty confers on a typically advantageous aspect of the daughter's situation is not inherent. That duty can be fulfilled without any bestowal of money (or of anything else that is typically beneficial) on the daughter. Just as Doris might choose to fast for a week or to purchase her groceries from a supermarket rather than from the local shop, so too the sister of Xavier might choose to keep the payment of £100 for herself or might choose to confer it upon a charity instead of giving any of it to her daughter. Hence, although the existence of Xavier's contractual duty may incidentally provide deontic protection to an aspect of the daughter's situation that is typically advantageous on balance for anyone like the daughter, the protection is indeed incidental rather than inherent.

Bentham's Test, naturally, generates the same conclusion about the sister's daughter. No set of facts minimally sufficient to constitute a breach of Xavier's contractual duty will include the fact that the daughter has not received any money. Such a fact about the daughter would be redundant, since every set of facts minimally sufficient to constitute a breach of the duty will include either the fact that a payee has not received a due amount of money from Xavier or the fact that Xavier has not done what his contractual duty requires him to have done. The inclusion of one or the other of those latter two facts is essential for the sufficiency of the overall set of facts, but it renders superfluous any fact about the daughter. In combination with various background facts, but without any fact about the daughter, the fact about a payee's not receiving from Xavier a due amount of money or the fact about Xavier's not having done what the terms of his binding contract require is sufficient to constitute a breach of his contractual duty. A set containing the background facts plus either one (but not both) of the two additional facts just mentioned will be minimally sufficient to constitute such a breach. Were a fact about the daughter to be added, the set would not any longer be a *minimally* sufficient set. Thus, Bentham's Test with its focus on minimal sufficiency excludes the daughter as a holder of a claim-right correlative to Xavier's contractual duty, even while it affirms that such a claim-right is held by the brother and by the sister.

Of course, the votaries of the Will Theory such as Hart and Cornell will continue to regard the Interest Theory as overexpansive in its ascriptions of claim-rights, because they will look askance at the notion that the sister as well as the brother of Xavier holds a legal claim-right correlative to Xavier's contractual duty. However, as has been remarked in my rejoinders to Cornell in Chapter 3, the status of the sister as a holder of such a claim-right—like the status of the brother as a holder of such a claim-right—is perfectly straightforward under the criterion laid down by the Interest Theory of right-holding. Given that the ascription to the sister of a claim-right is something that follows smoothly from the Interest Theory and is something discountenanced by the Will Theory, the germaneness of such an ascription is really settled by the competing merits of those two accounts of right-holding. Later in this chapter, I shall endeavor to vindicate the Interest Theory by mustering an array of objections against the Will Theory. Thus, my present discussion is in part a prolegomenon to this chapter's critique of the Will Theory.

4.1.3 The Underinclusiveness of the Interest Theory?

In addition to charges of overinclusiveness, allegations of underinclusiveness have beset the Interest Theory from time to time. Just as Sreenivasan has advanced some of the shrewdest objections of the first kind, so too he has advanced some thought-provoking objections of this latter kind. For some illustrations of the pertinence and limits of Bentham's Test, we should look at a couple of the efforts by Sreenivasan to show that the Interest Theory is underinclusive.

4.1.3.1 A Third Illustration of Bentham's Test: Another Vignette from Sreenivasan

Sreenivasan envisions a situation in which Muhammad Ali and Joe Frazier are participating in a boxing match (2017, 144–6). Outside the confines of a boxing match, Ali owes Frazier a duty not to punch him unprovokedly, and Frazier owes Ali a cognate duty. Each of them is therefore the holder of a claim-right correlative to the other's duty. In the context of the boxing bout between the two men, however, each of them has waived the other's duty for the duration of each round within the bout. Consequently, the claim-right of each man not to be punched unprovokedly by the other man is suspended for the duration of each round.

This unremarkable description of the fight between Ali and Frazier does not appear to pose any problems for the Interest Theory as an account of the holding of claim-rights. Nevertheless, Sreenivasan attempts to parlay it into an attack on the Interest Theory as he observes that the detriment which Frazier undergoes through being punched by Ali does not depend on whether the punch occurs during or after a round of the bout. Sreenivasan writes as follows (2017, 145, emphases in original):

> If Muhammad punches Joe, Joe will suffer some specific detriment; that is, some interest of Joe's will be set back (it does not matter which one). Let us call his detriment, "being stung." Crucially, the timing of Muhammad's punch makes *no* difference to Joe's interest. Whether Muhammad punches Joe during the round or after the bell, the detriment Joe will suffer is exactly the same.... Joe's having been stung cannot itself "suffice to establish" that Muhammad breached his duty, even if it occurs after the bell, since if it had occurred during the round there would have been no such breach to establish. Properly to establish a breach of Muhammad's duty, one has explicitly to include the fact that Joe was stung *after the bell* (or before the clapping of hands). Alternatively, if Joe was stung after the bell, and the fact that he was stung is taken, without reference to its timing, as sufficient to establish a breach of Muhammad's duty, then the fact that Joe was stung during the round must similarly be taken as sufficient to establish a breach of Muhammad's duty. But this, of course, would be the wrong result.

Despite what Sreenivasan presumes, his scenario of Frazier and Ali is handled with consummate ease by Bentham's Test. Every set of facts minimally sufficient for a violation of Ali's duty not to punch Frazier unprovokedly will include the fact that the duty has not temporarily or permanently gone out of existence at the time of the conduct that constitutes the violation. Sreenivasan is correct in asserting that Frazier's having been jolted by a punch from Ali is not itself sufficient to establish that Ali has transgressed the duty which I have just mentioned, but Sreenivasan errs in thinking that that point is somehow problematic for Bentham's Test. Suppose first that the jolting punch by Ali occurs after the bell has rung to signal the end of a round in the Frazier/Ali bout. When the fact about Frazier's being hit unprovokedly by Ali is combined with various background facts and with the fact that Ali's duty to refrain from punching Frazier unprovokedly was not temporarily or permanently inexistent at the time when the punch was thrown, the combined set of facts will be minimally sufficient to constitute a breach of Ali's duty. Now suppose instead that the stinging punch by Ali has occurred during a round of the boxing match. When the fact about Frazier's being hit unprovokedly by Ali is combined with various background facts and with the fact that Ali's duty to refrain from punching Frazier unprovokedly had temporarily gone out of existence at the time when the punch was thrown, the combined set of facts will not be sufficient—and will therefore not be minimally sufficient—to constitute a transgression of Ali's duty to refrain from punching Frazier unprovokedly.

Of course, in each of these two cases, Frazier undergoes a detriment by dint of being thwacked with a punch from Ali. However, only in the first of the two cases is his undergoing of that detriment encompassed within a set of facts minimally sufficient for a breach of Ali's duty not to punch Frazier unprovokedly. In the second of the two cases there is no such set, because Ali's duty does not exist in that second case. Thus, only in the first of the two cases—namely, the situation where Frazier's undergoing of a detriment is an element in a set of facts minimally sufficient for a transgression of Ali's duty—does Frazier hold a claim-right, a breached claim-right, that is correlative to Ali's duty. In the second of the two cases Frazier does not hold such a claim-right, because Ali's duty not to punch him unprovokedly has temporarily ceased to exist in that second case.

In sum, contrary to what Sreenivasan has supposed, Bentham's Test yields exactly the correct conclusions about Frazier and Ali. It generates the conclusion that, when Ali throws his punch after a round of the boxing match has ended, the punch contravenes a claim-right held by Frazier vis-à-vis Ali not to be hit unprovokedly. Bentham's Test likewise generates the conclusion that, when Ali throws his punch during a round of the boxing match, the punch has not contravened any claim-right held by Frazier. These correct conclusions emerge straightforwardly because Bentham's Test maintains that every set of facts minimally sufficient for a violation of Ali's duty to refrain from hitting Frazier unprovokedly will include the fact that that duty has not temporarily or permanently ceased to exist at the time of the specified violation. Because this fact about the non-cessation and non-suspension of the duty is fully taken into account by Bentham's Test, someone who has recourse to that test can readily see that the timing of any punch thrown by Ali is crucial in determining whether the punch has contravened a claim-right held by Frazier. In other words, the very consideration which Sreenivasan himself highlights as pivotal—the consideration of timing—is central to the way in which the exponents of Bentham's Test will come to grips with the scenario of Frazier and Ali. Sreenivasan has gone astray in presuming otherwise.[3]

4.1.3.2 Bentham's Test and the Personal/Vicarious Distinction

In an earlier article, Sreenivasan has expanded on Hart's scenario of a third-party-beneficiary contract in a manner that will lead me here to follow through on what has been said in the opening sentence of §4.1.2 above. That is, to rise to the challenge posed by Sreenivasan's embellishment of Hart's scenario, I shall need to elaborate on the evaluative premises of the Interest Theory. In his version of the Hartian scenario, Sreenivasan envisages a situation in which a person *X* has entered into a contract with her brother that obligates her to pay £100 to their sister (2005, 263-4). Like Hart, Sreenivasan believes that the Interest Theory does not handle this basic third-party-beneficiary contract adequately, but his innovation here—like his innovation in the third-party scenario involving Xavier, which we have already examined—arises from his going beyond the three parties in the situation to a fourth party. He asks his readers to suppose that those three parties have a grandmother. Now, as far as the terms of the contract are concerned, the grandmother can remain wholly unaware of the existence of the contract, and she can remain wholly unaware of the fulfillment or breaching of the contractual promise by *X*. In addition, the terms of the contract do not require that the grandmother undergo any personal benefit from the fulfillment of those terms. Her standing as a moral agent, in contrast with the standing of the brother as a moral agent to whom a promise has been made, is not at stake in *X*'s keeping or breaking of that promise. Nor must the grandmother be made financially better off in any respect through the keeping of that promise. Instead, the sole way in which the keeping of the promise will inherently benefit her is that it will benefit a close relative of hers (namely, her granddaughter). If *X* reneges on the promise, she will have deprived the grandmother of that benefit. Hence, according to Sreenivasan, Bentham's Test will conclude that the grandmother holds a claim-right to the fulfilling of the contractual duty by *X*. After all, every set of facts minimally sufficient to constitute a breach of that duty by *X* will include the fact that *X* has not paid the money to the sister which *X* has promised to pay. Thus, every such set of facts will include a fact that can be construed as the imposition of a detriment upon the grandmother, and so she might appear to qualify under Bentham's Test as a holder of a claim-right to *X*'s paying the sister the promised amount of money.

In a highly incisive article, Kurki has submitted that Sreenivasan's line of reasoning can be parried through a proper application of Bentham's Test. Kurki writes as follows (2018, 441–2, emphases in original):

[3] As Kurki has rightly observed (2018, 441 n. 41), the main reason why Sreenivasan stumbles is that he concentrates in 2017 on my earliest version of Bentham's Test without showing any awareness of my reformulation of the test in 2010 to focus it on minimal sufficiency.

> Consider these two statements:
> (a) [*X*] has not paid the agreed-upon £100 to [her sister].
> (b) [The grandmother's] interests as a grandmother are set back because of (a).
> By establishing (b), we have also established (a). Establishing (b) is hence *sufficient* for establishing the contravention, but it is not *minimally* sufficient—we can do without (b) when establishing the breach of duty.

Kurki's argument is not adequate, however, to dispel Sreenivasan's challenge entirely. What Kurki does cogently establish is that any reference to the grandmother would be superfluous when we are ascertaining the conditions minimally sufficient for a breach of the promissory duty which *X* owes to her brother and to her sister, whose situations are inherently protected by the duty in some aspects that are typically advantageous on balance. However, that correct point by Kurki does not preclude the possibility that *X* owes the grandmother a fourth-party duty akin to the third-party duties which I have pondered in my critique of Cornell in Chapter 3. Let us recall here that, both as a matter of morality and as a matter of law in any jurisdiction where a wrongful-death statute protects people against being deprived of the companionship of their immediate relatives through the misconduct (such as drunken driving) of other people, the parties protected are holders of claim-rights against being so deprived. Those parties hold moral claim-rights, and—in any jurisdiction of the kind just broached—they hold legal claim-rights. So I have argued in opposition to Cornell, in Chapter 3.

Now, Bentham's Test does not in itself exclude the owing of a fourth-party duty to the grandmother by *X*. Instead, Bentham's Test simply enables us to recognize that—as Kurki contends—no reference to the grandmother is included in any set of facts minimally sufficient for a breach of the promissory duty owed by *X* to her brother and to her sister. If there were additionally a fourth-party duty owed by *X* to the grandmother, then at least one set of facts (indeed, every set of facts) minimally sufficient for a violation of that extra duty would have to include the fact that the violation has affected the situation of a close relative of the grandmother in a way that is typically detrimental on balance for anybody like that relative and thus typically detrimental on balance for anybody like the grandmother. Bentham's Test is consistent with the existence of such a duty, though it is also of course consistent with the absence of such a duty. Bentham's Test tells us how to identify the holder of a claim-right that is correlative to any specified duty, but it does not in itself tell us whether some particular specified duty actually exists.

Accordingly, contrary to what Kurki suggests, the question whether the grandmother holds a relevant claim-right vis-à-vis *X* in Sreenivasan's scenario is not settled by Bentham's Test. Bentham's Test does not per se tell us whether a duty owed by *X* to the grandmother in that scenario actually exists or not. Like Kurki and Sreenivasan, I believe that no such duty exists and that the grandmother therefore does not hold any claim-right to the benefiting of her granddaughter through the fulfilling of *X*'s promissory commitment. By contrast, I have argued in Chapter 3 that the parents of a child who is killed by the careless driving of an inebriated motorist have held claim-rights vis-à-vis the motorist not to be deprived of their child through the motorist's misconduct. Why is there such a difference between the holding of relevant claim-rights vis-à-vis the motorist by the parents as third parties and the absence of any relevant claim-right held vis-à-vis *X* by the grandmother as a fourth party? Bentham's Test does not provide an answer to this question, which is instead answerable by reference to a distinction that I first drew nearly two decades ago: a distinction between personal benefits and purely vicarious benefits (Kramer and Steiner 2007, 302–4).

In Sreenivasan's scenario as I am construing it here, the promissory duty incumbent on *X* does not require her to make the grandmother aware of the existence or fulfillment of that duty in any way, and it does not require *X* or anyone else to confer financial benefits or any other benefits upon the grandmother. Instead, the duty only requires *X* to keep her promise by paying £100 to her sister. Hence, as I have said above, the sole aspect of the situation of the grandmother that is inherently protected by the existence of *X*'s duty is the benefiting of someone who is closely related to the grandmother (namely, her granddaughter). That aspect of the situation of the grandmother resides wholly in the fact that a typically advantageous aspect of someone else's situation is furthered. Such an aspect of the situation of the grandmother, however, is insufficient to qualify her under the Interest Theory as a holder of a claim-right correlative to a fourth-party duty borne by *X*. What is needed under the Interest Theory is a personal interest, rather than a purely vicarious interest, in the existence and fulfillment of a specified duty. The mere fact that the fulfillment of *X*'s promissory duty D would affect the situation of a person other than the grandmother in a fashion that is typically beneficial on balance for anyone like that other person, coupled with the fact that the other person is a close relative of the grandmother, does not suffice to endow the grandmother with any personal interest—any non-vicarious interest—in the benefiting of that other person through the fulfillment of D. If the grandmother is to hold a claim-right correlative to a fourth-party duty, her inherent stake in the benefiting of her granddaughter through the fulfillment of D must go beyond the fact that the granddaughter herself has an inherent stake in the fulfillment of D.

Of course, to say as much is not to say that the grandmother's inherent stake in the benefiting of her granddaughter through the fulfillment of D would have to be selfish in any way. A variant of Sreenivasan's scenario can serve to underscore this point. Suppose that *X* has promised her brother not only to pay her sister £100 but also to inform their grandmother that such a payment has been made. *X* owes her brother two duties: a duty to make the payment (D_1), and a duty to inform the grandmother of the payment (D_2). The grandmother does not hold any claim-right correlative to D_1, since no typically advantageous aspect of her situation is inherently protected by D_1. She does not have any non-vicarious stake in the fulfillment of that duty. She does, however, hold a claim-right correlative to D_2. She has a direct personal interest in the fulfillment of that latter duty, since it is normally beneficial on balance for a human being to receive true information about some good fortune undergone by a close relative. In this situation, nonetheless, the personal stake of the grandmother in the matter may very well be entirely altruistic. She may very likely expect no financial gain or other material benefit for herself whatsoever, as the only benefit accruing to her through her receipt of the information is the gratification derived from knowing that her granddaughter has fared well. All the same, an altruistic stake in the matter is a personal stake of the sort required for the holding of a claim-right. It is not a purely vicarious interest, for it goes beyond the sheer fact that the granddaughter will have been made better off through the payment of £100 from *X*. The situation of the grandmother herself will typically have been improved on balance through the fulfillment of D_2, even if the improvement consists solely in the altruistic gratification which the news about her granddaughter will elicit in her. (Quite immaterial for my purposes here, incidentally, is the fact that D_2 cannot be fulfilled unless D_1 is fulfilled. I could easily modify the scenario to eliminate that feature of it. For example, *X* could have promised her brother not only to pay £100 to their sister but also to inform their grandmother that the sister has now fully recovered after a long spell of illness.)

When we take on board the distinction between personal benefits and purely vicarious benefits—or personal interests and purely vicarious interests—we can readily discern the difference between Sreenivasan's scenario of the promise by *X* and Cornell's scenario of the child killed by a drunken motorist. In the version of the former scenario on which we have been principally concentrating here, the lone interest of the grandmother inherently protected by the existence of *X*'s promissory duty is a purely vicarious interest. That is, it resides wholly in the fact that the receipt of £100 by the sister is typically beneficial on balance for anyone like her. No typically advantageous aspect of the situation of the grandmother, apart from the purely vicarious aspect just mentioned, is inherently protected by the existence of the promissory duty. Consequently, there is no basis for the proposition that the grandmother holds a fourth-party claim-right to the benefiting of her granddaughter through the fulfilling of that promissory duty. By contrast, in Cornell's scenario the aspect of the situation of each parent that is inherently protected through the existence of the third-party duty owed by the motorist to each parent is a desideratum that consists in not being deprived of the companionship of a child through the negligence or other wrongdoing of somebody else. That aspect of the situation of each parent goes far beyond the mere fact that the situation of the child will inherently have been affected in a typically beneficial way by the fulfillment of the motorist's duty not to kill the child through negligent driving. Rather, the aspect of the situation of each parent that is inherently protected by the existence of the motorist's third-party duty is a major personal stake in the fulfillment of that duty. Whereas the duty owed by *X* to her brother and sister in Sreenivasan's vignette can be fully satisfied without affecting the personal situation of an existent grandmother in any non-vicarious way that is typically beneficial on balance, the satisfaction of the duty owed by the motorist to the child in Cornell's vignette would inherently affect not only the personal situation of the child but also the personal situation of any existent parent in a fashion that is normally beneficial on balance. Only by fulfilling the duty owed to the child can the motorist fulfill the duty owed to each parent not to deprive him or her of the companionship of the child through drunken negligence. Not being deprived of the companionship of one's child through somebody else's misconduct is a precious personal benefit indeed. Worth emphasizing again, however, is that my characterization of it as a personal benefit does not imply that the orientation of a person in undergoing it is perforce self-centered. On the contrary, the status of that benefit as personal is entirely consistent with the likelihood that the orientation of each parent in Cornell's scenario is exclusively or predominantly altruistic. Even so, somebody who possesses such an orientation in undergoing a personal benefit is still thereby undergoing a personal benefit.

Would Sreenivasan be warranted if he were to allege that I have resorted to an arbitrary stipulation when I contend that, under the Interest Theory, the holding of a claim-right by some person does not follow from the fact that a purely vicarious interest of that person is inherently protected through the existence of a duty incumbent on someone else? Is the distinction between personal benefits and purely vicarious benefits arbitrarily stipulative? No such retort by Sreenivasan would be warranted, and no such retort from him is likely—since my recourse to the personal/vicarious distinction has drawn on an insight about right-holding that is also drawn upon by him in his critique of Joseph Raz's interest theory of rights. Sreenivasan maintains that Raz's account of rights "fails to take the *status* of right-holder seriously enough." He proclaims: "Assignments of this status—that is, the vesting of an individual with a given claim-right—should reflect nothing apart from the *intrinsic* standing of the individual who is to possess it" (2005, 266, emphases in original). To be sure, Sreenivasan is like Raz in concentrating on the justifications for the existence of duties. By contrast, as has been affirmed in my opening chapter and as will be discussed further in this chapter, my own reflections on claim-rights and other entitlements are non-justificatory. Nonetheless, Sreenivasan's point about the integral connection between the holding of a claim-right by some party and the standing of that party as an individual or a collectivity or a non-human animal is likewise central to my own account of the holding of claim-rights. When supporters of the Interest Theory ascribe to some party P a claim-right correlated with a specified duty D, they are presuming that D inherently protects some aspect of P's situation that on balance is typically of personal benefit for P rather than typically of benefit for P in a purely vicarious manner only. Those supporters are not presuming, or are not merely presuming, that D inherently protects a typically beneficial aspect of the situation of some party other than P. An interest that accounts for an ascription to P of a claim-right—an interest that might be altruistically oriented, of course—has to be one of P's own interests rather than one of the interests of somebody else.

On the one hand, I can happily grant that there is a sense of the word "interest" such that a benefit conferred on a close relative or a close friend of P is in P's interest simply by dint of the benefit's occurrence (and thus independently of P's ever learning of the occurrence or ever deriving any personal gratification or gain from it). On the other hand, a purely vicarious interest of that sort is not what is covered by the Interest Theory with its reference to some aspect of P's situation that is typically advantageous on balance for anyone like P. I have not in this subsection been trying to propound a linguistic thesis about the word "interest." Rather, I am propounding a substantive thesis about the distinctiveness of claim-rights and of other entitlements that are commonly designated as "rights." As Sreenivasan has aptly insisted in his rejoinder to Raz, any felicitous attribution to P of a claim-right will regard P as more than a sheer extension of somebody else. Any ascription to P of a claim-right considers P in his or her own right, so to speak. I agree with Sreenivasan on that point, and I therefore conclude that his scenario of *X*'s promise does not depict a situation in which the grandmother holds a claim-right that is correlative to a fourth-party duty borne by *X*. There is no such duty, and there is no such claim-right. Although the grandmother might conceivably benefit personally in some way from *X*'s compliance with the promissory obligation owed to the brother and to the sister, any such benefit to the grandmother is incidental rather than inherent to the compliance. The sole aspect of the situation of the grandmother that is inherently protected by the existence of *X*'s promissory obligation is something imputable to her only as an extension of her granddaughter. Accordingly, that aspect of the situation of the grandmother is not sufficient for her holding of any claim-right correlated with any fourth-party duty borne by *X* to benefit the granddaughter by fulfilling the aforementioned promissory obligation. Again, there is no such fourth-party duty.

As an appendix to this subsection, I should note that Siegfried van Duffel has proffered a scenario that prefigures Cornell's vignette of the inebriated motorist and the parents of the slain child (Van Duffel 2012, 110). Suppose that some person Q has been culpably killed by some other person R. Van Duffel maintains that Interest Theorists are committed to the conclusion that R has not only contravened a moral claim-right held by Q but has also contravened some moral claim-rights held by Q's intimates, such as her parents and spouse and children. Van Duffel brands such a conclusion as "counterintuitive." He is correct in submitting that champions of the Interest Theory will endorse the conclusion which he broaches, but his riposte to that conclusion nicely epitomizes the unsatisfactoriness of intuition-mongering as a means of coming to grips with the complexities of right-holding. Just as the parents of the slain child have held claim-rights vis-à-vis the intoxicated motorist in the situation recounted by Cornell, so too the parents and spouse and children of Q in the situation recounted by van Duffel have held claim-rights vis-à-vis R. If there is a wrongful-death law in the relevant jurisdiction which extends to homicides like that inflicted on Q by R and which covers the very close relatives of decedents like those just mentioned, then each of Q's very close relatives has held a legal claim-right vis-à-vis R. Each of them has held a legal claim-right not to be deprived of the companionship of Q through R's wrongdoing. In any event, whether or not each of those immediate relatives has possessed a legal claim-right with that content vis-à-vis R, each of them vis-à-vis R has held a moral claim-right with that content. R has owed each of them a moral duty not to eliminate the companionship of Q through wrongdoing. Unlike the grandmother in Sreenivasan's scenario with regard to the promissory duty of *X*, each of the immediate relatives of Q has had an inherent personal stake rather than just a purely vicarious stake in the fulfillment of the duty owed by R to Q. Each of them has held a claim-right that could be fulfilled only through the fulfillment of that duty.

Maybe van Duffel would frown upon these ascriptions of claim-rights as "counterintuitive." If so, he has done nothing to explain or justify his dismissive stance on the matter. If he believes that the very close relatives of Q have not held any relevant moral claim-rights vis-à-vis R, then either he believes that R has not morally wronged those relatives by killing Q culpably or else he rejects the No Wrongs Without Claim-Rights Proposition (which I have sustainedly defended in the second half of Chapter 3). Appeals to dubious intuitions are not adequate as a basis for embracing either of those unpalatable commitments, yet van Duffel has not furnished any other basis.

Perhaps the reason why van Duffel has saddled himself with a choice between the two unappealing commitments just mentioned is that he has overlooked a point which I have made in the final paragraph of §3.10.6.3 of Chapter 3. Although the duty owed by R to Q is satisfiable by the same pattern of conduct that will satisfy the relevant duty owed by R to each of Q's immediate relatives—namely, a pattern of conduct that consists in R's not killing Q culpably—any set of facts minimally sufficient to constitute a violation of the duty owed by R to Q is not the same as any set of facts minimally sufficient to constitute a violation of the duty owed by R to each of Q's immediate relatives. Every fact comprised by a set of the former sort will be included in a set of the latter sort, but also included in each of the latter sets is the fact that the person culpably killed was a child or spouse or parent or sibling of the person whose status as a holder of a relevant claim-right is under consideration. Although facts about any of the immediate relatives would be excluded as superfluous from every set of facts minimally sufficient to constitute a violation of the duty owed by R to Q, a fact about the connection between Q and some immediate relative is included in every set of facts minimally sufficient to constitute a violation of the duty owed by R to that relative. Without such a fact about the familial connection to Q, a set of facts would not be sufficient (and would thus not be minimally sufficient) for a violation of the duty owed by R to any immediate relative of Q. As can be inferred from §3.10.6.3, the content of the relevant duty owed by R to any very close relative of Q is not quite the same as the content of the relevant duty owed by R to Q, even though compliance with the latter duty is both necessary and sufficient for compliance with the former duty. Whereas the duty owed by R to Q is a duty not to kill her culpably, the duty owed by R to any immediate relative of Q is a duty not to deprive that relative of the companionship of Q through R's culpable killing of her.

Hence, although van Duffel would be correct in looking askance at the notion that the relevant duty *d* owed to Q by R is somehow correlated with a claim-right held by a very close relative of Q, he goes astray in failing to recognize that a duty with a somewhat different content that includes the content of *d* is owed by R to each very close relative of Q and is therefore correlated with a claim-right held by each such relative. In regard to a duty with the somewhat different content just mentioned, one of the elements in any set of facts minimally sufficient for a contravention of the duty is the fact that the culpable slaying of Q by R has taken away any future companionship of Q from this or that immediate relative of hers. Given the existence of such a duty, the Interest Theory unequivocally classifies each immediate relative of Q as a holder of a moral claim-right vis-à-vis R. By recognizing that each such relative holds such a claim-right, we obviate the need for choosing between the two untenable commitments broached in my penultimate paragraph above. Van Duffel with his intuitions does have to choose between those commitments, or else he must abandon his intuition-peddling and must instead rely upon a properly theoretical comprehension of the holding of claim-rights.

4.1.4 The Inordinate Flexibility of the Interest Theory?

Before we move on to the Interest Theory in connection with the holding of moral claim-rights, we should ponder a couple of versions of an additional criticism that has sometimes been pressed against the Interest Theory in general. That is, the Interest Theory has sometimes been accused of excessive flexibility or manipulability almost to the point of vacuity. As will be observed from an investigation of the two main forms of this objection, each of them as an objection is misconceived.

4.1.4.1 The Misplacing of a Quantifier

Leif Wenar has misunderstood or misrepresented the Interest Theory of right-holding by incorrectly placing the pleonotetic quantifier that is operative in my formulation of the theory. Let us recall that my formulation affirms that any specified duty with its correlative claim-right deontically and inherently protects some aspect of the situation of the claim-right-holder that is typically beneficial on balance for a being like the claim-right-holder. Wenar retorts that "interest theorists have framed their theories around weak generalizations, which only attempt to explain some but not all rights.... Kramer presents his theory in terms of what is '*generally* beneficial for any *typical* human being or collectivity or non-human creature'.... The qualifications ... 'generally' and 'typical' limit the domain of rights that [Kramer's theory] will attempt to explain to a domain with certain rights (specifically, the counterexamples) removed." Wenar adds: "Weak generalizations are unsatisfying because of their lack of comprehensiveness. A linguist studying English will not rest content with the rule that *in all normal circumstances, 'i' comes before 'e'.* Nor will a toxicologist be satisfied with the thesis that *mushrooms are generally harmless when eaten*. It is unlikely that the best theory of rights takes the form: 'All rights have feature F (except for those that lack feature F).'"[4]

Wenar repeats his misunderstanding or misrepresentation in a later essay of his (2013, 204–5), but I will concentrate here on the statements just quoted. One preliminary point to be noted is that my formulation of the Interest Theory in this book is quite different from the wording in my 2007 article which Wenar quotes. However, the differences are inconsequential in the present context; I will therefore ignore them and concentrate on my current formulation of the Interest Theory.

Wenar has misplaced the pleonotetic quantifier—the quantifier rendered as "typically" within my formulation of the Interest Theory—in his strictures against my account of right-holding. He proceeds as if I had worded the relevant portion of the Interest Theory as follows: "Typically, a necessary condition for the holding of a claim-right by *X* is the fact that the duty correlative to the claim-right deontically and inherently protects some aspect of *X*'s situation that on balance is beneficial for a being like *X*." Had the relevant portion of the Interest Theory been formulated in that manner, it would have deserved Wenar's sneering. However, my actual formulation of the Interest Theory is very different, with the pleonotetic quantifier located correctly. Consequently, Wenar's dismissive remarks are themselves to be dismissed. Contrary to what Wenar contends, the Interest Theory ascribes a property to every instance of the holding of legal claim-rights rather than only to certain such instances. The main quantifier in my formulation of the theory, an implicit quantifier, is universal rather than pleonotetic. There is of course a pleonotetic quantifier in the formulation, but it governs the content of the ascribed property—the property of being beneficial on balance for someone like *X*—instead of governing the whole ascription of that property to instances of the holding of claim-rights. At the level of the ascription, rather than at the level of the content of the ascribed property, the quantifier is universal (distributively universal).

Wenar persists in his mistaken understanding when he writes as follows in a footnote: "It is of course possible to try to recapture universal application by

[4] Wenar 2008, 257, italics in original. The quotation inside the quotation is from Kramer and Steiner 2007, 290 (emphasis added by Wenar).

specifying some property specially rigged for the purpose, for example 'all rights share the property of belonging to a set whose members generally have feature F'. But the weak spot in the generalization will always remain" (2008, 257 n. 8). In this rigged formulation as well as in his other pronouncements on this matter, Wenar stumbles by presuming that the pleonotetic quantifier governs the ascription of F rather than the content of F. When his elementary logical error on that point is rectified, his complaint about the Interest Theory crumbles completely.

Though the Interest Theory is not at all vulnerable to Wenar's mockery about weak generalizations, his own theory of right-holding is. Wenar has left himself exposed here to a "*tu quoque*" riposte. When he unfurls his theory of right-holding in an article published in 2013, he formulates its third tenet as follows: "Enforcement of this duty [namely, the duty correlative to the claim-right that is held] is appropriate, ceteris paribus" (2013, 209, 219). Wenar nowhere tells us how to determine whether the "*ceteris paribus*" qualification is satisfied, and indeed he makes no effort whatsoever to elucidate that qualification. His account of right-holding therefore takes the form which he derides in the passage that I have quoted from his 2008 essay above: "All rights have feature F (except for those that lack feature F)."

4.1.4.2 The Matter of Categorization

Another potential focus for queries about the supposedly inordinate flexibility in my formulation of the Interest Theory is the wording "typically beneficial on balance for a being like *X*." That phrasing gives rise to a need for categorizing a party whenever we are seeking to ascertain whether the party holds a claim-right correlative to some specified duty. A critic of the Interest Theory might worry that the matter of categorization is largely open-ended. However, any such worry is baseless. For the most part, as has been suggested already in this chapter's ruminations on the evaluative premises of the Interest Theory, the categorizing of a party is conducted at a high level of abstraction. If "*X*" designates an individual human being whose status as a holder of a claim-right correlative to some duty is being ascertained, then normally *X* is aptly categorized simply as an individual human being. Normally, no greater level of concreteness is necessary or appropriate. Likewise, if "*X*" designates a collectivity of human beings whose status as a holder of a claim-right is being ascertained, then normally *X* is aptly categorized simply as a collectivity of human beings. Similarly, if "*X*" designates a non-human animal of some kind, then normally *X* is aptly categorized simply as a non-human animal or else as a non-human animal of a certain species or genus. These soaringly abstract levels of classification are distinctively germane in the large preponderance of cases.

Nevertheless, as has been observed in §4.1.1.1 above, there are some cases in which greater levels of concreteness can be pertinent. I ponder there a situation in which a masochist enters into a legally binding contract with someone else who is legally obligated under the contract to subject the masochist to torture. I also reflect there afresh on Kurki's scenario of anarchists who democratically gain control over a system of governance with an electoral manifesto that commits them to dismantling the system—a scenario which I have initially probed in §3.2.1.3 of Chapter 3. For each of those cases, and for any similar case, two main approaches are available. Let us briefly mull over those approaches again in connection with the situation of the masochist, and let us then contemplate a further example.

On the one hand, the masochist can be categorized simply as an individual human being. A typically advantageous aspect of the situation of a person on balance is his or her attainment of what he or she keenly desires, and that aspect of the situation of the masochist is inherently protected by the legal duty incumbent on his contractual partner to administer torture to the masochist. Under this approach, an ascription to the masochist of a legal claim-right—a claim-right correlated with the legal duty of the contractual partner—goes ahead straightforwardly while the masochist is categorized at the normally high level of abstraction. On the other hand, an alternative approach would also readily recognize that the masochist holds a legal claim-right to be subjected to torture, while further recognizing that the most salient trait of the masochist evinced in his formation of the contract is the anomalousness of his sexual inclinations and desires. Given the salience of that feature of the masochist and its manifestation through his entering into the contract, an Interest Theorist who analyzes the upshot of the contract can aptly categorize the masochist not just as an individual human being but much more concretely as a masochist. When the masochist is so categorized, Interest Theorists can smoothly conclude that the contract (if legally valid) endows him with a legal claim-right to be tortured by his contractual partner. For somebody like a masochist, being consensually subjected to torture is typically on balance a beneficial aspect of one's situation.

An approach of either type just outlined can likewise be entirely appropriate in response to a cognate example. Suppose that some psychologists and social reformers have prevailed upon a system of criminal justice to replace punishments with therapeutic techniques whereby malefactors are treated medically instead of being subjected to penal sanctions.[5] After a fairly short period of time, the convicted miscreants feel aggrieved about being treated as objects for psychological manipulation and management rather than as deliberative agents whose dignity lies partly in their accountability for their conduct. Bristling at the disrespect of being treated as patients with maladies that need to be cured or controlled, the convicts and their advocates outspokenly assert their "rights to be punished." In so doing, the convicts are condemning the system of criminal justice for wrongly declining to engage with their deliberative agency. Every such system is morally duty-bound

[5] This scenario is modeled quite closely on the situation in the 1950s and 1960s to which Morris 1968 was a classic response.

to uphold the dignity of the wrongdoers who come through the system's workings, and the institutions against which the convicts and their advocates are inveighing have failed to abide by that duty. Such is the message which the convicts and their advocates are proclaiming.

An Interest Theorist can come to grips with this scenario in either of the two ways that have been sketched above. On the one hand, the convicts can be categorized by such a theorist simply as individual human beings. For any such being who is endowed with sufficient mental faculties to qualify as a deliberative agent, the recognition of his or her status as such an agent is typically beneficial on balance in that it typically enhances his or her life more than would the withholding of such recognition. Because the recognition of that status in a certain context is inherently protected by the moral duty incumbent on a system of criminal justice to engage with the deliberative agency of convicts by punishing them rather than by treating them as objects of medical manipulation, a moral claim-right to be punished is something that can intelligibly be ascribed to each sound-minded convict under the Interest Theory. It is something that can intelligibly be asserted by each sane convict.

On the other hand, each such convict can be categorized by Interest Theorists more concretely as a sound-minded person who is resisting the non-consensual subjection of him or her to medical treatment. Because each such convict in this context has been found guilty of the criminality which he or she has perpetrated, the sole alternative to the administering of medical treatment is the administering of some punishment(s). Thus, when the sound-minded convicts invoke their moral claim-rights to be punished, they are demanding an alternative to the non-consensual plying of manipulation by doctors. They are contending that the system of criminal justice which has tried and convicted them is morally obligated not to subject them to such manipulation without their consent. Since not being subjected to such manipulation non-consensually is an aspect of the situation of a sane adult that is typically beneficial on balance, the moral duty incumbent on the system of criminal justice is correlated with a moral claim-right held by each sane convict—a moral claim-right not to be so subjected, which in the circumstances is tantamount to a moral claim-right to be punished. Again we arrive at the conclusion that Interest Theorists can aptly and intelligibly ascribe to each sane convict a claim-right to be punished.

What is most noteworthy here is that the anomalous ascriptions of claim-rights in these cases—and in some similarly unusual cases which I have discussed elsewhere (2001, 81–9; 2017b, 67–9)—do not involve any troublesome flexibility or indeterminacy in the Interest Theory of right-holding. In each case an Interest Theorist can remain at a highly abstract level when categorizing the party to whom a claim-right is being ascribed, and can take account of the fact that the fulfillment of keen desires is on balance a typically advantageous aspect of the situation of any human being. And in each case an Interest Theorist can move to a greater level of concreteness when categorizing the party to whom a claim-right is being ascribed, and can take account of the fact that the desires or inclinations of that party are in some respects aberrant. Either of those approaches will deliver the same upshot as the other in any of these unusual cases. There is some flexibility in the Interest Theory in its handling of such cases, as I have suggested earlier in §4.1.1.1 when recounting a subjective element in the objective evaluative premises of the Interest Theory. However, far from being inordinate, the flexibility involved in the theory's analyses of these exceptional cases is precisely what is needed for acknowledging the full range of propensities that human beings can and do exhibit. An account of right-holding is inadequate if it cannot make any sense of a situation in which a convict insists upon his moral claim-right to be punished rather than treated as an object of medical manipulation, or in which a masochist invokes his contractual claim-right to be tortured.

4.2 The Interest Theory in Connection with the Holding of Moral Claim-Rights

Although most of what has been said in this chapter about the Interest Theory in connection with the holding of legal claim-rights is also true *mutatis mutandis* of the Interest Theory in connection with the holding of moral claim-rights, there are some divergences across the law/morality divide. Most notably, as has been signaled in §4.1.1.2 and also in §§3.2.1.2 and 3.2.2, the evaluative premises of the Interest Theory in connection with the holding of moral claim-rights include the proposition that acting in conformity to the requirements of the correct principles of morality is typically beneficial on balance for a person who so acts. By contrast, as we have seen, that proposition about compliance with the correct principles of morality is excluded from the evaluative premises of the Interest Theory in connection with the holding of legal claim-rights.

4.2.1 An Additional Clause?

Alongside this divergence pertaining to the evaluative underpinnings of the Interest Theory, is there a division within the Interest Theory itself? In some previous work (Kramer 2022, 377–9), I have incorrectly suggested that the answer to this question is affirmative. I have there inappositely submitted that my formulation of the Interest Theory is in need of amplification when it is brought to bear on the realm of morality. Specifically, I have there propounded the following version of the theory:

> **Interest Theory For The Holding Of Moral Claim-Rights**: A party P holds a moral claim-right correlative to a moral duty D if and only if (1) D deontically and inherently protects some aspect of P's situation that on balance is typically beneficial for a being like P, and (2) the existence of D is not due to some moral wrong(s) perpetrated by P, and (3) P belongs to the class of potential holders of claim-rights.

As is evident, the first and third prongs of this ill-advised Interest Theory For The Holding Of Moral Claim-Rights correspond to the two prongs of the Interest Theory. By contrast, the second element in the Interest Theory For The Holding Of Moral Claim-Rights is not paralleled in the Interest Theory itself. In some of my previous work I mistakenly thought that the amplified version of the Interest Theory was needed to reflect the fact that, although there can be legal claim-rights that are correlated with legal duties which exist because of morally impermissible actions by the parties who hold the legal claim-rights, there cannot be moral claim-rights of that kind. I had in mind an example of the following sort.

Suppose that some thuggish officials in a highly oppressive system of governance commandeer several ordinary people and put them to work as slave laborers in a difficult and dangerous endeavor whereby the conscripts have to carry heavy objects from one location to another each day. The officials admonish the commandeered people that, if any one of them fails to carry out the task assigned to him or her on any given day, all of them will be killed. Under these circumstances, each of the conscripts owes a moral duty to each of the other conscripts to fulfill the task that has been assigned to him or her. Because any slacking will carry such dire consequences for everybody else among the press-ganged people, a moral duty is owed by every one of them to everybody else among them—a moral duty that obligates each of them not to slack in the performance of his or her labors. Nevertheless, although each of the dragooned people owes a moral duty with that content to each of the other dragooned people, no moral duty with that content is owed by any of them to the officials in the oppressive system of governance. Consequently, although each of the press-ganged people holds a moral claim-right that is correlated with the moral duty owed to him or her by each of the other press-ganged people, no moral claim-right to industriousness on the part of those people is held by any of the thuggish officials either individually or collectively. Nor is any such moral claim-right held by their system of governance. Neither the officials nor their system of governance will have been morally wronged by the failure of any hostage to complete the task that has been assigned to him or her.

In some of my earlier work I erroneously thought that, if the Interest Theory For The Holding Of Moral Claim-Rights did not include its second prong, it would generate the conclusion that each of the officials in my scenario holds a moral claim-right to industriousness on the part of the hostages. I presumed that that theory would similarly generate the conclusion that such a moral claim-right is held by the system of governance in whose service the officials are acting. After all, each of the enslaved people owes a moral duty of industriousness to every one of the other enslaved people. Not only does that duty inherently protect an aspect of the situation of each subjugated person that is normally advantageous on balance, but in addition it inherently protects an aspect of the situation of each official that is normally advantageous for anyone in a dictatorial position—and an aspect of the situation of the officials' brutal system of governance that is normally advantageous for an odious system. As has been contended in §3.2.1 of Chapter 3, compliance with the mandates laid down by a system of governance is typically beneficial on balance for such a system. Likewise, compliance with the directives issued by legal-governmental officials is an aspect of the situation of the officials that is typically advantageous on balance for people in their positions. Since the moral duty owed by each of the hostages in my scenario to every one of the other hostages is such that it requires compliance with the mandates of the regnant system of governance, that duty inherently protects a typically advantageous aspect of the situation of the system. And since the moral duty owed by each hostage requires compliance with the directives issued by the officials who have commandeered the labor of the hostages, that duty also inherently protects an aspect of the situation of each official that is typically advantageous for anyone in such a domineering position. Thus I thought that, were the second clause of the Interest Theory For The Holding Of Moral Claim-Rights not included therein, the theory would saddle its proponents with the conclusion that the moral duty borne by each dragooned person in my scenario is owed not only to each of the other dragooned people but also to the oppressive system of governance and to each of the officials directly involved.

I misguidedly supposed that the second clause in the Interest Theory For The Holding Of Moral Claim-Rights would articulate a necessary condition for the holding of a moral claim-right. Stated in full, that putatively necessary condition would be as follows:

> A party P holds a moral claim-right correlative to a moral duty D only if the existence of D is not due to some moral wrong(s) perpetrated by P.

In my vignette of the press-ganged laborers and the domineering officials, the moral duty of industriousness owed by each laborer to every one of the other laborers has been brought into existence through the wrongful coercion that has been wielded against all of them by the officials and by the system of governance in whose service the officials are acting. Consequently, when the ostensibly necessary condition above for the holding of a moral claim-right is brought to bear on the situation depicted in the vignette, it yields the conclusion that no moral claim-right correlative to the moral duty of industriousness is held by any of the officials or by their system of governance. That moral duty of industriousness incumbent on each of the hostages is not owed to any of the officials and is not owed to the officials' system of governance. It is owed to every one of the other hostages only. A moral claim-right correlative to that duty incumbent on each hostage is held by every one of the other hostages (and by each hostage himself or herself) but not by any of the officials. These conclusions, about the deontic relationships that are operative in the plight of the hostages, follow from the Interest Theory For The Holding Of Moral Claim-Rights with its second prong.

On the one hand, the Interest Theory For The Holding Of Moral Claim-Rights does generate the correct conclusions when it is applied to my scenario of the enslaved laborers and the thuggish officials. On the other hand, that amplified version of the Interest Theory is both superfluous and untenable. Before we examine why that amplified version is unsustainable, let us glancingly ponder how the Interest Theory itself will handle my scenario in regard to the holding of legal claim-rights. If we assume that the directives issued by the officials to the commandeered people are expressive of legal requirements—an assumption in accordance with my references to the fact that the officials are acting in the service of their system of governance, rather than on a lawless escapade of their own, when they dragoon their victims—we shall conclude that the officials and their system of governance hold legal claim-rights correlative to the legal duties of industriousness borne by the commandeered people. Because of the separability of legal duties and moral duties, the holding of those legal claim-rights by the officials and their system of governance is entirely consistent with their not holding any moral claim-rights that are correlative to the moral duties of the hostages. Thus, although the Interest Theory in the realm of law generates many conclusions parallel to those generated by the Interest Theory in the realm of morality, it leads to divergent conclusions about the legal entitlements and the moral entitlements that obtain in any predicament relevantly akin to the one sketched here.

4.2.2 An Additional Evaluative Premise

We can recognize that the Interest Theory For The Holding Of Moral Claim-Rights is superfluous when we recall that the Interest Theory itself in the realm of morality is underlain by an additional evaluative premise. For reasons that have been explained in §4.1.1.2 above, the Interest Theory in the realm of law is not associated with any evaluative premise about the goodness of acting in conformity to the objectively correct principles of morality. By contrast, as has been observed in §3.2.2 of Chapter 3, the Interest Theory in the realm of morality is indeed associated with just such an evaluative premise. In that latter realm, the theory takes account of the fact that compliance with those principles of morality is typically more important than anything else in determining whether the quality of one's life has been enhanced or impaired. Although the thin evaluative assumptions that inform the Interest Theory include a subjective element, they are predominantly objective. As an objective matter, courses of action that abide by requirements under the correct principles of morality typically improve the quality of a person's life more than would courses of action that clash with such requirements—even where the morality-flouting courses of action would carry significant benefits such as material enrichment or widespread popularity. Hence, the morality-flouting courses of action typically detract on balance from the quality of a person's life, whereas courses of action that are necessary for upholding the correct principles of morality are typically advantageous on balance.

In §3.2.2, my main concern has been to show that this evaluative premise about the goodness of conforming to the correct principles of morality is supportive of the Correlativity Axiom. Because every moral duty borne by a person is inherently protective of an aspect of her own situation that is typically advantageous on balance for a human being—scilicet, the aspect that consists in complying with the correct principles of morality—every moral duty is correlated with a moral claim-right held by the party who bears the duty. (Nearly all moral duties are also correlated with moral claim-rights held by other parties, of course.) Here my concern lies elsewhere. Instead of seeking to vindicate the Correlativity Axiom afresh, I shall show that the Interest Theory For The Holding Of Moral Claim-Rights is wholly superfluous.

Let us look again at the scenario of the repressive officials and the subjugated laborers. In that scenario, the officials and their system of governance are acting at variance with the correct principles of morality rather than in accordance therewith. Their crude coercion wielded against the hostages is transgressive of elementary principles of political morality. Although the moral duties engendered by the coercion (moral duties owed by the hostages to one another) do inherently protect an aspect of the situation of each official that is typically advantageous—an aspect consisting in obedience to the officials' directives—the advantageousness of that aspect is more than offset by the extent to which the immorality of the officials' conduct detracts from the quality of each official's life and from the ethical quality of their system of governance. Hence, contrary to initial appearances, the compliance of the hostages with the officials' behests is not typically advantageous *on balance* for the officials. It is typically detrimental *on balance* for them.[6] That compliance sustains a situation in which the officials are sullying the quality of their own lives through the immorality of the thuggish coercion which they wield in their interaction with the hostages. Thus the Interest Theory, in combination with its evaluative

[6] In the third paragraph of §4.2.1 above, where I explain why I earlier thought that the second clause of the Interest Theory For The Holding Of Moral Claim-Rights was essential for analyzing my scenario of the officials and the commandeered laborers adequately, I have deliberately omitted the phrase "on balance" whenever I have said that the obedience of the laborers to the behests of the officials is typically advantageous for the officials. Such obedience is typically beneficial for the officials in one evident respect, but—because the behests are grossly immoral—the obedience is not typically beneficial for the officials *on balance*.

premise about the typical on-balance goodness of acting in conformity to the correct principles of morality, will appositely yield the conclusion that none of the officials holds a moral claim-right correlative to the moral duty borne by each of the conscripted laborers.

Of course, that conclusion is also generated by the Interest Theory For The Holding Of Moral Claim-Rights via its second prong. However, my point here is precisely that that amplified version of the Interest Theory is unnecessary for the correct verdict on my scenario of the officials and the hostages. Given that acting at odds with the correct principles of morality is typically detrimental on balance for a person who so acts, any immoral conduct like that of the officials in my scenario will not give rise to any moral claim-rights held by the people who have engaged in such conduct. Although the issuance of the dictates by the officials does impose moral duties on the enslaved workers (moral duties owed by the workers to one another), and although those duties inherently protect an aspect of the situation of the officials that is typically beneficial on balance for them when no immorality is involved, the issuance of the directives by the officials in my scenario does involve blatantly immoral coercion. Hence, compliance by the workers with those directives is typically detrimental *on balance* for the situation of each of the officials, and accordingly the officials do not hold any moral claim-rights to such compliance vis-à-vis the workers. Such is the apt conclusion generated by the Interest Theory and its evaluative presuppositions in the realm of morality. Any recourse to the Interest Theory For The Holding Of Moral Claim-Rights would be redundant.

4.2.3 A Misconceived Criterion

Not only is the Interest Theory For The Holding Of Moral Claim-Rights completely dispensable as a supplement to the Interest Theory itself, but furthermore it is untenable as a criterion for the identifying of holders of moral claim-rights. It handles correctly my vignette of the repressive officials and the downtrodden laborers, but it arrives at badly mistaken verdicts when it is applied to some other sets of circumstances. Let us consider the following simple case.

Larry is a teenager who sneaks into an orchard to steal some apples from the trees, after the orchard has been closed to members of the public for the night. He ascends one of the trees and embarks on his thievery of the apples. While doing so, he slips and falls out of the tree and tumbles over the perimeter fence. He lands on the pavement outside the fence, where he lies supinely with a broken leg. A passer-by, Camilla, encounters Larry as he is groaning on the pavement. She is under a moral duty to provide assistance to him, especially if she possesses any medical expertise but even if she does not possess any such expertise. Her moral duty is owed not only to herself but also to Larry, who thus holds a moral claim-right correlative to her duty. These moral positions of the parties in this scenario are quite straightforward. Yet the second prong of the Interest Theory For The Holding Of Moral Claim-Rights would exclude Larry as the holder of any moral claim-right correlative to Camilla's moral duty of assistance. After all, the existence of her moral duty is due to his immoral conduct as a trespasser and a thief. Had he not engaged in that wrongful conduct, her moral duty of assistance would not have existed. Consequently, although the Interest Theory For The Holding Of Moral Claim-Rights would assess correctly the situation of the repressive officials and the subjugated laborers by denying that the officials hold moral claim-rights correlative to the laborers' moral duties of industriousness, it would assess the situation of Larry and Camilla in a seriously erroneous fashion by denying that Larry holds a moral claim-right correlative to Camilla's moral duty of assistance.

No doubt, the second clause of the Interest Theory For The Holding Of Moral Claim-Rights could be tweaked so that it would then handle the scenario of Larry and Camilla correctly. However, even in the unlikely event that the tweaked version of the clause would not have to be further modified in response to further counter-examples, any efforts to refine the Interest Theory For The Holding Of Moral Claim-Rights would not rescue it from its superfluousness. As an alternative to the two-clause Interest Theory (including the evaluative premises of the Interest Theory within the realm of morality), the three-clause Interest Theory For The Holding Of Moral Claim-Rights is redundant. Any cruxes aptly addressed by the middle clause of that amplified theory are satisfactorily addressed by the evaluative premises of the original theory.

4.3 The Interest Theory of Right-Holding versus the Razian Interest Theory of Rights

As has been remarked since my opening chapter, this book does not grapple with justificatory questions about the types of legal duties that should be borne by people or about the conditions under which those duties should be imposed. And, as has been made clear in Chapter 3 and especially in this chapter, the Interest Theory is a non-justificatory account of the holding of claim-rights. It lays down a criterion that enables us to differentiate between parties who hold claim-rights correlative to a specified duty and parties who do not hold claim-rights correlative to that duty. The criterion articulated by the Interest Theory does not pertain to the justifications for sundry claim-rights and their correlative duties. It focuses instead on evaluative matters concerning the aspects of people's situations that are inherently protected by the existence of specified duties. My elaboration of that criterion is a contribution to legal philosophy and to moral philosophy, as it helps to elucidate the nature of some key deontic relationships within the realm of law and the realm of morality. Moreover, as is apparent, my non-justificatory account of the holding of claim-rights is smoothly consistent with the Hohfeldian analysis of legal and moral positions (albeit a version of that analysis shorn of the obfuscatory dogmas with which Hohfeld encumbered his own insights). It is indeed vitally supportive of the Hohfeldian analysis, as we have beheld in Chapter 3 where the Interest Theory has figured saliently in my vindication of the Correlativity Axiom. In keeping with Hohfeld's own strictures, the Interest Theory distinguishes clearly between the interests of various parties and the claim-rights that are inherently protective of those interests.

In all these respects, my Interest Theory of right-holding differs from the so-called interest theory of rights propounded by Raz in the 1980s and beyond. Raz developed his theory not as a contribution to legal philosophy but instead as a contribution to political philosophy. Far from being non-justificatory in its orientation, his interest theory of rights is justificatory through and through. Its account of rights is an account of the conditions under which the imposition of duties on other parties is morally justified. Instead of differentiating between claim-rights and interests, Raz's theory conceives of rights as interests that serve to justify the imposition of duties on other parties. What is more, Raz presented his theory largely in opposition to the Hohfeldian analysis of claim-right/duty relationships and as an alternative thereto. We have seen at some length in Chapter 3 the multiple points of contention between the Razian understanding of rights and my Hohfeldian analysis of claim-right/duty relationships.

Most of the points of contention to which I have just referred are explored sustainedly in my third chapter and are not in need of being pursued afresh here. As has been observed there, Razians go astray when they presume that justificatory priorities are somehow inconsistent with the correlativity—the existential and logical parity—of claim-rights and duties. Razians likewise err when they suppose that the concretization of general legal claim-rights through the establishing of further legal claim-rights at greater levels of specificity is somehow at odds with the existential simultaneity of every claim-right and its correlative duty. Further mistaken is the conflation of interests and claim-rights by Raz and his followers, as well as their assumption that the Hohfeldian account of claim-right/duty relationships cannot accommodate the fact that the emergence of various legal claim-rights and other legal entitlements often proceeds through stages.

Instead of focusing anew on the points of controversy that have been covered in Chapter 3, my rather brief engagement with Raz here will concentrate on the justificatory orientation in his explication of the nature of rights. To that end, we should look at his chief encapsulation of that nature (Raz 1986, 166):

> *Definition:* "X has a right" if and only if X can have rights, and, other things being equal, an aspect of X's well-being (his interest) is a sufficient reason for holding some other person(s) to be under a duty.

Quite unexceptionable is the first component of this explication, which indicates that the possession of any claim-right by X is dependent on the inclusion of X in the class of potential holders of claim-rights. That component corresponds to the second prong in my own formulation of the Interest Theory of right-holding. My fifth chapter will endeavor to demarcate the class of potential holders of claim-rights, and will ruminate at times on Raz's approach to the demarcation of that class (an approach that superficially resembles my own in a few respects). At present, my concern is with the remaining portion of Raz's formulation above.

Raz's wording has to be understood somewhat differently between the realm of law and the realm of morality. In application to legal claim-rights, his reference to a sufficient reason for holding somebody to be under a duty is properly construable as a reference to a sufficient reason for arriving at an official decision—a decision by legislators or adjudicators or administrators—that places somebody under a legal duty. In other words, the reason in question is a reason for performing an official action that involves the exercising of legal powers which will alter the legal positions of somebody by imposing a legal duty upon him or her. As a matter of justification and as a matter of the operations in a system of legal governance, that legal duty is derivative of the Razian right which has called for the imposition of the duty. It is posterior to the Razian right both justificatorily and existentially.

In application to moral claim-rights, Raz's reference to a sufficient reason has to be construed differently. After all, except where a moral duty of compliance is engendered by the enactment of a morally binding legal mandate, the sway of a moral duty is not dependent on any actions of officials that would confer actuality upon the duty by authoritatively bringing it into existence. Hence, we should conclude that Raz's wording in application to moral claim-rights is pleonastic. In the realm of morality, apart from the exception just mentioned, a Razian right is not a reason for some official(s) to exercise some moral power(s) that will bring a moral duty into existence. Instead, a Razian right is a reason for the existence of a moral duty. Rowan Cruft makes this point deftly, though he omits to notice that it is applicable distinctively to moral duties and not to legal or institutional duties: "It is better to read Raz as saying that X is owed a duty if and only if X's interest is a sufficient reason for the existence of that duty, where 'reason' is not here essentially about the directing of reasoning, but rather indicates a ground. In this sense a sufficient reason for the existence of a duty is something sufficient to make it the case that the duty exists, that is, that someone is duty-bound" (2019, 15).

One obvious shortcoming of the Razian conception of rights is that it runs together claim-rights and interests. Indeed, its conflation of those two categories is its raison d'être. A closely related shortcoming is that the Razian conception of rights is starkly non-Hohfeldian in that it presents claim-rights as existentially prior to duties. Although the justificatory priority of claim-rights over duties in Raz's theory is compatible with the Hohfeldian Correlativity Axiom, the existential priority of claim-rights over duties in Raz's theory is squarely inconsistent with the

Hohfeldian analysis. My third chapter has already taken exception to these facets of Raz's ruminations on rights and has explained why they are so objectionable. Let us here mull over a few other weaknesses in those ruminations.

4.3.1 On Balance versus Typically

As has been emphasized at several junctures in this chapter, my formulation of the Interest Theory maintains that the holding of a claim-right by X inherently protects some aspect of X's situation that is *typically* beneficial *on balance* for anyone like X. The property of being typically beneficial and the property of being beneficial on balance are of course combinable but are not equivalent. In Raz's theorizing, however, those two properties are run together. We should particularly examine the following passage (Raz 1986, 180):

> Though rights are based on the interests of the right-holders, an individual may have rights which it is against his interest to have. A person may have property which is more trouble than it is worth. It may be in a person's interest to be imprisoned, even while he has a right to freedom. The explanation of this puzzle is that rights are vested in right-holders because they possess certain general characteristics: they are the beneficiaries of promises, nationals of a certain state, etc. Their rights serve their interests as persons with those characteristics, but they may be against their interests overall.

Most of this passage is focused on the fact that the possession of a claim-right is typically beneficial on balance, but not invariably beneficial on balance, for anyone like the party who holds the claim-right. Raz explained that point quite well, but the final sentence of the passage then suggests that what has been under discussion is the distinction between something that is beneficial *pro tanto* and something that is beneficial overall or on balance. On the contrary, what has been under discussion in the passage—as I have just said—is the distinction between something that is typically beneficial and something that is invariably beneficial.

Raz obscured the difference between those two distinctions partly because he did not include any "on balance" qualification in his formulation of his interest theory of rights.[7] Perhaps he presumed that his theory with its justificatory orientation was not in need of any such qualification, since something typically detrimental on balance (though typically beneficial *pro tanto*) would not play the justificatory role which he envisaged in his theory. In any event, whatever may have underlain Raz's elision of the difference between the two aforementioned

[7] In a later essay (1994, 46 n 2), Raz explicitly eschewed any such qualification.

distinctions, the inclusion of an "on balance" qualification in my own formulation of the Interest Theory of right-holding is crucial. As has been remarked near the outset of §4.1 above, the Interest Theory would be almost entirely undiscriminating if it lacked such a qualification. Thus, although proponents of the Interest Theory of right-holding are at one with Raz in having to accentuate the importance of the contrast between what is typically beneficial and what is invariably beneficial, they need to eschew his conflation of that contrast with the distinction between what is beneficial *pro tanto* and what is beneficial on balance. Each of those two dichotomies is operative in my Interest Theory of right-holding.

4.3.2 Raz's Commitment to the Justificatory Priority of Victims' Interests

My Interest Theory of right-holding does not train its attention at all on the justifications that underpin the existence of moral claim-rights and their correlative duties, nor on the justifications that do underpin or should underpin the establishment of legal claim-rights and their correlative duties. It leaves entirely open the nature of the relevant justifications, and it is therefore not committed to any position(s) in the debates over justificatory foci that have been recounted in §3.3 of Chapter 3. By contrast, Raz's interest theory of rights with its thoroughly justificatory orientation is a contribution to those debates. Any defender of the Razian theory is committed by it to the proposition that the justifications for the moral duties owed to individuals are centered on the interests of those individuals—that is, on the various aspects of the well-being of those individuals. To be sure, Raz's conception of rights does leave open some justificatory matters. For example, it does not in itself commit its devotees to some specific account(s) of the well-being of individuals, and in particular it does not indicate whether well-being is to be understood objectively or subjectively. Nevertheless, the Razian theory of rights does commit its exponents firmly to a position in the debates over justificatory foci that have been touched upon in §3.3. By the reckoning of a Razian, the moral duties owed to individuals are all justificatorily grounded on the interests of those individuals.

We should now ponder the unwisdom of the Razians in plighting themselves—through their conception of rights—to their stance concerning the justificatory grounds for the existence of any moral duties owed to individuals. An analysis of rights, or of the holding of claim-rights, should not carry such a commitment. Admittedly, as Raz proclaimed in the opening chapter of *The Morality of Freedom*, his analyses of major political concepts were expositions of principles of political morality (1986, 16):

> Much that is presented as conceptual analysis is really much more and includes advocacy of principles of political freedom. Moral and political philosophy has for long embraced the literary device (not always clearly recognized as such) of presenting substantive arguments in the guise of conceptual explorations. One may even say that the whole purpose of this book is to defend a concept of political freedom. It is only important to remember that that concept is a product of a theory or a doctrine consisting of moral principles for the guidance and evaluation of political actions and institutions. One can derive a concept from a theory but not the other way round.

Raz was on a solid footing when he insisted that explications of concepts of political morality must themselves be theses of political morality, but his correctness in insisting on that point did not warrant his putative analysis of the concept of moral claim-rights—an analysis presented as a thesis affirming the justificatory priority of the interests of claim-right-holders. Although any analysis of the concept of moral claim-rights has to be a doctrine of political morality, it should not be invested with such a problematic commitment. Let us explore how problematic that commitment is.

4.3.2.1 Punitive Torture and Monstrous Wrongdoers

As I have argued at length in my book on the morality of torture (2014, 203–9), the perpetration of punitive torture is always and everywhere morally wrong. There are no exceptions to the bindingness of the moral duty incumbent on everyone to refrain from the perpetration of such torture. Consequently, everyone at all times is possessed of a moral claim-right vis-à-vis everyone else not to be subjected to punitive torture. Now, if the Razian interest theory of rights were correct, that moral claim-right held unfailingly by everybody vis-à-vis everybody else would be grounded on the interests of each person as a holder of the claim-right. Such an implication of the Razian theory is belied by the fact that the moral claim-right in question is held even by any deeply iniquitous malefactor whose interests are of no positive moral force whatsoever. Let us here glance at an example which I have adduced elsewhere (Kramer 2017a, 143, 262–3; 2022, 389–90).

Suppose that Josef Mengele—directly responsible for hundreds of thousands of deaths and gruesome atrocities at Auschwitz—had been captured and brought to justice after the Second World War instead of being sheltered by Argentina and Paraguay and Brazil. Given that Mengele had perpetrated many thousands of acts of grisly torture, the subjection of him to punitive torture would have been richly deserved. Nonetheless, he had a moral claim-right not to be subjected to such torture. His moral claim-right was justificatorily traceable not to the importance of his interest in being free from excruciating pain (an interest that was of no positive ethical weight whatsoever), but instead to the importance of upholding the moral integrity of any system of governance whose officials had managed to apprehend him. By stooping to afflict Mengele with the torture which he thoroughly deserved, the officials in that system of governance would have degraded its moral integrity and their own moral integrity by using the system's punitive mechanisms to cater to urges for revenge. Though Mengele could legitimately have been executed and should have been executed, the subjection of him to torture would have turned the process of punishment into an enterprise of overweeningly sadistic self-indulgence. Mengele deserved no better; still, had a system of governance eschewed all normal restraints for the purpose of giving him torturously what he deserved, it would have debased itself by shaping its punitive measures to conform vindictively to his monstrousness. Extenuatingly understandable and primally satisfying though such measures would have been, they would have overstepped the bounds within which a system of governance must remain if it is to differentiate its own workings from the gross unrestraint to which its punitive responses would be addressed. Even in application to someone as demonic as Mengele, the indulgence of an urge for vengeance by a system of governance would have degraded the system's moral integrity—because the indulgence of such an urge would have manifested and exacerbated the system's own weakness through its failure to bring about adequately the conditions under which its citizens can warrantedly harbor ample levels of self-respect on the basis of their own individual and collective achievements. A system of governance that is ethically healthy enough to adhere to a pattern of self-restraint will operate its punitive mechanisms without inclining its citizens to derive gratification from the infliction of agony on other people. Given that one's deriving of gratification from the agony of other people is akin to sadism, a system of governance which caters to that impulse through punitive torture would be ignominiously presupposing that its citizens are partly dependent on the extreme adversities and littleness of others for their own self-esteem.

Thus, Mengele had a moral claim-right not to be subjected to punitive torture, even though his interest in being free from excruciating pain and terror and humiliation did not contribute at all to the justification for his having such a claim-right. Justificatorily, that claim-right was entirely derivative of the moral duties borne by the officials who might have captured Mengele. Its justification lay in the furtherance of their moral probity and the moral probity of their system of governance, rather than in the furtherance of his well-being.

4.3.2.2 Purposes of Perpetrators versus Interests of Victims

As has been argued in my 2014 book on torture, all instances of most types of torture are morally impermissible. However, as is also argued there, two types of torture are sometimes morally permissible. Most notably in the present context, some instances of ephemerally incapacitative torture are morally permissible (Kramer 2014, 186–7). The phrase "ephemerally incapacitative torture" refers to the deliberate affliction of a malefactor with severe pain for the purpose of inducing him to desist from his ongoing performance of a very seriously wrongful action, where the agonizing effects of the torture are neither intended to last permanently nor likely to last permanently. If the infliction of the severe pain is the least harmful means that is feasible as a way of preventing the completion of the seriously wrongful action, it can be morally legitimate.

Consider for example the following scenario, which recounts a variant of a situation broached initially by Uwe Steinhoff and discussed at some length by me in my book on torture (Kramer 2014, 87–8; Steinhoff 2009, 44). When a rapist assails a young woman and begins to tear her clothes off, she manages to stomp on his foot with one of her stiletto heels three or four times in order to afflict him with exquisite pain. Her hope is that the searingness of the pain will induce him to desist from his act of rape, as he loses his ability to concentrate on his ravishing of her and is instead absorbed by the consumingness of his own agony. He does indeed involuntarily cease to clutch her, and she escapes from her hellish predicament while he writhes in anguish. Her wielding of ephemerally incapacitative torture is unequivocally permissible in the circumstances.

Now, what is of the utmost importance here is that a Razian victim-focused assessment will not enable us to explain why the young woman's act of ephemerally incapacitative torture is morally permissible whereas no act of interrogational torture is ever morally permissible.[8] After all, even though the harmful effects of her stomping on the rapist's foot are neither intended to persist permanently nor likely to persist permanently, those effects—which might include some broken bones or other significant injuries as well as the anguish—are undoubtedly more severe than the harmful effects of some instances of interrogational torture. Thus, if we analyze the situation from a Razian victim-focused perspective that concentrates on the interests of a tortured person in being free from excruciating pain and injuries, we will not be able to fathom the following combination of facts: (1) the fact that the young woman's repelling of her attacker through the deliberate infliction of severe pain is morally permissible, and (2) the fact that the deliberate infliction of severe pain for the purpose of extracting information that can help to avert some calamity is never morally permissible. The combination of those two facts will be baffling from a Razian victim-focused perspective, since some instances of calamity-averting interrogational torture foreseeably cause less damage to the interests of their victims than the damage foreseeably caused by the young woman's use of ephemerally incapacitative torture.

Consequently, to grasp why the wrongness of interrogational torture is absolute whereas the wrongness of ephemerally incapacitative torture is not, we need

[8] To forestall any misunderstandings, I should note that the victim of the ephemerally incapacitative torture is the perpetrator of the crime of attempted rape whereas the perpetrator of the torture is the victim of the crime of attempted rape. Because my distinction here between a victim-focused perspective and a perpetrator-focused perspective is drawn in relation to the torture rather than in relation to the attempted rape, the person relevantly classifiable as the perpetrator is the young woman while the person relevantly classifiable as the victim is her assailant.

to shift to a perpetrator-focused viewpoint. When we switch to such a viewpoint, we can see that a pivotal matter for differentiating between the morality of interrogational torture and the morality of ephemerally incapacitative torture is the act/omission distinction. While torture of the former kind is aimed at inducing an information-imparting action, torture of the latter kind is aimed at inducing an omission by thwarting a seriously wrongful action. Given as much, and given the demarcation of the act/omission dichotomy—which is expounded rigorously and sustainedly in my *Torture and Moral Integrity* (2014, 77–97, 193–6)—interrogational torture is far more minutely controlling, with far more fine-grained direction of the victim's behavior, than is ephemerally incapacitative torture. Hence, the outlook associated with the perpetration of torture of the former kind is overweening in ways in which the outlook associated with the perpetration of torture of the latter kind is not. Some instances of ephemerally incapacitative torture are consistent with an ethic of self-restraint, whereas every instance of interrogational torture is not.

Of course, the assertions in the preceding paragraph merely gesture toward the relevant line of argument in my 2014 book instead of providing any full-blown line of argument here. However, again, the specifics of that lengthy line of reasoning—and in particular the complexities of drawing the act/omission distinction rigorously—are well beyond the scope of the present chapter. My point here is simply to underscore the significance of a shift from a Razian victim-focused perspective to a perpetrator-focused perspective. Only from that latter perspective, with its concentration on the moral integrity of the perpetrator(s) of torture, does the morally decisive difference between interrogational torture and ephemerally incapacitative torture become visible. Torture of either type can set back the interests of victims as much as torture of the other type, but the perpetration of interrogational torture involves grandiosely god-like controllingness that is not always characteristic of the perpetration of ephemerally incapacitative torture. Such controllingness is both degrading and extravagant, as it is impelled by desperation in its very striving to efface the opacity that stems from the separateness of individuals. We can discern as much from a perpetrator-focused perspective, which alerts us to the key divergence between interrogational torture and ephemerally incapacitative torture—a divergence that accounts for the absolute wrongness of the former and the variability of the moral status of the latter.

4.3.2.3 The Inappositeness of Raz's Justificatory Focus

As has frequently been remarked by commentators on Raz's interest theory of rights, there are numerous instances of claim-rights held by individuals whose interests are not sufficient to justify the existence of the duties that are correlative to the claim-rights. I have adduced some striking examples in the preceding two subsections from the philosophy of torture, but there are many other examples as well. Indeed, Raz himself adverted forthrightly to some. For instance, he mentioned a couple of such claim-rights in the following paragraph (1994, 50):

> Welfare law provides many similar examples. I, as a parent, have, in English law, a right to a periodic payment known as child benefit, which I receive because I am a parent and because benefiting me is a good way of benefiting my child. People who support invalid parents or spouses have similar rights to reductions in their tax liability, and there are many other examples. In all of them the weight of the right does not match the right-holder's interest which it serves, because in all of them the right is justified by the fact that by serving the interest of the right-holder it serves the interest of some others, and their interest contributes to determining the weight due to the right.

Among the numerous other examples that could be marshaled are the claim-rights of legal-governmental officials—held vis-à-vis members of the public—to be unprevented from carrying out their ordinary responsibilities as officials. Although the possession of such a claim-right inherently protects an aspect of the situation of each official that is typically advantageous on balance for anyone like him or her, the justification for the existence of the claim-right and its correlative duty pertains not to the interests of each official but instead to the interests of the public as a whole.

By modifying or reinterpreting his theory of rights, Raz attempted to accommodate these examples and other examples of claim-rights held by individuals whose interests are not sufficient to justify the existence of the correlative duties. He submitted that, in these cases, "the right-holders' interests are only part of the justifying reason for many rights. The interests of others matter too. They matter, however, only when they are served by serving the right-holders' interests, only when helping the right-holder is the proper way to help others" (1994, 51). One thing to be noted here is that Raz's modification of his account of rights is wholly unavailing for anyone who wants to come to grips with my examples from the philosophy of torture. As I have underscored, the interests of Mengele in being free from excruciating pain and humiliation and fear—pain and humiliation and fear of the sort which he had inflicted on so many thousands of his innocent victims—did not contribute at all to the moral justification for the fact that any system of governance which managed to apprehend him would have been morally obligated not to subject him to punitive torture. Morally, his interests were of negative weight only. Likewise, the interests of people who might be subjected to interrogational torture or to ephemerally incapacitative torture do not play any role in accounting for the difference between the absolute wrongness of the former and the potential legitimacy of the latter. The justificatory basis for that difference pertains to the moral integrity of the potential perpetrators of torture rather than to the interests of the potential victims.

Moreover, through his modification or reconception of his theory of rights, Raz turned that theory into a variant of my own Interest Theory of right-holding. Despite his apparent focus on the justifications for the existence of duties, Raz removed that focus in his effort to accommodate the various cases where the interests of holders of claim-rights contribute little or nothing to such justifications. In the first of my two quotations from him in this subsection, he suggested that his theory would suitably cover such cases if "the right [in each case] is justified by the fact that by serving the interest of the right-holder it serves the interest of some others." In the second of my quotations from him in this subsection, he contended in a similar vein that frequently the interests of people other than the holders of claim-rights constitute the justifications for the existence of the duties correlative to the claim-rights—though "only when [the interests of those other people] are served by serving the right-holders' interests, only when helping the right-holder is the proper way to help others." Instead of redeeming the criterion for the holding of claim-rights which he had propounded in *The Morality of Freedom*, Raz here abandoned that criterion.

On the one hand, there is of course a moral justification for the existence of any genuine moral duty, and the interests of others can indeed constitute the justification for this or that particular moral duty. Furthermore, every moral duty inherently protects what is on balance a normally beneficial aspect of the situation of the person who holds the correlative moral claim-right—or, in Razian terminology, every moral duty justified by reference to the interests of people other than the holder of the correlative moral claim-right will serve the interests of those others by serving the interests of the holder of the claim-right. However, all of those points are fully consistent with my own exposition of the holding of claim-rights and are indeed a variant of my exposition. No longer in the Razian theory are the interests of the holder of a moral claim-right necessarily playing any non-derivative justificatory role in accounting for the existence of the moral duty that is correlative to the claim-right. As a justificatory matter, the role of the interests of the claim-right-holder can be entirely derivative of the interests of other people. Those interests of others can be the decisive factors in justifying the existence of the duty. For example, in a liberal democracy, the interests of the citizenry as a whole can be the decisive factors in justifying the existence of moral duties incumbent on members of the public to refrain from thwarting the fulfillment of ordinary public responsibilities by legal-governmental officials. Any such moral duty inherently protects an aspect of the situation of an official that is typically beneficial on balance for somebody like him or her, but the on-balance benefit to the official plays no role—or no more than a minuscule role—in forming the justification for the existence of the duty.

By trying to accommodate the numerous claim-rights that do not fit with his canonical formulation of his interest theory of rights, then, Raz forsook his theory and opted instead for a variant of my own Interest Theory of right-holding. Cruft, in a valuable critique of Raz's ruminations on rights, summarizes this point forcefully: "Raz's theory ends up as a theory which says that a duty is owed to any being or body whose interests are necessarily served by its fulfilment. This is actually Kramer's theory of rights, the pertinent difference being the presentational point that Kramer explicitly abandons Raz's claim that duties can only be owed to beings whose interests ground them, while Raz maintains this notion of grounding by interpreting it too broadly to mean anything distinctive" (2019, 19 n. 29).

Cruft actually understates here the weakness of Raz's account of rights, because that account is only a variant of my Interest Theory of right-holding and is not my theory itself. In at least three respects, Raz afflicted his theory of rights with shortcomings that do not similarly mar my own Interest Theory of right-holding. In the first place, as I have complained in §3.8 of Chapter 3, Raz persistently conflated claim-rights and interests. By contrast, my solidly Hohfeldian Interest Theory makes clear that claim-rights are deontic protections of interests and are not the interests themselves. Second, whereas Raz completely neglected the role of the moral integrity of duty-bearers as something that can justify the existence of the moral duties which the bearers owe to parties who hold the correlative claim-rights, my espousal of the Interest Theory is combined with my insistence (in my books of political philosophy and moral philosophy) that the moral integrity of duty-bearers is what vitally underlies the absoluteness of various deontological moral prohibitions. Third, although I have correctly referred to claim-rights and duties as correlative throughout my discussion of Raz here, he himself denied their correlativity—as I have observed in §3.7 of Chapter 3. As I have shown there, he erred in thinking that certain important features of claim-rights and duties are inconsistent with the correlativity of claim-rights and duties. Consequently, his justificatory interest theory of rights does not partake of any strengths that might somehow offset its egregious failings. A non-justificatory alternative, which enables us to identify the holders of claim-rights correlative to specified duties and which does not per se commit us to any thesis about the factors that justify the existence of those duties, is what my present book has expounded.

4.4 The Capacious Version of the Interest Theory of Right-Holding

In my explication of the Interest Theory so far, I have presented it as an account of the holding of claim-rights. It has indeed been developed as just such an account. However, I have repeatedly referred to it as the Interest Theory of right-holding to leave open the possibility of extending it to the other Hohfeldian entitlements. Having explored that possibility in a couple of my previous publications (Kramer 2017b *passim*; Kramer and Steiner 2007, 288–94) I shall here mull over it afresh before returning in §4.5 to my focus on the holding of claim-rights. (In that next main section of this chapter, I will reinforce the Interest Theory by exposing the untenability of the rival Will Theory of right-holding.)

A capacious version of the Interest Theory that comprehends all four categories of Hohfeldian entitlements must obviously be formulated differently from the way in which I have formulated the Interest Theory specifically with reference to claim-rights and their correlative duties. One thing to be noted at the outset is that I am not aiming to present a version of the Interest Theory that would encompass every instance of each of the four broad Hohfeldian entitlements. Such an aim would be bootless, for reasons that can be inferred from my reflections on the evaluative open-endedness of powers and immunities in Chapter 2 and from my remarks on the term "entitlements" in that same chapter. Although the Interest Theory in its principal form (the form that has been expounded hitherto in the current chapter) applies to every claim-right, there might be some Hohfeldian liberties that are beyond the scope of the capacious version of the Interest Theory which will be expounded in this section, and there are numerous Hohfeldian powers and immunities beyond the scope of that capacious version.

To arrive at the expansive version of the Interest Theory, we should ponder the sorts of entitlements in each Hohfeldian category that are aptly designated as "rights." As should be evident straightaway, many instances of the entitlements in the two higher-order categories of Hohfeld's schema are not aptly so designated. Let us recall, for example, my scenario in Chapter 2 of a malefactor who alters his own legal positions and the legal positions of constables or other law-enforcement officials through his perpetration of a crime. In that scenario, the miscreant has exercised some Hohfeldian powers through his perpetration of a crime, but in any ordinary circumstances those powers cannot aptly be characterized as "rights." Quite ludicrous in any ordinary circumstances is the notion that the miscreant has exercised some rights by perpetrating his criminality, through which he has rendered himself liable to be arrested and placed on trial. That scenario, which illustrates the breadth of the Hohfeldian category of legal powers, can also alert us to the basis for differentiating between Hohfeldian entitlements that are appositely classifiable as "rights" and Hohfeldian entitlements that are not appositely classifiable in that manner. In other words, it can alert us to the criterion that should be encapsulated in a capacious version of the Interest Theory of right-holding:

> **Capacious Version of the Interest Theory**: A party *X* holds a right if and only if (1) *X* is endowed with a Hohfeldian claim-right or liberty or power or immunity of some kind, and (2) being endowed with a Hohfeldian claim-right or liberty or power or immunity of that kind is typically beneficial on balance for anyone like *X*.

Note that this formulation does not need to include a third clause which would affirm that *X* belongs to the class of potential holders of Hohfeldian entitlements. After all, the first clause presupposes that *X* does indeed belong to that class.

At a level of high generality, this wide-ranging version of the Interest Theory enables us to discern which Hohfeldian entitlements count as "rights" and which such entitlements do not so count. For instance, by recourse to it we can easily conclude that the legal powers of a wrongdoer to alter his legal positions detrimentally through his transgression of a criminal-law prohibition are not legal rights. Precisely because the possession of those powers is typically disadvantageous on balance for somebody like the wrongdoer, his possession of them is not an instance of any holding of legal rights on his part. Although this verdict serves to ratify any credible pre-theoretical understanding of the scenario of the wrongdoer, the Capacious Version of the Interest Theory fortifies such an understanding by distilling what underlies it.

Like the Interest Theory in its principal form, the Capacious Version of the Interest Theory has to be accompanied by evaluative premises. Without such premises to distinguish between the typically beneficial and the typically detrimental, the theory could never be brought to bear on any situations. My ruminations on the relevant evaluative assumptions earlier in this chapter with reference to the main version of the Interest Theory are not fully applicable *mutatis mutandis* to the capacious version of the theory. On the one hand, in the context of any inquiry whether a party holds some specified *legal* right(s), the evaluative premises associated with the Capacious Version of the Interest Theory are the same as those associated with the principal form of the Interest Theory. Specifically, they do not include any tenet about the goodness of acting in conformity to the requirements of the correct principles of morality. In application to the realm of law, the exclusion of such a tenet from the relevant evaluative premises—for the expansive version of the Interest Theory as much as for the chief version—is essential in an account of right-holding that duly acknowledges the separability of legal rights and moral rights.

On the other hand, the evaluative presuppositions that inform the Capacious Version of the Interest Theory with regard to the holding of *moral* rights are not always the same as the evaluative presuppositions that inform the main version of the Interest Theory with regard to the holding of moral claim-rights. In connection with moral rights on the left-hand half of the Hohfeldian table—that is, moral claim-rights and moral liberty-rights—the evaluative underpinnings of the Capacious Version of the Interest Theory are the same as the evaluative underpinnings of the main version of the Interest Theory in the realm of morality. In other words, the relevant underpinnings do include a tenet about the goodness of acting in conformity to the correct principles of morality. However, in connection with moral rights on the right-hand half of the Hohfeldian table (moral power-rights and moral immunity-rights), such a tenet is excluded from the evaluative premises of the Capacious Version of the Interest Theory. The exclusion of that tenet is made necessary by the evaluative open-endedness of the two categories of entitlements on the right-hand side of Hohfeld's schema.

4.4.1 Wenar's First Worry about the Capacious Version of the Interest Theory

Wenar has submitted that a capacious version of the Interest Theory will be woefully inadequate, as he declares that "[t]here are many rights the purpose of which is not to further the well-being of the rightholder, even in the general case." He elaborates (2005, 241):

> A judge has a (power) right to sentence criminals, but this right is not designed to benefit the judge. Rather, judges are ascribed this right as part of a system of justice that protects the members of the community. A traffic warden has a (power) right to issue parking tickets; but the point of this right is to improve the lives of motorists, not the life of the warden. Similarly, an army captain may have the (power) right to order units, including his own, into battle; yet the specific aim of the rule that confers this right is not to further the captain's well-being.

Unlike Raz's interest theory of rights, my Interest Theory of right-holding both in its principal form and in its capacious form is non-justificatory. It focuses not on the justifications for the existence of certain legal or moral positions but instead on the normative effects of the existence of those positions. Hence, whatever the pertinence of Wenar's remarks when they are construed as directed against a Razian theory, they are entirely misconceived insofar as they are directed against my own theorizing.

In response to Wenar's examples, we should not be asking whether the laws envisaged there are aimed at benefiting judges or traffic wardens or army captains. Instead, we should be asking whether the holding of the specified legal power by the judge or the traffic warden or the army captain would typically be advantageous on balance for anyone like each of them. Wenar apparently assumes that a proponent of the Capacious Version of the Interest Theory will answer the latter question negatively, but his assumption on that point is quite mysterious. If we are asking whether a judge will typically benefit on balance by possessing a general legal power to sentence criminals instead of lacking such a power, the answer is straightforwardly affirmative. Devoid of such a power, a judge will be unable to fulfill many of the responsibilities incumbent on her in her role as a judge. Her interest in being able to carry out those responsibilities effectively will be gravely set back if that general legal power is removed or withheld from her. Parallel observations apply to the general legal power of a traffic warden to impose penalties on motorists through the issuance of tickets or through other fitting means. If the warden lacks that general power, then at best he will have to rely on somebody else to fulfill his responsibilities for him. Such a state of dependence for the execution of one's tasks is typically detrimental on balance for anyone reduced to it. In any ordinary circumstances, the interest of a warden in being able to discharge the obligations of his role effectively will be furthered if he is vested with a general legal power to levy penalties on motorists who have contravened laws that regulate driving and parking. Even more obviously, a captain in an army will typically be far more proficient in the performance of her office if she possesses rather than lacks a legal power to obligate units of soldiers to enter into battle. If she does not possess any such legal power, then at best her prosecution of her responsibilities as a captain will depend on the issuance of the relevant orders by some other officer(s). Her being endowed with the power herself to issue such orders bindingly will in any ordinary circumstances benefit her on balance by enabling her to do smoothly what she is legally duty-bound to do. It will also typically benefit her on balance because the inclusion of that power among the legal prerogatives of her office bespeaks respect for her military judgment—whereas the exclusion of that power from the prerogatives of her office would bespeak remarkable disrespect for her military judgment.

In short, an exponent of the Capacious Version of the Interest Theory can easily handle every one of Wenar's examples focused on powers that belong to occupational roles. Every such example involves someone who will typically benefit on balance from being able to discharge a set of role-centered obligations capably and who will therefore typically benefit on balance from being endowed with legal powers that indispensably facilitate the capable fulfillment of those obligations. When somebody takes on an array of responsibilities that partly constitute an occupational role, the vesting of her with legal entitlements which enable the satisfactory execution of those responsibilities is something that will almost always redound to her advantage on balance. Contrary to what Wenar strangely appears to think, people typically have vital interests in being able to pursue their occupations adroitly. Indeed, the falsity of his stance on this matter could be underscored with countless additional examples: the legal power of a judge to obligate certain witnesses to testify, through the issuance of subpoenas; the legal power of a headmaster of a school to debar obstreperous students from attending their lessons; the legal power of the chief purchasing officer in a hospital to enter into contracts with firms for the provision of supplies; and so forth. In each case, somebody engaged in an occupation will generally stand to benefit on balance from being endowed with legal powers that are crucial for the fulfillment of his or her professional responsibilities. Just about any occupant of a professional role will have an interest in being possessed of the abilities that are requisite for performing the role efficaciously. Accordingly, those abilities as legal powers are aptly classified as legal rights by the Capacious Version of the Interest Theory of right-holding.

4.4.2 A Second Set of Complaints by Wenar

We can reach broadly similar conclusions about other examples that Wenar adduces. He refers to the legal liberty of a policeman to detain a suspect whom the policeman has been ordered to apprehend, and the paired legal liberties of a parent to choose between punishing a recalcitrant child and not punishing the child, and the paired legal liberties of a citizen to choose between restraining someone who attacks a third party and not restraining the attacker (2005, 248). Let us briefly contemplate how each of these examples is readily accommodated by the Capacious Version of the Interest Theory.

If the policeman were without a legal liberty to detain a suspect whom he has been ordered to take into custody, he would be under a legal duty to apprehend the suspect and simultaneously under a legal duty to abstain from doing so. In such circumstances, the policeman would be liable to incur legal penalties irrespective of how he might opt to behave. It is evident that the situation of the policeman will typically be improved on balance through his instead having an unpaired legal liberty to detain the suspect. He can thus fulfill his legal duty to perform an act of detention without thereby breaching a conflicting legal duty and hence without exposing himself to legal penalties for so doing. In any ordinary circumstances, his possession of that liberty will on balance make him better off than would his lacking it. In sum, far from drawing attention to an entitlement that is not classifiable as a legal right by the Capacious Version of the Interest Theory, Wenar's scenario of the policeman involves an entitlement that is straightforwardly so classifiable.

Much the same is true of a parent's paired legal liberties to choose between disciplining and not disciplining a refractory child. It is not clear from Wenar's text what the implicit contrast in this example is. Is the parent's possession of a liberty-to-punish and a liberty-to-abstain-from-punishing here contrasted with her possession of only the latter liberty, or is it instead contrasted with her possession of neither of those liberties? Whichever of those two contrasts is the *point d'appui* for the implicit comparison in Wenar's example, the typical on-balance advantageousness of the parent's possession of the legal liberty-to-punish is palpable. If the parent were to be deprived of that liberty, she would be under a legal duty to refrain from disciplining her child; any recourse by her to disciplinary measures would breach that duty and would consequently render her liable to undergo any applicable legal penalties. In any typical circumstances, her situation is plainly improved if she holds rather than lacks the legal liberty to discipline her child. In general, she will on balance be better off through her not having to worry about being subjected to legal sanctions for taking disciplinary steps which she reasonably believes to be necessary for the effective discharge of her responsibilities as a parent. When we bring to bear the Capacious Version of the Interest Theory upon her situation, the legal liberty-to-punish held by the parent is unproblematically construable as a legal right. Similarly construable, of course, is the parent's legal liberty to abstain from punishing her child on occasions when the child is disobedient. Normally, the situation of a parent is improved on balance through her not facing the prospect of legal sanctions for having chosen the path of forbearance on such occasions.

We can draw cognate conclusions when we mull over the paired legal liberties of a citizen to choose between restraining and not restraining somebody who is assailing a third party. Once again, the implicit contrast in Wenar's example is not entirely clear. Let us assume that the intended contrast is between the presence of the citizen's legal liberty-to-restrain-the-assailant and the absence of that particular legal liberty on the part of the citizen. A person P who lacks such a liberty will, of course, bear a legal duty not to apprehend anyone who is assailing somebody else. Whenever P does seek to fend off an attack against somebody else, she will have rendered herself liable to the imposition of legal sanctions (unless her legal duty is wholly unenforceable). Since being legally liable to undergo sanctions is usually detrimental on balance for a human being, P will usually on balance be better off if she possesses a legal liberty-to-restrain-an-assailant than if she does not possess such a liberty. Her general interest in not being subjected to legal penalties will be furthered through her possession of that legal liberty.

To be sure, there are some circumstances (not wholly outlandish) in which a citizen might on balance be worse off as a result of being endowed with a legal liberty to restrain someone who is unprovokedly attacking a third party. Suppose that, when *and only when* John is possessed of such a legal liberty, he will feel inclined to intervene if he espies an assault against an innocent third party. John will then be exposing himself to dangers which he would not have undergone in the absence of his legal liberty to apprehend the assailant through the use of force. Thus, his holding of that legal liberty might conceivably make him on balance worse off, as the benefit of penalty-free latitude might be more than offset by the detriment of the risks that he will be hazarding. Let us recall that, when the Capacious Version of the Interest Theory is brought to bear on one's possession of a legal liberty-right rather than on one's possession of a moral liberty-right, its evaluative underpinnings do not include any premise about the goodness of acting in conformity to the requirements of the correct principles of morality.

However, as Wenar himself is aware, the Capacious Version of the Interest Theory does not submit that every legal entitlement aptly classifiable as a legal right is *invariably* advantageous on balance for someone like the party who holds it. Rather, the theory maintains that every entitlement so classifiable is *typically* advantageous on balance for someone like the party who holds it. Given as much, the Capacious Version of the Interest Theory can easily accommodate a citizen's legal liberty-to-restrain-an-assailant—that is, can easily classify such a liberty as a legal right—even in the circumstances outlined by the preceding paragraph. Although a legal liberty with that content in those circumstances might be more detrimental than beneficial for its holder, such a legal liberty will be beneficial on balance for someone like its holder in most circumstances (indeed, in nearly all credible circumstances). Hence, an exponent of the Capacious Version of the Interest Theory should readily conclude that the legal liberty held by John is a legal right even in the exceptional circumstances delineated above.

4.4.3 Conflating Non-Justificatory Questions with Justificatory Questions

Broaching afresh in a later essay his examples of a judge's legal power to impose sanctions on criminals and a policeman's legal liberty to detain a suspect, Wenar muses as follows (2008, 259):

> [C]onsider the fact that a judge's power to sentence criminals is properly classified as a right. It would sound odd to say that this fact is explained by the fact that the possession of this power is generally beneficial for the judge. Similarly with the fact that a policeman's liberty to detain a suspect is properly classified as a right. One might not think that this fact is explained by the fact that the possession of such a liberty is generally beneficial for the policeman.

Strictly speaking, Wenar characterizes the *explanandum* accurately in each of his two rehashed examples. What is to be explained in the first of those examples is not the fact that the judge is endowed with a legal power to sentence criminals, but instead the fact that the judge's power is correctly classifiable as a legal right. What is to be explained in the second example is not the fact that the policeman is legally at liberty to detain a suspect, but instead the fact that the policeman's legal liberty is correctly classifiable as a legal right. However, although Wenar has stated each *explanandum* accurately, the persuasiveness of his queries about the handling of each of his examples by the Capacious Version of the Interest Theory is dependent on his readers' misidentifying each of the actual *explananda*.

If we ask whether the justification for the vesting of a judge with the legal power to sentence criminals is that her being so vested is generally beneficial on balance for someone like her, the answer to that question is obviously negative. If we instead ask whether the basis for classifying a judge's legal power-to-sentence-criminals as a legal right held by the judge is that the possession of such an entitlement is generally beneficial on balance for someone who bears the legal responsibilities of a judicial office, the answer to this second question is affirmative. If Wenar thinks otherwise, he will have to present arguments rather than sheer assertions. Given the absence of any arguments in his terse objection to the Capacious Version of the Interest Theory, he appears to be relying on his readers to think that the theory addresses the first of these two questions rather than the second. In other words, he is relying on his readers to neglect the fact that the Capacious Version of the Interest Theory—like the main version of the Interest Theory—is non-justificatory in its tenor.

Much the same can be said about the other example brandished by Wenar. If we ask whether the justification for endowing a policeman with the legal liberty to detain a suspect is that his being so at liberty is generally beneficial on balance for someone like him, the answer to that question is obviously negative. If we instead ask whether the basis for classifying a policeman's legal liberty-to-detain-a-suspect as a legal right is that the possession of such an entitlement is generally beneficial on balance for someone who bears the responsibilities of a policeman, the answer is affirmative. Again, if Wenar thinks otherwise, he will have to adduce some arguments to substantiate his position. Sheer assertions are scarcely sufficient. He once again appears to be relying on his readers to conflate the second of these two questions with the first. That is, he again appears to be trying to steer his readers toward mistakenly thinking that my Capacious Version of the Interest Theory is focused on the justifications for the various legal entitlements which it categorizes as legal rights.

While continuing to concentrate on the examples of the judge and the policeman, Wenar declares that my "line of reasoning [about the judge's legal power to sentence and the policeman's legal liberty to detain] simultaneously relies upon and misunderstands the norms that are roles." He elaborates as follows (2008, 260, footnote omitted):

> It is not as though there is a coherent role described as "judge who has the responsibility to sentence but no power to sentence"—and then we make a separate determination that the life of someone filling that role would go better if they gained the power to sentence. The original description makes no sense: a role that assigns a responsibility to ϕ but with no normative ability to ϕ is not a role that fits into any recognizable human practice. Similarly with the patrolman. There is no intelligible job that is "policeman who has the duty not to detain suspects whenever he has the duty to detain suspects." Such a job could be imagined only at the edges of a fantasy, if there; speculation about the interests of such a job-holder is moot. In reality, offices such as "judge" and "policeman" always pair the responsibilities of office with the normative abilities appropriate for carrying out these responsibilities. "Rights of office" are not optional add-ons that help a person do a job; rather, rights of office are an integral part of every job's description.

Nothing in this passage has any bearing on the ways in which the Capacious Version of the Interest Theory applies to the examples of the judge and the policeman. Wenar's remarks would have such a bearing if the relevant *explananda* were the fact that the judge possesses legal powers of sentencing and the fact that the policeman possesses legal liberties to detain suspects. If I were trying to explain those facts, my explanations which advert to the interests of the office-holders would be ludicrous for the reasons indicated by Wenar in the quoted passage. However, once again, those facts are not the relevant *explananda*. Rather, the Capacious Version of the Interest Theory is aiming to explain why the legal powers of the judge are properly classifiable as legal rights and why the legal liberties of the policeman are properly classifiable as legal rights. I am addressing not a question concerning why the judge and the policeman hold certain entitlements, but instead a question concerning the status of those entitlements as rights. Wenar's observations do not bear on that latter question nor on my answer to it.

Wenar's inadvertent or deliberate jumbling of the irrelevant *explananda* with the relevant *explananda* is epitomized in a slightly later pair of statements: "An interest-theoretical approach such as [the Capacious Version of the Interest Theory] cannot be the path toward understanding the rights of offices and positions. Rights of office cannot be explained by the interests of the individuals who occupy the office as currently defined" (2008, 262). These statements are tantalizingly ambiguous between the two sets of *explananda*. To any reader who is not unusually vigilant, Wenar will almost certainly appear to be indicating that I have sought to explain why some office-holders are vested with the entitlements which they possess. Whether Wenar has deliberately sought to foster such an impression or has instead simply neglected to avert it, the misdirectedness of his rejoinders to the Capacious Version of the Interest Theory will very likely go undiscerned by any readers who are not exceptionally vigilant against being misled.

4.4.4 The Discretion of a Parent Redux

Returning to his example of a parent who holds a legal liberty to discipline her child and a legal liberty not to discipline the child—an example to which I have responded in §4.4.2 above—Wenar asserts that the Capacious Version of the Interest Theory cannot "account for the fact that ... discretionary liberties are rights" (2008, 261). Wenar purports to summarize the gist of my explanation of the fact that the parent's paired legal liberties are indeed aptly classifiable as legal rights: "Imagine a world in which a parent has no liberty to punish her child (ie, she has a duty not to punish), but in which she retains the liberty not to punish her child. In such a world, Kramer says, the parent would be better off if she gained the liberty to punish her child because then she would no longer be liable to penalties whenever she did punish." He retorts: "In Kramer's imagined world parents are prohibited from punishing their children. In this world parents also have no duty to punish their children. Why in this world would a parent be better off if she gained a liberty to punish her child? She will be better off gaining a liberty to punish her child only if she has some reason to punish her child. Yet there is no reason that Kramer can depend upon here" (2008, 261). Wenar's riposte is badly misguided in more than one respect.

In the first place, Wenar errs in stating that a parent "will be better off gaining a liberty to punish her child only if she has some reason to punish her child." Indeed, this pronouncement by him ignores the chief point in my analysis of the situation. Even if *mirabile dictu* a parent has no reason to punish her child, she might punish her child—perhaps because she erroneously believes that she has a reason to do so. If she is legally at liberty to punish her child, she will not be classifiable as a lawbreaker for having done what she is legally at liberty to do. Contrariwise, if she is not legally at liberty to punish her child, she will be classifiable as a lawbreaker for having done what she is legally obligated not to do. Moreover, if her legal duty not to punish her child is enforceable, she will be liable to undergo legal sanctions for having contravened that duty. In those crucial respects as well as in virtually all other credible respects, her situation is made better by her possession of the specified legal liberty than by her lacking it.

Moreover, Wenar displays a paucity of imagination when he asserts that there are no reasons which I can attribute to the parent in this example. A parent might gain some peace and quiet by punishing her child for being unruly, or her infliction of a punishment might help to administer a moral education to the child both for his sake and for the parent's own sake. These considerations and other considerations that commonly militate in favor of punishing a child would not disappear if acts of punishing were to be legally proscribed. Given that such considerations will frequently be operative, the benefits to the parent from her being legally at liberty to punish her child are especially obvious. Decidedly peculiar is Wenar's apparent assumption that the existence of reasons for a parent to punish her child is dependent on her being under a legal duty to punish her child.

Wenar continues his discussion of the example of the parent with the following rejoinder to my analysis of the situation:

> Kramer appears to suggest that in his imagined world a parent would have a *role-based* reason to punish her child, and so would be better off with the liberty to punish. He says that with this liberty she would "not have to worry about being penalized for taking steps which she reasonably deems necessary for the effective performance of her role as a parent." Yet within this imagined world parents are prohibited from punishing their children, so their role is quite different than in our world. In this imagined world, the role of parent could at best be described as "raising one's children well, so far as one can do so without punishing them." Punishing one's child could not be a step reasonably deemed necessary for the

> effective performance of *that* role. In the imagined world, discipline is no part of a parent's job description. So Kramer has no role-based reason available to explain an interest in gaining the liberty to punish.[9]

Contrary to what is suggested by Wenar in this passage and in the other quoted passages about the scenario of the parent, I do not invoke the language of counterfactual worlds in my ruminations on that scenario. My focus, in coming to grips with the situation of the parent, has always lain preponderantly on the actual world. Of course, my analysis does have a counterfactual dimension—because I am pondering why a person's possession of the legal liberty to punish her offspring is generally beneficial on balance for somebody like that person, and because I therefore need to contemplate what the absence of that legal liberty would involve. However, given that my focus is on the actual world, the counterfactual world that serves as the point of comparison should differ as little as possible from actuality. In other words, the only significant difference should be the presence of a legal prohibition on punishing one's children in the counterfactual world, versus the absence of such a prohibition in the actual world. I am not asking whether the possession of the legal liberty to punish is generally beneficial on balance for a parent in comparison with a situation where that liberty is absent and where the role of a parent is very different. Rather, I am asking whether the possession of such a liberty is generally beneficial on balance for a parent in comparison with a situation where that liberty is absent and where the role of a parent is otherwise unchanged.[10] When the comparison is posed correctly in that fashion, we can arrive straightforwardly at my conclusion that the specified legal liberty is generally beneficial on balance for a parent. Quite baseless is Wenar's effort to block that conclusion by postulating additional contrasts between the actual world and the germane counterfactual world.

Wenar concludes his meditations on the example of the parent as follows (2008, 261–2, footnote omitted, emphasis in original):

[9] Wenar 2008, 261, citation omitted, emphases in original. The quotation within the quotation is from Kramer and Steiner 2007, 292. (The second portion between quotation marks in this passage is Wenar's own wording.)

[10] Perhaps Wenar is assuming that one's legal liberty to punish one's offspring is an essential constituent of one's role as a parent, such that any person who lacks a liberty of that kind is not performing the role of a parent even if she solicitously attends to her offspring exactly as a parent would. Let us leave aside the fact that Wenar does not offer any hint of an argument in support of such a wildly implausible assumption (an assumption which he might not be making). Even so, I could easily reformulate my remarks here to grant that implausible assumption *arguendo*. Instead of comparing the situation of a parent who possesses the legal liberty-to-punish and the situation of a parent who does not possess such a liberty, I would compare the situation of a parent who possesses such a liberty and the situation of a quasi-parent whose conduct and legal entitlements and responsibilities are the same as those of a parent except that the quasi-parent lacks a legal liberty-to-punish.

> Kramer might instead venture that a parent in his imagined world would have some *nonrole-based* reason to discipline her child. Yet this depends entirely on how we imagine this world to be. For example, in this imagined world where parents have no duty to discipline their children and indeed are prohibited from doing so, the responsibility for disciplining children might well be (indeed likely would be) assigned to someone else. Were we to posit that parents have an interest in punishing their children even when someone else is effectively doing so, we would seem to be making parents out to be simply cruel. Or again: parents in Kramer's imagined world might be just as glad, all things considered, to be legally prohibited from punishing their children. They might think that gaining the liberty to punish would result in their having endless headaches (familiar from our world) that they would just as soon avoid.

Until the final two sentences of this latest passage, Wenar simply repeats some missteps which I have already exposed as such. He again fails to recognize that the key question is not whether a parent typically has an interest in punishing her child, but is instead whether a parent typically has an interest in not being under a legal duty that requires her to refrain from punishing her child. And he again is unimaginative as he fails to come up with any of the reasons which a parent might credibly have for punishing her child even though she is not under a legal duty to punish.

Having committed those errors afresh, Wenar introduces a new line of thought in the closing two sentences of this passage. He suggests there that a parent legally prohibited from punishing her child might on balance benefit from the prohibition because she will no longer have to decide whether to punish her child in any given situation. The problem for such a line of thought is that a parent will indeed continue to face decisions whether to punish her child or not in sundry circumstances, only now with the added complication that she might be subjected to legal penalties if she does elect to go ahead in any of those circumstances. After all, a mode of conduct prohibited is not a mode of conduct precluded; a parent will still be able to punish her child even if she is not legally permitted to punish, and she will therefore still have to choose whether to exert that ability or not. Moreover, even in the extremely unlikely event that the legal prohibition disinclines a parent ever to consider whether to punish her child, she will then confront all the difficulties that ensue from the non-subjection of her child to discipline (or from her needing to rely on the clumsy device of having someone else punish her child, in a bizarre situation where other people are legally permitted to punish children while parents are not). Wenar has done nothing to make credible the notion that parents in scenarios of this kind will typically benefit on balance from being deprived of the legal liberty to punish their children. On the contrary, that notion is outlandish.

4.4.5 Some Further Putative Counter-examples

Wenar marshals a couple of peculiar scenarios which he perceives as counter-examples to the Capacious Version of the Interest Theory: "We get warnings of trouble in cases like the right of the bomb squadder to disarm bombs, the right of the kamikaze to his allocation of fuel, and so on" (2013, 205). It is quite unclear what Wenar has in mind when he refers to the right of a soldier in a bomb squad to disarm bombs. Perhaps he has in mind the legal liberty of the soldier to disarm bombs, or perhaps he has in mind the soldier's legal claim-right against being obstructed from carrying out the task of disarming bombs, or perhaps he has in mind both the legal liberty and the legal claim-right. However we are supposed to construe the example, it is completely unavailing as an objection to the Capacious Version of the Interest Theory. A soldier in a bomb squad is under a legal duty to proceed with the task of disarming bombs. If he is not legally at liberty to proceed with that task, he will be breaking the law when he does what he is legally duty-bound to do. Hence, his being vested with a legal liberty to carry out his work will affect his situation in a way that is typically beneficial on balance for someone like him.

If Wenar instead has in mind a claim-right against being obstructed from carrying out the task of disarming bombs, then he again is envisaging an entitlement that will affect the soldier's situation in a way that is typically beneficial on balance for someone like the soldier. After all, as I have remarked in the preceding paragraph, the soldier is under a legal duty to disarm the bombs. If he does not hold any legal claim-right against the disruption of his performance of that task, then he is legally unprotected against the thwarting of his efforts to fulfill his legal duty. A legal claim-right against his being thwarted will protect those efforts and will thus affect his situation in a way that is typically beneficial on balance for someone like him. (Of course, the relevant branch of the military will also hold a claim-right correlative to any duty of non-obstruction, as will the overall system of governance to which that branch of the military belongs.)

Wenar might seek to retort by surmising that the soldier will on balance be better off if he lacks a claim-right against obstruction, because he will then be spared from the dangerous task of disarming bombs. Any such retort would be problematic in several respects. First, whether actions of obstruction would spare the soldier from dangers is a matter that depends heavily on the nature of the obstruction. Many such actions would increase rather than diminish the hazardousness of his situation. Second, even if other people were somehow legally at liberty to disrupt the soldier's endeavors, each of them might lack any inclination to exercise such a legal liberty—especially since steps would very likely be taken to ward off any disruption robustly. In that event, the soldier would not be spared from any perils by the meddling of outsiders with his efforts. Third, any diversion of the soldier from his task would involve his contravening his enforceable legal duty to carry out that task. Unless he could raise a legal excuse that would shield him from legal sanctions for his non-fulfillment of his responsibilities, he would be liable to undergo such sanctions. Altogether dubious is the proposition that the diversion will on balance have made the soldier better off; the dishonor of his failure to fulfill his responsibilities and the possible sanctions for that failure would very likely surpass the benefit of being spared temporarily from a dangerous mission. Fourth, even if the three foregoing points are put aside, and thus even if we assume *arguendo* that obstruction would occur and that it would affect the situation of the soldier in a way that is typically beneficial on balance for someone like him, the example of the soldier is fully consistent with my Interest Theory of right-holding. After all, the example would then involve duties of non-obstruction that do not correlate with any claim-right held by the soldier.[11] By reference to the Interest Theory, we should conclude that those legal duties are correlated with legal claim-rights held solely by the regnant system of governance and by the relevant branch of the military. In other words, if all the risibly far-fetched assumptions that underlie Wenar's example are credited *arguendo*, the Interest Theory of right-holding will generate the conclusion that Wenar has misattributed the claim-rights that are correlated with the aforementioned duties of non-obstruction. Those duties are owed exclusively to the prevailing system of governance and to the relevant branch of the military rather than to the soldier.

A full analysis of the example of the kamikaze pilot would be closely similar to my analysis of the example of the soldier in the bomb squad. Hence, I will confine myself here to the chief difference between the two examples. Whereas the full success of the task of disarming bombs does not involve the death of the person who undertakes that task, the full success of a kamikaze mission does involve the death of the person who undertakes it. Hence, the third of my four points in the preceding paragraph might seem to be inapplicable to the example of the kamikaze pilot. However, anyone who draws that conclusion is ignoring what I have said earlier in this chapter about the evaluative premises of the Interest Theory. Although the germane evaluative stance for applying the Interest Theory (in either its principal form or its capacious form) is predominantly objective, it allows that "one of the interests of a typical person resides in being [able] to satisfy his or her strongly felt desires."[12] Anyone who is disposed to fly a kamikaze mission will very likely be fanatically devoted to the cause for which he is prepared to die,

[11] Wenar's ascription to the soldier of a legal claim-right (a claim-right against hindrances) presupposes that at least one other person is under a legal duty to abstain from hindering the soldier's performance of the task. Because such a duty is almost certainly owed by everyone else, I refer in the text to multiple duties that are correlated—through distributive universal quantification—with the specified claim-right.

[12] Kramer 2003, 435–6. The strength of desires is a property that pertains both to their intensity and to their tenacity. A desire is strong in the sense of being tenacious if it would continue to be harbored after the elimination of any misconceptions or ignorance relating to the physical and psychological facts that bear on the fulfillment of the desire.

and he would thus regard the dishonor of a foiled mission as worse than the loss of his life. Given as much, and given the importance of one's being able to satisfy one's strongly felt desires, my ascription to the kamikaze pilot of a legal claim-right against impediments will be apposite; the fulfillment of the duties correlative to the claim-right will affect the pilot's situation in a way that is generally beneficial on balance for someone like the pilot.

4.4.6 Arrangements for Marriages

In his scattershot objections to the Capacious Version of the Interest Theory, Wenar next cogitates on the existence of legal rights to arrange marriages (2008, 205): "In some societies, parents have a legal right to arrange marriages. That statement is clearly true, and remains true, even if it is also true that the human beings who are parents will normally be better off when parents have no legal right to arrange marriages (perhaps this is stressful or fuels resentment)." Wenar is here again taking aim at the Capacious Version of the Interest Theory, since the legal entitlements primarily involved are powers and liberties. If the parents are not under any legal duties to exercise those legal powers and liberties, then the possession of the powers and liberties will affect the situation of the parents in a way that is typically beneficial on balance for people like them. In such circumstances, after all, the parents are legally at liberty to exercise their powers and legally at liberty not to exercise their powers. If they sense that exercising those powers would be stressful or resentment-inducing, they can exercise their liberties not to exercise those powers.

By contrast, if the parents are under legal duties to exercise their legal powers and liberties to arrange marriages, they are legally required to proceed even if they sense that their doing so will be stressful or resentment-inducing. However, what are burdensome for the parents in such circumstances are not the liberties and powers but instead the duties. As for the legal liberties and powers themselves, they are pertinently classifiable as legal rights. After all, without those legal powers, the parents would be unable to fulfill their legal duties and would thus be breaking the law by dint of not exercising the powers which they do not possess. Without the legal liberties to exercise those legal powers, the parents would be under legal duties not to exercise the powers and would thus be confronted with deontic conflicts in which they are legally obligated to arrange the marriages of their children and legally obligated not to arrange such marriages. For anyone like the parents, not being faced with deontic conflicts of that kind is typically better on balance than being faced with them. Hence, *pace* Wenar, the legal powers and liberties of parents to arrange marriages are properly classifiable as legal rights under the Capacious Version of the Interest Theory even in the circumstances which he envisions (circumstances where parents would typically do well to refrain from effecting the arrangements for the marriages of their children, if the parents were not legally duty-bound to proceed with such arrangements).

Continuing to focus on entitlements pertaining to marriages, Wenar adduces an example that cuts in the other direction. He floats the following suggestion (2013, 205): "[I]n some societies, adults have a legal right to choose their own marriage partners. Yet it could be that adults would normally be better off were marriages arranged by parents (perhaps parents choose better partners)." As can be inferred from much of what I have said already, Wenar's parenthetical comment on the factors at stake in this example is simplistic and unavailing. Even in the improbable event that parents would generally choose better marriage partners for their offspring than would the offspring themselves, the vesting of people with legal liberties and powers to choose their own partners will uphold their dignity and will lessen the control which their parents are able to exert over them. Moreover, if somebody wishes to abide by her parents' choice of a partner for her, she will be legally at liberty to do so. Hence, even in a fanciful society where adults would generally fare better through the choosing of marriage partners for them by their parents than through their choosing of marriage partners for themselves, the vesting of people with legal liberties and legal powers to arrange their own marriages would typically be beneficial on balance for the people who are vested therewith.

4.4.7 The Message to Be Gathered

Wenar sums up the message which he has attempted to convey through his onslaughts against the Capacious Version of the Interest Theory: "What legal rights there are does not depend on what makes a human life go well, so we cannot make the analysis of the former turn on the truth about the latter" (2013, 205). If this maxim is an affirmation of the legal-positivist insistence on the separability of law and morality, then it is correct—but, insofar as it is supposed to be admonishing me, it is utterly superfluous. Over the past few decades, I have championed legal positivism as steadfastly and sustainedly as I have championed the Hohfeldian analysis. If the maxim by Wenar is instead asserting that the justifications for various legal entitlements are not always focused on improving the lives of the holders of those entitlements, then he is once again failing to engage with my theorizing. Like the main version of my Interest Theory of right-holding, the Capacious Version of the Interest Theory is not concerned with the justifications for legal entitlements. Yet another possibility is that Wenar is here contending that the holders of legal rights can be identified without any evaluations of the sort required under the Capacious Version of the Interest Theory. If his assertion is indeed to be construed along those lines, then it is an *ipse dixit* whose only "support" stems from the aforementioned onslaughts which I have rebutted in the preceding several subsections.

Wenar tries to provide further support in a footnote by invoking Jean-Jacques Rousseau and Karl Marx and Jesus of Nazareth (2013, 205 n. 9):

> Or consider the legal rights of property owners. Both Rousseau and Marx insist that it is bad for humans to own private property, because of the antagonistic relations and antisocial attitudes this brings. Jesus adds the thesis that it is worse to be rich than poor. These claims may be true or false, but no analysis of rights should make the existence of property rights within, say, the Swiss legal system turn on the truth or falsity of humanist critiques of capitalism, or on the truth or falsity of the thesis that the rich man shall hardly enter into the kingdom of heaven.

4.4.7.1 Rousseau and Marx

Let us begin with Rousseau and Marx. One important distinction blurred by Wenar here is the difference between the overarching institution of private property and the particular instances of rights that can be acquired within that institution, and another important distinction obfuscated here by Wenar is the difference between what is generally beneficial or detrimental for humanity and what is generally beneficial or detrimental for a particular owner of property. Although Rousseau and Marx regarded the institution of private property as detrimental on balance for humanity, each of them could recognize that there is a straightforward sense in which a particular owner of assets is on balance typically better off by virtue of her ownership than she would be in the absence of that status. This point becomes clear when we recall that the relevant evaluative judgments—the judgments concerning whether somebody like an owner Q will on balance typically be better off through holding the legal entitlements of an owner—are to be reached via a contrast with a nearby possible world rather than via a contrast with a preposterously remote world (a world that might not even be metaphysically possible). That is, we need to draw a contrast between a state of affairs in which Q possesses some rights of ownership and an otherwise similar state of affairs in which Q altogether lacks such rights. Although Q may be worse off in each of those states of affairs than she would be in some putative communist utopia, people like Q in the actual world and in any proximate counterfactual worlds are typically on balance better off with some rights of ownership than without any. Even someone who (unlike me) regrets the inexistence of the aforementioned utopia can recognize as much.

4.4.7.2 Jesus of Nazareth

Jesus, in his responses to the rich young ruler and in a number of his other adages and in some of his parables, contended that people are decisively worse off by dint of being vested with abundant rights of ownership. That is, by laying up treasures on earth, they are failing to lay up treasures in heaven. Thus, Jesus and his followers might appear to be committed to the proposition that legal rights of ownership are generally on balance detrimental for anyone who holds them in abundance. Notwithstanding, Jesus and his followers could recognize that such legal rights are indeed legal rights. Or so Wenar has apparently reasoned.

Now, given that Jesus emphasized that his kingdom is not of this world and that his followers should render to Caesar what is Caesar's, he could readily accept that the holding of legal rights is to be gauged by reference to the concerns and practices of this earthly vale of tears. After all, legal rights are decidedly earthly entities. At any rate, whatever Jesus may have thought, the philosophers who ruminate on such matters should recognize that the holding of legal rights is a worldly phenomenon whose instances are to be ascertained by reference to worldly evaluations rather than by reference to the eschatological preoccupations of Jesus. Accordingly, in the evaluative judgments through which we determine whether legal entitlements of ownership are typically detrimental or typically beneficial on balance for the people who hold them, we should be prescinding from supramundane considerations and should be concentrating instead on terrestrial matters. When our evaluative judgments are so oriented, we shall conclude that legal entitlements of ownership are typically beneficial on balance for the parties who hold them.

4.4.8 Some Problematic Legal Liberties

In the medley of scenarios broached by Wenar which I have examined so far, he has failed to come up with any examples of legal liberties that are not typically beneficial on balance for the parties who hold them. However, in a passage which I have not yet quoted here, he gestures toward some legal liberties that initially appear to be more problematic than those which I have considered heretofore in this chapter. Moreover, I myself in an earlier article have pointed to some legal liberties that are genuinely more complex in their bearings than are any of the legal liberties which this chapter has hitherto plumbed. Let us here first mull over the seemingly difficult class of cases detected by Wenar.

4.4.8.1 Paternalistic Legal Prohibitions

In a footnote, Wenar asserts that "reflection on paternalistic legislation gives further reason to doubt Kramer's [position]. Paternalistic legislation is just an attempt to make people better off by instituting a legal prohibition that disinclines them from doing something risky or difficult that they would otherwise do. For Kramer to establish that it is extremely rare for a legal prohibition to further the interests of those restricted by it, he would need to show that it is extremely rare for paternalistic legislation to achieve its aims" (2008, 262 n. 16). Unlike the other situations which Wenar adduces, the example of paternalistic legislation initially appears to involve some Hohfeldian liberties that are not typically beneficial on balance for the people who hold them. However, the example is much more complicated than Wenar suggests, and it turns out to yield a conclusion sharply at odds with his. Moreover, even if the superficial appearance of the example had been well founded, the conclusion drawn by Wenar therefrom would have been invalid.

4.4.8.1.1 Inconclusiveness at Best

For several reasons, the implications of paternalistic legislation are not nearly as clear-cut as Wenar suggests. Let us designate a paternalistically prohibited activity as "Z." Wenar appears to presume that the relevant contrast is between (1) a situation in which Z is legally prohibited and in which very few people do Z and (2) a situation in which Z is legally unprohibited and in which many people do Z. He also appears to presume that, if doing Z is on balance detrimental for most people and if the removal of each person's legal liberty-to-do-Z will incline everyone or nearly everyone against doing Z, the removal of each person's legal liberty-to-do-Z is on balance beneficial for most people.

Now, there are multiple ways in which a paternalistic prohibition can be detrimental on balance for most people. For one thing, legislators might err in thinking that doing Z would on balance be detrimental for most people who are inclined to do it. For another thing, the contrast which Wenar poses may be inapposite. Z might be an activity which hardly anyone is disposed to undertake even in the absence of a legal ban, or it might be an activity which most people are disposed to undertake even in the presence of a legal ban.

Furthermore, even if the legislators are correct in thinking that doing Z is on balance detrimental for most people who do it, and even if the legal proscription of Z will incline nearly everyone against pursuing that activity which nearly everyone would otherwise have pursued, the proscription will most likely be detrimental on balance for most people. After all, the germane contrast is not simply between doing Z and abstaining from doing Z. Rather, the germane contrast is also between being legally free to do Z and being legally unfree to do Z. Because the state of being legally unfree to do Z is imposed on each person for paternalistic reasons, it involves indignity for any sane adult whose legal freedom to do Z has been removed (especially if the paternalism is hard rather than soft—something which Wenar does not specify). Even if soft paternalism is sometimes morally permissible, the indignity of being subjected to a paternalistic restriction is always an ethical reason against the imposition of the restriction. *Pro tanto*, such indignity detracts from the quality of the life of a sane adult who undergoes it. As an evaluative matter concerning the goodness of someone's life, the negative upshot of such indignity may well surpass the importance of any considerations that favor the soft-paternalistic restriction.

Even more obviously, somebody who is not legally at liberty to do Z will face the prospect of legal sanctions for doing Z—save in the unlikely event that the legal duty to abstain from doing Z is wholly unenforceable. Whether or not the abstention of people from doing Z is typically better on balance for them than is their doing Z, their not being liable to undergo legal sanctions for doing Z is typically better on balance for them than is their being liable to undergo such sanctions for doing Z. Wenar writes as if the only difference between the existence and the inexistence of a legal prohibition on doing Z is that the existence of the prohibition will incline people not to do Z (an activity which he assumes to be harmful or risky for people who do it). However, the most salient difference is that people are liable to incur legal penalties for doing Z when an enforceable legal prohibition on doing Z is operative in their jurisdiction, whereas they are not liable to incur those penalties when no such legal prohibition is in existence there. That key difference is doubtless what chiefly accounts for the classification of one's legal liberty-to-do-Z as a legal right.

Moreover, as Ian Carter has argued persuasively—in Carter 1999, 31–67—freedom is possessed of content-independent value. (Carter trains his arguments mainly on modal freedom as abilities rather than on legal freedom as permissions. However, the factors that he invokes can be extended *mutatis mutandis* to freedom of the latter type.) The inherent value and constitutive value and instrumental value attributed by Carter to freedom will be at stake when paternalistic prohibitions are being contemplated. Someone who adverts only to the contrast between doing Z and not doing Z is overlooking much that is lost when the legal liberty to do Z is removed.

Finally, if the paternalism that impels a legal ban is hard rather than soft, it runs afoul of my arguments elsewhere in which I contend that hard paternalism is always morally wrong (Kramer 2017a, 251–96). Adopting a predominantly government-focused perspective rather than a predominantly citizen-focused perspective, I have maintained that hard-paternalist mandates bespeak a quidnunc mentality that undermines the moral legitimacy of those mandates. Such legal edicts are at once overweening and degrading for the system of governance that promulgates them. Someone who concentrates solely on the differences for citizens between doing Z and not doing Z will have neglected this government-focused consideration altogether.

Wenar does concentrate solely on those differences, as if nothing else is at stake when paternalistic legislation is being contemplated. Once we move beyond his strangely monocular focus, and once we take into account the sundry considerations that have been summarized in this subsection, we can recognize that his example of paternalistic legislation is far less impressive than he takes it to be. We can recognize that the contrast between being legally at liberty to do Z and being legally obligated not to do Z is a much more complicated matter than the contrast between doing Z and not doing Z. Of course, the considerations adduced here have been merely limned rather than fully elaborated. Some of them would require quite a bit of supportive argumentation—argumentation that has been supplied elsewhere by me or by Carter. Here my purpose has simply been to show that there are numerous factors which militate in favor of the idea that each person's legal liberty to do Z (a legal liberty that is lost when the doing of Z is prohibited) is a legal right. Together those factors make cogent the proposition that, even if not doing Z is typically better on balance for human adults than is doing Z, being legally at liberty to do Z is typically better on balance for human adults than is not being legally at liberty to do Z. Wenar complacently errs in thinking that his example tells straightforwardly against the classifiability of the legal liberty-to-do-Z as a legal right under the Capacious Version of the Interest Theory. On the contrary, to the extent that the example is straightforward, the conclusion generated by it is in favor of classifying the legal liberty-to-do-Z as a legal right. Given the ethical importance of being treated with dignity by one's system of governance, and given the prudential importance of not being liable to undergo legal sanctions for one's adoption of some specified course of conduct, we can safely conclude that being legally at liberty to do Z is typically better on balance for sane human adults than is being legally obligated not to do Z. That conclusion holds notwithstanding that the abstention of people from doing Z may very well typically be better on balance for them than would their doing of Z.

4.4.8.1.2 An Invalid Conclusion

Even if Wenar had been correct in presuming that the elimination of certain legal liberties by paternalistic legislation is on balance typically beneficial for the people from whom those liberties have been removed, he would have been mistaken in inferring that such an upshot belies the Capacious Version of the Interest Theory of right-holding. Instead of serving as counter-examples to the Capacious Version of the Interest Theory, the legal liberties extinguished by the paternalistic legislation would have been counter-examples to the proposition that every legal liberty is typically beneficial on balance for anyone like the party who holds it. However, that latter proposition is not entailed or presupposed by the Capacious Version of the Interest Theory. Rather, as has already been indicated, the Capacious Version of the Interest Theory affirms that every legal liberty *pertinently classifiable as a legal right* is typically beneficial on balance for anyone like the party who holds it. Whereas the main version of the Interest Theory submits that every claim-right inherently protects some aspect of the situation of its holder that is typically beneficial on balance for anybody like the holder, the expansive version of the theory does not advance any comparably sweeping contention (*mutatis mutandis*) about each of the other Hohfeldian entitlements. Indeed, it is framed as it is to take account of the fact that powers and immunities as general categories of entitlements are evaluatively neutral. Hence, fully consistent with the Capacious Version of the Interest Theory is the possibility that the legal liberties extirpated by some paternalistic legal ban were typically detrimental on balance for the people who held those liberties. Although that possibility is probably never actualized, its actualization would not cast any doubt upon the Capacious Version of the Interest Theory at all. A defender of that theory would simply have to conclude that the legal liberties squelched by some special paternalistic legal prohibition—legal liberties which, *ex hypothesi*, were typically detrimental on balance for their holders—were not pertinently classifiable as legal rights.

4.4.8.2 Legal Liberties in a Dire Condition

Although Wenar has not managed to come up with any examples of liberties that are typically detrimental on balance for their holders, I myself in an earlier article have contemplated a possible example (Kramer and Steiner 2007, 293–4). Suppose that, under the law of some jurisdiction J, each terminally ill person is legally at liberty to end his or her life at any time. Suppose further that the possession of such a legal liberty is something that leads most terminally ill people in J to feel under pressure to end their lives in order to relieve their families of the expenses and burdens of caring for them. Were the legal liberty-to-commit-suicide withheld from each terminally ill person, few such people (or, at any rate, only a minority of such people) would experience any sense of pressure to commit suicide. Now, although the empirical conditions posited here are unlikely to obtain anywhere, they are not utterly fanciful. We can take for granted that those conditions do obtain in the jurisdiction J that is under consideration. In J, then, the legal liberty to end one's life might typically be detrimental on balance for the terminally ill people who are each endowed with that liberty. Given as much, such a legal liberty might not aptly be classifiable as a legal right within J under the Capacious Version of the Interest Theory.

As we have done with Wenar's example of paternalistic legislation, we need here to attend to the sundry complexities that bear upon the upshot of holding the legal liberty which we are pondering. Some of those complexities have been handled stipulatively, through my positing of the empirical conditions—conditions pertaining to the inclinations of a substantial majority of terminally ill people—that are assumed here to obtain in J. Unlikely though those conditions are to obtain in actuality, they are not so preposterous that we can dismiss the prospect of their ever emerging somewhere in any credibly possible world.

We can further assume that those conditions are known to the officials who run the system of governance which presides in J, and that the officials have responded by outlawing acts of suicide on the part of terminally ill people. In other words, the factor impelling the officials to proscribe acts of suicide by terminally ill people is a concern to prevent large numbers of such people from feeling under pressure to end their lives prematurely. In that event, the attitude bespoken by the legal prohibition on such conduct is not that of disrespect for the deliberative agency of terminally ill people. Hence, although being treated with disrespect seriously detracts from the quality of someone's life, the outlawing of suicide in the envisaged circumstances does not treat terminally ill people in J with disrespect and therefore does not in that manner detract from the goodness of their lives. In this regard, the situation here diverges from the situation broached by Wenar. Ordinary paternalistic prohibitions, such as mandatory seatbelt-wearing laws or restrictions on the availability of high-fat snacks, do disrespect the deliberative agency of the sane adults who are covered by those prohibitions. On matters where the infliction of harm upon others is not at issue, such prohibitions legally require some of those adults to act against their preferences. Contrastingly, the law that prohibits suicide by terminally ill people in J has been enacted to enable those unfortunate people to realize the fulfillment of their preferences. Although a legal prohibition on suicide would normally be overweening as a display of disrespect for the deliberative agency of the sane adults to whom it is addressed, the very special circumstances in J that have led to the enactment of the suicide-proscribing statute there are such that the statute does not evince any disrespect for the deliberative agency of terminally ill adults. Whether or not the statute is morally justified, it is not high-handed. Hence, one of the chief considerations in favor of classifying any paternalistically extinguished legal liberties as legal rights—namely, the fact that being treated with disrespect typically detracts on balance from the goodness of a person's life—is not similarly applicable to the legal liberties removed by the statute in J that forbids suicide.

Cutting strongly in the other direction, however, are at least two main overlapping considerations. First, in any credibly possible world, not all the terminally ill adults in J will harbor the dispositions that have been stipulatively ascribed here to a majority of those adults. Some of the terminally ill people will be devoid of suicidal inclinations irrespective of whether they are legally at liberty to act upon such inclinations, as their holding of legal liberties-to-commit-suicide will not make them feel under pressure to exercise those liberties. Some others will be suicidally inclined regardless of whether they are legally at liberty to end their lives or not. A statute that prohibits them from committing suicide will make no beneficial difference to their lives.

Second, not only will such a statute fail to make any beneficial difference to the lives of those terminally ill people; it will in fact make a significantly detrimental difference. Those suicidally disposed people, or their estates, will now be liable to undergo the imposition of legal sanctions for ending their lives prematurely or attempting to end their lives prematurely (unless the legal duties imposed on them by the statute are wholly unenforceable). Indeed, in that regard, the legal ban on suicide will affect detrimentally the lives of all the terminally ill people who are subject to the ban. Even the terminally ill people who do not harbor any suicidal impulses will now face the prospect of legal sanctions if they ever develop such impulses and act upon them. In this general respect, the legal liberties removed from terminally ill people by the envisioned statute are like other legal liberties. One major reason why nearly all legal liberties are aptly classifiable as legal rights is that the holders of those liberties do not face the prospect of legal sanctions for exercising them. When a legal liberty to φ is removed from anybody, the prospect of legal sanctions for her φ-ing then looms (unless her new legal duty to forbear from φ-ing is wholly unenforceable—in which case she will still face the prospect of becoming a lawbreaker through her φ-ing). *Pro tanto*, her life has been worsened by the removal of that liberty.

Still, although the life of every terminally ill person in J has been worsened by the suicide-forbidding statute in the way just outlined, that fact is not per se sufficient to establish that the lives of most terminally ill people in J have been worsened *on balance* by that statute. Indeed, as has become evident, no conclusion about the on-balance effects of the statute will apply uniformly to the terminally ill people in J. A more nuanced conclusion is requisite here, for the on-balance effects are the focus of the Capacious Version of the Interest Theory. Any terminally ill person spared by the statute from feeling under pressure to end prematurely his or her life has been deprived of certain legal liberties by the statute but not of any legal rights. On balance, the legal liberties extinguished by the statute would have made the life of such a person worse. Accordingly, those liberties are not aptly classifiable as legal rights.

A quite different conclusion is warranted when we turn our attention to each terminally ill person in J whose inclination or disinclination to commit suicide has not been affected by the statute which forbids any conduct of that sort. On balance the life of each such person has been worsened by the statute, as the legal liberties taken away by the statute would on balance have improved the life of each such person if those liberties had been retained. Whether or not each such person in J is at all disposed to undertake any suicidal actions, each such person will now be a lawbreaker if he or she does undertake any actions of that kind. Consequently, the legal liberties that have been withdrawn from each such person by the statute are properly classifiable as legal rights of which he or she has been deprived.

On the one hand, then, the Capacious Version of the Interest Theory leads to the conclusion that the terminally ill people in J saved by the suicide-proscribing statute from feeling under pressure to terminate their lives are not deprived of any legal rights by the statute—though they are of course deprived of some legal liberties by it. On the other hand, the Capacious Version of the Interest Theory equally leads to the conclusion that the terminally ill people in J whose suicidal inclinations or disinclinations remain unaffected by the statute have lost some legal rights through its enactment. With regard to those latter people, the legal liberties removed by the statute are aptly classifiable as legal rights. The intricacy of this combination of conclusions is due to the intricacy of the situation about which the conclusions are reached. In application to circumstances where the lives of most terminally ill people in J are typically enhanced on balance by a suicide-proscribing statute and where the lives of some terminally ill people in J are typically worsened on balance by that statute, the evaluative judgments that inform the Capacious Version of the Interest Theory will be divided. Although the relevant evaluative judgments could be made univocal through a heavy emphasis on the adverb "typically" in my formulation of the theory—where such an emphasis would generate the evaluative verdict that the legal liberties extinguished by the suicide-outlawing statute were typically detrimental on balance for the terminally ill people in J and were thus not appropriately classified as legal rights for any such person—an approach along those lines would gloss over the anfractuosity of the situation in J. To capture that anfractuosity, we need to adopt the combination of verdicts which I have summarized in this paragraph and the preceding couple of paragraphs. A suitably nuanced approach to the dividedness of the circumstances that prevail in J is bound to be untidy.

4.4.9 Claim-Rights and Other Entitlements

Although the Capacious Version of the Interest Theory is valuable as an account of when and why the sundry Hohfeldian entitlements are properly designated as "rights," the version of the Interest Theory presented near the outset of this chapter (and near the outset of Chapter 3) is the principal version. Both the Interest Theory of right-holding and the Will Theory of right-holding—which will be explored at length in §4.5 below—are primarily accounts of what constitutes the holding of a claim-right. Before we move on to investigate the Will Theory and its shortcomings, we should briefly ponder why the Interest Theory of right-holding has been propounded chiefly in connection with claim-rights.

Though Wenar has subsequently published an article focused entirely on the holding of claim-rights (Wenar 2013), his 2005 article "The Nature of Rights" condemns any such restricted focus. In that early publication, his foremost worry about the circumscription of a theory of right-holding is that any such limitation runs against ordinary uses of the language of "rights." Here we return to a strain throughout his work which we have encountered in a general methodological context in §1.3 of Chapter 1. He submits that participants in everyday discourse would be inclined to classify any number of Hohfeldian entitlements as rights, and he thus contends that any philosopher who narrows the ambit of an account of right-holding is thereby "withdrawing [the account] from ordinary language." A cabined exposition of right-holding would be "incorrect for 'rights' as commonly understood" (2005, 243). Accordingly, such an exposition would fail to satisfy the standard for theoretical success which Wenar commends: "The test of a theory of the functions of rights is how well it captures our ordinary understanding of what rights there are" (2005, 238).

As I have fleetingly suggested in §1.3.1 of Chapter 1, an obvious drawback of the extremely heavy reliance by Wenar on what he perceives as ordinary usage is that there does not exist any single "ordinary understanding of what rights there are." Instead, there are multiple ordinary understandings which are inconsistent with one another on quite a few points. As Hohfeld disclosed with a myriad of quotations, even professional jurists tend to employ the terminology of "rights" in confusedly incompatible ways. Wenar himself readily acknowledges that that terminology is "systematically ambiguous," and he further acknowledges that ordinary speakers and writers frequently stumble into fallacies as a result (2005, 236). However, he repeatedly endeavors to defuse such observations with assurances that are curiously disconcerting: "Ordinary rights-talk can be entirely rigorous and error-free, provided that speakers understand how assertions of rights map onto the Hohfeldian [entitlements]" (2005, 237).

Wenar's assurances are far from reassuring, given that each of them carries a patently unsatisfied proviso. Such affirmations are not much more comforting and illuminating than a statement of the following sort: "Any laws against murder in this country can safely be eliminated entirely, provided that nobody in this country will try henceforth to perpetrate any act of murder." Indeed, Wenar's provisos attached to his commendations of ordinary rights-talk can tellingly be countered with a commendation that contains an alternative proviso: "Ordinary rights-talk can be entirely rigorous and error-free, provided that speakers and writers restrict the term 'rights' to Hohfeldian claim-rights (combined with immunities)." When Hohfeldian philosophers frown upon the looseness of the language of "rights" in quotidian discourse, they are distancing themselves from the ways in which laypeople and professional jurists *do* discuss various Hohfeldian entitlements. How those laypeople and jurists *would* discuss Hohfeldian entitlements in a world free of confusion is neither here nor there. Whatever might occur in that counterfactual world, the blanket use of the terminology of "rights" in the actual world to cover all the Hohfeldian entitlements is strongly conducive to muddles in people's thinking and argumentation. Muddles do not ensue inevitably, but they do occur readily and frequently. Hohfeld, with his efforts to expose the paralogisms committed by jurists and legal scholars, aimed to highlight the prevalence of the missteps spawned by the commonly incautious use of the language of "rights."

At any rate, Hohfeldian philosophers are not seeking to issue terminological ukases for everyday communications and contexts. Any such dictates would be quixotic and misconceived. Instead of engaging in such a ridiculously futile enterprise, the exponents of Hohfeld's schema have striven to develop a perspicuous and precise vocabulary within which the debates among philosophers about the nature of rights and right-holding can be conducted rigorously. Those philosophical debates are what the Hohfeldians have essayed to refine. Of course, some of the elements in people's ordinary uses of the language of "rights" are essential as points of departure for these endeavors of refinement, since such endeavors cannot begin from nowhere. If the terminology favored by Hohfeldians were unrecognizable to anyone beyond their circles, it would be obfuscatory and mystifying rather than illuminating and salutary. Predictably, then, and fortunately, each of the labels for each of the Hohfeldian entitlements—"claim-right," "liberty," "power," "immunity"—is indeed familiar to anyone who is competent to ruminate on the nature of rights and right-holding. Each of those labels has a grounding in everyday discourse. For example, the statement "A judge has the legal power to sentence a criminal" is at least as smoothly understandable as is the statement "A judge has the legal right to sentence a criminal." Still, although some of the elements of ordinary usage are indispensable as points of departure for the striving of Hohfeldians to transcend the inadequacies of ordinary usage, they are only points of departure. Some regimentation of the terminology is inevitable if the requisite degree of precision for disputes among philosophers is to be attained. Contrary to what Wenar intimates with his proviso-laden assurances, ordinary discourse includes the stumbles into which people are led when their modes of expression are insufficiently discriminating. Philosophers who hope to eschew those missteps, and who aspire to keep in view many subtle distinctions that are largely or entirely obscured in the conversations of everyday life, are well advised to avail themselves of a much more exact vocabulary for their own argumentation. Indeed, Wenar himself with his provisos is engaging obliquely in the regimentation of quotidian patterns of speaking and writing. He is avouching, however reluctantly, that the rigor of a philosophical theory cannot be attained if those quotidian patterns are taken on board without any purification.

Given the need for some regimentation, the confinement of the term "rights" to claim-rights accompanied by immunities is aptly warranted in most contexts. In fact, the foremost reason for adopting such a tack is itself grounded in the presuppositions of everyday usage. As Hohfeld's investigations tended to confirm, an assumption which ordinarily underlies the wielding of the noun "right" is that the holder of an entitlement denoted by that noun is owed a duty with some specified content. An assumption to that effect will be fully apt when the Hohfeldian entitlement under consideration is a claim-right—since every claim-right held by P vis-à-vis Q is correlated with a duty owed by Q to P, where the claim-right and the duty have the same content—but is otherwise prone to be false. Hence, reserving the term "rights" predominantly for claim-rights (coupled with immunities) is singularly appropriate. Although that regimentation along those lines might diverge from some of the modes of classification in everyday discourse and juristic discourse at a superficial level, it is in keeping with those modes of classification at a deeper level. It is in keeping with the main consideration that drives them.

A key factor behind the frequency with which Hohfeldian liberties and powers are categorized as "rights" is that virtually all instances of such entitlements are accompanied by claim-rights against many ways of preventing people from exercising those entitlements. As has been argued in §2.5.3 of Chapter 2, the accompaniment of legal liberties and legal powers by legal claim-rights against various ways of thwarting people from exercising those liberties or powers is a matter of metaphysical necessity. Likewise, the accompaniment of moral liberties and moral powers by moral claim-rights against various means of precluding people from exercising those powers and liberties is a matter of moral necessity (Kramer 2009a, 157–61). Here the point to be accentuated is that the accompaniment of liberties and powers by such claim-rights is indispensable for the appositeness of categorizing those Hohfeldian entitlements as "rights." For example, if a liberty to walk down Grange Road were *mirabile dictu* somehow unaccompanied by any claim-rights against some major ways of foiling the exercise of that liberty, it could not germanely be classified as a "right." Only because one's legal liberty to walk down Grange Road will always be accompanied by some legal claim-rights against major ways in which one's exercise of that liberty could be stymied, is the liberty itself properly classifiable as a legal right in the capacious sense. What carries a large share of the burden of earning the label "right" for that liberty is the protective ambit of one's elementary claim-rights that are held in conjunction with the liberty. Purely on its own, the liberty is not sufficient to warrant that label. By contrast, a claim-right does not need such supplementation to be aptly classifiable as a right. It is itself an instance of protection against interference or uncooperativeness, and it is itself thus appropriately categorizable as a right both within ordinary discourse and within the Hohfeldian analysis of legal and moral positions.

To be sure, as has been emphasized in §2.7.2 of Chapter 2, the very existence of a claim-right depends on its being accompanied by immunities against the extinguishing of the claim-right through the modes of behavior that would violate it, and the substantiveness (as opposed to hollowness) of a claim-right depends on its being accompanied by immunities against the extinguishing of the claim-right through sundry humdrum modes of behavior. If John vis-à-vis Peter supposedly has a legal claim-right not to be prevented from entering a certain edifice, and if Peter can divest John of that claim-right by smiling at him or by saying something to him or by waving at him, John's legal claim-right vis-à-vis Peter is hollow rather than substantive. However, the lesson to be drawn here is not really that the concomitant immunities against divestiture are necessary for the existence and substantiveness of John's legal claim-right as a legal *right*. Rather, the presence of the concomitant immunities is necessary for the existence and substantiveness of his claim-right as a legal *entitlement* or legal *position* of any kind. There cannot ever be a legal entitlement of any kind that is wholly unaccompanied by legal immunities against its termination. Claim-rights are no different from other Hohfeldian entitlements in that respect.

In short, the role played by the elementary immunities that accompany John's claim-right—an existence-sustaining and hollowness-averting role—is on a par with the role played by the elementary immunities that accompany other entitlements. Quite different is the vital role played by the elementary claim-rights that accompany any liberties or powers. That latter role consists not in sustaining the very existence of a liberty or power but instead in sustaining the classifiability of each of them as a legal or moral right. Because liberties and powers are almost always coupled with claim-rights that inherently protect the abilities of the holders of the liberties and powers to exercise their respective entitlements, the liberties and powers can pertinently be classified as "rights" under the Capacious Version of the Interest Theory. (Of course, whether they will be classified as "rights" is dependent on their satisfaction of the requirement that is specified in the Capacious Version of the Interest Theory itself.) Given that the accompaniment of legal liberties and legal powers by elementary legal claim-rights is a matter of metaphysical necessity, and given that the accompaniment of moral liberties and moral powers by elementary moral claim-rights is a matter of moral necessity, the Capacious Version of the Interest Theory does not expressly indicate that Hohfeldian liberties and powers properly classifiable as "rights" are conjoined with claim-rights against many of the ways in which people can be prevented from exercising those entitlements. Instead, it safely presupposes that such entitlements always will be so conjoined.

Since claim-rights are distinctive in sustaining the classifiability of other Hohfeldian entitlements as "rights" in the capacious sense, the singling out of claim-rights as rights in the principal version of the Interest Theory—the version formulated near the outset of this chapter and near the outset of Chapter 3—is scarcely an arbitrary stipulation. Inasmuch as the Interest Theory and the rival Will Theory are indeed explications of the conditions under which claim-rights are held, the key issue between them is puzzlingly put aside by Wenar: "Notice here that B's duty is not simply to perform the action.... It is a duty that is owed to or directed toward A. Explaining the 'direction' of duties is not simple, and I put this issue to one side here" (2005, 229 n. 7). As should already be manifest, and as will become evident still further in the rest of this chapter, the matter brushed aside by Wenar in this quotation is at the heart of the wrangling between the proponents of the Interest Theory and the proponents of the Will Theory. By setting forth the necessary and sufficient conditions for the holding of a claim-right, each theory is pinning down the location(s) of the party or parties to whom a correlative duty is owed. Advocates of the Will Theory contend that the direction of any legal or moral duty is determined by the location of the legal or moral powers through which the existence and enforcement of the duty can be controlled, whereas advocates of the Interest Theory maintain that the direction of any duty is determined by the location(s) of the typically beneficial effects that are inherent to the fulfillment of the duty. These competing theses generate the multiple points of controversy over which the Interest Theorists and the Will Theorists have long quarreled. We shall encounter those points of contention in the rest of this chapter. Wenar himself addresses some of those points of contention in his 2005 article and in a couple of his subsequent essays, yet in the quotation above he seems not to apprehend that the tussles between Interest Theorists and Will Theorists derive from the divergences between their answers to the question about the directionality of duties. Having prescinded from that question in the quoted pronouncement, Wenar obscures the central impetus that animates the Interest/Will disputation which he purports to resolve and transcend. That impetus returns to view when we recognize that the Interest Theory and the Will Theory are focused on claim-rights (accompanied by immunities), which are always correlated with duties that are owed to the holders of the claim-rights. Far from being an arid stipulation, my insistence that those theories are focused on claim-rights is crucial for making full sense of the philosophical scuffling in which both Wenar and I are participants.

4.5 Objections to the Will Theory of Right-Holding

In this final main section of Chapter 4, we return to the Interest Theory in its principal form by examining the foremost rival to it. For many decades, the Interest Theory's account of the necessary and sufficient conditions for the holding of a claim-right has been contested chiefly by the supporters of the rival Will Theory. To be sure, in recent times there have arisen some alternative theories that purport to bring together the strengths of the Interest Theory and the Will Theory. However, because I have elsewhere sought to expose some of the fatal weaknesses of those hybrid theories (Kramer 2013, 258–62; 2022, 394–401; Kramer and Steiner 2007, 308–10), and because Sreenivasan and Mark McBride as the two leading champions of those hybrid approaches are currently producing book-length expositions of their respective doctrines, I will not engage here with their attempts to devise their alternative accounts of right-holding. Instead, the rest of this chapter will do battle with the Will Theory in defense of the Interest Theory.

Like the Interest Theory, the Will Theory has emerged over the years in more than one form. Nevertheless, the gist of the Will Theory in its multiple incarnations can be summarized as follows:

> **Will Theory**: Both necessary and sufficient for the holding by *X* of a claim-right correlative to some specified duty is that *X* is competent and authorized to control the existence and enforcement of that duty.

This formulation of the Will Theory is in need of some elucidation and amplification. Straightaway, however, the inconsistencies between the Will Theory and the Interest Theory should be palpable. Although the extension of the Will Theory's criterion overlaps considerably with that of the Interest Theory's criterion, the two theories generate divergent conclusions in quite a few cases. Their extensional intersection falls well short of extensional equivalence. Even more clearly, the two theories diverge intensionally. Conditions singled out by either theory as necessary and sufficient for the holding of a claim-right are markedly different from those singled out by the rival theory.

In my formulation of the Will Theory, the notion of competence refers to the basic mental and physical abilities through which a party can make the sorts of choices that are involved in controlling the existence and enforcement of a specified duty. A party who lacks those abilities is not capable of holding claim-rights, by the reckoning of the Will Theorists. (We shall return to the matter of competence shortly.) The notion of authorization in my formulation of the Will Theory refers to the fact that a party is endowed with the Hohfeldian powers through which the existence and enforcement of a specified duty can be controlled. Such powers will have had to be conferred upon a party by some relevant law(s) or by some relevant moral principle(s), if that party is to qualify as a holder of a legal or moral claim-right that is correlated with the legal or moral duty to which the powers pertain. Or so the Will Theorists insist. Hence, those theorists are submitting that any holder of a claim-right CR is possessed of Hohfeldian powers to control the existence and enforcement of the duty that is correlated with CR, and that any holder of CR is endowed with sufficient cognitive and physical abilities to make choices between exercising and not exercising those powers. Intellectual abilities and normative abilities are constitutive of the holding of claim-rights, by the reckoning of the Will Theorists.

Further elucidation of the central tenet of the Will Theory can best proceed through some amplification. We need to fathom what is involved in the controlling of a duty through the exercising of Hohfeldian powers. On this point, Hart—the pre-eminent champion of the Will Theory in the twentieth century—valuably shed some light. He differentiated among three main stages at which the powers of control are held: the pre-violation stage, the post-violation stage, and the post-judgment stage (1982, 183–4). At each of these stages, a holder of a claim-right possesses two relevant Hohfeldian powers through which the holder can exercise control over a duty. For most duties, the first of the three stages is the only one that is ever reached. That is, because most duties go unviolated, there do not arise any occasions for legal proceedings or other measures through which those duties are enforced and the violations are rectified. Hence, the pre-violation phase of a duty's existence is the sole phase for most duties, and it is of course the stage in which *every* actual duty exists (perhaps for an indefinite duration) at some time or another. At that pre-violation juncture, according to the Will Theory, the holder of a claim-right correlative to a specified duty is endowed with a Hohfeldian power to keep the duty in existence and with a Hohfeldian power to extinguish the duty.

Subsequent stages of control over a duty materialize only when the duty in question has been contravened. At the post-violation juncture, according to the Will Theory, the holder of a claim-right correlative to a specified duty is endowed with a Hohfeldian power to waive any enforcement of the duty and with a Hohfeldian power to initiate and pursue such enforcement. (Each of the powers mentioned here can in fact be multiple powers, as we shall see.) If the party who holds the claim-right does exercise his or her power to effectuate the duty by going ahead with a process of enforcement, and if that process is pursued successfully, it will lead to a prescribed remedy. The Will Theorists contend that, at the post-judgment stage where a remedy has been prescribed, the holder of a claim-right correlative to the contravened duty is endowed with a Hohfeldian power to insist upon the implementation of the remedy and with a Hohfeldian power to waive the implementation of the remedy. At each of the three stages delineated by Hart, then, a holder of a claim-right correlative to a specified duty is—according to the Will Theory—endowed with a pair of Hohfeldian powers (or a pair of sets of Hohfeldian powers) through which the existence and effectuation of the duty can be controlled. Although many a duty will never go beyond the first of those three stages, a party is not a holder of a claim-right correlative to a given duty unless he or she would hold the Hohfeldian powers of control over that duty at each stage that might arise. Such are the tenets of the Will Theory of right-holding. Hart famously articulated the kernel of that theory as follows: "The idea is that of one individual being given by the law exclusive control, more or less extensive, over another person's duty so that in the area of conduct covered by that duty the individual who has the right is a small-scale sovereign to whom the duty is owed" (1982, 183).

4.5.1 A First Set of Objections

In the philosophical literature, the most familiar objections to the Will Theory are question-begging in that each of them presupposes the fallaciousness of that theory. Each of those standard objections rests on the premise that the Will Theory's analysis of the holding of claim-rights is incorrect. To say as much, however, is scarcely to say that such criticisms of the Will Theory are misguided or that they are lacking in trenchancy. On the contrary, each of them is very powerful indeed, and together they constitute a devastating indictment of the Will Theory. Hence, this chapter will begin its critiques of the Will Theory with these oft-voiced complaints before it moves on to some critiques which are more innovative and which are not question-begging. (Of course, when I characterize these opening complaints as very powerful, I am not suggesting that they will perforce be dialectically effective as means of convincing the votaries of the Will Theory to abandon their allegiances. Precisely because these initial criticisms beg the question against the Will Theory, their effectiveness as means of persuasion will typically be limited. Still, anybody not already enamored of the Will Theory should recognize the forcefulness of this opening volley of objections, and in any event this chapter will presently pose some objections against the Will Theory that are not question-begging.)

4.5.1.1 A Claim-Right Not to Be Murdered or Rendered Comatose

Under the Will Theory, nobody can ever hold a claim-right against being murdered by anyone else. Likewise, nobody can ever hold a claim-right against being subjected to a violent attack that will leave him or her permanently comatose. By the reckoning of the Will Theorists, the notion of a claim-right not to be murdered or a claim-right not to be rendered comatose is unsustainable. No one can ever hold a claim-right with such a content—by the reckoning of those theorists—because anybody who is a victim of a murder or of a coma-inducing attack will be incompetent to exercise any Hohfeldian powers at the second and third stages of enforceability which Hart delineated. Thus, the Will Theorists are committed to concluding that an act of murder or a coma-inducing attack does not contravene any legal or moral claim-rights of its victim. They are similarly committed to denying that a legal or moral duty to abstain from such an extreme crime is ever owed by a potential perpetrator to any potential victim of the crime.

Far from being rejected or grudgingly accepted by a staunch supporter of the Will Theory, these corollaries of the theory are welcomingly embraced. Hart, for example, wrote that "nothing seems to be gained in significance or clarity by translating, e.g. the statement that men are under a legal duty not to murder, assault, or steal from others into the statement that individuals have a right not to be murdered, assaulted, or stolen from, or by saying, when a man has been murdered, that his right not to be killed has been violated" (1982, 182). In part, Hart's meditations on this matter stemmed from something which I have criticized in §3.4 of Chapter 3: namely, from his correct but untenably one-sided insistence that every instance of the holding of a claim-right by P vis-à-vis Q is redescribable as the bearing of a duty by Q vis-à-vis P. Indeed, that insistence by Hart arose from his dismissal of a crude version of the Interest Theory. In addition, however, his commendation of the peculiar conclusions which I have synopsized here was due to his espousal of the Will Theory. Somebody not so besotted with the Will Theory should grasp how obfuscatory those peculiar conclusions are. They obscure the fact that claim-rights fundamentally are deontic protections.

4.5.1.2 No Claim-Rights of Victims under the Criminal Law

Hart's insistence that individuals do not hold any claim-rights against being murdered or rendered comatose was partly an offshoot of his broader insistence that the institutions of criminal law do not bestow any legal claim-rights upon individuals or groups. Hart observed correctly that a victim of a crime does not hold the pairs of Hohfeldian powers which would enable the victim to control the existence and enforcement of the legal duty that has been breached by the perpetration of the crime. As Hart wrote: "A person protected only by the criminal law has no power to release anyone from its duties, and though, as in England, he may in theory be entitled to prosecute along with any other member of the public he has no unique power to determine whether the duties of the criminal law should be enforced or not" (1982, 184). Indeed, Hart here understated the matter. Not only does a person protected by criminal-law prohibitions have no legal powers to *waive* most of the duties imposed by those prohibitions, but in addition such a person has no legal powers to *keep* the duties in existence. Those legal duties persist not because of any actions performed by such a person, but instead because of legal immunities which accompany the duties and which prevent them from being extinguished. Moreover, at the post-violation stage the vast majority of criminal-law proceedings in a jurisdiction such as that of England are pursued by public prosecutors rather than by the individuals who have been victimized by crimes. It is the prosecutors rather than the victims who hold the relevant Hohfeldian powers. Furthermore, the rare prosecutions pursued privately in England cannot usually go ahead without the assent of the Director of Public Prosecutions. At the post-violation stage, then, a victim of a crime is decidedly not furnished with sovereign control over the duty that has been contravened by the perpetrator of the crime. Similarly, at the post-judgment stage, a victim of a crime in a jurisdiction such as England typically does not have any Hohfeldian powers to determine whether the sentence pronounced by the judge will be implemented or not. In short, at none of the three stages outlined by Hart—much less at each of the three stages—do potential victims of crimes in most jurisdictions possess Hohfeldian powers of control over the duties incumbent on potential malefactors. Consequently, by the reckoning of Will Theorists such as Hart, the criminal-law prohibitions in most jurisdictions do not confer any legal claim-rights upon the parties who might be victimized by transgressions of those prohibitions. No such claim-rights are held by individuals under the criminal law of most jurisdictions, or so the Will Theorists insist.

4.5.1.3 Minimum-Wage Laws

Under most minimum-wage laws, which require employers to pay their workers at or above some specified levels of remuneration, prospective employees are not legally empowered to waive the duties owed by the employers. An employer continues to be legally obligated to pay each laborer at or above the legally specified level, even if a new laborer has agreed to accept a lower amount of remuneration. Minimum-wage obligations are typically made unwaivable in this fashion because a minimum-wage scheme would be highly precarious in the absence of such unwaivability. If some prospective employees are willing to toil for lower wages, and if they exercise legal powers to waive the legally prescribed minimum of remuneration, the prospective employees who would not otherwise agree to work at the lower rates will come under great pressure to do so—insofar as they wish not to remain unemployed. Very rapidly in most credible circumstances, then, a minimum-wage scheme would become inefficacious if the legal obligations imposed by it on employers were waivable. Accordingly, to uphold the protective purpose of such a scheme, a system of governance that introduces it will typically make unwaivable the legal duties which it establishes. Any prospective employee therefore lacks one of the key legal powers that would enable him or her to exercise control over a minimum-wage duty. (Any prospective employee also lacks most of the other legal powers that would enable such control, but I am here concentrating only on the power of waiver at the pre-violation stage.) Yet, because individuals will each lack that key power to control the duty owed by an employer, the champions of the

Will Theory have to conclude that any typical minimum-wage law does not confer claim-rights upon individuals to be paid at or above a certain level.

If a lawyer who adheres to the Will Theory is asked by a client whether the client has a legal claim-right to receive a minimum level of remuneration from his or her new employer, the theoretical allegiances of the lawyer call for a negative answer even though a minimum-wage statute is operative in the jurisdiction where the question has been posed. Of course, the lawyer can endeavor to alleviate the joltingness and peculiarity of such an answer—or perhaps to intensify its joltingness and peculiarity—by adding that the relevant employer is under a legal duty to remunerate the client at or above the minimum level. Maybe the exponents of the Will Theory regard such a response to the client's question as illuminating and perceptive, but anyone not enamored of the theory should be struck by the obtuseness of the response. Once again, the Will Theory's obfuscation of the fundamentally protective role of claim-rights is promotive of confusion rather than of insight.

4.5.1.4 The Class of Potential Holders of Claim-Rights

Although my next chapter will sustainedly grapple with the challenges involved in demarcating the class of potential holders of claim-rights, we need to contemplate that class more briefly here to descry one of the gravest shortcomings of the Will Theory. What has drawn more outspoken condemnation than any other feature of the theory is its exclusion of various types of beings from the category of potential holders of claim-rights. Because the Will Theorists insist that competence to make the sorts of choices required for controlling the duties of others is essential to the status of anyone as a potential holder of claim-rights, they are committed to affirming that only human adults of sound mind can ever hold any claim-rights. Among the beings excluded by the Will Theory from the category of potential holders of claim-rights are babies, infants, most children, insane people, people afflicted with dementia, permanently comatose people, foetuses, dead people, future generations, and all non-human animals. No such beings are capable of holding any claim-rights, because no such beings are capable of choosing non-fortuitously between exercising Hohfeldian powers and refraining from exercising those powers.

A diehard supporter of the Will Theory will be inclined to applaud the restrictions imposed by that theory on the class of potential holders of claim-rights. For example, specifically with reference to babies and non-human animals as potential holders of claim-rights in the realm of morality, Hart grasped the nettle as follows (1955, 181):

> These considerations should incline us not to extend to animals and babies whom it is wrong to ill-treat the notion of a [moral] right to proper treatment, for the moral situation can be simply and adequately described here by saying that it is

> wrong or that we ought not to ill-treat them or, in the philosopher's generalized sense of "duty," that we have a [moral] duty not to ill-treat them. If common usage sanctions talk of the rights of animals or babies it makes an idle use of the expression "a right," which will confuse the situation with other different moral situations where the expression "a right" has a specific force and cannot be replaced by... other moral expressions.

Other staunch admirers of the Will Theory, such as Nigel Simmonds, concur with Hart on this point (1998, 226 n. 138): "As regards moral rights, there is surely much merit in the claim that our moral concern for very small children is based on a concern for their welfare quite independently of their choices; as they grow older, some of our duties towards them come to be contingent upon their will. Is not this moral difference aptly reflected by the Will Theory of rights?"

Still, regardless of how confident the Will Theorists have generally been in the correctness of their position on this matter, the most frequent source of dissatisfaction with the Will Theory is the insistence by its proponents that infants and demented people and sundry others do not hold any moral or legal claim-rights. Indeed, as I have remarked elsewhere (1998, 69–70), Hart eventually retreated somewhat from his emphatic rejection of the idea of claim-rights held by babies and infants. In his final major essay on the topic of rights and right-holding, partly in response to remonstrations from Neil MacCormick and other philosophers about the holding of claim-rights by children, Hart allowed that legal claim-rights can properly be ascribed to infants (1982, 184 n. 86):

> Where infants or other persons not *sui juris* have rights, [the Hohfeldian powers of control over the correlative duties] are exercised on their behalf by appointed representatives and their exercise may be subject to approval by a court. But since (a) what such representatives can and cannot do by way of exercise of such power[s] is determined by what those whom they represent could have done if *sui juris* and (b) when the latter become *sui juris* they can exercise these powers without any transfer or fresh assignment; the powers are regarded as belonging throughout to them and not to their representatives, though they are only exercisable by the latter during the period of disability.

Hart stopped short here of repudiating the Will Theory, but he did plainly distance himself from one of the theory's many disconcerting implications.

Though Simmonds declares that Hart's attempt to reconcile the Will Theory with the holding of legal claim-rights by infants is "quite persuasive" (1998, 226 n. 138), what is noteworthy here is the feebleness of that attempt. Hart was of course correct in acknowledging that legal claim-rights can be held by infants, but he did not succeed in establishing that his acknowledgment of that point could be squared with his continued espousal of the Will Theory. Of the two reasons which he adduced for accepting that infants can hold legal claim-rights, the first would be applicable to each of the types of beings mentioned in the opening paragraph of this subsection. For any of those beings, the Hohfeldian powers exercisable by parties appointed to represent them in furtherance of their interests are the Hohfeldian powers that would be exercisable by the beings themselves if they were *sui juris*. If permanently comatose people or non-human animals or any of the other listed beings were *sui juris*, they would be able to exercise the powers that are in fact exercised on their behalf by the parties appointed to represent them. Of course, none of those beings is actually *sui juris*, because none of them possesses the competence—the basic cognitive and communicative abilities—on which the status of a being as *sui juris* depends. However, the same is obviously true of the infants whom Hart was discussing. Thus, Hart eviscerated the Will Theory with the first of his reasons for avowing that infants can hold legal claim-rights, as his reasoning would impel us to conclude that all the beings apparently excluded by that theory from the category of potential holders of claim-rights are instead within the confines of that category.

Of course, Hart did not present the first of his two reasons in isolation. He conjoined it with his second reason. Did that second consideration serve Hart's purposes any better than the first? The answer to this question is negative, for the second consideration is like the first in that it can apply to any of the beings whom the Will Theorists have purported to exclude from the category of potential holders of claim-rights. Admittedly, most of those beings never will become *sui juris*, because most of them never will develop the elementary cognitive and communicative abilities that are prerequisite to that status. However, the same is true of some human infants, and in any event the second reason adduced by Hart does not submit that infants are potential holders of legal claim-rights because they will eventually become *sui juris*. It instead submits that infants are potential holders of legal claim-rights because, when they become *sui juris*, they will thereby be able to exercise the Hohfeldian powers that are currently exercisable on their behalf by the parties appointed to represent them. No further transaction or appointment will be necessary for the exercisability of the specified powers by an erstwhile infant. Such a thesis is entirely consistent with the possibility that some infants will never become *sui juris* (a possibility that will be an actuality for some infants). Infants who do not eventually become *sui juris* are nonetheless included in the class of potential holders of legal claim-rights because, if they were to become *sui juris*, they would thereby be able to exercise the Hohfeldian powers that are currently exercisable only by their appointed representatives. Similarly, other beings who do not eventually become *sui juris* are includable in the class of potential holders of legal claim-rights because, if they were ever to become *sui juris*, they too without further legal formalities could be able to exercise the Hohfeldian powers that are currently exercisable on their behalf by the parties appointed to represent them. To be sure, as a jurisdiction-specific matter, there might not exist any arrangements—in this or that particular society—for accommodating those other beings as holders of legal powers and claim-rights. Nonetheless, as a matter of credible possibility anywhere rather than as a matter of jurisdiction-specific actuality here or there, Hart's second consideration can encompass any of the beings traditionally excluded by the Will Theory from the class of potential holders of claim-rights.

Defenders of the Will Theory might retort by pointing out that most human infants do eventually develop the competence which the Will Theory regards as essential for the holding of claim-rights. By contrast, dead people and non-human animals and permanently comatose people and people suffering from severe dementia never develop or redevelop such competence. Now, even if a rejoinder along those lines were apposite, it would leave intact my argumentation in the preceding couple of paragraphs with reference to foetuses and future generations and insane people. Most foetuses and most members of future generations do acquire cognitive abilities that are constitutive of competence, and some insane people recover those abilities. Accordingly, contrary to what the champions of the Will Theory have generally presumed, their theory as Hart elaborated it through his ruminations on the legal claim-rights of infants is fully consistent with the holding of legal claim-rights by foetuses and future generations and insane people.

In fact, furthermore, the posited riposte by the devotees of the Will Theory—the riposte focused on the fact that most infants come to be endowed with the cognitive abilities involved in the exercising of legal powers—is inapposite. It is an *ignoratio elenchi*. Hart, in the second of his reasons for granting that infants can hold legal claim-rights, did not rest his case on the proposition that most infants will eventually become endowed with the aforementioned cognitive abilities. He instead rested his case on the proposition that, when the infants do grow up and become so endowed in certain jurisdictions such as England, the exercisability of legal powers by them does not have to be preceded by any legal formalities. In those jurisdictions, the exercisability of the powers is an automatic legal appurtenance of one's gaining the cognitive abilities through which one can meaningfully make choices. Now, for any of the beings whom the Will Theorists have thought to exclude from the category of potential holders of claim-rights, there can be in place a legal arrangement of the kind Hart envisaged (as I have already suggested).

For example, the legislators in some jurisdiction J might superstitiously believe that dead people can be brought back to life through certain talismanic rituals like those administered by Elijah and Elisha in the Hebrew Scriptures or by Jesus in the gospels. Consequently, the legislators in J enact a statute which provides that any dead people magically revived through such rituals are thereafter automatically able to exercise the legal powers that are currently exercisable on their behalf by parties appointed to represent their interests. In the jurisdiction of J, then, dead people are holders of legal claim-rights that would have to be recognized as such by Hartian Will Theorists. Since dead people are *actual* holders of legal claim-rights in J, they belong everywhere to the class of *potential* holders of legal claim-rights that would have to be recognized as such by the Hartian Will Theorists. Or suppose that the legislators in a jurisdiction K wish to take account of the fact that some people presumed to be permanently comatose might somehow regain consciousness along with the psychological capacities that are constitutive of the competence of anyone who holds claim-rights by the reckoning of the Will Theorists. In accordance with that concern, the legislators in K enact a statute which applies to comatose people in much the same way in which the statute enacted by J's legislators is applicable to dead people. Hence, in the jurisdiction of K, permanently comatose people are holders of legal claim-rights that would have to be recognized as such by the Hartian Will Theorists. And since comatose people are actual holders of legal claim-rights in K, they belong everywhere to the class of potential holders of legal claim-rights that would have to be recognized as such by the Hartian Will Theorists. Or suppose that the legislators in another jurisdiction L think that non-human animals can occasionally acquire high levels of cognitive sophistication. Thinking as much, the legislators enact a statute which provides that any non-human animals who do acquire such sophistication are automatically thenceforward able to exercise the legal powers that are currently exercisable on their behalf by parties appointed to represent their interests. In the jurisdiction of L, therefore, non-human animals are holders of legal claim-rights that would have to be recognized as such by the Hartian Will Theorists. Given that non-human animals are actual holders of legal claim-rights in L, they too belong everywhere to the class of potential holders of legal claim-rights that would have to be recognized as such by the Hartian Will Theorists.

In sum, Hart's two reasons for acknowledging the possibility and actuality of the holding of legal claim-rights by infants will have undermined the Will Theory. *Malgré lui*, Hart with his reasoning expanded the category of potential holders of legal claim-rights to comprise all the beings whom the Will Theorists have long perceived as beyond the confines of that category. His followers such as Simmonds continue to undermine the Will Theory by endorsing his reasoning. If adherents of the Will Theory want to keep their doctrine extensionally distinguishable from the Interest Theory when they delimit the class of potential holders of legal claim-rights, they will have to re-embrace the unflinchingness of Hart in 1955 as he brusquely dismissed the idea of legal claim-rights held by infants. Of course, the disagreeableness of rejecting that idea outright is what led Hart to adopt his concessionary posture in his later work. However, his effort to limit the damaging implications of his concession cannot withstand scrutiny. If Hartian Will Theorists wish to remain Will Theorists, they cannot eschew their insistence that babies and infants never hold any legal or moral claim-rights.

In fairness to the Will Theorists, I should close this subsection with a caveat. As I have always readily acknowledged (Kramer 1998, 69; 2001, 29–30), the fact that the Will Theorists dissociate themselves from the idea of claim-rights held by infants or insane people or non-human animals does not mean that those theorists have committed themselves in any way to opposing the conferral of legal protections upon such beings. On the contrary, with perfect consistency they can favor the conferral of wide-ranging legal protections upon such beings—as all or virtually all Will Theorists do. Thus, for example, Simmonds as an impassioned environmentalist does not exhibit any inconsistency when he as a Will Theorist stoutly discountenances the notion of claim-rights held by non-human animals. Environmentalist manifestos prescribe the extent to which and the ways in which the interests of animals should be legally protected, but they can leave open the question whether the duties imposed through the relevant legal protections are correlated with claim-rights held by the non-human animals. Here we encounter afresh the distinction drawn in Chapter 1 between justificatory matters and non-justificatory matters that pertain to rights and right-holding. Will Theorists *qua* Will Theorists are taking stands on some central non-justificatory questions that pertain to the holding of claim-rights, but *qua* Will Theorists they are not taking stands on justificatory questions of the sorts that are addressed by most environmentalist credos. Hence, Simmonds is not deviating from the Will Theory at all when he calls for the well-being of animals to be stringently protected through legislation. Though the Will Theory certainly does not commit its defenders to espousing the tenets of an environmentalist creed with abundant solicitude for the well-being of animals, it is unproblematically consistent with such tenets. (Nothing in this paragraph should be taken to suggest that the matter broached in this subsection—the matter of delimiting the category of potential holders of claim-rights—is without any significant ethical dimension. On the contrary, as will become clear in my next chapter, any efforts to demarcate the category of potential holders of claim-rights must tackle some profound ethical issues. One reason for looking askance at the Will Theory is that it mishandles and oversimplifies the subtleties of those ethical issues. However, in my criticism of the Will Theorists along those lines, I am condemning their ethical glibness rather than any errors of logical inconsistency. That criticism is entirely compatible with my acknowledgment here that the account of right-holding propounded by the Will Theorists does not entail any positions in justificatory debates over the types and magnitude of the legal protections that should be bestowed on the interests of various beings. Such an account of right-holding does not entail or bespeak any stance of grim unconcern for those beings on the part of the Will Theorists.)

4.5.1.5 Fundamental Rights

Many of the claim-rights and other Hohfeldian entitlements possessed by people can be waived or transferred or forfeited. However, both as a matter of law in most jurisdictions and as a matter of the correct principles of morality, not all such entitlements are relinquishable in those ways. One's claim-right not to be subjected to lethal torture, for example, is insusceptible to being waived or forfeited. Similarly, one's claim-right against the lopping off of one's limbs by anybody else is insusceptible to being forfeited or waived (except in circumstances of medical exigency where the amputation of one's limbs is necessary for saving one's life). Likewise, one's claim-right and immunity against being sold permanently into slavery cannot ever be waived or forfeited. These claim-rights and certain other claim-rights are accompanied not by powers of waiver and forfeiture but instead by disabilities and their correlative immunities. So accompanied, the claim-rights are entrenchedly fortified against being extinguished or suspended during the life of each person who possesses them. Precisely because of the entrenchedness of those claim-rights, however, the Will Theorists are committed by their doctrine to denying that those entitlements are genuine claim-rights at all. As has been observed, the Will Theorists contend that the holder of any claim-right is vested with paired Hohfeldian powers of waiver and retention or enforcement at each of the three stages of a duty/claim-right relationship. For any claim-right like the ones mentioned here, the holder of the claim-right does not possess any power of waiver—or forfeiture or transfer—at the pre-violation stage of the claim-right's existence. Consequently, the Will Theorists have to conclude that each such apparent claim-right is not really a claim-right. (Of course, any holder of a claim-right not to be subjected to lethal torture will have ceased to exist at the post-violation and post-judgment stages of enforceability and will therefore lack any Hohfeldian powers at those stages. Accordingly, as I have maintained in §4.5.1.1 with reference to the broader claim-right against being murdered, any Will Theorists who concentrate on those subsequent stages of enforceability will contend that a claim-right against being subjected to lethal torture is not genuinely a claim-right. Here, however, I am concentrating on the pre-violation phase of a duty's existence. With a focus on that phase, the Will Theorists will reach the same conclusion about a claim-right against being subjected to lethal torture, but they will also reach that conclusion with reference to the other unwaivable claim-rights which have been mentioned here and indeed with reference to any unwaivable claim-rights.)

MacCormick forcefully derided the views of the Will Theorists on the status of these fundamental inalienable claim-rights (1977, 195–9). As he pointed out, such claim-rights inherently protect the vital interests of the parties who hold them, whereas many alienable claim-rights inherently protect some considerably less important aspects of one's situation such as one's possession of paltry gewgaws in one's residence. Yet the Will Theorists perceive those latter claim-rights as veritable claim-rights while insisting that the inalienable claim-rights which inherently protect vital interests are not properly classified as claim-rights at all. Now, although the Will Theorists are correct in thinking that one's legal and moral claim-rights against being deprived of one's gewgaws are genuine claim-rights, they go badly astray in presuming that the entrenchedness of certain fundamental duties which inherently protect the basic interests and autonomy of individuals is such that the individuals inherently protected by those duties do not hold any correlative claim-rights.

As has been stated, the entrenchedness of those fundamental duties and their correlative claim-rights is due to immunities (and their correlative disabilities) that prevent the duties and claim-rights from being extinguished even by the choices of the people who hold the claim-rights. I might thus seem to be overlooking the fact that Hart adopted an approach to immunities which differed significantly from his approach to claim-rights. Within Hart's cogitations, the dissimilarities between those approaches surfaced precisely in connection with the fundamental interests and autonomy of individuals. Whereas Hart dismissed as redundant the notion that individuals hold claim-rights vis-à-vis one another under the criminal law of any jurisdiction, he was far from dismissive in allowing that the immunities conferred upon individuals by many of the provisions in constitutional bills of rights are properly classified as rights: "But this accusation of redundancy is no longer pertinent when what is to be considered are not rights under the ordinary law, but fundamental rights which may be said to be against the legislature, limiting its powers to make (or unmake) the ordinary law, where so to do would deny to individuals certain freedoms and benefits now regarded as essentials of human well-being, such as freedom of speech and of association, freedom from arbitrary arrest, security of life and person, education, and equality of treatment in certain respects" (1982, 190). In a like vein, he remarked: "The chief, though not the only employment of this notion of an immunity from adverse legal change which we may call an 'immunity right' is to characterize distinctively the position of individuals protected from such adverse change by constitutional limitations or, as Hohfeld would say, by disabilities of the legislature. Such immunity rights are obviously of extreme importance to individuals and may usually be asserted in the form of justifiable claims that some purported enactment is invalid because it infringes them" (1982, 191, footnote omitted). Given these statements by Hart, my strictures in this subsection might seem to be unfair to him and to other Will Theorists. He might seem to have placed himself beyond the reach of those strictures, because he might seem to have granted already—long ago—that the fundamental legal protections for the vital interests and autonomy of individuals are aptly classifiable as rights.

Any such complaint about the supposed unfairness or inappositeness of my objections to the Will Theory in this subsection would itself be misguided. Hart, in his comments on the legal immunities conferred by many of the provisions in constitutional bills of rights, was not talking about the legal immunities to which I have mainly been referring in this subsection. He was instead talking about legal immunities of the kinds which I have pondered in §2.7.1 of Chapter 2. In line with what I have said there, Hart was correct when he submitted that many of the provisions in constitutional bills of rights bestow legal immunities on citizens which shield some of their legal liberties and other legal entitlements from being abridged by the enactments of legislatures or administrative agencies. Moreover, he was correct when he explained why those immunities are accurately classifiable as legal rights—for his explanation was very much in harmony with my Capacious Version of the Interest Theory. As he wrote: "[P]lainly, even in the loosest usage, the expression 'a right' is not used to refer to the fact that a man is ... immune from an *advantageous* change; the facts that the City Council cannot legally, i.e. has 'no power,' to award me a pension, and my neighbour has no power to exempt me from my duty to pay my income-tax, do not constitute any legal rights for me. An individual's immunity from legal change at the hands of others is ... a right only when the change in question is *adverse*, that is, would deprive him of legal rights of other kinds" (1982, 191, emphases in original). Still, these correct observations by Hart do not affect my criticisms of the Will Theory in this subsection.

As Hart indicated explicitly, he was adverting here to legal immunities held by citizens vis-à-vis their system of governance or vis-à-vis particular organizations within their system of governance. By contrast, I in this subsection have been adverting to immunities held by citizens vis-à-vis themselves, and I have been adverting to certain fundamental claim-rights held by citizens vis-à-vis one another. These latter immunities secure the fundamental claim-rights from being extinguished or suspended by the actions of the people who hold those claim-rights. Exactly because those claim-rights are secured against being discontinued by the choices of the people who hold them, however, any proponent of the Will Theory is committed to denying that they really are claim-rights. Though the fact that those claim-rights are insusceptible to being waived or forfeited is a hallmark of their centrality in any morally decent human interaction, that feature of insusceptibility or entrenchedness removes those claim-rights from the category of claim-rights in the eyes of the Will Theorists. Some or all adherents of the Will Theory might be in favor of the legal unwaivability and unforfeitability of the legal duties that are correlated with those claim-rights—and some or all adherents of the Will Theory might recognize that the legal immunities which establish the unwaivability and unforfeitability are properly classifiable as legal rights—but they will insist that the duties are not correlated with any claim-rights vested in the individuals whose basic interests are inherently protected by the duties. The outlandishness of their insistence is not offset at all by the pertinence of Hart's comments on the constitutional immunities broached in my penultimate and antepenultimate paragraphs above.

4.5.2 The Near-Eliminativism of the Will Theory

Correct and forceful though the foregoing objections to the Will Theory are, their dialectical effectiveness is curtailed by the fact that each of them begs the question against the Will Theory. In the course of reaching the conclusion that the Will Theory is fallacious, each of the foregoing objections is premised expressly or enthymematically on the proposition that the Will Theory is fallacious. As a result, most of the Will Theorists tend to be unfazed by each such criticism. To be sure, as is evidenced by Hart's retreat on the question whether infants are capable of holding legal claim-rights, not all Will Theorists are wholly insensitive to the potency of the reproaches that have been outlined so far. Nevertheless, the persuasiveness of those reproaches in the eyes of the Will Theorists is quite predictably lessened by the fact that each such reproach presupposes the unsoundness of the Will Theory.

Let us, then, proceed to a novel query about the Will Theory that is not question-begging. This new critique will show that the Will Theory is nearly eliminativist in its implications. That is, it will show that the analysis of right-holding propounded by the Will Theorists is generative of the conclusion that there are very few instances of the holding of claim-rights anywhere. Of course, the Will Theorists have always insisted that there are far fewer instances of the holding of claim-rights than the champions of the Interest Theory have supposed. When the Will Theorists discount the criticisms of their theory that have been marshaled hitherto, they are in effect contending that the people who advance those criticisms have greatly overestimated the numerousness of the situations in which legal duties are correlated with legal claim-rights that are vested in the parties whose interests are inherently protected by the duties. Even so, the Will Theorists have certainly not been propounding a conception of right-holding that is deliberately eliminativist. They have not sought to come up with an analysis of the holding of claim-rights which entails the conclusion that there are hardly any instances of the holding of claim-rights. On the contrary, the Will Theorists such as Simmonds believe that their account of the holding of claim-rights is illuminatingly and distinctively applicable to the realm of private law in any jurisdiction (Simmonds 1998, 141–5). Whereas the Will Theorists dismiss the notion that legal claim-rights are conferred upon individuals by criminal-law prohibitions or by regulatory statutes such as minimum-wage laws, they proclaim that the legal duties imposed within the institutions of private law in any jurisdiction are correlated with legal claim-rights held by the individuals whose interests are inherently protected through the duties. Admittedly, unlike the Interest Theorists, a Will Theorist does not maintain that the reason for classifying those individuals as holders of the specified legal claim-rights is that their interests are inherently protected by the correlative legal duties. Rather, a Will Theorist submits that the reason for so classifying those individuals is that the institutions of private law endow them with legal powers of control over the existence and enforcement of the correlative duties. As Simmonds declares: "[R]ights are primarily characteristic of private law: they exist within public law only in those special contexts (such as the conferment of welfare benefits) where public law is employed to secure particular benefits for individuals. The concept of a 'right,' on this account, is strongly linked to the value of individual choice, and to the primacy of private law in protecting such choices" (1998, 141–2).

My critique in this subsection will demonstrate that, under the Will Theory's explication of what the holding of a claim-right consists in, the institutions of private law confer very few legal claim-rights. By the reckoning of the Will Theorists, *malgré eux*, the vast majority of the legal duties imposed by those institutions are not correlated with legal claim-rights vested in individuals. By the reckoning of the Will Theorists, in other words, there are very few instances of the holding of claim-rights in the realm of private law. And since the Will Theorists contend that private law is the sphere in which instances of the holding of claim-rights distinctively occur, they turn out to be committed to the proposition that there are very few such instances anywhere. Their theory is nearly eliminativist in its implications. Moreover, that aspect of the Will Theory can be highlighted here without any begging of the question.

4.5.2.1 Two Default Rules

Instead of proceeding explicitly or implicitly from the premise that the Will Theory is fallacious, my critique of that theory begins with two default rules. Any legal duty imposed by a system of governance will be within the scope of one or the other of these two background rules. (While it is always true that one or the other of the two default rules is operative in relation to any given legal duty, it is not always true that one or the other of the two rules has been consciously adopted as such by legal officials or by anyone else beforehand. The operativeness of the default rule applicable to any particular duty might become apparent only after the duty has been breached.) Although my critique of the Will Theory will eventually concentrate on the pre-violation stage of a duty's existence, we should start with formulations of the two default rules that are focused on the post-violation stage:

> **Default Rule 1**: The non-exercise of a power of enforcement in the aftermath of a violation of a duty shall result in the non-effectuation of the duty.
> **Default Rule 2**: The non-exercise of a power of waiver in the aftermath of a violation of a duty shall result in the effectuation of the duty.

One point of terminology should be elucidated at the outset. A legal duty D is effectuated if either of the following conditions is met: (i) violations of D are averted through preventative steps taken by legal officials or by anyone else; or (ii) although D is violated, the violation is subsequently rectified through the application of some remedial measure(s) such as punishment, compensation, or restitution.

A terse illustration of the workings of the two default rules will be salutary here. Suppose that John breaches a legal duty which he owes to Mary. Mary does not do anything that would count as her exercising either a legal power of enforcement or a legal power of waiver. Now, either the duty will be enforced or it will be unenforced. There is no intermediate upshot whereby the duty is neither enforced nor unenforced. If the breached duty is enforced through the administering of some remedial measure(s), then Default Rule 2 is applicable to that duty. If the duty is instead left unenforced, then Default Rule 1 is applicable to it. Of course, a legal system need not rely solely on one type of default rule to the exclusion of the other. It can employ one of the two default rules for some legal duties and the remaining default rule for other legal duties. For every legal duty, however, there must be operative some default rule—perhaps not knowable beforehand—concerning what should happen if the duty is breached and if a party legally empowered to waive or seek enforcement of the duty does not do anything that would count as an exercise of her legal power of waiver or enforcement.

4.5.2.2 Two Situations Governed by the First Default Rule

Although the main focus of this critique of the Will Theory will lie on the pre-violation phase of a duty's existence and on a modified version of Default Rule 2, we can best approach that matter by initially considering a couple of scenarios in which Default Rule 1 is operative at the post-violation stage of enforceability. Each of these opening two scenarios does pose a challenge to the Will Theory, but in each case the challenge can easily be defused by the proponents of that theory.

4.5.2.2.1 A Limited Time for a Lawsuit

Suppose that, as a result of contravening a legal duty which inherently protects some aspect of the situation of Mary that is typically beneficial on balance for someone like her, John is now liable to be sued successfully by her. That is, he has incurred a Hohfeldian liability (or a set of Hohfeldian liabilities) to undergo the changes in his legal positions that would be brought about through her pursuit of legal proceedings. Suppose that Mary has two years during which she can exercise her power to sue John in order to enforce the duty which he has breached. If she exercises that power, she will alter his current legal positions. If she does not exercise her power of enforcement within the two-year period, John's liability to be sued successfully will cease to exist. However, the non-exercise of the power of enforcement by Mary in such circumstances does not amount to her exerting a power of waiver at the point when sufficient time for the exercise of the power of enforcement has run out. Rather, the cessation of the existence of John's liability is due to the operation of a general statute of limitations; it is due to the operation of a quasi-power.

Of course, Mary might hold a power of waiver whereby she can remove John's liability at any time before the expiration of the two years. If so, she holds a legal power of enforcement and a legal power of waiver until she exerts one of them—before the two-year period has elapsed—or until she loses those powers through the operation of the quasi-power that has just been mentioned. If and only if she does hold that power of waiver, it is paired with her power of enforcement until she exercises one of them or until she is deprived of both of them by the workings of the statute of limitations.

Devotees of the Will Theory have to conclude that, unless Mary does hold the power of waiver that has been broached in the preceding paragraph, she does not hold any legal claim-right correlative to the legal duty which John has contravened. Such a conclusion would be troublesome for the Will Theory if, within the realm of private law, human adults of sound mind were generally not endowed with legal powers of waiver over the enforcement of legal duties that inherently protect their interests. However, since human adults of sound mind are generally endowed with such legal powers in the realm of private law, the supporters of the Will Theory can shrug off this first scenario of John and Mary. They can rightly retort that the situation depicted in the scenario would be problematic for the Will Theory only if the realm of private law were markedly different from what it distinctively is. One of the hallmarks of that realm is its vesting of individuals with legal powers of waiver over the enforcement of legal duties that inherently protect their interests.

4.5.2.2.2 Unlimited Time for a Lawsuit

Let us now suppose that John's Hohfeldian liability to be sued successfully by Mary—like her correlative legal power to sue him successfully—is temporally unlimited. In that improbable event, the non-exercise of Mary's legal power of enforcement will for an indefinite period not alter anyone's legal positions. Thus, there are two reasons why her non-exercise of her legal power of enforcement is not itself an exertion of a legal power of waiver. First, it is never the case that the sheer fact of not exercising a power of enforcement amounts to an exertion of a power of waiver; one's exercise of a power always consists in one's performing some specified action(s) rather than purely in one's not performing some specified action(s). Second, any exercise of a legal power has to involve a change in someone's legal positions, yet the non-exercise of Mary's legal power of enforcement does not produce any such change when John's legal liability is of an unlimited duration. In such circumstances, her legal power of enforcement might not be accompanied by any legal power of waiver at the post-violation stage. Of course, even when John's legal liability to be sued successfully is not temporally limited, Mary might hold a legal power of waiver which enables her to terminate that liability at any particular time. Unless she does possess a distinct legal power of that sort, however, her legal power of enforcement is not coupled with any legal power of waiver.

Just as the Will Theorists can shrug blithely in response to the first scenario above, so too they should feel undismayed by this second scenario. For one thing, as has already been noted in connection with my opening vignette, private-law institutions do usually endow individuals such as Mary with discrete legal powers of waiver over the enforcement of legal duties that inherently protect their interests. In the realm of private law, the holding of legal powers of waiver by individuals at the post-violation stage of the enforceability of duties is commonplace and is indeed one of the distinctive features of that realm. Another factor that should reassure the Will Theorists in their contemplation of this second scenario is that a person harmed by a contravention of a private-law duty hardly ever enjoys an unlimited period during which she can successfully pursue legal proceedings for the rectification of the contravention. Statutes of limitations for such proceedings are routine in the realm of private law. For the Will Theory, then, any problematic implications of my second vignette are meager.

4.5.2.3 Two Situations Governed by Versions of the Second Default Rule

So far, things are going well for the defenders of the Will Theory. My delineation of Default Rule 1 has not disclosed any significant shortcomings in that theory as a representation of the jural relationships in the realm of private law. We now turn to Default Rule 2. For the moment, my exploration of that second default rule will continue to focus on the post-violation stage of the enforceability of a duty. As we shall behold, Default Rule 2 in application to that stage is unworrisome for the Will Theorists. We shall then consider a version of Default Rule 2 with a focus on the *pre*-violation stage of the existence of a duty—at which point the unflappableness of the Will Theorists should be at an end.

4.5.2.3.1 The Second Default Rule at the Post-Violation Stage

Under Default Rule 2, a contravened legal duty is to be enforced unless a relevant legal power of waiver is exercised by the person who has control over the enforcement of the duty. Suppose once again that John breaches some private-law duty which inherently protects a typically beneficial aspect of Mary's situation. Given the existence of the specified default rule, Mary does not hold any legal power of enforcement—since the enforcement of the duty will proceed automatically unless she exercises her legal power of waiver. Any notion of a legal power of enforcement held by Mary in combination with her legal power of waiver is chimerical in such a situation, since a putative legal power is no legal power at all if it does not make any difference to anyone's legal positions. Under Default Rule 2, John has rendered himself liable to undergo enforcement proceedings as a result of his breach of duty. Mary can terminate his liability by exercising her legal power of waiver, but otherwise the officials who operate the mechanisms of enforcement in the presiding system of governance will exercise their legal powers to impose compensatory or injunctive or restitutionary duties on John. The transformation of his liability into duties is undertaken by the officials rather than by Mary. If she does not alter his legal status by waiving his liability, then she herself does not alter his legal status at all. Her non-exercise of her power of waiver is not the exercise of a power of enforcement, partly because the non-exercise of a power of waiver is never itself the exercise of a power of enforcement, and partly because that non-exercise leaves John in precisely the position in which he has placed himself: namely, in a position of being liable to undergo enforcement proceedings at the hands of the officials.

A Hohfeldian legal power is an ability to effect changes in legal relations, rather than an ability to leave legal relations entirely as they are. Consequently, Mary's ability to leave John's legal posture wholly unmodified is no Hohfeldian legal power at all. Accordingly, if the duty breached by John is governed by Default Rule 2, the power of waiver possessed by Mary is not coupled with any power of enforcement held by her. Though a power to enforce that duty also exists, of course, it is held not by her but by some legal-governmental official(s).

In short, were the post-violation stage of the enforceability of a duty always or almost always governed by Default Rule 2 within the realm of private law, the Will Theory would be eliminativist or nearly eliminativist as a representation of the holding of claim-rights within that realm. Whereas the Will Theory contends that any holder of a claim-right is endowed with paired powers of control over the correlative duty at each stage limned by Hart, the applicability of Default Rule 2 to a legal duty at the post-violation stage would withhold a legal power of enforcement from the person apparently vested with the correlative legal claim-right and would assign that power instead to legal-governmental officials. Within the sway of Default Rule 2 at the post-violation stage, the apparent holder of a legal claim-right possesses only a legal power of waiver and not any legal power of enforcement. Thus, if Default Rule 2 were indeed always determinative at the post-violation stage of enforceability within the realm of private law, the Will Theory would entail the conclusion that there are not any holders of legal claim-rights within that realm. If nobody ever holds both a legal power of waiver and a legal power of enforcement at the post-violation phase of the enforceability of any legal duty, then the Will Theorists have to conclude that nobody ever holds a legal claim-right correlative to any legal duty. Proponents of the Will Theory would be propounding an eliminativist account of the holding of claim-rights.

In response to what has just been said, the Will Theorists can germanely defend themselves by pointing out that Default Rule 2 does not in fact govern the post-violation phase of the enforceability of duties in the realm of private law. A distinctive feature of that realm is that the legal power to enforce a legal duty at the post-violation stage is vested in the party whose interests are inherently protected by the existence of the duty. (There are exceptions, of course, for parties who are mentally incapacitated. However, this chapter has already criticized the Will Theory for its exclusion of claim-rights held by such parties. Here I am concentrating on the question whether the Will Theory furnishes a correct account of the holding of claim-rights by sane human adults within the purview of private law.) In the realm of private law, a party who has been culpably harmed by the conduct of someone else is possessed of the legal power to pursue legal proceedings for the rectification of the harm. Such a party, in the aftermath of the infliction of any duty-contravening harm, is legally empowered to control the enforcement of the duty by going ahead with legal proceedings and is also legally empowered to control the enforcement of the duty by waiving the occurrence of any such proceedings. To say as much is to say that the post-violation phase of the enforceability of a private-law duty is not governed by Default Rule 2. Hence, although the Will Theory would be an eliminativist account of the holding of claim-rights if Default Rule 2 were indeed always applicable to duties of private law in that post-violation phase, the Will Theorists can insouciantly observe that Default Rule 2 is seldom if ever applicable to private-law duties at that juncture. They will presumably feel confident that their account of the holding of legal claim-rights does not carry any eliminativist implications.

4.5.2.3.2 A Variant of the Second Default Rule at the Pre-Violation Stage

We should now explore why any such sense of confidence on the part of the Will Theorists is unfounded. Here we have to shift our attention from the post-violation phase of enforceability to the pre-violation phase of a duty's existence. As has already been noted, the pre-violation stage is especially important because every duty is in that stage at some point and because most duties (by dint of being uncontravened) do not ever go beyond that stage. For an investigation of the entitlements that surround an unviolated duty, the formulation of Default Rule 2 has to be modified. In application to an unviolated duty, the rule is as follows:

> **Default Rule 2A**: The non-exercise of a power to cancel or suspend the existence of a duty shall result in the continued existence of the duty.

Here the default rule is not about the enforcement of a duty but is instead about the retention of a duty in existence. It prescribes that, unless a power of cancellation or suspension is exercised, the duty is to persist as a duty.

Under the sway of Default Rule 2A, no one has a legal power to keep this or that legal duty in existence; a Hohfeldian legal power is an ability to change some legal positions, rather than an ability to keep all positions unchanged. An ability to keep positions completely unchanged is a Hohfeldian immunity rather than a Hohfeldian power. Thus, when a duty in the realm of private law at the pre-violation stage is within the sway of Default Rule 2A (as is almost always the case), a power to terminate or suspend the duty is not coupled with any power to retain the duty in existence.

At the pre-violation juncture, where a private-law duty has not been contravened, the party whose interests are inherently protected by the duty—or a representative of that party—will almost always be vested with a legal power to cancel or suspend the continued existence of the duty. However, that legal power of cancellation or suspension is very rarely accompanied by any converse legal power of retention. Usually no power of the latter sort is involved, because the persistence of a duty through the non-exercise of one's power of waiver is not itself due to the exercise of any power of retention. A Hohfeldian legal power is an ability to *alter* some legal relations, whereas the persistence of a legal duty usually involves the *retention* of all legal relations as they are. Thus, instead of being due to the exercise of a legal power, the persistence of a private-law duty over time is normally attributable to a legal immunity or an array of legal immunities. It consists in leaving things entirely as they are, rather than in changing things. In sum, because a power of retention if exercised would transform legal relationships, the notion of any such power at the pre-violation stage of the existence of a private-law duty is usually a phantasm—since the preservation of a duty at that stage usually consists in leaving legal relationships wholly unchanged. Consequently, at the pre-violation stage, the party whose interests are inherently protected by the existence of a private-law duty is endowed with a power of waiver over the duty but not normally with any power of retention.

What is so disquieting for the Will Theorists is that these reflections on the pre-violation stage of any duty's existence are applicable to nearly all private-law duties. Unlike my reflections on the post-violation stage of the enforceability of a duty, which have turned up difficulties for the Will Theory only in relation to some fanciful schemes of private law, my remarks on the pre-violation stage of a duty's existence have pointed to a difficulty that encompasses just about every duty in every system of private law. A proponent of the Will Theory maintains that the holder of a claim-right correlative to any private-law duty is vested with paired powers of waiver and retention (concerning that duty) at the pre-violation stage of the duty's existence. However, because it is very seldom true that somebody endowed at the pre-violation stage with a power of waiver over a duty in any system of private law is endowed with a power of retention concerning that duty at that stage, the proponents of the Will Theory have committed themselves to the proposition that very few legal claim-rights are established by any system of private law. Without paired powers of waiver and retention in the hands of any single person at the pre-violation stage of a duty's existence, there is no claim-right recognizable as such by the Will Theory. A theory which treats the realm of private law as its special sphere of application has turned out to generate the nearly eliminativist conclusion that very few legal claim-rights are conferred by any institutions of private law.

Admittedly, the Will Theory's account of the holding of claim-rights is nearly eliminativist rather than thoroughly eliminativist, because some legal duties within the realm of private law are kept in existence through the exercising of legal powers rather than solely through legal immunities. For example, the owner of a private road in England typically has to perform certain actions periodically for the purpose of keeping in place the legal duties incumbent on members of the public to refrain from using the road as a thoroughfare. Churchill College (Cambridge) as the owner of a private road has to obstruct it at least once a year in order to retain the status of the road as private. When the porters of Churchill College block off the road with traffic cones on Christmas Day each year, they are exercising some legal powers on behalf of the college to keep in existence the legal duties borne by members of the public. In so doing, the porters are altering the legal positions of the college by removing some quasi-liabilities—some quasi-liabilities of the college to undergo the loss of certain legal entitlements—and by replacing them with a set of legal immunities. *Pari passu*, the porters are altering the legal positions of members of the public by removing some quasi-liabilities (some quasi-liabilities of members of the public to gain certain legal entitlements) and by replacing them with legal disabilities. Such changes in the existing legal relationships are necessary for keeping in existence the legal claim-rights and other legal entitlements that are possessed by Churchill College as the owner of a private road. Hence, the college is vested not only with legal powers to waive those claim-rights and other entitlements but also with legal powers to retain them.

Nonetheless, although there are some claim-rights in the realm of private law which are of that type—where the holders of the claim-rights are endowed both with legal powers to terminate or suspend the correlative legal duties and with legal powers to keep those duties in existence—most claim-rights in the realm of private law are not of that type. With regard to the large majority of the claim-rights that obtain in the realm of private law, their holders possess legal powers to terminate or suspend the correlative legal duties but not any legal powers to preserve those duties in existence. Instead, what preserve the duties in existence are various legal immunities. For example, my claim-right not to be defamed by anyone or my claim-right not to be harmed by somebody else's negligence is scarcely kept in existence through my wiggling of my fingers or my dancing of a jig. Rather, each of those claim-rights remains in existence through the presence of sundry legal immunities that avert the extinguishing of each of those claim-rights (and through my not having performed any action that would constitute the waiving of either of those claim-rights). In that respect, each of those claim-rights is like nearly every one of my other claim-rights in the realm of private law.

4.5.2.3.3 Steiner and the Conflation of Powers and Immunities

Some Will Theorists such as Hillel Steiner have failed to grasp the key distinction between legal *powers* through which legal duties can be extinguished and legal *immunities* through which legal duties are kept in existence. Quoting Hart on the three phases of a duty's existence and enforcement, Steiner writes as follows (1998, 239–40, emphases in original):

> In a deservedly famous passage, [Hart] identifies the fundamental structural components of the [holding of a claim-right].... Hart suggests that these components are best understood as the several ingredients jointly constituting the *control* that one person can have over the duty of another.... These ingredients of control [at each juncture of a duty's existence or enforcement] are ... Hohfeldian *powers*.... Hart enumerates these powers in "either-or" pairs. To further sharpen the analysis of the control they are said to confer, and to illuminate some often

overlooked aspects of it that are of the utmost importance, let's set his powers out in a slightly more partitioned list. With respect to the duty owed to a right-holder, he or she confronts the following menu of options:

(1) to waive compliance with the duty (ie extinguish it);
(2) to leave the duty in existence (ie demand compliance with it).

Steiner goes on to enumerate four further legal powers, which are respectively operative at the post-violation and post-judgment stages of the enforceability of a duty. However, we are concerned here with the pre-violation phase of a duty's existence, and we are thus concerned only with Steiner's opening pair of powers or putative powers. Indeed, what is of interest here is solely the second element of that pair. Contrary to how Steiner frames the matter, the legal position that should be specified in his option 2 is a Hohfeldian immunity rather than a Hohfeldian power. He misses that distinction because he wrongly treats "leave the duty in existence" and "demand compliance with it" as interchangeable predicates. In fact, only the former of those two expressions is apposite; it correctly captures the essentially passive character of an immunity. By contrast, the latter of those two predicates incorrectly suggests that the performance of some specified type of action is typically needed for the preservation of a private-law duty. Mary does not need to demand anything in order to keep in place John's duty to refrain from defaming her, or his duty not to injure her through negligence, or his duty to pay her the contractually specified price for the goods which she has delivered to him. On the contrary, each of those duties will persist so long as Mary does not do anything sufficient to constitute a waiver of any of those duties. Her non-exercise of her power of waiver does not have to be combined with a demand or with any other active exertion. The pre-violation persistence of each of those duties is ascribable to immunities rather than to any powers that Mary needs to exercise through actions. When we steer clear of Steiner's conflation of immunities and powers, we can discern the untenability of his insistence that every legal claim-right consists in paired legal powers at each of the three principal stages of the existence and enforcement of a correlative legal duty. In particular, we can discern that his insistence is untenable in application to the first of those stages.

4.5.2.3.4 No Begging of the Question

Before we ponder a couple of rejoinders that might be mounted by the Will Theorists, we should note afresh that my critique of the Will Theory as a nearly eliminativist account of the holding of claim-rights does not beg any questions. That critique unfolds from my exposition of the two default rules, an exposition that does not presuppose the fallaciousness of the Will Theory in any way. I originally developed the gist of that exposition in quite a different context, without any reference to the Will Theory and its weaknesses and without my yet having realized that my sketch of the two default rules could be turned against the Will

Theory. Indeed, that original presentation is in an article to which Steiner's name is attached as a notional co-author.[13] My discussion there of the default rules does not proceed from any assumptions about the necessary and sufficient conditions for the holding of a claim-right, but instead simply proceeds from observations concerning the conditions under which various legal duties are preserved or eliminated or effectuated. Those observations can then get parlayed into an attack on the Will Theory's analysis of the holding of a claim-right—as has been done in this chapter—but they do not themselves presuppose anything about the nature of claim-rights or about the nature of the holding of claim-rights. Furthermore, the conclusion directly drawn from those observations is not even that the Will Theory is fallacious. Rather, the conclusion directly drawn from them is that the Will Theory is nearly eliminativist as an account of the holding of claim-rights. Of course, from the fact that the Will Theory is nearly eliminativist as such an account, I believe that one can soundly infer that the Will Theory is fallacious. Still, the proponents of the Will Theory could seek somehow to defend the proposition that their analysis of the holding of claim-rights is correct in being nearly eliminativist.

This point about my not having begged any questions is noteworthy, for the criticisms leveled by Interest Theorists and Will Theorists against each other are often perceived (and are quite often correctly perceived) as question-begging. Partly because the charges traded between the two camps in the Interest/Will debates have seemed question-begging to quite a few onlookers, the debates themselves have struck those onlookers as irresolvably deadlocked. Appeals for the discontinuation and transcendence of the Interest/Will disputation have ensued, with attempts to develop hybrid approaches of the sorts which I have touched upon earlier. Accordingly, by presenting a far-reaching critique of the Will Theory that plainly does not beg any relevant questions, this chapter has gone some way not only toward resolving the Interest/Will debates but also toward establishing that they have been worthwhile.

4.5.2.3.5 Some Possible Rejoinders

Steiner has been especially emphatic among the Will Theorists in insisting that the holding of a claim-right must involve the holding of paired powers at each of the three stages in the existence and enforcement of a correlative duty (Steiner 1994, 68–73; 1998, 239–47). He cannot jettison his insistence on that point without a major transformation of his version of the Will Theory. When he delineates the paired powers that will supposedly be possessed by the holder of a claim-right at each of the three stages in the existence and enforcement of a correlative duty, he quotes the famous passage by Hart in which a holder of a claim-right is

[13] Kramer and Steiner 2007, 286–8. The ideas and prose in the 2007 article are mine, but Steiner played a key role in urging me to write it, and he read it carefully in advance of my submission of it for publication.

characterized as a small-scale sovereign. If Steiner were to retreat from the notion that a claim-right consists in three sets of paired powers over a correlative duty, he would be abandoning his rationale for the Will Theory. That is, he would be abandoning his contention that the holder of any claim-right is a small-scale sovereign with exclusive control over the duty that is correlative to the claim-right. Thus, although my critique of the Will Theory of right-holding is focused on points that may seem quite arcane, it tells devastatingly against the most prominent versions of that theory.

Admittedly, although Steiner is unyielding in his insistence that the holding of a claim-right must consist in the holding of paired powers at each of the three stages of a duty's existence and enforceability, Hart's approach was slightly less heavy-handed. In the passage which I have mentioned just above, where Hart envisaged the holder of a claim-right as a small-scale sovereign, he stated that such a holder is "given by the law exclusive control, *more or less extensive*, over another person's duty" (1982, 183, emphasis added). With the wording which I have italicized, Hart left room for instances of the holding of claim-rights where not all six of the legal powers outlined by Steiner are operative. Hart added in a footnote: "The right-holder will have less than the full measure of control if, as in the case of statutory duties, he is unable to release or extinguish the duty or if principles of public policy prevent him, even after breach of the duty, making a binding agreement not to sue for injury caused by its breach.... In such cases the choice left to him is only to sue or not to sue" (1982, 183 n. 85). Hart here accepted that someone can hold a legal claim-right without holding a legal power of waiver over the correlative legal duty at the pre-violation stage of the existence of the duty. He likewise accepted that someone can hold a legal claim-right without holding a legal power of waiver over the enforcement of the correlative legal duty at the post-violation stage. He here conceded some ground to the Interest Theory of right-holding, but he clearly believed that his concessions pertained to exceptional or marginal instances of right-holding only. Neither here nor elsewhere did he glimpse the nearly eliminativist implications that follow from his account of the holding of claim-rights.

Still, Hart left some leeway for Will Theorists to espouse versions of their theory with attenuated ambitions. Perhaps the most obvious way of circumscribing the ambit of the Will Theory is to confine its theses to the pre-violation phase of any duty's existence. A proponent of such a scaled-down version of the Will Theory would affirm that the holding of a claim-right consists in the holding of a power of waiver and a power of retention over the correlative duty at the pre-violation stage of the duty's existence. Unlike Hart and Steiner, this modest rendering of the Will Theory would not advert to the post-violation and post-judgment stages of the enforcement of a duty. Even so, this diluted version of the Will Theory would beget the conclusion that individuals are possessed of hardly any legal claim-rights; after all, as we have seen, individuals at the pre-violation stage do not hold legal powers of retention over most of the legal duties that are owed to them. Nearly all such duties are kept in existence through the sway of legal immunities rather than through the exercising of legal powers.

Let us, then, mull over a second tack through which the Will Theorists might try to rein in their reflections on the holding of claim-rights. Advocates of the Will Theory might contend that the core of their theory resides in the idea that the holder of a claim-right can determine through his or her choices whether the duty correlative to the claim-right continues to exist (and whether the duty will be enforced in the event of its having been contravened). Such advocates might point out that, although every person holds very few legal powers to keep in existence the private-law duties which inherently protect aspects of her situation that are typically beneficial on balance for someone like her, any sane human adult in the realm of private law does hold legal powers to terminate or suspend the existence of most such duties. As a consequence of my being legally empowered to discontinue or suspend the existence of any particular private-law duty that is owed to me, my choices determine whether that duty at the pre-violation stage will persist or not. If I choose to terminate or suspend the existence of the duty, then it will permanently or temporarily cease to exist. If I choose not to terminate or suspend the existence of the duty, then it will persist indefinitely. Its continuing indefinitely is due to the operations of legal immunities rather than to my exercising of any legal powers, but its continuing indefinitely is dependent on my choices. Hence, the Will Theorists might conclude, their account of the holding of claim-rights is not a nearly-eliminativist account after all. Though the Will Theorists have to abandon Hart's and Steiner's picture of paired powers at each stage of a duty's existence or enforcement, they might hope to maintain that the existence or enforcement of a private-law duty is a product of choices made by the person who holds the legal claim-right correlative to that duty. Supporters of the Will Theory might contend that that feature of choice-dependence is the key to identifying the holder of any claim-right in the realm of private law. When we endeavor to ascertain who holds any particular claim-right in that realm, we should not be asking whose interests are inherently protected by the existence of the correlative legal duty; instead, we should be asking whose choices determine whether the duty remains in existence. Or so the Will Theorists might declare. Such is the way in which they might strive to accommodate and defuse my critique of their doctrine. They would take themselves to be renouncing the extravagance of the Hartian/Steinerian version of their theory in order to salvage their central thesis that the holding of a claim-right consists in the possession of control over the existence and enforcement of a duty.

Unfortunately for the devotees of the Will Theory, however, such a tack amounts to the abandonment of the theory rather than to the redemption of it. Although the second posited riposte to my critique of the Will Theory is much more subtle than the first, and although it is indeed probably the best retort that can be advanced by a proponent of the Will Theory, it reaffirms a central insight of the Interest Theory rather than the core of the Will Theory. According to the Interest Theory, claim-rights are fundamentally passive entitlements. A claim-right consists in being inherently protected by the existence of a legal or moral duty. Whereas a legal or moral power produces its effects through the performance of some action(s) by the holder of the power, a claim-right's typically advantageous effects are realized through some action(s) or omission(s) on the part of somebody other than the holder of the claim-right. (Four caveats should be entered here. First, as has been argued in §2.4.1 of Chapter 2, there can be claim-right/duty relationships with contents that do not make reference to the conduct of the duty-bearers. Those contents can make reference to the conduct of third parties or to natural phenomena such as meteorological conditions. In extravagantly weird cases, the contents can even make reference solely to the conduct of the holders of the claim-rights. Like the much more common claim-right/duty relationships with contents that are focused on the conduct of the duty-bearers, however, the vast majority of these other claim-right/duty relationships supply protection whose typically advantageous effects are not consummated through any actions by the holders of the claim-rights. A second caveat pertains to claim-rights that are held by a party vis-à-vis himself or herself. As has been discussed in Chapters 2 and 3, an analysis of any claim-right held by someone vis-à-vis himself or herself has to differentiate between a party *qua* holder of the claim-right and that same party *qua* bearer of the correlative duty. Some conduct by the party in his or her latter capacity as the bearer of the duty is what is involved in the fruition of the typically advantageous effects of the protection conferred by the claim-right that correlates with the duty. Third, numerous claim-rights protect the abilities of their holders to engage in actions of various sorts. However, the typically advantageous effects of the protection furnished by any such claim-right are consummated through the conduct of the bearer of the correlative duty rather than through an action of the claim-right-holder whose ability to perform that action is protected by the claim-right. For example, if Mabel holds a claim-right vis-à-vis Lancelot against some way in which he could prevent her from φ-ing, the typically advantageous effects of the protection furnished by her claim-right are consummated through his non-prevention rather than through her own φ-ing. A final caveat is that, although the Interest Theorists submit that claim-rights are fundamentally passive entitlements, those theorists of course recognize that claim-rights very often are combined and very often should be combined with Hohfeldian powers of waiver and enforcement possessed by the parties who hold the claim-rights.)

As fundamentally passive entitlements, claim-rights are similar to immunities and are in contrast with powers. Now, given that the Will Theorists contend that the holding of a claim-right is equivalent to the holding of certain powers, they disagree with the Interest Theorists by construing claim-rights as fundamentally active entitlements. As Hart wrote, "it is hard to think of rights [claim-rights] except as capable of *exercise* and this conception of rights [claim-rights] correlative to obligations as containing legal powers accommodates this feature" (1982, 184, emphasis in original). Indeed, the Will Theory's whole conception of one's holding of a claim-right as one's possession of control over the correlative duty is redolent of this vision of claim-rights as active entitlements. In the eyes of a Will Theorist, claim-rights produce their effects through actions performed by their holders—since claim-rights, in the eyes of a Will Theorist, always comprise powers that can be exercised through actions by their holders which produce changes in legal relationships.

If the Will Theorists adopt the rejoinder posited in the antepenultimate paragraph above, however, they are accepting that claim-rights at the pre-violation stage in the realm of private law (as well as in other realms) are fundamentally passive entitlements. Although the continued existence of a claim-right at the pre-violation stage in the realm of private law is dependent on the will of its holder, the dependence is a purely passive or negative dependence. That is, the continuation of a claim-right requires the non-performance of certain actions—rather than the performance of certain actions—by the holder of the claim-right. Specifically, it requires the non-performance of any actions by the holder of the claim-right that would bring about the termination or suspension of the claim-right. It requires omissions rather than actions by the holder of the claim-right. On the one hand, because the holder of a claim-right in the realm of private law is legally empowered to terminate or suspend the existence of the claim-right, a claim-right will not continue to obtain unless the holder of it refrains from performing any actions through which her legal power to discontinue the existence of the claim-right would be exercised. On the other hand, because the holder of any claim-right in the realm of private law is very seldom legally empowered to keep her claim-right in existence (since the continuation of a claim-right over time is almost always due to legal immunities rather than to exercises of legal powers), the persistence of a claim-right as such is hardly ever dependent on the performance of any actions by its holder. It is dependent on the holder's not performing certain actions, rather than on her performing any specific actions. It is dependent on the declinatory aspect of the will of the claim-right-holder rather than on the affirmative aspect of her will.

In that respect, the continued existence of a claim-right in the realm of private law is similar to the continued existence of the statuette of Abraham Lincoln that sits on my desk. Through various actions which I am capable of performing, I could terminate the existence of that statuette by smashing it to pieces. Its continued existence is dependent on my not performing any of those actions. It is dependent on the declinatory aspect of my will. At the same time, it is not dependent on the affirmative aspect of my will at all. The persistence of the statuette through time does not hinge on my performing any specific action(s). I do not need to wiggle my fingers at it or dance a jig around it or intone some esoteric phrasing. Irrespective of whether I perform any such superfluous actions, the statuette will persist only if I abstain from doing what is sufficient to terminate its existence.

Hence, the continuation of the statuette in existence is dependent on my choices, but the dependence is purely passive rather than active. My not making certain choices is what is crucial. No active exertions of my volition are needed.

Thus, if the Will Theorists seek to avail themselves of the fact that the continuation of the existence of any claim-right held by a party P in the realm of private law is dependent on P's not choosing to cancel or suspend the claim-right, they will be conceding that claim-rights even in the realm of private law are fundamentally passive entitlements. Those claim-rights with their protective effects continue to exist not through actions performed by their holders, but instead through the passivity of their holders in regard to any actions that would terminate or suspend the claim-rights. Contrary to what Hart wrote in my most recent quotation from him above, the exercising of legal powers is not integral to the existence and protective effects of a claim-right in the realm of private law; rather, what is integral to the existence and protective effects of such a claim-right is the *non*-exercising of certain legal powers. Indispensable is the passivity of the claim-right-holder with regard to the exercising of those powers. Consequently, if the Will Theorists retort to my critique of the nearly eliminativist implications of their doctrine by adverting to the fact that the existence of just about every claim-right in the realm of private law is dependent on the declinatory aspect of the will of the person who holds the claim-right, they will be replacing the core of their theory with the core of the Interest Theory. They will be acknowledging that claim-rights in the realm of private law are fundamentally passive entitlements. They will be acknowledging that the role of the choices of a claim-right-holder in sustaining the existence and effects of her claim-right at the pre-violation stage is fundamentally the same as the role of my choices in sustaining the existence of the statuette of Abraham Lincoln on my desk. Their vision of an active claim-right-holder who exercises his or her claim-rights at the pre-violation stage in the realm of private law will thus have given way to the Interest Theory's vision of a claim-right. It will have given way to the thesis that the central function or import of a claim-right consists in the bestowal of deontic protection.

4.5.3 A Further Critique of the Will Theory

This chapter will close with a further critique of the Will Theory wherein we return to the matter of unenforceable duties that has been explored in §2.4.4 of Chapter 2. Will Theorists are clearly committed by their doctrine to denying that there are any unenforceable legal claim-rights. If for example a statute in some jurisdiction J provides that every school in J is legally obligated to supply a free and nutritious lunch daily to each of its students, and if the statute does not establish any means of enforcing its requirement through public-law procedures, and if the courts (when faced with lawsuits pursued by famished students against their schools) decide that no private-law remedies are available for enforcing the statutory duty incumbent on every school, then the Will Theorists have to conclude that the statute has not conferred any legal claim-right upon each student in J. Despite the terms of the statute, the Will Theorists will insist that no student in J has any legal claim-right whatsoever to be presented with a free and nutritious lunch daily. A wholly unenforceable legal claim-right to be provided with a lunch is no legal claim-right at all, by the reckoning of the Will Theorists.

In line with my exposition of unenforceable legal duties in §2.4.4, my terse remarks here have concentrated on legal duties for which there are no legal powers of enforcement. Proponents of the Will Theory deny that such duties are correlated with any legal claim-rights, because their theory affirms that a necessary condition for one's holding of a legal claim-right correlative to a specified legal duty is one's being legally authorized (empowered) to press forward with the enforcement of that duty. However, the matter of authorization is not the only thing covered by the Will Theory. In addition to being legally empowered to proceed with the enforcement of a specified legal duty, the holder of a legal claim-right correlative to that duty must—by the reckoning of the Will Theorists—be *competent* to proceed with the enforcement of the duty. That additional insistence by the advocates of the Will Theory is an opportunity for another critique of their doctrine.

To embark upon that critique, we should briefly contemplate the class of regularly unenforced legal duties. Some of the duties in that class are regularly unenforced because there are not any legal powers in existence for the enforcement of them. I have offered an example in the penultimate paragraph above, with my scenario of the statute that legally obligates every school in J to provide a free and nutritious lunch daily to each of its students. Some other legal duties are regularly unenforced not because legal powers of enforcement for them are absent, but instead because the legal powers of enforcement that do exist for those duties are left unexercised. For example, suppose that the local government in some city enacts an ordinance that legally forbids jaywalking on any of the city's streets. The ordinance legally empowers the municipal officials to give effect to the anti-jaywalking prohibition through procedures of enforcement. Suppose further that numerous people in the city commit acts of jaywalking and that they are never or almost never subjected to any processes of enforcement. No warnings or sanctions or other remedial measures ever materialize in response to the contraventions of the ordinance. Although each person in the city owes a legal duty to the local government to refrain from acts of jaywalking, the frequent transgressions of that duty go unrectified by the municipality's officials. Why are those violations of the duty left unrectified?

In many credible contexts, the absence of any measures of enforcement by the city's officials will be due to their having chosen to forbear from exercising the legal powers of enforcement with which they are equipped. Although those powers exist, and although the officials are capable of exercising them, the officials implicitly or explicitly choose to leave the ordinance unenforced. Notwithstanding that the officials are aware of the violations of the ordinance or could readily gain such awareness, they elect not to issue any warnings or penalties. In these circumstances, as has been recounted in §2.4.4 (where the example of anti-jaywalking ordinances has likewise been adduced), there is enforceability without enforcement. Perhaps explicitly, or more likely implicitly, the officials who run the municipal government regularly acquiesce in the propensities of people to contravene the duties that have been imposed by the anti-jaywalking ordinance. Though the officials are legally empowered to pursue enforcement of those duties and are cognitively and physically competent to exercise their powers, they continually forbear in these circumstances—no doubt, often very wisely—from undertaking the procedures of law-enforcement which they are authorized and competent to undertake. Hence, while the legal duty of each person in the municipality not to jaywalk is an enforceable obligation, it is regularly unenforced. Legal powers held by officials to effectuate that duty are unwielded rather than absent.

Because some regularly unenforced legal duties are nonetheless enforceable, the Will Theorists are not committed by their doctrine to the proposition that all genuine legal duties and the correlative legal claim-rights are regularly given effect. Whereas some followers of the nineteenth-century legal philosopher John Austin did endeavor to explicate the concept of a legal duty by reference to the probability of the imposition of sanctions, the votaries of the Will Theory need not similarly insist that a vanishingly small likelihood of the imposition of legal sanctions for one's φ-ing is per se inconsistent with the existence of one's legal duty to refrain from φ-ing and the existence of a legal claim-right correlative to that duty. Although the Will Theorists cannot make sense of an unenforceable legal claim-right—that is, a legal claim-right in respect of which no one is authorized and competent to pursue enforcement—they can happily acknowledge the existence of legal claim-rights that are enforceable but regularly unenforced. So long as a legal claim-right is accompanied by legal powers of enforcement and waiver in the hands of a competent holder of the claim-right, the possession of those entitlements will in combination be classified by the Will Theorists as the possession of a legal claim-right. For the Will Theorists, such a classification applies regardless of whether the holder of the legal claim-right opts for enforcement or for waiver or for sheer inaction. Somebody who counts as a holder of a legal claim-right CR under the terms of the Will Theory might persistently abstain from doing anything about breaches of the duty D that is correlative to CR, but that persistent inaction does not negate the determinative control which the holder of CR possesses over D. Such an element of control, rather than the plying of the control in a specific direction, is what the Will Theory singles out as the essence of anyone's holding of a legal claim-right. Supporters of the Will Theory are not deviating from their doctrine when they allow for the existence of legal claim-rights that are enforceable but chronically unenforced.

Nevertheless, although the champions of the Will Theory can readily accept that some legal claim-rights are regularly unenforced, they cannot accept that any such claim-rights are unenforceable. Furthermore, their theoretical commitment to denying the existence of any unenforceable legal claim-rights is applicable regardless of whether the unenforceability derives from the absence of authorization or from the absence of competence. In my examples of unenforceability heretofore, such as the scenario of the statutory school-lunch obligation in J, the decisive factor has been the absence of authorization. When there do not exist any legal powers through which some specified legal claim-right could be enforced, the claim-right is not recognizable as a legal claim-right at all by the proponents of the Will Theory. Even where such legal powers do exist, however, those proponents remain committed by their theory to denying the existence of a legal claim-right when the party who holds the powers of enforcement is not capable of exercising them. To apprehend the import of this point, we should look afresh at the example of an ordinance that prohibits jaywalking.

Some contraventions of an anti-jaywalking ordinance are undetectable even in a society ruled by a highly repressive system of governance and *a fortiori* in a society where the presiding system of governance is liberal-democratic. When a person crosses a sleepy street (a street with no legally countenanced points for crossing) in order to visit a neighbor, her infraction of a local anti-jaywalking mandate may well lie beyond the monitoring capacity of any system of governance that does not have unlimited resources for policing. Even a totalitarian system of governance cannot keep abreast of every instance of conduct that occurs in the country where it holds sway. If there are myriad minor infractions of an anti-jaywalking ordinance on the sleepy streets of a town in the course of each day, it is virtually certain that some of those infractions will have lain beyond the capacity of the local government to monitor the conduct of the town's residents. In regard to the undetectable contraventions of the ordinance, the officials in the municipal government are incapable of exercising their legal powers of enforcement and are thus on a par with individuals who possess some legal powers while being mentally incapacitated from exercising those powers. Although the officials on numerous occasions are fully capable of exercising their legal powers to enforce the anti-jaywalking ordinance—even if on many occasions they are aptly inclined to forbear from doing so—they are incapable of exercising those powers on some other occasions, because any system of governance will have failed to espy some contraventions of its own mandates. When the officials do not proceed with any measures of enforcement in response to infractions of the anti-jaywalking ordinance which they have not been able to notice, their inaction is not deliberately chosen. They certainly have not exercised any powers of waiver, nor have they even elected to refrain from exercising their powers of enforcement. Instead, their inaction is a product of their epistemic limitations. In this respect, their inaction is like that of a mentally incapacitated person who does not do anything to exercise her legal powers to enter into contracts (in a jurisdiction where she is vested with such powers); her not taking any steps to enter into contracts is a product of her epistemic limitations rather than of any deliberate choices. Now, since the conditions specified in the Will Theory as necessary for the holding of a legal claim-right by X include the fact that X is competent as well as authorized to exercise legal powers of enforcement over the correlative legal duty, the devotees of the Will Theory have to conclude that the legal claim-right of the municipal government to compliance by each citizen with its anti-jaywalking mandate is suspended in any context where a contravention of that mandate is undetectable. In any such context, the municipal government is incapable of exercising its power to proceed with enforcement of the mandate and its power to waive enforcement of the mandate—because its epistemic limitations prevent it from becoming aware that a transgression of the mandate has occurred. In any such context, then, the legal duty imposed on some citizen by the anti-jaywalking ordinance is unenforceable rather than merely unenforced. It is unenforceable because the party endowed with the legal power to enforce it is incapable of exercising that power.

With reference to any context like the one just mentioned, where the local government is incapable of detecting a breach of its anti-jaywalking ordinance and is therefore incapable of responding to that breach, the Will Theorists must deny that the local government has held any legal claim-right to compliance with the ordinance. Hence, the Will Theorists also must deny that a citizen who commits an undetectable breach of the ordinance has on that occasion been under any legal duty to eschew the act of jaywalking that constitutes the breach. Indeed, given that the legal duty imposed by the ordinance is not incumbent on that citizen on that occasion, the ostensible breach of the ordinance is not such a breach at all. By engaging in an instance of jaywalking that is not detectable, a person will have temporarily relieved herself of her legal duty to forbear from jaywalking. Because the legal claim-rights conferred upon the municipal government through its anti-jaywalking ordinance are existent (by the reckoning of the Will Theorists) only when the legal duties of citizens correlative to those claim-rights are enforceable, the claim-rights and their correlative duties temporarily lapse in any contexts where acts of jaywalking are undetectable and are thus not susceptible to processes of enforcement.

Champions of the Will Theory such as Simmonds might respond that this critique of their doctrine overlooks the fact—or, rather, the putative fact—that the Will Theory and the Hohfeldian analysis are distinctively applicable to the realm of private law. Outside that realm, Simmonds might insist, the correlations between legal claim-rights and legal duties do not obtain or do not always obtain. Consequently, although the Will Theorists are committed to denying that the municipal government holds a legal claim-right to compliance by a citizen with its anti-jaywalking ordinance in any context where a transgression of the ordinance by that citizen is undetectable, they are not committed to denying that the citizen in question is under a legal duty of compliance even in such a context. After all, the duty is a public-law duty rather than a private-law duty. Such is the rejoinder of which a Will Theorist like Simmonds might seek to avail himself when confronted with the foregoing critique of the Will Theory.

Now, I of course do not accept that the Hohfeldian analysis of legal positions is confined to the realm of private law. However, even if the confinement of the analysis to that realm is granted *arguendo*, my critique of the Will Theory remains fully telling. My critique is thoroughly generalizable to the realm of private law as well as to the realm of public law. In the former realm as much as in the latter, some undetectable contraventions of legal duties can and do occur. For example, even if the owner of a sizeable plot of land expends large amounts of resources on monitoring and deterring acts of trespassing, there will almost inevitably occur some such acts that escape scrutiny. Likewise, slanderous utterances are frequently not ascertainable by the people who have been defamed through those utterances. If slanderous statements about some person P lower the reputation of P in the eyes of the addressees of those statements, and if the addressees are firmly disinclined to reveal what they now baselessly believe about P, the uttering of the defamatory statements will have been undetectable by P. In those cases and sundry other cases of unascertainable violations of legal obligations in the realm of private law, the parties who have been legally wronged by the violations are not capable of pursuing enforcement proceedings (because they do not know and cannot know about the violations). In such cases, then, those parties at the post-violation stage of enforceability lack the competence that is perceived by the Will Theorists as prerequisite to the holding of claim-rights. In regard to such cases, the Will Theorists are committed to denying that the apparently wronged parties have held legal claim-rights which would deontically protect those parties against the ostensible violations that have occurred. And since those ostensible violations have occurred in the realm of private law—a realm where claim-rights and duties are always mutually entailing, as even Simmonds and other Will Theorists acknowledge—the absence of any legal claim-right held by an ostensibly wronged party entails the absence of any correlative legal duty owed to that party. Thus, a trespasser who carries out his encroachment undetectably has on that occasion thereby freed himself from his legal duty not to engage in the encroachment. The Will Theorists have to accept that the undiscoverability of his act of trespassing removes its unlawfulness and its very status as an act of trespassing. On the occasion of his intrusion, his legal duty to abstain from intrusions has been suspended by his surreptitiousness. Similarly, the slanderer who traduces P in a manner that cannot be detected by P has thereby temporarily disburdened herself of her legal duty to refrain from defaming P. Her furtiveness has kept her from contravening the law as she maligns P, even though her maligning of him would have been illegal if it had been performed less stealthily.

In short, the Will Theory turns out to commit its supporters to the proposition that tortfeasors who are cleverly secretive in committing their misdeeds have managed to free themselves temporarily from the legal duties that would otherwise have been transgressed by those misdeeds. So long as the perpetrators of torts are sufficiently shrewd to ensure that their misconduct will not be espied through even the utmost endeavors of monitoring by their fellow citizens and the police, they will have avoided any breaches of legal duties—since the legal duties that would have been breached are suspended by the success of the perpetrators in concealing their misconduct. Whenever a tortfeasor is adroit at dissimulation in the undertaking of his misbehavior, he thus ensures that the misbehavior does not contravene any legal duties which it would have contravened if it had been perpetrated less covertly. Having deftly kept his harmful conduct from being discoverable, or having kept himself from being identifiable as the perpetrator of the harmful conduct, he is not classifiable by the Will Theorists as a tortfeasor at all. Because his apparently flouted legal duty is unenforceable on such an occasion, he has not flouted any legal duty whatsoever by the reckoning of those theorists. Not only has he managed to escape the burdens of owing compensation or restitution or indemnification, but in addition—so we are asked to think—he through the furtiveness of his harmful conduct has released himself from the legal obligation in connection with which any of those legal remedies would have been levied. Such is the ridiculous conclusion to which the Will Theory commits its proponents.

4.6 A Short Summary

This chapter has endeavored to elaborate and defend both a primary version and a capacious version of the Interest Theory of right-holding, and to expose the untenability of the Will Theory of right-holding. In so doing, the chapter has indispensably supplemented the Hohfeldian analysis of legal and moral positions by addressing a question or set of questions which that analysis does not answer. Moreover, as has been remarked at the outset of the chapter, my defense of the Interest Theory not only supplements the Hohfeldian schema but also crucially supports it by serving to vindicate the Hohfeldian Correlativity Axiom. My championing of that axiom in Chapter 3 has rested in part on the Interest Theory of right-holding. At the same time, while serving to bolster the Hohfeldian analytical framework, my exposition of the Interest Theory has drawn vitally upon that framework. Both when elaborating the main version of the Interest Theory for the holding of claim-rights and when elaborating the more capacious version for the holding of any Hohfeldian entitlements as rights, this chapter has proceeded with the categories delineated by Hohfeld. Differentiating correctly and precisely among those categories has been central to my discussions throughout the chapter.

For example, in my critique of the nearly eliminativist character of the Will Theory, the distinction between legal powers and legal immunities has been salient.

There remain, however, some matters—at the heart of the Interest Theory of right-holding—that have only fleetingly been touched upon in this chapter. Those matters are distilled in the second enumerated clause of the main version of the Interest Theory. As is evident from that clause, the correctness of any proposition that ascribes to some party P a claim-right will depend on the status of P as a potential holder of claim-rights. That is, it depends on the inclusion of P in the class of beings who are capable of holding claim-rights at all. Hitherto, in the course of expounding and upholding the Interest Theory, I have largely prescinded from questions about that class of beings. Nonetheless, any complete account of the non-justificatory aspects of rights and right-holding has to ponder those questions, and indeed they are some of the most salient points of contention in the contemporary philosophical and juristic debates over rights and right-holding. Accordingly, the final chapter of this book will now turn to those questions.

5
Potential Holders of Claim-Rights

This final chapter of *Rights and Right-Holding* explores some of the most prominent and controversial issues addressed by philosophers and jurists and ordinary people in their reflections on the holding of claim-rights. As has been remarked at the end of Chapter 4, the Interest Theory of right-holding affirms that a necessary condition for the holding of any claim-right by some party P is the inclusion of P in the class of potential holders of claim-rights. In other words, P cannot hold any claim-rights unless P is a being of a sort in whom claim-rights can be vested. Operative here is a distinction between the class of potential holders of claim-rights and the class of actual holders of claim-rights. Although every being in the latter class is also in the former class, the converse does not perforce obtain in the realm of law. For example, suppose that animals of a certain species are potential holders of claim-rights and that those animals are nonetheless not legally protected at all in some jurisdiction J. No typically beneficial aspects of the situation of any such animal are inherently protected by the legal duties which the system of governance in J has established. Within J, then, animals of the species envisaged here are not actual holders of any legal claim-rights even though they are potential holders of such claim-rights. If some on-balance typically advantageous aspects of their situations were inherently protected by legal duties in J, then these animals would hold legal claim-rights correlative to the duties. However, because no such aspects of their situations are in fact inherently protected by any legal duties that have been established there, the status of these animals as potential holders of legal claim-rights is not matched in J by their status as actual holders of legal claim-rights. The fact that they would hold legal claim-rights within J if they were inherently protected by laws there is due to their inclusion in the class of potential holders of claim-rights; the fact that they do not actually hold any legal claim-rights in J is due to the specifics of the duty-imposing laws there, which do not furnish any inherent protection for aspects of the situations of these animals that are typically advantageous for them on balance.

To be sure, in the realm of *morality* there is not ever any similar incongruity between the extension of the class of potential holders of claim-rights and the extension of the class of actual holders of claim-rights. Everyone included in the former class is also included in the latter; every being who can hold claim-rights at all is inherently protected, under the objectively correct principles of morality, against various forms of mistreatment. Even so, the distinction between the two classes is as important in the realm of morality as in the realm of law. My concern in this

Rights and Right-Holding. Matthew H. Kramer, Oxford University Press. © Matthew H. Kramer 2024.
DOI: 10.1093/oso/9780198891222.003.0005

chapter is to demarcate the class of potential holders of claim-rights—an endeavor that cuts across the distinction between the two aforementioned realms, since everyone who can hold moral claim-rights is also a potential holder of legal claim-rights and vice versa. Neither in regard to the purview of law nor in regard to the purview of morality is this chapter concerned to chart the *actual* holding of claim-rights. Within the realm of law, the actual holding of claim-rights is an empirical and evaluative matter pertaining to the contents of the sundry duty-imposing laws in each jurisdiction. Within the realm of morality, the actual holding of claim-rights is a justificatory matter that pertains to the vast array of duties imposed by the objectively correct principles of morality. A project of pinning down the actual holding of moral claim-rights would involve a complete exposition of those principles—something well beyond the scope of this book. As this volume has made clear since its opening chapter, it sets aside justificatory questions (which I have tackled in several of my other books) in order to concentrate on the fundamental non-justificatory features of rights and right-holding. Among the non-justificatory cruxes with which this book wrestles, the considerations that shape the category of potential holders of claim-rights are the final main set of issues yet to be addressed.

As has already been emphasized at more than one juncture, the fact that this chapter aligns with the previous chapters in prescinding from justificatory questions does not mean that its cogitations on the class of potential holders of claim-rights are devoid of ethical significance. On the contrary, some deep matters of ethics will inform my ruminations throughout this chapter, and the conclusions reached by those ruminations will carry further ethical implications. Indeed, as has been signaled in the opening paragraph of Chapter 4, some of the ethical argumentation in this chapter will be akin to a few of the lines of thought in several of my recent books on topics in political and moral philosophy. Hence, although the present chapter does not share the justificatory orientation of those recent books, it profits from some of their insights in its meditations on the beings who are capable of holding claim-rights.

One additional preliminary point of clarification is advisable here. As will be emphasized subsequently, the category of potential holders of claim-rights is not necessarily coextensive with the category of beings who are thought to be potential holders of claim-rights in this or that society. Misconceptions can lead people astray in either of two directions. Jurists and other people in some society might incorrectly think that certain beings in the class of potential holders of claim-rights are not within that class, or alternatively jurists and other people might err by thinking that certain beings outside that class are in fact within it. A misconception of the former type would obtain, for example, in a society where all non-human animals or some human beings are believed to be incapable of holding any claim-rights. A misconception of the latter type would obtain in a society where inanimate entities such as rivers or insentient organisms such as trees are believed to be capable of holding claim-rights. Misconceptions of each kind are not figments of my imagination. They have occurred in many actual societies, and in various forms they continue to occur. This chapter will delve into such mistaken perceptions and will explain why they are indeed mistaken. At this stage, we should simply note that the contours of the class of potential claim-right-holders are not determined by what the people in any particular society take those contours to be. Determinative of the scope of that class are objective ethical and conceptual considerations, rather than the variable perceptions to which people cling. Whereas the patterns of actual right-holding are of course variable across societies and across historical periods, the breadth of the category of potential claim-right-holders—the topic of this chapter—is not similarly a jurisdiction-specific matter. We shall return to this point in due course.

5.1 The Need for This Chapter

Unlike the Interest Theory, the Will Theory of right-holding in itself delimits the class of beings who are recognizable by the theory as potential holders of claim-rights. Given the tenor of the Will Theory, with its insistence on competence as a precondition for the holding of any claim-rights, the class of potential holders of such entitlements is confined to human adults who are of sound mind. Only sane human adults possess the cognitive and deliberative faculties that are constitutive of the competence which the devotees of the Will Theory regard as essential for the holding of claim-rights. Only such adults are capable of making the moderately sophisticated choices that are involved in exercising powers of control over the existence and enforcement of duties. Consequently, as has been recounted in §4.5.1.4 of Chapter 4, the advocates of the Will Theory believe that all beings other than sane human adults are excluded from the category of potential holders of claim-rights. Babies and infants and embryos and foetuses and demented people and insane people and permanently comatose people and dead people and future generations and non-human animals are all perceived by the Will Theorists as falling outside that category. Hence, a book-length exposition of the Will Theory would not need any chapter like the present one—though it would of course need to attempt to defend the way in which it delimits the category of potential holders of claim-rights, since its severe narrowing of that category has elicited more consternation over the past several decades than has any other feature of the Will Theory. No chapter of the present kind would be required, because any elaboration of the Will Theory would already demarcate the class of potential holders of claim-rights. A restrictive demarcation of that class is internal to the main tenet of the Will Theory, in combination with some elementary empirical observations about the cognitive and deliberative capacities of various types of beings.

By contrast, the Interest Theory in itself leaves open how broad or cabined the range of potential holders of claim-rights is. The Interest Theory is consistent with a highly circumscribed range such as that which is integral to the Will Theory, but it is also consistent with a much more expansive range. Interest Theorists usually maintain that the category of potential holders of claim-rights does extend far more broadly than the Will Theorists allow; I am unaware of any Interest Theorist who has endorsed the Will Theory's insistence that only human adults of sound mind are capable of holding claim-rights. Still, the Interest Theory per se is consistent with any answers to questions about the confinedness or embracingness of the class of potential holders of claim-rights.

Precisely because the Interest Theory itself can indeed be conjoined with any such answers, the current chapter is needed. My presentation of the Interest Theory will not be complete and satisfactory unless the second enumerated clause of the theory has been explicated adequately. To grasp vividly the need for a disquisition on the breadth or narrowness of that clause, we should ponder some contrasts between certain types of legal mandates. Consider first a law that prohibits the perpetration of unprovoked violence by any human being against any other human being. Correlated with the legal duty borne by each person in the jurisdiction under such a law is a legal claim-right held by every one of his or her fellows, a legal claim-right not to be subjected to unprovoked violence. After all, the existence of that legal duty inherently protects an aspect of the situation of each human being—an aspect that consists, of course, in not being subjected to such violence—which is typically beneficial on balance for people. What is more, although the inclusion of every human being in the class of potential holders of claim-rights will be confirmed and explained later in this chapter, it can here safely be taken as given. Hence, the deontic upshot of the statute that prohibits the perpetration of unprovoked violence is the conferral of a legal claim-right upon every human being in the jurisdiction vis-à-vis everyone else there. Such a conclusion about the upshot of that statute is fully in accordance with the Interest Theory of right-holding and is likewise in accordance with most credible pre-theoretical understandings of the matter. (At least in application to mentally incapacitated human beings, the aforementioned conclusion goes beyond what the proponents of the Will Theory would acknowledge. Whether the Will Theorists would accept that each sane human adult Q holds a legal claim-right vis-à-vis every one of his or her fellows under the statute is dependent on whether Q holds legal powers of control over the existence and enforcement of the duty incumbent on every one of his or her fellows not to subject Q to unprovoked violence.)

Let us now ponder an ordinance in some municipality that legally forbids people to walk upon the grass in the areas of a public park that have been marked with signs. Under the ordinance, each person in the jurisdiction bears a legal duty to refrain from walking on the grass in any of the designated areas. Correlated with that legal duty of each person is a legal claim-right to compliance held by the system of governance that has enacted the ordinance. By deontically requiring each person to conform with a mandate which that system of governance has promulgated, the duty borne by each person inherently protects an aspect of the situation of the system that is typically advantageous for it on balance. Does any other party hold a legal claim-right correlative to the legal duty imposed by the ordinance on every member of the public? Such a duty inherently protects an aspect of the situation of the grass in the park—an aspect that consists in not being trampled upon—which is typically advantageous on balance for organisms like the grass. Indeed, the chief effect of the ordinance resides in its promotion of the flourishing of the grass. Should we therefore conclude that the grass holds a legal claim-right correlative to the legal duty imposed on each person by the ordinance? Should we conclude that each individual blade of grass holds such a claim-right?

Let us now contemplate a law that prohibits the defacement or culpable damaging of Old Master paintings. Under such a law, every person in the relevant jurisdiction bears a legal duty to refrain from defacing or otherwise culpably damaging any master painting. A duty with that content inherently protects an aspect of the situation of each painting that is typically beneficial on balance for such an object. Each painting will be in a better condition if the duty of every person which pertains to it is fulfilled than if that duty is contravened. Should we therefore conclude that the Old Master paintings are holders of legal claim-rights correlated with the duties borne by members of the public under the envisaged law? Instead of merely pertaining to those works of art, are the duties owed to them?

A final law to be pondered at this juncture is a statute that proscribes the perpetration of vandalism. Such a statute imposes a duty on every person in the jurisdiction to forbear from culpably inflicting damage on buildings or other structures. A duty of that sort inherently protects an aspect of the situation of a building that is typically beneficial on balance for any such erection. Myriads of actions that would worsen the condition of a building are made legally wrong by the interdictory sway of the statute. Should we conclude that each edifice in the jurisdiction holds a legal claim-right correlative to the legal duty imposed on every person by the anti-vandalism law? Is that duty owed by every person to each edifice, as well as to the system of governance that has imposed the duty?

Of central importance here is that the Interest Theory does not in itself settle any of the questions posed in the last few paragraphs. In each of the scenarios in those paragraphs, the first enumerated clause of the Interest Theory is satisfied in application to entities of a certain kind (grass, paintings, or buildings). Thus, the questions in the scenarios are in effect asking whether the second enumerated clause of the Interest Theory is also satisfied. As is evident, my formulation of the Interest Theory does not without amplification enable us to judge whether the second clause of the theory has been satisfied or not. Accordingly, the purpose of this chapter is to provide the amplification that is requisite for arriving knowledgeably at any judgments about the reach of that clause.

Very likely, most readers at a pre-theoretical level will concur with me in thinking that grass and paintings and buildings are not included in the class of potential holders of claim-rights. Most readers will probably likewise concur with me in thinking that human beings—at the very least, human adults of sound mind who are currently alive—are included in that class. Consequently, if my conjectures about the pre-theoretical inclinations of most readers are correct, those readers will share my sense that the law which forbids the perpetration of unprovoked violence against other people has conferred upon each person vis-à-vis every one of his or her fellows a legal claim-right not to be subjected to such violence. And those readers will also share my sense that the laws which prohibit vandalism and walking on the grass and defacement of Old Master paintings have not conferred any legal claim-rights upon buildings or grass or paintings. Still, however widely endorsed those conclusions may be, they are not sufficient for the purposes of this book. Until they are furnished with a theoretical basis, those conclusions do not lend themselves to generalization. Similarly, until they are furnished with such a basis, they cannot be adequately defended against challenges. Challenges are abidingly possible, of course, since very few conclusions in the philosophy of rights and right-holding are wholly uncontroversial. For example, although I am unaware of any philosophers who have endeavored to argue that paintings and buildings are among the potential holders of claim-rights, there have certainly been philosophers and jurists who have argued that insentient organisms such as grass and trees are among those potential holders. Just over half a century ago, for instance, Christopher Stone in a classic article contended that trees can and should hold legal rights (Stone 1972). Quite a few environmental ethicists have jousted with one another over the question whether certain inanimate natural entities such as rivers and stone formations can and should hold legal rights (Barkham 2021; Kramer 2017a, 136; Kurki 2019, 127–31; 2022b; Stockwell 2022). In sum, given the diversity of the verdicts that have been reached by philosophers and jurists on these issues and on related issues, and given the need for extrapolating from one's stances on certain matters to appropriate stances on quite different matters, a pre-theoretical comprehension of the upshots of the several laws sketched here is patently not enough for coming to grips with the complexities of differentiating between the beings who are capable of holding claim-rights and the beings that are not so capable. We need to move beyond pre-theoretical convictions in order to gain a principled understanding—a richly theoretical understanding—of the category of potential holders of claim-rights. That principled understanding is what this chapter seeks to impart.

5.2 An Expansive Conception of Interests

As is apparent from what has been said already in this chapter, and as should indeed be evident from my formulation and exposition of the Interest Theory heretofore in this book, the conception of interests or benefits or advantages to which I adhere throughout is expansive. That conception can apply not only to human beings and other conscious creatures but also to insensate organisms and multitudes of inanimate phenomena. It can apply to grass and paintings and buildings quite straightforwardly. Under my broad conception of interests, the occurrence of some event *e* is on balance in the interest of a being B if and only if the occurrence of *e* will on balance improve B's situation or will on balance avert a worsening of that situation. Alternatively stated, the occurrence of *e* is on balance beneficial or advantageous for B if and only if such an occurrence will on balance improve B's situation or will on balance avert a worsening of that situation. Thus, for example, the enactment and implementation of an anti-vandalism statute in some jurisdiction J may well be beneficial on balance for the buildings there by averting an on-balance decline in the condition of each such building. Precisely because this conception of interests or benefits or advantages is so expansive, there arises the problem to which the present chapter is addressed. Within my formulation of the main tenet of the Interest Theory, the first enumerated clause invokes the notion of benefits without any restrictions that would limit the applicability of such a notion to only certain types of beings. Consequently, that first clause is consistent with the proposition that the enactment and implementation of an anti-vandalism statute will bestow legal claim-rights upon edifices. If such a proposition is to be rejected—as it should be—the basis for rejecting it lies in the second enumerated clause of the Interest Theory rather than in the first clause.

Very broad conceptions of interests, like the conception that is operative in my Interest Theory of right-holding, have drawn flak from some philosophers. We should here examine the objections that have been posed by Joseph Bowen and Ronald Dworkin respectively. Whereas Bowen in a recent essay has concentrated on my own account of interests (Bowen 2022), Dworkin trained his fire on broad understandings of interests while he was participating sustainedly during the early 1990s in debates over the morality of abortion (Dworkin 1993).

5.2.1 Bowen's Worries about My Account of Interests

When Bowen expresses his doubts about my far-reaching conception of interests, he initially raises some terminological misgivings. He writes as follows: "I think it is implausible that interests are so capacious: to my ear, the grass does not have an interest in being watered, nor does my computer have an interest in having its RAM upgraded, nor does my house have an interest in having its painting touched up" (2022, 58 n. 28). Though the formulations in the quoted sentence are somewhat awkward, each of them can easily be reworded to eliminate the awkwardness while retaining the invocation of an interest: "It is in the interest of the grass that it be watered regularly; it is in the interest of your computer that its software be up-graded regularly; it is in the interest of your house that its paint be touched up."

In any event, the objection pressed here by Bowen is a superficial matter of terminology. One thing to be noted in response to such an objection is that my formulation of the principal tenet of the Interest Theory nowhere employs the term "interest" or "interests." Instead, as has already been remarked, it refers to what is typically beneficial on balance. Jeremy Bentham's account of the holding of legal rights has sometimes been designated as the "benefit theory" (Ferraro 2022, 45; Graham 1996; Hart 1982, 174; Lyons 1984, 728; Mullock 1975); although Bentham's account is markedly different in some salient respects from my own exposition of the holding of claim-rights, there are also some affinities between the two, and the label "Benefit Theory" would be as germane for my exposition as is the label "Interest Theory." Were the language of "benefits" to be substituted for the language of "interests" in Bowen's observations about the grass and the computer and the house, his terminological qualms would not have any purchase at all. Entirely idiomatic are the following formulations: "The grass will benefit from being watered regularly; the computer and its operations will benefit from the regular up-grading of its software; the house will benefit from the touching up of its paint." I am concerned chiefly with the substance of my account of right-holding rather than with the labeling of it. If the redesignation of my account as the "Benefit Theory" would avert any terminological squeamishness on the part of Bowen or others, then I would be content with the redesignation. Though such a maneuver strikes me as superfluous, it would be wholly unobjectionable as a substantive matter. Still, the crucial point here is that the notion of interests and the notion of benefits or improvements or advantages—as they are invoked in this book—are thoroughly interrelated and are equally broad. An interest of a being in the occurrence of some event is simply the susceptibility of that being to the betterment of its condition through such an occurrence.

5.2.1.1 Bowen's First Substantive Query: The Univocality of a Theory

In addition to giving voice to his terminological queasiness, Bowen advances a couple of substantive objections to my expansive understanding of interests. He states the first of those substantive worries as follows (2022, 59, emphasis in original):

> [I]f we define interests capaciously, but then say it is only a subset of interests that matter for rights, we are not really defending the *Interest* Theory of Rights. Rather, we are defending the Interest* Theory, where the asterisk denotes the subset of

> morally relevant interests. If we define interests more narrowly, we do not need to make such accommodations—it is interests in general that are doing the work.

Far from exposing any insurmountable difficulties that afflict my broad conception of interests, Bowen's argument on this point can help to reveal one of the chief reasons for embracing that conception. Let us here recall the thesis with which I encapsulate the Interest Theory of right-holding:

> **Interest Theory of Right-Holding**: Individually necessary and jointly sufficient for the holding of a claim-right by *X* are (1) the fact that the duty correlative to the claim-right deontically and inherently protects some aspect of *X*'s situation that on balance is typically beneficial for a being like *X*, and (2) the fact that *X* is a member of the class of potential holders of claim-rights.

As has already been noted in this chapter, the second enumerated clause of the Interest Theory does not specify its own extension. Instead, it simply indicates that beings cannot hold any claim-rights unless the beings are within that extension. Consequently, exponents of the Interest Theory can adopt divergent views on the ambit of its second enumerated clause even while they all subscribe wholeheartedly to the Interest Theory as a correct account of right-holding. When this feature of the Interest Theory is duly recognized, the futility of Bowen's first substantive objection to my expansive conception of interests should be apparent. Contrary to what is suggested in that objection, the advocates of the Interest Theory are not espousing distinct accounts of right-holding that have to be labeled separately when those advocates differ with one another over the range of beings whose interests are within the scope of the Interest Theory. Such disagreements among the devotees of the Interest Theory pertain not to the correct exposition of right-holding—on which the devotees all concur—but instead to the specific conclusions derivable from the criterion which the Interest Theory provides for identifying the holders of claim-rights. The divergences concern the extension of that criterion rather than its intension.

By contrast, the approach to these matters which Bowen commends will run afoul of exactly the problem of equivocality which he incorrectly imputes to my approach. For Bowen, the class of beings with interests is equivalent to the class of potential holders of claim-rights. Accordingly, any disagreement about either of those classes is a disagreement about the other. Ergo, insofar as Bowen's approach is followed, there is no univocal Interest Theory of right-holding on which various philosophers converge while differing with one another over the breadth of the class of potential claim-right-holders. Under Bowen's approach, controversies relating to the breadth of that class are controversies relating to the basic nature of interests and vice versa. Thus, instead of sharing a single account of right-holding, Bowenite philosophers would be propounding incompatible accounts that should be separately designated as the Interest-1 Theory and the Interest-2 Theory and so forth.

One major reason for combining my broad conception of interests with the Interest Theory of right-holding, then, is that such a combination renders the Interest Theory univocal while leaving ample room for proponents of the theory to quarrel at the extensional level about the width of the class of potential holders of claim-rights. Having raised the problem of equivocality, Bowen obviously and appositely attaches importance to the devising of a univocal theory of right-holding. He should therefore follow my approach to these matters—an approach consisting in the combination which I have just outlined—and should forswear his own approach.

5.2.1.2 A Second Substantive Objection by Bowen: No Justification

A second substantive criticism broached by Bowen is wholly misdirected. He submits that my Interest Theory, when combined with my capacious conception of interests, "offers an implausible account of the grounds of right-holding." He elaborates (2022, 59, emphasis in original):

> [E]ven if we go for [Kramer's non-justificatory version of] the Interest Theory . . ., we *are* offering an account of grounds of right-holding—we are offering an account of that in virtue of which one is a potential right-holder. If we endorse [a view of those grounds focused on a person's well-being], we have an intuitively compelling account of the grounds of right-holding. This is because how our lives go for us—what our wellbeing consists of—is obviously of importance. When one's wellbeing is the grounds of some duty *or* when one's wellbeing is necessarily, typically served by some duty (depending on whether we endorse the [Razian] Justificatory or [Kramerian] Nonjustificatory version of the Interest Theory, respectively), it is plausible that the duty would resultantly be owed to one. The same is true to a similar extent of the Stakes View of Interests (on that view, recall, interests are those things we care about and that we have reason to care about—so rights are grounded in those things we care about and have reason to care about). But once we move to Kramer's capacious view [of interests], it is just not clear to me why advancing something's condition, such as a painting's condition, would result in the duty being owed to that thing.

What makes this passage so puzzlingly misguided is that it completely overlooks the main point of my ruminations on the class of potential holders of claim-rights. As has been underscored in this chapter, the second enumerated clause of the Interest Theory does not in itself delimit the class of potential holders of claim-rights. Although sundry votaries of the Interest Theory can disagree over the amplitude of that class, every such votary has to delimit it in some way—because nobody could plausibly maintain that everything susceptible to improvement or deterioration is within the class of potential holders of claim-rights. I have long insistently underlined the preposterousness of the notion that the class of potential holders of claim-rights is equivalent to the class of beings endowed with interests (where interests are understood in accordance with my broad conception thereof). Yet Bowen proceeds in the quoted passage as if I had espoused that preposterous notion. Given that I in fact have sustainedly rejected it in my earlier work as well as in this volume, the second of his substantive objections to my expansive conception of interests is badly misdirected.

Indeed, Bowen himself straightaway avows as much: "At this stage, one might reply: but if we endorse Kramer's capacious view [of interests], we cannot conclude from one's interest being necessarily, typically served by some duty that this will result in the duty being owed to the interest-bearer. This is because, as Kramer makes clear, we then need to inquire as to the moral status of the interest-bearer" (2022, 59). Having admitted that his second substantive criticism is misconceived, Bowen goes on to conclude that either my broad conception or a narrower conception of interests can be serviceable for the task of demarcating the range of potential holders of claim-rights. He asserts that "if we want to discover whether some entity is a potential right-holder, it is unclear it matters whether we define interests narrowly or capaciously" (2022, 60). Though I welcome the concessionary tenor of Bowen's discussion at this juncture, I am disinclined to be equally concessionary in return. As I have indicated in my riposte to his first substantive query, anyone who aspires to propound the Interest Theory as a univocal account of right-holding should recognize that the choice between my broad view and a more constricted view of interests does matter.

In short, neither in his terminological quibbling nor in his substantive worries does Bowen expose any genuine shortcomings in my expansive conception of interests. Moreover, the first of his substantive criticisms has turned out to tell against his own understanding of interests, and it has helped to reveal why my expansive understanding is superior. Like the quip by Tranio directed against Petruchio in Act V of Shakespeare's *The Taming of the Shrew*, the critique by Bowen directed against my perspective on the nature of interests "did glance away from me, [and] 'tis ten to one it maim'd [Bowen] outright" (V.ii.61–2).

5.2.2 Dworkin on Foetuses and Interests

In his efforts to establish that the controversies over abortion in the United States pertain not to the rights of foetuses but instead to the intrinsic value of human life, Dworkin repeatedly declared that foetuses—at least in their zygotic and embryonic stages—cannot have any interests of their own and consequently cannot be endowed with any rights. He contended that "it is very hard to make any sense of the idea that an early fetus has interests of its own, in particular an interest in not being destroyed, from the moment of its conception," and he sneered at "the scarcely comprehensible idea that an organism that has never had a mental life can still have interests" (1993, 15, 20). Reiterating that "[i]t is a mistake to suppose that an early fetus has interests of its own," he proclaimed that "an early fetus has no interests and rights" (1993, 98, 73). Similar statements by Dworkin abound in *Life's Dominion*, but his only argumentation to buttress those numerous assertions is in his book's opening chapter. Having elsewhere impugned his implicit assumption that any claim-rights vested in foetuses would have to be justified by reference to their interests (Kramer 2017a, 141–4), I will here assail his central contention that foetuses cannot have any interests.

Dworkin took it to be evident that insentient beings cannot have any interests. He stated his view emphatically: "It makes no sense to suppose that something has interests of *its own*—as distinct from its being important what happens to it—unless it has, or has had, some form of consciousness: some mental as well as physical life" (1993, 16, emphasis in original). After recounting a few assessments and findings by some embryologists, Dworkin brought to bear his narrow conception of interests on the situation of foetuses. He trumpeted that "it seems beyond challenge that a fetus does not have the neural substrate necessary for interests of any kind until some point relatively late in its gestation," and he concluded that "an immature fetus cannot have interests and therefore cannot have an interest in surviving" (1993, 18).

One way in which some philosophers who oppose the lawfulness of abortion will be inclined to respond, of course, is to contest Dworkin's understanding of the embryological literature (Grisez 1970, 21–3, 281). I will not pursue that route at all here, partly because I am unsympathetic to it and partly because the embryological findings are better addressed by scientists than by philosophers. Instead, I will challenge the general premise on which Dworkin relies: his premise that insentient beings cannot have any interests. That premise is too controversial to be a mainstay of an approach to the problem of abortion that aspires and purports to be neutral among all reasonable religious and ethical credos, and it is not well supported by the arguments that Dworkin marshaled in defense of it.

5.2.2.1 An Excessively Controversial Position

In fairness to Dworkin, it should initially be noted that his conception of interests is shared by a number of other philosophers. That conception is naturally appealing to any hard-core utilitarian like Peter Singer, who avers that "[t]he capacity for suffering and enjoyment is *a prerequisite for having interests at all*, a condition that must be satisfied before we can speak of interests in a meaningful way" (1995, 7, emphasis in original). Singer elaborates: "A stone does not have interests because it cannot suffer. Nothing that we can do to it could possibly make any difference to its welfare. The capacity for suffering and enjoyment is, however, not only necessary but also sufficient for us to say that a being has interests" (1995,

8). Bonnie Steinbock, who differs with Singer on quite a few other points, is at one with him and with Dworkin in her thinking about this matter. Asserting that interests are "conceptually connected with sentience (the ability to experience pain and pleasure) or conscious awareness," she submits that "[m]ere things—rocks, planets, automobiles—are not conscious or sentient and so do not have interests. Nor do plants, although, unlike mere things, they are alive." Steinbock explains that "plants lack interests because it does not matter to plants what is done to them.... Whatever reasons we may have for preserving or protecting nonsentient beings, these reasons do not refer to their own interests. For without conscious awareness, beings cannot have interests" (1992, 5). Steinbock applies her conception of interests to the situation of foetuses: "Without thoughts or feelings or awareness of any kind, the embryo or fetus has no interests.... It has the potential to develop into the kind of being that will have interests, but ... this potential does not give it the actual interests necessary for moral standing" (1992, 6). Mary Anne Warren expressed a similar view of the situation of foetuses: "[P]rior to the initial occurrence of conscious experience, there is no being that suffers and enjoys, and thus has needs and interests that matter to it" (1997, 204). Other philosophers and theorists have embraced a similar conception of interests.[1]

Dworkin was not being highly idiosyncratic, then, when he insisted that foetuses cannot have any interests and therefore cannot have any rights. Nevertheless, his narrow conception of interests was far too controversial to be serviceable for his hopes of coming up with a solution to the problem of abortion that would be neutral among all reasonable religious and ethical creeds. For one thing, as has been acknowledged by both Steinbock and Warren, some environmental ethicists reject any conception of interests that is limited to conscious beings.[2] Even more important in the present context, the conservative opponents of the lawfulness of abortion will reject any conception of interests that is so limited—at least if they concur (as they should) with Dworkin and Singer and Steinbock and Warren in maintaining that a being B cannot ever possess claim-rights unless B is endowed with interests. In other words, by espousing his cabined conception of interests, Dworkin presupposed the falsity of the conservative Catholic stance on abortion (Shrage 2003, 30–1; Williams 2015, 39, 40). To be sure, he did supply a bit of argumentation to back up his cabined conception; we shall examine his argumentation shortly. However, the point here is that he needed to furnish such argumentation concerning substantive ethical and conceptual matters that directly bear on the status of foetuses as persons. He could not grapple with those matters from the creed-transcending perspective which he professed to adopt.

[1] See, for example, Berg 2007, 376; Feinberg 1984, 32–4; Sumner 1988, 164. See also De Marneffe 2010, 138; Tooley 1972, 45–7; Williams 2000, 208.

[2] Steinbock 1992, 16–21; Warren 1997, 67. For some examples of writings in which environmental ethicists reject a narrow conception of interests, see Rodman 1977, 89–90; Rolston 1988, 106–9; Taylor 1981, 199–200.

Dworkin's straitened conception of interests is, of course, at odds with the considerably more expansive conception which I have propounded in this chapter (and in my earlier work). I have contended that any being B has interests if and only if B's situation can be enhanced or worsened. Under that conception of interests, the occurrence of some event *e* is in the interest of B if the occurrence of *e* will either improve B's situation or avert a worsening of it. An entity is without any interests only if its condition is insusceptible to any enhancement or deterioration. Creatures capable of experiencing gratification or pain are endowed with interests, of course, but so too are many insentient entities such as rivers and trees and Old Master paintings and elegant buildings.

Particularly noteworthy in the present context is that my broad conception of interests has not been adopted in the service of any specific stand on the problem of abortion. That conception has obviously not been adopted in furtherance of a "pro-life" doctrine, given that I reject any such doctrine. On the contrary, one of my principal concerns in this chapter is to prescind from justificatory debates such as those over abortion—partly by differentiating between the question whether a being of some specified type has any interests and the question whether a being of that type can hold claim-rights. Although both of those questions are ethical as well as conceptual, the former is more abstract than the latter. Thus, unlike Dworkin, I am endeavoring to address the former question in ways that can accommodate a wide range of answers to the latter question. (Of course, the question whether a being of some specified type can hold legal claim-rights is itself more abstract than the question whether a being of that type does hold certain legal claim-rights, and it is considerably more abstract than the justificatory question whether a being of that type should hold certain legal claim-rights.) Hence, someone who shares Dworkin's ambition to achieve neutrality among all reasonable religious and ethical credos while wrestling with the matter of abortion is clearly best advised to adopt my broad conception of interests rather than Dworkin's narrow conception. Given his own aspiration to achieve neutrality, his narrow conception of interests was a non-starter. With that conception, Dworkin deviated from neutrality *ab initio*.

5.2.2.2 Dworkin's First Argument: Begging the Question and Missing the Point

Let us, then, examine the arguments which Dworkin adduced in his efforts to vindicate his restrictive conception of interests. His first ostensible line of reasoning was really just a reaffirmation of his central thesis. Beginning with the unexceptionable proposition that "[n]ot everything that can be destroyed has an interest in not being destroyed," Dworkin proceeded to argue: "A beautiful sculpture can be smashed, and that would be a terrible insult to the intrinsic value that great works of art embody and also very much against the interests of people who take pleasure in seeing or studying them. But a sculpture has no interests of its own; a savage act of vandalism is not unfair to *it*" (1993, 15–16, emphasis in original). We should initially note that the latter half of the final sentence in this quotation is irrelevant to the point at issue. The question whether a being B has interests is distinct from the question whether B is a potential holder of claim-rights, which in turn is distinct from the question whether B actually holds certain claim-rights. Thus, even though an act of vandalism would not be unfair to the sculpture against which it is perpetrated, the prevention of such an act would be in the interest of that sculpture under my broad conception of interests—because the prevention of such an act would avert a worsening of the sculpture's condition.

Even more important, Dworkin's opening line of reasoning either begs the question or misses the point. As a response to my very broad conception of interests, his line of reasoning is flagrantly question-begging. Under his narrow conception of interests, his assertion that a statue has no interests is of course correct. However, such an assertion is simply an assertion, which does not supply any reasons for proponents of my broader conception of interests to forsake their understanding of the matter and embrace Dworkin's. (As has already been noted, Dworkin's observation about the absence of any unfairness to the statue does not supply such reasons—since that observation is fully consistent with the attribution of interests to the statue. Even in relation to adult human beings of sound mind, interests are often appropriately ascribable in circumstances where the undergoing of unfairness is not. It is in my interest that the weather be warm and sunny in Cambridge today, yet I will not have suffered any injustice or unfairness if the weather instead turns out to be chilly and cloudy.)

My very broad conception of interests is not the lone alternative to Dworkin's straitened conception. Someone could propound an intermediate conception that allows for the attribution of interests to all animate beings, including all insentient animate beings such as plants and trees and fungi and embryos. As a response to an intermediate conception of that kind, Dworkin's first line of argument would be a badly missed encounter. Proponents of that intermediate conception would concur with Dworkin about the inappositeness of ascribing any interests to a statue, but their agreement with him on that point would be accompanied by their insistence on the appropriateness of ascribing interests to foetuses.

In short, Dworkin's initial line of reasoning begs the question against my very broad conception of interests, and it misses the point of the intermediate conception that has just been broached. His line of reasoning does not contribute at all to the reinforcement of his own cabined conception of interests.

5.2.2.3 Dworkin's Second Argument: Missing the Target

In his next line of argument, Dworkin did engage with the intermediate conception of interests: "Nor is it enough, for something to have interests, that it be alive and in the process of developing into something more mature—it is not against the interests of a baby carrot that it be picked early and brought to the table as a delicacy—nor even that it be something that will naturally develop into something different or more marvelous: a butterfly is much more beautiful than a caterpillar, but it is not better for the *caterpillar* to become one" (1993, 16, emphasis in original).

In his remark about baby carrots, Dworkin conflated the conditions under which a being has interests and the conditions under which a being's interests are set back. Let us grant (very readily) that the acts of picking and cooking and eating the baby carrot as a delicacy are not against its interests. Even so, that proposition is consistent with the proposition that a baby carrot is possessed of some interests. Indeed, the acts of picking and cooking and eating the carrot are in its interests—because it will then have optimally served the purpose which it can best fulfill. Its instrumental value will have been enhanced by the occurrence of those acts.

Dworkin fared no better in his remark about caterpillars. For one thing, he was on shaky ground in contending that the metamorphosis of a caterpillar into a beautiful butterfly is not in the interests of the caterpillar *qua* caterpillar. At any rate, even if his dubious verdict on that point is conceded *arguendo*, the metamorphosis will clearly be in the interests of the caterpillar *qua* organism. Moreover, Dworkin here conflated the conditions under which a being has interests and the conditions under which a being's interests are advanced. Even if it were true that the metamorphosis into a butterfly would somehow not be in the interests of the caterpillar *qua* organism, we could still correctly ascribe interests to the caterpillar. For example, it has an interest in not being squashed under someone's foot. Thus, like Dworkin's reference to baby carrots, his reference to caterpillars does not go any way toward vindicating his narrow conception of interests.

5.2.2.4 Dworkin's Third Argument: Begging the Question and Missing the Target Afresh

In his third line of argument, Dworkin committed some errors similar to those which we have already detected: "Nor is it enough, for something to have interests, that it might, if treated in the right way, grow or develop into a human being. Imagine that (as some scientists apparently think conceivable) doctors were able to produce a child from an unfertilized ovum, by parthenogenesis. Menstruation would still not be against an ovum's interests; a woman who used contraception would not be violating some creature's fundamental right every month" (1993, 16, footnote omitted). Let us start by noticing that the latter half of the final sentence in this quotation again conflates the question whether a being has an *interest* in the non-occurrence of some mode of conduct and the question whether a being has a *claim-right* to the non-occurrence of that mode of conduct. As I have already indicated, a negative answer to the latter question does not entail a negative answer to the former question.

Furthermore, even under my expansive conception of interests, not everything is endowed with interests. It is doubtful whether an unfertilized ovum—as opposed to the organism who contains the unfertilized ovum—is endowed with any interests. However, for present purposes, I will grant that even an unfertilized ovum is possessed of some interests if suitable parthenogenic technology is available. In that event, the first half of the final sentence in this quotation again begs the question against my broad conception of interests. Only in the latter half of that sentence did Dworkin make any effort to substantiate his comment about menstruation in the former half; and, as I have remarked, his pronouncement there about the absence of a claim-right (though correct in itself) is an *ignoratio elenchi*. Consequently, his assertion that menstruation would not be against an ovum's interests is a sheer assertion that is not backed up by any relevant argumentation.

5.2.2.5 Dworkin's Final Argument: Familiar Errors

In one further attempt to make a persuasive case for his circumscribed conception of interests, Dworkin conjured up a scenario in which Doctor Frankenstein has assembled a collection of bodily parts into an inanimate creature that can be brought to life through some Promethean technology: "Imagine that, just as Dr. Frankenstein reached for the lever that would bring life to the assemblage of body parts on his laboratory table, someone appalled at the experiment smashed the apparatus. That act, whatever we think of it, would not have been harmful or unfair to the assemblage, or against its interests" (1993, 16). The errors in this final line of reasoning by Dworkin are familiar. First, his reference to the absence of unfairness is correct but is beside the point, since the absence of unfairness does not entail the absence of interests that are set back. Second, if we assume that a life for the creature generated by Frankenstein's macabre technology will be better than no life at all, Dworkin again begged the question against my very broad conception of interests when he insisted that the smashing of the apparatus would not be against the inanimate creature's interests. (If a life brought about through the eerie technology would be worse for the creature than no life at all, Dworkin's assertion about the smashing of the apparatus would be correct. However, the correctness of his assertion would derive not from the absence of any interests that are ascribable to the creature, but instead from the fact that the destruction of the machinery will have advanced those interests.) Third, as a rejoinder to the intermediate conception of interests, Dworkin's scenario is another missed encounter. Proponents of that intermediate conception would agree that the inanimate creature is not possessed of any interests, even while they would affirm that embryos are very different precisely because the embryos are not inanimate.

In sum, every one of the endeavors by Dworkin to vindicate his narrow conception of interests has foundered. Of course, in saying as much, I am not purporting to have refuted his conception outright. The dialectical situation has not called for any refutation of that conception. Rather, I have sought to show that he in his understanding of interests markedly departed from his quest for neutrality among all reasonable religious and ethical doctrines, and I have likewise shown that he signally failed to clinch the case for his understanding of interests with his several thought-experiments.

Dworkin was quite misguided in his ambition to resolve a key point of controversy in the debates over abortion—the matter of the moral personhood of foetuses—by recourse to an account of the nature of interests. At the end of the opening chapter of *Life's Dominion* (1993, 28–9), he indicated that he would not be relying directly on any general theory of justice or morality that had been devised in isolation from the problem of abortion. Instead of connecting a general theory to that problem from the outside in, Dworkin professedly aimed to venture from the inside out by expounding and combining moral principles on the basis of his grappling with the specifics of the disputation over abortion. Yet he then proceeded to peddle a narrow conception of interests which led him to insist that many of the pronouncements by "pro-life" activists cannot be taken at face value. As he averred: "The scalding rhetoric of the 'pro-life' movement seems to presuppose the [deontological] claim that a fetus is from the moment of its conception a full moral person with rights and interests equal in importance to those of any other member of the moral community. But very few people—even those who belong to the most vehemently anti-abortion groups—actually believe that, whatever they say" (1993, 13). In other words, Dworkin foisted upon the anti-abortion zealots a conception of interests which led him to the conclusion that those zealots do not really credit what they themselves earnestly proclaim. Someone like Dworkin, professing to argue from the inside out, should have known better.

5.3 Distinct Issues

As has been seen, the expansive conception of interests (or benefits or advantages) favored in this book is invulnerable to the objections posed respectively by Bowen and Dworkin. Furthermore, that expansive conception should be embraced by anyone who shares Bowen's apt conviction that the univocality of the Interest Theory as an account of the holding of claim-rights is a desideratum. Likewise, that conception should be embraced by anyone who shares Dworkin's aspiration to address the problem of abortion in ways that are neutral among reasonable religious and ethical credos. It is also the conception of interests that should inform any account of the fundamental nature of right-holding, since it invaluably facilitates the disentangling of distinct questions.

One major distinction in this area, of course, is between the class of beings with interests and the class of beings who are capable of holding claim-rights. Such a distinction is essential for the univocality of the Interest Theory, as has been observed, and it is also crucial more generally for one's recognition that entities such as grass and paintings and buildings can inherently be affected in typically beneficial ways through various legally obligatory occurrences or states of affairs without belonging to the class of potential holders of claim-rights. Another major distinction, discussed at the outset of this chapter, is between the class of potential holders of claim-rights and the class of actual holders of claim-rights. Specifically with reference to legal claim-rights, a further distinction is between beings who *do* actually hold claim-rights and beings who *should* actually hold claim-rights. Whereas the extension of the class of beings who do actually hold legal claim-rights in a particular jurisdiction is a partly empirical and partly ethical and partly evaluative matter centered on the contents of the duty-imposing laws that exist therein, the extension of the class of beings who should actually hold legal claim-rights is a justificatory matter pertaining to the proper distribution and contents of the legal claim-rights in any jurisdiction.

Like the previous chapters of this book, the current chapter prescinds from justificatory questions even while it engages with the ethical cruxes involved in delimiting the class of potential holders of claim-rights. Those cruxes do not concern the extent to which or the ways in which the interests of various beings should be legally protected through the conferral of legal claim-rights. Instead, they concern the grounds for acknowledging that certain beings are parties to whom claim-rights can properly be ascribed when some on-balance typically beneficial aspects of the situations of those beings are inherently protected through the imposition of legal duties upon others. Distinguishing between beings who are among the potential holders of claim-rights and beings that are not among those potential holders is different from distinguishing between beings whose interests should receive stringent legal protection and beings whose interests should not receive such stringent legal protection.

Thus, for example, the following two propositions are perfectly consistent:

(1) Wherever legal norms impose duties on people not to abort any foetuses, those norms have thereby endowed the foetuses with legal claim-rights against being aborted.
(2) As a matter of substantive morality, first-trimester foetuses should not be legally protected against abortions in any jurisdiction (except where abortion-inducing actions are malicious or reckless or negligent).

Proposition 1 does not prescribe the extent to which or the ways in which the interests of foetuses should be legally protected. It does not prescribe in favor of the establishing of certain legal duties, nor does it prescribe against the establishing of those duties. It does not say anything about the moral justification for bringing any legal duties into existence, and it does not say anything about the moral justification for keeping any legal duties out of existence. No such justificatory matters are addressed by proposition 1. Instead, it addresses the non-justificatory question whether foetuses are included in the class of potential holders of claim-rights. It presupposes that the answer to that question is affirmative, as it declares that foetuses hold legal claim-rights-not-to-be-aborted wherever people are under legal duties not to abort foetuses. Those legal duties inherently protect aspects of the situations of foetuses that are typically beneficial on balance for such beings; consequently, because foetuses are capable of holding legal claim-rights, the specified duties are correlated with legal claim-rights held by foetuses in any jurisdiction where the duties exist. Such is the thesis articulated by proposition 1, which does not take any stance on the moral justifiability or unjustifiability of the specified duties.

By contrast, proposition 2 comes to grips with one of the chief justificatory matters from which proposition 1 prescinds. It affirms that legal duties requiring people to abstain from aborting first-trimester foetuses are morally unjustified (except where malice or recklessness or negligence is involved). It concerns the degrees to which and the ways in which the vital interests of foetuses should be legally protected. With its focus on such justificatory questions, it leaves unaddressed the non-justificatory issue tackled by proposition 1. That is, it leaves unaddressed the question whether any legal duties requiring people to abstain from aborting first-trimester foetuses would be correlated with legal claim-rights held by the foetuses. More generally stated, it leaves unaddressed the question whether foetuses are included in the class of potential holders of claim-rights or not.

Divergent though proposition 1 and proposition 2 are in their respective orientations, they are straightforwardly consistent. Neither of them entails the other, but neither of them excludes the other. Somebody can quite coherently endorse both of them or only one of them or neither of them. This chapter addresses only the matter broached by proposition 1, and it will indeed endorse proposition 1. The chapter does not mull over the justificatory topic with which proposition 2 engages, even though I would endorse proposition 2 if its topic were under consideration here.

Similarly consistent are the following two propositions:

(3) When the law in any jurisdiction secures arboreal welfare by placing people under legal duties not to engage in activities that are injurious to trees, those duties are not correlated with any legal claim-rights held by trees.
(4) Trees should be legally shielded against many injurious activities, as a matter of substantive morality, through the imposition of legal duties that obligate people not to undertake those activities.

Like proposition 1, proposition 3 does not address any justificatory questions. It does not take any stand on the extent to which or the ways in which the interests of trees should be legally safeguarded. It does not take any position on the moral justifiability or unjustifiability of the legal duties to which it refers. It instead speaks to the non-justificatory question whether insentient organisms such as trees are among the potential holders of claim-rights. It presupposes that the answer to that question is negative—by declaring that, when legal duties inherently protect aspects of the situations of trees that are typically beneficial on balance for such organisms, the trees do not hold any legal claim-rights correlated with those duties.

This negative answer to the question about the status of trees as potential holders of claim-rights is entirely consistent with proposition 4. Instead of pronouncing upon that non-justificatory question about the extension of the class of potential claim-right-holders, proposition 4 pronounces upon a justificatory matter. It asserts that the imposition of extensive legal duties on people to protect the well-being of trees is morally justified in any jurisdiction. Its expression of solicitude for trees is unproblematically compatible with proposition 3, as has been suggested at the end of §4.5.1.4 in Chapter 4 where I remark that a Will Theorist such as Nigel Simmonds can be (and is) an avid environmentalist. Simmonds's insistence that only sane human adults can hold claim-rights is readily conjoinable with his further insistence that natural organisms of virtually all types should receive stringent legal protection that will promote their flourishing. Each of those stances adopted by Simmonds is an ethical position, but the ethical issues on which he concentrates as a Will Theorist are quite distinct from the ethical issues on which he concentrates as a champion of environmentalist campaigns.

Keeping in view these distinctions between justificatory matters and non-justificatory matters that pertain to the holding of claim-rights, we can descry an additional dichotomy that is of cardinal importance for this chapter. That is, we need to differentiate between beings *for whom* various legal duties are imposed and beings merely *in regard to which* various legal duties are imposed. Beings of the former sort are the subjects, rather than only the objects, of legal relationships. Beings of the former sort are included in the class of potential holders of claim-rights. When on-balance typically advantageous aspects of their situations are inherently protected by legal duties that have been established, they hold legal claim-rights correlative to those duties.

As will be maintained in this chapter, all living human beings and all future generations of people and many dead human beings are among the subjects of legal relationships. They are beings for whom various legal duties are imposed upon others, as they hold legal claim-rights that are correlated with those duties. This chapter will also affirm that most non-human animals are among the subjects of legal relationships. Those animals too belong to the category of potential holders of claim-rights, and therefore they too hold legal claim-rights correlated with any legal duties which inherently protect aspects of their situations that are typically beneficial on balance for beings like them. Alongside human beings, most non-human animals are creatures of ultimate value. Their possession of such value is what qualifies them as subjects of legal relationships *for whom*—rather than solely *in regard to which*—those relationships are brought into existence.

5.4 A Discourse on Value

In light of what has just been said, this chapter obviously needs to provide a brief exposition of the nature of ultimate value. We can best approach this matter by first pondering some other kinds of value, from which ultimate value is to be distinguished.

5.4.1 Instrumental Value

An entity is possessed of instrumental value if and only if it is serviceable for the causing of good consequences. Tools and appliances are paradigmatic examples of entities that possess such value, which often is the only value that they possess. However, entities of sundry other sorts—including countless entities endowed with further types of value—also partake of instrumental value. Insofar as anything or anyone can be employed to bring about good effects (or to facilitate the bringing about of good effects), it or he or she partakes of instrumental value.

My use of the term "entity" or "entities" in the preceding paragraph should be construed expansively. That term refers not only to physical objects and organisms such as tools and appliances and rivers and metals and trees and animals and human beings, but also to events and properties and dispositions and states of affairs. Any such entities can possess instrumental value. For example, the disposition of John to help needy people whom he encounters is a trait that can be instrumentally valuable in multiple ways. Most obviously, by manifesting itself in John's furnishing of financial support to destitute individuals, it can contribute directly to the alleviation of their hardships. In addition, the generosity of John can inspire his fellow citizens to emulate him in their bountifulness toward the poor, and it can elicit feelings of gratitude and admiration toward him (both on the part of the people whom he assists and on the part of other people who are aware of his largesse). In these respects and in further respects, the disposition of John to be lavish in his almsgiving can partake of considerable instrumental value. As has already been suggested, its possession of such value does not exclude its also possessing value of some other kind(s).

Now, as should be evident, the fact that some entity E partakes of instrumental value is not sufficient for the inclusion of E in the class of potential holders of claim-rights. Hammers and nails and jigsaws and paintings and John's liberality are all endowed with instrumental value, but none of those things can ever hold any claim-rights. John himself is a potential holder (and an actual holder) of claim-rights, of course, but his generosity is not. Precisely because the class of things endowed with instrumental value is so vast, it is patently not equivalent to the class of potential holders of claim-rights. Large though the latter class is, it does not encompass any of the inanimate or insentient things that possess instrumental value.

Accordingly, this chapter's investigation of the nature of right-holding has to go beyond the instrumental value of entities to explore types of value that are not as wide-ranging in their applicability.

5.4.2 Constitutive Value

Whereas instrumental value is centered on the serviceability of entities for the causing of good effects, constitutive value is centered on the roles of entities in contributing non-causally to good upshots or states of affairs. Having discussed the chief differences between causal connections and constitutive connections elsewhere (Kramer 2018, 25–7; 2021, 16–18), I should touch upon them laconically here. When events or facts are causally connected to each other, they are logically distinct. Instead of being joined by ties of logical indisseverability, they are connected through laws of nature that are ascertainable empirically by physicists and chemists and biologists and other scientists. Those laws of nature conjoin events or facts causally in the operations of the material world.

Constitutive relationships are very different. Some event or fact X is constituted by some event or fact Y if and only if (1) Y, in combination with all the prevailing circumstances other than any causal laws of nature, logically entails X; and (2) without Y, the prevailing circumstances other than any causal laws of nature would not logically entail X. Whereas laws of nature are the foundations of causal relationships, they do not play any role in tying events or facts together constitutively. If one event or fact constitutes another, the two of them are linked conceptually or logically rather than through the operations of the material world.

In a constitutive relationship between Y and X, Y is endowed with constitutive value insofar as X is itself valuable. Consider, for example, the relationship between freedom and autonomy. Freedom consists in the range of the combinations of jointly exercisable opportunities that are available to a person at any given time. Autonomy as an ethical ideal of self-determination cannot be achieved by a person in the absence of a high level of freedom enjoyed by her. Without a high level of freedom, a person cannot exercise the declinatory aspect of her will adequately for the attainment of a high level of autonomy. This point has been made by Thomas Hurka in an important article published nearly four decades ago. Hurka asks his readers to envisage two situations (1987, 366–7), which I will slightly modify and embellish. Suppose that Rhonda in some situation S1 is faced with two options *b* and *c*, whereas in some other situation S2 she is faced not only with *b* and *c* but also with three additional options *d* and *e* and *f*. In all other respects, the two situations are the same. Suppose further that Rhonda prefers *b* over any of the other options available to her in S2, and that the option chosen by her in S2 (namely, *b*) is therefore the same as the option chosen by her in S1. Even so, S2 is constitutively more valuable for her than S1 in a key respect. Whereas she is responsible in S1 for bringing about *b* and not-*c*, she is responsible in S2 for bringing about *b* and not-*c* and not-*d* and not-*e* and not-*f*. Rhonda has therefore impressed her will on the world more in S2 than in S1. In S2 she "is responsible for more facts about her life [than in S1], and thus is more expansively an agent. To succeed as an agent is to make a difference in what the world does and does not contain, and this is more possible with more numerous options" (Hurka 1987, 366). As Ian Carter has commented when recounting how an increase in one's overall freedom augments the declinatory force of one's decisions: "What Hurka's example illustrates is the value ... [of] our ability [as agents] to make an impact on the world, by intervening in the causal chains which bring about events and states of affairs. A necessary condition for our being able to intervene in this way is that we be able to say no as well as yes.... The more times we are able to say no, the more impact we will have on the world when we *do* choose, and hence [*pro tanto*] the more [autonomy-constitutive] value there is in our situation" (1999, 42–3, emphasis in original).

Given that a high level of autonomy is itself of great value, a high level of freedom is of great value constitutively. A myriad of other examples of entities endowed with constitutive value could be adduced here, but what is clear already is that constitutive value is no more availing than instrumental value as a basis for the inclusion of entities in the class of potential holders of claim-rights. Though a person who enjoys a high level of freedom is of course included in that class, his or her high level of freedom is not itself so included. Inanimate entities such as the property of freedom—or any other properties—are not capable of holding claim-rights. Thus, since numerous properties are possessed of constitutive value and are not in the class of potential holders of claim-rights, this chapter's effort to demarcate that class will have to be centered on some other type of value.

5.4.3 Intrinsic Value

If something is of intrinsic value, it is valuable in itself. There are at least two main ways in which this notion of intrinsic value can be elaborated: a milder and largely uncontroversial way, and a more audacious and much more controversial way. First, and more familiar, is the idea that some things are valuable in themselves irrespective of whether they are also valuable in causing salutary effects or in constituting other benign phenomena. Even the utilitarians accept this understanding of intrinsic value, since they believe that utility—construed as the experiencing of gratification or as the satisfying of preferences or in some other fashion—is intrinsically good. Of course, the hard-core utilitarians believe that utility is the only intrinsic good; but anyone not enamored of utilitarianism can recognize that many other phenomena are intrinsically valuable in that their goodness is independent of the goodness of any consequences they are apt to cause or constitute. Masterly works of art and beautiful symphonic compositions and Shakespearean poetry and mighty rivers and redoubtable trees and magnificent stone formations are among the multitudinous things to which this type of value can accurately be ascribed. Such things are good whether or not they cause other good things to come into existence, and whether or not they are constitutive of other good things.

As will be seen, intrinsic value does play a role in the account of value on which this chapter's endeavors to delimit the category of potential holders of claim-rights will be centered. Nevertheless, in itself it is manifestly insufficient to serve as the *point d'appui* for the delimitation. None of the things just mentioned as possessed of intrinsic value is included in the class of potential holders of claim-rights. Great paintings and symphonies and poetry and rivers and trees and stone formations are all valuable in themselves independently of any other good things to which they can contribute causally or constitutively, but those inanimate entities are not capable of holding any claim-rights. Hence, like instrumental value and constitutive value, intrinsic value as consequence-independence is not suitable by itself as a cornerstone for this chapter's ruminations on the class of potential holders of claim-rights.

Let us, then, glance at the more audacious conception of intrinsic value. Though this second conception insists on the consequence-independence of value that is intrinsic, it goes further by maintaining that the value of some things is also experience-independent. That is, it submits that a world with grand natural entities such as those listed in my preceding two paragraphs is better than an otherwise similar world in which those entities do not exist, even if neither world contains any conscious beings (because such beings have been entirely whisked out of existence in each world, or because they never have existed in either world). In other words, the thesis is that the goodness of powerful rivers and majestic canyons and towering trees is not dependent on the existence of any creatures who are capable of experiencing the goodness of those things. Such goodness would withstand the disappearance of all conscious beings from the world. Now, I do not need here to defend this latter understanding of the notion of intrinsic value, nor do I need to reject it. What is clear is that this type of value is unsuitable for the purposes of this chapter, just as much as is intrinsic value *qua* consequence-independent goodness. After all, the entities that might possess experience-independent value are many of the same insentient entities that possess consequence-independent value. Because such entities do not ever hold any claim-rights, neither of the two understandings of intrinsic value is pivotal on its own for the class of potential holders of claim-rights.

5.4.4 Ultimate Value

And so we arrive finally at the notion of ultimate value.[3] As has already been indicated at the end of §5.3 above, ultimate value is the hallmark of the beings who are included in the category of potential holders of claim-rights. Such value is possessed by beings if and only if (1) they are *êtres pour eux-mêmes* and (2) the furtherance of their interests is intrinsically valuable. Several points are in need of elucidation here.

5.4.4.1 Foreign Wording

First, I have used a variant of the Sartrean French phrase "*être pour soi*" rather than the English phrase "conscious beings" mainly in order to leave open a certain question which I do not need to settle in this chapter. Specifically, my recourse to the French phrase leaves open the question whether artificial-intelligence mechanisms might at some time in the future become so sophisticated and adroit in their capacities for reflection upon themselves—and for the adaptation of themselves accordingly—that they will then be properly included in the class of potential holders of claim-rights even if they are not conscious in the manner of human beings and other animals. Any satisfactory exploration of that crux would have to delve into an array of matters ranging from technological prospects to ethical conundrums to issues in the philosophy of mind. This chapter would become derailed if it were to investigate all those matters in the depth required, since the chapter's concern with the category of potential holders of claim-rights is predominantly intensional rather than predominantly extensional. Although I will treat of many extensional details herein, my prime objective is to delineate the basis for the demarcation of that category. Thus, the best tack for this chapter in response to the development of artificial-intelligence mechanisms is to leave open the question whether some such mechanisms will eventually fall within the class of potential holders of claim-rights. Insightful meditations on that question have been published by certain other philosophers—for example, Chopra and White 2011; Kurki 2019, 175–89; Schwitzgebel and Garza 2015; Solum 1992—and, although I do not entirely agree with those meditations, I do not need to challenge any of them here. My use of a quasi-Sartrean French phrase in my explication of the notion of ultimate value signals my non-committal stance on the topic of artificial intelligences. (A further benefit of that non-committal stance is that I do not have to ponder the possibility of forms of intelligent life in the universe that are markedly different from any forms of life with which we are familiar on Earth. Given the

[3] My understanding of ultimate value is different from that in Raz 1986, 177–8. Raz did not distinguish between ultimate value and intrinsic value, though his terse remarks on them lead me to think that the divergences between his conception of ultimate value and my own conception are more taxonomical than substantive.

overwhelming vastness of the universe, there could conceivably exist beings who are self-reflectively intelligent but who are not conscious in the manner of human beings and other animals on Earth. Unlikely though such a prospect is, there is no need for me to rule it out here. If any such beings do exist somewhere, my conception of ultimate value could extend to them.)

5.4.4.2 No Specific Attitudes

Second, the phrase "*êtres pour eux-mêmes*" should obviously not be misconstrued as an indication that extravagant selfishness or solipsism is a key to the possession of ultimate value and thus to inclusion in the class of potential holders of claim-rights. Like the Sartrean wording of which it is a variant, my phrase simply indicates that a key to the possession of ultimate value—and thus to inclusion in the class of potential holders of claim-rights—is a level of self-reflective attunedness that is characteristic of conscious engagement with oneself and with the world. Though human beings and most animals are selfish or self-absorbed to varying degrees, dispositions of those kinds are not at issue in my conception of ultimate value and in my efforts to demarcate the category of potential holders of claim-rights. At issue instead are much more general faculties of self-reflection and contemplation and adaptability and sophisticated alertness to one's environs.

5.4.4.3 Some of the Main Exclusions

Third, if we leave aside the matter of artificial-intelligence mechanisms, we can easily discern that inanimate beings and insentient organisms do not possess ultimate value. Trees and grass and plants and fungi are all excluded from my conception of ultimate value, as are all the inanimate entities—such as paintings and symphonies and poems and rivers and canyons and hammers and nails and jigsaws and the property of freedom or generosity—which I have discussed above in connection with other types of value. Immensely valuable though many such entities are, they are not endowed with ultimate value and are therefore not potential holders of claim-rights. They are not *êtres pour eux-mêmes*. Legal duties can and should be established to protect many of those things, but the legal claim-rights correlated with any such duties are not held by those things themselves. Although the situations of inanimate or insentient beings are improved through the establishment of legal duties that inherently safeguard them, those beings are the objects to which the duties pertain rather than the subjects for whom the duties are introduced.

Of course, the exclusion of all insentient and inanimate phenomena from the class of potential holders of claim-rights is a corollary that follows from the first of the two components in my conception of ultimate value. That exclusion might thus seem arbitrarily stipulative. However, my next principal section—§5.5 below—will vindicate that conception of ultimate value by supplying a rationale for delimiting the class of potential holders of claim-rights along the lines envisaged here. Far from being arbitrarily stipulative, the two clauses in the formulation at the outset of §5.4 above are expressive of the deepest ethical import that underlies the inclusion of beings in the category of potential holders of claim-rights.

A rationale is clearly needed, for the exclusion of insentient and inanimate beings from the property of ultimate value and from the class of potential holders of claim-rights is not wholly uncontroversial. As has been observed in §5.1 above, quite a number of environmental ethicists have contended that insentient organisms such as trees and plants can hold claim-rights, and some legislatures as well as environmental ethicists have presumed that certain inanimate entities such as rivers and coral reefs can hold claim-rights. Laws that expressly purport to confer legal claim-rights upon such beings are now in existence in some jurisdictions.

To be sure, not all the exclusions of inanimate phenomena broached here are controversial. Nobody has ever seriously averred that entities such as the property of freedom and the property of generosity are potential holders of claim-rights, nor has anybody ever seriously argued that hammers and nails and jigsaws and the like are capable of holding claim-rights. On the one hand, Rowan Cruft in a recent essay appears to proclaim that there are virtually no limits on the range of the entities that can be vested with legal claim-rights by the legislature in any particular jurisdiction. His essay contains manifold declarations of the following sort: "[L]awmakers can create rights wherever they want, independently of the location of any interests" (2022, 38). He slightly later contends that lawmakers "have the power to determine which legal duties correlate with whose legal rights, untethered by the location of rights-independent interests. This seems most consonant with a legal positivism in which the shape of the law is fully up to us, within the constraints of logic. In particular, it seems to me that just as the creation of legal duties is up to us without being constrained by the location of interests, so such duties' status as rights should be similarly up to us" (2022, 42). Cruft does allow here that the Law of Non-contradiction curbs the range of the entities on which the legislature in any jurisdiction can confer legal claim-rights, but he appears not to envisage any additional constraints. On the other hand, he has assured me in private correspondence that his remarks should not be so construed. No more than anyone else, does he believe that entities of the kinds mentioned near the outset of this paragraph are potential holders of claim-rights. In the quoted statements, he has simply insisted—incorrectly—that lawmakers can bestow legal claim-rights on potential holders of claim-rights even if the correlative legal duties do not inherently protect any aspects of the situations of those holders that are typically beneficial on balance for them.

Still, although Cruft apparently does not cleave to any outlandishly expansive conception of the class of beings who can hold legal claim-rights, Michael Hartney has not been similarly circumspect. In an essay published somewhat over three decades ago, Hartney writes emphatically as follows (1991, 301–2):

> The utterance of a legal authority (legislature, official, court) that a right is being conferred is conclusive evidence that a legal right has been conferred. Whatever legal authorities say is a legal right, is a legal right, whether this agrees with what philosophers would say about moral rights. If a statute says that trees have rights, then trees have certain legal rights, whether we consider this to be morally defensible or even morally possible. The utterances of legal authorities constitute the raw data upon which our theory of legal rights must build. This theory must make room for all the rights and the kinds of rights which utterances of legal authorities say have been conferred.

Hartney does not elaborate on what he has said in this passage. His assertion that trees can hold legal claim-rights is not itself preposterous, even though it is at variance with my own contentions about the category of potential holders of claim-rights. Given that he does not mention any other sorts of beings to which the enactments of various legislatures might purport to assign legal claim-rights, one can only conjecture whether he would fully adhere to the substance of his quoted asseverations if he were to ponder whether hammers and nails and the property of generosity and the number six can be vested with legal claim-rights by lawmakers. If he would indeed adhere doggedly to the substance of those asseverations, then his position on the matter is fatuous. One can presume that instead he would blench at the absurdity of the implications of the quoted passage if he were to contemplate them.

In any event, regardless of whether Hartney would reject or embrace those implications if he were to ruminate upon them, neither he nor anyone else has ever seriously affirmed that hammers and nails and jigsaws and the property of generosity and the number six can hold legal claim-rights. To that extent, the conclusions inferable from my conception of ultimate value are uncontroversial. All the same, as I have readily acknowledged, some of the other conclusions inferable from that conception are controversial. Though many environmental ethicists will be pleased by this chapter's affirmation that most non-human animals are capable of holding claim-rights, some of them will be dismayed by the chapter's exclusion of insentient organisms and inanimate natural entities such as rivers from the category of potential holders of claim-rights. Because of the likelihood of such dismay, my vindication of the chapter's exclusions will be especially vital. Of course, in saying as much, I am not suggesting that any vindication will persuade everyone who looks askance at the concrete conclusions that are being upheld. My aim in §5.5 will not be to convince everyone who dissents from those concrete conclusions. People who disagree with me about the exclusion of insentient organisms and rivers and coral reefs from the category of potential holders of claim-rights, and also people who disagree with me about the inclusion of non-human animals or future generations or babies or insane people or many dead people within that category, will probably not shed their convictions as a result of being presented with a rationale for the concrete conclusions from which they dissent. Instead of pursuing the quixotic objective of eliciting a consensus on those conclusions, §5.5 will more sensibly aim to show that my conception of ultimate value and my delimitation of the class of potential holders of claim-rights follow from some deep ethical considerations. They are not peremptory stipulations. (Naturally, when I state here that the aforementioned conception and delimitation follow from some deep ethical considerations, I do not mean that they in all their specifics are logically entailed by those considerations. Somebody can accept the fundamental premises of §5.5 without thereby having to endorse every jot and tittle of my conclusions about the extension of the category of potential claim-right-holders. Those conclusions fit admirably well with those premises, but the relationship between them is not one of logical inseparability.)

Before we move on, we should glimpse one further exclusion of a set of beings from the class of potential holders of claim-rights. Suppose that the legislature in the country of Superstitia has enacted a statute which imposes a legal duty on every head of a household to sacrifice a goat annually to the god Apollo. Correlated with the legal duty incumbent on each head of a household, according to the terms of the statute, is a legal claim-right vested in the god Apollo. In other words, the legislators of Superstitia have presupposed that Apollo is a potential holder of claim-rights, and they have purported to confer upon him an array of actual legal claim-rights.

Now, the sheer fact that Apollo does not exist is per se insufficient to clinch my verdict that the Superstitian legislators have gone astray by presuming that he is included among the potential holders of claim-rights. After all, this chapter will be arguing that future generations of people and many dead people are so included, even though future generations do not yet exist and even though decedents no longer exist. Decisive instead is the mode of Apollo's inexistence. Unlike dead people, Apollo never has existed; and, unlike future generations, Apollo never will exist. His existence as a god is nomologically impossible and is probably also metaphysically impossible. Accordingly, he is not susceptible to any improvements in his condition, nor is he vulnerable to any worsening therein. By reference to the Interest Theory, then, we can discern that the vesting of him with claim-rights is a conceptual impossibility. Thus, the deontic upshot of the Superstitian statute does not consist in the instances of right-holding which the legislators in that country have aspired to produce. Sincere though the drafters of the statute may have been in professing to bestow legal claim-rights on the god Apollo, they have not genuinely managed to do so. Correlated with the legal duties imposed by the statute on heads of households are legal claim-rights held not by Apollo but instead solely by the Superstitian system of governance. Contrary to what the officials in that system of governance have presumed, impossible beings such as Apollo are not included in the class of potential holders of claim-rights.

5.4.4.4 Another Significant Exclusion

Fourth, given the second clause in the formulation of the nature of ultimate value at the outset of §5.4, there can exist conscious beings who are not of ultimate value and who are therefore not within the class of potential holders of claim-rights. That is, there can exist non-human animals in regard to which the furtherance of their interests is not of intrinsic value. Whether any non-human animals are of that sort is, patently, a substantive ethical question as well as an empirical question. Environmental ethicists and conservation biologists will be inclined to insist that every species of animals is such that the furtherance of the interests of the creatures within each species is intrinsically valuable. By contrast, this chapter's vindication of my conception of ultimate value will submit that there are some animals—cockroaches and tsetse flies, for example—in regard to which the furtherance of their interests is not intrinsically valuable. In many credible contexts, the furtherance of their interests can be instrumentally or constitutively valuable; but it is not valuable independently of the effects that will be caused or constituted by it.

Of course, from the fact that the furtherance of the interests of certain animals such as cockroaches and tsetse flies is not of intrinsic value, we cannot validly infer that there are no moral duties incumbent on people to abstain from mistreating those animals. On the contrary, everyone is always under a moral duty to refrain from subjecting animals such as cockroaches and tsetse flies to sadistic torture. Instead of presuming incorrectly that no such duty exists, we should recognize that the justificatory basis for it does not consist in the fact that the welfare of cockroaches and tsetse flies will be enhanced insofar as people refrain from subjecting those creatures to torture. Rather, the justificatory basis for the duty lies in the moral integrity of any potential perpetrator of sadistic torture. As I have argued elsewhere at length (2014, 72, 182, 210–12, 305–6; 2017a, 257–9, 286–7), the perpetration of sadistic torture is always and everywhere morally wrong because the attitude that impels it is both extravagantly overweening and ignominious. Indeed, this point has been signaled near the end of my brief discussion of punitive torture in Chapter 4 of this book. Torture conducted in satisfaction of sadistic urges is overweening because it treats its victims as playthings for the gratification of such urges, and because it is aimed at exerting the sort of control over those victims that would be plied by a malevolent deity—a type of control that stems from breaking down the opacity of the victims by enveloping their consciousness with the agony of severe and unremitting pain.[4] At the same time, such torture is thoroughly degrading for its perpetrator because it establishes that his own achievements and merits are insufficient for his contentment; his sense of contentment also has to derive from his awareness of the anguish that afflicts other creatures through his

[4] Here, as in the final paragraph of §4.3.2.2 in Chapter 4, my use of the term "opacity" deliberately echoes the discussion of "opacity respect" in Carter 2011, 550–60. However, Carter's perspective is closer to Rawlsianism and Kantianism than is my own perspective.

malign ministrations. His largeness in his own eyes is dependent on his perception of the littleness and misery of others. Hence, his perpetration of sadistic torture betokens not only his lack of elementary respect for others but also his lack of elementary respect for himself and his own accomplishments. His wielding of torture may bolster his sense of self-esteem, but it greatly lowers the level of self-esteem that he is warranted in harboring. It is a violation of moral duties which he owes to himself, as well as of moral duties which he owes to others.

The existence of a moral duty borne by each person to abstain from inflicting sadistic torture on creatures such as cockroaches and tsetse flies is very much in keeping with my observation that the furtherance of the interests of such creatures can be constitutively valuable. Given that a moral duty with the content just specified will inherently protect an aspect of the situation of any cockroach or tsetse fly that is typically beneficial on balance for such a creature, the furtherance of the interests of cockroaches and tsetse flies in accordance with the content of that duty is partly constitutive of the moral integrity of everyone who bears the duty. It is constitutively valuable as an element of the moral probity of each upright person. Of course, the furtherance of the interests of cockroaches and tsetse flies in the way(s) required by that duty is consistent with the setting back of their interests in manifold other ways. Moral duties that inherently safeguard aspects of the well-being of such creatures are not extensive. Still, some duties of that kind do exist, and compliance with them—which is nearly always beneficial on balance for such creatures—is valuable through its partly constituting the moral decency of anyone who bears the duties.

5.4.4.5 The Level of Application

Fifth, the most important point of clarification for my conception of ultimate value is the level at which the two components of the conception apply. This point is crucial particularly for one's understanding of how the conception pertains to the status of human beings as potential holders of claim-rights. Not every human being meets the criterion articulated by one or the other of the two clauses in my conception of ultimate value. Myriads of human beings are not *êtres pour eux-mêmes*: anencephalic infants, permanently comatose people, dead people, future generations. Nevertheless, as will be argued later, many dead people and all anencephalic infants and permanently comatose people and future generations of people are potential holders of claim-rights. Similarly, some human beings—flagitious evildoers of the likes of Josef Mengele, for example—are such that the furtherance of their interests is not intrinsically valuable. Even so, they too are included in the class of potential holders of claim-rights. Now, given that the ultimate value of creatures is the hallmark of their inclusion in the class of potential holders of claim-rights, and given that some human beings fall short of satisfying the two criteria for the possession of ultimate value, the inclusion of those human beings in the class of potential holders of claim-rights is obviously in need of explanation.

With regard to members of the human species, the requirements articulated in my formulation of the nature of ultimate value are applicable at the level of the species rather than at the level of each individual member of that species. In other words, in application to the category of human beings, the formulations of those requirements are to be construed as generics rather than as universally quantified propositions. Generic statements occur in many varieties (Leslie 2008), and the generics contained in my formulation of the nature of ultimate value—as applied to the human species—belong to the most common of those varieties, albeit in slightly differing ways.

When the second enumerated clause in my conception of ultimate value is applied to the human species, it articulates a generic proposition with a quite familiar tenor. As Sarah-Jane Leslie observes: "Many generics of the form 'Ks are F' hold of a large majority of the Ks, and their exceptions are often in some ways defective. Take, for example, 'tigers have four legs': it is only tigers with birth defects, or that have met with unfortunate accidents, that do not have four legs" (2008, 13, footnote omitted). Leslie's encapsulation of the tenor of these familiar generics is entirely pertinent with reference to the second clause in my conception of ultimate value, when that clause is applied to the members of the human species. For a large majority of the members of the human species, the furtherance of their interests in sundry ways is intrinsically valuable. Human beings who are exceptions to this proposition about the intrinsic value of furthering their interests—namely, the monstrous evildoers such as Mengele—are indeed exceptional rather than typical. Moreover, any such human beings are indeed grievously defective. Hence, the statement "Human beings are such that the furtherance of their interests is intrinsically valuable" is unproblematically a generic of the familiar kind which Leslie distills. It contains an implicit pleonotetic quantifier of broadly the sort to which I have adverted in §3.2.1.2 of Chapter 3. It ascribes to human beings a property which is characteristic of them but which is not universally shared by them.

Somewhat more complicated is the generic contained in the first enumerated clause of my conception of ultimate value as applied to the members of the human species. On the one hand, if the relevant domain comprises only the human beings who are currently alive, the proposition "Human beings are *êtres pour eux-mêmes*" is plainly a generic of the same kind which I have discussed in the preceding paragraph. It smoothly fits the pattern recounted by Leslie in my quotation from her. Governed by an implicit pleonotetic quantifier which ranges over the domain of human beings who are now alive, the proposition ascribes to such beings a property which is possessed by almost every one of them but which is not quite universally shared. Human beings who lack that property—for example, anencephalic infants and permanently comatose people—are defective in quite palpable ways. Thus, when our enquiry is confined to human beings who are alive at present, the genericity of "Human beings are *êtres pour eux-mêmes*" is on a par with the genericity of "Human beings are such that the furtherance of their interests is intrinsically valuable." So construed, each of those propositions contains an implicit pleonotetic quantifier that ranges over a domain which comprises the human beings now alive.

On the other hand, as has been adumbrated already and as will be explained hereafter, this chapter's meditations on the category of potential holders of claim-rights are not confined to human beings who are currently alive. Future generations of people and many dead people are also included in that category. Future generations are not yet *êtres pour eux-mêmes*, and dead people are no longer so. Although the dead human beings in the class of potential holders of claim-rights probably do not outnumber the currently living people in that class, the members of future generations vastly outnumber the currently living people in that class. Hence, in the context of this chapter's ruminations on the category of potential holders of claim-rights—ruminations in which the domain covered by a pleonotetic quantifier has to comprise not only the human beings currently alive but also many dead people and all members of future generations—the genericity of "Human beings are such that the furtherance of their interests is intrinsically valuable" appears to be different from the genericity of "Human beings are *êtres pour eux-mêmes*." Whereas the former proposition straightforwardly partakes of the structure attributed by Leslie to the most familiar generics, the proposition "Human beings are *êtres pour eux-mêmes*" is less straightforward. Within this chapter, a pleonotetic quantifier in that latter proposition will have to range over a domain that comprises mostly human beings who are not currently *êtres pour eux-mêmes*. Thus, unless the proposition is reconstrued, we shall have to conclude that its being governed by an implicit pleonotetic quantifier is inconsistent with its truth.

What should be reconsidered is not the implicit quantifier but instead the property that is ascribed by the proposition "Human beings are *êtres pour eux-mêmes*." That property does not pertain only to the present; it pertains also to the past and the future. It is a disjunctive property that can be fully formulated as "were *êtres pour eux-mêmes* or are *êtres pour eux-mêmes* or will be *êtres pour eux-mêmes*." That disjunctive property can aptly be predicated not only of human beings currently alive but also of dead human beings and future human beings. It is a characteristic feature of the members of the human species. Of course, not all living human beings are *êtres pour eux-mêmes* now, and not all dead human beings were *êtres pour eux-mêmes* in the past, and not all future human beings will be *êtres pour eux-mêmes* hereafter. Though a large majority of human beings were *êtres pour eux-mêmes* in the past or are *êtres pour eux-mêmes* now or will be *êtres pour eux-mêmes* in the future, a small minority of human beings—such as anencephalic infants—never have been *êtres pour eux-mêmes* and never will be. Accordingly, the implicit quantifier in "Human beings are *êtres pour eux-mêmes*" is distributively pleonotetic rather than distributively universal. In short, when the property ascribed by the proposition "Human beings are *êtres pour eux-mêmes*" is recognized as extending into the past and the future as well as throughout the present, we can see that that proposition fits the pattern of the most common generics encapsulated by Leslie.

Now, precisely because "Human beings are *êtres pour eux-mêmes*" is not to be construed as a universally quantified proposition and is instead to be construed as a generic proposition with an implicit pleonotetic quantifier, the human beings whose existence would falsify that proposition if it were universally quantified are nevertheless included in the class of potential holders of claim-rights. And precisely because "Human beings are such that the furtherance of their interests is intrinsically valuable" is not to be construed as a universally quantified proposition and is instead to be construed as a generic proposition with an implicit pleonotetic quantifier, the human beings whose existence would falsify that proposition if it were universally quantified are nonetheless included in the class of potential holders of claim-rights. Anencephalic infants and monstrous evildoers are so included, even though the former never have been and never will be *êtres pour eux-mêmes*, and even though the latter are not such that the furtherance of their interests is intrinsically valuable. Those human beings are within the class of potential holders of claim-rights by dint of their membership in the human species, notwithstanding that they each lack one or the other of the key properties that underlie the possession of ultimate value. As is evident, this inclusion of such human beings in the class of potential holders of claim-rights is in need of vindication, since it may seem objectionable as a form of "speciesism." Why should membership in the human species be a factor that qualifies these human beings for the status of potential holders of claim-rights, when they each lack one or the other of the two properties that together qualify non-human beings for that status? My answer to this question will emerge presently, in §5.5, when I explain why speciesism is inevitable to some degree in any satisfactory endeavor to delimit the class of potential holders of claim-rights.

Before we proceed to that endeavor, a caveat should be appended to this discussion. Although anencephalic infants and heinous evildoers are on a par with other human beings in that they belong to the category of potential holders of claim-rights, they are obviously very different from other people in the range and contents of the legal and moral entitlements which they hold. Through no fault of their own, anencephalic infants hold very few legal entitlements. They have legal and moral claim-rights against certain types of mistreatment, and they have legal and moral immunities against being deprived of those claim-rights. However, because they are wholly unable to perform actions and are thus wholly unable to exercise any legal or moral powers, they do not possess any such powers. Extravagantly evil wrongdoers, as a result of the turpitude of their own conduct, are likewise vested with relatively few legal and moral entitlements. They too hold moral claim-rights and should hold legal claim-rights against certain forms of mistreatment—such as their claim-rights against being subjected to punitive torture, on which I have expatiated in §4.3.2.1 of Chapter 4—and they too hold moral immunities and should hold legal immunities against being deprived of those claim-rights. Unlike anencephalic infants, of course, the horrific evildoers are fully capable of exercising any legal or moral powers that they possess, and they do indeed possess some such powers. Still, their moral entitlements are much more limited than those of ordinary people, and their legal entitlements should be much more limited. For one thing, they are morally liable and should be legally liable to undergo legal proceedings for the atrocities which they have perpetrated, and they will be morally liable and should be legally liable to undergo punishment in the event of their being convicted through such proceedings. Their moral liberties are curtailed far more than those of ordinary people, and their legal liberties should be curtailed far more. These and additional differences between their entitlements and the entitlements of their fellow citizens are entirely consistent with the inclusion of these people alongside their fellow citizens in the class of potential holders of claim-rights. Whereas the differences between the entitlements respectively held are justificatory matters concerning the extent to which and the ways in which the situations of various people should be legally protected, the parity of the members of the human species as beings who belong to the class of potential holders of claim-rights is a non-justificatory matter. Such parity does not in itself carry any implications for the extent to which and the ways in which the situations of various people should be legally protected.

5.4.4.6 Human Collectivities and Ultimate Value

Sixth, although not many philosophers in recent decades have contested the proposition that groups of human beings can hold claim-rights, a matter more often contested is whether the claim-rights held by groups are reducible to claim-rights held by the individuals who compose the groups. In §3.2.1.2 of Chapter 3, I have shown that the claim-rights held by collectivities of human beings are not so reducible. I have also there explored the quantification that is involved in the logical ties between any collectively held claim-right and any duty that is correlated with it. More will be said about that quantification in §5.5.2.8.3 below, specifically with reference to claim-rights held by future generations of people. Here the question to be addressed is why human collectivities are endowed with ultimate value. After all, beings of any type possess ultimate value—a property that is essential for their inclusion in the class of potential holders of claim-rights—only if they are *êtres pour eux-mêmes* and are such that the furtherance of their interests is intrinsically valuable. Can those constituents of ultimate value properly be ascribed to groups of human beings?

At this juncture, we can behold afresh the salutariness of two of the features in my account of ultimate value: my use of the phrase "*êtres pour eux-mêmes*" in lieu of the phrase "conscious beings"; and the fact that the two main components of the account apply as generics, rather than as universally quantified propositions, to humanity. Though human collectivities are not conscious in any straightforward sense, many of them are *êtres pour eux-mêmes* in that they can sophisticatedly undertake deliberations and reach decisions and form intentions and adjust their actions to the circumstances of their environments. This point is most obviously applicable to the group agents which I have discussed in §3.2.1.2, with their elaborate procedures for ruminations and for the reaching of collective choices. Group agents are the human collectivities most plainly included in the class of potential holders of claim-rights. However, this point also applies to many coalitions of the sort which I have discussed in §3.2.1.2, for they too can engage in collective deliberations and decision-making and actions—even though the procedures of a coalition for exercising its collective agency typically are ad hoc or episodic and are less sophisticated than the procedures employed by group agents. Human beings collectively, as well as individually, can perpend and resolve and act and reconsider as *êtres pour eux-mêmes*.

Are human collectivities such that the furtherance of their interests is intrinsically valuable? Here of crucial importance is the fact that the second requirement for the possession of ultimate value applies as a generic, rather than as a universally quantified proposition, to human beings. Quite a few groups of human beings, such as the Mafia or the Chinese Communist Party or the Ku Klux Klan, are clearly not such that the furtherance of their interests is of intrinsic value. They are nefarious variants of the innumerable human collectivities that do directly satisfy the second of the two requirements for the possession of ultimate value. In a complex fashion, decent collectivities gain their ultimate value from that of the human beings who are their members. On the one hand, as has been argued in §3.2.1.2, the interests of an organization of human beings are not reducible to the interests of any member or to the interests of any proper subset of its members. On the other hand, the continued existence of an organization is advantageous on balance for that organization only if a substantial proportion of its members stand to benefit on balance from the continuation of its existence. If hardly any of those members will benefit on balance from the continuation of their group, then the group itself will on balance be better off if it is terminated. In such circumstances, the members in their collective capacity—the members *qua* group—do not have any interest in the sustainment of that capacity.

Now, given that the interests of a collectivity of people in its continued existence and thriving are dependent on the fact that a substantial proportion of its members have interests in its existence and thriving, the central role of collectively held claim-rights—the role of such claim-rights in inherently protecting the interests of a collectivity—cannot be performed without furnishing inherent protection for interests of human individuals, each of whom is of ultimate value. Human organizations have interests that necessarily involve and incorporate certain interests of people, even though the interests of such an organization are never reducible to those of any proper subset of its members. Because of this dependence between the well-being of a collectivity and the well-being of human individuals, and because of the possession of ultimate value by every human individual, human collectivities are endowed with ultimate value and are therefore included in the class of potential holders of claim-rights. Furthering the interests of groups of people is intrinsically valuable because it involves the furtherance of the interests of people, who are such that the advancement of their interests is intrinsically valuable.

As has been noted, the inclusion of human collectivities in the category of potential holders of claim-rights extends even to nefarious collectivities—not because furthering the interests of such evil groups is intrinsically valuable, but instead because the second requirement for the possession of ultimate value (like the first requirement) applies as a generic rather than as a universally quantified proposition to human beings and their organizations. Just as extravagantly iniquitous human individuals are brought within the scope of my conception of ultimate value through quantification that is pleonotetic rather than universal, so too the iniquitous groups formed by some human beings are encompassed within that scope through such quantification. Hence, because group agents and coalitions satisfy each of the requirements for the possession of ultimate value either directly or on the coat-tails of ordinary group agents and coalitions, they are within the community of potential holders of claim-rights. (In my reflections on future generations of people in §5.5.2.8 below, I will broach a human collectivity that is neither a group agent nor a coalition: the human species as a whole. As will be explained there, the reason why the human species can hold claim-rights despite falling outside the category of *êtres pour eux-mêmes* is essentially the same as the reason why anencephalic infants can hold claim-rights despite falling outside that category. In each case, the ethically pregnant commonality among the members of the human species is such that it requires the inclusion of certain beings in the class of potential holders of claim-rights—which is why the first component of my conception of ultimate value is like the second component in that it applies as a generic, rather than as a universally quantified proposition, to humankind.)

5.5 Warranted Self-Respect and the Class of Potential Holders of Claim-Rights

Although the inclusion of beings in the class of potential holders of claim-rights is a non-justificatory matter, it scarcely is a non-ethical matter. On the contrary, as has been foreshadowed at more than one juncture in this book, the delimitation of that class is connected to the paramount moral responsibility borne by every system of governance and by each individual. That is, any accurate delimitation will hinge on what is required for establishing and sustaining the conditions under which everyone in a society can be warranted in harboring a strong sense of self-respect (where the relevant society can range from local to global in its scope). At the same time, while any delimitation of the class of potential claim-right-holders is indeed profoundly ethical, it is non-justificatory in the sense specified by this book. In other words, none of my conclusions herein about that class will prescribe how legal duties should be distributed among people, nor will those conclusions prescribe what the contents of any such legal duties should be. Similarly, my conclusions will not entail any thesis about the proper justificatory bases for any legal duties that are imposed. As has already been emphasized, there might justifiably be very few legal safeguards for the interests of some beings who are included in the class of potential holders of claim-rights, and there might justifiably be very extensive legal safeguards for the interests of some beings that are excluded from that class. Deeply ethical though my reasoning in this chapter (and especially in this portion of the chapter) has to be, it does not seek to tell us who should hold which legal claim-rights or who should bear which legal duties.

5.5.1 A Community without Institutions

Now, the key to pinning down the extension of the category of potential claim-right-holders is to grasp that that category itself amounts to a community. It is not a community with institutions or with a presiding system of governance—and is therefore not a polity (Letsas 2018)—but it is a community in that its members have certain ethical ties among them. Those ties consist precisely in the fact that the members share a fundamental status. On the basis of varying ethical considerations that are all centered on the paramount moral responsibility to bring about the conditions under which every member of a society can be warranted in harboring a robust sense of self-respect, certain beings are potential holders of claim-rights. Their shared status as potential holders of claim-rights is something which the paradigmatic members of the community are morally obligated to acknowledge, for only through the acknowledgment of the sharing of that status can the paradigmatic members comply with the paramount moral responsibility that has just been recapitulated. Unlike most of the other beings who belong to the community of potential holders of claim-rights, the paradigmatic members of the community are capable of recognizing the status which they share with those other beings; given their capability in that regard, they are morally obligated to accept that those other beings can hold claim-rights. (I should emphasize afresh that the question whether such beings can hold claim-rights is separate from the question whether they should hold any specific legal claim-rights.)

Who, then, are the paradigmatic members in the community of potential holders of claim-rights? They are paradigmatic or central in two senses. First, their status as members of that community is straightforward and uncontroversial. If there are any potential holders of claim-rights at all, these paradigmatic parties are among them. Second, they are paradigmatic or central in that their role within the community is pivotal. Incumbent on them are moral obligations—obligations to acknowledge that other beings are also potential holders of claim-rights—which serve to delimit the extension of the community.

As is manifest both from this chapter and from Chapter 4, these paradigmatic parties are human adults of sound mind. Even the proponents of the Will Theory of right-holding would agree and indeed insist that such adults are potential holders of claim-rights. Proponents of the Interest Theory naturally concur with the Will Theorists in classifying sane human adults as potential holders of claim-rights, though virtually every Interest Theorist departs from the Will Theorists by maintaining that certain other types of beings are also among the potential holders of claim-rights. Any credible account of right-holding will allow that sane human adults are able to hold claim-rights, which is one main reason why their status as potential holders of claim-rights is paradigmatic. Their possession of that status is uncontroversial. Another main reason for characterizing these adults as the paradigmatic possessors of such a status is that, unlike most of the other beings who belong to the class of potential holders of claim-rights, they are capable of grasping that those other beings do belong to that class. Whether these paradigmatic parties actually do grasp as much is a contingent matter, of course, but the ability to do so is possessed by any ordinary human adults of sound mind. Consequently, given that the contours of the community of potential claim-right-holders are fixed by what such adults are able to recognize and are morally obligated to recognize, those adults play a central role in sustaining the existence of that community.

My remarks in the preceding paragraph have pertained to all sane human adults. On the assumption that many extravagantly iniquitous malefactors are sane, those remarks therefore imply that many such malefactors are paradigmatically within the category of potential holders of claim-rights. Some readers might balk at that implication of my remarks. They might balk, that is, at the notion that somebody as depraved as Mengele was paradigmatically within the category just mentioned. While granting that such a rebarbative evildoer did belong to that category, these readers might nonetheless deny that his status within it was paradigmatic. After all, Mengele qualified as a being of ultimate value not because the furtherance of his own interests was intrinsically valuable—since the furtherance of his own interests was in fact not of any intrinsic value at all—but instead because most of his fellow human beings are such that the furtherance of their interests is intrinsically valuable. Given that the ultimate value of a man of such turpitude was dependent on speciesism, the status of such a vile miscreant as a potential holder of claim-rights might seem far from paradigmatic to quite a few readers.

Understandable though such a worry is, three principal considerations tell against it. First, especially important in this context is the distinction between justificatory matters and non-justificatory matters in connection with the holding of claim-rights. As has been underscored, the status of a being B as a potential holder of claim-rights is fully consistent with the proposition that very few typically advantageous aspects of B's situation should receive any inherent protection through the imposition of legal obligations on others. Even if B's status as a potential holder of claim-rights is paradigmatic, it is consistent with the proposition about meager legal protection. The paradigmaticity of that status is a non-justificatory matter, which per se leaves open any justificatory questions about the extent to which and the ways in which the interests of various beings should be legally protected through the establishment of legal duties. Thus, for example, the inclusion of an extreme evildoer among the paradigmatic members of the community of potential claim-right-holders is perfectly compatible with the proposition that any system of governance which manages to capture him should not impose any legal duties in furtherance of his interests except to the degree necessary for upholding its own moral integrity (and the moral integrity of its officials and of the citizens over whom it presides). When the separability of these matters is clearly taken on board, the classification of such an evildoer as someone who paradigmatically belongs to the community of potential holders of claim-rights is no longer disconcerting.

Second is a consideration focused directly on the property of paradigmaticity as it has been expounded here. As has been indicated in the penultimate paragraph above, my present remarks assume that many extravagantly wicked malefactors are sane. Insofar as that assumption is accurate, those malefactors are capable of recognizing the inclusion of certain other beings in the category of potential holders of claim-rights. Of course, whether any of those malefactors will actually exercise that ability is a contingent matter (as I have already suggested). Such people might be especially unlikely to exert that ability. Nevertheless, unlike beings that cannot understand the concept of the holding of claim-rights at all, these extreme evildoers are capable of grasping that concept and are able to draw upon their understanding of it to recognize that beings of some other types are also among the potential holders of claim-rights. Hence, one of the cardinal reasons for classifying sane human adults as paradigmatic members of the class of potential holders of claim-rights is applicable to sane human adults who have been egregiously reprehensible in their conduct. Like other sane human adults, those egregiously reprehensible evildoers are endowed with the cognitive abilities through which they can acknowledge that the status of potential holders of claim-rights is occupied not only by them but also by beings of certain other kinds.

Third is another consideration that pertains directly to the property of paradigmaticity. Not only are heinous wrongdoers capable of recognizing that some beings beyond sane human adults are potential holders of claim-rights, but in addition their own classifiability as holders of claim-rights is clear-cut whenever various legal duties inherently protect some on-balance typically advantageous aspects of their situations. Generally, of course, the heinous wrongdoers should enjoy far fewer legal protections than do their fellow citizens. However, my point here is not about that justificatory matter. Rather the point is that, whenever the interests of heinous wrongdoers are indeed inherently protected through the imposition of legal duties, there are no serious disputes over the fact that those duties are correlated with legal claim-rights held by the wrongdoers. For example, if legal duties are incumbent on the officials in a system of governance to refrain from subjecting iniquitous criminals to interrogational or punitive torture, the fact that the criminals hold legal claim-rights correlative to those legal duties is straightforward rather than doubtful. Similarly, if legal duties are incumbent on the people in a given jurisdiction not to injure others through negligence, and if the protective reach of those duties is not curtailed even where the victims of negligence have themselves previously perpetrated terrible crimes, the fact that extreme evildoers in the jurisdiction hold legal claim-rights not to be injured through the negligence of others is straightforward. In each of these contexts, the deontic upshot pertaining to extreme evildoers is very different from the deontic upshot pertaining to blades of grass under a "Keep Off the Grass" ordinance—or from the deontic upshot pertaining to edifices under an anti-vandalism statute. Whereas the blades of grass and the edifices are straightforwardly not potential holders of claim-rights and are therefore straightforwardly not vested with any legal claim-rights by the ordinance and the statute, the extreme evildoers are straightforwardly potential holders of claim-rights and are therefore straightforwardly vested with legal claim-rights by the laws envisaged above which forbid the use of torture and the injuring of people through negligence.

Thus, since the two main considerations that account for the paradigmaticity of sane human adults as members within the class of potential holders of claim-rights are applicable to such adults regardless of their benignity or malignity, we should conclude that extravagantly malevolent wrongdoers are paradigmatically within that class if they are sane. Such a conclusion about this non-justificatory matter is consistent with any answers to justificatory questions about the extent to which and the ways in which the interests of extravagantly malevolent wrongdoers should be legally protected. In particular, the conclusion about the non-justificatory matter of paradigmaticity is aptly conjoinable with a justificatory thesis affirming that legal duties inherently protective of the interests of those wrongdoers should be far fewer than the legal duties inherently protective of the interests of other people.

5.5.2 Non-Paradigmatic Members in the Community of Potential Holders of Claim-Rights

Whereas the advocates of the Will Theory believe that the paradigmatic members in the class of potential holders of claim-rights are the only members (perhaps along with human infants), virtually all proponents of the Interest Theory contend that certain other beings are also within that class. There is ample leeway, however, for the Interest Theorists to disagree among themselves over the precise extension of the category of potential claim-right-holders. There is no canonical specification of that extension which every Interest Theorist must endorse in order to remain an Interest Theorist. Although this chapter will endeavor to delineate the boundaries of the aforementioned category, my foremost objective herein is to elaborate the proper basis for the inclusion of beings within that category and for the exclusion of beings from it. Any Interest Theorist who disagrees with me over the specific locations of the boundaries can nonetheless concur with me on the basis for drawing them.

As has already been suggested, that basis resides in the paramount moral responsibility borne by every system of governance and by every individual. Paradigmatic members in the class of potential holders of claim-rights are morally obligated to recognize the inclusion of other beings within that class, insofar and only insofar as the bestowal of such recognition is necessary for the compliance of the paradigmatic members with their paramount moral responsibility to foster the conditions under which everyone in their societies can be warranted in harboring a strong sense of self-respect. Accordingly, in an enquiry aimed at demarcating the contours of that class, we need to ask whether the inclusion of various beings within those contours is integral to the fulfillment of that paramount moral responsibility or not. There are two chief dimensions to such an enquiry: the import of the inclusion or exclusion of certain beings for those beings themselves, and the import of the inclusion or exclusion of certain beings for the paradigmatic potential holders of claim-rights.

5.5.2.1 Inanimate and Insentient Entities

Let us begin with inanimate entities such as rivers and canyons and paintings, and with insentient organisms such as trees and grass. If we inquire about the import of the inclusion (or exclusion) of such entities and organisms for those entities and organisms themselves, we should conclude that there is no such import. Those entities and organisms are wholly without any awareness of their situations and are thus without any capacities to experience either gratification or consternation through such awareness. Because they entirely lack such awareness, they are not shown any disrespect when the paradigmatic potential holders of claim-rights take for granted that inanimate entities and insentient organisms are not the beings *for whom* any legal duties are imposed. Instead, those entities and organisms are beings *in regard to which* many such duties are established. Inanimate entities and insentient organisms are not shown any disrespect when they are aptly perceived as some of the objects of legal regulation rather than as the subjects thereof—for the perception of them as objects clear-sightedly grasps what they are.

Of course, nothing in the preceding paragraph implies that inanimate entities and insentient organisms are beings without any interests and are for that reason incapable of holding any claim-rights. On the contrary, given the capacious conception of interests that informs this chapter, inanimate entities such as rivers and canyons and paintings plainly do have interests. Much the same is true of insentient organisms such as trees and grass. The situations of those entities and organisms can improve or deteriorate in sundry ways. Events or states of affairs that enhance their situations are in furtherance of their interests, as is the non-occurrence of any events or states of affairs that would impair their situations. Hence, although lifeless entities and insentient organisms are incapable of holding any claim-rights, the reason for their inability is not that they lack any interests.

Also misconceived is the notion that the exclusion of inanimate entities and insentient organisms from the category of potential holders of claim-rights is somehow indicative of the ways in which and the extent to which the interests of those beings should receive legal protection. A thesis which ascribes great intrinsic value to certain inanimate entities or insentient organisms is entirely consistent with a thesis which denies that any such entities or organisms can ever hold any claim-rights. Whereas the former thesis is about the intrinsic value of certain beings, the latter thesis is about (or is a corollary of) the fact that those beings lack any ultimate value. Notwithstanding that those beings lack any ultimate value—because they are not *êtres pour eux-mêmes*—the fact that they are endowed with great intrinsic value is very likely sufficient to warrant the imposition of stringent legal duties which will inherently protect some aspects of the situations of those beings that are typically advantageous on balance for them. Justificatory theses about the appropriateness and moral obligatoriness of establishing such legal duties are smoothly compatible with the non-justificatory proposition that those duties will not be correlated with any legal claim-rights held by the inanimate entities or insentient organisms which the duties inherently safeguard. Thus, on top of the fact that such a non-justificatory proposition does not manifest any disrespect for the inanimate entities and insentient organisms through its exclusion of them from the category of potential holders of claim-rights, it does not affirm or entail any conclusions that are inimical to the interests of those entities and organisms.

Admittedly, as a contingent matter, there can be contexts in which the imposition of stringent legal protections for the interests of such entities and organisms is rendered more likely insofar as the supporters of those protections succeed in propagating the view that the entities and organisms are potential holders of claim-rights. Indeed, such a tactical consideration doubtless lies behind many of the efforts by environmental activists to get rivers and trees and other natural phenomena officially classified as holders of legal entitlements. (I have referred briefly to some of those efforts in the final paragraph of §5.1 above.) Still, although there can certainly be contexts of this kind—in which the safeguarding of various aspects of natural phenomena will be made more probable if activists are successful in persuading legal-governmental officials to endorse the proposition that such phenomena are capable of holding claim-rights—the tactical judgments to be reached in those contexts are not a basis from which we can soundly infer that inanimate entities and insentient organisms are genuinely within the class of potential holders of claim-rights. After all, there can be numerous contexts in which the attaining of certain results is facilitated through the dissemination of misconceptions. For example, the shielding of various aspects of trees and rivers from harm could be made more likely in quite a few circumstances through the peddling of the notion that such phenomena are endowed with souls or with magical properties. Circumstances of that sort are credibly possible, but their possibility is no basis at all from which we can soundly infer that souls or magical properties do infuse natural phenomena. Whatever judgments might be reached in such circumstances by tacticians, a philosophical theory should not countenance falsehoods about souls or magical properties in trees and rivers. Similarly, whatever might be the judgments reached by tacticians who try to prevail upon legal-governmental officials to embrace the idea that inanimate entities or insentient organisms are potential holders of claim-rights, a philosophical theory should not have any truck with that idea.

Let us, then, turn our attention to the paradigmatic potential holders of claim-rights. What is the import for them of the exclusion of inanimate entities and insentient organisms from the category of potential holders of claim-rights? Would their affirmation of that exclusion bespeak high-handedness or effrontery or insecurity on their part? The answer to the latter question is negative, for such an affirmation by the paradigmatic potential holders of claim-rights would simply instead evince their recognition that inanimate entities and insentient organisms never have been able and never will be able to participate as subjects in the community of potential holders of claim-rights.[5] Numerous claim-right/duty relationships among the subjects in that community do pertain to such entities and organisms, but only as objects of those relationships and not as subjects thereof. Inanimate or insentient things are not the beings *for whom* such relationships exist, even though they often are the beings *in regard to which* those relationships are established. No such things ever have been or ever will be endowed with any awareness of their situations. When the paradigmatic potential holders of claim-rights take as given that inanimate and insentient things are without any such awareness, and when they consequently take as given that there is a fundamental ethical difference between those things and themselves, they are not manifesting any attitudes of high-handedness or effrontery or insecurity. They do not thereby slight any beings whose ethically pregnant features they fail to notice, nor are they overlooking any profound affinities between those beings and themselves. On the contrary, even while the paradigmatic potential holders of claim-rights discern undeludedly that inanimate entities and insentient organisms are far-reachingly different from

[5] As has already been noted, this chapter remains non-committal on the question whether some artificial-intelligence mechanisms in the future will become so sophisticatedly self-reflective that they gain the status of *êtres pour eux-mêmes* despite their inanimateness. My whole discussion here prescinds from the possibility of such a development.

themselves, they can attend to any ethically pregnant features of those entities and organisms that justify the ascription of intrinsic value thereto.

In short, we can safely conclude that inanimate entities and insentient organisms are excluded from the class of potential holders of claim-rights. Both when we ponder the import of their exclusion for those entities and organisms themselves, and when we ponder the import of it for the paradigmatic potential holders of claim-rights, we find that the exclusion of the inanimate and insentient beings does not detract in any way from the conditions under which everyone in a society can be warranted in sustaining an ample sense of self-respect. Those entities and organisms never have been capable and never will be capable of experiencing any sense of self-respect, and they are thus not set back at all when the fact that they fall outside the category of potential holders of claim-rights is clearly and pervasively recognized. Conversely, sane human adults do not display any attitudes of overbearingness or self-indulgence or insecurity when they take for granted that those entities and organisms indeed cannot ever hold any claim-rights. That is, the sane human adults do not display any attitudes that would warrant the lowering of their own levels of self-respect. Accordingly, since the exclusion of inanimate and insentient things from the class of potential holders of claim-rights does not impair the fulfillment of the paramount moral responsibility incumbent on the paradigmatic members of that class, and since the exclusion in fact advances the fulfillment of that responsibility by upholding the fundamental divide between inanimate or insentient things as objects and *êtres pour eux-mêmes* as subjects, the paradigmatic potential holders of claim-rights are both morally permitted and morally obligated to accept that exclusion. They thus affirm that the class of potential holders of claim-rights is a community.

To close this discussion, a caveat should be attached. As readers might infer from my example involving the god Apollo in §5.4.4.3 above, a system of governance can purport to confer legal claim-rights on inanimate or insentient things even though such things are not among the potential holders of claim-rights. With regard to any such occurrence, we should conclude that what the relevant system of governance professes to have done is not what it has actually done. Suppose for example that the legislature in the country of Arborea enacts a statute which professes to bestow legal claim-rights upon leaves that have fallen from trees. Under the terms of the statute, each homeowner in Arborea is legally obligated to gather any leaves that have fallen onto an adjoining sidewalk from trees located on the homeowner's land. Raked-up leaves are to be stored in sacks, so that they can be taken away for use in compost heaps or in similarly worthy ventures. By the reckoning of the legislators in Arborea, the legal duties imposed by the statute inherently protect some aspects of the situations of leaves that are typically advantageous on balance for such entities. Instead of rotting as piles of slippery mush on the sidewalks of Arborea, the leaves will end their existence in ways that serve valuable purposes. Consequently, the legislators designate their statute as the "Upholding the Rights of

Fallen Foliage Act." They sincerely believe that a correlate of the legal duty imposed on each homeowner under the statute is a legal claim-right held by each leaf or by the leaves collectively on each relevant portion of any sidewalk in Arborea. Now, when a philosopher seeks to gauge the deontic upshot of the Arborean enactment, he or she should not accept at face value the terms in which the enactment is drafted and the terms in which the legislators of Arborea characterize what they have done. A philosopher should cheerily grant that the legal duties imposed by the statute do inherently protect some aspects of the situations of leaves that are typically beneficial on balance for such entities, but a philosopher should insist that those duties are not correlated with legal claim-rights held by the leaves—because inanimate things such as fallen leaves cannot ever hold any claim-rights.

Not in doubt here is that the legislature of Arborea has enacted a genuine law that imposes legal duties on the homeowners in the country. Likewise not in doubt is that the legal duty incumbent on each homeowner under the statute is correlated with a legal claim-right or with an array of legal claim-rights. What *is* contested here is the notion that the fallen leaves in Arborea hold the claim-rights correlative to the duties imposed by the statute. Instead, those legal claim-rights are held by the Arborean system of governance and perhaps also by members of the public individually or collectively. Although the legislators in Arborea earnestly purport to have invested the fallen leaves of their country with legal claim-rights, the deontic upshot of their statute does not genuinely involve any holding of claim-rights by the leaves. The exclusion of those inanimate entities from the category of potential holders of claim-rights is not something that can be altered by the say-so of a legislature.

5.5.2.2 Non-Human Animals

Non-human creatures during their lifetimes are animate, and the large majority of them are sentient. Unlike lifeless phenomena and insentient organisms, then, most non-human animals are *êtres pour eux-mêmes*. Nearly every animal that is alive and non-comatose is endowed with one of the two properties that are necessary for the possession of ultimate value and thus for inclusion in the class of potential holders of claim-rights. As has already been contended, however, not every animal is such that the furtherance of its interests is intrinsically valuable. Some non-human animals are such that the furtherance of their interests is only instrumentally or constitutively valuable. Those latter non-human animals are therefore not of ultimate value, and are excluded from the category of potential holders of claim-rights. We need here to examine this matter in greater depth, with reference to the two main considerations that guide my reflections throughout the present section of this chapter. In other words, with regard to the inclusion of any specified animals in the class of potential holders of claim-rights or the exclusion of those animals from that class, we need to consider the import of the inclusion or exclusion for those animals themselves and the import of the inclusion or exclusion for the paradigmatic potential holders of claim-rights. In each case, we will be endeavoring to ascertain whether the inclusion or the exclusion is partly constitutive of the conditions under which everyone in a society can be warranted in harboring a strong sense of self-respect.

5.5.2.3 Non-Human Animals and Ultimate Value

In §5.4.4.4 above, as I have just remarked, this chapter has submitted that some animals such as cockroaches and tsetse flies are not of ultimate value. At the same time, the chapter has readily accepted that most animals are of ultimate value and are therefore among the potential holders of claim-rights. The furtherance of the interests of those latter animals is intrinsically valuable. Various aspects of the situations of those animals that are typically advantageous on balance for them are inherently protected by certain moral duties and are also inherently protected in many jurisdictions by certain legal duties. Accordingly, the animals in the class of potential holders of claim-rights are *actual* holders of claim-rights. Hence, this chapter overall is robustly supportive of the efforts by some philosophers and most environmentalists to maintain that non-human animals belong to the community of potential holders of claim-rights—even while the chapter remains noncommittal on the justificatory questions addressed by those philosophers and environmentalists, who exhort legislators and other governmental officials to introduce laws that will more amply safeguard the interests of animals. Still, although this chapter is firmly supportive of the proposition that non-human animals belong to the community of potential holders of claim-rights, it allows that some animals do not belong to that community. Thus, the basis for my affirmation of the status of non-human animals as potential holders of claim-rights must also be a basis for my insistence that some non-human animals do not occupy that status.

5.5.2.3.1 The Inclusion of Many Animals

When we concentrate on the import for non-human animals themselves of their inclusion in the category of potential holders of claim-rights (or the import for them of their exclusion from that category), we discover a major consideration that tells in favor of the inclusion of many such animals. On the one hand, unlike lifeless or insentient things, most non-comatose animals currently living are *êtres pour eux-mêmes*; and, given the understanding of self-respect as self-esteem which I have elaborated at length elsewhere (Kramer 2017a, 299–340; 2017c, 336–7; 2021, 129–30), most non-human animals can experience self-respect to varying degrees and can be warranted in so doing. Most non-human animals can undergo pain or consternation and can likewise undergo gratification. Some non-human animals can grasp deontic concepts at rudimentary levels. Not entirely beyond their ken is the notion that some patterns of behavior are morally forbidden or morally obligatory (Bekoff and Pierce 2009; Rowlands 2012).

On the other hand, although many non-human animals are partly comparable to human beings in the ways just recounted, they are not sufficiently sophisticated to fathom the difference between their inclusion in the category of potential holders of claim-rights and their exclusion from that category. After all, as has been underscored at many junctures in this book, the matter of falling within that category or falling outside it is separate from the matter of the extent to which and the ways in which the interests of beings are morally protected and should be legally protected. Whereas the extent of any legal protections for the interests of non-human animals and the specific contents of those protections can affect the lives of animals palpably enough for them to descry, the sheer fact that the animals of some species are included in the class of potential holders of claim-rights or excluded from that class is not similarly discernible by those animals themselves. As far as any non-human animals can grasp, then, the difference between inclusion and exclusion does not make a difference. Consequently, their levels of self-respect will not be impaired by their exclusion from the class of potential holders of claim-rights and will not be increased by their inclusion in that class. Nevertheless, the levels of self-respect which they can *warrantedly* harbor are impaired by their exclusion from that class and are increased by their inclusion. Albeit such effects on the warrantedness or unwarrantedness of their levels of self-esteem are not due to anything which the animals themselves are capable of detecting, the fact that their inclusion will raise the levels of self-esteem which they can warrantedly harbor is something that—at least *prima facie*—places a moral duty on the paradigmatic holders of claim-rights to recognize that many non-human animals are also potential holders of claim-rights. To be sure, this consideration is not in itself decisive, since it presupposes that many non-human animals are within the domain covered by the universal quantifier in my formulation of the content of the paramount moral responsibility borne by each person: the responsibility to strive for the conditions under which *everyone* in a society can be warranted in experiencing a sturdy sense of self-respect. However, the consideration adduced in this paragraph can become decisive through the substantiation of what it presupposes.

We shall find the requisite substantiation and shall thus find decisive grounds for the status of many non-human animals as potential holders of claim-rights, when we shift our attention squarely to the paradigmatic potential holders of claim-rights. What is the import for sane human adults of the inclusion of non-human animals in the category of potential holders of claim-rights, and what is the import for sane human adults of the exclusion of non-human animals from that category? Unlike the non-human animals themselves, sane human adults are capable of grasping the relatively sophisticated deontic concepts involved in any proposition which affirms that animals are among the potential holders of claim-rights. Sane human adults are also capable of understanding whether the levels of self-respect enjoyed by animals are warranted or not. In that regard as well, those adults are different from the non-human animals themselves. Both the differences and the affinities between sane human adults and non-human animals are crucial as we inquire whether the paramount moral obligation borne by the human adults requires them to recognize that many of the non-human animals are potential holders of claim-rights.

Whereas the paradigmatic potential holders of claim-rights are morally on a solid footing when they recognize the fundamental divide between themselves and inanimate or insentient things, they would not be morally or scientifically on a solid footing if they were to posit any comparably far-reaching divide between themselves and non-human animals. There are important differences between sane human adults and non-human animals, of course, but nearly all of those differences are matters of degree rather than wholesale matters of kind. In the antepenultimate paragraph above, I have recounted some of the chief resemblances between human beings and animals. Sane human adults, as they seek to frame the terms of their interaction with non-human animals in the course of endeavoring to comply with the paramount moral duty that is incumbent on every such adult, are morally obligated to acknowledge the resemblances between themselves and the non-human creatures. They are morally obligated to recognize that many such creatures belong to the domain covered by the universal quantifier in my formulation of the content of that paramount moral duty: the duty to promote the social and political and economic conditions under which *everyone* in a society can be warranted in sustaining a high level of self-respect. Of course, as has been remarked, the non-human animals themselves are not able to understand that paramount moral duty or the notion of being warranted in one's level of self-respect. Still, although they cannot meaningfully strive to fulfill that duty, many of them are inherently among its beneficiaries. The inclusion of many of them as inherent beneficiaries of that duty is a principal mark of the divergence between creatures capable of experiencing self-respect and the countless inanimate or insentient things which are not so capable. It is also a mark of the fundamental affinities between non-human animals and human beings as organisms able to harbor feelings of self-respect. Though the factors that undergird the self-respect of animals are obviously not equivalent to the factors that undergird the self-respect of human beings, the ability to form and sustain attitudes of self-respect is something that aligns human beings with non-human animals as *êtres pour eux-mêmes* in contradistinction to inanimate entities and insentient organisms which of course lack any such ability. Sane human adults, who shoulder the paramount moral responsibility pertaining to the conditions for warrantedly high levels of self-respect, are not morally permitted to disregard the fundamental alignment between themselves and non-human animals—an alignment centered on the capacity for self-respect—as they endeavor to fulfill that paramount responsibility.

Now, the considerations that account for the inclusion of most non-human animals as members of the societies which comprise human beings are also considerations that group non-human animals and human beings together as members of the overall community of potential claim-right-holders. When we strive to differentiate between the beings who belong to that latter community and the beings that do not, we are distinguishing between the beings who are potentially subjects of deontic relationships and the beings that are only ever the objects of deontic relationships. We are distinguishing between the beings *for whom* certain legal duties might be established and the beings merely *in regard to which* certain legal duties might be established. Any credible way of cashing out the distinction between subjects and objects, or the distinction between the beings for whom legal protections exist and the beings merely in regard to which such protections ever exist, will make reference to the beings on the former side of each of those distinctions as *êtres pour eux-mêmes* who can feel consternation or gratification and who can experience levels of self-respect. Those factors, which of course are common to human beings and non-human animals and which distinguish them from lifeless entities and insentient organisms, are not only of key importance for inclusion in the domain covered by the universal quantifier in my formulation of the content of the paramount moral duty borne by each person; in addition, those factors are of key importance for inclusion in the class of potential holders of claim-rights. Paradigmatic potential holders of claim-rights are morally obligated to attend to those factors when reaching judgments about the inclusion of other beings in the category of potential holders of claim-rights.

As is apparent from the preceding two paragraphs, there is some convergence or congruity between certain justificatory questions and certain non-justificatory questions in this area—albeit at a lofty level of abstraction. Here the relevant justificatory questions, pertaining to the ways in which and the extent to which the interests of various beings should receive legal protection, are centered on the scope of the domain covered by the universal quantifier in my formulation of the content of the paramount moral duty borne by each person. And here the relevant non-justificatory questions are centered on membership in the class of beings who are capable of holding claim-rights. Considerations of vital importance for addressing the former set of questions are also of vital importance for addressing the latter set of questions. This overlap between some justificatory matters and some non-justificatory matters is genuine, but in three ways it is quite limited.

First, the specified justificatory questions are only some of the myriads of justificatory questions that can be posed about the extent to which and the ways in which the interests of various beings should receive legal protection. For example, numerous beings such as paintings and buildings and trees and coral reefs are not inherently among the beneficiaries within the scope of the paramount moral responsibility incumbent on every system of governance and on every person, yet they are in need of stringent legal protection. Left entirely open by the considerations adduced in the penultimate and antepenultimate paragraphs above are questions about the extent to which and the ways in which the interests of paintings and buildings and trees and reefs (and the interests of multitudinous other inanimate or insentient things) should be protected through the imposition of legal obligations.

Second, as has been noted, the convergence between certain justificatory matters and certain non-justificatory matters is occurrent at a very high level of abstraction. Throngs of justificatory questions at tiers of greater specificity will remain to be addressed, even after people have accepted that most non-human animals as well as every human being are inherently comprehended within the protective scope of the paramount moral duty borne by each person. Although human beings and non-human animals are alike in their possession of the fundamental features on which I have concentrated in the preceding several paragraphs, they are manifestly divergent in multiple characteristics that affect the extent to which and the ways in which their respective interests should be legally safeguarded. Notwithstanding that most of the divergences are differences of degree, the disparities of degree are often very considerable. Hence, the elementary affinities between human beings and non-human animals that have been highlighted in this subsection—hugely significant though they are—will be perfectly consistent with the justifiability of major differences between human beings and animals in their respective legal entitlements. Exactly what those respective entitlements should encompass is a question not settled at all by the existence of the elementary affinities just mentioned.

Third, as will be pondered imminently in the next subsection, the fundamental similarities between non-human animals and human beings—coupled with the fact that every human being who exists at any given time is then of ultimate value and is therefore a potential holder of claim-rights—do not oblige us to infer that all non-human animals are comprehended within the class of potential holders of claim-rights. After all, the status of any creatures as *êtres pour eux-mêmes* is a necessary but insufficient condition for their possession of ultimate value. To possess such value, non-human creatures must also be such that the furtherance of their interests is intrinsically valuable. Though the fundamental similarities between non-human animals and human beings are naturally consistent with the proposition that every non-human animal alive at any given time is of ultimate value and is therefore a potential holder of claim-rights, they are also consistent with the proposition that some animals are not of ultimate value and are therefore not potential holders of claim-rights. Non-human animals excluded from the class of potential holders of claim-rights will not be subjects of legal regulation and will instead only ever be objects thereof. This chapter has already affirmed that some non-human animals are indeed excluded from that class. A defense of my stance on that matter must obviously go beyond the main considerations about non-human animals and human beings that have been invoked in the opening several paragraphs of this subsection, given that those highlighted considerations assimilate animals and human beings as *êtres pour eux-mêmes* who can experience feelings of self-respect. At the same time, such a defense will be unproblematically consistent with those considerations—for they can be fully acknowledged even as my next subsection dwells countervailingly on factors which constitute some major differences between human beings and certain non-human animals. These countervailing factors are the basis for the exclusion of certain non-human animals from the community of potential holders of claim-rights.

5.5.2.3.2 The Exclusion of Certain Animals

To understand why certain non-human animals fall outside the class of potential holders of claim-rights, we should recall that the extension of that class comprises all and only the beings whom the paradigmatic potential holders of claim-rights are morally obligated to acknowledge as members of it. Those paradigmatic potential holders are morally duty-bound to reach judgments about the inclusion of other beings in a community, albeit a community without institutions. Such judgments will be oriented in large part toward the prevalent patterns of interaction between human beings and other animals, and toward the remoteness or proximity between the characteristics of human beings and the characteristics of any animals who are under scrutiny. Those two foci substantially determine whether the specified animals are indeed alongside human beings in a community which the paradigmatic potential holders of claim-rights are morally obligated to recognize as such.

A pair of caveats should be stated clearly at the outset. First, this subsection does not aim to pin down an exact extension for the category of potential holders of claim-rights. There is certainly no need here for any systematic survey of various creatures to gauge whether they are inside or outside that extension. Instead my concern is to explain at a general level why, although many non-human animals are included in the class of potential holders of claim-rights, not all non-human animals are so included. Wherever the demarcation lies between the animals who are included and the animals who are excluded, the general fact that such a demarcation exists is what this subsection seeks to illuminate.

A second preliminary caveat pertains to the justificatory/non-justificatory distinction that has been accented repeatedly in this book. Here, as elsewhere, the non-justificatory question under investigation—the question why some non-human animals are excluded from the category of potential holders of claim-rights—is not to be conflated with justificatory questions about the extent to which and the ways in which the interests of the excluded animals should be legally protected. In much the same manner in which the interests of some inanimate entities and insentient organisms should be stringently shielded through the imposition of legal duties even though those entities and organisms are not holders of any claim-rights correlative to the duties that inherently protect some aspects of their situations which are typically advantageous on balance for them, so too there can be grounds for legally protecting certain interests of the animals who are excluded from the category of potential holders of claim-rights.

Still, in two ways, this second caveat should itself be hedged about. For one thing, the basis for the exclusion of certain animals from the class of potential holders of claim-rights is importantly unlike the basis for the exclusion of all inanimate entities and insentient organisms from that class. Whereas all inanimate or insentient things are excluded because they are not *êtres pour eux-mêmes* even though some of them are such that the furtherance of their interests is intrinsically valuable, certain non-human animals are excluded because the furtherance of their interests is not intrinsically valuable even though those animals are *êtres pour eux-mêmes*. The inherent protection bestowed by certain legal duties upon some on-balance typically beneficial aspects of the situations of great paintings and elegant edifices and magnificent coral reefs and towering trees is intrinsically valuable because the sound condition of each such intrinsically good entity is itself intrinsically valuable. By contrast, with regard to any of the non-human animals excluded from the class of potential holders of claim-rights, the inherent protection bestowed by certain legal duties upon some on-balance typically beneficial aspects of their situations is not intrinsically valuable. At most, that protection is instrumentally or constitutively valuable—because the sound condition of any of the excluded creatures is itself never more than instrumentally or constitutively valuable. Consequently, the grounds for establishing some stringent legal duties which inherently protect the interests of any of those excluded creatures are generally fewer than the grounds for establishing some stringent legal duties which inherently protect the interests of inanimate or insentient things that are intrinsically valuable.

Another rider attached to my second caveat is that the considerations which determine whether species of animals are included in the class of potential holders of claim-rights—namely, the prevalent patterns of interaction between human beings and other animals, and the remoteness or proximity between the traits of human beings and the traits of other animals—are also considerations that bear upon decisions about safeguarding the interests of non-human animals through the imposition of legal duties. If those factors call for the exclusion of some species of animals from the class of potential holders of claim-rights, they are also likely to militate against the notion that the interests of the animals in that species should be stringently shielded. There are no logical entailments between answers to the non-justificatory question about the potential holding of claim-rights and answers to justificatory questions about the suitable modes of legal protection, but negative answers to the non-justificatory question for certain species of animals will very likely signal that stringent legal safeguards for the interests of those animals are unwarranted.

Let us, then, turn to the considerations that are determinative for the non-justificatory question about the community of potential holders of claim-rights. Certain species of animals such as cockroaches and tsetse flies, frequently labeled as "vermin," are predominantly if not unalloyedly inimical to human flourishing.

They are predominantly, if not unalloyedly, injurious to human health and destructive of human endeavors. As I have stated in my first caveat above, there is no need for me here to catalogue the roster of creatures that should be classified as vermin. What is crucial here instead is the general point that some animals are accurately so classified. Animals to which that classification applies are not properly recognizable by sane human adults as belonging to the community of creatures who are capable of holding claim-rights. Even though that community lacks any institutions and is decidedly diffuse, its nature as a community in even the most modest sense would be undermined if it were to comprehend creatures that are systematically hostile to the interests of the paradigmatic members of the community. Those paradigmatic members are morally obligated to contribute to the social and political and economic conditions that enable everyone in their societies to be warranted in harboring a strong sense of self-respect. They cannot fulfill that obligation if they abase themselves by taking themselves to be in a community—even a very loosely-knit community—with vermin.

Like some of my reflections in §5.4.4.5 above, my meditations at this stage of the chapter will doubtless elicit complaints about "speciesism" from some readers. After all, not only are the paradigmatic members of the class of potential claim-right-holders identified as such in a manner that might strike some readers as smacking of speciesism; so too, the non-human animals excluded from the class of potential claim-right-holders are identified in a manner that might seem even more disconcertingly speciesist. Animals fall outside that class if they are vermin, and they are categorized as vermin by reference to the destructiveness of their interaction with human beings. Some readers might balk at the idea that the elementary interests of human beings are pivotal in determining whether non-human animals can hold claim-rights. However, any misgivings along those lines can be put to rest when we recall that the extension of the category of potential claim-right-holders comprises all and only the beings whom sane human adults are morally obligated to acknowledge as belonging to the diffuse community of potential claim-right-holders. Moral duties of acknowledgment borne by sane human adults in this matter are derivative of their paramount moral responsibility which I have invoked at the end of the preceding paragraph (as well as at many previous junctures in this chapter). Given the nature of the judgments to be reached by the paradigmatic potential holders of claim-rights, those judgments will inevitably be speciesist. As has already been explained in §5.5.1, sane human adults are central to the whole community of potential holders of claim-rights not only because they belong to that community straightforwardly but also because they are the point of reference for the inclusion or exclusion of other beings. If the embracing of certain other creatures as members of that community by the paradigmatic members would be inconsistent with the fulfillment of the paramount moral responsibility incumbent on each of those paradigmatic members, then the other creatures are excluded. The inclusion of those other creatures might bolster the levels of self-respect which they are warranted in experiencing, but it would lower the levels of self-respect that are warranted for the paradigmatic potential holders of claim-rights—since it would degrade the community of potential holders of claim-rights by stretching the contours thereof to encompass creatures that are persistently noxious to the flourishing and needs of human beings. For these reasons, certain non-human animals are not among the potential holders of claim-rights. Such reasons are of course speciesist, but they have to be if the community of potential holders of claim-rights is to exist as a community in even the most modest sense.

Let us now mull over the second chief consideration that guides this enquiry: the remoteness or proximity between the characteristics of human beings and the characteristics of non-human animals. Some non-human animals are perhaps not vermin but are nonetheless so markedly different from human beings that they are unrecognizable as fellow members of a community in even the most modest sense. Again, there is no need for me here to try to pin down exactly which non-human creatures are excluded on this ground from the community of potential holders of claim-rights. Some primitive forms of life, such as earthworms and slugs, would no doubt be among those creatures. Such beings are morally protected against various types of mistreatment and should be legally protected commensurately, but the moral and legal duties that inherently safeguard them are not correlated with any claim-rights held by them. Instead, the legal duties are correlated with legal claim-rights held by the system of governance that has established the duties, and the moral duties are correlated with moral claim-rights held by each person who bears the duties. Those moral duties—prohibiting the infliction of torture on earthworms and slugs, for example—inherently protect the moral integrity of anyone on whom the duties are incumbent.

As can be gathered from the preceding few sentences (and from my underscoring of the justificatory/non-justificatory distinction throughout this book), the non-justificatory matter tackled by this subsection is distinct from questions about the extent to which and the ways in which the interests of earthworms and slugs should be legally safeguarded. Still, as has already been observed, the considerations invoked in this subsection's ruminations on vermin are germane not only for explaining why some non-human animals are excluded from the class of potential holders of claim-rights, but also for pondering the extent to which and the ways in which the interests of the animals excluded from that class as vermin should be legally protected. More specifically, those considerations call for any legal protections to be quite meager. Because vermin are inimical to human flourishing and are not of ultimate value—since the furtherance of their interests is not intrinsically valuable—legal duties that inherently shield any typically advantageous aspects of the situations of such creatures should be limited to the duties that are necessary for upholding the moral integrity of the duty-bearers.

5.5.2.3.3 Holding Claim-Rights and Bearing Duties

Before we move on, I should rebut a complaint that has sometimes been leveled against the proposition that non-human animals can hold claim-rights. Some philosophers and legal theorists have argued that, because animals cannot bear any duties, they cannot hold any claim-rights.[6] "Rights bring with them responsibilities" is a slogan often voiced in this connection. According to such a line of thought, no being B is ever a holder of claim-rights unless B can bear duties. Proceeding from the premise that non-human animals are incapable of bearing any duties, such a line of thought concludes that those animals are therefore also incapable of holding any claim-rights. That conclusion supposedly rests on the indisseverability of claim-rights and duties.

At least four considerations tell fatally against any objection along these lines to the proposition that non-human animals are among the potential holders of claim-rights. First, such an objection conflates a party's bearing of a duty and a party's fulfilling of a duty. Even if it were true that non-human animals are never capable of understanding and fulfilling any duties incumbent upon them, they would be capable of bearing duties. One's status as a potential bearer of a duty D does not entail one's ability to comply with what D requires, nor does it entail one's ability to understand what D requires. Even if every non-human animal lacked each of those abilities, many such animals could be placed under legal duties by legal norms. Whereas a legal norm that purports to impose legal duties on desks or tables or sunflowers would *pro tanto* be nonsensical, a legal norm that purports to impose legal duties on horses or dogs or cattle does indeed make those creatures the bearers of such duties. If a law calls for certain animals to abide by some specified constraints or else incur legal penalties, the animals in question are under legal duties to abide by those constraints—regardless of their ability or inability to understand what is required. Admittedly, the imposition of such duties on animals who are incapable of understanding them would be both silly and cruel. Medieval practices of subjecting non-human animals to trials and punishments for the perpetration of crimes are aptly nowadays perceived as weird and repugnant. Still, the silliness and cruelty of imposing legal duties on animals would not amount to impossibility or unintelligibility. In contrast with a law that professes to place inanimate objects under legal obligations, a law that places some animals under legal obligations might be dubious ethically but is not dubious conceptually.

Second, the philosophers who peddle the "Rights bring with them responsibilities" line of reasoning are mistaken in their assumption that all non-human animals are incapable of understanding and fulfilling any duties. Most

[6] See, for example, Carruthers 1992, 98–105; Cupp 2009, 66–9; Duckler 2008, 191–8; Huss 2002, 60–1; Kelch 1999, 8; Rawls 1999, 441, 448; Scruton 2000; Sumner 1987, 203. For some predominantly sympathetic reflections on a version of this line of thought in Kant's moral philosophy, see O'Neill 1998. For my previous riposte to argumentation of this sort, see Kramer 2001, 42–5.

animals that are susceptible to domestication are capable of grasping the existence of some duties and are capable of adjusting their behavior to conform with what is required of them by those duties. Of course, even domesticable animals are not capable of grasping the contents of intricate or subtle duties and are not capable of complying therewith. Their deontic comprehension is rudimentary rather than comparable to the sophistication of ordinary human adults. Nonetheless, the philosophers opposed to the idea of claim-rights held by non-human animals proceed far too sweepingly insofar as they assume that such animals cannot ever manage to discern the existence of duties or to adopt patterns of behavior deliberately in keeping with the requirements laid down by those duties.

Third, the "Rights bring with them responsibilities" objection smacks strongly of the Will Theory of right-holding. Although the specific focus of the objection is different from that of the Will Theory, what is common to them is the notion that no being B is ever included in the class of potential holders of claim-rights unless B is endowed with the deliberative faculties of an ordinary human adult. Given this significant convergence between the Will Theory and the aforementioned objection, the latter inherits many of the egregious shortcomings of the former (which I have expounded in Chapter 4).

Fourth, and most important, the "Rights bring with them responsibilities" line of thought is based on a grievous misunderstanding or misrepresentation of the Hohfeldian Correlativity Axiom. Except when a duty is owed by oneself to oneself, the holder of the correlative claim-right is some other party. Although the holding of a claim-right entails the shouldering of a correlative duty, it does not entail the shouldering of a duty by the party who holds the claim-right (save where a duty is owed by oneself to oneself). When a party P holds a legal or moral claim-right vis-à-vis some other party Q, P is legally or morally entitled to Q's φ-ing.[7] In such a situation, Q as a party required to φ obviously bears a duty to do so; but whether P bears any duties is an entirely separate matter. Hence, even if non-human animals were somehow unable to bear any duties or fulfill any duties, they could perfectly well hold legal and moral claim-rights—claim-rights correlated with duties borne by human individuals or human collectivities. Non-human animals do in fact hold many moral claim-rights, and they should hold some legal claim-rights in any jurisdiction.

Doubtless, the officials in some system of governance can elect to make anyone's possession of certain legal claim-rights depend on his or her fulfillment of certain legal duties. In that event, one's holding of those claim-rights does depend on one's fulfilling of those duties. However, such a state of affairs is a wholly contingent product of the particular system of governance in which it obtains, and is therefore

[7] As I have argued in §2.4.1 of Chapter 2, some duties have contents that are not focused on any conduct of the duty-bearers. However, I can prescind from such duties here, since my taking them into account would not serve in any way to fortify the "Rights bring with them responsibilities" line of thought.

not something that follows from the very nature of right-holding. Indeed, even within the jurisdiction of that system of governance, it is overwhelmingly likely that only some claim-rights are bestowed conditionally in this fashion. Virtually any credible system of governance will establish some legal duties which inherently protect certain aspects of the situations of animals that are normally advantageous on balance for such creatures. Given as much, the animals hold claim-rights correlative to the duties irrespective of whether the officials in the prevailing system of governance have identified correctly the parties in whom those claim-rights are vested. Having already noted that the say-so of the officials in any system of governance cannot ever manage to bestow legal claim-rights upon entities (such as fallen leaves) that are incapable of holding any claim-rights, I am adding here that the say-so of any officials is likewise inefficacious in the opposite direction. Non-human animals hold legal claim-rights correlative to any legal duties which inherently protect aspects of their situations that are normally beneficial on balance for such creatures, even if the officials who have imposed the duties wrongly believe that all non-human animals are excluded from the class of potential holders of claim-rights.

In short, the "Rights bring with them responsibilities" worry is unfounded in multiple respects. Worst of all is its gross misunderstanding or misrepresentation of the correlativity of claim-rights and duties. Except where a duty is owed by oneself to oneself, the holding of a claim-right always involves the owing of a correlative duty not by the holder of the claim-right but instead by some other party. When we fathom this elementary corollary of Hohfeld's analysis of claim-right/duty relationships, we can readily see that the "Rights bring with them responsibilities" mantra does not cast any doubt upon the prospect of claim-rights held by non-human animals.

5.5.2.4 Infants and People with Mental Incapacities

Sane human adults are the paradigmatic members in the class of potential holders of claim-rights, but also included in that class are all other human beings who are alive at any given time. Infants and people with serious mental incapacities are not paradigmatic members, partly because their status as potential holders of claim-rights is controversial and partly because they are not able to comprehend what the holding of claim-rights involves. Their status as potential holders of claim-rights has of course been challenged by the proponents of the Will Theory (even though some of those proponents, such as H.L.A. Hart and Nigel Simmonds, have adopted a concessionary stance with regard to infants). By contrast, the Interest Theory is smoothly consistent with the proposition that infants and mentally incapacitated people can hold claim-rights, and such a proposition is quite clearly sustainable by reference to the factors that have served as the lodestars of my reflections on non-paradigmatic potential holders of claim-rights. That is, here as elsewhere when we contemplate whether certain beings are within the class of potential holders of claim-rights, we have to ask about the import of their inclusion in that class for those beings themselves and about the import of their inclusion in that class for the paradigmatic potential holders of claim-rights.

Infants and people with serious mental incapacities (severe dementia, severe mental retardation, and the like) are incapable of understanding whether they are included in the category of potential holders of claim-rights or not. Their inclusion in that category will not boost the levels of self-esteem which they experience, and their exclusion from that category would not detract from those levels. Nonetheless, their inclusion does elevate the levels of self-esteem which they are *warranted* in sustaining. Hence, like the inclusion of many non-human animals—who are similarly incapable of grasping the reasons for the increases in the levels of self-respect which they are warranted in feeling—the status of infants and mentally incapacitated people as potential holders of claim-rights is something which the paradigmatic potential holders of claim-rights are morally obligated to acknowledge. Only thus can the paradigmatic potential holders comply with the paramount moral responsibility that is incumbent upon them.

That conclusion is reinforced when we turn to concentrate sustainedly on the paradigmatic potential holders of claim-rights themselves. They have to be attentive to their own patterns of interaction with infants or mentally incapacitated people, and they likewise have to be attentive to the proximity or remoteness between their own elementary characteristics and the elementary characteristics of infants or mentally incapacitated people. Whereas some species of animals are vermin whose interaction with human beings is profoundly baneful, the patterns of interaction between sane human adults and infants or mentally incapacitated people are generally far more benign. Neither babies nor people with serious mental incapacities are deeply antagonistic to the flourishing of sane human adults, to say the least. What is more, the proximity between the elementary traits of infants or mentally incapacitated people and the elementary traits of sane human adults is manifest. All the beings on each side of any such comparison are members of the human species and are easily discernible as such. Markedly different from earthworms or slugs or other primitive creatures are the beings on either side of the comparison. Of course, infants and mentally incapacitated people are saliently unlike human adults of sound mind, in that they are mentally undeveloped or mentally infirm. However, that divergence redounds upon justificatory questions about the types of legal entitlements with which infants and mentally incapacitated people should be endowed, rather than upon this chapter's non-justificatory question about the inclusion of such people in the community of potential holders of claim-rights.

Were the paradigmatic members of that community to disregard the far-reaching likenesses between themselves and these non-paradigmatic members, they would be contravening their paramount moral obligation in more than one way. They would of course be lowering the levels of self-respect which the infants and mentally incapacitated people are warranted in harboring, since those levels are affected not only by the actual inclusion of such beings in the class of potential holders of claim-rights but also by the recognition of their inclusion on the part of sane human adults. Admittedly, as has been observed in §5.5.2.3.1 with regard to non-human animals, my contention in this paragraph about a breach of the paramount moral obligation incumbent on every sane human adult is in need of substantiation—because my contention *presupposes* that infants and mentally incapacitated people are among the beings whose interests are inherently protected by that paramount moral obligation, and because my contention therefore cannot itself *establish* that infants and mentally incapacitated people are indeed so protected. However, that presupposition can be substantiated when we observe how the paradigmatic potential holders of claim-rights would be aggrandizing and degrading themselves if they were to deny that infants and mentally incapacitated people are also potential holders of claim-rights.

Those paradigmatic potential holders would be aggrandizing themselves by dissociating themselves from other human beings, whom they would in effect deem to be so far beneath their own status as not even to belong to the exceedingly modest community of potential holders of claim-rights. (Let us remember here that even some of the Will Theorists have balked at the notion that infants do not belong to that community. Let us also remember that the status of a being as a potential holder of claim-rights is consistent with the possibility that that being holds very few actual claim-rights.) There genuinely are differences between sane human adults and infants or mentally incapacitated people, of course, but those differences are scarcely a basis for perceiving the infants and mentally incapacitated people as if they are on a par with inanimate entities and mushrooms and earthworms and slugs. Further, any such perception of infants and mentally incapacitated people would be degrading not only for them but even more for the sane human adults who would cleave to such a perception. Just as human beings who are aptly confident about their own strengths and accomplishments will suitably acknowledge the accomplishments and strengths of other people and will suitably abide the foibles of those other people instead of belittling them—because human beings aptly confident about their own achievements and strengths will not need to resort to the disparagement of others for the sake of magnifying those achievements and strengths—so too any sane human adults aptly aware of the distinctiveness of their status as deliberative agents will suitably acknowledge the commonalities that place them alongside infants and mentally incapacitated people as potential holders of claim-rights. Their distinctiveness as agents is duly manifested in the sundry legal entitlements that are held uniquely by them in any jurisdiction, whereas their affinities with other human beings as ultimately valuable *êtres pour eux-mêmes* from the same species are duly reflected in the fact that every one of those human beings is a potential holder of claim-rights. Only if sane human adults are not aptly confident about their distinctiveness, will they be inclined to assert that distinctiveness by denying that other human beings are included with them in the class of potential holders of claim-rights. Any such denial would be degrading as a product of insecurity and weakness. Consequently, when sane human adults fulfill their paramount moral obligation to strive for the conditions under which everyone in a society can be warranted in feeling a strong sense of self-respect, they will acknowledge that infants and mentally incapacitated people are indeed potential holders of claim-rights. Complying with that paramount moral obligation, human adults of sound mind subscribe to the Terentian aphorism: "*Homo sum, humani nihil a me alienum puto.*"

5.5.2.5 Permanently Comatose People and Anencephalic Infants

As will be recalled from §5.4.4.5 above, each of the components in my conception of ultimate value as applied to members of the human species is a generic proposition with an implicit pleonotetic quantifier. Given my conception of ultimate value, then, permanently comatose people are of such value even though they are not any longer *êtres pour eux-mêmes*, and anencephalic infants are of such value even though they never have been and never will be *êtres pour eux-mêmes*. Accordingly, any permanently comatose people and anencephalic infants are in the class of potential holders of claim-rights. Legal or moral duties that inherently protect some aspects of their situations that are typically advantageous on balance for them are correlated with legal or moral claim-rights held by them.

Differences between sane human adults and permanently comatose people or anencephalic infants are obviously more gaping than the differences between sane human adults and ordinary infants or mentally incapacitated people. However, the accentuation of the disparities is properly reflected in the meagerness of the claim-rights and other entitlements actually held by permanently comatose people or anencephalic infants, rather than in the exclusion of them from the class of potential holders of claim-rights. Though the fact that they are not *êtres pour eux-mêmes* is a consideration that sharply curtails the range of the legal claim-rights and other legal entitlements with which such human beings should be vested, it is not something that undoes the applicability of Terence's apothegm to their status as potential holders of claim-rights. They qualify for that status as human beings who are currently alive, even though they lack any awareness of their lives.

Here the basis for the inclusion of certain beings in the class of potential holders of claim-rights does not reside at all in the import for those beings of their inclusion or exclusion. They are not capable of knowing about their inclusion any more than they are capable of knowing about anything else, and they are likewise wholly unable to harbor any sense of self-respect. Though the levels of self-respect warranted for these people would be increased if they were able to experience any self-respect, they cannot experience anything. Hence, the inclusion of them in the class of potential holders of claim-rights is due entirely to the import of that inclusion for the paradigmatic members of the class. Those paradigmatic members are morally obligated to recognize that permanently comatose people and anencephalic infants belong to the community of potential holders of claim-rights as fellow human beings.

To an especially great extent, the inclusion of these non-paradigmatic members in the community of potential holders of claim-rights is overtly speciesist. Sane human adults are morally obligated to grasp that permanently comatose people and anencephalic infants, as human beings, are not outside that community on a par with inanimate objects and insentient non-human organisms. Devoid of consciousness though these human beings are, the fact that they belong to the human species is sufficient to lay a moral duty on sane human adults to acknowledge that these unfortunates are fundamentally similar to the other members of that species—including, of course, sane human adults. Unlike the non-human animals that are accurately classifiable as vermin, permanently comatose people and anencephalic infants are patently not antagonistic to the health and flourishing of sane human adults. And unlike earthworms and slugs, permanently comatose people and anencephalic infants are not alienly unrecognizable as fellow members of a very modest community without institutions.

Resemblances between the properties of sane human adults and the properties of these other human beings are relatively straightforward in regard to permanently comatose people, the vast majority of whom were *êtres pour eux-mêmes* at earlier stages of their lives. Their inclusion in the class of potential holders of claim-rights is clinched not only by their continued existence as members of the human species who are currently alive, but also by the subsumption of the no-longer-conscious phase of each of them into the overall trajectory of his or her life. If human adults of sound mind were to decline to acknowledge the inclusion of such people in the class of potential holders of claim-rights—and if they were thus to decline to accommodate the misfortunes of fellow human beings who are no longer *êtres pour eux-mêmes*—they in their aggrandizement of themselves would be debasing themselves by evincing a lack of due confidence about their own distinctiveness as sophisticated deliberative agents. Endowed with such confidence, human adults of sound mind can readily accept that their distinctiveness (real and important though it is) does not set them apart by excluding the unfortunates of their species from the community of potential holders of claim-rights. The distinctiveness of sane human adults does of course set them apart from those unfortunates in numerous other ways, but not in regard to the elementary capacity for the holding of claim-rights. Because the deontic protectedness involved in the holding of a claim-right does not in itself require any active exertions, the inability of permanently comatose people to engage in such exertions is no bar to their status as potential possessors of claim-rights.

Resemblances between sane human adults and anencephalic infants are obviously more tenuous than the resemblances between the former and permanently comatose people. Unlike the vast majority of permanently comatose people, anencephalic infants never have been conscious. Nor will they ever be conscious. Their affinities with sane human adults are confined to their shared membership in the human species. Still, as has been submitted in the preceding paragraph—where one ground for the inclusion of permanently comatose people in the category of potential holders of claim-rights is the sheer fact that they are human beings who are currently alive—the membership of anencephalic infants in the human species is just enough to undergird their status as potential holders of claim-rights during their short lives. Though any claim-rights and other Hohfeldian entitlements held by such an infant will of course be far fewer than the entitlements held by any sane adult or indeed by any ordinary infant, the paradigmatic potential holders of claim-rights would be acting ignominiously if they were to flout the status of anencephalic infants as human beings by deeming those infants to be on a par with inanimate entities. Such a perception of those infants as ethically tantamount to inanimate objects would underlie any denial of their inclusion in the community of potential holders of claim-rights. Sane human adults cannot deny the inclusion of those infants in that community without demeaning the cardinal characteristic which they have in common with those infants: namely, their membership in the human species. Ergo, insofar as any sane human adults fulfill their paramount moral responsibility to strive for the realization of conditions under which everyone in any society can be warranted in sustaining a sturdy sense of self-respect, they will have recognized that the humanity of anencephalic infants is sufficient—barely sufficient, but sufficient—for the inclusion of those infants in the community of potential holders of claim-rights. Although the domain covered by the universal quantifier in the content of that paramount moral responsibility does not comprise the anencephalic infants (since they cannot ever harbor any feelings of self-respect), it does of course comprise every sane human adult along with many other human beings and non-human creatures. Thus, since sane human adults will have denigrated their own humanity if they suppose that anencephalic infants are outside the community of potential holders of claim-rights, they cannot fulfill their paramount moral responsibility without abandoning any such supposition.

Admittedly, we have here encountered one of the outermost bounds that delimit the category of potential holders of claim-rights. Anencephalic infants are of ultimate value only because they are members of the human species (a species to which the preconditions for ultimate value apply as generics rather than as universally quantified propositions), and their status as potential holders of claim-rights is therefore likewise due to their membership in that species. Here the speciesism that imbues my efforts to delimit the category of potential holders of claim-rights is at its starkest, but—as this chapter has already observed—the speciesism is made inevitable by the fact that the endeavor of delimitation requires us to ask which beings the paradigmatic members of the community of potential holders of claim-rights are morally obligated to recognize as also members of that community. Because sane human adults would disparage their own humanity if they were to decline to acknowledge the inclusion of anencephalic infants in the community of potential holders of claim-rights, their acknowledgment of that inclusion is necessary for their compliance with their paramount moral obligation. Since the paradigmatic potential holders of claim-rights are human beings who are morally obligated to reach judgments about the community of potential holders of claim-rights that will accord with their paramount moral responsibility, and since those judgments so oriented will have to ascribe special importance to the humanity of any beings whose inclusion in that community is under examination (because any failure to ascribe special importance thereto would slight the humanity of the people who are reaching those judgments), the speciesism is a central feature of the endeavor rather than a flaw therein. Anybody troubled by it should note that it is entirely consistent with the inclusion of most non-human animals in the community of potential holders of claim-rights.

5.5.2.6 Foetuses

Though the topic of foetuses as potential holders of claim-rights is particularly prominent because of its connection to the tempestuous debates over the lawfulness and morality of abortion, my reflections on it here can be very brief—for the difficulties of the topic are addressed *mutatis mutandis* by what this chapter has already said about the nature of interests and about anencephalic infants and permanently comatose people. Here the term "foetus" refers to an antenatal human organism at various stages of development, including the zygotic and embryonic stages. Given as much, foetuses in the early stages of their development are not yet *êtres pour eux-mêmes*. At much later stages of their development, they do acquire rudimentary awareness and rudimentary capacities to experience pain and gratification. In the final stages of their development, their mental capacities are essentially the same as those of newborn babies.

In §5.2.2 above, we have scrutinized a medley of arguments advanced by Dworkin in his opposition to the idea that foetuses are potential holders of claim-rights. He contended that foetuses cannot possess any claim-rights, because they are not endowed with any interests that would be inherently protected by the claim-rights. As I have maintained there, Dworkin's narrow conception of interests is unfounded both in general and in the specific context—the context of disputation over the morality and lawfulness of abortion—with which Dworkin was engaging. Under a properly expansive conception, for which I have argued throughout §5.2, interests are straightforwardly ascribable to foetuses. Sundry on-balance typically advantageous aspects of the situation of any foetus can be furthered or set back through actions or omissions by other people as well as through natural events. A foetus has an interest in the performance of any action that will promote one or more of those on-balance typically beneficial aspects of its situation, and an interest in the non-occurrence of any action that would impair one or more of those aspects. Thus, Dworkin's reservations about the inclusion of foetuses in the category of potential holders of claim-rights—reservations grounded on his insistence that foetuses lack any interests—were misjudged.

Still, while firmly rejecting Dworkin's cabined conception of interests and while accepting that foetuses do possess interests that can be inherently protected through the imposition of legal duties, somebody might nevertheless think that foetuses are not potential holders of claim-rights. Somebody who clings to such misgivings will presume that, although legal duties inherently protective of the interests of foetuses are correlated with legal claim-rights, the claim-rights are not held by the foetuses themselves. Worries of this kind are most likely focused on the early stages of foetal development, which forego the emergence of the portions of the brain that generate consciousness. However, given that anencephalic infants are properly included in the class of potential holders of claim-rights, foetuses even in their zygotic and embryonic stages are included *a fortiori*. After all, unlike anencephalic infants, the vast majority of foetuses will become *êtres pour eux-mêmes* in due course. With regard to membership in the community of potential holders of claim-rights, the zygotic and embryonic phases of a human being are subsumed into the overall trajectory of his or her existence as a living human organism (inversely to the way in which the closing phase of the life of a permanently comatose person is subsumed into the overall trajectory of his or her existence as a living human organism). Hence, both by dint of belonging to the human species and by dint of emerging as the initial incarnations of beings who are sophisticatedly conscious for most of their existence, foetuses qualify for membership in the community of potential holders of claim-rights. My arguments in the preceding subsection in support of such membership for anencephalic infants and permanently comatose people are applicable here *mutatis mutandis*.

Even more than for my other discussions in this chapter, the distinction between non-justificatory matters and justificatory matters is hugely important for any cogitations on the status of foetuses. What this subsection has pondered is the non-justificatory question whether foetuses can be endowed with claim-rights at all. Neither an affirmative answer nor a negative answer to that question entails any answers to justificatory questions about the extent to which and the ways in which the interests of foetuses should be legally protected. I have sought to underline this point in §5.3 above by juxtaposing the following two propositions, which are smoothly consistent with each other:

(1) Wherever legal norms impose duties on people not to abort any foetuses, those norms have thereby endowed the foetuses with legal claim-rights against being aborted.
(2) As a matter of substantive morality, first-trimester foetuses should not be legally protected against abortions in any jurisdiction (except where abortion-inducing actions are malicious or reckless or negligent).

The present subsection has been concerned solely with the non-justificatory matter that is addressed by proposition 1, whereas it has not tackled the justificatory matter addressed by proposition 2 at all. Nor has it tackled any other justificatory matters pertaining to how much or how little the interests of foetuses should be legally protected.

In particular, readers should not suppose that the inclusion of foetuses in the community of potential holders of claim-rights is equivalent to their moral personhood as envisaged by the opponents of the lawfulness of abortion. Moral personhood has been understood by philosophers in numerous different ways in a variety of contexts, but in debates over abortion it is invoked frequently as a property that justifies the banning of all or nearly all abortions. It is a property ascribed to foetuses by almost all opponents of the lawfulness of abortions, whereas most defenders of the lawfulness of abortions deny that foetuses are properly classified as moral persons. To be sure, some "pro-choice" philosophers—most famously Judith Jarvis Thomson (1971)—have prescinded from questions about moral personhood by granting *arguendo* that foetuses are moral persons. However, because I have shown elsewhere the limitedness of the "pro-choice" conclusions which those philosophers succeed in establishing when they forbear from denying that foetuses are moral persons (Kramer 2017a, 125–32), and because in any event a large majority of philosophers and other people on the "pro-choice" side of the disputation over abortion do deny that foetuses are such persons, moral personhood is a property that bears directly on justificatory questions about the morality of abortion. As I have declared elsewhere, the question whether foetuses are included in the category of moral persons is "tantamount to the question whether foetuses should be endowed with the same basic legal rights as those that are properly conferred on human beings who have already been born.... If foetuses are such persons, they are endowed with basic moral rights against sundry types of harm, and they should be endowed with basic legal rights that correspond to those moral entitlements" (2017a, 108, 109). In other words, moral personhood is a property that pertains to the substance and extent of the legal protections which every system of governance is morally obligated to provide for any being who is endowed with that property. Thus, if the matter of the inclusion of foetuses in the class of potential holders of claim-rights were equivalent to the matter of their inclusion in the class of moral persons, this subsection's affirmative stand on the former issue would be a "pro-life" stand in the controversies over the morality of abortion. In fact, however, those two matters are quite distinct. I actually adhere to a complex "pro-choice" doctrine that will be elaborated at length in my next book *Abortion and the Limits of Governance*, and here I have neither been anticipating the arguments of that book nor been deviating from them. This subsection has not put forward any contentions about the morality of abortion or about other justificatory matters concerning the interests of foetuses. Its contentions instead about the non-justificatory matter of the inclusion of foetuses in the category of potential holders of claim-rights can and should be endorsed by fervent supporters of the lawfulness of abortion as well as by people who believe that abortion should be strictly outlawed.

5.5.2.7 Dead People

Even more complicated than the questions that have been explored heretofore in this chapter are questions about the status of dead people as potential holders of claim-rights. Unlike the beings whom I have contemplated hitherto, dead people no longer exist when we ponder whether they are capable of holding any claim-rights. We therefore have to ask whether anyone who has ceased to exist at some time t can be vested with claim-rights at some subsequent time $t + n$. Equivalently, we have to ask whether anyone can owe a duty at $t + n$ to somebody who has ceased to exist at t.[8]

In coming to grips with this topic, we should keep in mind that the holding of a claim-right is a relational property. My formulation of the Interest Theory of right-holding explicates the nature of that property, which obtains as a relationship between a duty borne by one party and some typically on-balance advantageous aspect of the situation of another party. (When a duty is owed to oneself, the two parties mentioned here are a single human being or a single collectivity in two distinct statuses.) Given that any claim-right and its correlative duty are always strictly coeval, the two sides of the relationship involved in the holding of a claim-right must be coexistent or co-occurrent whenever the duty correlative to the claim-right is fulfilled. In other words, the typically on-balance beneficial aspect of the situation of a party P that is inherently protected by a duty incumbent on some other party Q has to exist at the same time as the duty itself whenever the duty is fulfilled. To say as much, however, is scarcely to say that P and Q have to exist at the same time or that Q's duty and P have to exist at the same time.

5.5.2.7.1 The Overall Trajectory of a Life

If dead people are included in the class of potential holders of claim-rights, then the situation of each dead person P has to extend beyond his existence as a living organism. It has to encompass some span of time after P's death. That span of time, in combination with the span of time during which P existed as a living organism, constitutes the overall trajectory of his life. That overall trajectory, rather than solely the period during which P was alive, is what would be charted by a

[8] For some writings that are directly relevant to this topic, from quite a variety of perspectives, see Aas 2020; Bahn 1984; Baier 1981; Belliotti 1979; Boonin 2019; Bowen 2022; Brecher 2002; Callahan 1987; Da Silva 2015; Fabre 2008; Feinberg 1974, 57–60; Feinberg 1984, 79–95; Glannon 2001; Grover 1989; Kelch 1999, 9; Kramer 2001, 29–31, 49–52; 2022, 375–84; Levenbook 1984; 1985; Luper 2004; 2013; Marquis 1985; Mulgan 1999; Nelkin and Andrews 1998; Partridge 1981; Persad 2019; Pitcher 1984; Portmore 2007; Quay 1984; Ridge 2003; Scarre 2003; Smolensky 2009; Solomon 1976; Sperling 2008; Taylor 2005; Wellman 1995, 146–57; Wilkinson 2002; Wisnewski 2009; Yoshida 2003.

satisfactory biography of P. Such a biography would not abruptly terminate after recounting the moment of P's death. Instead, it would additionally delineate the aftermath of P's biological existence to report on the ways in which the sundry strands of his life have developed after his death. One's investigation of such matters will contribute crucially to one's gauging how successful or discommendable the life of P has turned out to be.

Attentiveness to the posthumous unfolding of the strands of P's life is indispensable for an informed assessment of that life, because the upshot of many of those strands will not fully materialize until quite some time after P has died. In numerous instances, his projects and wishes and aspirations will reach fruition or frustration not during his lifetime but instead long afterward. His life overall will be enhanced or diminished in its quality as a result of the post-mortem occurrences whereby his projects and wishes and aspirations are realized or thwarted. For example, suppose that P after his death undergoes a precipitous decline in his reputation either because of his having been persuasively traduced by somebody or because of the release of some highly embarrassing information about him which he had managed to keep concealed while alive. Whereas P was widely esteemed at the time of his death, the admiration thereafter dissipates and is replaced by contempt and derision elicited through the posthumous defamation or revelation. Although P is of course not able to experience the contumely that is now heaped upon him, the lasting damage to his reputation greatly detracts from the overall tenor of his life. It greatly detracts from the extent to which the overall trajectory of his life can be accurately appraised as successful.

Or suppose that P is a professional artist who keenly aspires to revolutionize the styles of painting that have come to be dominant at the time when he embarks upon his career. Devoting himself sedulously to the pursuit of that ambition, he produces numerous acclaimed works of art during the decades of his life, and he delivers proselytizing talks that inspire quite a few of his younger contemporaries to follow his preferred style of artistry. At the time of his death he experiences considerable pride in what he has accomplished, and he looks upon his life as a success. Were a biography of P to stop abruptly after recounting the day of his death, it too would assess his life as triumphant. Not long after the demise of P, however, his favored style of painting fades from prominence and quickly falls into permanent oblivion. Artists once inspired by him now shift their allegiances to markedly different modes of painting that are much closer to those which P longed to supplant. Both P and his work are forgotten, as his imprint upon the artistic world has proved to be highly ephemeral. Hence, the overall trajectory of his life—which includes not only the years of his existence as a living organism but also the aftermath of those years—is marked not predominantly by success but instead predominantly by failure. His aspirations, which were fulfilled transiently during his lifetime, have been mortifyingly dashed thenceforth. A satisfactory biography that takes account of the full trajectory of his life will conclude that that trajectory sloped sharply and conclusively downward after a period of ascent.

Or suppose that P before his death has indicated to his heirs how he wishes to divide his estate among them. He tells them that he wants to set aside some of his assets for a specified charity, and he details the ways in which his other assets should be apportioned among the heirs. They readily and sincerely assure him that they will comply with his wishes on these matters. P does not create any formal will, because he confidently trusts in his heirs to abide by the oral undertakings which they have proffered in response to his instructions. After P has died, his heirs flout his wishes as they abandon the intentions which they once sincerely articulated in their colloquy with P. Instead of channeling any of his assets to his favored charity, they keep all the assets for themselves. And instead of distributing the rest of his wealth in line with his instructions, they distribute it very differently. They reason that P will never know about their defiance of his wishes. Now, although P will indeed never know what they have done, their perfidy has significantly tarnished the overall arc of his life. He has been detrimentally affected both by the sheer fact of having been betrayed and by the fact that the elements of his estate have been allotted in ways that are at variance with what he wished and prescribed.

Many more examples could be adduced here, of course. What each of the scenarios in the preceding three paragraphs has illustrated is a posthumous occurrence that detracts from the goodness of a decedent's life. In the first scenario, the damage done to the goodness of P's life resides in the sullying of his reputation; in the second scenario, the damage lies in the thwarting of P's hopes and ambitions; in the third scenario, the damage consists in the breaking of promises made to P by some of his close relatives. Though each of those post-mortem developments has not affected what P experienced during his existence as a living organism, it has greatly affected the estimableness of his life overall. In each vignette, there has posthumously been a serious deterioration in the situation of P—through the emergence of widespread disdain toward him among his once-admiring contemporaries, or through the foundering of his central artistic objectives, or through the betrayal of his trust by people whom he loved. P's situation was susceptible to being worsened in each of those ways. Conversely his situation would have been posthumously improved if his reputation had been burnished rather than besmirched, or if his paintings and his favored styles of artistry had continued to enjoy acclaim, or if his instructions to his legatees had been faithfully implemented.

In my first scenario the posthumous worsening of P's situation has very likely involved some contraventions of duties, and in my third scenario the posthumous worsening of his situation has unequivocally involved some such contraventions. Of course, we cannot yet conclude that the duties in either of those scenarios were owed to P as a holder of correlative claim-rights. Such a conclusion would presuppose that a dead person like P is included in the class of potential holders of claim-rights—which is exactly the proposition that is under investigation here. Still, even though we cannot yet presume that the duties breached by the posthumous infliction of damage on P's situation are owed to P, the point here is that each such duty is coeval with the aspect of P's situation that is inherently affected by the fulfillment or violation of the duty. After the death of P, his heirs are under moral duties to abide by his wishes for the disposition of his assets. Those duties inherently protect an aspect of the situation of P that is normally advantageous on balance for anyone like him. Being treated with respect and fidelity posthumously, especially by one's heirs, will normally enhance the goodness of the overall life of a person. Similarly, after the death of P, anyone who proceeds to defame him baselessly is under a moral duty (and, in some jurisdictions, under a legal duty) to refrain from doing so. That moral duty inherently protects an aspect of the situation of P that is typically beneficial on balance for anyone like him. Posthumously as well as during one's lifetime, the sustainment of one's favorable reputation is typically on balance promotive of the goodness of one's overarching life—where, again, the overarching trajectory of one's life comprises not only the period of one's existence as a living organism but also the aftermath of that period.

To be sure, the duties just mentioned were not existent during P's lifetime. Moral duties incumbent on his heirs to comply with his instructions for the division of his estate are borne by them after his death rather than before. Similarly, a moral duty incumbent on everyone to abstain from defaming P posthumously is borne by everyone after the death of P rather than before (though of course a homologous duty was borne by everyone during P's lifetime). Nonetheless, the Interest Theory of right-holding does not require simultaneity between the existence of a duty and the lifetime of the holder of a claim-right correlative to that duty. Rather, what is required for the holding of a claim-right under the Interest Theory is simultaneity between the existence of a duty and any aspect of the situation of a party that will inherently be affected by the fulfillment or contravention of that duty. As has just been maintained in the preceding paragraph, simultaneity of the latter kind is operative when P's heirs after his death bear moral duties to follow his instructions for the apportioning of his assets, and it is likewise operative when everyone after the death of P bears a moral duty and perhaps a legal duty not to libel or slander him. Co-occurrent with the fact that P's legatees after his death are under moral duties to heed his wishes is the aspect of the overarching path of P's life that will inherently be affected in typically beneficial ways on balance if his legatees heed those wishes. Likewise, co-occurrent with the fact that everyone after the death of P bears a moral duty and perhaps a legal duty not to libel or slander him is the aspect of the overarching path of his life that will be affected in typically advantageous ways on balance if he is not libeled or slandered after his death. In regard to the situation of a dead person such as P, simultaneity of the sort required by the Interest Theory for the holding of claim-rights is straightforwardly satisfied.

5.5.2.7.2 Do Dead People Belong to the Community of Potential Holders of Claim-Rights?

In the preceding subsection, I have addressed a worry that troubles some philosophers as they contemplate the idea of claim-rights held by dead people. That is, they are puzzled at the thought that someone can hold a claim-right when he or she no longer exists. I have sought to dispel any such puzzlement by emphasizing that the holding of a claim-right is a relational property and that the relevant relation can obtain posthumously. Events that occur after the end of the existence of some person P as a living organism can increase or decrease the goodness of the overall bent of P's life, and a legal or moral duty-to-φ borne by Q can coincide in time with the aspect of the overarching trajectory of P's life that will inherently be affected in typically advantageous ways on balance if Q does indeed φ. Thus, if dead people are included in the community of potential holders of claim-rights, they actually do hold many claim-rights—since the relationship involved in the holding of a claim-right is a relationship in which a dead person can straightforwardly be a party. Not yet answered, however, is the question whether dead people do belong to the community of potential holders of claim-rights.

We need to proceed here in the same general manner in which we have proceeded throughout §5.5 of this chapter. In other words, when we are inquiring whether dead people are included in the class of potential holders of claim-rights, we need to ask about the import of their inclusion for dead people themselves and about the import of their inclusion for the paradigmatic potential holders of claim-rights. For dead people themselves, the import of their inclusion manifestly does not lie in any experienced gratification. Neither gratification nor anything else is experienced by such people. They are no longer *êtres pour eux-mêmes*. Rather, the import lies in the augmentation of the goodness of each such person's life through his or her inclusion posthumously among the potential holders of claim-rights. Though a dead person obviously does not harbor any sense of self-respect, the vast majority of dead people were quite sophisticated *êtres pour eux-mêmes* during their lifetimes. They did harbor levels of self-respect while they were alive, and the levels of self-respect warranted for them were lifted by the fact that each person would remain within the community of potential holders of claim-rights after his or her death. Quite immaterial is whether or not people were aware that they would be included posthumously in that community; what matters is the upshot for the levels of self-respect they were warranted in experiencing, rather than the upshot for the levels which they actually did experience.

When we concentrate on the people who belong paradigmatically to the community of potential holders of claim-rights, we find that the import for them of the inclusion of decedents in that community is multifaceted. In the first place, as has just been suggested, the level of self-respect warranted for each paradigmatic potential holder of claim-rights—namely, for each sane human adult currently alive—is bolstered by the fact that he or she will remain in the aforementioned community throughout some span of time after his or her death. Moreover, when we ask whether the inclusion of dead people in the class of potential holders of claim-rights is something which the paradigmatic members of that class are morally obligated to acknowledge in fulfillment of their paramount moral duty to strive for the conditions under which everyone in a society can be warranted in feeling a strong sense of self-respect, the answer is affirmative. As has been observed in earlier portions of this chapter, one's reply to such an inquiry should focus on the basic interaction between the people who paradigmatically belong to the community of potential holders of claim-rights and the other beings whose status as members of that community is under consideration; and one's reply should also focus on the proximity or remoteness between the characteristics of the people who paradigmatically belong and the characteristics of the other beings.

Whereas the basic patterns of interaction between vermin and human beings are marked by hostility that is often lethal, there is no such hostility in the basic relationships between the living and the dead. Contrary to myths of malign spirits who haunt and persecute the living, there are not genuinely any visitations by the dead. Death is indeed the undiscover'd country from whose bourn no traveler returns. Of course, although there are not genuinely any ghosts that stalk the living in order to prey upon them, there are patterns of interaction between the dead and the living in a more expansive sense. Dead people have bequeathed countless things, some of which are welcome and some of which are unwelcome, to the people who succeed them. In turn, the currently living people can enhance or debase the overall trajectories of the lives of dead people in a host of ways suggested by §5.5.2.7.1 above. Admittedly, sometimes the relationships between the dead and the living are onerous for the latter. Portia in Shakespeare's *The Merchant of Venice* expresses this point with her usual poutiness and self-indulgence when she laments that "the will of a living daughter [is] curb'd by the will of a dead father" (I.ii.24–5). Still, although living people sometimes chafe at restrictions or burdens laid upon them by the dead, there is no systematic pattern of antagonism between the living and the dead. In that regard as well as in other respects, dead people are decidedly not assimilable to vermin such as tsetse flies and cockroaches.

Furthermore, the closeness between the characteristics of dead people and the characteristics of living people is unmistakable. Obviously, the one main difference—the only main difference—between the dead and the living is that the former no longer exist as animate organisms. Notwithstanding this evident difference between those who are deceased and those who are alive, the place of each dead person for a certain period in the community of potential holders of claim-rights is secured through the fact that the aftermath of each such person's biological existence is subsumed into the overall trajectory of her life. Although a dead person no longer exists as a living organism, she continues to be present in a multiplicity of ways. Her continued presence obtains through her influence on other people and on the unfolding of various events, and through the memories of her in the minds of relatives and friends and other contemporaries, and through any belongings and assets which she accumulated and then transmitted to legatees. In these forms and in other forms, the presence of a dead person during the aftermath of her lifetime is real and multifaceted. In addition to the persistence of the influence of a dead person on the doings and thoughts and fortunes of people who have outlived her is the deceased person's own susceptibility to actions and decisions undertaken by those people. That susceptibility of dead people to the posthumous intensification or diminution of the goodness of their lives through such actions and decisions by their successors is something which I have explored in §5.5.2.7.1. In that regard, as well as through the ways in which dead people continue to shape the conduct and outlooks and circumstances of the living, the deceased are meaningfully present in interaction with the living. By way of that interaction, dead people belong to the community of potential holders of claim-rights. The paradigmatic members of that community are morally obligated to acknowledge the extent to which they are enmeshed with the dead, by recognizing that the dead are members as well.

5.5.2.7.3 How Long?

As has been contended in the preceding subsection, each dead person belongs for a certain period to the community of potential holders of claim-rights. How long is the period in question? As should be manifest, there is no single answer to this inquiry; the length of the period will vary from one deceased person to the next. Nor is there a highly precise answer to that inquiry for anyone. We are not able to specify in seconds or minutes or hours exactly when the status of a dead person as a potential holder of claim-rights has ceased to obtain. Nonetheless, although there is not any talismanic point of cessation any more than there is a particle-by-particle point of transition between a single grain of sand and a heap of multitudinous grains of sand, the status of each deceased person as a potential holder of claim-rights does eventually terminate.

The cessation of that status for each dead person will occur because the considerations that undergird the inclusion of him or her in the community of potential holders of claim-rights will themselves change. Those considerations, which subsume the aftermath of the biological existence of a decedent into the overall arc of his or her life, pertain chiefly to the interaction between the dead and the living which I have outlined at the end of the preceding subsection. For each deceased person DP, as that interaction fades into history, so too does the overall arc of his or her life. People with memories of DP as a contemporary, rather than simply with knowledge of him or her as a historical figure, gradually die out. Similarly, people who have acquired assets directly from DP—rather than only from his or her descendants—gradually die out. Much the same is true of people whose conduct and situations have been affected directly through any actions or decisions undertaken by DP during his or her lifetime. As the direct formative influences of DP on his or her contemporaries (including any descendants born during his or her lifetime) evolve into historically mediated influences on successive generations, the overall trajectory of the life of DP reaches its terminus. When that transition has occurred, the place of DP in the community of potential holders of claim-rights has ceased. People thereafter might still be under moral or legal duties to abide by DP's wishes concerning various matters or to show respect for DP in other ways, but the claim-rights correlative to those duties are no longer held by DP.

As is apparent, the transition just limned will take place more speedily for some dead people than for others. Some people produce far fewer lasting effects on the world and their contemporaries than do other people. Some people, who die in obscurity and who are rather quickly forgotten by their small circles of acquaintances, posthumously occupy the status of potential holders of claim-rights for relatively short periods. Their interaction with the living is transitory. By contrast, other deceased people will occupy the status of potential holders of claim-rights throughout the lifetimes of the many contemporaries who remember them or who have been discernibly influenced by them in other ways. For relatively long spans of time, dead people of this latter kind are assimilable to the living people who they once were, and they therefore continue to be included for those spans of time in the community of potential holders of claim-rights. Disparities of these sorts among dead people with regard to the durability of their inclusion in that community are inevitable but are not extravagantly vast. After all, although some decedents during their lifetimes heavily and lastingly influenced myriads of their contemporaries, they will have become purely historical figures—no longer included in the community of potential holders of claim-rights—by the time those contemporaries have all died out.

5.5.2.7.4 Bowen's First Objection

I can best amplify and clarify my account of the status of dead people as potential holders of claim-rights by probing a few objections which Bowen in a recent essay has leveled against my ruminations on this matter. Bowen, who himself argues in favor of the proposition that dead people can hold claim-rights, has of course engaged with some of my previous writings—especially my 2001 essay "Getting Rights Right"—rather than with the lines of reasoning in this chapter. Still, although my present lines of reasoning are both more detailed than those in my previous writings and significantly different from them, there is naturally quite a bit of overlap between what I have argued previously and what I am arguing now. Hence, my rejoinders to some of Bowen's criticisms will suitably reinforce and illuminate the meditations in the preceding three subsections of this chapter.

Bowen focuses his attention chiefly on my observations about the posthumous persistence of any dead person through the sundry ways in which he or she has influenced the situations of contemporaries who are still alive. Bowen does not doubt the correctness of those observations themselves, of course, but he insists that they are not pertinent as a basis from which we can validly draw conclusions about the status of dead people as potential holders of claim-rights. He delivers his first onslaught as follows (2022, 62, emphasis in original):

> An initial limitation of Kramer's argument is that it cannot be relied upon by a defender of the Justificatory version of the Interest Theory [that is, a defender of the Razian interest theory]. This is because, on that version of the view, for one to be owed a duty and hold a right correlative to that duty, one's interests need to be the grounds of that duty. And, though the fact that the dead figure in the lives of the living may well be the grounds of duties that we treat the dead in certain ways, those duties will not be grounded in the interests of the dead—rather, they will be grounded in the interests of the living, the people whose lives the dead figure in. On the Justificatory version of the Interest Theory, then, Kramer's argument is able only to justify the living holding rights whose content refers to the dead, rather than the dead being holders of rights *themselves.*

Bowen here goes astray in two interrelated ways. In the first place, there is no basis for his supposition that my focus on the presence of the dead in the conduct and outlooks of the living would somehow commit me to the thesis that all duties pertaining to the dead are grounded in the interests of the living. In my discussions of dead people as potential holders of claim-rights, the duties correlative to the claim-rights inherently protect aspects of the situations of decedents that are typically advantageous on balance for them, and those duties are often burdensomely contrary to the interests of the living people on whom the duties are incumbent. Admittedly, that fact alone does not suffice to establish that the duties are grounded at least partly on the interests of the dead people. Nonetheless, it warrants our inferring quite confidently that in many cases the grounds for the duties are indeed located at least partly in those interests. *Pace* Bowen, nothing in this chapter or in my earlier "Getting Rights Right" essay excludes such a grounding.

A second and connected shortcoming in the reasoning by Bowen is that he conflates two ethical issues, or two sets of ethical issues, which I have taken pains to distinguish both in this chapter and in "Getting Rights Right." When I contemplate the influence of any dead person on the conduct and outlooks of the living, my reason for doing so is that such traces of a dead person in the lives of people who survive him or her are some key determinants of the length of time during which that person posthumously occupies the status of a potential holder of claim-rights. Those traces are such determinants because, as an ethical matter, they render a dead person partly assimilable to the person who he or she was during his or her lifetime. They thereby procure a place for a dead person in the community of potential holders of claim-rights. In the passage just quoted, Bowen is not grappling with this non-justificatory question about the span of time during which each dead person is a potential holder of claim-rights. He is instead broaching the distinct justificatory issue of the extent to which—or the conditions under which—the interests of the dead, or of the living, should be legally protected. According to the adherents of the Razian interest theory, the interests of dead people should be legally protected insofar as those interests are sufficiently weighty to justify morally the imposition of legal duties on people who are still alive. In taking such a position, the Razians are not addressing my non-justificatory question about the status of dead people as potential holders of claim-rights; instead, they are addressing the distinct justificatory issue that has just been broached. At a very high level of abstraction, they are indicating the extent to which—or the conditions under which—the interests of the dead should be legally protected through the imposition of duties.

Note that this second rejoinder to Bowen's argument is not simply pointing out that Raz's interest theory of rights, with its justificatory tenor, differs from my non-justificatory Interest Theory of right-holding. After all, any full exposition of right-holding in the Razian theory has to come to grips with the status of dead people and of other beings as potential holders of claim-rights. Raz did indeed touch upon that matter at the outset of his explication of what is involved in the holding of a claim-right: "'X has a right' ... only if X can have rights" (1986, 166). At an uninformatively high level of abstraction, that element of Raz's explication focuses on the question whether various beings are included in the class of potential holders of claim-rights. Such a question, in one of its applications, is what I am pondering in my reflections on dead people. However, in the passage from Bowen which I have quoted above, he prescinds from that opening element in Raz's theory of rights. He concentrates instead on the distinct issue about the extent to which—or the conditions under which—certain interests should be legally protected. That latter issue is of course addressed (at a high level of abstraction) by Raz's justificatory account of rights, but it is separate from the non-justificatory matter addressed by the opening element of his account, and it is therefore separate from the non-justificatory matter addressed by my ruminations on the presence of dead people in the outlooks and conduct of the living. Consequently, Bowen commits a non sequitur when he contends that the tenor of my ruminations is somehow inconsistent with the Razians' approach to questions about the extent to which—or the conditions under which—certain interests should be legally protected.

5.5.2.7.5 A Second Line of Attack by Bowen

Bowen next trains his fire directly on my attentiveness to the presence of the dead in the conduct and outlooks of the living (2022, 63–4):

> Kramer's methodology is to begin with what he takes to be paradigmatic right-holders, "mentally competent human adults," and then to look at the similarities and differences between such right-holders and the class of putative potential

> right-holders under examination. We then need to attend to the moral significance of these similarities and differences. And, it looks like Kramer thinks the salient similarities between the dead and the living is [*sic*] that the dead figure prominently in the lives of the living. But that just seems beside the point. Lots of things figures in the lives of the living.

Bowen is assailing a ridiculous straw man in this passage. Neither in my "Getting Rights Right" essay nor in the present chapter have I ever suggested that the status of dead people as potential holders of claim-rights is grounded on the sheer fact that dead people figure prominently in the lives of people who survive them. Had I been foolish enough to adopt such a position, I would have been committing myself to the thesis that earthquakes and volcanic eruptions are potential holders of claim-rights—since those natural calamities, as well as countless other natural events and entities, figure prominently in the lives of people who have been affected by them. Rather, the purpose of my focus on the presence of the dead in the outlooks and conduct of the living is to ascertain the length of time during which each dead person is ethically assimilable to the person he or she was while still alive. Any typical dead person was paradigmatically within the class of potential holders of claim-rights while still alive, and even the exceptional dead people who were not paradigmatic members of that class during their lifetimes were nonetheless of ultimate value and were therefore also potential holders of claim-rights. That aspect of the situation of each dead person crucially differentiates her from an earthquake or a volcanic eruption or a river. Whereas the effects of a dead person on the conduct and outlooks of living people are due to what she did or said or intended while she was a potential holder of claim-rights, the effects of an inanimate occurrence or entity on the conduct and outlooks of living people are not similarly analyzable. At no point has a river or an earthquake or a volcanic eruption ever occupied the status of a potential holder of claim-rights. Hence, there is no purchase for any question about the ethical assimilability of such a natural entity or event to some previous phase when it occupied that status. By contrast, I am grappling with that very question about a dead person when I seek to ascertain how long she will remain a potential holder of claim-rights.

Bowen goes on to assert that "it is just not clear why focusing on the various ways in which the dead figure in the lives of the living amounts to a morally relevant similarity to Kramer's paradigm right-holders" (2022, 64). Bowen's bafflement is itself baffling. I have just recounted in a nutshell why I devote so much attention to the influence of the dead on the outlooks and conduct of the living, and I have explained that matter at considerably greater length in some of the preceding subsections of this chapter and also in "Getting Rights Right." What Bowen and I agree upon is that living people have interests in the occurrence or non-occurrence of sundry events that will emerge (if at all) after their deaths. The overall trajectory of the life of a person would be enhanced by the occurrence of some of those events and by the non-occurrence of others.[9] What is less evident, and what is therefore also addressed by my cogitations on dead people in this chapter and in "Getting Rights Right," is the length of time during which the interests of each decedent will be inherently protectable through claim-rights held by him or her posthumously. Bowen apparently thinks that he does not need to wrestle with that question. As we shall see, his neglect of it results in some preposterous implications for his own account of the post-mortem holding of claim-rights.

5.5.2.7.6 A Third Line of Attack by Bowen

Bowen next adverts to something which I myself have highlighted in §5.5.2.7.3 above—namely, the fact that people figure prominently in the lives of their successors for varying periods. Some people will posthumously remain potential holders of claim-rights longer than will others. Bowen thinks that that corollary of my approach to this matter is problematic (2022, 65):

> [H]ow much one figures in the lives of the living is going to depend on how influential one is. No matter how successful I could hope to be in my philosophical career, for example, it is very likely that Shakespeare will figure more in the lives of others than I. This means that Shakespeare will be a potential right-holder for far longer than I. But, this might strike one as implausible. Suppose Shakespeare and I were to have been contemporaries—then, our status as potential right-holders should have been morally equal; yet, this equality breaks down after we die.

As we shall discover anon, the worry expressed by Bowen in this passage is deeply ironic. His own preferred approach to the matter of posthumous right-holding will call for extreme inequalities among the spans of time during which various dead people are included in the class of potential holders of claim-rights.

How telling is Bowen's complaint against my account of posthumous right-holding? Two main responses to this question are appropriate here. First is a point made repeatedly in this chapter and throughout this book, in one form or another. Non-justificatory questions about the span of time during which a dead person remains a potential holder of claim-rights are distinct from justificatory questions about the extent to which and the ways in which the interests of a dead person should be legally protected. With perfect consistency, an expansive viewpoint on the matters covered by the former set of questions can be combined with a highly restrictive viewpoint on the matters covered by the latter set of questions, and vice versa. Accepting that some person P after death will remain a potential holder of claim-rights for quite a lengthy period is entirely compatible with insisting that the interests of P should receive very little inherent protection through the

[9] For one of the many passages in Shakespeare's plays where this point is recognized, see *The Comedy of Errors*, III.i.98–106.

establishment of legal duties. Conversely, accepting that some person P after death will remain a potential holder of claim-rights for quite a short span is fully compatible with insisting that certain interests of P should be amply and prolongedly safeguarded through the establishment of legal duties. When we keep in mind this distinction between the non-justificatory questions and the justificatory questions, we can see that the prospect of inequalities among dead people in the sustainedness of their classifiability as potential holders of claim-rights is far less troubling than it might at first appear. Those disparities do not entail any disparities among the degrees to which—or the ways in which—the interests of various dead people should be inherently furthered through the imposition of legal duties. Disparities of the latter kind might obtain, of course, but they never follow simply by dint of the fact that disparities of the former kind obtain.

Second is a point which I have already made in §5.5.2.7.3. That is, although there will undoubtedly be some inequalities among dead people in the lengths of the periods during which they will remain potential holders of claim-rights, those inequalities are not vast. This point relates to my criticism of Bowen for his erroneous assertion that my account of posthumous right-holding attaches determinative importance to the sheer fact that decedents figure saliently in the outlooks and conduct of people who are still alive. Of crucial significance is not the sheer salience of the influence of the dead, but the mode of that influence. My focus on the presence of dead people in the conduct and outlooks of the living is aimed at ascertaining the assimilability or unassimilability of each decedent to the person who he or she was while alive. Accordingly, the modes of influence investigated by such an enquiry are akin to the influence of a living person on his or her contemporaries. Memories of a dead person P on the part of his or her contemporaries (including much younger contemporaries, and contemporaries who never met P) are obviously among those modes of influence, as are the inheritance of assets from P and any other direct ways in which P has affected his or her contemporaries. After a few generations have passed, however, any familiarity with the life of P on the part of people in later generations is historical knowledge rather than veritable memories. Somebody can of course feel great admiration for her ancestors or for other people from the past, but such attitudes after a few generations are harbored toward those people as historical figures rather than as coevals. Likewise, the bequest of property by P to his or her direct heir(s) is very different from the bequest of that property two or three generations later by a descendant of P to the descendant's own legatees. Whereas the former bequest is a direct connection to P on the part of the heir(s), the latter bequest is a historical connection to P.

Whenever P's presence in the minds and conduct of her successors is sufficient to ground her status as a potential holder of claim-rights, that presence consists in the relatively direct connections between P and her coevals (again, including those who are much younger and those who never met her). By contrast, when P's presence consists only in historical connections—because all her contemporaries have ceased to exist—her status as a potential holder of claim-rights no longer obtains. Moreover, even when some of her contemporaries are still alive, P may have ceased to be a potential holder of claim-rights because nobody any longer recalls P or anything that she said or did or intended. Thus, although dead people will remain potential holders of claim-rights for varying amounts of time, the disparities among those lengths of time will be quite limited.

My emphasis here on the distinction between temporally proximate connections and temporally remote connections is vital for any satisfactory project through which we demarcate the extension of the class of potential holders of claim-rights. Pursuing such a project, we have to determine which sorts of beings the paradigmatic members in the community of potential holders of claim-rights are morally obligated to acknowledge as additional members of that community. Just as the qualitative remoteness between the traits of certain primitive animals and the traits of human beings is inconsistent with the membership of those animals alongside sane human adults in the community of potential holders of claim-rights, so too the temporal remoteness between decedents and distant successors is inconsistent with the membership of the decedents in that community during the lifetimes of those distant successors. Even a minimal community requires some modicum of proximity to keep it together as a community. Sane human adults in the present day do not conduct themselves highhandedly or invidiously or degradingly when they recognize that Plato and Aristotle and Cicero and Thomas Hobbes and John Locke are not any longer among the potential holders of claim-rights.

A caveat should be attached here, however, since the import of the factor of temporal remoteness is to some degree variable across societies. In some societies (whether actual or credibly possible), the presence of distant ancestors is felt much more intensely than in modern Western countries. People who lived long ago are perceived not only as worthy of esteem and gratitude but also as actively overseeing the fortunes of the current inhabitants of these societies. In such circumstances, the remote ancestors are aptly classifiable as potential holders of claim-rights. Within these societies, the inclusion of the distant ancestors in the class of potential holders of claim-rights is due to their being widely and vividly perceived as still actively present. So perceived, the ancestors are some of the beings whom the paradigmatic members in the community of potential holders of claim-rights are morally obligated to acknowledge as also belonging to that community.

5.5.2.7.7 A Query Borrowed from Kurki

One of the most interesting queries in Bowen's essay is posed not by Bowen himself but by Visa Kurki. Bowen writes as follows (2022, 65 n. 45): "Visa Kurki has raised some additional complications in private communication. Following Shakespeare's death, the living's picture of him could well have gradually shifted from what he was actually like. At the limiting case, someone could die and the living could have a completely false view of them." As will be evident to anyone acquainted with the literature in the philosophy of language that has developed from the work of Saul Kripke and Hilary Putnam and David Lewis and others, the germane response to Kurki's conundrum will depend on the referential intentions of the contemporaries of Shakespeare who contemplate him after his death. If their referential intentions are *de re*, and if there is not any radical reference failure in their discourses about Shakespeare—a failure that would consist in their talking unwittingly about someone who has never actually existed—then their unfounded attributions to him of sundry accomplishments and traits do not prevent their utterances from referring to him. In such circumstances, he is present in the outlooks and conduct of his surviving contemporaries (albeit in decidedly peculiar ways), and he therefore continues to possess the status of a potential holder of claim-rights. By contrast, if the referential intentions of those contemporaries are *de dicto*, then their sweeping mistakenness about the traits and doings of Shakespeare is such that he no longer genuinely impinges on their thoughts and conduct. In these extreme circumstances, the descriptions of Shakespeare by his contemporaries actually pick out someone else—perhaps Francis Bacon or Edward de Vere—to whom those erroneous descriptions apply. If none of the coevals of Shakespeare is referring to him *de re*, and if none of them has any accurate recollections of what Shakespeare did or said or intended, then he is no longer present among them and is therefore no longer a potential holder of claim-rights.

5.5.2.7.8 Purposes Mistook and Fall'n on the Inventor's Head

Bowen complains that my account of posthumous right-holding classifies dead people as potential holders of claim-rights for disparate lengths of time. As has been observed, however, the inequalities among dead people in that respect are quite modest under my account. By contrast, the inequalities among them under Bowen's preferred approach to posthumous right-holding are vast—indeed, virtually limitless. Bowen supposes that well-being either is a matter of satisfying one's desires or is a matter of attaining worthwhile objectives, and he argues as follows for the status of dead people as potential holders of claim-rights (2022, 67):

> Now, many of my desires may be satisfied after I die. Many of the potential accomplishments that are relevant for the Objective List [of worthy attainments] can be affected after I die. (In fact, it is plausible that many of my most strongly held desires and most important accomplishments survive my death. For example, how my loved ones fare.) Because of this, both Desire and Objective List Theories [of well-being] can say that things can be good or bad for us (can affect our wellbeing) after we die. If we endorsed the Wellbeing View of Interests, this means the dead are bearers of interests, and so potential right-holders on the Interest Theory. This is because our interests can be served or potentially ground duties after we die.

I will here concentrate on just one major difficulty that afflicts Bowen's line of reasoning. Whereas the contents of some people's desires or of their worthwhile objectives extend far into the future, the contents of some other people's desires or of their worthwhile objectives extend little if at all into the future. One person might desire that human beings continue to live and flourish on the planet Earth until it is ultimately engulfed by the sun hundreds of millions of years hence, and she might pursue various endeavors that will conduce to the realization of her desire. Another person might desire simply that she herself will enjoy a comfortable existence until she eventually dies, and she might give nary a thought to the prospect of human survival and flourishing long after her demise. Under Bowen's approach to the posthumous holding of claim-rights, the first of these people will qualify as a potential holder of claim-rights for hundreds of millions of years. In sharp contrast, the second person will qualify as a potential holder of claim-rights for only quite a short time after her death. Countless other attitudes and objectives harbored by people are likewise possible, of course, with contents that reach into the future even further or at diverse intermediate levels. Hence, anybody who endorses Bowen's analysis of the posthumous holding of claim-rights is thereby committed to accepting that there can be (and almost certainly will be) gaping inequalities among dead people in regard to the lengths of time during which they are potential holders of claim-rights. Bowen has lumbered himself with such a conclusion precisely because he does not engage in the sorts of enquiries which he derides me for undertaking.

5.5.2.8 Future Generations

This chapter will close by investigating whether claim-rights can be held by future generations of people.[10] Instead of grappling with justificatory questions about the extent to which or the ways in which the interests of future generations should be inherently protected through the imposition of legal duties, my reflections here will grapple with the non-justificatory question whether such duties would be correlated with legal claim-rights held now by the future generations of people themselves. Regardless of how generous or niggardly the legal safeguards for the interests of unconceived people should be, the safeguards involve the holding of legal claim-rights by those people if and only if the sane human adults currently alive are morally obligated to accept that those not-yet-existent people belong now to the community of potential holders of claim-rights. In coming to grips with this non-justificatory matter, we encounter a temporal complexity that is the inverse

[10] For some writings that broach this topic, from a variety of perspectives, see Bandman 1982; Beckerman and Pasek 2001; Bell 2011, 104–10; Bränmark 2016; Bruhl 2002; De George 1981; De-Shalit 1992; 1995; Düwell and Bos 2016; Earl 2011; Elliot 1989; Fabre 2009; Feinberg 1974, 64–8; Gosseries 2008; Griffith 2017; 2018; Herstein 2009; Hiskes 2009; Kramer 2001, 52–7; Macklin 1981; Palombella 2023; Partridge 1990; Perry 2009, 554–80; Pletcher 1981; Reichenbach 1992, 212–17; Steiner 1983; Sterba 1980; Woods 2016.

of the complexity encountered in §5.5.2.7 during my ruminations on the status of dead people as potential holders of claim-rights. There we have had to probe into the past to explore whether people who no longer exist are nonetheless still present in forms which assimilate the decedents to their erstwhile selves and which therefore bring them within the community of potential holders of claim-rights. Here we have to probe instead into the future to ascertain whether human beings who do not yet exist are nonetheless present in forms which assimilate them to the people they will become and which therefore bring them now within the aforementioned community.

With regard to future generations of people as much as with regard to dead people, of course, the temporal complications arise from the fact that the people in question do not currently exist. In that respect, the complexities of the holding of claim-rights by future generations are parallel to the complexities of the holding of claim-rights by decedents. Nonetheless, because the current inexistence of future people foreruns rather than follows their existence, the complexities of the holding of claim-rights by them may seem to be greater in a major respect than are the complexities of the holding of claim-rights by dead people. Whereas dead people have existed as particular human beings prior to their current inexistence, future people have not yet existed and are therefore not yet particularized at all. Hence, when we contemplate whether future people can hold any claim-rights now, we may seem to confront some formidable problems of individuation that do not similarly bedevil one's posing of cognate questions about decedents as potential holders of claim-rights. Thus, although my enquiry into the status of unconceived people as potential holders of claim-rights will significantly resemble my enquiry into the status of dead people as potential holders of claim-rights, it will also have to broach some knotty questions that have not emerged heretofore in this chapter.

5.5.2.8.1 Are Future Generations Assimilable Now to the People They Will Be?

When one asks whether future generations of people are sufficiently present now to be assimilable to the human beings they will eventually become, one's outlook of course has to be prospective rather than retrospective. Consequently, some of the modes of presence applicable to dead people are obviously inapplicable to future people. For example, nobody currently has any memories of people who have not yet existed, nor has anybody inherited assets or genes from such people or been influenced by their doings and accomplishments. Those traces of the past in successive times are manifestly not what we shall discover when we attend to the ways in which future people are present now. Still, although the prospective orientation of this discussion is the inverse of the retrospective orientation of my cogitations in §5.5.2.7, those previous cogitations shed light on one key route by which the people of future generations are present as influences on the lives of people now.

As has been recounted in §5.5.2.7.1 with a few examples, the goodness or badness of the overall life of any person P now in existence will be partly determined by how people in the future perceive and treat him or her. Although my remarks on the posthumous bettering or worsening of P's life through the actions of people after his or her death have pertained mainly to people whose lifetimes overlap with the lifetime of P, the general point made by those remarks is pertinent also in connection with people who have not yet been conceived and born at the time when P dies. Such people can affect the goodness or badness of the overall life of P in any of the ways plumbed by §5.5.2.7.1, and in numerous other ways. For example, when lauding the adeptness of some professional actors, Hamlet declares that "they are the abstract and brief chronicles of the time. After your death you were better have a bad epitaph than their ill report while you live" (*Hamlet*, II.ii.524–6). Albeit Hamlet refers here to the maligning of someone during her lifetime, he could equally well have referred to the maligning of someone posthumously—as indeed he does when he mentions the effects of an unfavorable epitaph on the reputation of somebody who has died. Moreover, although he is here speaking about some actors who are his contemporaries, he could equally well have been speaking about actors in the future who are not yet conceived and born. People now alive can be harmed posthumously through ill reports or unfavorable epitaphs, and they can benefit posthumously through commendatory reports or favorable epitaphs. Damage inflicted on the reputation of P after her death will have lessened the goodness of the overall arc of her life, and the enhancement of her reputation after her death will have strengthened the goodness of the overall arc of her life. Any such damage will thus have decreased the levels of self-esteem which P during her lifetime is warranted in harboring, and any such enhancement will have increased those levels. Because P is susceptible in these ways and other ways to the detrimental or beneficial effects of actions performed by people who are conceived after her death, the inexistence of those people during her lifetime does not exclude their presence then as potential influences on the goodness or badness of her life.

Plaudits or condemnations bestowed in the future upon a currently living person by people unconceived during her lifetime are only one set of ways in which the not-yet-conceived people can affect the levels of self-respect which somebody now alive is warranted in sustaining. I have contemplated a few additional sets of ways in §5.5.2.7.1, and there are likewise numerous other kinds of actions through which people who are conceived after someone's death can augment or impair the goodness of the overall trajectory of her life. A perhaps even deeper sense in which future generations of people are present as influences on people currently alive is fascinatingly highlighted by Samuel Scheffler in a quite recent book, *Death and the Afterlife* (2013). Whereas the term "death" in Scheffler's title refers to the demise of each individual human being, the term "afterlife" does not refer to a state of ethereal immortality or to any other conscious existence of an individual in the period following his or her demise. Scheffler has no truck with pie-in-the-sky-when-you-die superstitions. Instead, the term "afterlife" in his title refers to the fact that successive generations of human beings will continue to emerge indefinitely after the death of each human being in any generation. In other words, the afterlife envisaged by Scheffler is a property of humankind—namely, the persistence of humankind indefinitely—rather than a property of any particular person. What Scheffler maintains is that the meaningfulness of most pursuits undertaken by people who currently exist is dependent on the afterlife in the specified sense. It is dependent on the fact that, indefinitely into the future, generations of people will continue to emerge.

Scheffler marshals two main thought-experiments in support of his contentions. In the first of these, a person (whom I shall designate as "Minerva") somehow learns that all life on Earth will be wiped out through a collision with a gigantic asteroid thirty days after her death at a normal age. Though Scheffler does not mention King Hezekiah in ancient Judah at all, the situation of Minerva is roughly akin to that of Hezekiah when he is told by God through the prophet Isaiah that all the people and wealth of Judah will be carried away into captivity by the Babylonians not too long after the death of Hezekiah from natural causes (2 Kings 20:14–19; Isaiah 39:5–8). Scheffler prods his readers to contemplate how Minerva would be likely to react to what she has learned. He contends that "few of us would be likely to say, if told that the earth would be destroyed thirty days after our death: 'So what? Since it won't happen until thirty days after my death, and since it won't hasten my death, it isn't of any importance to me. I won't be around to experience it, and so it doesn't matter to me in the slightest'" (2013, 19). Now, admittedly, Hezekiah in the Biblical story does respond with such nonchalance to the revelation from Isaiah (2 Kings 20:19): "Then said Hezekiah to Isaiah, 'The word of the LORD which you have spoken is good.' For he thought, 'Why not, if there will be peace and security in my days?'" However, the calamity foretold to Hezekiah did not come close to involving the destruction of all human beings and other living creatures on Earth, and in any event the reply by Hezekiah to the prophecy of that calamity was probably included by the Biblical author as evidence of the king's moral degeneracy. Scheffler is undoubtedly on a solid footing when he declares that a typical person furnished with knowledge like that of Minerva "would respond to the doomsday scenario with what I will generically call, with bland understatement, profound dismay" (2013, 21). As he further asserts, "[t]he upshot is that many types of projects and activities would no longer seem worth pursuing, or as worth pursuing, if we were confronted with the doomsday scenario" (2013, 25).

Scheffler adduces a second thought-experiment to eliminate some features of the first one that might distract attention from the chief point conveyed by it. Drawing upon the fictional background circumstances depicted in the novel *The Children of Men* by P.D. James (1992), he sketches a scenario in which every human being has somehow become entirely infertile (Scheffler 2013, 38–40). Unlike his first doomsday scenario, this second vignette does not involve any premature or abrupt or violent deaths. It involves simply the gradual but quite rapid extinction of humankind, as individual human beings die of natural causes without any prospect of successors. Procreation has altogether ceased. Scheffler is again persuasive when he muses that "I find it plausible to suppose that such a world would be a world characterized by widespread apathy, anomie, and despair; by the erosion of social institutions and social solidarity; by the deterioration of the physical environment; and by a pervasive loss of conviction about the value or point of many activities" (2013, 40).

Scheffler provides many piquant observations and arguments as he elaborates upon his responses to the thought-experiments which he delineates, and as he convincingly fends off objections that might be posed against those responses. We do not need to delve here into the details of his argumentation and into the subtleties of the many distinctions which he draws. For my purposes, what is most valuable about his book is that it underscores a major facet of the influence of future human beings on people who are currently alive. The fact that future generations will continue to emerge indefinitely is something presupposed by the doings and ambitions and outlooks of people who exist now. Without the prospect of the emergence of those generations indefinitely into the future, countless projects of people now alive would be deprived of their meaningfulness, and countless ambitions harbored and pursued by people now alive would be deprived of their motivatingness. Future generations of people thus serve to impel much of the striving of their predecessors who are living today. Though the future generations do not yet exist, they are pervasively present today as the mainstays that undergird the purposefulness of the lives and endeavors and outlooks of those predecessors.

Let us ponder one additional facet of the influence of unconceived human beings on people who are currently alive. Unconceived people shape the conduct and expectations of people today, not only by imbuing their lives generally with purposefulness but also by inducing various anticipatory adjustments in the conduct and attitudes of the currently living. Such adjustments consist in sacrifices undertaken for future generations. At the level of individuals, those sacrifices can be quite highly specific in their orientation. For example, Juan might endure the hardships of a difficult job so that he can amass sufficient wealth to secure a comfortable upbringing for the children or grandchildren or great-grandchildren whose future existence he envisions. Even before such offspring eventually materialize, their influence has been formatively registered in the preparedness of Juan to undergo adversities for their sake. He will be disposed to brave further hardships for their sake when they do exist in the future, and he is willing to brave hardships for them now in anticipation of their future existence. Because their presence in this fashion is actively felt in advance of their materializing, they are—for the purposes of my reflections on their status as potential holders of claim-rights—assimilable now to the people they will be in the future. Vital is the fact that each expected descendant who does eventually emerge will exist as a human being, most likely as a conscious human being who will develop into an adult of sound mind. That upshot of eventual existence as a human being is what makes the pre-existence of each descendant assimilable to the existence of a potential holder of claim-rights. Were it not for that upshot, the sacrifices endured by Juan for the sake of those future offspring would not warrant the inclusion of those offspring now in the community of potential holders of claim-rights (any more than the solicitude shown by him toward inanimate entities or insentient organisms would warrant the inclusion of *them* in that community).

At a societal or species-wide level, too, the prospect of future generations is sufficient to incline many people to adjust their behavior now in the hope of benefiting those generations through conscientious frugality. Insofar as people today do adopt some degree of abstemiousness in their conduct out of a concern to improve the circumstances in which the generations of the future will live, those successive generations are present now through their eliciting of such adjustments in the lifestyles of the current inhabitants of the world. By inspiring the moral concern that leads to those self-denying adjustments on the part of the current inhabitants, future generations of people are present now as discernible patterns in the actions and aspirations of the currently living. *Pro tanto*, they occupy positions vis-à-vis the currently living that are cognate with the positions which they will occupy vis-à-vis one another when they have eventually materialized. People in any given society endure hardships for the sake of one another as they interact, and likewise many people at any given time endure hardships for the sake of successive generations—at a societal or species-wide level as well as at an individualized level. Those successive generations are ethically assimilable now to the living people they will become.

In several prominent respects, then, future generations of people are present now as influences on the fortunes and activities and purposefulness of people who are currently alive. Because the future generations are present today in those forms, they are included today in the loose-knit community of potential holders of claim-rights. Just as dead people for certain periods are members of that community despite the fact that they no longer exist, so too the future generations are members of that community despite the fact that they do not yet exist. Of course, the inclusion of future generations of people in the class of potential holders of claim-rights does not in itself mean that the future generations actually hold any extensive moral claim-rights or that they should hold any extensive legal claim-rights. Once again, the distinction between non-justificatory matters and justificatory matters is crucial. My discussion in this subsection has been addressing the former matters; specifically, it has been addressing the non-justificatory question whether future generations of people are ethically assimilable now to the living people they will become. I have argued that those generations are indeed present now in ethically significant ways through their influence on the actions and outlooks and striving of people who are alive today. Still, although my affirmative answer to that non-justificatory question does not per se entail any verdicts on justificatory matters about the extent to which or the ways in which the interests of future generations of people should be furthered through the imposition of legal duties on people who are currently alive, the considerations that underpin my affirmative answer—especially the considerations adduced by Scheffler—very likely do warrant the imposition of some stringent legal duties that will inherently protect the interests of those future generations.

5.5.2.8.2 When Are the Claim-Rights of Future Generations Held?

Any claim-right is always strictly coterminous with the duty to which it correlates. Neither of those positions can ever exist at any time *t* unless the other position likewise exists at *t*. Hence, if any moral duties or legal duties that inherently protect various interests of future generations of people are incumbent now on human beings who are currently alive, the correlative claim-rights held by the future people are existent now. Some readers might balk at the notion that claim-rights can be held now by people who do not yet exist. However, any air of mystery or imponderability is dispelled when we recall something that has been emphasized in the second paragraph of §5.5.2.7 above. That is, we should recall that the holding of a claim-right is a relational property. It is relevantly similar to the relational property of being spoken about by somebody else. If I speak about Ronald Reagan at some time *t*, he acquires at *t* the property of being spoken about by me then. He has gained that property posthumously rather than at any point during his lifetime. Similarly, if I speak at *t* about my first grandson who is born thirty years later, then he at *t* acquires the property of being spoken about by me then. He does not acquire that property thirty years later, long after I have desisted from talking about him and have perhaps died. Of course, at *t* I am not able to refer to him *de re*; any reference to him at that time has to be *de dicto*. I cannot pick out at *t* a particular person who does not yet exist then. In that regard, my speaking about my future grandson is different from my speaking about Ronald Reagan. Whereas I can refer to Reagan either *de dicto* or *de re*, I cannot refer to my future first grandson in the latter fashion. Even so, I can perfectly well refer to my future first grandson *de dicto*, such that my assertions will be applicable to anyone who eventually occupies the status designated by the phrase "Matthew Kramer's future first grandson."

Like the property of being spoken about by somebody else, the property of holding a claim-right is a relational property. Somebody who has not yet been conceived can partake of that property. As has been noted at the outset of §5.5.2.7, the relationship involved in the holding of a claim-right—a relationship of inherent protection between a duty borne by some party and a typically on-balance advantageous aspect of the situation of some other party, who holds a correlative claim-right—is articulated by my Interest Theory of right-holding. When unconceived people hold claim-rights vis-à-vis people who are currently alive, the latter people owe duties to the former. Although the holders of the claim-rights and the bearers of the duties are not contemporaneous, the holding of the claim-rights and the bearing of the duties are contemporaneous. Precisely because the duties are owed now, the claim-rights are held now. Each duty is owed when and only when its correlative claim-right is held. A duty is owed by some party P to a future person Q at *t* if and only if a duty incumbent on P at *t* is inherently protective of some aspect of Q's situation that is typically advantageous on balance for somebody like Q, who consequently at *t* holds a claim-right correlative to the duty.

As is evident, some assertions about the vesting of claim-rights in not-yet-existent people will turn out to be unfounded, in that the envisaged people—to whom the ascriptions of the claim-rights refer *de dicto*—never materialize. In such circumstances the ascriptions of those claim-rights are false or else are neither true nor false, like statements which assert that the current King of France is bald. Still, many intelligible statements about the future are vulnerable in this respect to being falsified or to being rendered truth-inapt. For instance, if Pamela says that everyone who patronizes her restaurant on the opening night will enjoy the exotic new dishes which she has devised, and if nobody in fact shows up at the restaurant on that opening night, then the prediction by Pamela has proved to be false or else has proved to be neither true nor false. Difficulties along these lines are by no means confined to statements which affirm that various unconceived people hold claim-rights. Assertions about people who will patronize a restaurant on a certain night are not rendered enigmatically unintelligible by the fact that such assertions will turn out to be unfounded if the restaurant in question does not attract any customers on that night. Similarly, statements about the holding of claim-rights now by unconceived people are not rendered enigmatically unintelligible through the fact that such statements will prove to be unfounded if there never materialize the unconceived people whose eventual existence is presupposed by the statements. To be sure, Pamela's prediction is about something that will occur in the future, whereas a statement which ascribes to unconceived people certain claim-rights that correlate with duties borne now by individuals or organizations is about the holding of those claim-rights now. Notwithstanding, what Pamela's prediction and the statement about the holding of claim-rights by unconceived people have in common is their susceptibility to being falsified or to being rendered truth-inapt through future developments. (Worth noting also is that the general sorts of difficulties recounted in this paragraph are not limited to statements about the future. If Drucilla says that the first customer who patronized Pamela's restaurant last week received a free bottle of wine, and if in fact nobody showed up as a customer last week at the restaurant—unbeknownst to Drucilla—her pronouncement about the receipt of a free bottle of wine is false, or else it is neither true nor false.)

Complexities of the kind recounted in the preceding paragraph largely disappear when we shift from the level of individuals or small groups to a societal or species-wide level. At the latter level, there is a markedly lower probability that any ascriptions of claim-rights will be falsified or rendered truth-inapt as a result of the inexistence of the party or parties to whom the claim-rights are ascribed. After all, when claim-rights are ascribed to the not-yet-existent people who in the future will make up a country or the whole of the human species as the members thereof, the likelihood of the inexistence of the country or the species is far lower than the likelihood of the inexistence of any individual who fits the description "Matthew Kramer's future first grandson" or the description "someone who will be a customer at Pamela's restaurant next week." Admittedly, even at the level of the human species, the likelihood is not zero. A gigantic asteroid might collide with the planet Earth, or some other extinction-inducing catastrophe might occur. Still, although the occurrence of such a catastrophe is not impossible, it is far less likely than a situation in which no grandson is ever descended from me or in which nobody turns up as a customer at Pamela's restaurant next week.

5.5.2.8.3 Universal Quantification in the Holding of Claim-Rights

In the preceding paragraph, we have shifted our attention from the level of individuals or small groups to the level of a society or the human species. At the latter level, universal quantification is clearly involved in the owing of duties and the holding of their correlative claim-rights, but we should here briefly mull over the specifics of that universal quantification. In many cases a moral or legal duty D is such that the holder of a correlative claim-right is a society as a whole or the human species as a whole, even though not every member of the society or species holds a homologous claim-right. A deontic relationship of that kind obtains where the existence of D inherently protects some aspect of the situation of a society or of the human species that is typically advantageous on balance, and where the inherent protection bestowed by D is typically beneficial on balance for a preponderance of the members of the society or of the species but not for every member. In such circumstances, two main types of quantification are involved in the holding of the relevant claim-rights. First, D is correlated with the claim-right held by the society or the species through aggregative universal quantification. That is, a proposition ascribing D to the current bearer(s) of that duty entails—and is entailed by—a proposition ascribing to the society or species a correlative claim-right, where the latter ascription treats the society or species as a collective entity by universally quantifying over its members in an aggregative fashion. (My next two paragraphs will say more about the aggregative universal quantification.) Second, through distributive pleonotetic quantification, D is correlated with a claim-right held by each member of the society or species for whom the inherent protection bestowed by D is typically beneficial on balance. That is, a proposition ascribing D to the current bearer(s) of that duty entails—and is entailed by—a proposition ascribing to each such typically benefited member of the society or species a correlative claim-right, where the latter ascription pleonotetically quantifies in a distributive manner over a domain that comprises every member of the society or species.

When the party to whom we ascribe a claim-right correlated with D is a society as a whole, the aggregative universal quantification involved in the ascription is very much in keeping with what has been said about collectivities as holders of claim-rights in §3.2.1.2 of Chapter 3. In other words, the society is a collectivity with governmental institutions and other institutions that constitute its status as a group agent. That status is reflected in the fact that the society is recognized as an overarching unit by the aforementioned ascription of a claim-right correlated with D—an ascription that universally quantifies over the society's members in an aggregative fashion. By contrast, when the party that holds a claim-right correlated with D is the human species as a whole, the status of that party as an overarching unit is more tenuous than the status of either a group agent or a coalition (the two types of collectivities discussed in §3.2.1.2). Although diverse international institutions coordinate the activities and policies of countries on quite a number of issues, those institutions are too rudimentary and scattered to constitute a global system of governance, and they fall short of encompassing the whole of the human species within their regulatory reach. Any characterization of the human species as a group agent would be overblown. Nor is the human species even a coalition of the sort envisioned in §3.2.1.2, for the members of a coalition act concertedly to achieve some shared aim(s). Instead, the human species is a community in the attenuated sense attached to that notion by this chapter when I have styled the class of potential holders of claim-rights as a community. In other words, the human species is a collective entity not only biologically but also ethically in that any of its members who can understand the existence of the species as such are morally obligated to acknowledge their commonality with the other members thereof. They are morally obligated to acknowledge the commonality because any denial of it by them—any denial of the truth of the Terentian epigram which I have invoked at the end of §5.5.2.4 above—would degrade not only their fellow members of the species but also themselves in an ignominious display of insecurity about their own strengths and distinctiveness. By dismissing the significance of the humanity which so saliently aligns them with the other members of the species, they would demean themselves as beings who partake of that humanity. They would thus run athwart the paramount moral obligation of each person to strive for the conditions under which everyone in a society can be warranted in feeling a strong sense of self-respect.

Whether at the level of a society or at the level of the whole human species, the aggregative universal quantification contemplated here is importantly different in one further regard from the aggregative universal quantification contemplated in §3.2.1.2. Here we are concentrating on collectivities in their future incarnations rather than in their current incarnations. Accordingly, here the quantification in any given context ranges over a domain comprising the future members of a society or the future members of humankind. Because those members do not yet exist as particular beings, the inclusion of each of them in that domain has to be effected through a placeholder designation. That is, because the specification of the domain cannot refer to each of the future members *de re*, it has to refer to each of them *de dicto* through a placeholder description such as "a human being at *t*, arbitrarily classified as *n*." Here the "*t*" variable is filled in for each designation as a specified time in the future, and the "*n*" variable is filled in for each designation as a particular number. Each member of a society or of the human species at the specified time can then be arbitrarily assigned to a unique numerical value for "*n*," which will distinguish him or her from everyone else at that time. The beings in the domain over which the quantification ranges are human beings (rather than possibilities of human beings), but they are differentiated one from another in a placeholder fashion through designations that bespeak their current inexistence.

Let us close this discussion of quantification by briefly considering any state of affairs where a moral or legal duty D is such that a correlative claim-right is held by a society as a whole or the human species as a whole, and where additionally a correlative claim-right is held by every member of the society or species. A deontic relationship of that kind obtains where the existence of D inherently protects some aspect of the situation of a society or the situation of the human species that is typically advantageous on balance, and where the inherent protection bestowed by D is also typically beneficial on balance for the situation of every member of the society or of the species. In such circumstances, two types of universal quantification are involved in the holding of the relevant claim-rights. Once again, of course, the correlation between D and the claim-right vested in the society or species as a whole is structured by aggregative universal quantification. Once again, a proposition ascribing D to the current bearer(s) of that duty entails—and is entailed by—a proposition ascribing to the society or species a correlative claim-right, where the latter ascription treats the society or species as a collective entity by universally quantifying over its members in an aggregative fashion. However, the aggregative universal quantification involved in the holding of a correlative claim-right by the society or species is co-occurrent here with the distributive universal quantification involved in the holding of a correlative claim-right by every member of the society or species. A proposition ascribing D to the current bearer(s) of that duty entails—and is entailed by—a proposition ascribing to every member of the society or species a correlative claim-right. Hence, whereas aggregative universal quantification is co-occurrent with distributive *pleonotetic* quantification in any circumstances of the sort broached by the first paragraph of this subsection, aggregative universal quantification is co-occurrent with distributive *universal* quantification in any circumstances of the sort broached by this paragraph.

5.5.2.8.4 The Non-Identity Conundrum?

Readers familiar with the work of Derek Parfit might worry that, insofar as we ascribe to future people various claim-rights which those people hold now as the correlates of currently existing duties, we will run afoul of the non-identity problem that was brilliantly highlighted by Parfit in the final main Part of his *Reasons and Persons* (1984, 351–79). As a prolegomenon to mulling over some cruxes in the philosophy of population ethics, Parfit highlighted the ways in which changes in the world at certain junctures would lead to significant changes at later junctures. After presenting a certain thesis about the sameness of a person across possible worlds, Parfit concluded that major alterations in the behavior of people during a certain period of time would bring about some far-reaching alterations in the world at subsequent periods to such an extent that the individuals who come into existence during those considerably later periods will not be the same as the individuals who would have come into existence then if the alterations during the earlier period had not occurred. Parfit's reflections have engrossed population ethicists and environmental ethicists for the past several decades, but here my concern with those reflections is naturally focused instead on the question whether future generations of people can hold claim-rights now.

Whenever we apply the Interest Theory of right-holding to ascertain whether some party P holds a claim-right with a certain content, we have to engage explicitly or implicitly in an evaluative comparison. Whether explicitly or implicitly, we have to compare the situation of P in the presence of some specified duty D and the situation of P in the absence of D. If and only if the content of D is such that it cannot be fulfilled without affecting P's situation in some way that is typically beneficial on balance for anybody like P, P holds a claim-right correlative to D. For P, then, a world containing D is typically better than an otherwise indistinguishable world that does not contain D. Let us now assume that D is a legal duty of which the fulfillment will momentously affect the climatic conditions wherein future generations of people will live. When somebody invokes Parfit's non-identity problem to impugn the notion that claim-rights correlative to D can be held at present by future generations of people, he or she is presumably contending that the requisite comparison between a world that currently contains D and an otherwise similar world that currently lacks D is not meaningful—since the current presence or absence of D, as a legal duty of far-reaching import when regularly heeded and effectuated, will sweepingly affect the identities of the people in the future generations who are said to hold currently existent claim-rights correlative to D. Hence, somebody who adverts in this context to the non-identity problem will be complaining that we cannot compare like with like when we ponder whether future generations of people hold claim-rights at present that are correlative to D.

Such a worry is baseless, however, for two reasons. First, as has already been indicated, the holding of claim-rights by future generations of people will involve aggregative universal quantification. Claim-rights are held by a future generation as an overarching collective entity, or by future generations as successions of overarching collective entities. A proposition affirming the existence of D entails (and is entailed by) a proposition affirming that a legal claim-right correlative to D is vested in each future generation as an overarching entity. Because the individuals who make up any future generations do not yet exist as such, the aggregative universal quantification involved in treating any future generation as a collective unit is operative over a domain whose members are differentiated one from another through placeholder designations of the sort which I have delineated in the penultimate paragraph of §5.5.2.8.3. Those designations leave entirely unspecified the identities of the members, whose identities do not yet exist. Hence, claim-rights vested in each future generation *en masse* are not rendered imponderable at all by Parfit's non-identity problem.

Second, even when ascriptions of claim-rights held by future people are focused on the level of individuals rather than on the level of future generations as overarching entities, the ascriptions are undamaged by the non-identity problem. If legal duties are incumbent now on human beings to undertake far-reaching adjustments in their behavior that will inherently affect the situations of future people in ways that are typically advantageous on balance, legal claim-rights correlative to those duties are vested now in the not-yet-existent people whose interests are inherently protected by the duties. What we can infer from Parfit's ruminations on the non-identity problem is that, if those legal duties had *not* been incumbent on human beings and heeded by human beings at present, the people who would have come into existence in the future would be different from the people who will actually come into existence (given that the duties are actually incumbent on human beings and heeded by human beings at present). Hence, the existence of those legal duties at present is in two respects inherently promotive of the interests of the future people who currently hold legal claim-rights correlative to those duties. It inherently protects the interests of those people in good climatic conditions and other good environmental conditions for their eventual lives on Earth, and it also serves to ensure that they rather than alternative possible people are the ones who will actually materialize to lead such lives. Accordingly, by the reckoning of the Interest Theory of right-holding, those future people are straightforwardly now the holders of legal claim-rights correlated with the aforementioned legal duties.

Of course what can also be inferred from Parfit's ruminations is that, if those legal duties were *not* incumbent on human beings now to undertake far-reaching adjustments in their behavior that will inherently affect the situations of future people in ways that are typically advantageous on balance—and if consequently no such adjustments were to occur—the interests of the people who would come into existence in the future would thereby be "protected." Their interests would be "protected" because the non-existence of the duties and the non-occurrence of the behavioral alterations would mean that over time the people coming into existence would be different from the people who will in fact come into existence in the actual world where the wide-ranging legal duties do exist and where the commensurately wide-ranging behavioral alterations do occur. Since the people who would come into existence in the counterfactual world would benefit on balance by so doing in comparison with their never existing at all, they would on balance be better off through the absence of any wide-ranging legal duties in place now for the benefit of future generations. Even so, although the future people who would eventually materialize would thereby on balance be made better off than they are as never-existent people in the actual world, the "protection" conferred upon them by the absence of the wide-ranging legal duties would not be deontic in character. It would not be correlated with any legal duties, since no relevant legal duties would obtain. It therefore would not consist in any legal claim-rights, since there would not be any legal duties with which the claim-rights would be correlated. In sum, the only circumstances in which future generations of people currently hold legal claim-rights are circumstances in which some legal duties currently require human beings to undertake far-reaching adjustments in their behavior that will inherently affect the situations of future people in ways that are typically advantageous on balance. In the absence of such duties, no correlated legal claim-rights are held now by future generations—even though the absence of such duties can constitute the strange sort of "protection" described in this paragraph.

5.6 A Laconic Conclusion

This chapter has had to omit quite a few fascinating issues that pertain to the occupancy of Hohfeldian positions by parties of various kinds. Such omissions have been inevitable as the chapter has concentrated on the potential holding of claim-rights. An exploration of the occupancy of other Hohfeldian positions (including the bearing of duties by parties of various kinds) would require at least one further long chapter. Still, notwithstanding the omissions, this chapter has endeavored to plumb the deep moral matters to which any satisfactory account of rights and right-holding must address itself. In that regard, Chapter 5 has fittingly brought to a close this book as a whole. My meditations on rights and right-holding have tackled some knotty analytical and logical questions but have also tackled some complicated ethical questions. Those topics have been interwoven throughout this volume, even while topics of one kind have predominated at certain junctures whereas topics of a different kind have predominated at other junctures. An enquiry into the nature of rights and right-holding has to be variegated, because the phenomena under investigation are themselves highly variegated—as the Hohfeldian table serves to accentuate. Moreover, the diverse strands of such an enquiry are interwoven because the phenomena under investigation are themselves intricately interrelated. We have seen as much in every chapter, where I have time and again drawn attention to the interdependence between a full exposition of the Hohfeldian analysis and a full defense of the Interest Theory of right-holding. Furthermore, in the current chapter even more clearly than in any previous chapters, we have found that my answers to the non-justificatory questions addressed by this volume are partly dependent on my answers to some of the justificatory questions which I have addressed in several of my other books. At the same time, they are also partly dependent on some of the technical points of logic developed in Chapters 2 and 3. *Rights and Right-Holding* is a complex assemblage of analytical theses and ethical theses brought together to illuminate the matters encapsulated in the book's title.

References

Aas, Sean. 2020. “Some Notes on the Nature and Limits of Posthumous Rights: A Response to Persad.” 46 *Journal of Medical Ethics* 345–6.
Adams, David. 1985. “Hohfeld on Rights and Privileges.” 71 *ARSP: Archiv für Rechts- und Sozialphilosophie* 84–95.
Alchourrón, Carlos and Bulygin, Eugenio. 1971. *Normative Systems*. Vienna: Springer-Verlag.
Altham, J.E.J. 1991. “Plural and Pleonotetic Quantification.” In Harry Lewis (ed.), *Peter Geach: Philosophical Encounters*. Dordrecht: Springer, pp 105–19.
Anderson, Alan Ross. 1962. “Logic, Norms, and Roles.” 4 *Ratio* 36–49.
Anscombe, G.E.M. 1958. “Modern Moral Philosophy.” 33 *Philosophy* 1–19.
Bahn, Paul. 1984. “Do Not Disturb? Archaeology and the Rights of the Dead.” 1 *Journal of Applied Philosophy* 213–25.
Baier, Annette. 1981. “The Rights of Past and Future Persons.” In Ernest Partridge (ed.), *Responsibilities to Future Generations*. Buffalo, NY: Prometheus Books, pp 171–83.
Bandman, Bertram. 1982. “Do Future Generations Have the Right to Breathe Clean Air?” 10 *Political Theory* 95–102.
Barkham, Patrick. 2021. “Should Rivers Have the Same Rights as People?” *The Observer*, July 25, 2021. URL = https://www.theguardian.com/environment/2021/jul/25/rivers-around-the-world-rivers-are-gaining-the-same-legal-rights-as-people.
Beckerman, Wilfred and Pasek, Joanna. 2001. *Justice, Posterity, and the Environment*. Oxford: Oxford University Press.
Bekoff, Marc and Pierce, Jessica. 2009. *Wild Justice: The Moral Lives of Animals*. Chicago, IL: University of Chicago Press.
Bell, Derek. 2011. “Does Anthropogenic Climate Change Violate Human Rights?” 14 *Critical Review of International Social and Political Philosophy* 99–124.
Belliotti, Raymond. 1979. “Do Dead Human Beings Have Rights?” 60 *The Personalist* 201–10.
Benditt, Theodore. 1978. *Law as Rule and Principle*. Hassocks: Harvester Press.
Berg, Jessica. 2007. “Of Elephants and Embryos: A Proposed Framework for Legal Personhood.” 59 *Hastings Law Journal* 369–406.
Biasetti, Pierfrancesco. 2014. “Rights, Duties, and Moral Conflicts.” 16 *Ethics & Politics* 1042–62.
Bobbitt, Philip. 2008. *Terror and Consent*. London: Allen Lane.
Boonin, David. 2019. *Dead Wrong: The Ethics of Posthumous Harm*. Oxford: Oxford University Press.
Bowen, Joseph. 2022. “The Interest Theory of Rights at the Margins: Posthumous Rights.” In Visa Kurki and Mark McBride (eds), *Without Trimmings: The Legal, Political, and Moral Philosophy of Matthew Kramer*. Oxford: Oxford University Press, pp 51–71.
Brännmark, Johan. 2016. “Future Generations as Right-Holders.” 19 *Critical Review of International Social and Political Philosophy* 680–98.
Brecher, Bob. 2002. “Our Obligation to the Dead.” 19 *Journal of Applied Philosophy* 109–19.
Bruhl, Aaron-Andrew. 2002. “Justice Unconceived: How Posterity Has Rights.” 14 *Yale Journal of Law and the Humanities* 393–439.
Bulygin, Eugenio. 2013. “Kelsen on the Completeness and Consistency of Law.” In Luis Duarte d’Almeida, John Gardner, and Leslie Green (eds), *Kelsen Revisited*. Oxford: Hart Publishing, pp 225–43.
Callahan, Joan. 1987. “On Harming the Dead.” 97 *Ethics* 341–52.
Carruthers, Peter. 1992. *The Animals Issue*. Cambridge: Cambridge University Press.
Carter, Ian. 1999. *A Measure of Freedom*. Oxford: Oxford University Press.

Carter, Ian. 2011. "Respect and the Basis of Equality." 121 *Ethics* 538–71.
Chopra, Samir and White, Laurence. 2011. *A Legal Theory for Autonomous Artificial Agents*. Ann Arbor, MI: University of Michigan Press.
Cohen, G.A. 1983. "The Structure of Proletarian Unfreedom." 12 *Philosophy and Public Affairs* 3–33.
Conee, Earl. 1982. "Against Moral Dilemmas." 91 *Philosophical Review* 87–97.
Cornell, Nicolas. 2015. "Wrongs, Rights, and Third Parties." 43 *Philosophy and Public Affairs* 109–43.
Cruft, Rowan. 2019. *Human Rights, Ownership, and the Individual*. Oxford: Oxford University Press.
Cruft, Rowan. 2022. "Rights, Positivism, and the Vice of Self-Puffery: Why Kramer's Interest Theory Is Nearly Right." In Mark McBride and Visa Kurki (eds), *Without Trimmings: The Legal, Moral, and Political Philosophy of Matthew Kramer*. Oxford: Oxford University Press, pp 36–49.
Cupp Jr, Richard. 2009. "Moving beyond Animal Rights: A Legal/Contractualist Critique." 46 *San Diego Law Review* 27–84.
Curzer, Howard. 2006. "Admirable Immorality, Dirty Hands, Ticking Bombs, and Torturing Innocents." 44 *Southern Journal of Philosophy* 31–56.
Da Silva, Michael. 2015. "On Barbara Baum Levenbook's 'Harming Someone after His Death.'" 125 *Ethics* 1160–3.
De George, Richard. 1981. "The Environment, Rights, and Future Generations." In Ernest Partridge (ed.), *Responsibilities to Future Generations*. Buffalo, NY: Prometheus Books, pp 157–66.
De Marneffe, Peter. 2010. *Liberalism and Prostitution*. Oxford: Oxford University Press.
De-Shalit, Avner. 1992. "Community and the Rights of Future Generations." 9 *Journal of Applied Philosophy* 105–15.
De-Shalit, Avner. 1995. *Why Posterity Matters*. London: Routledge.
Donohue, Laura. 2022. "Correlation and Constitutional Rights." In Mark McBride and Visa Kurki (eds), *Without Trimmings: The Legal, Moral, and Political Philosophy of Matthew Kramer*. Oxford: Oxford University Press, pp 3–36.
Dowding, Keith. 2011. "Republican Freedom, Rights, and the Coalition Problem." 10 *Politics, Philosophy & Economics* 301–22.
Duarte d'Almeida, Luis. 2016. "Fundamental Legal Concepts: The Hohfeldian Framework." 11/10 *Philosophy Compass* 554–69.
Duckler, Geordie. 2008. "Two Major Flaws of the Animal Rights Movement." 14 *Animal Law* 179–200.
Düwell, Marcus and Bos, Gerhard. 2016. "Human Rights and Future People—Possibilities of Argumentation." 15 *Journal of Human Rights* 231–50.
Duxbury, Neil. 1995. *Patterns of American Jurisprudence*. Oxford: Oxford University Press.
Dworkin, Ronald. 1978. *Taking Rights Seriously*. Cambridge, MA: Harvard University Press.
Dworkin, Ronald. 1993. *Life's Dominion*. New York, NY: Alfred Knopf.
Dworkin, Ronald. 2006. *Justice in Robes*. Cambridge, MA: Harvard University Press.
Dworkin, Ronald. 2011. *Justice for Hedgehogs*. Cambridge, MA: Harvard University Press.
Earl, Dennis. 2011. "Ontology and the Paradox of Future Generations." 3 *Public Reason* 60–72.
Edmundson, William. 2012. *An Introduction to Rights*. Second Edition. Cambridge: Cambridge University Press.
Eleftheriadis, Pavlos. 2008. *Legal Rights*. Oxford: Oxford University Press.
Elliot, Robert. 1989. "The Rights of Future People." 6 *Journal of Applied Philosophy* 159–69.
Erk, Christian. 2017. *Moral Philosophy*. Neunkirchen-Seelscheid: Editiones Scholasticae.
Fabre, Cécile. 2008. "Posthumous Rights." In Matthew Kramer, Claire Grant, Ben Colburn, and Antony Hatzistavrou (eds), *The Legacy of H.L.A. Hart*. Oxford: Oxford University Press, pp 225–38.
Fabre, Cécile. 2009. "Preconception Rights." In Stephen de Wijze, Matthew Kramer, and Ian Carter (eds), *Hillel Steiner and the Anatomy of Justice*. New York, NY: Routledge, pp 53–69.

Feinberg, Joel. 1970. "The Nature and Value of Rights." 4 *Journal of Value Inquiry* 243–60.
Feinberg, Joel. 1973. *Social Philosophy*. Englewood Cliffs, NJ: Prentice-Hall.
Feinberg, Joel. 1974. "The Rights of Animals and Unborn Generations." In William Blackstone (ed.), *Philosophy and Environmental Crisis*. Athens, GA: University of Georgia Press, 43–68.
Feinberg, Joel. 1980. *Rights, Justice, and the Bounds of Liberty*. Princeton, NJ: Princeton University Press.
Feinberg, Joel. 1984. *Harm to Others*. Oxford: Oxford University Press.
Ferraro, Francesco. 2022. "Utility, Predictability, and Rights: Bentham's Utilitarianism and Constitutional Entitlements." 35 *Ratio Juris* 38–54.
Finnis, John. 1972. "Some Professorial Fallacies about Rights." 4 *Adelaide Law Review* 377–88.
Fitch, Frederic. 1967. "A Revision of Hohfeld's Theory of Legal Concepts." 10 *Logique et Analyse* 269–76.
Flathman, Richard. 1976. *The Practice of Rights*. Cambridge: Cambridge University Press.
Fraassen, Bas van. 1973. "Values and the Heart's Command." 70 *Journal of Philosophy* 5–19.
Fuller, Lon. 1969. *The Morality of Law*. Revised Edition. New Haven, CT: Yale University Press.
Geach, P.T. 1980. *Logic Matters*. Berkeley and Los Angeles, CA: University of California Press.
Geras, Norman. 2009. "Games and Meanings." In Stephen de Wijze, Matthew Kramer, and Ian Carter (eds), *Hillel Steiner and the Anatomy of Justice*. New York & London: Routledge, pp 185–200.
Gilbert, Margaret. 2018. *Rights and Demands*. Oxford: Oxford University Press.
Glannon, Walter. 2001. "Persons, Lives, and Posthumous Harms." 32 *Journal of Social Philosophy* 127–42.
Goldberg, John and Zipursky, Benjamin. 2022. "Hohfeldian Analysis and the Separation of Rights and Powers." In Shyamkrishna Balganesh, Ted Sichelman, and Henry Smith (eds), *Wesley Hohfeld a Century Later*. Cambridge: Cambridge University Press, pp 366–85.
Gosseries, Axel. 2008. "On Future Generations' Future Rights." 16 *Journal of Political Philosophy* 446–74.
Graham, Paul. 1996. "The Will Theory of Rights: A Defence." 15 *Law and Philosophy* 257–70.
Green, Michael. 2021. "Permissions, Deontic Voids, and the Karamazov Argument." 66 *American Journal of Jurisprudence* 291–307.
Griffith, Aaron. 2017. "The Rights of Future Persons and the Ontology of Time." 48 *Journal of Social Philosophy* 58–70.
Griffith, Aaron. 2018. "Intergenerational Rights and the Problem of Cross-Temporal Relations." 83 *Erkenntnis* 693–710.
Grisez, Germain. 1970. *Abortion: The Myths, the Realities, and the Arguments*. New York, NY: Corpus Books.
Gross, Oren. 2004. "Are Torture Warrants Warranted? Pragmatic Absolutism and Official Disobedience." 88 *Minnesota Law Review* 1481–555.
Grover, Dorothy. 1989. "Posthumous Harm." 39 *Philosophical Quarterly* 334–53.
Halpin, Andrew. 1997. *Rights and Law: Analysis and Theory*. Oxford: Hart Publishing.
Halpin, Andrew. 2019. "Choosing Axioms of Correlativity." 64 *American Journal of Jurisprudence* 225–58.
Halpin, Andrew. 2020. "No-Right and Its Correlative." 65 *American Journal of Jurisprudence* 147–66.
Hare, R.M. 1972. "Rules of War and Moral Reasoning." 1 *Philosophy and Public Affairs* 166–81.
Hare, R.M. 1981. *Moral Thinking*. Oxford: Oxford University Press.
Hare, R.M. 1989. *Essays in Ethical Theory*. Oxford: Oxford University Press.
Hart, H.L.A. 1955. "Are There Any Natural Rights?" 64 *Philosophical Review* 175–91.
Hart, H.L.A. 1982. *Essays on Bentham*. Oxford: Oxford University Press.
Hart, H.L.A. 1994. *The Concept of Law*. Second Edition. Oxford: Oxford University Press.
Hartney, Michael. 1991. "Some Confusions Concerning Collective Rights." 4 *Canadian Journal of Law and Jurisprudence* 293–314.
Heinze, Eric. 2003. *The Logic of Liberal Rights*. London: Routledge.

Herstein, Ori. 2009. "The Identity and (Legal) Rights of Future Generations." 77 *George Washington Law Review* 1173–215.
Hill, Thomas. 1996. "Moral Dilemmas, Gaps, and Residues: A Kantian Perspective." In H. E. Mason (ed.), *Moral Dilemmas and Moral Theory*. Oxford: Oxford University Press, pp 167–98.
Himma, Kenneth. 2007. "Assessing the Prohibition against Torture." In Steven Lee (ed.), *Intervention, Terrorism, and Torture: Contemporary Challenges to Just War Theory*. Dordrecht: Springer, pp 235–48.
Hiskes, Richard. 2009. *The Human Right to a Green Future*. Cambridge: Cambridge University Press.
Hohfeld, Wesley. 1923. *Fundamental Legal Conceptions*. New Haven, CT: Yale University Press.
Holton, Richard. 2002. "Principles and Particularisms." 76 *Aristotelian Society Supplementary Volume* 191–209.
Holton, Richard. 2010. "The Exception Proves the Rule." 18 *Journal of Political Philosophy* 369–88.
Hughes, G.E. and Cresswell, M.J. 1996. *A New Introduction to Modal Logic*. London: Routledge.
Hull, N.E.H. 1997. *Roscoe Pound and Karl Llewellyn*. Chicago, IL: University of Chicago Press.
Hurd, Heidi and Moore, Michael. 2018. "The Hohfeldian Analysis of Rights." 63 *American Journal of Jurisprudence* 295–354.
Hurd, Heidi and Moore, Michael. 2019. "Replying to Halpin and Kramer: Disagreements and No-Agreements." 64 *American Journal of Jurisprudence* 259–74.
Hurka, Thomas. 1987. "Why Value Autonomy?" 13 *Social Theory and Practice* 361–82.
Husik, Isaac. 1924. "Hohfeld's Jurisprudence." 72 *University of Pennsylvania Law Review* 263–77.
Huss, Rebecca. 2002. "Valuing Man's and Woman's Best Friend: The Moral and Legal Status of Companion Animals." 86 *Marquette Law Review* 47–106.
James, P.D. 1992. *The Children of Men*. London: Faber and Faber.
James, Susan. 2003. "Rights as Enforceable Claims." 103 *Proceedings of the Aristotelian Society* 133–47.
Jones, Peter. 1994. *Rights*. Basingstoke: Macmillan Press.
Kanger, Stig and Kanger, Helle. 1966. "Rights and Parliamentarism." 32 *Theoria* 85–115.
Kelch, Thomas. 1999. "The Role of the Rational and the Emotive in a Theory of Animal Rights." 27 *Boston College Environmental Affairs Law Review* 1–42.
Kelsen, Hans. 1945. *General Theory of Law and State*. Translated by Anders Wedberg. Cambridge, MA: Harvard University Press.
Kelsen, Hans. 1967. *Pure Theory of Law*. Translated by Max Knight. Berkeley, CA: University of California Press.
Kennedy, Duncan and Michelman, Frank. 1980. "Are Property and Contract Efficient?" 8 *Hofstra Law Review* 711–70.
Kocourek, Albert. 1922. "Non-Legal-Content Relations." 4 *Illinois Law Quarterly* 233–9.
Kramer, Matthew. 1991. *Legal Theory, Political Theory, and Deconstruction*. Bloomington, IN: Indiana University Press.
Kramer, Matthew. 1997. *John Locke and the Origins of Private Property*. Cambridge: Cambridge University Press.
Kramer, Matthew. 1998. "Rights without Trimmings." In Matthew Kramer, N. E. Simmonds, and Hillel Steiner, *A Debate over Rights*. Oxford: Oxford University Press, pp 7–111.
Kramer, Matthew. 1999. *In Defense of Legal Positivism*. Oxford: Oxford University Press.
Kramer, Matthew. 2000. "On the Nature of Legal Rights." 59 *Cambridge Law Journal* 473–508.
Kramer, Matthew. 2001. "Getting Rights Rights." In Matthew Kramer (ed.), *Rights, Wrongs, and Responsibilities*. Basingstoke: Palgrave Macmillan, pp 28–95.
Kramer, Matthew. 2003. *The Quality of Freedom*. Oxford: Oxford University Press.
Kramer, Matthew. 2004. *Where Law and Morality Meet*. Oxford: Oxford University Press.
Kramer, Matthew. 2005. "Moral Rights and the Limits of the 'Ought'-Implies-'Can' Principle: Why Impeccable Precautions Are No Excuse." 48 *Inquiry* 307–55.
Kramer, Matthew. 2007. *Objectivity and the Rule of Law*. Cambridge: Cambridge University Press.

Kramer, Matthew. 2008. "Rights in Legal and Political Philosophy." In Keith Whittington, Daniel Kelemen, and Gregory Caldeira (eds), *The Oxford Handbook of Law and Politics*. Oxford: Oxford University Press, pp 414–27.
Kramer, Matthew. 2009a. *Moral Realism as a Moral Doctrine*. Oxford: Wiley-Blackwell.
Kramer, Matthew. 2009b. "Consistency is Hardly Ever Enough: Reflections on Hillel Steiner's Methodology." In Stephen de Wijze, Matthew Kramer, and Ian Carter (eds), *Hillel Steiner and the Anatomy of Justice*. New York, NY: Routledge, pp 201–13.
Kramer, Matthew. 2010. "Refining the Interest Theory of Rights." 55 *American Journal of Jurisprudence* 31–9.
Kramer, Matthew. 2011. *The Ethics of Capital Punishment*. Oxford: Oxford University Press.
Kramer, Matthew. 2012. "What Is Legal Philosophy?" 43 *Metaphilosophy* 125–34.
Kramer, Matthew. 2013. "Some Doubts about Alternatives to the Interest Theory of Rights." 123 *Ethics* 245–63.
Kramer, Matthew. 2014. *Torture and Moral Integrity*. Oxford: Oxford University Press.
Kramer, Matthew. 2015. "The Purgative Rationale for the Death Penalty: Replies to Steiker and Danaher." 9 *Criminal Law and Philosophy* 379–94.
Kramer, Matthew. 2016. "Moral Conflicts, the 'Ought Implies Can' Principle, and Moral Demandingness." In Marcel van Ackeren and Michael Kühler (eds), *The Limits of Moral Obligation*. London: Routledge, pp 163–84.
Kramer, Matthew. 2017a. *Liberalism with Excellence*. Oxford: Oxford University Press.
Kramer, Matthew. 2017b. "In Defence of the Interest Theory of Right-Holding: Rejoinders to Leif Wenar on Rights." In Mark McBride (ed.), *New Essays on the Nature of Rights*. Oxford: Hart Publishing, pp 49–83.
Kramer, Matthew. 2017c. "On Political Morality and the Conditions for Warranted Self-Respect." 21 *Journal of Ethics* 335–49.
Kramer, Matthew. 2018. *H.L.A. Hart: The Nature of Law*. Cambridge: Polity Press.
Kramer, Matthew. 2019. "On No-Rights and No Rights." 64 *American Journal of Jurisprudence* 213–23.
Kramer, Matthew. 2021. *Freedom of Expression as Self-Restraint*. Oxford: Oxford University Press.
Kramer, Matthew. 2022. "Looking Back and Looking Ahead: Replies to the Contributors." In Mark McBride and Visa Kurki (eds), *Without Trimmings: The Legal, Moral, and Political Philosophy of Matthew Kramer*. Oxford: Oxford University Press, pp 363–592.
Kramer, Matthew. 2024. "Incorporationism, Inclusivism, and Indeterminacy." In Thomas Bustamante, Saulo De Matos, and André Coelho (eds), *Law, Morality, and Judicial Reasoning: Essays on W.J. Waluchow's Jurisprudence and Constitutional Theory*. Berlin: Springer.
Kramer, Matthew and Steiner, Hillel. 2007. "Theories of Rights: Is There a Third Way?" 27 *Oxford Journal of Legal Studies* 281–310.
Kurki, Visa. 2017. "Legal Competence and Legal Power." In Mark McBride (ed.), *New Essays on the Nature of Rights*. Oxford: Hart Publishing, pp 31–47.
Kurki, Visa. 2018. "Rights, Harming, and Wronging: A Restatement of the Interest Theory." 38 *Oxford Journal of Legal Studies* 430–50.
Kurki, Visa. 2019. *A Theory of Legal Personhood*. Oxford: Oxford University Press.
Kurki, Visa. 2022a. "Are Legal Positivism and the Interest Theory of Rights Compatible?" In Mark McBride and Visa Kurki (eds), *Without Trimmings: The Legal, Moral, and Political Philosophy of Matthew Kramer*. Oxford: Oxford University Press, pp 73–91.
Kurki, Visa. 2022b. "Can Nature Hold Rights? It's Not as Easy as You Think." 11 *Transnational Environmental Law* 525–52.
Leslie, Sarah-Jane. 2008. "Generics: Cognition and Acquisition." 117 *Philosophical Review* 1–47.
Letsas, George. 2018. "Law and Polity: Some Philosophical Preliminaries." 16 *International Journal of Constitutional Law* 1242–50.
Levenbook, Barbara Baum. 1984. "Harming Someone after His Death." 94 *Ethics* 407–19.
Levenbook, Barbara Baum. 1985. "Harming the Dead, Once Again." 96 *Ethics* 162–4.
Lewis, David. 2002. *Convention*. Oxford: Blackwell Publishing. First published in 1969.

Luper, Steven. 2004. "Posthumous Harm." 41 *American Philosophical Quarterly* 63–72.
Luper, Steven. 2013. "Retroactive Harms and Wrongs." In Ben Bradley, Fred Feldman, and Jens Johansson (eds), *The Oxford Handbook of the Philosophy of Death*. Oxford: Oxford University Press, pp 317–35.
Lyons, David. 1984. "Founders and Foundations of Legal Positivism." 82 *Michigan Law Review* 722–39.
MacCormick, Neil. 1977. "Rights in Legislation." In Peter Hacker and Joseph Raz (eds), *Law, Morality, and Society*. Oxford: Oxford University Press, pp 189–209.
MacCormick, Neil. 1982. *Legal Right and Social Democracy*. Oxford: Oxford University Press.
MacCormick, Neil. 2008. *H.L.A. Hart*. Second Edition. Stanford, CA: Stanford University Press.
Macklin, Ruth. 1981. "Can Future Generations Correctly Be Said to Have Rights?" In Ernest Partridge (ed.), *Responsibilities to Future Generations*. Buffalo, NY: Prometheus Books, pp 151–6.
Makinson, David. 1986. "On the Formal Representation of Rights Relations: Remarks on the Work of Stig Kanger and Lars Lindahl." 15 *Journal of Philosophical Logic* 403–25.
Marcus, Ruth Barcan. 1980. "Moral Dilemmas and Consistency." 77 *Journal of Philosophy* 121–36.
Marmor, Andrei. 1997. "On the Limits of Rights." 16 *Law and Philosophy* 1–18.
Marquis, Don. 1985. "Harming the Dead." 96 *Ethics* 159–61.
Mayo, Bernard. 1965. "Human Rights." 39 *Proceedings of the Aristotelian Society, Supplementary Volumes* 219–36.
McBride, Mark. 2021. "The Dual Reality of No-Rights." 66 *American Journal of Jurisprudence* 39–48.
McCain, John. 2006. "It's about Us." 33 (# 1) *Human Rights* 20–2.
McConnell, Terrance. 2010. "Moral Dilemmas." In Edward Zalta (ed.), *Stanford Encyclopedia of Philosophy (Summer 2010 Edition)*. URL = http://plato.stanford.edu/archives/sum2010/entries/moral-dilemmas.
Moore, Michael. 1982. "Moral Reality." 1982 *Wisconsin Law Review* 1061–156.
Moore, Michael. 1992. "Moral Reality Revisited." 90 *Michigan Law Review* 2424–533.
Moore, Michael. 2007. "Patrolling the Borders of Consequentialist Justifications: The Scope of Agent-Relative Restrictions." 27 *Law and Philosophy* 35–96.
Moore, Michael. 2009. *Causation and Responsibility*. Oxford: Oxford University Press.
Morris, Herbert. 1968. "Persons and Punishment." 52 *The Monist* 475–501.
Morris, Madeline. 1993. "The Structure of Entitlements." 78 *Cornell Law Review* 822–98.
Mulgan, Tim. 1999. "The Place of the Dead in Liberal Political Philosophy." 7 *Journal of Political Philosophy* 52–70.
Mullock, Philip. 1971. "The Hohfeldian Jural Opposite." 13 *Ratio* 158–65.
Mullock, Philip. 1972. "Holmes on Contractual Duty." 33 *University of Pittsburgh Law Review* 471–82.
Mullock, Philip. 1975. "The Choice Theory of Legal Rights." 14 *Western Ontario Law Review* 241–62.
Nascimento, Daniel. 2018. "Hohfeld on the Duties in Privileges and Claims." 19 *Unisinos Journal of Philosophy* 150–5.
Nascimento, Daniel. 2019. "Hohfeld on Privileges and Liberties." 24 *Philosophos—Revista de Filosofia* 55–67.
Nelkin, Dorothy and Andrews, Lori. 1998. "Do the Dead Have Interests? Policy Issues for Research after Life." 24 *American Journal of Law and Medicine* 261–91.
Nussbaum, Martha. 2000. "The Costs of Tragedy: Some Moral Limits of Cost-Benefit Analysis." 29 *Journal of Legal Studies* 1005–36.
Oliveira Lima, Joao Alberto de, Griffo, Cristine, Almeida, Joao Paulo, Guizzardi, Giancarlo, and Aranha, Marcio. 2021. "Casting the Light of the Theory of Opposition onto Hohfeld's Fundamental Legal Concepts." 27 *Legal Theory* 2–35.
O'Neill, Onora. 1996. *Towards Justice and Virtue*. Cambridge: Cambridge University Press.

O'Neill, Onora. 1998. "Kant on Duties Regarding Nonrational Nature: Necessary Anthropocentrism and Contingent Speciesism." 72 *Proceedings of the Aristotelian Society, Supplementary Volumes* 211–28.

Palombella, Gianluigi. 2023. "Irreversible Choices and Future Generations' Rights." 10 *Kutafin Law Review* 110–36.

Parfit, Derek. 1984. *Reasons and Persons*. Oxford: Oxford University Press.

Partridge, Ernest. 1981. "Posthumous Interests and Posthumous Respect." 91 *Ethics* 243–64.

Partridge, Ernest. 1990. "On the Rights of Future People." In Donald Scherer (ed.), *Upstream/Downstream: Issues in Environmental Ethics*. Philadelphia, PA: Temple University Press, pp 40–66.

Paskins, Barrie. 1976. "What's Wrong with Torture?" 2 *British Journal of International Studies* 138–48.

Penner, James. 1997. "The Analysis of Rights." 10 *Ratio Juris* 300–15.

Penner, James. 2017. "Legal Powers and the Will and Interest Theories of Rights." In Mark McBride (ed.), *New Essays on the Nature of Rights*. Oxford: Hart Publishing, pp 99–126.

Persad, Govind. 2019. "Authority without Identity: Defending Advance Directives via Posthumous Rights over One's Body." 45 *Journal of Medical Ethics* 249–56.

Perry, Ronen. 2009. "Correlativity." 28 *Law and Philosophy* 537–84.

Pettit, Philip. 2009. "The Reality of Group Agents." In C. Mantzavinos (ed.), *Philosophy of the Social Sciences*. Cambridge: Cambridge University Press, pp 67–91.

Petti, Philip and List, Christian. 2011. *Group Agency*. Oxford: Oxford University Press.

Pitcher, George. 1984. "The Misfortunes of the Dead." 21 *American Philosophical Quarterly* 183–8.

Pletcher, Galen. 1981. "The Rights of Future Generations." In Ernest Partridge (ed.), *Responsibilities to Future Generations*. Buffalo, NY: Prometheus Books, pp 167–70.

Portmore, Douglas. 2007. "Desire Fulfillment and Posthumous Harm." 44 *American Philosophical Quarterly* 27–38.

Posner, Eric and Vermeule, Adrian. 2006. "Should Coercive Interrogation Be Legal?" 104 *Michigan Law Review* 671–707.

Posner, Richard. 1990. *The Problems of Jurisprudence*. Cambridge, MA: Harvard University Press.

Quay, Paul. 1984. "Utilizing the Bodies of the Dead." 28 *Saint Louis University Law Journal* 889–928.

Rawls, John. 1999. *A Theory of Justice*. Revised Edition. Oxford: Oxford University Press.

Raz, Joseph. 1972. "Voluntary Obligations and Normative Powers." 46 *Proceedings of the Aristotelian Society, Supplementary Volumes* 79–102.

Raz, Joseph. 1984. "On the Nature of Rights." 93 *Mind* 194–214.

Raz, Joseph. 1986. *The Morality of Freedom*. Oxford: Oxford University Press.

Raz, Joseph. 1990. *Practical Reason and Norms*. Second Edition. Princeton, NJ: Princeton University Press.

Raz, Joseph. 1994. *Ethics in the Public Domain*. Oxford: Oxford University Press.

Reichenbach, Bruce. 1992. "On Obligations to Future Generations." 6 *Public Affairs Quarterly* 207–25.

Ridge, Michael. 2003. "Giving the Dead Their Due." 114 *Ethics* 38–59.

Rodman, John. 1977. "The Liberation of Nature?" 20 *Inquiry* 83–145.

Rolston III, Holmes. 1988. *Environmental Ethics*. Philadelphia, PA: Temple University Press.

Rowlands, Mark. 2012. *Can Animals Be Moral?* Oxford: Oxford University Press.

Saunders, Kevin. 1990. "A Formal Analysis of Hohfeldian Relations." 23 *Akron Law Review* 465–506.

Scarre, Geoffrey. 2003. "Archaeology and Respect for the Dead." 20 *Journal of Applied Philosophy* 237–49.

Schauer, Frederick. 2022. "Hohfeld on Legal Language." In Shyamkrishna Balganesh, Ted Sichelman, and Henry Smith (eds), *Wesley Hohfeld a Century Later*. Cambridge: Cambridge University Press, pp 99–111.

Scheffler, Samuel. 2013. *Death and the Afterlife*. Edited by Niko Kolodny. Oxford: Oxford University Press.

Schlegel, John Henry. 2022. "Wesley Newcomb Hohfeld: On the Difficulty of Becoming a Law Professor." In Shyamkrishna Balganesh, Ted Sichelman, and Henry Smith (eds), *Wesley Hohfeld a Century Later*. Cambridge: Cambridge University Press, pp 494–517.

Schwitzgebel, Eric and Garza, Mara. 2015. "A Defense of the Rights of Artificial Intelligences." 39 *Midwest Studies in Philosophy* 98–119.

Scruton, Roger. 2000. "Animal Rights." *City Journal*, Summer 2000. URL = https://www.city-journal.org/article/animal-rights.

Shakespeare, William. 1974. *The Riverside Shakespeare*. Edited by G. Blakemore Evans. Boston, MA: Houghton Mifflin Company.

Shrage, Laurie. 2003. Abortion *and* Social Responsibility. Oxford: Oxford University Press

Simester, Andrew. 2008. "Necessity, Torture, and the Rule of Law." In Victor Ramraj (ed.), *Emergencies and the Limits of Legality*. Cambridge: Cambridge University Press, pp 289–313.

Simmonds, N.E. 1998. "Rights at the Cutting Edge." In Matthew Kramer, N.E. Simmonds, and Hillel Steiner, *A Debate over Rights*. Oxford: Oxford University Press, pp 113–232.

Simpson, Thomas. 2017. "The Impossibility of Republican Freedom." 45 *Philosophy and Public Affairs* 27–53.

Singer, Peter. 1995. Animal Liberation. Second Edition. London: Pimlico.

Smolensky, Kirsten Rabe. 2009. "Rights of the Dead." 37 *Hofstra Law Review* 763–803.

Solomon, Robert. 1976. "Is There Happiness after Death?" 51 *Philosophy* 189–93.

Solum, Lawrence. 1992. "Legal Personhood for Artificial Intelligences." 70 *North Carolina Law Review* 1231–87.

Spena, Alessandro. 2012. "The Strange Case of the Protective Perimeter: Liberties and Claims to Non-Interference." 31 *Law and Philosophy* 161–84.

Sperling, Daniel. 2008. *Posthumous Interests*. Cambridge: Cambridge University Press.

Sreenivasan, Gopal. 2005. "A Hybrid Theory of Claim-Rights." 25 *Oxford Journal of Legal Studies* 257–74.

Sreenivasan, Gopal. 2017. "Public Goods, Individual Rights, and Third-Party Benefits." In Mark McBride (ed.), *New Essays on the Nature of Rights*. Oxford: Hart Publishing, pp 127–48.

Steinbock, Bonnie. 1992. *Life before Birth*. Oxford: Oxford University Press.

Steiner, Hillel. 1983. "The Rights of Future Generations." In Peter Brown and Douglas MacLean (eds), *Energy and the Future*. Totowa, NJ: Rowman & Littlefield, pp 151–65.

Steiner, Hillel. 1994. *An Essay on Rights*. Oxford: Blackwell.

Steiner, Hillel. 1998. "Working Rights." In Matthew Kramer, N. E. Simmonds, and Hillel Steiner, *A Debate over Rights*. Oxford: Oxford University Press, pp 233–301.

Steinhoff, Uwe. 2009. "Justifying Defensive Torture." In Bev Clucas, Gerry Johnstone, and Tony Ward (eds), *Torture: Moral Absolutes and Ambiguities*. Baden-Baden: Nomos, pp 39–60.

Sterba, James. 1980. "Abortion, Distant Peoples, and Future Generations." 77 *Journal of Philosophy* 424–40.

Stockwell, Billy. 2022. "The Rights of Rivers." *The Ecologist*, August 9, 2022. URL = https://theecologist.org/2022/aug/09/rights-rivers.

Stone, Christopher. 1972. "Should Trees Have Standing?—Toward Legal Rights for Natural Objects." 45 *Southern California Law Review* 450–501.

Sumner, L.W. 1987. *The Moral Foundation of Rights*. Oxford: Oxford University Press.

Sumner, L.W. 1988. "Animal Welfare and Animal Rights. 13 *Journal of Medicine and Philosophy* 159–75.

Taylor, James Stacey. 2005. "The Myth of Posthumous Harm." 42 *American Philosophical Quarterly* 311–22.

Taylor, Paul. 1981. "The Ethics of Respect for Nature." 3 *Environmental Ethics* 197–218.

Thompson, Jack Clayton. 2018. "The Rights Network: 100 Years of the Hohfeldian Rights Analytic." 7 *Laws* 1–15.

Thomson, Judith Jarvis. 1971. "A Defense of Abortion." 1 *Philosophy and Public Affairs* 47–66.

Tooley, Michael. 1972. "In Defense of Abortion and Infanticide." 2 *Philosophy and Public Affairs* 37–65.

Tuomela, Raimo. 2013. *Social Ontology: Collective Intentionality and Group Agents.* Oxford: Oxford University Press.
Twining, William and Miers, David. 2010. *How to Do Things with Rules.* Fifth Edition. Cambridge: Cambridge University Press.
Valentini, Laura. 2021. "The Natural Duty of Justice in Non-Ideal Circumstances: On the Moral Demands of Institution Building and Reform." 20 *European Journal of Political Theory* 45–66.
Vallentyne, Peter. 1987. "Prohibition Dilemmas and Deontic Logic." 117–18 *Logique et Analyse* 113–22.
Vallentyne, Peter. 1989. "Two Types of Moral Dilemmas." 30 *Erkenntnis* 301–18.
Van Duffel, Siegfried. 2012. "The Nature of Rights Debate Rests on a Mistake." 93 *Pacific Philosophical Quarterly* 104–23.
Van Duffel, Siegfried. 2017. "Adequacy Constraints for a Theory of Rights." In Mark McBride (ed.), *New Essays on the Nature of Rights.* Oxford: Hart Publishing, pp 187–202.
Waldron, Jeremy. 1984. "Introduction." In Jeremy Waldron (ed.), *Theories of Rights.* Oxford: Oxford University Press, pp 1–20.
Waldron, Jeremy. 1988. *The Right to Private Property.* Oxford: Oxford University Press.
Waldron, Jeremy. 1990. *The Law.* London: Routledge.
Waldron, Jeremy. 1993. *Liberal Rights.* Cambridge: Cambridge University Press.
Warren, Mary Anne. 1997. *Moral Status.* Oxford: Oxford University Press.
Wellman, Carl. 1995. *Real Rights.* Oxford: Oxford University Press.
Wenar, Leif. 2005. "The Nature of Rights." 33 *Philosophy and Public Affairs* 223–53.
Wenar, Leif. 2008. "The Analysis of Rights." In Matthew Kramer, Claire Grant, Ben Colburn, and Antony Hatzistavrou (eds), *The Legacy of H.L.A. Hart.* Oxford: Oxford University Press, pp 251–73.
Wenar, Leif. 2013. "The Nature of Claim-Rights." 123 *Ethics* 202–29.
Westen, Peter. 2018. "Poor Wesley Hohfeld." 55 *San Diego Law Review* 449–67.
Wilkinson, T.M. 2002. "Last Rights: The Ethics of Research on the Dead." 19 *Journal of Applied Philosophy* 31–41.
Williams, Andrew. 2000. "The Alleged Incompleteness of Public Reason." 6 *Res Publica* 199–211.
Williams, Glanville. 1956. "The Concept of Legal Liberty." 56 *Columbia Law Review* 1129–50.
Williams, Jeremy. 2015. "Public Reason and Prenatal Moral Status." 19 *Journal of Ethics* 23–52.
Wisnewski, Jeremy. 2009. "What We Owe the Dead." 26 *Journal of Applied Philosophy* 54–70.
Woods, Kerri. 2016. "The Rights of (Future) Humans *Qua* Humans." 15 *Journal of Human Rights* 291–306.
Yoshida, Masayuki. 2003. "Rights of the Dead." PhD dissertation. University of Sheffield School of Law. URL = https://etheses.whiterose.ac.uk/14754/1/274997_vol1.pdf.

Index

Note on index: For the benefit of digital users, this index has been compiled with paragraph numbers (which are converted here to page numbers). Thus, an indexed item in a paragraph which spans two pages is listed here with both of those pages even though it might appear on only one of them.

Aas, Sean 359n.8
abortion 310–11, 357–59
Abraham Lincoln statuette 283–84
absence of duties owed to future generations 386–87
abstraction in categorizing claim-right-holders 205, 206, 207–8
action-guidance 32–33
  role of claim-rights in 164–74
  from unenforceable duties 41–43
actions
  differentiated from omissions 77–78
  powers exercised by 77–78
act-omission dichotomy 221–22, 272, 273–74, 281–84
actual holders of claim-rights 292, 293–94, 305–6, 309–10, 339
Adams, David 46–48
aftermath of dead person's lifespan 364–66, 369–72
aggregative universal quantification 58–59, 61–62, 64, 106–9, 327, 382–84, 385–86
Alchourrón, Carlos 30n.8, 68n.20
Altham, J. E. J. 108
anarchism, illusoriness of 111
anarchists 109–11, 182–83, 205–6
Anderson, Alan Ross 4n.1, 30n.8
Andrews, Lori 359n.8
Andromeda Galaxy 66–67
anencephalic infants 323, 326–27
Anscombe, Elizabeth 150–53
anticipatory adjustments in current behavior 378–79
Apollo 68–69, 104, 321, 337–38
Arborea 337–38
Aristotle 372
arranging of marriages 240–41
artificial intelligence 317–18, 336n.5
assimilability of future generations now to people they will become 374–80
asteroid in collision with Earth 377, 381–82
attempted rape, scenario of 220–22
Austin, John 115, 286
  Hart's critique of 95
authorization 255–56, 285, 287
autonomy, constituted by freedom 314–15
auxiliary verb "should" 169

babies and infants
  Will Theory rights not held by 12, 260–65, 274–75, 294
baby carrots 306–7
Bacon, Francis 372–73
Bahn, Paul 359n.8
Baier, Annette 359n.8
  "on balance" 180
  conflated by Raz with "typically" 217–18
Bandman, Bertram 374n.10
Barkham, Patrick 297
basketball 180
Beckerman, Wilfred 374n.10
begging of question
  avoided by critique of near-eliminativism of Will Theory 278–79
  dialectical effectiveness impaired by 257, 268–69, 278–79
  by Dworkin against broad conception of interests 305–6, 307–8
beings for whom legal duties are established 312, 318, 341–42
beings merely in regard to which legal duties are established 312, 318, 334, 336–37, 341–42
Bekoff, Marc 339
Belliotti, Raymond 359n.8
Benditt, Theodore 130–31
"Benefit Theory," alternative label for Interest Theory 299
Bentham, Jeremy 33n.9, 188
  account of right-holding by 299

Bentham's Test 188–203
applied to Frazier/Ali bout 194–96
applied to scenario of Doris and her employer 189–90
applied to Sreenivasan's third-party-beneficiary contract 190–93
formulation of 188
and fourth-party beneficiaries 196–203
Hart on 188
Kurki on 188
and multiple minimally sufficient sets of facts 189, 192
notational variation of Interest Theory 188–89, 191
Berg, Jessica 304n.1
Biasetti, Francesco 120n.3
Bible
Isaiah 377
2 Kings 377
biconditional entailment, correlativity as 21–22, 25–26, 77, 99–177, 349–50, 380
bills of rights 90–91
immunities conferred by 93–97, 267–68
legislative disabilities imposed by 94–97
Bobbitt, Philip 30n.8
Boonin, David 359n.8
Bos, Gerhard 374n.10
Bowen, Joseph 298–302, 309, 359n.8, 366–74
and conflation of potential right-holders with beings that have interests 301–2
terminological worries about broad conception of interests 298–99
on univocality of a theory 299–301
Brännmark, Johan 374n.10
Brecher, Bob 359n.8
Bruhl, Aaron-Andrew 374n.10
Bulygin, Eugenio 30n.8, 35, 68n.20
Bush, George W. 114

Callahan, Joan 359n.8
capacious version of Interest Theory 17, 18, 79–80, 178–79, 225–55, 267–68
evaluative premises of 227–28, 231, 239–40, 243
formulation of 226
Wenar's attacks on 228–47
Cardozo, Benjamin 154–55
Carruthers, Peter 348n.6
Carter, Ian 245–46
on declinatory force of one's decisions 314–15
on opacity respect 322n.4
categorizing of holders of claim-rights
abstract in most cases 205, 206, 207–8
concrete in anomalous cases 205–8
caterpillars, Dworkin on 306–7
causal/constitutive distinction 314
central-instance methodology 5–6
ceteris paribus qualifier 205
chess 180
Chinese Communist Party 328
choice-dependence of existence of pre-violation duties 281
Chopra, Samir 317–18
Churchill College Private Road
Cicero 372
civil-rights campaigns 93–94
claim-right-focused justifications 113–18
claim-right not to be amputated 265–66
claim-right not to be enslaved 265–66
claim-right not to be murdered 257–58
claim-right not to be tortured lethally 265–66
claim-right not to be tortured punitively 219–20, 223
claim-right to be punished 206–8
claim-right to be tortured, held by masochist 182–83, 205–6, 207–8
"claim-rights," as term rooted in ordinary usage 8
claim-rights 24–43
dependent on immunities for existence and substantiveness 253–54
evaluatively non-neutral 82–83
exercises of liberties protected by 51–55
fundamental passivity of 281–84
held by collectivities 25
held vis-à-vis oneself 25, 26–27, 80, 111–13, 122, 281–82, 347, 349, 359
interests differentiated from 128–31
liberties not entailed by 55–57
main version of Interest Theory confined to 250–55
not always justified by interests of holders 222–25
not conferred by criminal law, according to Will Theorists 258–59, 269
not entailed by liberties 24, 53, 55
perceived by Hart as exerted by actions 282–83, 284
"rights" best restricted to 9
Wenar on 9
class of potential holders of claim-rights
actual right-holders all belong to 227
incongruities with perceived classes of potential holders 293–94, 319, 321
Raz on 216
underlain by ethical considerations 264–65, 291, 292–387
Will Theory's restrictive conception of 260–65, 294, 349

cluster-concept methodology 5–6
coalitions 106–7, 382–83
  as *êtres pour eux-mêmes* 327–28
cockroaches
  not of ultimate value 322–23, 339, 345–46
  sadistic torture of always wrong 322–23
  as vermin 345–47, 351, 354, 364
Cohen, G. A. 59n.16
collectively held claim-rights
  aggregative universal quantification in 106–9, 327, 382–84, 385–86
  denied by Hohfeld 61–62, 64, 99–100, 104–9, 122, 327
collectivities
  as holders of claim-rights 25, 61–62, 64, 99–100, 104–9, 327, 382–84
  ultimate value of 327–29
comatose people 9–10, 12
The Comedy of Errors 370n.9
community of potential holders of claim-rights
  not a community if historical links are too remote 372
  not a community if vermin are included 345–47
  without institutions 330–33, 382–83
competence 255–56, 260–65, 284–90, 294
competence-focused critique of Will Theory 284–90
comprehensiveness of Hohfeld's schema
  limits on Hohfeldian positions 66–70, 72–73, 76–77
  quasi-powers outside 86–87
concession on claim-rights of infants, by Hart 261–64
concrete entitlements, generated by abstract entitlements 125–28
concreteness in categorizing of right-holders 205–8
Conee, Earl 30n.8
consequence-independent value 315–16
consequentialism, denial of moral conflicts by 31–32
conservative Catholic stance on abortion 304
constitutive relationships, general nature of 314
constitutive value 314–15
content-independent value of freedom 245
contents of claim-rights
  accurate specifications of 55–56
  hardly ever focused chiefly on conduct of right-holders 26–28, 57
contents of duties 26–28
  not always focused on conduct of duty-bearers 281–82, 349n.7
contents of liberties
  not always focused on conduct of liberty-holders 49–51
contractual powers
  and disjunctive universal quantification 90
  limited by disabilities 90–91
contradictions 34–39
  distinguished from deontic conflicts 34–36
contradictories, distinguished from contraries 28
contradictoriness, distinguished from duality 77, 92
contraries, distinguished from contradictories 28
conventional moral codes 161–62
convicts, as holders of claim-rights to be punished 206–8
Cornell, Nicolas 189–90
  and allegation of overexpansiveness of Interest Theory 187–89
  on claim-rights in guiding conduct 164–74
  Correlativity Axiom impugned by 153–54, 177
  deontic overdetermination disregarded by 170
  on deprivation of companionship 163–64, 165–73
  on *Flanders v Cooper* 155–58
  general theoretical reflections by 164–76
  Interest Theory badly misunderstood by 174–75, 179
  on *Julius Caesar* 161–62
  on loss of consortium 164–66
  on motivation versus obligation 166–67
  on *Much Ado about Nothing* 159–61
  No Wrongs Without Claim-Rights Proposition rejected by 135–77
  and overproliferation of wrongs 175–76
  on *Palsgraf v Long Island Railroad* 154–58
  on patriarchal familial prerogatives 164–66
  on *Randi W. v Muroc*
  rights and interests conflated by 130
  and scenario of the cheated prizewinner 142–46
  and scenario of drunken motorist 162–64, 197–98, 199–200, 201–2
  and scenario of overheard falsehood 146–54
  and scenario of recreational fireworks 167–69
  on Shakespeare 158–62
  on third-party-beneficiary contracts 138–42, 174–76
  thought-experiments by 136
  on unforeseeable harms 150
  on *White v Jones* 144–45

Cornell, Nicolas (*cont.*)
Will Theory embraced by 136, 138–42, 154, 171, 174–75, 176, 193
on wrongful-death statutes 165–67
wrongness/gravity distinction disregarded by 168–69, 170–71, 172–73
correctness, distinguished from moral permissibility 32–33
"correlates," as umbrella term 18–19, 21
correlates, biconditionally entailed by entitlements 19, 21–22, 25–26, 77, 99–177, 349–50, 380
correlativity 126–27
between entitlements and correlates 19, 21–22, 25–26, 77, 99–177, 349–50, 380
not across Hohfeldian columns 24
Correlativity Axiom 22, 43–44, 64, 99–177, 349, 380
axiomaticity of 102–13
dynamic aspect of rights consistent with 125–28
formulation of 99–100, 120–21, 127
Interest Theory in defense of 100–2, 108–13, 121–22, 131–32, 178
Kurki on 102
not dogmatic 100, 102–13
rejection of No Wrongs Without Claim-Rights Proposition consistent with 135–36
and Scottish intestate law 123–25
and self-directedness of every moral duty 212
counterfactual worlds 236
Cresswell, M. J. 30n.8
crimes against humanity 151–52
Cruft, Rowan 52
on collapse of Raz's interest theory into Kramer's Interest Theory 224–25
on eleemosynary duties 120n.3
on limits on range of potential right-holders 319
on Razian rights 216
Cupp Jr, Richard 348n.6
Curzer, Howard 30n.8

Da Silva, Michael 359n.8
dead people 12, 68–69
direct ties fade into historical ties 365–66, 371–72
as potential holders of claim-rights 312, 323, 325, 359–65
ultimate value of 323, 325
Will Theory rights not held by 260–65, 294
declinatory aspect of the will 283, 284
de dicto/*de re* distinction 91–92, 372–73, 380, 383–84
defacement of Old Master paintings 296
default rule at pre-violation stage 275–77
default rules
formulations of 270
De George, Richard 374n.10
de Marneffe, Peter 304n.1
demented and insane people 12
Will Theory rights not held by 260–65, 274–75, 294, 295
democratic legitimacy 97
deontic auxiliary verbs 35n.10
deontic categories, distinguished from modal categories 81
deontic conflicts 4, 24, 28–34, 48–49, 111–13, 168–69, 172, 183–84, 240–41
action-guidance in 32–33
contradictions distinguished from 34–36
denied by consequentialists 31–32
denied by Kant 31–32, 34
denied by standard deontic logic 30–34
remedial obligations inevitable in 32–33
unfairness of in some cases 29–30, 34
deontic freedom, distinguished from modal freedom 44
deontic logic
denial of deontic conflicts by 30–34
distinguished from modal logic 32
deontic overdetermination 170
deontic protection conferred by duties 25, 179–80
deontology versus consequentialism 31–32
deprivation of companionship 201–3
derivativeness of third-party claim-rights 170–74
De-Shalit, Avner 374n.10
deterrence, through enforcement of duties 25
de Vere, Edward 372–73
diagonal relationships 22–24
dialectical effectiveness 257, 268–69, 278–79
direct ties between dead and living fade into historical ties 365–66, 371–72
directionality
of duties and claim-rights 133–34, 145–46, 178, 254–55
of power/liability relationships 91–92
and quantification 133–34
Director of Public Prosecutions 258–59
disabilities 92–98
as limits on legislative and contractual powers 90–91
disjunctive properties 325–26
disjunctive universal quantification 58–64, 65–66, 87–88, 89–91, 99–100, 120–22, 124n.4, 143–44

distinguished from existential quantification 59–63
in eleemosynary duties 120–22
over sets of changes in legal relationships 89–91
disparities among spans during which dead people can hold rights 365–66, 370–72, 373–74
distributive pleonotetic quantification 108–9, 324–26, 382, 384
distributive universal quantification 58–59, 62–63, 64–66, 87–88, 91–92, 108–9, 145–46, 151–52, 204, 239n.11, 384
over potential bearers of liabilities 91–92
Donohue, Laura 85
Doris and her employer, scenario of 175–76
Bentham's Test applied to 189–90, 192
Interest Theory applied to 189–90, 192
Dowding, Keith 106–7
drunken motorist scenario 162–64, 197–98, 199–200, 201–2
duality, distinguished from contradictoriness 77
Duarte d'Almeida, Luis 4–5, 48–49, 64–65
Duckler, Geordie 348n.6
duties 24–43
contents of 26–28
contents of not always focused on conduct of duty-bearers 281–82, 349n.7
as deontic protections 25, 179–80
enforcement of 25
owed to oneself 25, 26–27, 80, 111–13, 122, 281–82, 347, 349, 359
owed posthumously to dead person 361–63
possibly requiring some conduct by holder of correlative right 28
retained in existence by immunities 258–59
"duty," synonymous with "obligation" v
duty-bearer's conduct, sometimes not included in content of duty 281–82, 349n.7
duty-focused justifications 113–18
Düwell, Marcus 374n.10
Duxbury, Neil 16n.1
Dworkin, Ronald 30n.8, 32–33
on baby carrots and caterpillars 306–7
and conflation of no unfairness with no interests 305–6, 307, 308
denial of foetal interests by 302–9, 356–57
on Frankenstein 308–9
and futile aim for neutrality among reasonable creeds 303, 304, 305, 308–9
on inside-out argumentation 309
on interests and abortion 298, 302–9, 356–57
on justificatory priorities 114–15, 116
dynamic aspect of rights
consistent with Correlativity Axiom 125–28
MacCormick on 125–28
Raz on 125–28
Waldron on 127–28

Earl, Dennis 374n.10
earthworms 347, 351, 352–53, 354
Edmundson, William 120n.3
effectuation of legal duties, explication of 270
Eleemosynary Obligation Proposition 60–61, 63
eleemosynary obligations 60–61, 63–64, 120–22
owed to oneself 121
Eleftheriadis, Pavlos 23n.4
Elijah and Elisha 263–64
eliminativism (nearly) of Will Theory 268–84
Elliot, Robert 374n.10
empirical conjectures by Wenar 9–10, 12–13
empirical matters, versus philosophical matters 3
enforcement of duties 25, 179–80
physical protection conferred by 179–80
typically *ex post* 179–80
"entitlement"
as technical term 226
as umbrella term 17–19
entitlements
biconditionally entailed by correlates 19, 21–22, 25–26, 77, 99–177, 349–50, 380
dependent on concomitant immunities 97–98
"entity" construed very broadly 313
environmentalism, championed by Simmonds 264–65
environmentalist ethicists
broad conception of interests favored by 304
rights ascribed to inanimate natural phenomena by 319, 320–21
ephemerally incapacitative torture 220–22
Erk, Christian 120n.3
essentialist methodology 5–13
established legal entitlements 131–34
ethical basis for class of potential right-holders 12
êtres pour eux-mêmes 317–18
evaluative comparisons in ascriptions of claim-rights 385
evaluative neutrality
of liabilities and disabilities 18–19
of powers and immunities 17–19, 226, 227–28, 246–47
of powers and liabilities 80, 81–83
evaluative premises
of capacious version of Interest Theory 227–28, 231, 239–40, 243

evaluative premises (*cont.*)
for holding of legal claim-rights 181–87, 208, 211–12, 227, 231
of Interest Theory 11–12, 111–13, 121–22, 178–79, 180, 181–87, 196–203, 208–14, 227–28, 239–40
objectivity of 182–83, 211–12, 239–40
personal/vicarious distinction in 196–203
subjective element in 182–83, 206, 207–8, 211–12, 239–40
thinness of 180–81
exclusive disjunctive universal quantification 89–90
executors of estates 123–25
exercises of liberties 51–55
existence-conditions of duties, versus fulfillment-conditions 33
existential quantification 58–63
in ascriptions of legal powers 88–89
different from disjunctive universal quantification 59–63
expansive conception of interests 298–312, 334–35, 356–57
neutral among reasonable creeds 305
experience-independent value 316
explicability, versus reducibility 106
extraterrestrial creatures 317–18
extravagant evil 150–53

Fabre, Cécile 359n.8, 374n.10
factory owner and fishermen, scenario of 55–57
facts minimally sufficient for breaches of duties 163–64
fallen leaves 337–38
family resemblances 5–6
Fatal Accidents Act 165–67
Feinberg, Joel 30, 120n.3, 304n.1, 359n.8, 374n.10
Ferraro, Francesco 299
Finnis, John 26n.6
First Amendment 93, 97–98
immunities conferred by 95
first-order/higher-order distinction 19–21
fishermen and factory, scenario of 55–57
Fitch, Frederic 4n.1, 30n.8
Flanders v Cooper 155–58
Flathman, Richard 44–45
foetuses 12, 356–57
and justificatory/non-justificatory distinction 310–11
Will Theory rights not held by 260–65, 294
formal/substantive distinction 1–2
formalization in analyses of rights 3–5
dependent on philosophical assumptions 4, 30
fourth-party beneficiaries
Kurki on 196–98
Sreenivasan on 196–203
Francis of Assisi 181n.1
Frankenstein 308–9
Frazier/Ali bout, Bentham's Test applied to 194–96
freedom
autonomy constituted by 314–15
content-independent value of 245
freedom of expression, principle of 94–97
free morpheme 70
fulfillment-conditions, versus existence-conditions 33
Fuller, Lon 29, 35
fundamental inalienable rights
denied by Will Theory 265–68
entrenched by immunities 265–66, 267–68
MacCormick on 266
future generations 12, 68–69
assimilable now to the people they will become 374–80
not yet particularized 375, 383–84
as potential holders of claim-rights 312, 323, 325, 374–87
rights held now by 380–82
ultimate value of 323, 325
Will Theory rights not held by 260–65, 294

games, analysis of 6, 25n.5
Garza, Mara 317–18
Geach, Peter 108
general entitlements 125–28
general norms as quasi-powers 86–87
general theoretical reflections by Cornell 164–76
generic statements 324–26, 328, 329, 353
generosity 313–14
Geras, Norman 6n.2
Gilbert, Margaret 26n.6
Glannon, Walter 359n.8
Goldberg, John 145–46
goodness of moral uprightness 109, 111–13
not taken into account for holding of legal rights 109, 111–12, 183–87, 208, 211–12, 227, 231
taken into account for holding of moral rights 111–13, 183–84, 186, 187, 208–14, 227–28
Gosseries, Axel 374n.10
Graham, Paul 299
gravity/wrongness distinction 168–69, 170–71, 172–73
Griffiths, Aaron 374n.10
Grisez, Germain 303

Gross, Oren 30n.8
group agents 106–7, 382–83
as *êtres pour eux-mêmes* 327–28
Grover, Dorothy 359n.8

Halpin, Andrew 22n.3, 52–53n.14, 57, 69n.21
Hamlet 375–76
hard paternalism 244, 245
Hare, R. M. 30n.8, 31
harming, versus wronging 140–41, 156, 158, 159–60
Hart, H. L. A.
on active character of claim-rights 282–83, 284
on Bentham's account of right-holding 299
on Bentham's logic of the will 33n.9
and Bentham's Test 188
on class of potential holders of rights 260–65
on collectively held claim-rights 61–62, 64, 99–100, 104–9, 122
concession on claim-rights of infants by 261–64, 268–69, 350–51
critique of Austin by 95
and denial of claim-right not to be murdered 258
and denial of claim-rights under criminal law 258–59
on fundamental immunities 267–68
on minimum content of natural law 41, 53–54, 111
on nullity versus sanctions 95–96
powers analyzed by 78
on putative priority of duties over claim-rights 119–20, 258
on right-holder as small-scale sovereign 256–57
robust but not extreme in adherence to Will Theory 279–81
on stages of a duty's existence and enforcement 256, 277–78
on third-party-beneficiary contracts 138–42, 174–75, 176, 187–88, 196
Will Theory championed by 193
Hartney, Michael 319–21
having interests, versus capable of holding rights 301–2, 305, 309–10, 334–35
Hebrew Scriptures 263–64, 377
Heinze, Eric 4n.1
Henry V 167
Herstein, Ori 374n.10
Hezekiah 377
Hill Jr, Thomas 30n.8
Himma, Kenneth 30n.8
Hiskes, Richard 374n.10
Hobbes, Thomas 372
Hohfeld, Wesley 1, 4–5, 10–11, 16–98, 99–177
and disambiguation of "rights" 8
explicability conflated with reducibility by
interests and rights distinguished by 130
on multital duties 62–63, 145–46
one-to-one correlations insisted upon by 61–64, 99–100, 120
and ordinary usage 8, 10–11, 250–52
use of "privileges" by 8n.3
on quasi-powers 83
Hohfeldian analysis 16–98, 99–177
applicable to ancient Roman society 161–62
applicable to conventional moral codes 161–62
applicable to language 25n.5
applicable to medieval honor societies 160
comprehensiveness of 16, 86–87
formalization of 3–5
indeterminacy as a limit on 67–68
limits on 66–70, 72–73, 76–77
misuse of "no-right" by 71–72
past defenses of by Kramer 13–15
Raz's opposition to 215, 216–17, 225
Hohfeldian Table of Legal Positions 16*t*, 17
left-hand half versus right-hand half 23–24, 81–83
hollowness of entitlements without immunities 97–98
honor societies 160, 161
Hughes, G. E. 30n.8
Hull, N. E. H. 16n.1
human species
as collectivity of ultimate value 329
as ethical community without institutions 382–83
Hurd, Heidi 4n.1, 30n.8, 69–70, 72–77
on moral significance of liberties 74–77
typographical errors by 73n.22
Hurka, Thomas 314–15
Husik, Isaac 69n.21
Huss, Rebecca 348n.6
hybrid theories 255, 279

ignoratio elenchi 263, 307–8
immediate relatives of dead victims 163–64, 165–73
"immunities," rooted in ordinary usage 8
immunities 92–98
conferred by bills of rights 93–97
conferred by First Amendment 93, 95
essential for any duty's existence 258–59, 275–78, 280–81
essential for claim-rights as "rights" 98
essential for other entitlements 97–98, 253–54
Hart on 267–68
often unnoticed 50–51

import for beings of their inclusion among potential right-holders 334–36, 337, 338–40, 350–51, 353–54, 363
import for paradigmatic right-holders of including other beings 334, 336–37, 338–39, 340–42, 345–47, 350–54, 355–56, 363–65
inanimate and insentient things 66–67, 293–94, 298, 302–10, 311–12, 313–14, 315–16, 318, 334–38
inchoate legal entitlements 131–34
inclusive disjunctive universal quantification 61
Inclusive Legal Positivism 130–31
income tax 103
incongruities between genuine right-holders and perceived right-holders 335–36, 337–38, 349–50
Incorporationism 130–31
indeterminacy 67–68
infants 12
  benignity of interaction with human adults 351
  proximity between their traits and those of human adults 351
  as potential holders of rights 350–53
  self-respect, warranted levels for 351
infinitive verb phrase 71–72
inherency 101, 174–75, 179, 189–90, 192
"and inherently" 188–89
insane people 12
insentient forces and entities, as quasi-powers 83–85
in sensu composito, versus *in sensu diviso* 59
inside-out argumentation 309
instrumental value 313–29
"interest," explication of v
  broad sense of that covers purely vicarious stakes 201
Interest Theory of right-holding
  applied to scenario of Doris and her employer 189–90
  applied to third-party-beneficiary contract 190–91, 192
  capacious version of 17, 18, 79–80, 178–79, 225–55, 267–68
  class of potential right-holders left open by 294–97, 333–34
  defense of 178–291
  in defense of Correlativity Axiom 100–2, 108–13, 121–22, 131–32, 178
  in defense of No Wrongs Without Claim-Rights Proposition 136, 138–42, 163, 174–75
  and disjunctive universal quantification 63
  evaluative premises of 11–12, 111–13, 121–22, 178–79, 180–81, 182–87, 196–203, 208–14, 227–28, 239–40
  evaluative premises of for holding legal rights 181–87, 208, 211–12, 227, 231
  formulation of 101, 179–208
  and inherency of protection 101, 174–75, 179, 188–90, 192
  "inherently" in formulation of 101
  inordinate flexibility imputed to 203–8
  and John's duties concerning his parents 82
  legal positivism consistent with 184–87
  main version of confined to claim-rights 250–55
  misguided variant of for moral claim-rights 208–14
  notational variation of Bentham's Test 188–89, 191
  overinclusiveness imputed to 174–75, 179, 187–93
  past defenses of by Kramer 13–15
  protection under not always beneficial 175
  subjective element in evaluative premises of 182–83, 206, 207–8, 211–12, 239–40
  underinclusiveness imputed to 193–203
  univocality of 299–301, 302, 309
  Wenar on 6–11
  Will Theory opposed by 178–79, 193, 225–26, 250, 254–91
interest theory of rights, Raz's version of 116, 128–29, 131–32, 134–35, 200–1, 214–25, 228, 367–68
interests
  in attaining one's keen desires 110–11
  benefits and advantages interconnected with 299
  expansive conception of 298–312, 334–35, 356–57
  intermediate conception of 306–7, 308–9
  rights distinguished from 128–31, 214–15, 216–17, 225
  specified objectively 110–11
interference, understood broadly 24–26, 252–53
interrogational torture 332–33
  absolute wrongness of 220–22
  claim-right against 128
  justifications for banning of 114, 116
intrinsic value 315–16
  as consequence-independent value 315–16
  as experience-independent value 316
intuition-mongering 201–3
Ireland, Supreme Court of 4–5

James, P. D. 377–78
James, Susan 133n.6
jaywalking ordinance 39–40
  enforceable but regularly unenforced 285–88
  undetectable violations of 287–89

Jesus of Nazareth 242–43, 263–64
John's duties pertaining to his parents 81–83
Jones, Peter 120n.3
Julius Caesar 161–62
jurists, as readers of this book 4–5
justificatory account of rights, Raz's version of 2–3, 116, 128–29, 131–32, 134–35, 200–1, 214–25, 228, 367–68
justificatory matters 2–3, 11, 12, 178, 200–1, 214–15, 218, 228, 232–34, 264–65, 292–93, 305, 309–10, 312, 326–27, 329–32, 333, 335, 342–45, 347, 357–59, 367–68, 370–71, 374–75, 379–80
justificatory/non-justificatory distinction 2–3, 11, 12, 178, 200–1, 214–15, 218, 228, 232–34, 264–65, 292–93, 305, 309–10, 312, 326–27, 329–32, 333, 335, 342–45, 347, 357–59, 367–68, 370–71, 374–75, 379–80
justificatory priorities
  correlativity of rights and duties consistent with 113–18, 215, 216–17
  Dworkin on 114–15, 116
  logical and existential parity consistent with 113–18
  MacCormick on 115–16
  Marmor on 116
  Waldron on 115–16

Kanger, Helle 4n.1
Kanger, Stig 4n.1
Kant, Immanuel 348n.6
Kantianism 31–32, 322n.4
Kelch, Thomas 348n.6, 359n.8
Kelsen, Hans 35–38
Kennedy, Duncan 18n.2
King of France 381
Kocourek, Albert 44–45, 47–48
Kramer, Matthew, previous work of v, 13–15
Kripke, Saul 372–73
Ku Klux Klan 328
Kurki, Visa
  on anarchists 109–11, 182–83, 205–6
  on artificial intelligence 317–18
  on Bentham's Test 188
  conception of powers by 79
  on Correlativity Axiom 102
  on eleemosynary duties 120n.3
  on fourth-party beneficiaries 196–98
  on inanimate entities 297
  on reformulation of Bentham's Test 196n.3
  on Shakespeare 372–73

Latvian cousin 150–53
law-administration 93–94
"laws," ambiguity of 37
legal claim-rights
  and evaluative premises of Interest Theory 181–87, 208, 211–12, 227, 231
  goodness of moral uprightness not taken into account for 109, 111–12, 183–87, 208, 211–12, 227, 231
  as metaphysically necessary concomitants of other legal entitlements 53–55, 252–54
  moral claim-rights contrasted with 143–44
  stages of emergence of 131–35
legal disabilities
  as remedies for breaches of moral duties 95–97
  sometimes functionally akin to sanctions 96
  suitable for democratic legitimacy 97
legal duties
  owed only to presiding system of governance 103–4
  owed to presiding system of governance 60, 61, 81–82, 102–11, 121–22, 238–39, 287–88, 295–96, 347
legal liberties, not classifiable as rights in some extreme circumstances 247–50
legal positions existent only within system of legal governance 66
legal positivism 241
  consistent with Interest Theory 184–86, 187
legal powers
  to activate quasi-powers 84–85
  of enforcement 176
legal prohibition on defacement of Old Master paintings 296
legal prohibition on unprovoked assaults 295
legal prohibition on vandalism 296, 298, 332–33
legal prohibition on walking on grass 295–96, 332–33
legal rights, versus moral rights 11–12, 66
legislative bad faith 96–97
legislative bodies, broad understanding of 96n.29
legislative disabilities 94–97
legislative powers 89–91
length of time for subsumability of aftermath of lifespan into lifespan 365–66, 369–72
leprechauns 68–69
Leslie, Sarah-Jane 324–26
Letsas, George 330
Levenbook, Barbara Baum 359n.8
Lewis, David 59n.16, 372–73
liabilities 80
  borne vis-à-vis oneself 80
liabilities and disabilities, evaluative neutrality of 18–19
"liability," as technical term 80

liberties 43–70
claim-rights not logically entailed by 24, 53, 55
contents of 49–51
exercise of protected by claim-rights 51–55
and metaphysical necessity of concomitant claim-rights 53–55
moral significance of dismissed by Hurd and Moore 74–77
paired versus unpaired 45–49
as permissions 44
reality of 69–70
unentailed by claim-rights 55–57
unnoticed frequently 49–51
"liberties," rooted in ordinary usage 8
liberty to commit suicide 247–50
limits on Hohfeldian positions 66–70, 72–73, 76–77
List, Christian 106n.1
living human beings 312, 350–51
Locke, John 372
logic of the will 33n.9
logical contradictoriness 22–24
logical duality 22–24, 44–45, 71
limits on 22
logical equivalence consistent with justificatory priorities 113–18
logical notation 3–5
loss of consortium 164–66
lost property 86
Luper, Steven 359n.8
Lyons, David 299

MacCormick, Neil
on children's claim-rights 261
on dynamic aspect of rights 125–28
on fundamental inalienable claim-rights 266
on Hart's conception of legal powers 78n.25, 79–80
on inchoate legal entitlements 131–32
on justificatory priorities 115–16
on putative priority of duties over rights 119–20
rights and interests conflated by 128–31, 134
on Scottish intestate law 123–25
Macklin, Ruth 374n.10
Mafia 328
Makinson, David 4n.1
mandatory seatbelt laws 247–48
Marcus, Ruth Barcan 34
Marmor, Andrei 30, 116
Marquis, Don 359n.8
masochist 182–83, 205–6, 207–8
Mayo, Bernard 120n.3
McBride, Mark 22n.3, 255
McCain, John 114
McConnell, Terrance 30n.8, 32–33
medieval trials of animals 348
Mengele, Josef
as holder of claim-right not to be punitively tortured 219–20, 223
as paradigmatic potential holder of claim-rights 331–33
ultimate value of 323, 324
mentally incapacitated people 350–53
The Merchant of Venice 364
metaphysical impossibility of Marxist utopia 242
metaphysical necessity 53–55, 252–54
metaphysics, distinguished from logic 75–76
methodology 5–13
Michelman, Frank 18n.2
Miers, David 37–38
military conscription 103
Milky Way Galaxy 66–67
mind-control 27–28
minimal sufficiency 163–64
in Bentham's Test 189
of facts for enabling legal changes 88–89
minimum-wage laws 259–60, 269
misery-averting law 118
misplacing of quantifier by Wenar 203–5
modal categories 81
modal freedom 44
modal logic, versus deontic logic 32
monstrous evildoers 326–27
Moore, Michael 4n.1
on deontic conflicts 30n.8, 34
on moral significance of liberties 74–77
naturalistic dogmas of 76n.24
on reality of liberties 69–70
on reality of no-rights 72–77
typographical errors by 73n.22
moral claim-rights
goodness of uprightness taken into account for 111–13, 183–84, 186, 187, 208–14, 227–28
moral necessity of as accompaniments of other moral entitlements 252–54
moral duties, always owed to oneself 111–13, 122, 183–84, 212, 347
moral integrity of duty-bearers
basis for absolute wrongness of sadistic torture 322–23
ignored by Raz 225
moral necessity 252–54
moral permissibility, versus correctness 32–33
moral personhood 358–59

moral rights, versus legal rights 11–12, 66, 143–44
moral uprightness, goodness of 109, 111–13
Morris, Herbert 206n.5
Morris, Madeline 18n.2
motivation, contrasted with obligation 166–67
Much Ado about Nothing 159–61
Mulgan, Tim 359n.8
Mullock, Philip 4n.1, 30n.8, 299
multiple minimally sufficient sets of facts 189, 192
multital duties 62–63, 145–46
mythical or imaginary parties 68–69, 104, 321

Nascimento, Daniel 48n.13, 120n.3
naturalistic dogmas 76n.24
natural-law jurisprudence 184–87
natural necessity, as metaphysical necessity 53–54
near-eliminativism, versus thorough eliminativism 276–77
Nelkin, Dorothy 359n.8
neutrality among reasonable creeds 303, 304, 305, 308–9
no-liberties 75
nominalized verb phrase 71–72
nomological impossibility 321
non-human animals 12, 25
  capable of bearing duties 348
  if domesticable, capable of fulfilling some duties 348
  most as potential holders of rights 312, 322–23, 338–50
  ultimate value lacking for some 322–23, 339–50
  warranted level of self-respect higher through inclusion among right-holders 340–42, 343
  Will Theory rights not held by 260–65, 294
non-identity problem 384–87
non-justificatory matters 2–3, 11, 12, 178, 200–1, 214–15, 218, 228, 232–34, 264–65, 292–93, 305, 309–10, 312, 326–27, 329–32, 333, 335, 342–45, 347, 357–59, 367–68, 370–71, 374–75, 379–80
"no-right," as neologism 70, 71, 72
no-rights 43–77
  content shared with correlative liberty 71
  "no-rights" versus "no rights" 70–77
  reality of 72–77
norms, versus norm-formulations 35–39
norm-formulations, versus norms 35–39
No Wrongs Without Claim-Rights Proposition 202
  defense of against Cornell 135–77
  Interest Theory's role in defending 136, 138–42, 163, 174–75
nullity
  sanctions different from 95

Nussbaum, Martha 32–33

objections to Will Theory 257–91
objectivity of Interest Theory's evaluative premises 182–83, 211–12, 239–40
obligatedness, *tout court* 65–66
obligation
  motivation contrasted with 166–67
"obligation," synonymous with "duty" v
Old Master paintings 296, 305
Oliveira Lima, Joao 4n.1, 48n.13, 68n.20
omissions
  actions contrasted with 77–78
  powers not exercised by 86
O'Neill, Onora 133n.6, 348n.6
one-to-one correlations 61–64, 99–100, 120
opacity respect 322n.4
ordinary usage
  looseness and imprecision of 7–13, 250–52
  Wenar's excessive reliance on 6–13, 250–51
"ought" 35n.10
overheard falsehood, scenario of 146–54
overinclusiveness, imputed to Interest Theory 174–75, 179, 187–93
oxygen in atmosphere of Earth 49–50, 98

paired liberties 45–49
  in Wenar's examples 230–32, 234–37
Palombella, Gianluigi 374n.10
Palsgraf v Long Island Railroad 154–58
paradigmatic potential right-holders 330–33
  morally obligated to recognize other potential right-holders 331, 332, 334, 382–83
paramount moral responsibility
  as determinant of inclusion among potential right-holders 329–83
  universal quantifier in content of 340–42, 343, 354–55
Parfit, Derek 384–87
parthenogenesis 307–8
Partridge, Ernest 359n.8, 374n.10
Pasek, Joanna 374n.10
Paskins, Barrie 30n.8
passivity of claim-rights and immunities 281–84
paternalistic legal prohibitions 243–47
  disrespectfulness of 247–48
  Wenar on 243–47
patriarchal familial prerogatives 164–66
patriarchal honor societies 160, 161
patterns of interaction with sane human adults
  benign for infants and mentally incapacitated people 351
  benign for many non-human animals and antagonistic for some 344–47

patterns of interaction with sane human adults (*cont.*)
  non-antagonistic for the anencephalic and the permanently comatose 354
  non-antagonistic for dead people 363–64
Paul Bunyan 68–69
Penner, James 52, 130
permanently comatose people
  ultimate value of 323
  Will Theory rights not held by 260–65, 274–75, 294
permissibility *tout court* 64–66
Perry, Ronen 374n.10
Persad, Govind 359n.8
personal interests
  possible altruism of 198–99, 200–1
personal/vicarious distinction
  in evaluative premises of Interest Theory 196–203
  in scenario of fourth-party beneficiary 196–203
  Sreenivasan's apparent endorsement of 200–1
Pettit, Philip 106n.1
philosophy, versus social science 3
Pierce, Jessica 339
Pitcher, George 359n.8
placeholder designations 383–84, 385–86
Plato 372
pleonotetic quantification 108–9, 329, 353, 382, 384
  in many familiar generics 324–26
  Wenar's misunderstanding of 203–5
Pletcher, Galen 374n.10
Portmore, Douglas 359n.8
Posner, Eric 30n.8
Posner, Richard 130
posthumous betrayal of trust 361
posthumous defamation 360, 361
posthumous disclosure of embarrassing information 360, 361
posthumous harms and benefits 359–63, 369–70, 373–74, 375–76
posthumous loss of acclaim 360–61
posthumous presence of dead person 364–72
post-judgment stage of enforcement of duty 256–57, 258–59, 265–66, 270, 271–75, 278
post-violation situation with official enforcement 273–75
post-violation situation without statute of limitations 272–73
post-violation situation with statute of limitations 271–72
potential holders of claim-rights, class of
  actual holders of claim rights contrasted with 292, 293–94, 305–6, 309–10
  ethical basis of 12, 178, 264–65, 291, 292–387
  for legal claim-rights, not all are actual holders 292
  for moral claim-rights, all are actual holders 292
powers
  as abilities to change legal or moral relationships 77–92
  exercised only through actions 77–78, 272, 273–74
  Hart's conception of 78, 79–80
  Hohfeld's broad understanding of 78–80
  Kurki's conception of 79
  Raz's conception of 78–79
"powers," rooted in ordinary usage 8
powers and immunities
  conflated by Steiner 277–78
  evaluative neutrality of 17–19, 226, 227–28, 246–47
powers and liabilities 77–92
  evaluative neutrality of 80, 81–83
powers of enforcement 39
presence of future generations now 374–80
  as mainstays of current purposefulness 376–78, 379–80
  through ability to worse or improve lives posthumously 375–76
  through anticipatory adjustments in current behavior 378–79
pre-theoretical understandings, inadequacy of 7–13, 201–3, 227, 297
pre-violation powers to keep duties in existence 275–78, 280–81
pre-violation stage of duty's existence 256–57, 258–60, 265–66, 271, 275–84
primary goods 181–82
primary natural goods 181
primary social goods 181
private law
  perceived by Will Theorists as their distinctive realm 269–70, 288–89
  post-violation powers of waiver pervasive in 272–73
  powers of enforcement pervasive in 274–75
  statutes of limitations pervasive in 272–73
  undetectable violations of duties in 289, 290
private property as an institution 242
private road of Churchill College 276–77
"privileges"
  misleadingness of 8n.3, 46–48
  and unpaired permissions 46–48
  used by Wenar 8n.3
promises about the conduct of third parties 137
proximity of traits with those of sane human adults
  anencephalic infants in lessened proximity 354–55

dead people in close proximity 363–65
infants and mentally incapacitated people in close proximity 351
most but not all non-human animals in fairly close proximity 344, 347, 372
permanently comatose people in close proximity 354
public duties 103
punishment, versus therapeutic manipulation 206–8
punitive torture 219–20, 223, 326–27, 332–33
Putnam, Hilary 372–73

quantification 3–4, 22, 43–44, 46, 58–66, 87–92, 133–34, 382–84
aggregative universal 58–59, 61–62, 64, 106–9, 327, 382–84, 385–86
disjunctive universal 58–64, 65–66, 87–88, 89–91, 99–100, 120–22, 124n.4, 143–44
distributive pleonotetic 108–9, 324–26, 382, 384
distributive universal 58–59, 62–63, 64–66, 87–88, 91–92, 108–9, 145–46, 151–52, 204, 239n.11, 384
existential 58–63
over bearers of liabilities 91–92
over bearers of no-rights 64–66
over parties 58–66
over sets of changes in legal relationships 89–91
over sets of conditions for changes in legal relationships 88–89
pleonotetic 108–9, 329, 353, 382, 384
quasi-liabilities 83–87, 276–77
quasi-parents 236n.10
quasi-powers 66–67, 83–87
as applicability of general norms 86–87
comprehensiveness of Hohfeld's matrix compromised by 86–87
sometimes due to intentions or culpability 84–85, 143–44
Quay, Paul 359n.8
question-begging objections to Will Theory 257–68
quidnunc mentality 245

Randi W. v Muroc 147–48
Rawls, John 348n.6
on primary natural goods 181
on primary social goods 181
on the thin theory of the good 11–12, 181–82
Raz, Joseph
on analyses of political concepts 218–19
"on balance" and "typically" conflated by 217–18
claim-rights conflated with interests by 128–31, 134, 215, 216–17, 225
on class of potential holders of rights 216
and collapse of his interest theory into Kramer's Interest Theory 222–25
on deontic conflicts 30n.8
on dynamic aspect of rights 125–28
Hohfeldian analysis opposed by 215, 216–17, 225
on inchoate legal entitlements 131–32
justificatory account of rights by 2–3, 116, 128–29, 131–32, 134–35, 200–1, 214–25, 228, 367–68
justificatory focus on interests of right-holders 218–25, 228
moral integrity of duty-bearers ignored by 225
on nature of legal powers 78–79
on ultimate value 317n.3
Razian rights
Cruft on 216
as reasons for existence of moral duties, in realm of morality 216
as reasons for official actions, in realm of law 216
Razian victim-focused perspective 220–22, 223
Reagan, Ronald 380
reasons for parent to punish child 235, 237
recreational fireworks 167–69
redescribability of claim-rights in terms of duties 258
reducibility, conflated by Hohfeld with explicability 106
reductionism 104–9
regimentation of philosophical terminology 251–55
regularly unenforced legal duties 39–43, 285–86
Reichenbach, Bruce 374n.10
Reinhard's stolen sculptures 184–86
rejoinder by Will Theorists to critique of their near-eliminativism 281
and rebuttal of the rejoinder 281–84
relationality
of Hohfeldian positions, as correlativity 16, 19, 21–22, 25–26, 64–65, 77, 99–177, 349–50, 380
and quantification 64–66
remedial obligations 32–33
Ridge, Michael 359n.8
right to an education 132–34
"right to commit a wrong" 57
right-holding as a relational property 359–63, 380–81

"rights"
ambiguity of 1, 5–6, 7–13, 17–19, 57
apt label for other entitlements because of concomitant claim-rights 252–55
restricted to claim-rights plus immunities 9, 24–25, 98
"rights bring with them responsibilities" 348–50
Rodman, John 304n.2
role-centered responsibilities and prerogatives 228–29, 230, 233–34, 235–36, 236n.10
Rolston III, Holmes 304n.2
Rousseau, Jean-Jacques 242
Rowlands, Mark 339
rule of law 6

sadistic torture 322–23
sanctions, versus nullity 95
sane human adults
morally obligated to recognize other potential right-holders 331, 332, 334, 382–83
as paradigmatic potential right-holders 330–33
Will Theory rights held only by 260–65, 294, 312, 331, 333–34, 349
Saunders, Kevin 4n.1, 26n.6, 87–88
scalar properties 125
Scarre, Geoffrey 359n.8
Schauer, Frederick 11
Scheffler, Samuel 376–78, 379–80
Schlegel, John Henry 16n.1
Schmofeld 75
school doors 40–41, 43
Schwitzgebel, Eric 317–18
Scottish intestate law 123–25
Scruton, Roger 348n.6
self-aggrandizement and self-degradation 351–53, 354, 355–56
self-defense 54–55
self-directed duties 25, 26–27, 80, 111–13, 122, 281–82, 347, 349, 359
self-reflective responsiveness and adaptability 318
September 11 atrocities 150–53
sets of facts minimally sufficient for breaches of duties
different for duties with different contents 202–3
Shakespeare, William 175, 370
The Comedy of Errors 370n.9
Cornell on 158–62
Hamlet 375–76
Henry V 167
Julius Caesar 161–62
The Merchant of Venice 364
mistaken recollections of 372–73
Much Ado about Nothing 159–61
The Taming of the Shrew 302
Shrage, Laurie 304
Simester, Andrew 30n.8
Simmonds, Nigel 103
as avid environmentalist 264–65, 312
Hart's concession on infants endorsed by 261–62, 264, 350–51
on private law as distinctive realm of Will Theory 269, 288–89
and restrictive class of potential right-holders 260–65
Simpson, Thomas 106–7
Singer, Peter 303–4
slope, upward and downward inclination of 117, 119
slugs 347, 351, 352–53, 354
small-scale sovereign, Hart's vision of right-holder as 279–80
Smolensky, Kirsten Rabe 359n.8
social science versus philosophy 3
societal variability in import of temporal remoteness 372
Solomon, Robert 359n.8
Solum, Lawrence 317–18
sorites problems 365
speciesism 326, 331, 346–47, 354, 355–56
Spena, Alessandro 52–53n.14, 53
Sperling, Daniel 359n.8
Sreenivasan, Gopal
on fourth-party beneficiaries 196–203
on Frazier/Ali boxing match 194–96
hybrid theory by 255
overinclusiveness imputed to Interest Theory by 187–93, 196–203
personal/vicarious distinction apparently accepted by 200–1
on third-party beneficiary contracts 187–93, 196–203
underinclusiveness imputed to Interest Theory by 193–203
stages of duty's existence and enforcement 256, 277–78
stages of emergence of legal claim-rights 131–35
statuette of Abraham Lincoln 283–84
status of potential right-holder, different from moral personhood 358–59
statutes of limitations
pervasive in private law 272–73
as quasi-powers 86
Steinbock, Bonnie 303–4
Steiner, Hillel 8, 13n.5, 225–26, 236n.9, 278–79, 374n.10
on deontic conflicts 30

extremeness in adherence to Will Theory 279–81
powers and immunities conflated by 277–78
Steinhoff, Uwe 221
Sterba, James 374n.10
Stockwell, Billy 297
Stone, Christopher 297
strength of desires 239n.12
subjective element in evaluative premises of Interest Theory 182–83, 206, 207–8, 211–12, 239–40
subordinate clause 71–72
suicide, liberty to commit 247–50
Sumner, L. W. 26n.6, 30, 304n.1, 348n.6

tactical judgments, versus philosophical theses 335–36
The Taming of the Shrew 302
Taylor, James Stacey 359n.8
Taylor, Paul 304n.2
temporal remoteness, societal variability in import of 372
Terentian aphorism 352–53, 382–83
theoretical success, standards for 6–13
therapeutic manipulation 206–8
thin theory of good 11–12, 181–82
third-party-beneficiary contracts
Cornell on 138–42, 174–76
Hart on 138–42
Sreenivasan on 187–93, 196–203
third-party claim-rights
derivativeness of 170–74
van Duffel on 201–3
third-party complaints about wrongs 148–49
Thompson, Jack Clayton 120n.3
Thomson, Judith Jarvis 358–59
thought-experiments 3
by Cornell 136
thuggish officials and enslaved laborers, scenario of 209–13
timing, in Frazier/Ali bout 195–96
Tooley, Michael 304n.1
torture
claim-right against 128
justifications for ban on 114, 116
non-essentialist analysis of 6
trajectory of a life, with aftermath of a lifespan 359–62, 363, 364–72
trees, and justificatory/non-justificatory distinction 311–12
truth-inaptitude 381
tsetse flies
of no ultimate value 322–23, 339, 345–46
sadistic torture of always wrong 322–23
as vermin 345–47, 351, 354, 364
Tuomela, Raimo 106n.1
tu quoque riposte 205
Twining, William 37–38
two default rules for post-violation stage 270–75
typically beneficial rather than invariably beneficial 110, 175, 180
"typically" quantifier in capacious Interest Theory 249–50

ultimate value 312, 313, 317–29
of anencephalic infants 353
of collectivities 327–29
formulation of 317
of non-human animals, some excluded from 322–23, 339–50
of permanently comatose people 353
Raz on 317n.3
uncooperativeness, broad understanding of 24–26, 252–53
underinclusiveness, imputed to Interest Theory 193–203
undetectable violations of legal duties 284–90
in realm of private law 289–90
unenforceability entailed by undetectability 287–90
unenforceability, versus mere unenforcedness 39–43
unenforceable legal duties
in contradictions 43
genuineness of 40–43
voluntary guidelines contrasted with 42–43
Will Theorists' blindness to 284–90
unfairness, versus logical impossibility 29–30, 34
unforeseeable harms 150
Anscombe on 150–53
unfoundedness of some ascriptions of rights to future people 381–82
universal quantification 58–66
three varieties of 58–66
univocality of a theory 299–301, 302, 309
unpaired liberties 45–49
unprovoked assaults, ban on 295
unwaivability of minimum-wage duties 259–60

Valentini, Laura 120n.3
Vallentyne, Peter 30n.8
vandalism, ban on 296, 298, 332–33
van Duffel, Siegfried 65n.18, 120n.3
on deprivation of companionship 201–3
liberties and exercises of liberties conflated by 52
van Fraassen, Bas 31–32

Vermeule, Adrian 30n.8
vermin 345–47, 351, 354, 364
voluntary guidelines, versus unenforceable duties 42–43

Waldron, Jeremy
on dynamic aspect of rights 127–28
on eleemosynary duties 120n.3
on justificatory priorities 115–16
on putative priority of duties over claim-rights 119–20
rights and interests conflated by 130
walking on grass, ban on 295–96, 332–33
warranted level of self-respect, affected by posthumous occurrences 375–76
warranted self-respect, conditions for 152, 322–23
impaired by use of punitive torture 219–20
and inclusion of dead people among potential right-holders 363
and inclusion of infants among potential right-holders 351
and inclusion of mentally incapacitated people among potential right-holders 351
paramount moral duty to promote 329–83
Warren, Mary Anne 303–4
water-boarding 128
Wellman, Carl 359n.8
Wenar, Leif
on arranging of marriages 240–41
capacious Interest Theory attacked by 228–47
and carping about focus on claim-rights 250–51
on claim-rights 9
on comatose people 9–10
elementary logical error by 203–5
empirical conjectures by 12–13
on Interest Theory and Will Theory 6–11
on Jesus of Nazareth 242–43
on kamikaze pilot 238–40
on legal liberty of policeman to detain suspects 230–34
on legal power of judge to sentence criminals 228–29, 232–34
on legal powers of army captain 228–29
on legal powers of traffic warden 228–29
misleading specifications of *explananda* by 232–34
on ordinary usage 6–13, 250–51
on paired liberties to choose between defending and not defending a victim 230–32
on parent's paired liberties to choose between punishing and not punishing 230–32, 234–37
on paternalism 243–47
peculiar provisos by 250–52
on Rousseau and Marx 242
on soldier's right to disarm bombs 238–40
tu quoque riposte to 205
Westen, Peter 52
White, Laurence 317–18
White v Jones 144–45
Wilkinson, T. M. 359n.8
Will Theory
no begging of question against 268–79
Cornell's adherence to 136, 138–42, 154, 171, 174–75, 176, 193
and denial of claim-right not to be murdered 257–58
and denial of claim-rights under criminal law 258–59, 269
and denial of claim-rights under minimum-wage laws 259–60, 269
exposition of 255–57
formulation of 255
Hart and Cornell as proponents of 193
Interest Theory's opposition to 178–79, 193, 225–26, 250, 254–91
near-eliminativism of 268–84
objections to 13, 257–91
question-begging objections to 257–68
and restrictive conception of class of potential right-holders 260–65, 294, 349
Wenar on 6–11
Williams, Andrew 304n.1
Williams, Glanville 26n.6, 29
Williams, Jeremy 304
Wisnewski, Jeremy 359n.8
Wittgenstein, Ludwig 6
Wittgensteinian methodology 5–6
Woods, Kerri 374n.10
wrongful-death statutes 165–67, 197, 201–2
wronging, versus merely harming 140–41, 156, 158, 159–60
wrongness, versus gravity of wrongness 168–69, 170–71, 172–73

Yoshida, Masayuki 359n.8

Zipursky, Benjamin 145–46

The manufacturer's authorised representative in the EU for product safety is Oxford University Press España S.A. of el Parque Empresarial San Fernando de Henares, Avenida de Castilla, 2 – 28830 Madrid (www.oup.es/en or product.safety@oup.com). OUP España S.A. also acts as importer into Spain of products made by the manufacturer.

www.ingramcontent.com/pod-product-compliance
Ingram Content Group UK Ltd.
Pitfield, Milton Keynes, MK11 3LW, UK
UKHW020843150926
475595UK00004B/133

* 9 7 8 0 1 9 8 8 9 1 2 2 2 *